National Party Conventions
1831–2004

National Party Conventions
1831–2004

CQ PRESS

A DIVISION OF CONGRESSIONAL QUARTERLY INC.
WASHINGTON, D.C.

CQ Press
1255 22nd Street, NW, Suite 400
Washington, DC 20037

Phone: 202-729-1900; toll-free, 1-866-427-7737 (1-866-4CQ-PRESS)

Web: www.cqpress.com

Illustration credits: Most of the photographs and engravings appearing in *National Party Conventions 1831–2004* were obtained from the collection of the Library of Congress or the White House. Other photos and their sources are the following: 17 and 168 (right and left)—no credit; 19 and 174 (right)—AP/Wide World Photos; 39—Dennis Brack/Landov; 79 (right), 81 (right), and 85—National Portrait Gallery, Smithsonian Institution, Washington, D.C.; 110 (left) and 113 (left)—New York State Historical Society; 113 (left center)—Harry S. Truman Library; 168 (center)—Billy Suratt, UPI.

Cover design: Malcolm McGaughy
Cover photos: *Bottom left:* National Museum of American History; *all others:* AP/Wide World Photos.

♾ The paper used in this publication exceeds the requirements of the American National Standard for Information Sciences—Permanence of Paper for Printed Library Materials, ANSI Z39.48-1992.

Printed and bound in the United States of America

09   08   07   06   05   1   2   3   4   5

Cataloging-in-Publication data are available from the Library of Congress.

ISBN: 1-56802-982-9

Contents

Preface

One of the enduring images of American political life is that of a cavernous hall filled with loyal delegates waving banners and cheering as a party leader or presidential nominee recites the party's cherished political beliefs. The national nominating convention is a uniquely American institution. Since the 1830s all major U.S. political parties and a host of prominent minor parties have chosen presidential and vice-presidential candidates at national conventions. Although television viewership of conventions has declined during the past two decades, the convention continues to evolve and remains an integral part of the presidential selection process through its adaptability and multiplicity of functions.

The convention system, which has now been in continuous use for 173 years, was not mentioned in the Constitution. The Founders established the Electoral College as the sole mechanism in selecting the president. But the Founders also did not foresee the rise of political parties; and when competing parties developed in the nation's formative years, a nominating method had to be devised. In the early nineteenth century party leaders first employed congressional caucuses to nominate presidential candidates. But as the desire for increased democracy swept the nation, the exclusive caucuses proved unsatisfactory and a way had to be found to involve mass citizen participation.

The new method turned out to be the convention and was initiated by the Anti-Masonic Party in September 1831. Its gathering was small by modern standards, attracting 116 delegates from thirteen states. The delegates adopted an address to the people (a forerunner of the modern platform) and nominated William Wirt for the presidency. Although Wirt fared poorly in the general election and the Anti-Masonic Party failed to survive the decade, the success of the convention as a nominating mechanism led to its adoption by other parties.

The Democratic Party held its first convention in 1832 and without interruption has held a national convention every four years since then. The Democrats' gathering in Boston in July 2004 was the party's forty-fifth (the party convened twice in 1860). The Republicans held their first convention in 1856, two years after the party's formation, and their 2004 convention in New York was their thirty-eighth national meeting.

Through a century of massive political, social, and technological changes, the survival of the convention is a tribute to both its adaptability and importance in the nomination of presidential candidates. Since its beginning, the convention has had a number of functions—foremost, the selection of a national ticket, the adoption of a platform, the discussion of party affairs, and the building of party unity. The conduct and setting of the convention have changed dramatically over the years, but the major functions have remained unaltered.

Before the Civil War, conventions were held in relative obscurity. At most, several hundred delegates attended the early conventions. Delegate selection was often informal, and participation was open to anyone with the motivation to chance the nation's uncertain transportation system.

Improved transportation and communication provided conventions with greater national attention and placed them under closer scrutiny. The selection of delegates was formalized, and the drive for increased democratization produced the presidential primary, now the major method of delegate selection. In 2004, thirty-seven states and the District of Columbia held either a Republican, Democratic, or combined presidential primary.

Advances in radio and television enabled conventions in the post–World War II years to become media spectaculars. The thousands of delegates, spectators, and media representatives who attended the Democratic and Republican conventions of 2004 offered a marked contrast to the relatively informal conventions of the 1830s.

The national party convention is on the verge of change once again. With presidential primaries stealing the suspense of who the eventual party nominee will be, television networks no longer provide gavel-to-gavel coverage of conventions. Party leaders now strive to avoid what were common occurrences of conventions past—the unscheduled interruptions by the delegates, the spontaneous demonstrations for candidates, and the bitter floor fights over rules and platforms. Conventions have become, as evidenced by the smoothly run 2004 gatherings, carefully choreographed television presentations, timed to fill one or two hours each night and focused on the successful marketing of the party's presidential ticket.

About This Book

National Party Conventions 1831–2004 is an up-to-date collection of historical data and facts covering all major nominating conventions from the first Anti-Masonic convention in 1831 to the major national conventions of 2004—the Republican convention that nominated President George W. Bush and the Democratic convention that nominated Sen. John Kerry.

The volume begins with a discussion of the presidential nominating process in the preconvention years, from 1789 to 1828 (Chapter 1). It covers the origins of the American party system and the reliance on the congressional caucus during this period as the principal nominating method. The decline of the caucus and the rise of the convention system are also discussed.

The next chapter discusses the origins and development of the presidential primary, which has assumed preeminent importance in the presidential selection process. The primary, which by the 1970s had supplanted the caucus method of choosing delegates to a national convention, has become the national stage where the major parties' presidential candidates are chosen. In the past decade, however, more and more states have held their primaries earlier and earlier in the campaign season—with the result in 2004 of both major party nominations being wrapped up by early March. This effect has not been altogether welcomed, and both parties now are considering reforms that might extend the primary season.

Chapter 3 provides an overview of the functions and development of the national convention. It focuses on various aspects of the convention—delegate selection, party rules, credentials disputes, the platform, and convention officers—as well as basic changes in the conduct of conventions. This section contains many useful tables and figures, such as the list of all officers and keynote speakers at Democratic and Republican national nominating conventions. A chronological table of national party convention highlights completes the section.

The heart of the volume is Chapter 4, which describes the conventions of all parties that received at least 2 percent of the popular vote in any presidential election since 1831. Included are all Democratic, Republican, and Whig conventions, as well as those of leading third parties. Within each brief convention history are discussions of the contest for the presidential and vice-presidential nominations, all significant roll calls, and an overiew of the party platform. Excerpts from the party's platform on leading issues of that particular campaign are included.

The next chapter augments the convention chronology with charts of key convention ballots, showing the vote of each state and territory on major roll calls at all Democratic, Republican, and Whig conventions. In addition to ballots for the presidential nominees, important votes on rules and credentials disputes are also provided.

The appendix provides a variety of information on political parties and candidates. It includes historical profiles of all parties whose conventions are described in the convention chronology, as well as other parties, such as Reform, Green, and Libertarian parties that are active today; a biographical directory of all presidential and vice-presidential candidates who received electoral votes; and a comprehensive roster of presidential and vice-presidential nominees from 1831 to 2004 that lists minor as well as major party candidates.

The book concludes with a bibliography, which provides the starting point for further reading about conventions and the nominating process, and a comprehensive index.

CHAPTER 1

Preconvention Politics, 1789–1828

For more than a century and a half the United States has had an established two-party system. The Framers of the Constitution, however, never envisioned such a system. They in fact viewed the existence of political parties with suspicion.

In his Farewell Address, written in 1796, President George Washington warned the American people of "the danger of parties." He went on to state:

There is an opinion that parties in free countries are useful checks upon the administration of the government, and serve to keep alive the spirit of liberty. This within certain limits is probably true; and in governments of a monarchical cast patriotism may look with indulgence, if not with favor, upon the spirit of party. But in those of the popular character, in governments purely elective, it is a spirit not to be encouraged. . . . A fire not to be quenched, it demands a uniform vigilance to prevent its bursting into a flame, lest, instead of warming, it should consume.

Other early American leaders shared Washington's suspicion of parties. Alexander Hamilton remarked in 1787, "[N]othing could be more illjudged than that intolerant spirit which has at all times characterized political parties." Two years later Thomas Jefferson declared: "If I could not go to heaven but with a party, I would not go there at all." Even a generation later, after the establishment of a U.S. party system, two early nineteenth-century presidents continued to speak out against the existence of political parties. Andrew Jackson, twelve years before he was elected president, wrote in 1816: "Now is the time to exterminate the monster called party spirit." In 1822, after his unopposed 1820 election victory, President James Monroe characterized parties as "the curse of the country."

Early American leaders were heavily influenced in their attitude by a dominant antiparty theme in European political philosophy, which equated parties with factions and viewed both negatively. Thomas Hobbes (1588–1679), David Hume (1711–1776), and Jean Jacques Rousseau (1712–1778)—three European philosophers whose views strongly influenced the Founders—regarded parties as threats to state government. In England there was no formal party system until the 1820s, several decades after the formation of parties in the United States. In colonial America there were no parties, and there were none in the Continental Congress or under the Articles of Confederation.

The Constitution did not provide authority for political parties or prohibitions against them. Historians have pointed out that most of the Framers had only a dim understanding of the function of political parties and thus were ambivalent, if not hostile, toward parties when they laid down the foundation of the new government. Nevertheless, the delegates to the Constitutional Convention and their successors in Congress ensured a role for parties in the government when they gave protection to civil rights and the right to organize. The Founders set up what they regarded as safeguards against excesses of party activity by providing an elaborate governmental system of checks and balances. The prevailing attitude of the convention was summed up by James Madison, who wrote in *The Federalist* that the "great object" of the new government was "to secure the public good and private rights against the danger of such a faction [party], and at the same time to preserve the spirit and the form of popular government."

Madison's greatest fear was that a party would become a tyrannical majority. This could be avoided, he believed, through the republican form of government that the proponents of the Constitution advocated. In *The Federalist* Madison wrote, "Among the numerous advantages promised by a well-constructed Union, none deserved to be more accurately developed than its tendency to break and control the violence of faction." A republic, as understood by Madison, was an elected body of wise, patriotic citizens, while a democracy was equated with mob rule. Madison dismissed the democratic form of government as a spectacle of "turbulence and contention."

Ironically, in this setting two competing parties grew up quickly. They developed as a result of public sentiment for and against adoption of the Constitution. The Federalist Party—a

Sources

Chambers, William N. *Political Parties in a New Nation: The American Experience, 1776–1809*. New York: Oxford University Press, 1963.

Key, V. O., Jr. *Politics, Parties and Pressure Groups*. 5th ed. New York: Crowell, 1964.

Nichols, Roy F. *The Invention of the American Political Parties*. New York: Free Press, 1972.

Roseboom, Eugene H. *A History of Presidential Elections: From George Washington to Jimmy Carter*. 4th ed. New York: Macmillan, 1979.

Schlesinger, Arthur M., Jr. *History of U.S. Political Parties*. Vol. 1. 1973. Reprint. New York: Chelsea House, 1981.

Stanwood, Edward. *History of the Presidency*. Vol. 1. 1921. Reprint. New York: Kelley, 1975.

Stimpson, George W. *A Book About American Politics*. New York: Harper, 1952.

"[N]othing could be more illjudged than that intolerant spirit which has at all times characterized political parties."

—Alexander Hamilton, 1787

loose coalition of merchants, shippers, financiers, and other business interests—favored the strong central government provided by the Constitution, while their opponents (at first called Anti-Federalists or Jeffersonians and later known as Democratic-Republicans) were intent upon preserving the sovereignty of the states. Underlying the controversy was the desire of the interests represented by the Federalists to create a government with power to guarantee the value of the currency (and thus protect the position of creditors) and the desire of the agrarians and frontiersmen who made up the Anti-Federalists to maintain easy credit conditions and the power of state legislatures to fend off encroachments by a remote federal government.

Unlike the Federalist Party, which was never more than a loose alliance of particular interests, the Anti-Federalists achieved a high degree of organization. The Federalists, in fact, never considered themselves a political party but rather a gentlemanly coalition of interests representing respectable society. What party management there was, they kept clandestine, a reflection of their fundamental suspicion of parties.

There is no precise date for the beginning of parties, although both Thomas Jefferson and Alexander Hamilton (a Federalist) referred to the existence of a Jeffersonian republican "faction" in Congress as early as 1792.

While party organization became more formalized in the 1790s and early 1800s, particularly among the Jeffersonians, the parties never acquired nationally accepted names. The Jeffersonians most commonly referred to themselves as Republicans. Their opponents labeled them as Anti-Federalists, disorganizers, Jacobins (after the radical democrats in France) and Democrats—the latter an unflattering term in the early years of the Republic. To many Americans in the late eighteenth century, a democrat was considered a supporter of mob rule and revolution and often ideologically identified with the bloody French Revolution of 1789.

The designation Democrat-Republican was used by the Jeffersonians in several states but was never widely accepted as a party label. However, historians often refer to the Jeffersonians as the Democratic-Republicans, to avoid confusion with the later and unrelated Republican Party, founded in 1854.

Although the early American political leaders acknowledged the development of parties, they did not foresee the emergence of a two-party system. Rather, they often justified the existence of their own party as a reaction to an unacceptable opposition. Jefferson defended his party involvement as a struggle between good and evil: "[When] the principle of difference is as substantial and as strongly pronounced as between the republicans and the Monocrats of our country, I hold it as honorable to take a firm and decided part, and as immoral to pursue a middle line, as between the parties of Honest men, and Rogues, into which every country is divided."

Presidential Politics

The rise of parties forced an alteration in the presidential selection method envisioned by the creators of the Constitution. Delegates to the Constitutional Convention of 1787 had sought a presidential selection method in which the "spirit of party" would play no part. The Electoral College system they finally settled on was a compromise born of a basic distrust in the political abilities of the populace, the complexities of the separation of powers system and the diversity in the states—slavery in the South and rivalries between the big and small states.

Rather than have the people vote directly for president, the choice was to be entrusted to presidential "electors," who the Founders hoped would be wise leaders in the separate states, able to choose the one person best qualified to be president. Under the Electoral College system, states were to choose electors as they saw fit; the electors would meet in their separate states some time after their selection to pick the next president.

While it seems odd that the leaders of a new democracy would choose to bypass the general populace, the decision was not so far out of line with conditions of the day as it might appear. The electors would merely be a somewhat more sophisticated version of the eighteenth-century electorate, which was quite different from the voting population of today. The Constitution left it to the states to determine voting requirements. In all states only men could vote. Many states also limited voting rights to property owners. Indeed, property qualifications had existed in all the colonies and endured in several states, although the exact requirements differed among states.

Some states allowed personal property or the payment of taxes as a substitute for holding real estate. By 1800 four states had established universal manhood suffrage. But property requirements of one sort or another were not abandoned by all the states until 1856. While they lasted, such requirements were restrictive, but their effect can be overstated. Because the United States was predominantly a middle-class society with fairly widespread ownership of property, such qualifications were not so significant a limit as they at first might appear. And since women and many men already were excluded from voting, restricting presidential selection to an elite group did not have the effect that it would today under universal suffrage.

Caucus System

While the Electoral College retained the power to *elect* the president, the state electors soon lost the authority to *nominate* the candidates and thus determine the field from which to choose a president. Strong political parties developed and removed the nomination process from the electors' hands. The parties created instead the first informal nominating device for choosing a president: a caucus of each party's members in Congress.

From 1796 until 1824, congressional caucuses—when a party had enough representatives to form one—chose almost all the candidates for president; the electors then chose from the party nominees. Only twice—in 1800 and 1824—as a result of a failure of any candidate to receive a majority of electoral votes, were presidential elections decided by the House of Representatives, and even in those two cases political parties were instrumental in the election of the president.

ELECTION OF 1789

In the first presidential election, held in 1789 shortly after the ratification of the Constitution, the nominating and electing process centered in the Electoral College. Electors chosen in the various states were, under the Constitution, entitled to cast two votes and required to cast each vote for a different person. The individual receiving votes of a majority of the electors was named president and the person receiving the second highest total was named vice president.

There were no formal nominations in 1789, but public opinion centered on George Washington of Virginia for president. He received sixty-nine electoral votes, the maximum possible. John Adams of Massachusetts was the leading second choice, although he did not enjoy the degree of unanimity that surrounded Washington. Adams easily won the vice presidency, receiving thirty-four electoral votes.

ELECTION OF 1792

The Federalists and Democratic-Republicans were emerging as competitive parties by the election of 1792. As a result, the Republic experienced the first modification in the presidential nominating process. No attempt was made to displace President Washington, but the Democratic-Republicans mounted a challenge to Vice President Adams. Meeting in Philadelphia in October 1792, a group of Democratic-Republican leaders from the Middle Atlantic states and South Carolina endorsed Gov. George Clinton of New York for the vice presidency, bypassing Sen. Aaron Burr of the same state. While Adams emerged victorious in the Electoral College, Clinton's endorsement by a meeting of party politicians was a milestone in the evolution of the presidential nominating process and a step away from the original Electoral College system.

ELECTION OF 1796

The election of 1796 brought further modifications in the nominating method, evidenced by the appearance of the congressional caucus.

There was no opposition to Thomas Jefferson as the Democratic-Republican presidential candidate, and he was considered the party's standard-bearer by a consensus of party leaders. A caucus of Democratic-Republican senators, however, was unable to agree on a running mate, producing a tie vote be-

tween Burr and Sen. Pierce Butler of South Carolina that ended with a walkout by Butler's supporters. As a result, there was no formal Democratic-Republican candidate to run with Jefferson.

The Federalists held what historian Roy F. Nichols described as a "quasi caucus" of the party's members of Congress in Philadelphia in May 1796. The gathering chose Vice President Adams and Minister to Great Britain Thomas Pinckney of South Carolina as the Federalist candidates.

ELECTION OF 1800

The election of 1800 was the first where both parties used the congressional caucus as the nominating body. Neither party, however, desired much publicity for the process, gathering in secret to deliberate. The proceedings were sketchily described by private correspondence and occasionally referred to in newspapers of the day. Unlike the public national conventions of later years, privacy was a hallmark of the early caucuses.

Although the actual dates of the 1800 caucuses are hazy, it is believed that both caucuses were held in May. The Democratic-Republican caucus was held in Marache's boardinghouse in Philadelphia, where forty-three of the party's members of Congress selected Aaron Burr to run with Thomas Jefferson, the latter again the presidential candidate by consensus and not formally nominated by the caucus.

Federalist members of Congress met in the Senate chamber in Philadelphia and nominated President Adams and Gen. Charles Cotesworth Pinckney of South Carolina. Pinckney, the

Presidents, 1789–1829

Term	President	Vice President
1789–1793	George Washington (FED)	John Adams (FED)
1793–1797	George Washington (FED)	John Adams (FED)
1797–1801	John Adams (FED)	Thomas Jefferson (D-R)
1801–1805	Thomas Jefferson (D-R)	Aaron Burr (D-R)
1805–1809	Thomas Jefferson (D-R)	George Clinton (D-R)
1809–1813	James Madison (D-R)	George Clinton (D-R)
1813–1817	James Madison (D-R)	Elbridge Gerry (D-R)
1817–1821	James Monroe (D-R)	Daniel D. Tompkins (D-R)
1821–1825	James Monroe (D-R)	Daniel D. Tompkins (D-R)
1825–1829	John Q. Adams (D-R)	John C. Calhoun (D-R)

KEY: FED—Federalist; D-R—Democratic-Republican

"If I could not go to heaven but with a party, I would not go there at all."
—Thomas Jefferson, 1789

"Among the numerous advantages promised by a well-constructed Union, none deserved to be more accurately developed than its tendency to break and control the violence of faction."

—James Madison, 1787

elder brother of the Federalist vice-presidential candidate in 1796, was placed on the ticket at the insistence of Alexander Hamilton, who believed one of the South Carolina Pinckneys could win. Although the deliberations of the Federalist caucus were secret, the existence of the meeting was not. It was described by the local Democratic-Republican paper, the *Philadelphia Aurora,* as a "Jacobinical conclave." Further denunciations by the paper's author, Benjamin F. Bache, earned him a personal rebuke from the U.S. Senate.

ELECTION OF 1804

The 1804 election was the first one held after the Twelfth Amendment to the Constitution went into effect, requiring electors to cast separate votes for president and vice president. The amendment was designed to avoid the unwieldy situation that had developed in 1800, when the two leading Democratic-Republican candidates, Jefferson and Burr, both received the same number of electoral votes. The unexpected tie vote threw the presidential election into the House of Representatives, where thirty-six ballots were cast before Jefferson finally won. With ratification of the amendment, parties in 1804 and thereafter specifically designated their presidential and vice-presidential candidates.

The Democratic-Republicans retained the caucus system of nomination in 1804, as they did for the next two decades, and for the first time they publicly reported their deliberations. The party caucus was held in February and attracted 108 of the party's senators and representatives. President Jefferson was renominated by acclamation, but Vice President Burr was not considered for a second term. On the first nominating roll call publicly reported in American political history, Gov. Clinton of New York was chosen to run for vice president. He received sixty-seven votes to easily defeat Sen. John Breckinridge of Kentucky, who collected twenty votes. To "avoid unpleasant discussions" no names were placed in nomination, and the vote was taken by written ballot.

Before adjourning, the caucus appointed a thirteen-member committee to conduct the campaign. A forerunner of party national committees, the new campaign group included members of both the House and Senate, but with no two individuals from the same state.

The Federalists dropped the congressional caucus as their nominating method. Federalist leaders in 1804 informally chose Charles Cotesworth Pinckney for president and Rufus King of New York for vice president. But the details of how they formulated this ticket are not known. There is no record in 1804 of any Federalist meeting to nominate candidates.

ELECTION OF 1808

The Democratic-Republican caucus was held in January 1808. For the first time a formal call was issued. Sen. Stephen R. Bradley of Vermont, the chairman of the 1804 caucus, issued the call to all 146 Democratic-Republicans in Congress and several Federalists sympathetic to the Democratic-Republican cause. His authority to call the caucus was questioned by several party leaders, but various reports indicate that eighty-nine to ninety-four members of Congress attended.

As in 1804 the balloting was done without the formal placing of names in nomination. For president, Jefferson's handpicked successor, Secretary of State James Madison of Virginia, was an easy winner with eighty-three votes. Vice President Clinton and James Monroe of Virginia each received three votes. For vice president the caucus overwhelmingly renominated Clinton. He received seventy-nine votes, while runner-up John Langdon of New Hampshire collected five. Even after the Democratic-Republicans renominated him for vice president, Clinton's supporters continued to hope that the Federalists would nominate their man for president later in the year. But their hopes were dashed when the nomination ultimately went to Pinckney.

As in 1804 the Democratic-Republican caucus appointed a committee to conduct the campaign. Membership was expanded to fifteen House and Senate members and it was formally called the "committee of correspondence and arrangement." The committee was authorized to fill any vacancies on the national ticket, should any occur.

Before adjournment a resolution was approved defending the caucus system as "the most practicable mode of consulting and respecting the interest and wishes of all." Later caucuses adopted similar resolutions throughout the history of the system.

The resolution was meant to stem the rumblings of opposition to the caucus system. Seventeen Democratic-Republican members of Congress signed a protest against Madison's selection and questioned the authority of the caucus as a nominating body. Vice President Clinton, himself selected by the caucus, wrote of his disapproval of the caucus system.

The Federalists in 1808 again altered their presidential selection process, holding a secret meeting of party leaders in August of that year to choose the ticket. The meeting, held in New York City, was initially called by the Federalist members of the Massachusetts legislature. Twenty-five to thirty party leaders from seven states, all north of the Potomac River except South Carolina, attended the national meeting. There was some discussion of choosing Vice President George Clinton, a dissident Democratic-Republican, for the presidency, but the meeting ultimately selected the Federalist candidates of 1804: Charles Cotesworth Pinckney and Rufus King.

ELECTION OF 1812

The Democratic-Republicans held their quadrennial nominating caucus in May 1812. Eighty-three of the party's 138 members of Congress attended, with the New England and New York delegations poorly represented. The New York delegation was sympathetic to the candidacy of the state's lieutenant governor, De Witt Clinton, who was maneuvering for the Federalist nomination, while New England was noticeably upset with the Madison foreign policy that was leading to war with England. President Madison was renominated with a near-unanimous total, receiving eighty-two votes.

John Langdon of New Hampshire was chosen for vice president by a wide margin, collecting sixty-four votes to sixteen for Gov. Elbridge Gerry of Massachusetts. But Langdon declined the nomination, citing his age (seventy) as the reason. In a second caucus, held in June, Gerry was a runaway winner with seventy-four votes.

In 1812, as four years earlier, the Federalists held a secret meeting in New York City. It was more than twice the size of the 1808 gathering, with seventy representatives from eleven states attending the three-day meeting in September. Delegates were sent to the conference by Federalist general committees, with all but nine of the delegates coming from the New England and Middle Atlantic states.

Debate centered on whether to run a separate Federalist ticket or to endorse the candidacy of De Witt Clinton, the nephew of George Clinton. The younger Clinton already had been nominated for the presidency by the New York Democratic-Republican caucus, and the Federalists ultimately adopted a resolution approving his candidacy and that of Jared Ingersoll. Ingersoll was a Pennsylvania Federalist who was initially nominated for vice president by a party legislative caucus in that state.

ELECTION OF 1816

The Federalist Party was nearly extinct by 1816 and did not hold any type of meeting to nominate candidates for president and vice president. As a result, nomination by the Democratic-Republican caucus was tantamount to election. Only fifty-eight members of Congress attended the first caucus in the House chamber. With the expectation of better attendance, a second caucus was held several days later in mid-March 1816 and drew 119 senators and representatives. By a vote of sixty-five to fifty-four, Secretary of State James Monroe was nominated for president, defeating Secretary of War William H. Crawford of Georgia. Forty of Crawford's votes came from five states: Georgia, Kentucky, New Jersey, New York, and North Carolina. The vice-presidential nomination went to New York governor Daniel D. Tompkins, who easily outdistanced Pennsylvania governor Simon Snyder, eighty-five to thirty.

The nominations of Monroe and Tompkins revived a Virginia-New York alliance that extended back to the late eighteenth century. With the lone exception of 1812, every Democratic-Republican ticket from 1800 until 1824 was composed of a candidate from Virginia and a vice-presidential candidate from New York.

While the collapse of the Federalists ensured Democratic-Republican rule, it also increased intraparty friction and spurred further attacks on the caucus system. Twenty-two Democratic-Republican members of Congress were absent from the second party caucus, and at least fifteen were known to be opposed to the system. Historian Edward Stanwood wrote that there were mass meetings around the country to protest the caucus system. Opponents claimed that the writers of the Constitution did not envision the caucus, that presidential nominating should not be a function of Congress and that the caucus system encouraged candidates to curry the favor of Congress.

ELECTION OF 1820

The 1820 election came during the "Era of Good Feelings," a phrase coined by a Boston publication, the *Columbian Centinel,* to describe a brief period of virtual one-party rule in the United States. With only one candidate, President James Monroe, there was no need for a caucus. One was called, but fewer than fifty of the Democratic-Republicans' 191 members of Congress attended.

The caucus voted unanimously to make no nominations and passed a resolution explaining that it was inexpedient to do so. Despite the fact that Monroe and Tompkins were not formally renominated, electoral slates were filed on their behalf. They both received nearly unanimous Electoral College victories.

Demise of the Caucus

In 1824 there was still only one party, but within this party there was an abundance of candidates for the presidency: Secretary of State John Quincy Adams of Massachusetts, Sen. Andrew Jackson of Tennessee, Secretary of War John C. Calhoun of South Carolina, House Speaker Henry Clay of Kentucky, and Secretary of the Treasury William H. Crawford. It was generally assumed that Crawford was the strongest candidate among members of Congress and would win a caucus if one were held; therefore, Crawford's opponents joined the growing list of caucus opponents.

In early February 1824, eleven Democratic-Republican members of Congress issued a call for a caucus to be held in the middle of the month. Their call was countered by twenty-four

"We must always have party distinctions."
—Martin Van Buren, 1827

other members of Congress from fifteen states who deemed it "inexpedient under existing circumstances" to hold a caucus. They claimed that 181 members of Congress were resolved not to attend if a caucus were held.

When the caucus convened in mid-February, only sixty-six members of Congress were present, with three-quarters of those attending from just four states—Georgia, New York, North Carolina, and Virginia. As expected, Crawford won the presidential nomination, receiving sixty-four votes. Selected for vice president was Albert Gallatin of Pennsylvania, who received fifty-seven votes.

The caucus adopted a resolution defending its actions as "the best means of collecting and concentrating the feelings and wishes of the people of the Union upon this important subject." A committee was appointed to write an address to the people. As written, the text of the address viewed with alarm the "dismemberment" of the Democratic-Republican Party.

The caucus nomination proved to be an albatross for Crawford as his opponents denounced him as the candidate of "King Caucus." Reflecting the increasing democratization of American politics, other presidential candidates relied on nominations by state legislatures to legitimize their presidential ambitions. However, in an attempt to narrow the field, the candidates had to negotiate among themselves.

Calhoun alone withdrew to become the vice-presidential candidate of all the anticaucus entries. Adams offered the vice presidency to Jackson as "an easy and dignified retirement to his old age." Jackson refused. Other maneuvers were equally unsuccessful, so that four presidential candidates remained in the field to collect electoral votes, subsequently throwing the election into the House of Representatives, where Adams won.

The election of 1828 proved to be a transitional one in the development of the presidential nominating process. The caucus was dead, but the national nominating convention was not yet born. Jackson was nominated by the legislature of his native Tennessee and in October 1825, three years before the election, accepted the nomination in a speech before the legislature. He accepted Vice President Calhoun as his running mate, after it was proposed in January 1827 by the *United States Telegraph,* a pro-Jackson paper in Washington. A Pennsylvania state convention paired President Adams with Secretary of the Treasury Richard Rush of Pennsylvania, a ticket that Adams' supporters in other states accepted. Both Jackson and Adams were endorsed by other legislatures, conventions, and meetings.

Trend Toward Conventions

The birth of the national convention system came in 1831, seven years after the death of the caucus. The caucus system collapsed when a field of candidates appeared who would not acquiesce to the choice of one caucus-approved candidate. But other factors were present to undermine the caucus system. These included changes in voting procedures and an expansion of suffrage. Between 1800 and 1824 the proportion of states in which the electors were chosen by popular vote rather than by the state legislature increased from four out of sixteen to eighteen out of twenty-four. In 1828 the popular vote reached 1.1 million, compared with fewer than 400,000 in 1824. A broader base of support than the congressional caucus became essential for presidential aspirants.

State legislatures, state conventions, and mass meetings all emerged in the 1820s to challenge the caucus. The trend to democratization of the presidential nominating process, as evidenced by the expansion of suffrage and increased importance of the popular vote for president, led shortly to creation of the national nominating convention. The convention system, initiated by the Anti-Masons in 1831, was adopted by all the major parties before the end of the decade.

The birth of the national nominating convention was a milestone in the evolution of the presidential nominating process. Political scientist V. O. Key Jr. summarized some of the major forces that brought about the rise of the convention system:

The destruction of the caucus represented more than a mere change in the method of nomination. Its replacement by the convention was regarded as the removal from power of self-appointed oligarchies that had usurped the right to nominate. The new system, the convention, gave, or so it was supposed, the mass of party members an opportunity to participate in nominations. These events occurred as the domestic winds blew in from the growing West, as the suffrage was being broadened, and as the last vestiges of the early aristocratic leadership were disappearing. Sharp alterations in the distribution of power were taking place, and they were paralleled by the shifts in methods of nomination.

With the establishment of the national convention came the reemergence of the two-party system. Unlike the Founders, who were suspicious of competitive parties, some political leaders in the late 1820s and 1830s viewed the existence of opposing parties favorably. One of the most prominent of these men, Martin Van Buren, a leading organizer of Jackson's 1828 election victory and himself president after Jackson, had written in 1827: "We must always have party distinctions."

CHAPTER 2

Presidential Primaries

THE QUADRENNIAL PROCESS of electing a president has two distinct parts—the nominating process and the general election. In contrast to the stable character of the general election—a one-day nationwide vote on the first Tuesday after the first Monday in November—the nominating process has changed many times in the nation's history.

Modifications in the nominating process have been dramatic—beginning with congressional caucuses in the early nineteenth century, through the heyday of the national conventions over the next century and a half, to the present nominating system, where conventions merely ratify the choices made months earlier by Democratic and Republican primary voters.

While originating in the Progressive Era in the early twentieth century, primaries were few and far between until after the 1968 election. The Democrats' tumultuous convention in Chicago that year encouraged both parties, but the Democrats in particular, to look for ways to open the nominating process to broader participation. Primaries quickly mushroomed—from fifteen in 1968, to thirty-six in 1980, to forty-four (including those in the District of Columbia and Puerto Rico) in 2000, declining slightly to thirty-five for Democrats in 2004, and more severely to thirty-one (including five cancelled uncontested primaries) for Republicans.

Their significance increased as well. Gone were the days when candidates could win their party's nomination without entering the primaries. No nominee of either major party has done so since Democrat Hubert H. Humphrey in 1968. Gone too were the days when candidates could win their party's nomination without first proving broad-based popularity among millions of voters. Since Democrat George McGovern in 1972, every major party nominee has first been his party's highest vote-getter in the primaries. In the process, the once climactic conventions have become little more than giant pep rallies, ratifying the choices of Democratic and Republican primary voters and providing the staging ground for the parties' general election campaigns.

The greater role of primary voters has also meant that the ability to mobilize voters has become more important than the bargaining skills of professional politicians. As a result, nominating campaigns now emphasize the skills of political consultants, the ability to use and influence the mass media, and the organizational clout of interest groups such as evangelical ministries and labor unions.

"Front-Loaded" Process

As the number of primaries has grown, more and more states have moved their primaries forward to dates near the be-ginning of the election year in a bid to heighten their influence (a process that has become known as "front-loading"). As a result, nominations have been settled earlier and earlier. In 1968 only New Hampshire's primary was held before the end of March. In 1980 ten states held primaries so early. By 1988 the number surpassed twenty. In 2004 the pace was accelerated: twenty-three states held primaries by the second week of March. Joined by states choosing delegates by party caucuses, two-thirds of the nation completed its actions by March 9. New Hampshire also moved its primary to January for the first time.

The result has been an increasingly truncated nominating process that has followed a clear pattern. Early votes in Iowa and New Hampshire have winnowed the field to a handful of candidates. Then, after a short period of unpredictability, one candidate has scored a knockout in the glut of March primaries—a victory ratified by a string of essentially meaningless primary votes over the spring months.

The campaigns of 2000 were typical. Among Republicans, Sen. John McCain of Arizona routed the GOP front-runner, Gov. George W. Bush of Texas, in New Hampshire and battled him in scattered primaries during February. But once the calendar flipped to March, Bush's superior organization and resources enabled him to win convincingly on March 7, when eleven primaries were held across the nation. Bush's triumphs—including the featured events in California, New York, and Ohio—drove McCain from the race. The Democratic presidential contest ended at the same time, as Vice President Albert "Al" Gore Jr. defeated former senator Bill Bradley of New Jersey in all eleven of the day's Democratic primaries.

The same pattern held in the 2004 Democratic contest. Although Gov. Howard Dean of Vermont led early opinion polls, he lost in January to Sen. John F. Kerry of Massachusetts in the Iowa caucuses and the New Hampshire primary. In nine scattered contests in February, Kerry won seven states, losing only Oklahoma to Gen. Wesley Clark and South Carolina to Sen. John Edwards of North Carolina. Kerry ensured his nomination by victories in eight of nine additional states on March 2, including the heavily populated states of California, New York, and Ohio, with Dean's Vermont being the only exception. Kerry cleared away all remaining opposition by winning four southern primaries a week later and Illinois on March 16.

Cut out of any meaningful role in the year's nominating process were fifteen states, including New Jersey, North Carolina, and Pennsylvania, as well as a dozen other states, which chose their delegates after the competitive stage of the primary season had ended. Other major states such as Florida, Illinois, and Texas had only a minor role, holding their primaries after

Types of Primaries and Procedures

In many respects, the presidential nominating process is similar to a modern-day Alice in Wonderland. Its basic dynamics do not always appear logical. Primaries and caucuses are strewn across the calendar from January to June, culminating with party conventions in the summer. A nomination is won by a candidate attaining a majority of delegates, an honor that is formally bestowed at the conventions but for decades has informally occurred much earlier during the primary season.

Size is less important in determining a state's importance in the nominating process than its tradition and place on the calendar (early is best). Hence the quadrennial starring role for Iowa and New Hampshire, and the bit parts frequently assigned to larger states, such as Pennsylvania or Texas.

States have different ground rules in the nominating process. Some have caucuses, many more have primaries. Almost all primaries currently allocate a state's delegates in line with the voters' presidential preference, but a few are nonbinding "beauty contests," with the delegates elected independently of the preference vote.

Rules on voter participation vary from state to state. Some states hold "closed" contests, which are open only to a party's registered voters. Some hold "semi-open" events, which allow independent voters to participate along with registered members of the party. About half the states have "open" primaries or caucuses, in which any registered voter can participate. The bulk of these states do not have party registration to begin with.

The parties themselves also have different playing fields. From 1980 to 2000, Democrats did not allow any states except Iowa, New Hampshire, and sometimes Maine to hold a primary or caucus before early March, but the party loosened these rules in 2004. Republicans have had no such restriction, and in some years a state or two on the GOP side has voted in advance of Iowa and New Hampshire.

Since 1984, Democrats have reserved between 10 and 20 percent of their delegate seats for high-level party and elected officials (such as Democratic governors, members of Congress, and members of the party's national committee). Often called "superdelegates," these automatic delegates do not have to declare a presidential preference, although they usually follow their state's primary vote. (Republicans did not have "superdelegates" until their 2004 convention.) Since 1992, Democrats have required states to distribute delegates among their candidates in proportion to their vote, statewide and in congressional districts, with 15 percent required to win a share.

Republicans, in contrast, allow a variety of delegate allocation methods, including proportional representation, statewide winner-take-all (in which the candidate winning the most votes statewide wins all the delegates), congressional district and statewide winner-take-all (in which the high vote-getter in a district wins that district's delegates and the high vote-getter statewide wins all the at-large delegates), or some combination of the three.

Still another method is the selection of individual delegates in a "loophole," or direct election, primary. In Republican caucus states, delegates often run as individuals and frequently are not officially allocated to any candidate.

How delegates are actually elected can vary from state to state. Most primary states hold presidential preference votes, in which voters choose among the candidates who have qualified for the ballot in their states. Although preference votes may be binding or nonbinding, in most states the vote is binding on the delegates, who are elected in the primary itself or chosen outside of it by a caucus process, by a state committee, or by the candidates who have qualified to win delegates.

For those primaries in which the preference vote is binding on delegates, state laws may vary as to the number of ballots through which delegates at the convention must remain committed. Delegates may be bound for as short as one ballot or as long as a candidate remains in the race. For the first time in 1980 national Democratic rules bound delegates for the first ballot unless released beforehand by the candidate they were elected to support. The rule became a flash point of controversy that year between the front-runner, President Jimmy Carter, and his major challenger, Sen. Edward M. Kennedy of Massachusetts. While Kennedy wanted the binding rule dropped, the Carter forces prevailed in having the rule sustained at the 1980 convention, allowing Carter to win the nomination after one ballot. During the quadrennial review of party rules after the election, the binding rule was dropped, but presidential candidates retained the right to replace disloyal delegates with more faithful ones.

Until 1980 the Republicans had a rule requiring delegates bound to a specific candidate by state law in primary states to vote for that candidate at the convention regardless of their personal presidential preferences. That rule was repealed at the party's 1980 convention.

The final authority on delegate selection is the party itself, at its national convention. Regardless of state law or previous procedures, the convention can decide which delegates to seat to represent a state, and that decision is binding on the courts. Disputes on delegate credentials have sometimes been critical in party conventions, for example in the Republican nomination of Dwight Eisenhower in 1952 and the Democratic nomination of George McGovern in 1972.

the decisive votes of March 2. Primaries were of no consequence for the Republicans in 2004, given the absence of competition to President Bush.

The last time that either the Democratic or Republican Party had an extended tug-of-war for its presidential nomination was 1984, when former vice president Walter F. Mondale and Sen. Gary Hart of Colorado battled into the final week of Democratic primaries before Mondale won the final delegates needed to secure his nomination. Neither party has had a nominating contest that was even vaguely competitive at the time of its national convention since the 1976 Republican race between President Gerald R. Ford and former governor Ronald Reagan of California.

"Front-loading" has worked to the advantage of the most prominent candidates. In the contemporary system, only aspirants who already have popular recognition and campaign money can realistically contest in what is almost a nationwide primary. In every contest since 1980 (with Dean in 2004 a possible exception), the eventual nominee has either led in opinion polls or raised the most money—and usually both—before, and often many months before, any voters have actually cast their primary ballots.

The need for early public recognition has resulted in the disappearance of the fabled "dark horse," a candidate of little prominence who develops strength over the course of the primary season. The large cost of widespread campaigning has further limited opportunities for surprises. As a result, candidates are withdrawing earlier in the nominating process, even before the first primary vote, as happened with Sen. Elizabeth Dole of North Carolina in the Republican 2000 race and Sen. Bob Graham of Florida in the Democratic 2004 race. The increasing cost of these campaigns has also undermined the system of public funding for presidential campaigns, with the most prominent candidates relying on private contributions rather than federal funds. These funds were first rejected by Bush in 2000; following his precedent, the most prominent Democrats in 2004—Dean and Kerry—relied only on private contributions for their extensive war chests.

An Evolutionary Process

During the early years of the nation, presidential nominations were decided by party caucuses in Congress (derided by their critics as "King Caucus"). At the dawn of the Jacksonian era in the 1830s, though, the nominating role shifted to national conventions, a broader-based venue where party leaders from around the country held sway.

In the early twentieth century, presidential primaries appeared on the scene, adding a new element of grassroots democracy and voter input. But for the next half century, the primaries were relatively few in number and played a limited advisory role. Nominations continued to be settled in the party conventions.

After World War II, American society became more mobile and media-oriented, and once-powerful party organizations began to lose their clout. An increasing number of presidential aspirants saw the primaries as a way to generate popular support that might overcome the resistance of party leaders. Both Republican Dwight D. Eisenhower in 1952 and Democrat John F. Kennedy in 1960 scored a string of primary victories that demonstrated their vote-getting appeal and made their nominations possible. Yet conventions continued to be the most important part of the nominating process until 1968.

LEGACY OF THE PROGRESSIVE ERA

Primaries may seem entrenched in the electoral process, but they are relatively recent replacements for the old smoke-filled rooms where party bosses once dictated the choice of presidential nominees. Presidential primaries originated as an outgrowth of the Progressive movement in the early twentieth century. Pro-

Democrat Hubert H. Humphrey in 1968 was the last candidate to win a major party's presidential nomination without entering the primaries.

gressives, fighting state and municipal corruption, objected to the links between political bosses and big business and advocated returning the government to the people.

Part of this "return to the people" was a turn away from what were looked on as boss-dominated conventions. It was only a matter of time before the primary idea spread from state and local elections to presidential contests. Because there was no provision for a nationwide primary, state primaries were initiated to choose delegates to the national party conventions (delegate-selection primaries) and to register voters' preferences on their parties' eventual presidential nominees (preference primaries).

Florida enacted the first presidential primary law in 1901. The law gave party officials an option of holding a party primary to choose any party candidate for public office, as well as delegates to the national conventions. However, there was no provision for placing names of presidential candidates on the ballot—either in the form of a preference vote or with information indicating the preference of the candidates for convention delegates.

Wisconsin's progressive Republican governor, Robert M. La Follette, gave a major boost to the presidential primary following the 1904 Republican National Convention. At that convention, the credentials of La Follette's progressive delegation were rejected and a regular Republican delegation from Wisconsin seated instead. Angered by what he considered unfair treatment, La Follette returned to his home state and began pushing for a presidential primary law. The result was a 1905 Wisconsin law mandating the direct election of national convention delegates.

Votes Cast and Delegates Selected in Presidential Primaries, 1912–2004

| | Democratic Party | | | Republican Party | | | Total | | |
Year	Number of primaries	Votes cast	Delegates selected through primaries (%)	Number of primaries	Votes cast	Delegates selected through primaries (%)	Votes cast	Delegates selected through primaries (%)
1912	12	974,775	32.9	13	2,261,240	41.7	3,236,015	37.3
1916	20	1,187,691	53.5	20	1,923,374	58.9	3,111,065	56.2
1920	16	571,671	44.6	20	3,186,248	57.8	3,757,919	51.2
1924	14	763,858	35.5	17	3,525,185	45.3	4,289,043	40.4
1928	16	1,264,220	42.2	15	4,110,288	44.9	5,374,508	43.5
1932	16	2,952,933	40.0	14	2,346,996	37.7	5,299,929	38.8
1936	14	5,181,808	36.5	12	3,319,810	37.5	8,501,618	37.0
1940	13	4,468,631	35.8	13	3,227,875	38.8	7,696,506	37.3
1944	14	1,867,609	36.7	13	2,271,605	38.7	4,139,214	37.7
1948	14	2,151,865	36.3	12	2,653,255	36.0	4,805,120	36.1
1952	16	4,928,006	38.7	13	7,801,413	39.0	12,729,419	38.8
1956	19	5,832,592	42.7	19	5,828,272	44.8	11,660,864	43.7
1960	16	5,687,742	38.3	15	5,537,967	38.6	11,224,631	38.5
1964	16	6,247,435	45.7	16	5,935,339	45.6	12,182,774	45.6
1968	15	7,535,069	40.2	15	4,473,551	38.1	12,008,620	39.1
1972	21	15,993,965	65.3	20	6,188,281	56.8	22,182,246	61.0
1976	27	16,052,652	76.0	26	10,374,125	71.0	26,426,777	73.5
1980	34	18,747,825	71.8	34	12,690,451	76.0	31,438,276	73.7
1984	29	18,009,217	52.4	25	6,575,651	71.0	24,584,868	59.6
1988	36	22,961,936	66.6	36	12,165,115	76.9	35,127,051	70.2
1992	39	20,239,385	66.9	38	12,696,547	83.9	32,935,932	72.7
1996	35	10,996,395	65.3	42	14,233,939	84.6	25,230,334	69.2
2000	40	14,045,745	64.6	43	17,156,117	83.8	31,201,862	70.8
2004	35	16,535,823	67.5	26	8,008,070	55.5	24,543,893	<<ADD>>

Source: Percentages of delegates selected are from Congressional Quarterly.

The law, however, did not include a provision for indicating the delegates' presidential preference.

La Follette's sponsorship of the delegate-selection primary helped make the concept a part of the progressive political program. The growth of the progressive movement rapidly resulted in the enactment of presidential primary laws in other states.

The next step in presidential primaries—the preferential vote for president—took place in Oregon. There, in 1910, Sen. Jonathan Bourne, a progressive Republican colleague of La Follette (then a senator), sponsored a referendum to establish a presidential preference primary, with delegates legally bound to support the primary winner. By 1912, with Oregon in the lead, fully a dozen states had enacted presidential primary laws that provided for either direct election of delegates, a preferential vote, or both. By 1916 the number had expanded to twenty-six states.

The first major test of the impact of presidential primary laws—in 1912—demonstrated that victories in the primaries did not ensure a candidate's nomination. Former president Theodore Roosevelt, campaigning in twelve Republican primaries, won nine of them, including Ohio, the home state of incumbent Republican president William Howard Taft. Roosevelt lost to Taft by a narrow margin in Massachusetts and to La Follette in North Dakota and Wisconsin.

Despite this impressive string of primary victories, the convention rejected Roosevelt in favor of Taft. With primaries confined to a quarter of the states, Taft supporters kept control through the Republican National Committee (RNC), which ran the convention, and the convention's credentials committee, which ruled on contested delegates. Moreover, Taft was backed by many state organizations, especially in the South, where most delegates were chosen by caucuses or conventions dominated by party leaders.

On the Democratic side, the convention more closely reflected the primary results. Gov. Woodrow Wilson of New Jersey and Speaker of the House Champ Clark of Missouri were closely matched in total primary votes, with Wilson only 29,632 votes ahead of Clark. Wilson emerged with the nomination after a long convention struggle with Clark.

DECLINE AND REVIVAL OF THE PRIMARIES

After the first wave of enthusiasm for presidential primaries, interest waned. By 1935, eight states had repealed their presidential primary laws. The diminution of reform zeal during the 1920s, the preoccupation of the country with the Great Depression in the 1930s, and war in the 1940s appeared to have been leading factors in this decline. Also, party leaders were not enthusiastic about primaries; the cost of conducting them was relatively high, both for the candidates and the states. Many presidential candidates ignored the primaries, and voter participation often was low.

But after World War II, interest picked up again. Some politicians with presidential ambitions, knowing the party leadership was not enthusiastic about their candidacies, entered the primaries to try to generate political momentum. In 1948 Harold Stassen, Republican governor of Minnesota from 1939 to 1943, entered presidential primaries in opposition to the Republican organization and made some headway before losing in Oregon to Gov. Thomas E. Dewey of New York. And in 1952 Sen. Estes Kefauver, D-Tenn., riding a wave of public recognition as head of the Senate Organized Crime Investigating Committee, challenged Democratic Party leaders by winning several primaries, including an upset of President Harry S. Truman in New Hampshire. The struggle between Gen. Dwight D. Eisenhower and Sen. Robert A. Taft for the Republican Party nomination that year also stimulated interest in the primaries.

In 1960 Sen. John F. Kennedy of Massachusetts challenged Sen. Hubert Humphrey of Minnesota in two primaries: Wisconsin, which bordered on Humphrey's home state, and West Virginia, a labor state with few Catholic voters. (Kennedy was Roman Catholic, and some questioned whether voters would elect a Catholic president.) After Kennedy won both primaries, Humphrey withdrew from the race. The efforts of party leaders to draft an alternative to Kennedy came to be viewed as undemocratic by rank-and-file voters. Primaries now significantly challenged approval by party leaders as the preferred route to the nomination. Similarly, Sen. Barry M. Goldwater, R-Ariz., in 1964 and former vice president Richard Nixon in 1968 were able to use the primaries to show their vote-getting and organizational abilities on the way to becoming their party's presidential nominees.

Party domination of presidential nominations ended in 1968, amid the turmoil of the Vietnam War. Although the Republicans calmly nominated Nixon with little concern for the primaries, the nominating process tore the Democrats apart. Sens. Eugene McCarthy of Minnesota and Robert F. Kennedy of New York used the handful of Democratic primaries that spring to protest the war in Vietnam, together taking more than two-thirds of the party's primary vote and driving President Lyndon B. Johnson from the race.

History might have been different if Kennedy had not been assassinated after his victory in the California primary that June. But without Kennedy on the scene, the party's embattled leadership was able to maintain a tenuous control of the convention that August in Chicago, nominating Vice President Humphrey, who had not competed in a single primary state.

But Humphrey's nomination came at a price. Extensive street demonstrations in opposition to Humphrey and the war were met by brutal police force. On the floor of the convention, insurgent delegations were rebuffed, amid televised curses and fist fights. For the first time in several generations, the legitimacy of the convention itself was thrown into question. As an outgrowth, a series of Democratic rules review commissions began to overhaul the presidential nominating process to encourage much greater grassroots participation.

Nominations Reform: Reversal of Fortune

Democrats and Republicans have considered and enacted reforms of the nominating process frequently since the 1960s. Typically, the party that has lost the presidential election is more active, hoping to improve its chances in the next election, while the winners bask in complacency.

The initial thrust toward reform came from the Democrats, after their narrow defeat in the 1968 election. A commission headed by Sen. George McGovern of South Dakota established standards for broader and timely participation in the nominating process, which resulted in widespread adoption of primaries in place of party caucuses. Republicans followed suit, although more cautiously and more slowly.

THE DEMOCRATS EXPERIMENT WITH NEW RULES

Despite the growing importance of primaries, party leaders until 1968 maintained some control of the nominating process. With only a handful of the fifteen to twenty primaries regularly contested, candidates could count on a short primary season. The primaries began in New Hampshire in March, then candidates tested their appeal during the spring in Wisconsin, Nebraska, Oregon, and California before resuming their courtship of party leaders. In 1968—admittedly an unusual year, with incumbent Democratic president Lyndon B. Johnson suddenly withdrawing from his race for reelection, and the leading Democratic candidate (Sen. Robert F. Kennedy of New York) assassinated a few weeks before the convention—Vice President Hubert H. Humphrey was able to gain the party's nomination without entering a single primary.

But after 1968, the Democrats began altering their nominating rules, in an effort to reduce the alienation of liberals and minorities from the political system and to allow voters to choose their leaders. Victors in 1968, and four of the five presidential elections that followed, the Republicans were slow to make any changes to their rules. (See boxes, "Changes in Democrats' Nominating Rules," p. 30; "GOP Primary Rules," p. 32.) The immediate result was a dramatic increase in presidential primaries that enhanced the chances of outsiders and produced Democratic presidential candidates such as McGovern, a liberal who lost in a landslide to Nixon in 1972, and Jimmy Carter, a former governor of Georgia who beat incumbent President Gerald R. Ford in 1976 but lost to Ronald Reagan in 1980.

In 1980 a then-record thirty-seven primaries, including those in the District of Columbia and Puerto Rico, provided more opportunity for mass participation in the nominating process than ever before. President Carter and Republican nominee Reagan were the clear winners of the long primary season. Although Carter received a bare majority of the cumulative Democratic primary vote, he was still more than 2.5 million votes ahead of his major rival, Sen. Edward M. Kennedy of Massachusetts. With no opposition in the late primary contests, Reagan emerged as a more one-sided choice of GOP primary voters. He finished nearly 4.8 million votes ahead of his closest competitor, George Bush.

Disheartened by Carter's massive defeat in 1980, the Democrats revised their nominating rules for the 1984 election. The party created a new bloc of so-called "superdelegates"—that is, delegate seats were reserved for party leaders who were not formally committed to any presidential candidate. This reform had

Selection by Caucus

In the current primary-dominated era of presidential politics, which began three decades ago, caucuses have survived in the quiet backwater of the nominating process. The impact of caucuses decreased in the 1970s as the number of primaries grew dramatically. Previously, a candidate sought to run well in primary states mainly to have a bargaining chip with which to deal with powerful leaders in the caucus states. Republicans Barry Goldwater in 1964 and Richard Nixon in 1968 and Democrat Hubert H. Humphrey in 1968 all built up solid majorities among caucus state delegates that carried them to their parties' nominations. Humphrey did not compete in a single primary state in 1968.

After 1968, candidates placed their principal emphasis on primaries. First George McGovern in 1972—and then incumbent Republican president Gerald R. Ford and Democratic challenger Jimmy Carter in 1976—won nomination by securing large majorities of the primary state delegates. Neither McGovern nor Ford won a majority of the caucus state delegates. Carter was able to win a majority only after his opponents' campaigns collapsed.

More recently, there has been an increase in the number of states employing caucuses to choose convention delegates, mostly in smaller states. The increase was slight among Democrats, but more extensive among Republicans in 2004, when the party saw little reason to spend money or time in an uncontested renomination of President George W. Bush. The primaries continue to be the major prizes and to receive the most attention from the media and the candidates.

Complex Method

Compared with a primary, the caucus system is complicated. Instead of focusing on a single primary election ballot, the caucus presents a multitiered system that involves meetings scheduled over several weeks, sometimes even months. There is mass participation at the first level only, with meetings often lasting several hours and attracting only the most enthusiastic and dedicated party members.

The operation of the caucus varies from state to state, and each party has its own set of rules. Most begin with precinct caucuses or some other type of local mass meeting open to all party voters. Participants, often publicly declaring their votes, elect delegates to the next stage in the process.

In smaller states such as Delaware and Hawaii, delegates are elected directly to a state convention, where the national convention delegates are chosen. In larger states such as Iowa, there is at least one more step, sometimes two. Delegates in Iowa are elected at the precinct caucuses to county conventions, which are followed by congressional district conventions and the state convention, the two levels where the national convention delegates are chosen.

Participation, even at the first level of the caucus process, is much lower than in primaries. Caucus participants usually are local party leaders and activists. Many rank-and-file voters find a caucus complex, confusing, or intimidating.

As a result, caucuses are usually considered tailor-made for candidates with a cadre of passionately dedicated supporters. That was evident as long ago as 1972, when a surprisingly strong showing in the Iowa precinct caucuses helped to propel Sen. George McGovern of South Dakota, an ardent foe of the Vietnam War, toward the Democratic nomination.

In a caucus state the focus is on one-on-one campaigning. Time, not money, is usually the most valuable resource. Because organization and personal campaigning are so important, an early start is far more crucial in a caucus state than in a primary. Because only a small segment of the electorate is targeted in most caucus states, candidates usually use media advertising sparingly.

---

two main goals. First, Democratic leaders wanted to ensure that the party's elected officials would participate in the nomination decision at the convention. Second, they wanted to ensure that these uncommitted party leaders could play a major role in selecting the presidential nominee if no candidate was a clear front-runner.

While the reforms of the 1970s were designed to give more influence to grassroots activists and less to party regulars, this revision was intended to bring about a deliberative process in which experienced party leaders could help select a consensus Democratic nominee with a strong chance to win the presidency.

The Democrats' new rules had some expected, as well as unexpected, results. For the first time since 1968, the number of primaries declined and the number of caucuses increased. The Democrats held only thirty primaries in 1984 (including the District of Columbia and Puerto Rico). Yet, as with McGovern in 1972 and Carter in 1976, Colorado senator Gary Hart used the primaries to pull ahead (temporarily) of former vice president Walter F. Mondale, an early front-runner whose strongest ties were to the party leadership and its traditional core elements. In 1984 the presence of superdelegates was important because about four out of five backed Mondale. (Still, Mondale wound up with more primary votes than Hart.)

A few critics regarded the seating of superdelegates as undemocratic, and there were calls for reducing their numbers. Yet to those of most influence within the party, the superdelegates had served their purpose. In the following years, the Democratic National Committee (DNC) set aside additional seats for party leaders, increasing the number of superdelegates from 14 percent of the delegates in 1984 to 18 percent in 1996. All members of the DNC were guaranteed convention seats, as were all Democratic governors and members of Congress.

The lone exception is Iowa. As the kick-off point for the quadrennial nominating process, Iowa has recently become a more expensive stop for ambitious presidential candidates, as they must shell out money for everything from straw votes to radio and TV advertising. But the accent in Iowa, as in other caucus states, is still on grassroots organization. That was underscored in 1996, when the late-starting campaign of wealthy publisher Malcolm S. "Steve" Forbes Jr. spent lavishly on an Iowa media blitz that netted only 10 percent of the Republican caucus vote.

Although the basic steps in the caucus process are the same for both parties, the rules that govern them are vastly different. Democratic rules have been revamped substantially since 1968, establishing national standards for grassroots participation. Republican rules have remained largely unchanged, with the states given wide latitude in drawing up their delegate-selection plans.

Caucuses

For both the Republican and Democratic parties, the percentage of delegates elected from caucus states was on a sharp decline throughout the 1970s. But the Democrats broke the downward trend and elected more delegates by the caucus process in 1980 than in 1976.

Between 1980 and 1984, six states switched from a primary to a caucus system; none the other way. Since 1984 the trend has turned back toward primaries. In 1996 primaries were held in forty-one states, the District of Columbia, and Puerto Rico. The Democrats elected 65.3 percent of their national convention delegates in primaries, against only 16.8 percent in caucuses. (The remaining 17.9 percent were "superdelegate" party and elected officials.) The Republicans in 1992 chose 84.6 percent of delegates in primaries and the rest by caucus or state committee, with no superdelegates. The proportions have stayed roughly the same since then.

A strong showing in the caucuses by Walter F. Mondale in 1984 led many Democrats—and not only supporters of his rivals—to conclude that caucuses are inherently unfair. The mainstream Democratic coalition of party activists, labor union members, and teachers dominated the caucuses in Mondale's behalf.

The caucus also came in for criticism in 1988. The Iowa Democratic caucuses were seen as an unrepresentative test dominated by liberal interest groups. The credibility of the caucuses was shaken by the withdrawal from the race of the two winners—Democrat Richard A. Gephardt and Republican Robert J. "Bob" Dole—within a month after the caucuses were held. Furthermore, several other state caucuses featured vicious infighting between supporters of various candidates.

Yet in 1996 and again in 2000, Iowa was back enjoying center stage. In both years, the campaigns of the Republican nominee—Dole and Gov. George W. Bush of Texas, respectively—were successfully launched in Iowa, as was the campaign of Vice President Albert "Al" Gore Jr. in 2000 on the Democratic side. In 2004 Iowa became an important turning point in the party's contest, when Sen. John F. Kerry overcame the initial enthusiasm for Gov. Howard Dean of Vermont. Kerry then went on to win the following primaries.

The major complaint about the caucus process is that it does not involve enough voters, and that the low turnouts are not so representative of voter sentiment as a higher-turnout primary. The combined turnout for both parties for the Iowa caucuses in 2000, for example, was roughly 150,000, less than half the number that turned out for the New Hampshire primary a week later. Additionally, Iowa's population is more than twice that of New Hampshire.

Staunch defenders, however, believe a caucus has party-building attributes a primary cannot match. They note that several hours at a caucus can involve voters in a way that quickly casting a primary ballot does not. Following caucus meetings, the state party comes away with lists of thousands of voters who can be tapped to volunteer time or money, or even to run for local office. While the multitiered caucus process is often a chore for the state party to organize, a primary is substantially more expensive.

MOVING THE WINDOWS

In the 1970s the primary calendar started slowly, giving little-known candidates the time to raise money and momentum after doing well in the early rounds. Most of the primaries then were held in May and June. But the schedule of the nominating process has been less favorable to dark horses since then. States began to move forward on the calendar in a bid to increase their influence, heightening the need for candidates to be well-organized and well-funded at the beginning of the primary season.

Democrats sought to put a brake on the calendar sprawl toward the beginning of the election year by instituting the "window," which prohibited any of the party's primaries or caucuses from being held before early March, with the exception of Iowa, New Hampshire, and, for a while, Maine.

Many states crept right up to this early March firewall, scheduling their primary in March—gradually at first, but then in tidal wave proportions in 1988, with the creation of a full-scale primary vote across the South on the second Tuesday in March that came to be known as "Super Tuesday." By doing so they hoped to steer the nomination toward a centrist son of the South, such as Sen. Albert "Al" Gore Jr. of Tennessee.

The Democratic "window" proved to be a confining brick wall for the Democrats in 2000. With no primaries scheduled for five weeks after New Hampshire, the party and its likely nominee, Gore—now vice president—disappeared from the news, while Republican George W. Bush continued to gain media attention. Attempting to recoup in 2004, Democrats allowed states to select delegates as early as a week after New Hampshire, and eighteen states—mostly small in population—took advantage of the opportunity to hold nine primaries and nine caucuses.

Choosing a Running Mate: The Balancing Act

In modern times, with presidential candidates wrapping up their party's nominations early in the primary season, the greatest suspense before a national convention has centered on the selection of a running mate. But this closely watched selection process is a recent development.

During the country's first years, the runner-up for the presidency automatically took the second slot, although that system did not last long. In 1800 Thomas Jefferson and Aaron Burr found themselves in a tie for electoral votes, even though Jefferson was the Democratic-Republicans clear choice to be the top of the ticket. Burr's supporters, however, were unwilling to settle for the lesser office. The deadlock went to the House of Representatives, where Jefferson needed thirty-six ballots to clinch the presidency. It also led to the Twelfth Amendment to the U.S. Constitution, ratified in 1804, providing for separate Electoral College balloting for president and vice president.

With the emergence of political parties after 1800, candidates ran as teams. Once party conventions began in 1831, delegates, with the guidance of party bosses, began to do the choosing. Sometimes the vice presidency was used as a bargaining chip, as when Franklin D. Roosevelt won the critical support of Texas by endorsing Rep. John Nance Garner for the second slot.

Only in 1940 did presidential nominees begin regularly handpicking their running mates. That year, after failing to persuade Secretary of State Cordell Hull to accept the vice presidency, Franklin D. Roosevelt forced Henry A. Wallace on a reluctant Democratic convention by threatening to not run a third time if Wallace was rejected. Four years later, Roosevelt turned to Sen. Harry S. Truman to replace Wallace. The only exception to the

practice that Roosevelt established came in 1956, when Democrat Adlai E. Stevenson left the choice up to the convention.

If the selection of a running mate often resembled an afterthought, it could be because the position itself was not especially coveted. John Adams, the first to hold the job, once complained, "My country has in its wisdom contrived for me the most insignificant office that ever the intention of man contrived or his imagination conceived." More than a century later Thomas R. Marshall, Woodrow Wilson's vice president, expressed a similarly dismal view: "Once there were two brothers. One ran away to sea; the other was elected Vice President. And nothing was ever heard of either of them again."

Writing in *Atlantic* in 1974, historian Arthur Schlesinger Jr. suggested the office be done away with. "It is a doomed office," he commented. "The Vice President has only one serious thing to do: that is, to wait around for the President to die." In fact, however, the vice presidency has become a significant office in more recent times, both within government and politically. There is now a reasonable chance that whoever fills the position will get a chance to move up, either by succession or election. In 1988 George Bush became the first vice president to be elected directly to the White House since Martin Van Buren in 1836. As of 2000, fourteen presidents had held the second-ranking post, seven in the twentieth century.

Also, since the mid-1970s the vice presidency has evolved from the somnolent office it once was; during this period five vice presidents enjoyed responsibility their predecessors did not. Nelson A. Rockefeller, who served under Gerald R. Ford, was given considerable authority in domestic policy coordination. Walter F.

Despite the diffusion of primaries over more weeks, Democrats remained dissatisfied with the concentration of selection at the beginning of the election year. There was too little time, critics said, for voters to consider alternatives and to test the campaign mettle of the declared candidates. After their defeat in the 2004 election, Democrats established a new reform group, the Commission on Presidential Nomination Timing and Scheduling. It was to report in late 2005 on arrangements for the 2008 nominating contests.

REPUBLICAN EFFORTS

The Republican Party was slower to change its nominating procedures: it did not guarantee delegate seats to its leaders until the 2000 convention voted to make members of the RNC automatic "superdelegates" at the party's convention in 2004. Republicans had not acted before that in part because their rules permit less rigid pledging of delegates, which generally has led to substantial participation by Republican leaders, despite the absence of guarantees.

When they were regularly winning the White House in the 1970s and 1980s, Republicans showed little interest in tinkering

with the nominating process; they were happy to leave that as a concern of the Democrats. But once the GOP began to lose presidential elections in the 1990s, many Republicans began to decry the "front-loaded" primary calendar that produced nominees within a few weeks of voting.

At their convention in San Diego in 1996, Republicans approved a rules change designed to help spread out the calendar. States were offered bonus delegates the later they held their primary or caucus, but the proposal received few takers in 2000. Yet in the wake of that year's Bush-McCain contest, a party commission headed by former Tennessee senator and national GOP chairman Bill Brock recommended that the presidential primary calendar be dramatically overhauled, so that small states would vote first in 2004 and large states would vote last.

States were to be grouped into four "pods" of roughly equal number, with each pod voting over the course of a month. The initial calendar called for voting from March to June, but in the course of discussion the calendar was moved up a month to start in February and end in May. Still, the fourth pod was to include the largest states, holding roughly half the delegates. The idea was to slow the rush to judgment evident in the "front-

Mondale and George Bush helped to set policy for their respective presidents. Bill Clinton placed Albert "Al" Gore Jr. in charge of a "reinventing government" task force as well as environmental and high-tech initiatives. George W. Bush gave Richard B. Cheney wide influence throughout the government, particularly in foreign and defense policy. Many aspiring politicians now see the office as the premier base from which to campaign for the presidency.

Yet whoever is selected is often scrutinized for how well the choice balances (or unbalances) the ticket. One important factor is geography, which Clinton of Arkansas used unconventionally in choosing Sen. Gore of Tennessee to form the first successful all-southern ticket in 164 years. Because George W. Bush and his vice-presidential choice, Cheney, both lived in Texas before their nominations, Cheney had to return to Wyoming to fulfill the constitutional requirement that the two executive officials come from different states. Other traditional factors weighed by nominees are religion and ethnicity. In modern national politics, however, those considerations seemed to be losing their place to race, gender, and age. In 1984, for example, the Democrats chose Rep. Geraldine A. Ferraro of New York to be their vice-presidential candidate, the first woman to receive a major party nomination.

Although no African American has so far been selected by either party, many Democrats thought that Jesse Jackson deserved second place on the ticket in 1988. Jackson had received 29 percent of the primary vote to 43 percent for Michael Dukakis. Instead, the fifty-four-year-old Dukakis chose Sen. Lloyd Bentsen of Texas, then sixty-seven, balancing the Democratic ticket by age as well as geographically and philosophically.

Age has become an important criterion with the rise of the "baby-boomer" generation. In 1988 George Bush surprised many by selecting Sen. James Danforth "Dan" Quayle of Indiana. Quayle was forty-one years old and had a relatively brief career in politics—two terms in the House of Representatives before his election to the Senate in 1980. Because of Quayle's youth and good looks, it was even suggested by some critics that Bush had selected him to appeal to young voters and women. For his running mate, the forty-six-year-old Clinton, in another unbalancing act, selected someone in his age group (Gore, forty-four) rather than an elder statesperson such as Bentsen.

In 2000 Texas governor George W. Bush also took age into consideration, but in the opposite direction from his father, in choosing a running mate. The younger Bush chose Cheney, an experienced Washington hand, who was a former Wyoming representative and defense secretary in the elder Bush's administration.

When it was his turn atop the ticket in 2000, Gore too broke new ground. Rather than pick a southern baby-boomer as Clinton had, Gore chose Sen. Joseph I. Lieberman of Connecticut, the fifty-eight-year-old chair of the centrist Democratic Leadership Council and the first member of the Jewish faith to win a place on the national ticket of either major party. The Democrats' attention to age, as well as region, became evident again in 2004, when presidential candidate John F. Kerry chose a young southerner, Sen. John Edwards of North Carolina.

Recent presidential candidates, such as Gore and Kerry, have also developed a new practice, when they announced their choice of a vice-presidential candidate even before the convention convened. In so doing, they demonstrated the final loss of independent power by the national convention. Delegates now had no function other than to be cheerleaders at the campaign launch of leaders who had been chosen without any deliberation by the party delegates.

loaded" primary system by making it mathematically impossible for a candidate to amass a majority of delegates before most, if not all, of the states had voted.

The idea, dubbed the "Delaware Plan" because of its state of origin, was controversial, particularly among the larger states, who feared a loss of influence if they were required to vote en masse at the end of the primary season. Still, it won the approval of the rules committee in May 2000 and the full RNC on the eve of the party's convention that summer.

But the plan was defeated in the convention rules committee July 28, after the Bush campaign shifted from a position of neutrality to opposition. Several reasons were cited for the eleventh hour change of heart, including complaints from the big states over their potential loss of influence and fears of a loss of control by the states over their primary or caucus dates if the "Delaware Plan" were imposed. But it was also obvious that the Bush campaign wanted a harmonious convention without any contested issues on the floor. There was no effort to change the Republican nominating schedule in 2004, and by 2005 there was little interest in doing so for 2008.

Indeed, Republicans took a different tack in 2004, with many states returning to selection by state party caucuses and conventions, or canceling the scheduled primaries. The change was probably only a temporary reflection of the lack of a challenge to incumbent President Bush that year.

Even if Republicans had approved the "Delaware Plan," it still would have faced an uncertain future. Earlier in 2000, the rules committee of the Democratic Party had expressed support for the status quo and urged Republicans to embrace the Democratic primary calendar, which allowed Iowa and New Hampshire to vote first but prohibited other states from voting before the first Tuesday in March. Likewise, the Democratic evaluation under way in 2005 may later affect both parties and require some degree of GOP acquiescence.

REGIONAL PRIMARIES AND SUPER TUESDAYS

In addition to internal party concerns with the nominating process, other critics often cited the length of the primary season (nearly twice as long as the general election campaign), the expense,

Presidents' Reelection Chances

The record of U.S. presidential elections in the twentieth century and at the start of the twenty-first indicates that a smooth path to renomination is essential for incumbents seeking reelection. Every president who actively sought renomination during this period was successful. Those who were virtually unopposed within their party won another term. But all the presidents who faced significant opposition for renomination ended up losing in the general election.

The following chart shows the presidents who sought reelection to a second term since 1900, whether they had "clear sailing" or "tough sledding" for renomination and their fate in the general election.

Theodore Roosevelt did not seek renomination in 1908, after the completion of almost two full terms, even though he was eligible to run. However, four years later, he did seek another Republican nomination. Although he won most primaries, he was defeated at the Republican convention and then ran, unsuccessfully, as the Progressive Party candidate. Tellingly, President William H. Taft, who won the bitter fight against Roosevelt for the Republican nomination, lost in the general election to Democrat Woodrow Wilson.

Another two presidents—Harry S. Truman in 1952 and Lyndon B. Johnson in 1968—faced significant opposition at the end of their tenure and declined to run for another term. Truman was eligible for a third term because he was exempted from the Twentieth Amendment to the Constitution, which established the two-term limit. Johnson came to the presidency in 1963, completing John Kennedy's term, and was eligible for another four years.

A president with an asterisk (*) next to his name was, such as George W. Bush in 2004, completing his first full four-year term when he sought reelection. A dash (—) indicates there were no presidential preference primaries. The primary vote for President Johnson in 1964 included the vote cast for favorite sons and uncommitted delegate slates; Johnson was subsequently nominated by acclamation at the Democratic convention. George Bush in 1992 had to fight off a significant challenge by Patrick J. Buchanan in the Republican primaries before he went on to win 95 percent of the convention delegates.

	Incumbent's Percentage of:		
	Primary vote	Convention delegates	General election result
'Clear Sailing'			
William McKinley (1900) *	—	100%	Won
Theodore Roosevelt (1904)	—	100	Won
Woodrow Wilson (1916) *	99%	99	Won
Calvin Coolidge (1924)	68	96	Won
Franklin D. Roosevelt (1936) *	93	100	Won
Franklin D. Roosevelt (1940)	72	86	Won
Franklin D. Roosevelt (1944)	71	92	Won
Harry S. Truman (1948)	64	75	Won
Dwight D. Eisenhower (1956) *	86	100	Won
Lyndon B. Johnson (1964)	88	100	Won
Richard Nixon (1972) *	87	99	Won
Ronald Reagan (1984) *	99	100	Won
Bill Clinton (1996) *	88	100	Won
George W. Bush (2004) *	98	100	Won
'Tough Sledding'			
William H. Taft (1912) *	34%	52%	Lost
Herbert Hoover (1932) *	33	98	Lost
Gerald R. Ford (1976)	53	53	Lost
Jimmy Carter (1980) *	51	64	Lost
George Bush (1992) *	72	95	Lost

the physical strain on the candidates, and the variations and complexities of state laws as problems of presidential primaries.

To deal with these problems, several states in 1974 and 1975 discussed the feasibility of creating regional primaries, in which individual states within a geographical region would hold their primaries on the same day. Supporters of the concept believed it would reduce candidate expenses and strain and would permit concentration on regional issues. The push toward regional primaries has generally been undermined by the more prominent development of "front-loading."

The regional primary idea achieved some limited success in 1976 when three western states (Idaho, Nevada, and Oregon) and three southern states (Arkansas, Kentucky, and Tennessee) decided to organize regional primaries in each of their areas. Attempts also were made in New England to construct a regional primary. But New Hampshire would not participate because its law required the state to hold its primary at least one week before any other state. Only Vermont joined Massachusetts in holding a simultaneous presidential primary, on March 2.

In 1980 and 1984, limited regional primaries were held again in several areas of the country. Probably the most noteworthy was the trio of southern states (Alabama, Florida, and Georgia) that voted on the second Tuesday in March in both years. It became the basis for "Super Tuesday," which became a full-blown southern-oriented regional primary in 1988.

Sixteen states—a dozen from the South—held primaries on Super Tuesday, March 8, 1988. The long-held goal of many southern political leaders to hold an early regional primary was finally realized. Most of the GOP primaries were winner-take-all, and when Vice President George Bush swept every Republican primary on Super Tuesday, he effectively locked up the GOP nomination. For the Democrats, Gov. Michael S. Dukakis of Massachusetts also fared well on Super Tuesday. But despite Dukakis's victories, the Rev. Jesse Jackson—the first serious African American candidate for a major party presidential nomination—kept the contest going into June.

"MARCH MADNESS"

By 1992 Super Tuesday had become part of a general rush among states to hold their primaries as early as possible. Dubbed "March Madness," the early clustering of primaries—seventeen states held primaries in February or March—was

Republican presidential candidates face off in debate before the 1996 primaries. Left to right: Alan Keyes, Morry Taylor, Steve Forbes, Robert Dornan, Bob Dole, Richard Lugar, Lamar Alexander, and Pat Buchanan.

viewed with dismay by some political analysts. They said it could lead to nominees being locked in before most voters knew what was happening, resulting in less informed and deliberative voting in the general election.

In 1996 the process was even more heavily weighted in favor of early primaries, as more than two-thirds of them were held before the end of March. The idea of regional primaries also came the closest to fruition in 1996. "Junior Tuesday Week" (March 2–7) featured primary voting in ten states (five of which were in New England); Super Tuesday (March 12) had seven primaries (six of which were in the South); and "Big Ten" Tuesday (March 19) had four primaries in the industrial Midwest—Illinois, Michigan, Ohio, and Wisconsin. By the time California (which had moved it primary forward in the hope of increasing its sway on the nominating process) had its primary on March 26 (along with two other western states—Nevada and Washington), Sen. Robert J. "Bob" Dole of Kansas had all but clinched the Republican nomination.

In 2000 there were not only a glut of early primaries, but a large concentration on a single day—March 7. The clustering on this date—the first Tuesday of the month—was not coincidental. It was the earliest date allowed by Democratic rules for states other than Iowa and New Hampshire to hold their primary or caucus. Eleven states scheduled primaries on March 7, 2000, creating a de facto national primary that became variously known as "Titanic Tuesday" or the new "Super Tuesday," although the large southern-oriented vote of the same name remained on the second Tuesday in March.

Political analysts predicted the huge volume of early primaries would result in both parties' nominations being decided by the ides of March, which is what occurred. George W. Bush and John McCain battled almost evenly through the seven states that held Republican primaries in February—Bush winning four, McCain, three. In March, Bush's well-financed campaign machine proved decisive as he dominated the vote March 7, and McCain withdrew soon afterwards.

With Democratic rules preventing a wholesale movement of states into February, the early Democratic calendar was quite different from the Republican one. The Democratic campaign essentially went "dark" from the early February voting in New Hampshire until the huge array of primaries March 7.

But the result was the same on the Democratic side as it was on the Republican, an early knockout by the front-runner. Vice President Gore was closely contested by his major challenger, Bill Bradley of New Jersey, in raising funds and drawing media attention during the long stretch before the primaries. But once the balloting began, Bradley proved no match for Gore. The vice president won the late January caucuses in Iowa decisively, the New Hampshire primary narrowly, and swept all the Democratic primaries and caucuses March 7, driving Bradley to the sidelines. Only half the states had voted by then, but the Democratic and Republican races were over.

The regional primary effort then declined. In 2004, while the bulk of the New England states continued to vote on the first Tuesday in March, only a four-state remnant of the South remained grouped together on the second Tuesday, and there was no cohesion among either states in the Midwest or West.

The most notable change was the dramatic movement toward a broad-based, coast-to-coast vote on the first Tuesday in March. The day's primaries and caucuses involved states with a third of the nation's population, including three of the seven most populous states—California, New York, and Ohio. When Kerry won all but Vermont that day (and the Minnesota caucuses), his nomination was assured. The remaining large states—Texas, Florida, and Illinois—followed in the next two weeks, confirming Kerry's dominance through overwhelming victories against limited competition, resulting in the formal withdrawal of all significant opponents.

VPs Who Have Become President

Fourteen men who served as vice president have become president: John Adams, Thomas Jefferson, Martin Van Buren, John Tyler, Millard Fillmore, Andrew Johnson, Chester A. Arthur, Theodore Roosevelt, Calvin Coolidge, Harry S. Truman, Richard M. Nixon, Lyndon B. Johnson, Gerald R. Ford, and George Bush.

Of those, all but Adams, Jefferson, Van Buren, Nixon, and Bush first became president on the death or resignation of their predecessor. Only two—Van Buren in 1836 and Bush in 1988—have been elected president at a time of widespread suffrage while they held the office of vice-president.

Nine vice presidents since 1900 have run unsuccessfully for president:

• Thomas R. Marshall, Democratic vice president under Woodrow Wilson from 1913 to 1921, failed to win the nomination in 1920.

• Charles G. Dawes, Republican vice president under Coolidge from 1925 to 1929, unsuccessfully sought the nomination in 1928 and 1932.

• John Nance Garner, Democratic vice president under Franklin D. Roosevelt from 1933 to 1941, ran unsuccessfully (against Roosevelt) for the nomination in 1940.

• Henry A. Wallace, Democratic vice president under Roosevelt from 1941 to 1945, was Progressive Party nominee in 1948.

• Alben W. Barkley, Democratic vice president under Truman from 1949 to 1953, failed to win the 1952 nomination.

• Nixon, Republican vice president under Dwight D. Eisenhower from 1953 to 1961, was the GOP nominee in 1960. (He won in 1968 and 1972.)

• Hubert H. Humphrey, Democratic vice president under Lyndon Johnson from 1965 to 1969, was the Democratic nominee in 1968.

• Walter F. Mondale, Democratic vice president under Jimmy Carter from 1977 to 1981, was the Democratic nominee in 1984.

• Al Gore, Democratic vice president under Bill Clinton from 1993 to 2001, was the Democratic nominee in 2000.

On the Republican side, there was a distinct movement away from primaries, which were held in only twenty-six states, a substantial drop from the forty-three held four years earlier. The reason for the decline was the lack of any challenge to incumbent president George W. Bush. States saw little reason to spend money on an uncontested race. Previous Republican primary battlegrounds such as Arizona, Virginia, and South Carolina turned to caucuses and party conventions, while scheduled primaries were cancelled in Connecticut, Florida, Mississippi, New York, and South Dakota.

Nominations Today

During the past decades, the country has established a distinct process for presidential nominations. Many issues remain under debate, about that process itself and about its effects on the general election.

THE CURRENT PROCESS

Even though much of the primary calendar has changed dramatically since the 1960s, the accepted starting points have remained Iowa and New Hampshire. The two states illustrate the two different types of delegate-selection processes that states have to choose from. Iowa is a caucus; New Hampshire is a primary. Primaries require voters only to cast a ballot, an exercise that usually takes just a few minutes. The deliberative nature of a neighborhood caucus, though, often requires the commitment of an afternoon or evening

Both states have made their early events into cottage industries with the help of candidates and the media. More than ever, Iowa and New Hampshire are about the only states left where candidates have some control over their destinies. They can woo voters one-on-one, whether in bowling alleys, coffee shops, or the frequent gatherings in neighborhood living rooms. Yet, as the importance of these contests has increased, they have also turned to extensive television advertisements to deliver their message more broadly. For if there is one thing that has become certain in recent years, once the New Hampshire primary is over and candidates must compete in several states simultaneously, there is a frenetic burst of tarmac-to-tarmac campaigning heavily dependent on media advertising.

To be taken seriously, candidates are expected to win at least one of these two early states, with New Hampshire the more important of the pair. With one exception, every presidential nominee since 1976 has won either Iowa or New Hampshire, and finished no lower than third in the other. However, the importance of these states has been questioned. Bill Clinton, in 1992, did not seriously contest Iowa in deference to the home-state appeal of Sen. Tom Harkin and finished second in New Hampshire behind a New Englander, former senator Paul E. Tsongas of Massachusetts. George W. Bush, in 2000, won the Iowa caucuses but lost to Sen. John McCain in New Hampshire.

CHANGE IN THE FUTURE

The many innovations in the nominating process over the years continue to stimulate ideas for further change. These include:

• Changes in timing of the state primaries, such as those of the Republican "Delaware Plan." A major motive behind these suggestions is to reduce the influence of Iowa and New Hampshire, often considered unrepresentative of the national parties' voters, especially among Democrats. Another purpose is to limit "front-loading," so as to provide more opportunities for less prominent candidates to make their case.

• A single national primary to allow all voters to have an equal impact on the presidential nomination. This change would require federal legislation, at least, and perhaps a constitutional amendment.

• A system of regional primaries, whose order would be rotated every four years, recommended by the secretaries of state of all fifty states. This plan would give the first region to vote a

Presidential candidate Howard Dean's primal scream after losing the 2004 Iowa Caucuses—seen on television and in newspapers across the country—may have contributed to his demise as front-runner and John Kerry's rise to take the Democratic nomination.

considerable advantage, although that power would shift from one region to another in each election.

• Revived power of the national convention to choose, or at least influence, the selection of the presidential and vice-presidential candidates. One suggestion along these lines is that the parties hold their conventions early, reduce the number of candidates to the most serious aspirants, to be followed by a national party primary.

Still, even without the Democrats or Republicans opting for bold changes, the nominating process is by nature evolutionary. Every four years at least a few states move their primary or caucus date, creating a new calendar; and nearly every four years, at least one of the parties makes a change in its rules that proves significant. That effect will surely be evident for the 2008 elections as well.

EFFECT ON ELECTIONS

Voters in presidential primaries are numerous but still represent only a small slice of the citizenry and may actually be unrepresentative of the national electorate. Voter turnout is usually much higher in a primary than a caucus, but even in primaries the turnout is much lower than in a general election. In New Hampshire, for instance, where interest in the presidential primary is probably greater than in any other state, nearly 400,000 voters turned out in February 2000 for the two presidential primaries, but that was still less than the general election turnout of 572,000. In 2004, when only the Democrats had a contest, 220,000 persons voted in the Democratic primary, but the total fall turnout was three times greater. The Iowa caucuses show

even greater differences—a Democratic caucus vote in 2004 of 124,000, compared to the party's general election vote of 742,000.

The disparity is greater in many other states. Roughly 31 million votes were cast in all the presidential primaries in 2000, when both parties had contests, and close to 17 million in the Democratic primaries of 2004. Meanwhile, turnout in the handful of states that held caucuses was no more than seven hundred thousand more voters. By comparison, 105 million voters turned out for the 2000 general election, and 123 million in 2004. Democrats and Republicans voting in the primaries and caucuses are making important decisions for the majority of their partisan colleagues.

Rules governing voter participation play a role in the comparatively low turnouts for the nominating process. Every primary is not as open as a general election, where any registered voter can participate. A number of states limit participation to registered Democratic and Republican voters. Some others allow independents to participate but list them on the voting rolls afterward as members of the party in which they cast their primary ballot.

Still, the vast majority of registered voters across the country can participate in a presidential primary or caucus if they want. The fact that more do not has generated the conventional wisdom that the nominating process is dominated by ideological activists—liberals on the Democratic side, conservatives on the Republican.

That is debatable in the primaries, where the winners in recent years generally have been from the mainstreams of both parties. Candidates perceived as more extreme such as Republican Pat Robertson in 1988 or Howard Dean in 2004 have had limited primary success. An ideological bent is usually more evident in the low-turnout world of the caucuses, where a small cadre of dedicated voters can significantly affect the outcome.

EVALUATION

The political community continues to debate whether the current primary-dominated nominating process is better than the old system, in which party leaders controlled the selection process. But it is a fact that the increased number of primaries helps provide valuable clues about the vote-getting potential of candidates in the general election. Nominees that have exhibited broad-based appeal among the diverse array of primary voters in the winter and spring have gone on to be quite competitive in the fall, while those nominees who have struggled through the primaries showing limited appeal among one or two of their party's major constituency groups have usually been buried under landslides in November.

It is also true that the current system results in quick decisions on the presidential candidates, which may come before their qualities are fully assessed by the voters, and that the process favors candidates who are already well-known and well-financed. The system of "front-loading" may also create, according to some critics, a "rush to judgment," which excludes a full evaluation of other talented aspirants. The diminished role of party politicians may mean that their expert skills and expert judgments are given too limited a role in choosing the next leaders of the nation. These questions are likely to induce continued changes in the American nominating process.

Growth of Presidential Primaries: More and More, Earlier and Earlier

In recent decades, there have been more and more states holding primaries earlier and earlier in the presidential election year. The result is that a nominating system that once featured primaries sprinkled across the spring is now front-loaded with the bulk of the primaries held during the winter months of February and March. In 2004 for the first time New Hampshire held its first-in-the-nation primary in January.

Following is a list of primaries held in each month of every nominating season from 1968 through 2004. Primaries included are those in the fifty states and the District of Columbia in which at least one of the parties permitted a direct vote for presidential candidates, or there was an aggregated statewide vote for delegates. Primaries in the U.S. territories, such as Puerto Rico, are not included.

	1968	1972	1976	1980	1984	1988	1992	1996	2000	2004
January	0	0	0	0	0	0	0	0	0	2
February	0	0	1	1	1	2	2	5	7	9
March	1	3	5	9	8	20	15	24	20	14
April	3	3	2	4	3	3	5	1	2	1
May	7	11	13	13	11	7	10	8	9	7
June	4	4	6	9	7	5	7	4	5	5
Total	15	21	27	36	30	37	39	42	43	38

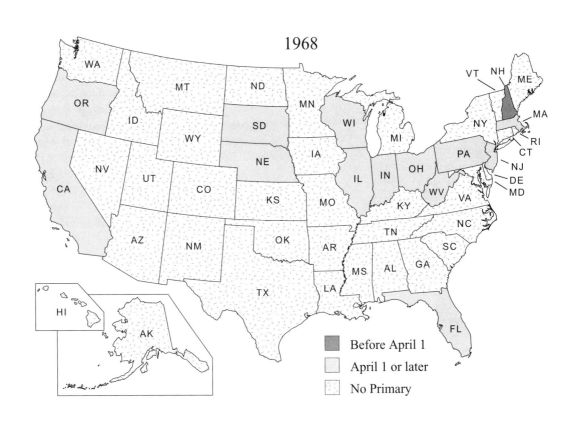

1968

Before April 1

April 1 or later

No Primary

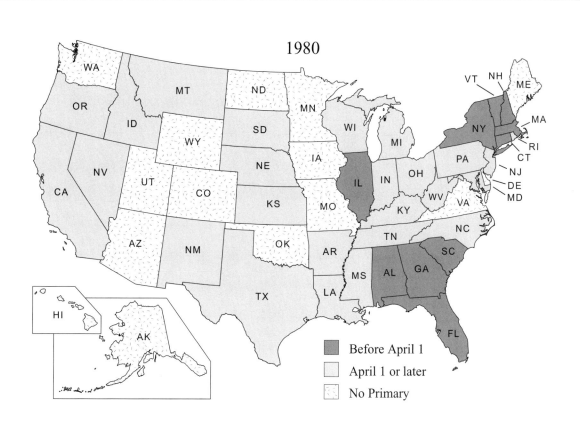

1980

Before April 1
April 1 or later
No Primary

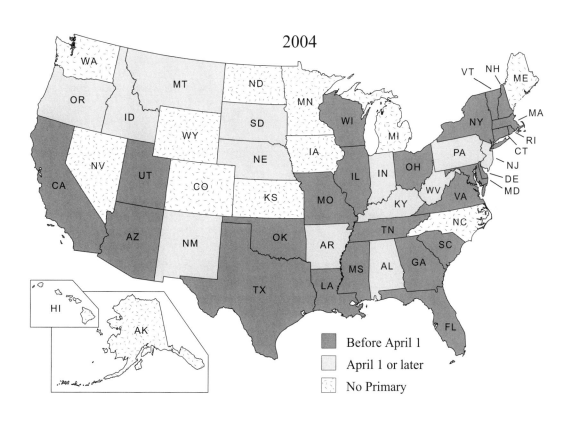

2004

Before April 1
April 1 or later
No Primary

CHAPTER 3

Nominating Conventions

Although the presidential nominating convention has been a target of criticism throughout its existence, it has survived to become a traditional fixture of American politics. The convention owes its longevity and general acceptance in large part to the multiplicity of functions that the convention uniquely combines.

The convention is a nominating body that the Democrats, Republicans, and most of the principal third parties have used since the early 1830s to choose their candidates for president and vice president. The convention also produces a platform containing the party's positions on issues of the campaign. Convention delegates form the supreme governing body of the party and as such they make major decisions on party affairs. Between conventions such decisions are made by the national committee with the guidance of the party chair.

The convention provides a forum for compromise among the diverse elements within a party, allowing the discussion and often the satisfactory solution of differing points of view. As the ultimate campaign rally, the convention also gathers together thousands of party leaders and rank-and-file members from across the country in an atmosphere that varies widely, sometimes encouraging sober discussion but often resembling a carnival. But even though the process has drawn heavy criticism, the convention has endured because it successfully performs a variety of actions.

The convention is an outgrowth of the U.S. political experience. Nowhere is it mentioned in the Constitution, nor has the authority of the convention ever been a subject of congressional legislation. Rather, the convention has evolved along with the presidential selection process. The convention has been the accepted nominating method of the major political parties since the election of 1832, but internal changes within the convention system have been massive since the early, formative years.

Convention Sites

Before the Civil War, conventions frequently were held in small buildings, even churches, and attracted only several hundred delegates and a minimum of spectators. Transportation and communications were slow, so most conventions were held in the late spring in a city with a central geographical location. Baltimore, Maryland, was the most popular convention city in this initial period, playing host to the first six Democratic conventions (1832 through 1852), two Whig conventions, one National Republican convention, and the 1831 Anti-Masonic gathering—America's first national nominating convention. With the nation's westward expansion, the heartland city of Chicago emerged as the most frequent convention center. Since its first one in 1860, Chicago has been the site of twenty-five major party conventions (fourteen Republican, eleven Democratic). The Democrats held their national convention in Chicago as recently as 1996. In 2004 the Democrats chose to meet in Boston, the first time the city had hosted a national party convention. The Republicans met in New York City, site of the Sept. 11, 2001, terrorist attacks on the World Trade Center. It was the Republicans' first convention in the city; Democrats had held five conventions there.

LOCATING AND FINANCING CONVENTIONS

Since 1976, presidential elections have been at least partially publicly funded. Early on, the newly created Federal Election Commission (FEC) ruled that host-city contributions to conventions are allowable, enabling the parties to far exceed the technical limit on convention spending. In 1988, for example, the FEC allotted the two major parties $9.2 million each in public funds for their conventions. The money came from an optional checkoff for publicly financing presidential campaigns on federal income tax forms. (Congress raised the original $1 checkoff to $3 per taxpayer, beginning in 1993.) In 1988 the Republicans, however, spent a total of $18 million on their New Orleans convention, while the Democrats spent $22.5 million in Atlanta. To attract the Democratic convention, Atlanta levied a special tax on hotel guests, which enabled the host committee to offer a package of $5 million in borrowed money. For both conventions, General Motors (with FEC permission) provided fleets of cars at an estimated cost of $350,000.

Costs continued to soar for subsequent conventions. In 1992 the Democrats spent $38.6 million on their New York City meeting, according to political scientist Herbert E. Alexander. For the 1996 conventions, the FEC allotted the two major parties $12.4 million each in public funds, but the total spending for both parties, according to Alexander, was at least twice that amount. In 2000 the federal money given each of the two major parties for their conventions reached $13.5 million. The Reform Party was given $2.5 million. In the wake of the 2001 terrorist attacks, huge amounts were spent on additional security in 2004; the federal government alone allocated up to $50 million in assistance for each major convention that year. In addition to the federal spending on security and the FEC grant money of $14.9 million given to each major party, the FEC reported that the Democrats raised an additional $56.8 million for their convention in Boston, while the Republicans raised $85.7 million for New York City.

Sites of Major Party Conventions, 1832–2004

The following chart lists the twenty-two cities selected as the sites of major party conventions and the number of conventions they have hosted from the first national gathering for the Demo-crats (1832) and the Republicans (1856) through the 2004 conventions. The Democrats have hosted a total of forty-five conventions; the Republicans, thirty-eight.

	Total conventions	Democratic conventions		Republican conventions	
		Number	Last hosted	Number	Last hosted
Chicago, Ill.	25	11	1996	14	1960
Baltimore, Md.	10	9	1912	1	1864
Philadelphia, Pa.	8	2	1948	6	2000
New York, N.Y.	6	5	1992	1	2004
St. Louis, Mo.	5	4	1916	1	1896
San Francisco, Calif.	4	2	1984	2	1964
Cincinnati, Ohio	3	2	1880	1	1876
Kansas City, Mo.	3	1	1900	2	1976
Miami Beach, Fla.	3	1	1972	2	1972
Cleveland, Ohio	2	0	—	2	1936
Houston, Texas	2	1	1928	1	1992
Los Angeles, Calif.	2	2	2000	0	—
Atlanta, Ga.	1	1	1988	0	—
Atlantic City, N.J.	1	1	1964	0	—
Boston, Mass.	1	1	2004	0	—
Charleston, S.C.	1	1	1860	0	—
Dallas, Texas	1	0	—	1	1984
Denver, Colo.	1	1	1908	0	—
Detroit, Mich.	1	0	—	1	1980
Minneapolis, Minn.	1	0	—	1	1892
New Orleans, La.	1	0	—	1	1988
San Diego, Calif.	1	0	—	1	1996

Besides the amounts spent on security, major outlays typically go for construction, administration, office space, convention committees, and regular police and fire personnel. Besides adequate hotel and convention hall facilities, safety of the delegates and other attendees is increasingly a major consideration in selection of a national party convention site. The island location of Miami Beach, for example, made it easier to contain protest demonstrators and reportedly was a factor in its selection by the Republicans in 1968 and by both parties in 1972.

For the party that controls the White House, often the over-riding factor in site selection is the president's personal preference—as in the GOP's decision to meet in 1992 in President George Bush's adopted home city of Houston, or the Democrats' decision to meet in Atlantic City in 1964, because President Lyndon Johnson wanted a site within helicopter distance of Washington and convenient to New York City. In 2004 the Republicans chose to meet in New York City, which had lost the World Trade Center in the 2001 terrorist attacks—a significant location for President George W. Bush, whose presidency had centered on responding to terrorism after Sept. 11, 2001.

The national committees of the two parties select the sites about one year before the conventions are to take place.

CALL OF THE CONVENTION

The second major step in the quadrennial convention process follows several months after the site selection with the announcement of the convention call, the establishment of the three major convention committees—credentials, rules, and platform (reso-lutions)—the appointment of convention officers, and finally the holding of the convention itself. While these basic steps have undergone little change during the past 170 years, there have been major alterations within the nominating convention system.

The call to the convention sets the date and site of the meeting and is issued early in each election year, if not before. The call to the first Democratic convention, held in 1832, was issued by the New Hampshire Legislature. Early Whig conventions were called by party members in Congress. With the establishment of national committees later in the nineteenth century, the function of issuing the convention call fell to these new party organizations. Each national committee currently has the responsibility for allocating delegates to each state.

Delegate Selection

Both parties have modified the method of allocating delegates to the individual states and territories. From the beginning of the convention system in the nineteenth century, both the Democrats and Republicans distributed votes to the states based on their electoral college strength.

The first major deviation from this procedure was made by the Republicans after their divisive 1912 convention, in which President William Howard Taft won renomination over former president Theodore Roosevelt. Taft's nomination was largely because of almost solid support from the South—a region vastly overrepresented in relation to its number of Republican voters. Before their 1916 convention the Republicans reduced the alloca-

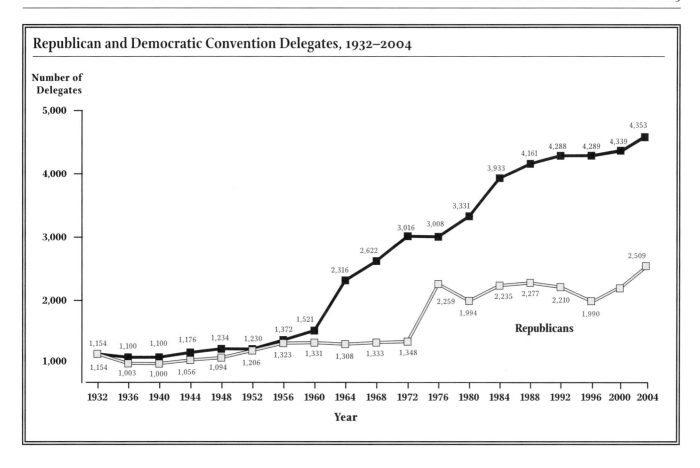

Republican and Democratic Convention Delegates, 1932–2004

Number of Delegates

tion of votes to the southern states. At their 1924 convention the Republicans applied the first bonus system, by which states were awarded extra votes for supporting the Republican presidential candidate in the previous election. The concept of bonus votes, applied as a reward to the states for supporting the party ticket, has been used and expanded by both parties since that time.

The Democrats first used a bonus system in 1944, completing a compromise arrangement with southern states for abolishing the party's controversial two-thirds nominating rule. Since then both parties have used various delegate-allocation formulas. At their 1972 convention the Republicans revised the formula and added more than 900 new delegate slots for 1976, increasing the size of the convention by two-thirds. The Ripon Society, an organization of liberal Republicans, sued to have the new rules overturned. They argued that because of the extra delegates awarded to states that voted Republican in the previous presidential election, small southern and western states were favored at the expense of the more populous but less Republican eastern states. The challenge failed when the Supreme Court in February 1976 refused to hear the case and thus let stand a U.S. Court of Appeals decision upholding the rules.

Only 116 delegates from thirteen states attended the initial national nominating convention held by the Anti-Masons in 1831, but with the addition of more states and the adoption of increasingly complex voting-allocation formulas by the major parties, the size of conventions spiraled. The 1976 Republican convention had 2,259 delegates, while the Democrats in the same year had 3,075 delegates casting 3,008 votes. (The number of delegate votes was smaller than the number of delegates because Democratic Party rules provided for fractional voting.)

The expanded size of modern conventions in part reflected their democratization, with less command by a few party leaders and dramatic growth among youth, women, and minority delegations. Increased representation for such groups was one of the major reasons given by the Republicans for the huge increase in delegate strength authorized by the 1972 convention (and effective for the 1976 gathering).

The Democrats adopted new rules in June 1978, expanding the number of delegates by 10 percent to provide extra representation for state and local officials. The new Democratic rules also required that women account for at least 50 percent of the delegates beginning with the 1980 convention. That party's national convention continued to grow throughout the next decades—from 3,331 delegate votes in 1980 to a record 4,353 (and 611 alternates) in 2004. In 2004 almost 40 percent of the Democratic delegates were members of minority groups, another record.

The 2004 Republican convention also convened a record number of participants with 2,509 delegates and 2,344 alternates. Of these delegates and alternates, 44 percent were women and 17 percent were minorities, the highest percentage ever at a GOP convention.

With the increased size of conventions has come a formalization in the method of delegate selection, which at first was often haphazard and informal. At the Democratic convention in 1835, for example, Maryland had 188 delegates to cast the state's ten

Democratic Conventions, 1832–2004

Year	City	Dates	Presidential nominee	Vice-presidential nominee	No. of pres. ballots
1832	Baltimore	May 21–23	Andrew Jackson	Martin Van Buren	1
1836	Baltimore	May 20–23	Martin Van Buren	Richard M. Johnson	1
1840	Baltimore	May 5–6	Martin Van Buren	—[1]	1
1844	Baltimore	May 27–29	James K. Polk	George M. Dallas	9
1848	Baltimore	May 22–25	Lewis Cass	William O. Butler	4
1852	Baltimore	June 1–5	Franklin Pierce	William R. King	49
1856	Cincinnati	June 2–6	James Buchanan	John C. Breckinridge	17
1860	Charleston	April 23–May 3	Deadlocked		57
	Baltimore	June 18–23	Stephen A. Douglas	Benjamin Fitzpatrick Herschel V. Johnson[2]	2
1864	Chicago	Aug. 29–31	George B. McClellan	George H. Pendleton	1
1868	New York	July 4–9	Horatio Seymour	Francis P. Blair	22
1872	Baltimore	July 9–10	Horace Greeley	Benjamin G. Brown	1
1876	St. Louis	June 27–29	Samuel J. Tilden	Thomas A. Hendricks	2
1880	Cincinnati	June 22–24	Winfield S. Hancock	William H. English	2
1884	Chicago	July 8–11	Grover Cleveland	Thomas A. Hendricks	2
1888	St. Louis	June 5–7	Grover Cleveland	Allen G. Thurman	1
1892	Chicago	June 21–23	Grover Cleveland	Adlai E. Stevenson	1
1896	Chicago	July 7–11	William J. Bryan	Arthur Sewall	5
1900	Kansas City	July 4–6	William J. Bryan	Adlai E. Stevenson	1
1904	St. Louis	July 6–9	Alton S. Parker	Henry G. Davis	1
1908	Denver	July 7–10	William J. Bryan	John W. Kern	1
1912	Baltimore	June 25–July 2	Woodrow Wilson	Thomas R. Marshall	46
1916	St. Louis	June 14–16	Woodrow Wilson	Thomas R. Marshall	1
1920	San Francisco	June 28–July 6	James M. Cox	Franklin D. Roosevelt	44
1924	New York	June 24–July 9	John W. Davis	Charles W. Bryan	103
1928	Houston	June 26–29	Alfred E. Smith	Joseph T. Robinson	1
1932	Chicago	June 27–July 2	Franklin D. Roosevelt	John N. Garner	4
1936	Philadelphia	June 23–27	Franklin D. Roosevelt	John N. Garner	Acclamation
1940	Chicago	July 15–18	Franklin D. Roosevelt	Henry A. Wallace	1
1944	Chicago	July 19–21	Franklin D. Roosevelt	Harry S. Truman	1
1948	Philadelphia	July 12–14	Harry S. Truman	Alben W. Barkley	1
1952	Chicago	July 21–26	Adlai Stevenson	John J. Sparkman	3
1956	Chicago	Aug. 13–17	Adlai Stevenson	Estes Kefauver	1
1960	Los Angeles	July 11–15	John F. Kennedy	Lyndon B. Johnson	1
1964	Atlantic City	Aug. 24–27	Lyndon B. Johnson	Hubert H. Humphrey	Acclamation
1968	Chicago	Aug. 26–29	Hubert H. Humphrey	Edmund S. Muskie	1
1972	Miami Beach	July 10–13	George McGovern	Thomas F. Eagleton R. Sargent Shriver[3]	1
1976	New York	July 12–15	Jimmy Carter	Walter F. Mondale	1
1980	New York	Aug. 11–14	Jimmy Carter	Walter F. Mondale	1
1984	San Francisco	July 16–19	Walter F. Mondale	Geraldine A. Ferraro	1
1988	Atlanta	July 18–21	Michael S. Dukakis	Lloyd Bentsen	1
1992	New York	July 13–16	Bill Clinton	Al Gore	1
1996	Chicago	Aug. 26–29	Bill Clinton	Al Gore	1
2000	Los Angeles	Aug. 14–17	Al Gore	Joseph Lieberman	1
2004	Boston	July 26–29	John F. Kerry	John Edwards	1

1. The 1840 Democratic convention did not nominate a candidate for vice president.

2. The 1860 Democratic convention nominated Benjamin Fitzpatrick, who declined the nomination shortly after the convention adjourned. On June 25 the Democratic National Committee selected Herschel V. Johnson as the party's candidate for vice president.

3. The 1972 Democratic convention nominated Thomas F. Eagleton, who withdrew from the ticket on July 31. On Aug. 8 the Democratic National Committee selected R. Sargent Shriver as the party's candidate for vice president.

votes. In contrast, Tennessee's fifteen votes were cast by a traveling businessman who happened to be in the convention city at the time. While the number of delegates and the number of votes allocated tended to be equal or nearly so later in the nineteenth century, a few party bosses frequently exercised domination of national conventions.

Two basic methods of delegate selection were employed in the nineteenth century and continued to be used into the twentieth: the caucus method, by which delegates were chosen by meetings at the local or state level, and the appointment method, by which delegates were appointed by the governor or a powerful state leader.

PRESIDENTIAL PRIMARIES

A revolutionary new mechanism for delegate selection emerged during the early 1900s: the presidential primary election in which the voters directly elected convention delegates.

Initiated in Florida at the turn of the century, the presidential primary by 1912 was used by thirteen states. In his first annual message to Congress the following year, President Woodrow

Chief Officers and Keynote Speakers at Democratic National Conventions, 1832–2004

Year	Chair national committee	Temporary chair	Permanent chair	Keynote speaker
1832		Robert Lucas, Ohio	Robert Lucas, Ohio	
1836		Andrew Stevenson, Va.	Andrew Stevenson, Va.	
1840		Isaac Hill, N.H.	William Carroll, Tenn.	
1844		Hendrick B. Wright, Pa.	Hendrick B. Wright, Pa.	
1848	Benjamin Hallet, Mass.	J.S. Bryce, La.	Andrew Stevenson, Va.	
1852	Robert M. McLane, Md.	Gen. Romulus M. Saunders, N.C.	John W. Davis, Ind.	
1856	David A. Smalley, Vt.	Samuel Medary, Ohio	John E. Ward, Ga.	
1860	August Belmont, N.Y.	Francis B. Flournoy, Ark.	Caleb Cushing, Mass.	
1864	August Belmont, N.Y.	William Bigler, Pa.	Horatio Seymour, N.Y.	
1868	August Belmont, N.Y.	Henry L. Palmer, Wis.	Horatio Seymour, N.Y.	
1872	Augustus Schell, N.Y.	Thomas Jefferson Randolph, Va.	James R. Doolittle, Wis.	
1876	Abram Stevens Hewitt, N.Y.	Henry M. Watterson, Ky.	John A. McClernand, Ill.	
1880	William H. Barnum, Conn.	George Hoadly, Ohio	John W. Stevenson, Ky.	
1884	William H. Barnum, Conn.	Richard B. Hubbard, Texas	William F. Vilas, Wis.	
1888	William H. Barnum, Conn.	Stephen M. White, Calif.	Patrick A. Collins, Mass.	
1892	William F. Harrity, Penn.	William C. Owens, Ky.	William L. Wilson, W.Va.	
1896	James K. Jones, Ark.	John W. Daniel, Va.	Stephen M. White, Calif.	
1900	James K. Jones, Ark.	Charles S. Thomas, Colo.	James D. Richardson, Tenn.	
1904	Thomas Taggart, Ind.	John Sharp Williams, Miss.	Champ Clark, Mo.	
1908	Norman E. Mack, N.Y.	Theodore A. Bell, Calif.	Henry D. Clayton, Ala.	
1912	William F. McCombs, N.Y.	Alton B. Parker, N.Y.	Ollie M. James, Ky.	
1916	Vance C. McCormick, Pa.	Martin H. Glynn, N.Y.	Ollie M. James, Ky.	
1920	George H. White, Ohio	Homer S. Cummings, Conn.	Joseph T. Robinson, Ark.	
1924	Clem Shaver, W.Va.	Pat Harrison, Miss.	Thomas J. Walsh, Mont.	
1928	John J. Raskob, Md.	Claude G. Bowers, Ind.	Joseph T. Robinson, Ark.	
1932	James A. Farley, N.Y.	Alben W. Barkley, Ky.	Thomas J. Walsh, Mont.	
1936	James A. Farley, N.Y.	Alben W. Barkley, Ky.	Joseph T. Robinson, Ark.	Alben W. Barkley, Ky.
1940	Edward J. Flynn, N.Y.	William B. Bankhead, Ala.	Alben W. Barkley, Ky.	William B. Bankhead, Ala.
1944	Robert E. Hannegan, Mo.	Robert S. Kerr, Okla.	Samuel D. Jackson, Ind.	Robert S. Kerr, Okla.
1948	J. Howard McGrath, R.I.	Alben W. Barkley, Ky.	Sam Rayburn, Texas	Alben W. Barkley, Ky.
1952	Stephen A. Mitchell, Ill.	Paul A. Dever, Mass.	Sam Rayburn, Texas	Paul A. Dever, Mass.
1956	Paul M. Butler, Ind.	Frank G. Clement, Tenn.	Sam Rayburn, Texas	Frank Clement, Tenn.
1960	Henry Jackson, Wash.	Frank Church, Idaho	LeRoy Collins, Fla.	Frank Church, Idaho
1964	John M. Bailey, Conn.	John O. Pastore, R.I.	John W. McCormack, Mass.	John O. Pastore, R.I.
1968	Lawrence F. O'Brien, Mass.	Daniel K. Inouye, Hawaii	Carl B. Albert, Okla.	Daniel K. Inouye, Hawaii
1972[1]	Lawrence F. O'Brien, Mass.		Lawrence F. O'Brien, Mass.	Reubin Askew, Fla.
1976	Robert S. Strauss, Texas		Lindy Boggs, La.	John Glenn, Ohio Barbara C. Jordan, Texas
1980	John C. White, Texas		Thomas P. O'Neill Jr., Mass.	Morris K. Udall, Ariz.
1984	Charles T. Manatt, Calif.		Martha Layne Collins, Ky.	Mario M. Cuomo, N.Y.
1988	Paul G. Kirk Jr., Mass.		Jim Wright, Texas	Ann W. Richards, Texas
1992	Ronald H. Brown, D.C.		Ann W. Richards, Texas	Bill Bradley, N.J. Zell Miller, Ga. Barbara C. Jordan, Texas
1996	Donald Fowler, S.C.		Thomas A. Daschle, S.D. Richard A. Gephardt, Mo.	Evan Bayh, Ind.
2000	Joe Andrew, Ind.		Barbara Boxer, Calif. Dianne Feinstein, Calif.	Harold E. Ford Jr., Tenn.
2004	Terry McAuliffe, N.Y.		Bill Richardson, N.M.	Barack Obama, Ill.

1. A rule change eliminated the position of temporary chair.

Wilson advocated the establishment of a national primary to select presidential candidates: "I feel confident that I do not misinterpret the wishes or the expectations of the country when I urge the prompt enactment of legislation which will provide for primary elections throughout the country at which the voters of several parties may choose their nominees for the presidency without the intervention of nominating conventions." Wilson went on to suggest the retention of conventions for the purpose of declaring the results of the primaries and formulating the parties' platforms.

Before any action was taken on Wilson's proposal, the progressive spirit that spurred the growth of presidential primaries died out. Not until the late 1960s and early 1970s, when widespread pressures for change touched both parties but especially the Democratic, was there a rapid growth in presidential primaries. In the mid-1980s some states reverted to the caucus method of delegate selection, but their revival soon abated. A record forty-four primaries were held in 2000, including those in the District of Columbia and Puerto Rico. In 2004, with an incumbent president running unopposed on the Republican

Republican Conventions, 1856–2004

Year	City	Dates	Presidential nominee	Vice-presidential nominee	No. of pres. ballots
1856	Philadelphia	June 17–19	John C. Fremont	William L. Dayton	2
1860	Chicago	May 16–18	Abraham Lincoln	Hannibal Hamlin	3
1864	Baltimore	June 7–8	Abraham Lincoln	Andrew Johnson	1
1868	Chicago	May 20–21	Ulysses S. Grant	Schuyler Colfax	1
1872	Philadelphia	June 5–6	Ulysses S. Grant	Henry Wilson	1
1876	Cincinnati	June 14–16	Rutherford B. Hayes	William A. Wheeler	7
1880	Chicago	June 2–8	James A. Garfield	Chester A. Arthur	36
1884	Chicago	June 3–6	James G. Blaine	John A. Logan	4
1888	Chicago	June 19–25	Benjamin Harrison	Levi P. Morton	8
1892	Minneapolis	June 7–10	Benjamin Harrison	Whitelaw Reid	1
1896	St. Louis	June 16–18	William McKinley	Garret A. Hobart	1
1900	Philadelphia	June 19–21	William McKinley	Theodore Roosevelt	1
1904	Chicago	June 21–23	Theodore Roosevelt	Charles W. Fairbanks	1
1908	Chicago	June 16–19	William H. Taft	James S. Sherman	1
1912	Chicago	June 18–22	William H. Taft	James S. Sherman Nicholas Murray Butler[1]	1
1916	Chicago	June 7–10	Charles E. Hughes	Charles W. Fairbanks	3
1920	Chicago	June 8–12	Warren G. Harding	Calvin Coolidge	10
1924	Cleveland	June 10–12	Calvin Coolidge	Charles G. Dawes	1
1928	Kansas City	June 12–15	Herbert Hoover	Charles Curtis	1
1932	Chicago	June 14–16	Herbert Hoover	Charles Curtis	1
1936	Cleveland	June 9–12	Alfred M. Landon	Frank Knox	1
1940	Philadelphia	June 24–28	Wendell L. Willkie	Charles L. McNary	6
1944	Chicago	June 26–28	Thomas E. Dewey	John W. Bricker	1
1948	Philadelphia	June 21–25	Thomas E. Dewey	Earl Warren	3
1952	Chicago	July 7–11	Dwight D. Eisenhower	Richard M. Nixon	1
1956	San Francisco	Aug. 20–23	Dwight D. Eisenhower	Richard M. Nixon	1
1960	Chicago	July 25–28	Richard M. Nixon	Henry Cabot Lodge	1
1964	San Francisco	July 13–16	Barry Goldwater	William E. Miller	1
1968	Miami Beach	Aug. 5–8	Richard M. Nixon	Spiro T. Agnew	1
1972	Miami Beach	Aug. 21–23	Richard M. Nixon	Spiro T. Agnew	1
1976	Kansas City	Aug. 16–19	Gerald R. Ford	Robert Dole	1
1980	Detroit	July 14–17	Ronald Reagan	George Bush	1
1984	Dallas	Aug. 20–23	Ronald Reagan	George Bush	1
1988	New Orleans	Aug. 15–18	George Bush	Dan Quayle	1
1992	Houston	Aug. 17–20	George Bush	Dan Quayle	1
1996	San Diego	Aug. 12–15	Robert Dole	Jack Kemp	1
2000	Philadelphia	July 31–Aug. 3	George W. Bush	Richard B. Cheney	1
2004	New York City	Aug. 30–Sept. 2	George W. Bush	Richard B. Cheney	1

1. The 1912 Republican convention nominated James S. Sherman, who died on Oct. 30. The Republican National Committee subsequently selected Nicholas Murray Butler to receive the Republican electoral votes for vice president.

side, only thirty-seven states held primaries along with the District of Columbia.

In many states participation in the presidential primary is restricted to voters belonging to the party holding the primary. In some states, however, participation by voters outside the party is allowed by state-mandated open primaries, usually with the caveat, though, that the party in which they cast a primary ballot is publicly recorded.

DEMOCRATIC RULES IN RECENT DECADES

In June 1982 the Democratic National Committee (DNC) adopted several changes in the presidential nominating process recommended by the party's Commission on Presidential Nominations, chaired by Gov. James B. Hunt Jr. of North Carolina. The Hunt Commission, as it came to be known, suggested revisions to increase the power of party regulars and give the convention more freedom to act on its own. It was the fourth time

in twelve years that the Democrats, struggling to repair their nominating process without repudiating earlier reforms, had rewritten their party rules. (See box, "Changes in Democrats' Nominating Rules," p. 30.)

One major change in the Democrats' rules was the creation of a new group of "superdelegates," party and elected officials who would go to the 1984 convention uncommitted and would cast about 14 percent of the ballots. The DNC also adopted a Hunt Commission proposal to weaken the rule binding delegates to vote for their original presidential preference on the first convention ballot. But the new rule also allowed a presidential candidate to replace any disloyal delegate with a more faithful one.

One of the most significant revisions was the Democrats' decision to relax proportional representation at the convention and end the ban on the "loophole" primary-winner-take-all by district. Proportional representation is the distribution of delegates among candidates to reflect their share of the primary or caucus vote, both statewide and in congressional districts. Man-

Chief Officers and Keynote Speakers at Republican National Conventions, 1856–2004

Year	Chair national committee	Temporary chair	Permanent chair	Keynote speaker
1856	Edwin D. Morgan, N.Y.	Robert Emmet, N.Y.	Henry S. Lane, Ind.	
1860	Edwin D. Morgan, N.Y.	David Wilmot, Pa.	George Ashmun, Mass.	
1864	Edwin D. Morgan, N.Y.	Robert J. Breckinridge, Ky.	William Dennison, Ohio	
1868	Marcus L. Ward, N.J.	Carl Schurz, Mo.	Joseph R. Hawley, Conn.	
1872	William Claflin, Mass.	Morton McMichael, Pa.	Thomas Settle, N.C.	
1876	Edwin D. Morgan, N.Y.	Theodore M. Pomeroy, N.Y.	Edward McPherson, Pa.	
1880	J. Donald Cameron, Pa.	George F. Hoar, Mass.	George F. Hoar, Mass.	
1884	Dwight M. Sabin, Minn.	John R. Lynch, Miss.	John B. Henderson, Mo.	
1888	B.F. Jones, Pa.	John M. Thurston, Neb.	Morris M. Estee, Calif.	
1892	James S. Clarkson, Iowa	J. Sloat Fassett, N.Y.	William McKinley Jr., Ohio	
1896	Thomas H. Carter, Mont.	Charles W. Fairbanks, Ind.	John M. Thurston, Neb.	
1900	Marcus A. Hanna, Ohio	Edward O. Wolcott, Colo.	Henry Cabot Lodge, Mass.	
1904	Henry C. Payne, Wis.	Elihu Root, N.Y.	Joseph G. Cannon, Ill.	
1908	Harry S. New, Ind.	Julius C. Burrows, Mich.	Henry Cabot Lodge, Mass.	
1912	Victor Rosewater, Neb.	Elihu Root, N.Y.	Elihu Root, N.Y.	
1916	Charles D. Hilles, N.Y.	Warren G. Harding, Ohio	Warren G. Harding, Ohio	
1920	Will H. Hays, Ind.	Henry Cabot Lodge, Mass.	Henry Cabot Lodge, Mass.	Henry Cabot Lodge, Mass.
1924	John T. Adams, Iowa	Theodore E. Burton, Ohio	Frank W. Mortdell, Wyo.	
1928	William M. Butler, Mass.	Simeon D. Fess, Ohio	George H. Moses, N.H.	
1932	Simeon D. Fess, Ohio	L. J. Dickinson, Iowa	Bertrand H. Snell, N.Y.	
1936	Henry P. Fletcher, Pa.	Frederick Steiwer, Ore.	Bertrand H. Snell, N.Y.	Frederick Steiwer, Ore.
1940	John Hamilton, Kan.	Harold E. Stassen, Minn.	Joseph W. Martin Jr., Mass.	Harold E. Stassen, Minn.
1944	Harrison E. Spangler, Iowa	Earl Warren, Calif.	Joseph W. Martin Jr., Mass.	Earl Warren, Calif.
1948	Carroll Reece, Tenn.	Dwight H. Green, Ill.	Joseph W. Martin Jr., Mass.	Dwight H. Green, Ill.
1952	Guy George Gabrielson, N.J.	Walter S. Hallanan, W.Va.	Joseph W. Martin Jr., Mass.	Douglas MacArthur
1956	Leonard W. Hall, N.Y.	William F. Knowland, Calif.	Joseph W. Martin Jr., Mass.	Arthur B. Langlie, Wash.
1960	Thruston B. Morton, Ky.	Cecil H. Underwood, W.Va.	Charles A. Halleck, Ind.	Walter H. Judd, Minn.
1964	William E. Miller, N.Y.	Mark O. Hatfield, Ore.	Thruston B. Morton, Ky.	Mark O. Hatfield, Ore.
1968	Ray C. Bliss, Ohio	Edward W. Brooke, Mass.	Gerald R. Ford, Mich.	Daniel J. Evans, Wash.
1972	Robert Dole, Kan.	Ronald Reagan, Calif.	Gerald R. Ford, Mich.	Richard G. Lugar, Ind. Anne L. Armstrong, Texas
1976	Mary Louise Smith, Iowa	Robert Dole, Kan.	John J. Rhodes, Ariz.	Howard H. Baker Jr., Tenn.
1980	Bill Brock, Tenn.	Nancy Landon Kassebaum, Kan.	John J. Rhodes, Ariz.	Guy Vander Jagt, Mich.
1984	Frank J. Fahrenkopf Jr., Nev.	Howard H. Baker Jr., Tenn.	Robert H. Michel, Ill.	Katherine Ortega, N.M.
1988	Lee Atwater, S.C.	Elizabeth Hanford Dole, N.C.	Robert H. Michel, Ill.	Thomas H. Kean, N.J.
1992	Richard N. Bond, N.Y.	Kay Bailey Hutchison, Texas	Robert H. Michel, Ill.	Phil Gramm, Texas
1996	Haley Barbour, Miss.	Christine Todd Whitman, N.J. George W. Bush, Texas	Newt Gingrich, Ga.	Susan Molinari, N.Y.
2000	Jim Nicholson, Colo.	Trent Lott, Miss.	J. Dennis Hastert, Ill.	Colin Powell, D.C.
2004	Ed Gillespie, N.J.	Linda Lingle, Hawaii	J. Dennis Hastert, Ill.	Zell Miller, Ga.

dated by party rules in 1980, it was blamed by some Democrats for the protracted primary fight between President Jimmy Carter and Sen. Edward M. Kennedy of Massachusetts. Because candidates needed only about 20 percent of the vote in most places to qualify for a share of the delegates, Kennedy was able to remain in contention. But while the system kept Kennedy going, it did nothing to help his chances of winning the nomination.

Although the Democrats' 1984 rules permitted states to re-tain proportional representation, they also allowed states to take advantage of two options that could help a front-running can-didate build the momentum to wrap up the nomination early in the year.

One was a winner-take-more system. States could elect to keep proportional representation but adopt a winner bonus plan that would award the top vote-getter in each district one extra delegate.

The other option was a return to the loophole primary, which party rules outlawed in 1980 (with exemptions allowing

Illinois and West Virginia to retain their loophole voting sys-tems). In the loophole states, voters balloted directly for dele-gates, with each delegate candidate identified by presidential preference. Sometimes several presidential contenders would win at least a fraction of the delegates in a given district, but the most common result is a sweep by the presidential front-runner, even if he has less than an absolute majority. Loophole pri-maries aid the building of a consensus behind the front-runner, while still giving other candidates a chance to inject themselves back into the race by winning a major loophole state decisively.

The DNC retained the delegate-selection season adopted in 1978, a three-month period stretching from the second Tuesday in March to the second Tuesday in June. But, in an effort to re-duce the growing influence of early states in the nominating process, the Democrats required Iowa and New Hampshire to move their highly publicized elections to late winter. Party rules maintained the privileged status of Iowa and New Hampshire before other states but mandated that their initial nominating

Changes in Democrats' Nominating Rules

Between 1972 and 1992 Democrats tinkered with their nominating rules every four years, producing a system that, if not better than before, was always different. Since 1992, however, the party left its rules basically unchanged. The following chart shows the ebb and flow of the Democratic Party's rules changes, with a "✔" indicating the years these major rules were in effect.

	1972	1976	1980	1984	1988	1992	1996	2000	2004
Timing: Restrict delegate-selection events to a three-month period (the "window").			✔	✔	✔	✔	✔	✔	✔
Conditions of Participation: Restrict participation in delegate-selection events to voters who declare themselves Democrats.		✔	✔	✔	✔	✔	✔	✔	✔
Proportional Representation: Ban all types of winner-take-all contests.			✔			✔	✔	✔	✔
Ban all types of winner-reward contests (where winner receives extra delegates).						✔	✔	✔	✔
Delegate Loyalty: Give candidates the right to approve delegates identifying with their candidacy.		✔	✔	✔	✔	✔	✔	✔	✔
Bind delegates to vote for their original presidential preference at convention on first ballot.			✔						
Party and Elected Officials: Expand each delegation to include pledged party and elected officials.			✔	✔	✔	✔	✔	✔	✔
Further expand each delegation to include unpledged party and elected officials ("superdelegates").				✔	✔	✔	✔	✔	✔
Demographic Representation: Encourage participation and representation of minorities and historically underrepresented groups (affirmative action).			✔	✔	✔	✔	✔	✔	✔
Require delegations to be equally divided between men and women.			✔	✔	✔	✔	✔	✔	✔

rounds be held only eight days apart in 1984. Five weeks had intervened between the Iowa caucuses and New Hampshire primary in 1980.

The DNC also retained rules requiring primary states to set candidate filing deadlines thirty to ninety days before the election and limiting participation in the delegate-selection process to Democrats only. This last rule eliminated cross-over primaries where voters could participate in the Democratic primary without designating their party affiliation. African Americans and Hispanics won continued endorsement of affirmative action in the new party rules. Women gained renewed support for the equal division rule, which required state delegations at the national convention to be divided equally between men and women.

The Democratic Party's 1988 presidential nominating process remained basically the same as that used in 1984. The rules adopted by the national committee included only minor modifications suggested by the party's rules review panel, the Fairness Commission.

The bloc of uncommitted party and elected officials (superdelegates) was expanded slightly to 16 percent and rearranged to reserve more convention seats for members of Congress, gov-

ernors, and the DNC; the rules restricting participation in Democratic primaries and caucuses to Democrats only was relaxed so the open primaries in Wisconsin and Montana could be conducted with the approval of the national party; and the share of the vote a candidate needed to win in a primary or caucus to qualify for delegates was lowered from the 20 percent level used in most places in 1984 to 15 percent.

Only the rule regarding the 15 percent "threshold" spawned much debate during the rules-writing process, and though the discussion of the issue seldom was acrimonious, it did reveal a yawning chasm in the party on what the proper role of the national convention should be.

Most party leaders, including DNC chairman Paul G. Kirk Jr., wanted a threshold of at least 15 percent because they thought it would help steadily shrink the field of presidential candidates during the primary and caucus season and ensure that the convention would be a "ratifying" body that confirmed the choice of the party's voters.

But civil rights leader and presidential candidate Jesse L. Jackson saw it differently, as did a cadre of liberal activists. They wanted a convention that was more "deliberative," and they complained that getting one was virtually impossible under the

NOMINATING CONVENTIONS 31

Political Party Organization and Rules

Political parties in the United States are loosely organized. Anyone of voting age can become a party member simply by signing up. Millions of Americans do just that, while many others shun formal partisan affiliations but think of themselves as Democrats or Republicans nonetheless.

Cowboy humorist Will Rogers used to get laughs by saying, "I am not a member of any organized party. I am a Democrat." But the same line could also be applied to the Republicans, even if they sometimes seemed to be less disorganized than their major rivals.

Both parties have the same fluidity of membership, with the rolls open to independents as well as to supporters of the other party. Formally registering as a Democrat or Republican has the advantage of permitting the member to participate in the party's nominating primaries and caucuses. Most states bar crossover voting in the other party's elections, largely for fear that members of one party would try to nominate the weakest candidates of the opposing party.

There is little evidence, however, that most rank-and-file voters are as concerned about parties as such. In recent elections, roughly three times as many voters have participated in the presidential election as have taken part in the parties' presidential primaries. In 1995, for the first time ever, a plurality of voters surveyed by the Gallup poll identified themselves as "other" (36 percent) rather than as Republican or Democratic (32 percent each). In 2004 the trend slightly dipped with 32 percent polled by Gallup identifying themselves as "other" with Republican or Democratic identification at 34 percent each.

Party Structure

Loose though it is, each major party has an organizational structure—a necessity for continuing as an institution, fundraising, and conducting election campaigns. Congress has officially recognized the role of the parties, and public funding is provided for their presidential nominating conventions. Some states also provide funding for election campaigns.

Beginning at the precinct or neighborhood level, a series of progressively larger units make up the national organization. Next up the line are city, county, legislative district, congressional district, and, just below the national committee, the state organizations.

There is no "chain of command." Each unit is more or less independent. The national chair exerts influence mainly through prestige and force of personality, rather than through any specified powers. The national committee elects the chair, but the president actually designates the chair of the party controlling the White House.

With approximately 440 members, the Democratic National Committee (DNC) is more than twice the size of the 165-member Republican National Committee (RNC). The smaller DNC executive committee includes a mix of party officers, regional representatives, "at-large" members elected by the DNC, and others representing Democratic affiliates.

Since 1984 the Democrats have occupied their $6.4 million national headquarters at 430 South Capitol Street, S.E., in Washington. Previous locations in New York and Washington (including the Watergate offices burglarized by the Republicans in 1972) were rented.

Besides the chair, eight other DNC officers are specified in the party charter and elected by the national committee: five vice chairs, treasurer, secretary, and national finance chair. Party organizations in the states and territories elect their DNC members for four-year terms, ending with the next convention. They are the state chair and the next highest-ranking member of the opposite sex. Another 200 votes are distributed on a population basis, with each state or territory guaranteed at least two, equally divided among men and women.

Other DNC members are two U.S. senators, two House members, two members of the College Democrats, and three representatives each from among Democratic governors, mayors, state legislators, county officials, municipal officials, Young Democrats, and the National Federation of Democratic Women, as well as two representatives each from among lieutenant governors, secretaries of state and state treasurers, and several dozen at-large members.

The RNC elects at least a dozen officers for two-year terms—the chair, cochair, eight vice chairs, secretary, treasurer, and any other officer deemed necessary. The party owns its national headquarters at 310 First Street, S.E., in Washington. The Republicans maintain a large field staff and generally have more money than the Democrats to dispense to campaigns.

Because of their large sizes, the full national committees seldom meet more than a few times during the four years between the national conventions, which are the parties' supreme governing bodies. In both parties, the day-to-day work of the national organization is done by the chair and the headquarters staff, under direction of the executive committee.

Operating Rules

The most important rules of both major parties deal largely with the selection of delegates to the quadrennial national nominating conventions. While the Democrats in the 1970s and 1980s experimented widely with these rules, mainly to give more representation to women, youth, and minorities, Republicans left their rules largely unchanged until the 1990s. *(See box, "GOP Primary Rules," p. 32.)*

Beginning with reforms proposed by Sen. George S. McGovern of South Dakota, who won the nomination himself in 1972, the Democratic Party attempted to "democratize" the process. A succession of commissions headed by Barbara A. Mikulski of Maryland (1972), Morley Winograd of Michigan (1976), Gov. James B. Hunt Jr. of North Carolina (1980), and Donald L. Fowler of South Carolina (1984) succeeded in gaining equal representation for women, requiring proportional representation of delegates among primary vote-getters, and giving convention votes to "superdelegate" party and elected officials.

For the 1992 convention, Democrats for the first time in two decades did not have a special commission intensively examining the nominating process. Since 1992 the Democratic Party has left its rules largely unchanged. *(See "Democratic Rules in Recent Decades," p. 28.)*

system as it existed because it discriminated against long-shot candidates and produced an artificial consensus behind one candidate.

Most Democratic leaders were satisfied with the way the nominating process operated in 1984, and they felt it would be a disaster for the party to go through a free-wheeling, multiballot convention. Not since 1952—at the beginning of the television age—has a national party taken more than one ballot to nominate its presidential candidate.

At the DNC meeting where the new rules were approved, some African American committee members joined with a few white liberal activists in proposing to eliminate the 15 percent threshold altogether. The proposal was rejected by voice vote. A second proposal to lower the threshold to 10 percent was defeated 92 to 178.

In 1990 the DNC made two basic changes that directly affected the delegate-selection process for the 1992 convention. One change moved forward the officially sanctioned start of the presidential primary season by one week, from the second Tuesday in March to the first. This was an invitation to California to move its 1992 primary from June to March 3. (California declined in 1992 but in 1996 moved its primary from June to late March. This was part of a desire by both parties in 1992 to speed up the nominating contest and settle it by April or early May, so that united parties could organize their conventions with eyes focused on the November election.) The second change banned winner-reward systems, which gave extra delegates to the winner of a primary or caucus. Fifteen states had used some form of a winner-reward system in 1988.

The Democrats required all states in 1992 and thereafter to divide their publicly elected delegates proportionally among candidates who drew at least 15 percent of the primary or caucus vote. The Democratic Party also continued to steadily increase the number of superdelegates, expanding their number to 802 for the 2000 convention (or 18.5 percent of the 4,339 delegate votes). In 2004 the number of superdelegates dropped slightly to 733, or 16.8 percent.

During the 1972–1996 period the Republican Party followed an entirely different approach and made few changes in its nominating rules. While the Democratic rules were revised somewhat for each presidential cycle, the GOP rules remained stable. For the year 2000, however, the Republicans changed their minds on the desirability of deciding the nomination contest by March or April; they provided a bonus for those states that chose their delegates to the 2000 GOP convention after the ides of March.

Before the 2000 convention was even held, though, Republicans were considering even more controversial solutions to spread out the primary calendar, which had become congested with events in February and March. The so-called "Delaware Plan" would have put the smallest states at the beginning of the nominating season in 2004, the largest states at the end. But after winning the approval of the Republican National Committee (RNC) at its preconvention meeting, the proposal was killed by the convention rules committee at the behest of the party standard-bearer, Gov. George W. Bush of Texas, who wanted to remove any semblance of controversy.

GOP Primary Rules

The Republican Party, wrote political scientist Nelson W. Polsby, "in many respects remains unreformed." Virtually anything has been permitted in the nominating process so long as it was not baldly discriminatory. That has been the way GOP leaders have wanted it—at least until recent years.

While the Democratic Party has a tightly crafted, nationalized set of rules that govern its nominating process, Republicans historically have shunned control by a central authority. The individual GOP state parties have been given wide latitude to determine how their delegates are selected, with guidelines from the national party kept to a minimum.

The result has been a nominating procedure with a simplicity and continuity that the Democrats lack. A more homogeneous party than the Democrats, the Republicans until the late 1990s had not felt the pressure for rules reform that had engulfed the Democrats as long as the GOP was winning presidential elections. No major rules changes were made by the Republicans between 1974 and 1996.

For the year 2000, though, the Republicans instituted bonus delegates for those states that chose their delegates to the national convention after the middle of March. The quickness of the 1996 decision convinced many party leaders that a longer selection process would be more desirable.

At the 2000 GOP convention, the party voted to eliminate the bonus delegates but added automatic "superdelegate" seats for Republican National Committee members at the 2004 convention as well as increased the base delegate vote total of every state. Yet even in earlier years when Republicans had a laissez faire approach to their nominating process, they were not able to operate totally in their own world. Campaign finance laws and the rising influence of mass media affected Republicans as well as Democrats. In states where legislatures accommodated the Democrats and created a presidential primary, the Republicans were dragged along.

The Republican Party held twenty primaries in 1972, but during the next three decades the number of primaries steadily increased. In 2000 the party held a record forty-four primaries, including those in the District of Columbia and Puerto Rico (the Democrats' record was forty primaries in 1992 and 2000). Primaries helped to select roughly 85 percent of delegates to the GOP convention in 2000. In 2004, with an incumbent president running unopposed for the nomination, the Republicans held only twenty-seven primaries in which a vote was recorded.

Republicans, however, made several changes in delegate-selection rules for 2004, including elimination of the bonus delegates and creation of automatic "superdelegate" seats for members of the RNC. *(See box, "GOP Primary Rules," above.)*

CREDENTIALS DISPUTES

Before the opening of a convention the national committee compiles a temporary roll of delegates. The roll is referred to the convention's credentials committee, which holds hearings on the challenges and makes recommendations to the convention, the final arbiter of all disputes.

Some of the most bitter convention battles have concerned the seating of contested delegations. In the twentieth century most of the heated credentials fights concerned delegations from the South. In the Republican Party the challenges focused on the power of the Republican state organizations to dictate the selection of delegates. *(See box, "Notable Credentials Fights," p. 442.)*

The issue was hottest in 1912 and 1952, when the party throughout most of the South was a skeletal structure whose power was restricted largely to selection of convention delegates. Within the Democratic Party the question of southern credentials emerged after World War II on the volatile issues of civil rights and party loyalty. Important credentials challenges on these issues occurred at the 1948, 1952, 1964, and 1968 Democratic conventions.

There were numerous credentials challenges at the 1972 Democratic convention, but unlike those at its immediate predecessors, the challenges involved delegations from across the nation and focused on violations of the party's newly adopted guidelines.

After their 1952 credentials battle, the Republicans established a contest committee within the national committee to review credentials challenges before the convention. After their divisive 1968 convention, the Democrats also created a formal credentials procedure to review all challenges before the opening of the convention.

Equally important to the settlement of credentials challenges are the rules under which the convention operates. The Republican Party adopts a completely new set of rules at every convention. Although large portions of the existing rules are enacted each time, general revision is always possible.

After its 1968 convention, the Democratic Party set out to reform itself and the convention system. The Commission on Rules and the Commission on Party Structure and Delegate Selection, both created by the 1968 convention, proposed many changes that were accepted by the national committee. As a result, a formal set of rules was adopted for the first time at the party's 1972 convention.

Controversial Rules

Although it did not have a formal set of rules before 1972, the Democratic Party had long operated with two controversial rules never used by the Republicans: the unit rule and the two-thirds nominating rule. The unit rule enabled the majority of a delegation, if authorized by its state party, to cast the entire vote of the delegation for one candidate or position. In use since the earliest Democratic conventions, the unit rule was abolished by the 1968 convention.

From their first convention in 1832 until the 1936 convention, the Democrats employed the two-thirds nominating rule, which required any candidate for president or vice president to win not just a simple majority but a two-thirds majority. Viewed as a boon to the South since it allowed that region a virtual veto power over any possible nominee, the rule was abolished with

---

Democrats' Two-Thirds Rule

At their first convention in 1832 the Democrats adopted a rule requiring a two-thirds majority for nomination. Two presidential candidates—Martin Van Buren in 1844 and Champ Clark in 1912—received majorities but failed to attain the two-thirds requirement.

On the first ballot in 1844 former president Van Buren received 146 of the 266 convention votes, 54.9 percent of the total. His total fell under a simple majority on succeeding roll calls, and on the ninth ballot the nomination went to a dark-horse candidate, former governor James K. Polk of Tennessee.

In 1912 from the tenth through the sixteenth ballots House Speaker Clark recorded a simple majority. He reached his peak on the tenth ballot, receiving 556 of the 1,094 convention votes, 50.8 percent of the total. The nomination, however, ultimately went to New Jersey governor Woodrow Wilson, who was selected on the forty-sixth ballot.

At their 1936 convention the Democrats voted to end the requirement for a two-thirds majority for nomination.

---

the stipulation that the South would receive an increased vote allocation at later conventions.

In its century of use the two-thirds rule frequently produced protracted, multiballot conventions, often giving the Democrats a degree of turbulence the Republicans, requiring only a simple majority, did not have. Between 1832 and 1932, seven Democratic conventions took more than ten ballots to select a presidential candidate. In contrast, in their entire convention history, the Republicans have had just one convention that required more than ten ballots to select a presidential candidate. *(See box, "Democrats' Two-Thirds Rule," above.)*

One controversy that surfaced during the 1980 Democratic Party convention concerned a rule that bound delegates to vote on the first ballot for the candidates under whose banner they had been elected. Supporters of Senator Kennedy had devoted their energy to prying the nomination from incumbent President Carter by defeating that rule. But the final tally showed 1,936.42 delegates favoring the binding rule and 1,390.58 opposing it. Passage of the binding rule ensured Carter's renomination, and shortly after the vote Kennedy announced that his name would not be placed in nomination.

Convention Officers

Credentials, rules, and platform are three of the major convention committees. Within the Republican Party, though, the committee on permanent organization ratifies the slate of convention officials. In the Democratic Party, the rules committee recommends the officials.

In both the Democratic and Republican parties, the presiding officer during the bulk of the convention is the permanent chairman. For much of the postwar period, the position has gone to the party's leader in the House of Representatives,

Notable Credentials Fights

1848, Democratic. Two rival New York state factions, known as the Barnburners and the Hunkers, sent separate delegations. By a vote of 126 to 125, the convention decided to seat both delegations and split New York's vote between them. This compromise suited neither faction: the Barnburners bolted the convention; the Hunkers remained but refused to vote.

1860, Democratic. Dissatisfaction with the slavery plank in the party platform spurred a walkout by several dozen southern delegates from the Charleston convention. When the tumultuous convention reconvened in Baltimore six weeks later, a credentials controversy developed on the status of the bolting delegates. The majority report of the credentials committee recommended that the delegates in question, except those from Alabama and Louisiana, be reseated. The minority report recommended that a larger majority of the withdrawing Charleston delegates be allowed to return. The minority report was defeated, 100½ to 150, prompting a walkout by the majority of delegates from nine states.

1880, Republican. Factions for and against the candidacy of former president Ulysses S. Grant clashed on the credentials of the Illinois delegation. By a margin of 387 to 353, the convention rejected a minority report that proposed seating pro-Grant delegates elected at the state convention over other delegates elected at a congressional district caucus. Three other votes were taken on disputed credentials from different Illinois districts, but all were decided in favor of the anti-Grant forces by a similar margin. The votes indicated the weakness of the Grant candidacy. The nomination went to a dark-horse candidate, Rep. James A. Garfield of Ohio, on the thirty-sixth ballot.

1912, Republican. The furious struggle between President William Howard Taft and Theodore Roosevelt for the presidential nomination centered on credentials. The Roosevelt forces brought seventy-two delegate challenges to the floor of the convention, but the test of strength between the two candidates came on a procedural motion. By a vote of 567 to 507, the convention tabled a motion presented by the Roosevelt forces barring any of the delegates under challenge from voting on any of the credentials contests. This procedural vote clearly indicated Taft's control of the convention. All the credentials cases were settled in favor of the Taft delegates, and the presidential nomination ultimately went to the incumbent president.

1932, Democratic. Two delegations favorable to the frontrunner for the presidential nomination, Franklin D. Roosevelt, came under challenge. However, in a show of strength, the Roosevelt forces won both contests: seating a Louisiana delegation headed by Sen. Huey P. Long by a vote of 638¾ to 514¼ and a Roosevelt delegation from Minnesota by an even wider margin, 658¼ to 492¾. Roosevelt won the nomination on the fourth ballot.

1952, Democratic. The refusal of three southern states—Louisiana, South Carolina, and Virginia—to agree to a party loyalty pledge brought their credentials into question. The Virginia delegation argued that the problem prompting the loyalty pledge was covered by state law. By a vote of 650½ to 518, the convention approved the seating of the Virginia delegation. After Louisiana and South Carolina took positions similar to that of Virginia, they were seated by a voice vote.

1952, Republican. Sixty-eight delegates from three southern states (Georgia, Louisiana, and Texas) were the focal point of the fight for the presidential nomination between Gen. Dwight D. Eisenhower and Sen. Robert A. Taft of Ohio. The national committee, controlled by forces favorable to Taft, had voted to seat delegations friendly to the Ohio senator from these three states. But by a vote of 607 to 531 the convention seated the Georgia delegation favorable to Eisenhower. It seated the Eisenhower delegates from Louisiana and Texas without roll calls. The general went on to win the presidential nomination on the first ballot.

1968, Democratic. A struggle between the anti–Vietnam War forces, led by Sen. Eugene J. McCarthy of Minnesota, and the party regulars, headed by Vice President Hubert H. Humphrey, dominated the seventeen cases considered by the credentials committee. Three of the cases, involving the Texas, Georgia, and Alabama delegations, required roll calls on the convention floor. All were won by the Humphrey forces. By a vote of 1,368¼ to 956¾, the regular Texas delegation headed by Gov. John B. Connally was seated. A minority report to seat the entire Georgia delegation led by black leader Julian Bond was defeated, 1,043.55 to 1,415.45. Another minority report to seat a McCarthy-backed, largely black delegation from Alabama was also rejected, 880¾ to 1,607. Humphrey, having shown his strength during the credentials contests, went on to win an easy first ballot nomination.

1972, Democratic. The first test of strength at the convention between South Dakota senator George McGovern's delegates and party regulars came over credentials. Key challenges brought to the convention floor concerned the South Carolina, California, and Illinois delegations. The South Carolina challenge was brought by the National Women's Political Caucus in response to alleged underrepresentation of women in the delegation. Although the caucus's position was supposedly supported by the McGovern camp, votes were withheld to avoid jeopardizing McGovern's chances of winning the important California contest. The caucus's challenge lost 1,429.05 to 1,555.75. The California challenge was of crucial importance to McGovern, because it involved 151 delegates initially won by the South Dakota senator in the state's winner-take-all primary, but stripped from him by the credentials committee. By a vote of 1,618.28 to 1,238.22, McGovern regained the contested delegates, thereby nailing down his nomination. With victory in hand, the dominant McGovern camp sought a compromise on the Illinois case, which pitted a delegation headed by Chicago's powerful mayor Richard Daley against an insurgent delegation composed of party reformers. Compromise was unattainable, and with the bulk of McGovern delegates voting for the reformers, a minority report to seat the Daley delegates was rejected.

National Party Chairs, 1848–2005

Name	State	Years of service
Democratic Party		
B. F. Hallett	Massachusetts	1848–1852
Robert McLane	Maryland	1852–1856
David A. Smalley	Virginia	1856–1860
August Belmont	New York	1860–1872
Augustus Schell	New York	1872–1876
Abram S. Hewitt	New York	1876–1877
William H. Barnum	Connecticut	1877–1889
Calvin S. Brice	Ohio	1889–1892
William F. Harrity	Pennsylvania	1892–1896
James K. Jones	Arkansas	1896–1904
Thomas Taggart	Indiana	1904–1908
Norman E. Mack	New York	1908–1912
William F. McCombs	New York	1912–1916
Vance C. McCormick	Pennsylvania	1916–1919
Homer S. Cummings	Connecticut	1919–1920
George White	Ohio	1920–1921
Cordell Hull	Tennessee	1921–1924
Clem Shaver	West Virginia	1924–1928
John J. Raskob	Maryland	1928–1932
James A. Farley	New York	1932–1940
Edward J. Flynn	New York	1940–1943
Frank C. Walker	Pennsylvania	1943–1944
Robert E. Hannegan	Missouri	1944–1947
J. Howard McGrath	Rhode Island	1947–1949
William M. Boyle Jr.	Missouri	1949–1951
Frank E. McKinney	Indiana	1951–1952
Stephen A. Mitchell	Illinois	1952–1954
Paul M. Butler	Indiana	1955–1960
Henry M. Jackson	Washington	1960–1961
John M. Bailey	Connecticut	1961–1968
Lawrence F. O'Brien	Massachusetts	1968–1969
Fred Harris	Oklahoma	1969–1970
Lawrence F. O'Brien	Massachusetts	1970–1972
Jean Westwood	Utah	1972
Robert Straus	Texas	1972–1977
Kenneth Curtis	Maine	1977–1978
John White	Texas	1978–1981
Charles Manatt	California	1981–1985
Paul Kirk	Massachusetts	1985–1989
Ronald H. Brown	Washington, D.C.	1989–1993
David Wilhelm	Illinois	1993–1994
Christopher Dodd (general chair)	Connecticut	1994–1997
Donald Fowler	South Carolina	1994–1997
Roy Romer (general chair)	Colorado	1997–1999
Steven Grossman	Massachusetts	1997–1999
Ed Rendell (general chair)	Pennsylvania	1999–2001
Joe Andrew	Indiana	1999–2001
Terrence McAuliffe	New York	2001–2005
Howard Dean	Vermont	2005–
Republican Party		
Edwin D. Morgan	New York	1856–1864
Henry J. Raymond	New York	1864–1866
Marcus L. Ward	New Jersey	1866–1868
William Claflin	Massachusetts	1868–1872
Edwin D. Morgan	New York	1872–1876

Name	State	Years of service
Republican Party (continued)		
Zachariah Chandler	Michigan	1876–1879
J. Donald Cameron	Pennsylvania	1879–1880
Marshall Jewell	Connecticut	1880–1883
D. M. Sabin	Minnesota	1883–1884
B. F. Jones	Pennsylvania	1884–1888
Matthew S. Quay	Pennsylvania	1888–1891
James S. Clarkson	Iowa	1891–1892
Thomas H. Carter	Montana	1892–1896
Mark A. Hanna	Ohio	1896–1904
Henry C. Payne	Wisconsin	1904
George B. Cortelyou	New York	1904–1907
Harry S. New	Indiana	1907–1908
Frank H. Hitchcock	Massachusetts	1908–1909
John F. Hill	Maine	1909–1912
Victor Rosewater	Nebraska	1912
Charles D. Hilles	New York	1912–1916
William R. Willcox	New York	1916–1918
Will Hays	Indiana	1918–1921
John T. Adams	Iowa	1921–1924
William M. Butler	Massachusetts	1924–1928
Hubert Work	Colorado	1928–1929
Claudius H. Huston	Tennessee	1929–1930
Simeon D. Fess	Ohio	1930–1932
Everett Sanders	Indiana	1932–1934
Henry P. Fletcher	Pennsylvania	1934–1936
John Hamilton	Kansas	1936–1940
Joseph W. Martin Jr.	Massachusetts	1940–1942
Harrison E. Spangler	Iowa	1942–1944
Herbert Brownell Jr.	New York	1944–1946
B. Carroll Reece	Tennessee	1946–1948
Hugh D. Scott Jr.	Pennsylvania	1948–1949
Guy George Gabrielson	New Jersey	1949–1952
Arthur E. Summerfield	Michigan	1952–1953
C. Wesley Roberts	Kansas	1953
Leonard W. Hall	New York	1953–1957
H. Meade Alcorn Jr.	Connecticut	1957–1959
Thruston B. Morton	Kentucky	1959–1961
William E. Miller	New York	1961–1964
Dean Burch	Arizona	1964–1965
Ray C. Bliss	Ohio	1965–1969
Rogers C. B. Morton	Maryland	1969–1971
Robert Dole	Kansas	1971–1973
George Bush	Texas	1973–1974
Mary Louise Smith	Iowa	1974–1977
William Brock	Tennessee	1977–1981
Richard Richards	Utah	1981–1983
Paul Laxalt (general chair)	Nevada	1983–1986
Frank Fahrenkopf Jr.	Nevada	1983–1989
Lee Atwater	South Carolina	1989–1991
Clayton Yeutter	Nebraska	1991–1992
Rich Bond	New York	1992–1993
Haley Barbour	Mississippi	1993–1997
Jim Nicholson	Colorado	1997–2001
James Gilmore	Virginia	2001–2002
Marc Racicot	Montana	2002–2003
Ed Gillespie	New Jersey	2003–2005
Ken Mehlman	Maryland	2005–

Sources: Hugh A. Bone, *Party Committees and National Politics* (Seattle: University of Washington, 1958), 241–243; Congressional Quarterly, *The President, the Public, and the Parties*, 2nd ed. (Washington, D.C.: Congressional Quarterly, 1997), 21; and various issues of *CQ Weekly Report*.

Major Platform Fights

1860, Democratic. A minority report on the slavery plank, stating that the decision on allowing slavery in the territories should be left to the Supreme Court, was approved, 165 to 138. The majority report (favored by the South) declared that no government—local, state, or federal—could outlaw slavery in the territories. The acceptance of the minority report precipitated a walkout by several dozen southern delegates and the eventual sectional split in the party.

1896, Democratic. The monetary plank of the platform committee, favoring free and unlimited coinage of silver at a ratio of 16 to 1 with gold, was accepted by the convention, which defeated a proposed gold plank, 626 to 303. During debate William Jennings Bryan made his famous "Cross of Gold" speech supporting the platform committee plank, bringing him to the attention of the convention and resulting in his nomination for president.

1908, Republican. A minority report, proposing a substitute platform, was presented by Sen. Robert M. La Follette of Wisconsin. Minority proposals included increased antitrust activities, enactment of a law requiring publication of campaign expenditures, and popular election of senators. All the proposed planks were defeated by wide margins; the closest vote, on direct election of senators, was 114 for, 866 against.

1924, Democratic. A minority plank was presented that condemned the activities of the Ku Klux Klan, then enjoying a resurgence in the South and some states in the Midwest. The plank was defeated 5427/20 to 5433/20, the closest vote in Democratic convention history.

1932, Republican. A minority plank favoring repeal of the Eighteenth Amendment (Prohibition) in favor of a state-option arrangement was defeated, 4602/9 to 69019/36.

1948, Democratic. An amendment to the platform, strengthening the civil rights plank by guaranteeing full and equal political participation, equal employment opportunity, personal security, and equal treatment in the military service, was accepted, 6511½ to 582½.

1964, Republican. An amendment offered by Sen. Hugh Scott of Pennsylvania to strengthen the civil rights plank by including voting guarantees in state as well as in federal elections and by eliminating job bias was defeated, 409 to 897.

1968, Democratic. A minority report on Vietnam called for cessation of the bombing of North Vietnam, halting of offensive and search-and-destroy missions by U.S. combat units, a negotiated withdrawal of U.S. troops, and establishment of a coalition government in South Vietnam. It was defeated, 1,041¼ to 1,567¾.

1972, Democratic. By a vote of 1,852.86 to 999.34, the convention rejected a minority report proposing a government guaranteed annual income of $6,500 for a family of four. By a vote of 1,101.37 to 1,572.80, a women's rights plank supporting abortion rights was defeated.

1980, Democratic. The platform battle, one of the longest in party history, pitted President Jimmy Carter against his persistent rival, Sen. Edward M. Kennedy of Massachusetts. Stretching over seventeen hours, the debate focused on Kennedy's economics plank, which finally was defeated by a voice vote. Yet Carter was forced to concede on so many specific points, including Kennedy's $12 billion antirecession jobs programs, that the final document bore little resemblance to the draft initially drawn up by Carter's operatives.

1992, Democratic. A tax fairness plank offered by former senator Paul E. Tsongas of Massachusetts was defeated by a vote of 953 to 2,287. The plank called for a delay in any middle-class tax cut and tax credit for families with children until the deficit was under control.

---

particularly at the GOP convention. *(See "National Party Chairs, 1848–2005" table, p. 35.)*

However, this loose precedent was broken in the Democratic Party by a rule adopted at the 1972 convention requiring that the presiding officer position alternate every four years between the sexes.

Party Platforms

The adoption of a party platform is one of the principal functions of a convention. The platform committee is charged with the responsibility of writing a party platform to be presented to the convention for its approval.

The main challenge before the platform committee has traditionally been to write a platform all party candidates can use in their campaigns. For this reason, platforms often fit the description given them by Wendell L. Willkie, Republican presidential candidate in 1940: "fusions of ambiguity." *(See box, "Major Platform Fights," above.)*

Despite the best efforts of platform-builders to resolve their differences in the comparative privacy of the committee room, they sometimes encounter so controversial a subject that it cannot be compromised. Under these conditions dissident committee members often submit a minority report to the convention floor. Open floor fights are not unusual and, like credentials battles, often reflect the strength of the various candidates.

When the party has an incumbent president, the platform often is drafted in the White House or at least has the approval of the president. Rarely does a party adopt a platform that is critical of an incumbent president of the same party. When Democratic delegates at their 1896 convention, inspired by William Jennings Bryan's "Cross of Gold" speech, repudiated President Grover Cleveland and his support for a gold standard for hard currency, and nominated Bryan for president on a "free silver" platform, they signaled a major sea change in American politics. A similar change took place in 1948, when Democratic delegates led by Mayor Hubert Humphrey of Minneapolis overturned a recommendation by the platform committee and precipitated a walk-

Chief Officers at Other National Party Conventions, 1831–1892

Year	Party	Temporary chair	Chair
1831	Anti-Masonic		John C. Spencer, N.Y.
1831	National Republican	Abner Lacock, Pa.	James Barbour, Va.
1839	Whig	Isaac Bates, Mass.	James Barbour, Va.
1844	Whig	Andrew F. Hopkins, Ala.	Ambrose Spencer, N.Y.
1848	Whig	John A. Collier, N.Y.	John M. Morehead, N.C.
1852	Whig	George C. Evans, Maine	John G. Chapman, Md.
1843	Liberty		Leicester King
1848	Free Soil		Charles Francis Adams, Mass.
1852	Free Soil (Free Democrats)		Henry Wilson, Mass.
1856	American (Know-Nothing)		Ephraim Marsh, N.J.
1860	Southern Democrat (Breckinridge)		Caleb Cushing, Mass.
1860	Constitutional Union		Washington Hunt, N.Y.
1872	Liberal Republican	Stanley Matthews, Ohio	Carl Schurz, Mo.
1880	Greenback	Gilbert De La Matyr, Ind.	Richard Trevellick, Mich.
1888	Prohibition	H. A. Delano, Conn.	John P. St. John, Kan.
1892	Prohibition	John P. St. John, Kan.	Eli Ritter, Ind.
1892	People's (Populist)	C. H. Ellington, Ga.	H. L. Loricks, S.D.

out of southern delegates by adopting a strong civil rights plank. Although overridden, President Harry S. Truman accepted the Humphrey plank—and won with it.

The first platform was adopted by the Democrats in 1840. It was a short document, fewer than 1,000 words. Since then the platforms with few exceptions have grown longer and longer, covering more issues and appealing to more and more interest groups. One of the exceptions to the growth trend was the 4,500-word Democratic platform of 1988—about one-tenth the length of the 1984 platform. In 2004 the Democratic platform was 19,500 words; the Republican platform was more than twice as long at almost 48,000 words.

THIRD PARTIES: RADICAL IDEAS

Throughout U.S. history, many daring and controversial political platforms adopted by third parties have been rejected as too radical by the major parties. Yet many of these proposals later have won popular acceptance and have made their way into the major party platforms—and into law. Ideas such as the abolition of slavery, prohibition, the graduated income tax, the popular election of senators, women's suffrage, minimum wages, Social Security, and the eighteen-year-old vote were advocated by Populists, Progressives, and other third parties long before they were finally accepted by the nation as a whole.

The radical third parties and their platforms have been anathema to the established wisdom of the day, denounced as impractical, dangerous, destructive of moral virtues, and even traitorous. They have been anti-establishment and more far-reaching in

their proposed solutions to problems than the major parties have dared to be. *(See box, "Third Parties Usually Fade Rapidly," p. 38.)*

MAJOR PARTIES: BROADER APPEAL

In contrast with the third parties, Democrats and Republicans traditionally have been much more cautious against adopting radical platform planks. Trying to appeal to a broad range of voters, the two major parties have tended to compromise differences or to reject controversial platform planks.

The Democratic Party has been more ready than the Republicans to adopt once-radical ideas, but there is usually a considerable time lag between their origin in third parties and their eventual adoption in Democratic platforms. For example, while the Democrats by 1912 had adopted many of the Populist planks of the 1890s, the Bull Moose Progressives of that year already were way ahead of them in proposals for social legislation. Not until 1932 were many of the 1912 Progressive planks adopted by the Democrats.

Similarly, it was not until the 1960s that Democratic platforms incorporated many of the more far-reaching proposals originally put forward by the 1948 Progressive Party in that year.

Filling Vacancies

Starting with the Democratic convention of 1848, and the Republican Party's first national organizing meeting in 1856, both major parties have elected national committees to run the day-to-day business of the parties between conventions.

Third Parties Usually Fade Rapidly

Most third-party movements are like shooting stars, shining brightly in one election and then quickly disappearing. Since 1832, eleven third parties—plus independents John B. Anderson in 1980 and H. Ross Perot in 1992—have drawn at least 5 percent of the popular vote in a presidential election.

As of 2004 none of these third parties or independents were able to maintain their footholds in the electoral process. Four had disappeared by the next election, six others drew smaller vote totals, and three endorsed one of the major parties. The Reform Party, which first received 8.5 percent of the vote in 1996 with Perot atop its ticket, confirmed this pattern in 2000 when its candidate Patrick J. Buchanan only received 0.4 percent. Perot had received his highest popular vote percentage (18.9 percent) in 1992

when he first ran for president as an independent. (Although Ralph Nader in 2000 and 2004 never received above 5 percent of the vote, his candidacy illustrated the same diminishing appeal when he received 2.7 percent of the popular vote in the first election but only 0.4 percent in the second.)

Each of the significant third parties, except the Socialists in 1912, made its best showing in its first election. (The Socialists, led by Eugene V. Debs, first ran in 1900, winning just 0.62 percent of the vote.) The following chart lists each party's presidential candidate and the percentage of the vote the party received in its most successful race and in the following election. A dash (–) indicates that the party had disappeared.

Party (candidate)	Year	Percentage of vote	Next election
Anti-Mason (William Wirt)	1832	7.8%	endorsed Whig
Free Soil (Martin Van Buren)	1848	10.1	4.9%
Whig-American (Millard Fillmore)	1856	21.5	–
Southern Democrats (John C. Breckinridge)	1860	18.1	–
Constitutional Union (John Bell)	1860	12.6	–
Populist (James B. Weaver)	1892	8.5	endorsed Democrat
Progressive (Bull Moose) (Theodore Roosevelt)	1912	27.4	0.2
Socialist (Eugene V. Debs)	1912	6.0	3.2
Progressive (Robert M. La Follette)	1924	16.6	–
American Independent (George C. Wallace)	1968	13.5	1.4
John B. Anderson (Independent)	1980	6.6	endorsed Democrat
H. Ross Perot (Independent)	1992	18.9	8.5 (Reform Party)
Reform Party	1996	8.5 (Perot)	0.4 (Buchanan)

Since their beginning, one of the most important functions of national committees has been to replace a candidate who dies or resigns after the convention adjourns, or after election day but before the electors cast their votes for president and vice president. This replacement power was assumed informally, but without controversy, at first. It was granted by several national conventions during the Progressive Era (1900–1912) and was made part of both parties' permanent standing rules by the 1920s.

There have been four such vacancies.

In 1860 the Democratic designee for vice president, Sen. Benjamin Fitzpatrick of Alabama, declined the nomination after the ruinously chaotic Baltimore convention of that year finally adjourned. The national committee then nominated former gov-

ernor Herschel V. Johnson of Georgia as Sen. Stephen A. Douglas's running mate.

In 1872 the Democratic nominee for president, Horace Greeley, founder of the *New York Tribune*, died shortly after election day. (Incumbent Republican president Ulysses S. Grant had won the election.) Greeley's dispirited party's national committee declined to select a replacement candidate, and the Democratic electors voted for four different candidates.

In 1912 Vice President James S. Sherman of New York died in office the week before election day. The Republican convention of that year had authorized the national committee to fill vacancies, and the committee quickly replaced Sherman. His name remained on state ballots as President William Howard Taft's

President George W. Bush waves to the crowd at the 2004 Republican National Convention in New York City.

running mate, but the eight Republican electors voted, as recommended by the committee, for the replacement candidate, Nicholas Murray Butler of New York, president of Columbia University. The Taft ticket did not win reelection.

Finally, in 1972, the Democratic nominee for vice president, Sen. Thomas Eagleton of Missouri, resigned his candidacy after the convention adjourned. The nominee for president, Sen. George McGovern, recommended R. Sargent Shriver of Illinois, former head of the Peace Corps, as his replacement running mate, and Shriver was selected by a special meeting of an expanded national committee.

Communications and the Media

Major changes in the national nominating convention have resulted from the massive advances in transportation and communication technologies during the twentieth century.

The revolution in transportation has affected the scheduling of conventions. In the nineteenth century, conventions were sometimes held a year or more before the election and at the latest were completed by late spring of the election year. With the ability of people to assemble quickly, conventions in recent years have been held later in the election year, usually in July or August. Advances in transportation also have affected site location. Geographic centrality is no longer a primary consideration in the selection of a convention city.

Radio coverage of conventions began in 1924, television coverage sixteen years later. One of the first changes inspired by the media age was the termination of the custom that a presidential candidate not appear at the convention but accept his nomination in a ceremony several weeks later. Franklin D. Roosevelt was the first major party candidate to break this tradition when in 1932 he delivered his acceptance speech in person before the

Democratic convention. Twelve years later, Thomas E. Dewey became the first Republican nominee to give his acceptance speech to the convention. Since then, the final activity of every Democratic and Republican convention has been the delivery of the acceptance speech by the presidential nominee.

Party leaders have also, in recent years, streamlined the schedule, with the assumption that the interest level of most of the viewing public for politics is limited. The result has been shorter speeches and generally fewer roll calls than at those conventions in the pretelevision era. At both conventions in 2004, the address of the vice-presidential candidate was delivered on the night before that of the presidential nominee.

Party leaders desire to put on a good show for the viewing public with the hope of winning votes for their party in November. The convention is a showcase, designed to present the party as both a model of democracy and an efficient, harmonious body. The schedule of convention activities is drawn up with an eye on the peak evening television viewing hours. There is an attempt to put the party's major selling points—the highly partisan keynote speech, the nominating ballots, and the candidates' acceptance speeches—on in prime time. (The effort to put acceptance speeches on in prime time has been especially strong since 1972, when Democratic nominee George S. McGovern was forced to wait until the wee hours of the morning to make his speech.) Conversely, party leaders try to keep evidence of bitter party factionalism—such as explosive credentials and platform battles—out of the peak viewing period.

Both the Republicans and Democrats went to extraordinary lengths to turn their 2000 conventions into tightly scripted, visually appealing television shows. But it seems that the harder the political parties try to win over American audiences, the less they have to show for their efforts. Many TV viewers voted with their remote controls—tuning out the 2000 conventions.

Highlights of National Party Conventions, 1831–2004

1831 First national political convention held in Baltimore by Anti-Masonic Party.

1832 Democratic Party met in Baltimore for its first national convention.

1839 Whig Party held its first national convention.

1840 Democrats set up committee to select vice presidential nominees, subject to approval of convention.

1844 Democrats nominated James K. Polk—first "dark-horse" candidate—after nine ballots. Silas Wright declined the vice-presidential nomination. First time a convention nominee refused nomination.

1848 Democrats established continuing committee, known as "Democratic National Committee."

1852 Democrats and Whigs both adopted platforms before nominating candidates for president, setting precedent followed almost uniformly ever since.

1856 First Republican national convention held in Philadelphia.

1860 Democrats met in Charleston, S.C. After ten days and deadlocked on a presidential nominee, delegates adjourned and reconvened in Baltimore. Benjamin Fitzpatrick, the Democrats' choice for vice president, became the first candidate to withdraw after convention adjournment and be replaced by a selection of the national committee.

First Republican credentials dispute took place over seating delegates from slave states and voting strength of delegates from states where party was comparatively weak.

1864 In attempt to close ranks during Civil War, Republicans used the name "Union Party" at convention.

1868 For the first time, Republicans gave a candidate (Ulysses S. Grant) 100 percent of vote on first ballot.

A letter from Susan B. Anthony was read before Democratic convention urging support of women's suffrage.

1872 Victoria Clafin Woodhull, nominated by the Equal Rights Party, was the first woman presidential candidate. Black leader Frederick Douglass was her running mate.

1880 Republicans nominated James A. Garfield for president on 36th ballot—party's all-time record number of ballots.

1884 Republican Rep. John Roy Lynch of Mississippi became first black elected temporary chairman of national nominating convention.

1888 Frederick Douglass was first black to receive a vote in presidential balloting at a major party political convention (Republican).

1900 Each party had one woman delegate.

1904 Florida Democrats selected delegates in first-ever presidential primary election.

1920 For first time, women attended conventions in significant numbers.

1924 Republicans adopted bonus votes for states that went Republican in previous election. GOP convention was first to be broadcast on radio.

John W. Davis was nominated by Democrats on record 103rd ballot.

1928 Democrats nominated Gov. Alfred E. Smith of New York for president—first time a Roman Catholic placed on national ticket by a major party.

1932 Republicans began tradition of appointing their party leader from House of Representatives as permanent convention chairman.

Democrat Franklin D. Roosevelt became first major party candidate to accept presidential nomination in person.

1936 Democratic Party voted to end requirement of two-thirds delegate majority for nomination.

1940 Republican convention was first to be televised.

1944 Democrats adopted bonus votes for states that went Democratic in previous election.

Thomas E. Dewey became first Republican candidate to accept nomination in person.

1948 Democrats began appointing Speaker of the House as permanent chairman. Republicans renominated Thomas E. Dewey—first time GOP renominated a defeated presidential candidate.

1952 Adlai E. Stevenson was chosen as Democratic nominee in one of few genuine "drafts" in history.

1956 Democrats used party loyalty provision in selecting delegates for first time.

1960 Democrats adopted civil rights plank that was strongest in party history.

Republican nominee Richard Nixon was party's first vice president nominated for president at completion of his term.

1964 Sen. Margaret Chase Smith was nominated for presidency at Republican convention—first time a woman placed in nomination by a major party.

1968 Democratic Party voted to end unit rule. Outside the Chicago convention, antiwar protests erupt in violence.

1980 Democratic delegates were composed of an equal number of men and women.

1984 Democrats nominated Rep. Geraldine A. Ferraro of New York for vice president—the first woman placed on national ticket by a major party.

1996 The Reform Party conducted its first convention in a two-stage process that allowed balloting by mail, electronic mail, or phone.

2000 Democrats nominated Sen. Joseph Lieberman of Connecticut for vice president—first time a person of Jewish faith placed on national ticket by a major party.

2004 First conventions held after the terrorist attacks of September 11, 2001.

By and large, ratings for the three major networks' broadcasts of the conventions have been on a steady decline for the past two decades. In 2004 the networks—ABC, CBS, and NBC—opted to broadcast only three hours of each four-day convention. Viewers, however, could tune to cable stations such as CNN, Fox, MSNBC, or C-SPAN to watch full coverage. Public broadcasting also provided additional coverage.

In the media age the appearance of fairness is important, and in a sense this need to look fair and open has assisted the movement for party reform. Some influential party leaders, skeptical of reform of the convention, have found resistance difficult in the glare of television.

Before the revolution in the means of transportation and communication, conventions met in relative anonymity. Today conventions are held in all the privacy of a fishbowl, with every action and every rumor closely scrutinized. They have become media events and as such are targets for political demonstrations that can be not only an embarrassment to the party but a security problem as well.

In spite of its difficulties, the convention system has survived. As the nation has developed during the past century and a half, the convention has evolved as well, changing its form but retaining its variety of functions. Criticism has been leveled at the convention, but no substitute has yet been offered that would nominate a presidential ticket, adopt a party platform, act as the supreme governing body of the party, and serve as a massive campaign rally and propaganda forum. In addition to these functions, a convention is a place where compromise can take place—compromise often mandatory in a major political party that combines varying viewpoints.

CHAPTER 4

Convention Chronology, 1831–2004

THIS CHAPTER contains brief descriptions of all presidential nominating conventions of major U.S. political parties and excerpts from party platforms. The chronology begins in 1831, when the Anti-Masonic Party held the first nominating convention in American history, and concludes with the national conventions of the Republican and Democratic parties in 2004.

The narrative includes conventions for all parties receiving at least 2 percent of the popular vote in the presidential election. Thus, conventions for the Socialist Party, which received at least 2 percent of the presidential popular vote in 1904, 1908, 1912, 1920, and 1932, are included. Socialist Party conventions for other presidential election years when the party received less than 2 percent of the popular vote do not appear. In 2000 the Green Party received 2.7 percent of the popular vote so its convention is included here.

The sources most frequently consulted in preparing the narrative were Richard C. Bain and Judith H. Parris, *Convention Decisions and Voting Records,* (Washington, D.C.: Brookings Institution, 1973); and various issues of the *CQ Weekly.*

BALLOT VOTE TOTALS

Throughout the narrative, vote totals appear for significant ballots on platform disputes and procedural issues and for presidential and vice-presidential balloting.

The source used for 1835–1972 vote totals was *Convention Decisions and Voting Records.* The sources for the 1976 through 2004 vote totals were *The Official Proceedings of the Democratic National Convention* and the Republican National Committee. Charts showing state-by-state voting on selected ballots appear in Chapter 5, Key Convention Ballots, pages 182–251. *(For details on these charts, see p. 181.)*

PLATFORM EXCERPTS

The source for the party platform excerpts that appear in the convention chronology was Kirk H. Porter and Donald Bruce Johnson, *National Party Platforms, 1840–1972* (Urbana: University of Illinois Press, 1973). For the Democratic and Republican platform excerpts for 1976 to 2004, the official texts of the platforms adopted by the two parties were used.

In adopting the material from *National Party Platforms, 1840–1972,* Congressional Quarterly has added boldface subheadings to highlight the organization of the texts. For example, excerpts from the 1844 Democratic Party platform appear on page 49. The boldface headings—Appeal to the Masses, Internal Improvements, Government Spending, etc.—do not appear in the text of the party platform as it was published in *National Party Platforms, 1840–1972.* In all other respects, Congressional Quarterly has followed the style and typography of the platform texts appearing in *National Party Platforms, 1840–1972.* In excerpting the material from the Democratic and Republican platforms from 1976 to 2004, Congressional Quarterly has also edited the boldface subheadings from the original platform documents.

1831–1832 Conventions

PRESIDENTIAL CANDIDATES

William Wirt
Anti-Mason

Henry Clay
National Republican

Andrew Jackson
Democrat

ANTI-MASONS

In September 1831 the Anti-Masonic Party held the first national nominating convention in American history. Thirteen states, none south of Maryland, sent 116 delegates to the gathering in Baltimore. They selected the party's presidential and vice-presidential candidates, adopted an address to the people (a precursor of the party platform), and established a national corresponding committee that created the framework for a national campaign organization.

Ironically, the Anti-Masons, whose keystone was opposition to Masonry, nominated a former Mason, William Wirt of Maryland, as their presidential standard-bearer. In spite of a rule requiring a three-fourths nominating majority, Wirt was an easy first-ballot winner and the nearly unanimous nominee of the convention.

He was not, however, the first choice of party leaders, who had been rebuffed in their earlier efforts to persuade Henry Clay and later Supreme Court justice John McLean to take the presidential nomination. Wirt himself was not an enthusiastic candidate, stating that he saw nothing repugnant about Masonry and that if his views did not suit the convention, he would willingly withdraw from the ticket. The delegates supported Wirt and chose Amos Ellmaker of Pennsylvania as his vice-presidential running mate.

NATIONAL REPUBLICANS

In December 1831 the National Republicans held a national convention in Baltimore. The National Republicans were united primarily in their opposition to incumbent President Andrew Jackson. The idea of a convention had been proposed by an anti-Jackson committee in New York City and approved by the leading National Republican newspaper, the *National Intelligencer*. There was no uniform method of delegate selection, with state conventions, legislative caucuses, and local meetings all being used.

Eighteen states sent 168 delegates to the National Republican convention, although nearly one-quarter were late in arriving due to inclement winter weather. Without any preestablished rules, it was agreed that the roll calls would be taken by announcing each delegate's name. Henry Clay of Kentucky was the convention's unanimous choice for president, and former representative John Sergeant of Pennsylvania was selected without opposition for vice president. Letters accepting their nominations were received from both candidates.

There was no formal platform, although the convention adopted an address to the people that criticized Jackson for dividing a previously harmonious country.

In May 1832 a convention of young National Republicans met in Washington, D.C., and passed a series of resolutions calling for a protective tariff, federal support of internal improvements, and recognition of the Supreme Court as the ultimate authority on constitutional questions. The last was a rebuke of Jackson for disregarding Supreme Court decisions concerning the Cherokee. Other resolutions criticized Jackson's use of the spoils system in distributing patronage and his handling of foreign policy with Great Britain. Although not a formal platform, the resolutions adopted by the convention of young National Republicans were the most definitive discussion of issues during the 1832 campaign.

DEMOCRATS

The Democrats held their first national convention in Baltimore in late May 1832. Representatives from twenty-three states attended. The call for a Democratic national convention had been made by Jacksonian members of the New Hampshire legislature, and their proposal was approved by prominent members of President Andrew Jackson's administration. The convention was called to order by a member of the New Hampshire legislature, who explained the intent of the gathering in these words:

... [The] object of the people of New Hampshire who called this convention was, not to impose on the people, as candidates for either of the two first offices of the government, any local favorite; but to concentrate the opinions of all the states. . . . They believed that the example of this convention would operate favorably in future elections; that the people would be disposed, after seeing the good effects of this convention in conciliating the different and distant sections of the country, to continue this mode of nomination." *(Reprinted from Convention Decisions and Voting Records, by Richard C. Bain, p. 17.)*

The convention adopted two rules that Democratic conventions retained well into the twentieth century. One based each state's convention vote on its electoral vote, an apportionment method unchanged until 1940.

A second rule established a two-thirds nominating majority, a controversial measure that remained a feature of Democratic conventions until 1936. The 1832 convention also adopted the procedure of having one person from each delegation announce the vote of his state.

The delegates did not formally nominate Jackson for the presidency. Instead they concurred in the various nominations he had received earlier from state legislatures. Jackson's choice for vice president, Martin Van Buren of New York, was easily nominated on the first ballot, receiving 208 of the 283 votes cast.

Instead of adopting a platform or address to the people, the convention decided that each state delegation should write its own report to its constituents. The convention also determined to establish in each state general corresponding committees that together would provide a nationwide organization for the campaign.

1835–1836 Conventions

PRESIDENTIAL CANDIDATES

Martin Van Buren
Democrat

Daniel Webster
Whig

Hugh L. White
Whig

William Henry Harrison
Whig

DEMOCRATS

The Democrats held their second national convention in Baltimore in May 1835. The early date had been set by President Andrew Jackson to prevent the emergence of opposition to his handpicked successor, Vice President Martin Van Buren. Delegates from twenty-two states and two territories attended, and the size of the delegations was generally related to their distance from Baltimore. Maryland sent 188 individuals to cast the state's 10 votes, but only one person attended from Tennessee—a visiting businessman who cast 15 votes. Alabama, Illinois, and South Carolina were unrepresented.

Two rival Pennsylvania delegations arrived, precipitating the first credentials dispute in convention history. It was decided to seat both delegations and let them share the Pennsylvania vote.

An effort to eliminate the rule requiring a two-thirds nominating majority initially passed by a margin of 231 to 210 (apparently counting individual delegates instead of state convention votes), but the two-thirds rule was reimposed by a voice vote. A question developed whether the nominating majority should be based on only the states represented or on all the states in the union. It was decided to base the majority on only those present.

Vice President Van Buren won the presidential nomination, winning all 265 votes. Richard M. Johnson of Kentucky barely reached the necessary two-thirds majority on the first vice-presidential ballot, receiving 178 votes, just one vote more than the required minimum. *(Table, p. 182.)*

Johnson, famous as the alleged slayer of the Native American chief Tecumseh, had aroused some disapproval because of his personal life. Johnson had lived with a mulatto mistress by whom he had two daughters.

Once again the Democrats did not write a formal platform, although an address to the people was published in the party newspaper, the *Washington Globe.* Van Buren wrote a letter of acceptance in which he promised to "tread generally in the footsteps of President Jackson."

WHIGS

During Jackson's second term, a new party, the Whigs, emerged as the Democrats' primary opposition. It contained remnants of the short-lived National Republican Party, as well as anti-Jackson elements in the Democratic and Anti-Masonic parties. Although the Whigs were a rising political force, the party lacked national cohesion in 1836. Instead of holding a convention and nominating national candidates, the Whigs ran regional candidates nominated by state legislatures. It was the hope of

Whig strategists that the regional candidates would receive enough electoral votes to throw the election into the House of Representatives, where the party could unite behind the leading prospect.

Sen. Daniel Webster of New Hampshire ran as the Whig candidate in Massachusetts; Sen. Hugh L. White of Tennessee was the party standard-bearer in the South; Gen. William Henry Harrison of Ohio was the Whig candidate in the rest of the country. The Whigs chose Francis Granger of New York as Harrison and Webster's running mate and John Tyler of Virginia to run with White.

1839–1840 Conventions

PRESIDENTIAL CANDIDATES

William Henry Harrison
Whig

Martin Van Buren
Democrat

WHIGS

By 1839 the Whigs had established themselves as a powerful opposition party, unified enough to run a national candidate against the Democratic president, Martin Van Buren. The call for the Whigs' first national convention was issued by a group of party members in Congress. Nearly 250 delegates responded, gathering in Harrisburg, Pa., in December 1839.

Three candidates were in contention for the presidential nomination: Generals William Henry Harrison of Ohio and Winfield Scott of Virginia and Sen. Henry Clay of Kentucky. After long debate, it was decided that each state would ballot separately, then select representatives who would meet and discuss the views and results of their delegation meetings with representatives of the other states. The unit rule would be in effect, binding the entire vote of each state to the candidate who received a majority of the state's delegates.

The nominating rules agreed to by the convention strongly favored the forces opposed to Clay. First, they negated substantial Clay strength in state delegations in which he did not hold a majority of the vote. Second, they permitted balloting in rela-

tive anonymity, so that delegates would be more likely to defect from the popular Kentuckian than they would if the balloting were public.

Clay led on the first ballot, but switches by Scott delegates on subsequent roll calls gave the nomination to Harrison. On the final ballot, Harrison received 148 votes to 90 for Clay and 16 for Scott. Harrison's vote was short of a two-thirds majority, but under Whig rules only a simple majority was needed to nominate.

To give the ticket factional and geographic balance, a friend of Clay, former Democrat John Tyler of Virginia, was the unanimous selection for vice president. The convention did not risk destruction of the tenuous unity of its anti-Democratic coalition by adopting a party platform or statement of principles.

DEMOCRATS

In May 1840 the Democrats held their national convention in Baltimore. The call once again was initiated by members of the New Hampshire legislature. Delegates from twenty-one states attended, while five states were unrepresented. Again, the size of the state delegations was largely determined by their distance from Baltimore. New Jersey sent fifty-nine people to cast the state's eight votes, while only one delegate came from Massachusetts to decide that state's fourteen votes.

To avoid a bitter dispute over the vice-presidential nomination, the convention appointed a committee to recommend nominees for both spots on the ticket. The committee's recommendation that Van Buren be renominated for president was passed by acclamation. On the touchier problem of the vice presidency, the committee recommended that no nomination be made, a suggestion that was also agreed to by the convention. Dissatisfaction with the personal life of Vice President Johnson had increased, leading to the decision that state Democratic leaders determine who would run as the vice-presidential candidate in their own states.

Before the nominating process had begun, the convention had approved the first party platform in American history. A platform committee was appointed "to prepare resolutions declaratory of the principles of the . . . party." The committee report was approved without discussion.

The first Democratic platform was a short document, fewer than 1,000 words long. Although brief by modern standards, the platform clearly emphasized the party's belief in a strict reading of the Constitution. It began by stating "that the federal government is one of limited powers" and spelled out in detail what the federal government could not do. The platform stated that the federal government did not have the power to finance internal improvements, assume state debts, charter a national bank, or interfere with the rights of the states, especially relating to slavery. The platform criticized the abolitionists for stirring up the explosive slavery question. The Democrats urged the government to practice economy, supported President Van Buren's independent treasury plan, and affirmed their belief in the principles expressed in the Declaration of Independence.

In addition to the platform, the convention adopted an address to the people, which was written by a separate committee. Much longer than the platform, the address discussed party principles, lauded Van Buren and Jackson for following these principles and warned of dire consequences if the opposition should be elected.

Following are excerpts from the Democratic platform of 1840:

Strict Construction. That the federal government is one of limited powers, derived solely from the constitution, and the grants of power shown therein, ought to be strictly construed by all the departments and agents of the government, and that it is inexpedient and dangerous to exercise doubtful constitutional powers.

Internal Improvements. That the constitution does not confer upon the general government the power to commence and carry on, a general system of internal improvements.

State Debts. That the constitution does not confer authority upon the federal government, directly or indirectly, to assume the debts of the several states, contracted for local internal improvements, or other state purposes; nor would such assumption be just or expedient.

Equality of Rights. That justice and sound policy forbid the federal government to foster one branch of industry to the detriment of another, or to cherish the interests of one portion to the injury of another portion of our common country—that every citizen and every section of the country, has a right to demand and insist upon an equality of rights and privileges, and to complete and ample protection of person and property from domestic violence, or foreign aggression.

Government Spending. That it is the duty of every branch of the government, to enforce and practice the most rigid economy, in conducting our public affairs, and that no more revenue ought to be raised, than is required to defray the necessary expenses of the government.

National Bank. That congress has no power to charter a national bank; that we believe such an institution one of deadly hostility to the best interests of the country, dangerous to our republican institutions and the liberties of the people, and calculated to place the business of the country within the control of a concentrated money power, and above the laws and the will of the people.

States' Rights, Slavery. That congress has no power, under the constitution, to interfere with or control the domestic institutions of the several states, and that such states are the sole and proper judges of everything appertaining to their own affairs, not prohibited by the constitution; that all efforts by abolitionists or others, made to induce congress to interfere with questions of slavery, or to take incipient steps in relation thereto, are calculated to lead to the most alarming and dangerous consequences, and that all such efforts have an inevitable tendency to diminish the happiness of the people, and endanger the stability and permanency of the union, and ought not to be countenanced by any friend to our political institutions.

Independent Treasury. That the separation of the moneys of the government from banking institutions, is indispensable for the safety of the funds of the government, and the rights of the people.

Democratic Principles. That the liberal principles embodied by Jefferson in the Declaration of Independence, and sanctioned in the constitution, which makes ours the land of liberty, and the asylum of the oppressed of every nation, have ever been cardinal principles in the democratic faith; and every attempt to abridge the present privilege of becoming citizens, and the owners of soil among us, ought to be resisted with the same spirit which swept the alien and sedition laws from our statute-book.

1843–1844 Conventions

PRESIDENTIAL CANDIDATES

James G. Birney
Liberty

Henry Clay
Whig

James K. Polk
Democrat

LIBERTY PARTY

The Liberty Party held its second national convention in Buffalo, N.Y., in August 1843. The party, born of the failure of the Whigs and the Democrats to make a strong appeal to abolitionist voters, had held its first national convention in April 1840 in Albany, N.Y. James G. Birney of Michigan, a former slave owner, was nominated for president and Thomas Earle of Ohio was chosen as his running mate. In the 1840 election the party polled 0.29 percent of the national popular vote.

At the 1843 convention, 148 delegates from twelve states assembled in Buffalo and renominated Birney for the presidency and chose Thomas Morris of Ohio as his running mate. The party platform was more than 3,000 words long, the lengthiest platform written by any party in the nineteenth century. In spite of its length, the platform discussed only one issue, slavery. In the 1844 election, the party received 2.3 percent of the national popular vote, its highest total in any presidential election. By 1848, most members of the party joined the newly formed Free Soil Party.

Following are excerpts from the Liberty Party platform of 1844:

Resolved, That the Liberty party . . . will demand the absolute and unqualified divorce of the General Government from Slavery, and also the restoration of equality of rights, among men, in every State where the party exists, or may exist.

Therefore, Resolved, That we hereby give it to be distinctly understood, by this nation and the world, that, as abolitionists, considering that the strength of our cause lies in its righteousness—and our hope for it in our conformity to the LAWS of GOD, and our respect for the RIGHTS OF MAN, we owe it to the Sovereign Ruler of the Universe, as a proof of our allegiance to Him, in all our civil relations and offices, whether as private citizens, or as public functionaries sworn to support the Constitution of the United States, to regard and to treat the third clause of the second section of the fourth article of that instrument, whenever applied to the case of a fugitive slave, as utterly null and void, and consequently as forming no part of the Constitution of the United States, whenever we are called upon, or sworn, to support it.

WHIGS

In a harmonious one-day session, the Whigs' national convention nominated for the presidency the party's former leader in Congress, Henry Clay. It was a final rebuff for President John Tyler from the party that had nominated him for the second spot on its ticket in 1840. Three years of bickering between the White House and Whig leaders in Congress had made Tyler, former Democrat, persona non grata in the Whig Party.

Delegates from every state were represented at the Whig convention, held in Baltimore on May 1, 1844. Clay was the unanimous nominee, and it was proposed that he be invited to address the convention the next day. However, the Kentuckian declined this opportunity to make the first acceptance speech in U.S. political history, stating in a letter that he was unable to reconcile an appearance with his "sense of delicacy and propriety." *(Table, p. 183.)*

Three potential candidates for the vice presidency sent letters of withdrawal before balloting for second place on the ticket began. Unlike the convention four years earlier, the Whigs abandoned their relatively secret state caucus method of voting and adopted a public roll call, with the chair calling the name of each delegate. Theodore Frelinghuysen of New Jersey won a plurality of the convention vote for vice president on the first ballot and went on to gain, on the third ballot, the required majority.

After the nominations, several resolutions were adopted, including one that defined Whig principles and served as the party's first platform. It was a brief document, fewer than 100 words long, and the only clear difference between it and the platform adopted later by the Democratic convention was on the issue of distributing proceeds from the sale of public land. The Whigs favored distribution of these revenues to the states; the Democrats opposed it believing the proceeds should be retained by the federal government. In a continued reaction to the Jackson administration, the Whigs criticized "executive usurpations" and proposed a single-term presidency. The rest of the Whig platform called for government efficiency, "a well-regulated currency" and a tariff for revenue and the protection of American labor.

Westward territorial expansion, particularly the annexation of Texas, was not mentioned in the Whig platform, but it was an explosive issue by 1844 that made a significant impact on the Democratic convention.

Following is an excerpt from the Whig platform of 1844:

Resolved, That these principles may be summed as comprising, a well-regulated currency; a tariff for revenue to defray the necessary expenses of the government, and discriminating with special reference to protection of the domestic labor of the country; the distribution of the proceeds of the sales of the public lands; a single term for the presidency; a reform of executive usurpations;—and, generally—such an administration of the affairs of the country as shall impart to every branch of the public service the greatest practicable efficiency, controlled by a well regulated and wise economy.

DEMOCRATS

Delegates from every state except South Carolina assembled in Baltimore in late May 1844 for the Democratic convention. The front-runner for the presidential nomination was former president Martin Van Buren, whose status was threatened on the eve of the convention by his statement against the annexation of Texas. Van Buren's position jeopardized his support in the South, and with a two-thirds majority apparently necessary, dimmed his chances of obtaining the presidential nomination. The question of requiring a two-thirds nominating majority was debated in the early sessions of the convention, and by a vote of 148 to 118 the two-thirds majority rule, initially adopted by the party in 1832, was ratified. *(Table, p. 182.)*

Van Buren led the early presidential balloting, actually receiving a simple majority of the vote on the first ballot. On succeeding roll calls, however, his principal opponent, Lewis Cass of Michigan, gained strength and took the lead. But neither candidate approached the 178 votes needed for nomination.

With a deadlock developing, sentiment for a compromise candidate appeared. James K. Polk, former speaker of the Tennessee House and former governor of Tennessee, emerged as an acceptable choice and won the nomination on the ninth ballot. It marked the first time in American history that a dark-horse candidate won a presidential nomination. *(Table, p. 182.)*

A friend of Van Buren, Sen. Silas Wright of New York, was the nearly unanimous nominee of the convention for vice president. But Wright refused the nomination, quickly notifying the delegates by way of Samuel Morse's new invention, the telegraph. After two more ballots, George M. Dallas of Pennsylvania was chosen as Polk's running mate.

Among its final actions, the convention appointed a central committee and recommended that a nationwide party organization be established—a forerunner of the national committee. The delegates did not adopt a platform but appointed a committee to draft resolutions.

The resulting document contained the same resolutions included in the party's 1840 platform, plus several new planks. The Democrats opposed the distribution of the proceeds from the sale of public lands; were against placing any restrictions on the executive veto power; and, to alleviate the sectional bitterness

aroused by the prospect of Western expansion, recommended the annexation of both Texas and Oregon.

President Tyler, although abandoned by the major parties, wanted to remain in office. Friends and federal officeholders gathered in Baltimore at the same time as the Democrats and nominated Tyler. However, it became apparent that the president's national vote-getting appeal was limited, and he withdrew from the race in favor of the Democrat, Polk.

Following are excerpts from the Democratic resolutions of 1844:

Appeal to the Masses. That the American Democracy place their trust, not in factitious symbols, not in displays and appeals insulting to the judgment and subversive of the intellect of the people, but in a clear reliance upon the intelligence, patriotism, and the discriminating justice of the American masses.

That we regard this as a distinctive feature of our political creed, which we are proud to maintain before the world, as the great moral element in a form of government springing from and upheld by the popular will; and we contrast it with the creed and practice of Federalism, under whatever name or form, which seeks to palsy the will of the constituent, and which conceives no imposture too monstrous for the popular credulity.

Internal Improvements. That the Constitution does not confer upon the General Government the power to commence or carry on a general system of internal improvements.

State Debts. That the Constitution does not confer authority upon the Federal Government, directly or indirectly, to assume the debts of the several states.

Government Spending. That it is the duty of every branch of the government to enforce and practice the most rigid economy in conducting our public affairs, and that no more revenue ought to be raised than is required to defray the necessary expenses of the government.

National Bank. That Congress has no power to charter a United States Bank, that we believe such an institution one of deadly hostility to the best interests of the country, dangerous to our republican institutions and the liberties of the people.

States' Rights. That Congress has no power, under the Constitution, to interfere with or control the domestic institutions of the several States; and that such States are the sole and proper judges of everything pertaining to their own affairs, not prohibited by the Constitution; that all efforts, by abolitionists or others, made to induce Congress to interfere with questions of slavery, or to take incipient steps in relation thereto, are calculated to lead to the most alarming and dangerous consequences.

Public Lands. That the proceeds of the Public Lands ought to be sacredly applied to the national objects specified in the Constitution, and that we are opposed to the laws lately adopted, and to any law for the distribution of such proceeds among the States, as alike inexpedient in policy and repugnant to the Constitution.

Executive Veto Power. That we are decidedly opposed to taking from the President the qualified veto power by which he is enabled, under restrictions and responsibilities amply sufficient to guard the public interest.

Western Expansion. That our title to the whole of the Territory of Oregon is clear and unquestionable; that no portion of the same ought to be ceded to England or any other power, and that the reoccupation of Oregon and the reannexation of Texas at the earliest practicable period are great American measures, which this Convention recommends to the cordial support of the Democracy of the Union.

1848 Conventions

PRESIDENTIAL CANDIDATES

Lewis Cass
Democrat

Zachary Taylor
Whig

Martin Van Buren
Free Soil

DEMOCRATS

Delegates from every state gathered in Baltimore in May 1848 for the Democratic Party's fifth national convention. A seating dispute between two rival New York delegations enlivened the early convention sessions. The conflict reflected a factional fight between a more liberal antislavery faction, known as the Barnburners, and a more conservative faction, known as the Hunkers. By a vote of 126 to 125, the convention adopted a compromise by which both delegations were seated and shared New York's vote. However, this compromise satisfied neither of the contesting delegations. The Barnburners bolted the convention. The Hunkers remained but refused to vote. *(Table, p. 183.)*

Before the presidential balloting could begin, the convention had to decide whether to use the controversial two-thirds rule. Consideration of the rule preceded the credentials controversy, which brought an objection from New York delegates who wanted their seating dispute settled first. But, by a vote of 133 to 121, the convention refused to table the issue. A second vote on adoption of the two-thirds rule was approved, 176 to 78. *(Table, p. 183.)*

The front-runner for the presidential nomination was Sen. Lewis Cass of Michigan. Although Cass was from the North, his view that the existence of slavery in the territories should be determined by their inhabitants (a forerunner of Stephen Douglas's "popular sovereignty") was a position acceptable to the South.

Cass received 125 votes on the first ballot, more than double the total of his two principal rivals, James Buchanan of Pennsylvania and Levi Woodbury of New Hampshire. Cass's vote total steadily increased during the next three roll calls, and on the fourth ballot he received 179 votes and was nominated. His vote was actually short of a two-thirds majority of the allotted convention votes, but the chair ruled that, with New York not voting, the required majority was reduced. *(Table, p. 183.)*

The vice-presidential nomination went on the second ballot to Gen. William O. Butler of Kentucky, who had 169 of the 253 votes cast. As in the earlier presidential balloting, Butler's two-thirds majority was based on votes cast rather than votes allotted. Butler's primary rival for the nomination was a military colleague, Gen. John A. Quitman of Mississippi.

One of the most significant acts of the convention was the formation of a national committee, with one member from each state, that would handle party affairs until the next convention four years later.

As in 1840 and 1844, the heart of the Democratic platform was a series of resolutions describing the party's concept of a federal government with limited powers. New resolutions emphasized Democratic opposition to a national bank and the distribution of land sales to the states, while applauding the independent treasury plan, the lower tariff bill passed in 1846, and the successful war against Mexico. An effort by William L. Yancey of Alabama to insert in the platform a plank on slavery that would prevent interference with the rights of slaveholders in states or territories was defeated, 216 to 36. The slavery plank written in the platform had the same wording as earlier versions in the 1840 and 1844 Democratic platforms. The plank was milder than Yancey's proposal, stating simply that Congress did not have the power to interfere with slavery in the states. The convention adopted the complete platform by a vote of 247 to 0.

Following are excerpts from the Democratic platform of 1848:

Mexican War. That the war with Mexico, provoked on her part by years of insult and injury, was commenced by her army crossing the Rio Grande, attacking the American troops, and invading our sister State of Texas; and that, upon all the principles of patriotism and laws of nations, it is a just and necessary war on our part, in which every American citizen should have shown himself on the side of his country, and neither morally nor physically, by word or by deed, have given "aid and comfort to the enemy."

Democratic Accomplishments. That the fruits of the great political triumph of 1844, which elected James K. Polk and George M. Dallas President and Vice President of the United States, have fulfilled the hopes of the Democracy of the Union—in defeating the declared purposes of their opponents to create a national bank; in preventing the corrupt and unconstitutional distribution of the land proceeds, from the common treasury of the Union, for local purposes; in protecting the currency and the labor of the country from ruinous fluctuations, and guarding the money of the people for the use of the people, by the establishment of the constitutional treasury; in the noble impulse given to the cause of free trade, by the repeal of the tariff in 1842 and the creation of the more equal, honest, and productive tariff of 1846.

WHIGS

Whig delegates from every state except Texas gathered in Philadelphia in June 1848. Although the Lone Star state was unrepresented, a Texas Whig state convention had earlier given a proxy for its votes to the Louisiana delegates. There was debate in the convention about the legality of the proxy, but it was ultimately accepted by the delegates.

The battle for the Whig's presidential nomination involved three major contenders, the party's respected aging statesman, Henry Clay of Kentucky; and two generals—Zachary Taylor and Winfield Scott, both of Virginia—whose political appeal was significantly increased by their military exploits in the recently completed Mexican War. Taylor led throughout the balloting, taking the lead on the first ballot with 111 votes, compared with 97 for Clay and 43 for Scott. Taylor increased his lead on subsequent roll calls, winning the nomination on the fourth ballot with 171 of the 280 votes cast. *(Table, p. 184.)*

Millard Fillmore of New York and Abbott Lawrence of Massachusetts were the prime contenders for the vice-presidential nomination. Fillmore led Lawrence, 115 to 109, on the first ballot and pulled away to win on the second ballot with 173 of the 266 votes cast.

A motion to make the presidential and vice-presidential nominations unanimous failed when several delegates objected, doubting Taylor's support of Whig principles.

The Whig convention did not formally adopt a party platform, although a ratification meeting held in Philadelphia after the convention adopted a series of resolutions. The resolutions avoided a discussion of issues, instead lauding the party's presidential nominee, Zachary Taylor, and affirming his faithfulness to the tenets of the party.

FREE SOILERS

Antislavery Whigs, New York Barnburners, and members of the Liberty Party gathered in Buffalo, N.Y., in August 1848 to form a new third party, the Free Soilers. While opposition to slavery was a common denominator of the various elements in the new party, the dissident Democrats and Whigs also were attracted to the Free Soil Party by the lack of influence they exerted in their former parties. The call for a Free Soil convention was made by the New York Barnburners at their state conclave in June 1848 and by a nonpartisan gathering in Columbus, Ohio, the same month. The latter assembly, organized by Salmon P. Chase, was entitled a People's Convention of Friends of Free Territory and was designed to set the stage for a national Free Soil convention.

Eighteen states (including the slave states of Delaware, Maryland, and Virginia) sent 465 delegates to Buffalo for the birth of the Free Soil Party. Because of the large number of delegates, convention leaders determined that delegates from each state would select several members to form a Committee on Conference, which would conduct convention business. The rest of the delegates would sit in a large tent and listen to campaign oratory.

Martin Van Buren, the former Democratic president and a favorite of the Barnburners, was chosen as the new party's standard-bearer on the first ballot. Van Buren received 244 votes to defeat John P. Hale of New Hampshire, who had 181 votes. Hale had been nominated by the Liberty Party in October 1847, but with Van Buren's nomination he withdrew from the race. The vice-presidential nomination went to a former Whig, Charles Francis Adams of Massachusetts.

While the Free Soil platform opposed the extension of slavery into the territories, the party did not feel the federal government had the power to interfere with slavery in the states. Although this position was significantly stronger than the position adopted by the Democrats, it was milder than the all-out opposition to slavery expressed by the Liberty Party four years earlier. The Free Soilers also adopted positions on a variety of other issues, supporting free land for settlers, a tariff for revenue purposes, cheap postage, and federal spending for river and harbor improvements. Basically, the Free Soil platform expressed belief in a federal government with broader powers than that conceived by the Democrats.

Following are excerpts from the Free Soil Party platform of 1848:

Slavery. That Slavery in the several States of this Union which recognize its existence, depends upon the State laws alone, which cannot be repealed or modified by the Federal Government, and for which laws that Government is not responsible. We therefore propose no interference by Congress with Slavery within the limits of any State.

Resolved, THAT IT IS THE DUTY OF THE FEDERAL GOVERNMENT TO RELIEVE ITSELF FROM ALL RESPONSIBILITY FOR THE EXISTENCE OR CONTINUANCE OF SLAVERY WHEREVER THAT GOVERNMENT POSSESS CONSTITUTIONAL POWER TO LEGISLATE ON THAT SUBJECT, AND IS THUS RESPONSIBLE FOR ITS EXISTENCE.

Resolved, That the true, and, in the judgment of this Convention, the *only* safe means of preventing the extension of Slavery into territory now free, is to prohibit its existence in all such territory by *an act of Congress.*

Government Administration. That we demand CHEAP POSTAGE for the people; a retrenchment of the expenses and patronage of the Federal Government; the *abolition* of all *unnecessary* offices and salaries; and the election by the People of all civil officers in the service of the Government, so far as the same may be practicable.

Internal Improvements. That *river* and *harbor improvements,* when demanded by the safety and convenience of commerce with foreign nations, or among the several States, are objects of *national concern;* and that it is the duty of Congress, in the exercise of its constitutional powers, to provide therefor.

Homesteading. That the FREE GRANT TO ACTUAL SETTLERS, in consideration of the expenses they incur in making settlements in the wilderness, which are usually fully equal to their actual cost, and of the public benefits resulting therefrom, of reasonable portions of the public lands, under suitable limitations, is a wise and just measure of public policy, which will promote, in various ways, the interest of all the States of this Union; and we therefore recommend it to the favorable consideration of the American People.

Tariff. That the obligations of honor and patriotism require the earliest practical payment of the national debt, and we are therefore in favor of such a tariff of duties as will raise revenue adequate to defray the necessary expenses of the Federal Government, and to pay annual installments of our debt and the interest thereon.

Party Motto. *Resolved,* That we inscribe on our banner, "FREE SOIL, FREE SPEECH, FREE LABOR, AND FREE MEN."

1852 Conventions

PRESIDENTIAL CANDIDATES

Franklin Pierce
Democrat

Winfield Scott
Whig

John P. Hale
Free Soil

DEMOCRATS

In spite of the efforts of the major politicians of both parties, the explosive slavery question was fast becoming the dominant issue in American politics and was threatening the tenuous intersectional alliances that held together both the Democratic and Whig parties. Under the cloud of this volatile issue, the Democratic convention convened in Baltimore in June 1852.

The delegates were called to order by the party's first national chairman, Benjamin F. Hallett of Massachusetts. Hallett's first action was to limit the size of each state delegation to its electoral vote, dispatching members of oversized delegations to the rear of the hall. Retention of the two-thirds rule provoked little opposition, unlike the disputes at the 1844 and 1848 conventions, and an effort to table the rule was soundly beaten, 269 to 13.

With a degree of orderliness, the convention disposed of procedural matters, clearing the way for the presidential balloting. There were four major contenders for the nomination: Sen. Lewis Cass of Michigan, James Buchanan of Pennsylvania, and William L. Marcy of New York—all three more than sixty years old—and the rising young senator from Illinois, Stephen A. Douglas, thirty-nine. Each of the four challengers led at one point during the numerous ballots that followed.

Cass jumped in front initially, receiving 116 votes on the first ballot. Buchanan trailed with 93, while Marcy and Douglas were far back with 27 and 20 votes, respectively. Cass's vote dropped after the first few roll calls, but he was able to hold the lead until the twentieth ballot, when Buchanan moved in front. Buchanan led for several roll calls, followed by Douglas, who edged into the lead on the thirtieth ballot, only to be quickly displaced by Cass on the thirty-second ballot. Marcy made his spurt between the thirty-sixth and forty-eighth ballots, and took the lead on the forty-fifth and forty-sixth ballots. But in spite of the quick changes in fortune, none of the four contenders could win a simple majority of the votes, let alone the two-thirds required. (*Table, p. 185.*)

With a deadlock developing, on the thirty-fifth ballot the Virginia delegation introduced a new name, Franklin Pierce of New Hampshire. Although formerly a member of both houses of Congress, Pierce was little known nationally and not identified with any party faction. Pierce's relative anonymity made him an acceptable alternative in the volatile convention. Pierce received fifteen votes on the thirty-fifth ballot and gradually gained strength on subsequent ballots, with the big break coming on the forty-ninth roll call. Nearly unanimous votes for Pierce in the New England states created a bandwagon effect that resulted in his nomination on this ballot with 279 of the 288 votes cast. The forty-nine ballots took two days.

Beginning the vice-presidential roll call, a spokesperson for the Maine delegation suggested that second place on the ticket go to a representative of the South, specifically mentioning Sen. William R. King of Alabama. King moved into a strong lead on the first ballot with 125 votes and easily won nomination on the second roll call with 277 of the 288 votes cast.

The platform adopted by the Democratic convention contained the same nine resolutions that had been in all party platforms since 1840, detailing the Democratic concept of a limited federal government. The platform included a plank supporting the Compromise of 1850, the congressional solution to the slavery question. Actually, both the Whigs and Democrats endorsed the compromise of 1850. The major point of dispute between the two parties was over the issue of internal improvements, with the Whigs taking a broader view of federal power in this sphere.

Following are excerpts from the Democratic platform of 1852:

Compromise of 1850. *Resolved,* . . . the democratic party of the Union, standing on this national platform, will abide by and adhere to a faithful execution of the acts known as the compromise measures settled by the last Congress—"the act for reclaiming fugitives from service or labor" included; which act, being designed to carry out an express provision of the constitution, cannot, with fidelity thereto be repealed nor so changed as to destroy or impair its efficiency.

Resolved, That the democratic party will resist all attempts at renewing, in congress or out of it, the agitation of the slavery question, under whatever shape or color the attempt may be made.

Democratic Principles. That, in view of the condition of popular institutions in the Old World, a high and sacred duty is devolved, with increased responsibility upon the democratic party of this country, as the party of the people, to uphold and maintain the rights of every State, and thereby the Union of the States, and to sustain and advance among us constitutional liberty, by continuing to resist all monopolies and exclusive legislation for the benefit of the few at the expense of the many, and by a vigilant and constant adherence to those principles and compromises of the constitution, which are broad enough and strong enough to embrace and uphold the Union as it was, the Union as it is, and the Union as it shall be, in the full expansion of the energies and capacity of this great and progressive people.

WHIGS

Although in control of the White House, the Whigs were more sharply divided by the Compromise of 1850 than were the Democrats. The majority of northern Whigs in Congress opposed the Compromise, while most southern members of the party favored it. Faced with widening division in their ranks, Whig delegates convened in Baltimore in June 1852. The call for this national convention had been issued by Whig members of Congress, and delegates from all thirty-one states attended.

The convention sessions were often lively and sometimes raucous. When asked to present its report the first day, the credentials committee responded that it was not ready to report and "didn't know when—maybe for days." A minister, invited to the hall to deliver a prayer to the convention, never had his chance. The delegates debated when the prayer should be delivered and finally decided to omit it.

A heated debate occurred on how many votes each state would be apportioned on the platform committee. By a vote of 149 to 144, the delegates adopted a plan whereby each state's vote on the committee would reflect its strength in the electoral college. Strong protests from southern and small northern states, however, brought a reversal of this decision, and although no formal vote was recorded, representation on the platform committee was changed so that each state received one vote.

The northern and southern wings of the Whig Party were nearly equally represented at the Baltimore convention, and the close split produced a prolonged battle for the party's presidential nomination. The two major rivals for the nomination, President Millard Fillmore and Winfield Scott, had nearly equal strength. Ironically, the basic appeal of Fillmore of New York was among southern delegates, who appreciated his support of the Compromise of 1850.

Although a native of Virginia, Scott was not popular in the South because of his ambivalence on the Compromise and the active support given him by a leading antislavery northerner, Sen. William H. Seward of New York. Scott's strength was in the northern and western states. A third candidate in the field was Daniel Webster, the party's elder statesman, whose appeal was centered in his native New England.

On the first ballot, Fillmore received 133 votes, Scott had 132, and Webster collected 29. This nearly equal distribution of the vote between Fillmore and Scott continued with little fluctuation through the first two days of balloting. Midway through the second day, after the thirty-fourth ballot, a motion was made to adjourn. Although it was defeated by a vote of 126 to 76, other motions were made to adjourn throughout the rest of the session. Finally, amid increasing confusion, after the forty-sixth ballot, delegates voted by a margin of 176 to 116 to adjourn. *(Table, p. 186.)*

Commotion continued the next day, with southern delegates trying unsuccessfully to expel Henry J. Raymond, the editor of the *New York Times,* who was also a delegate by proxy. In an article, Raymond had charged collusion between party managers and southern delegates, with the South getting its way on the platform while Scott received the presidential nomination.

Amid this uproar, the leaders of the Fillmore and Webster forces were negotiating. Fillmore was willing to release his delegates to Webster, if Webster could muster 41 votes on his own. As the balloting continued, it was apparent that Webster could not; and enough delegates defected to Scott to give the Mexican War hero a simple majority and the nomination on the fifty-third ballot. On the final roll call, Scott received 159 votes, compared with 112 for Fillmore, and 21 for Webster.

Several individuals placed in nomination for the vice presidency refused it immediately. The chairman of the convention finally declared Secretary of the Navy William A. Graham of North Carolina to be the unanimous selection. No formal roll-call vote was recorded.

For only the second time in their history, the Whigs adopted a party platform. Like their Democratic adversaries, the Whigs supported the Compromise of 1850 and perceived the federal government as having limited powers. Additional planks called for a tariff on imports to raise revenue and for an isolationist foreign policy that avoided "entangling alliances." The platform was adopted by a vote of 227 to 66, with all the dissenting votes cast by delegates from the North and West.

Following are excerpts from the Whig platform of 1852:

Strict Construction. The Government of the United States is of a limited character, and it is confined to the exercise of powers expressly granted by the Constitution, and such as may be necessary and proper for carrying the granted powers into full execution, and that all powers not granted or necessarily implied are expressly reserved to the States respectively and to the people.

Foreign Policy. That while struggling freedom everywhere enlists the warmest sympathy of the Whig party, we still adhere to the doctrines of the Father of his Country, as announced in his Farewell Address, of keeping ourselves free from all entangling alliances with foreign countries, and of never quitting our own to stand upon foreign ground, that our mission as a republic is not to propagate our opinions, or impose on other countries our form of government by artifice or force; but to teach, by example, and show by our success, moderation and justice, the blessings of self-government, and the advantages of free institutions.

Tariff. Revenue sufficient for the expenses of an economical administration of the Government in time of peace ought to be derived from a duty on imports, and not from direct taxation.

Internal Improvements. The Constitution vests in Congress the power to open and repair harbors, and remove obstructions from navigable rivers, whenever such improvements are necessary for the common defense, and for the protection and facility of commerce with foreign nations, or among the States, said improvements being, in every instance, national and general in their character.

Compromise of 1850. That the series of acts of the Thirty-first Congress—the act known as the Fugitive Slave Law, included—are received and acquiesced in by the Whig Party of the United States as a settlement in principle and substance, of the dangerous and exciting question which they embrace; and, so far as they are concerned, we will maintain them, and insist upon their strict enforcement, until time and experience shall demonstrate the necessity of further legislation.

FREE DEMOCRATS (FREE SOILERS)

After the 1848 election, the New York Barnburners returned to the Democratic Party, and the rest of the Free Soilers were ready to coalesce with either the Democrats or the Whigs. But the process of absorption was delayed by the Compromise of 1850. It was viewed as a solution to the slavery question by the two major parties but was regarded as a sellout by most antislavery groups.

Responding to a call for a national convention issued by a Cleveland, Ohio, antislavery meeting, delegates gathered in Pittsburgh in August 1852. Antislavery Whigs and remnants of the Liberty Party were in attendance at what was termed the Free Soil Democratic Convention.

John P. Hale of New Hampshire unanimously won the presidential nomination, and George W. Julian of Indiana was selected as his running mate.

Although the platform covered a number of issues, the document focused on the slavery question. The Free Soil Democrats opposed the Compromise of 1850 and called for the abolition of slavery. Like both major parties, the Free Democrats expressed the concept of a limited federal government, but they agreed with the Whigs that the government should undertake certain river and harbor improvements. The Free Democrats went beyond the other parties in advocating a homestead policy, extending a welcome to immigrants and voicing support for new republican governments in Europe and the Caribbean.

Following are excerpts from the Free Democratic platform of 1852:

Strict Construction. That the Federal Government is one of limited powers, derived solely from the Constitution, and the grants of power therein ought to be strictly construed by all the departments and agents of the Government, and it is inexpedient and dangerous to exercise doubtful constitutional powers.

Compromise of 1850. That, to the persevering and importunate demands of the slave power for more slave States, new slave Territories, and the nationalization of slavery, our distinct and final answer is—no more slave States, no slave Territory, no nationalized slavery, and no national legislation for the extradition of slaves.

That slavery is a sin against God and a crime against man, which no human enactment nor usage can make right; and that Christianity, humanity, and patriotism, alike demand its abolition.

That the Fugitive Slave Act of 1850 is repugnant to the Constitution, to the principles of the common law, to the spirit of Christianity, and to the sentiments of the civilized world. We therefore deny its binding force upon the American People, and demand its immediate and total repeal.

Homesteading. That the public lands of the United States belong to the people, and should not be sold to individuals nor granted to corporations, but should be held as a sacred trust for the benefit of the people, and should be granted in limited quantities, free of cost, to landless settlers.

Internal Improvements. That river and harbor improvements, when necessary to the safety and convenience of commerce with foreign nations or among the several States, are objects of national concern, and it is the duty of Congress in the exercise of its constitutional powers to provide for the same.

1856 Conventions

PRESIDENTIAL CANDIDATES

John C. Fremont
Republican

Millard Fillmore
Know-Nothing

James Buchanan
Democrat

REPUBLICANS

With the decline of the Whigs and the increasing importance of the slavery issue, there was room for a new political party. Officially born in 1854, the new Republican Party moved to fill the vacuum.

The party's first meeting was held in Pittsburgh in February 1856, with delegates from twenty-four states attending. United in their opposition to the extension of slavery and the policies of the Pierce administration, the gathering selected a national committee (with one representative from each state), which was empowered to call the party's first national convention.

The subsequent call was addressed not to Republicans but "to the people of the United States" who were opposed to the Pierce administration and the congressional compromises on slavery. Each state was allocated six delegates at the forthcoming convention, with three additional delegates for each congressional district.

When the first Republican National Convention assembled in Philadelphia in June 1856, the gathering was clearly sectional. There were nearly 600 delegates present, representing all the northern states, the border slave states of Delaware, Maryland, Virginia, and Kentucky, and the District of Columbia. The territory of Kansas, symbolically important in the slavery struggle, was treated as a state and given full representation. There were no delegations from the remaining southern slave states.

Under convention rules, the roll call was to proceed in alphabetical order, with each state allocated three times its electoral vote. In response to a question, the chair decided that a simple majority would be required and not the two-thirds majority mandated by the Democratic convention. This was an important rule that distinguished the conventions of the two major parties well into the twentieth century.

Two major contenders for the Republican presidential nomination, Salmon P. Chase of Ohio and William H. Seward of New York, both withdrew before the balloting began. Another contender, Supreme Court Justice John McLean of Ohio, withdrew briefly but then reentered the race. However, McLean could not catch the front-runner, John C. Fremont of California. Although briefly a U.S. senator, Fremont was most famous as an explorer, and he benefited from being free of any ideological identification.

The other contenders were all identified with one of the factions that had come to make up the new party. Fremont won a preliminary, informal ballot, receiving 359 votes to 190 for McLean. On the formal roll call, Fremont won easily, winning 520 of the 567 votes. *(Table, p. 187.)*

A preliminary, informal ballot was taken for the vice presidency as well. William L. Dayton, a former senator from New Jersey, led with 253 votes, more than twice the total received by an Illinois lawyer, Abraham Lincoln, who had served in the House of Representatives 1847–1849. On the formal ballot, Dayton swept to victory with 523 votes. His nomination was quickly made unanimous.

The Republican platform was approved by a voice vote. It was a document with sectional appeal, written by northern delegates for the North. Unlike the Democrats, the Republicans opposed the concept of popular sovereignty and believed that slavery should be prohibited in the territories. Specifically, the platform called for the admission of Kansas as a free state.

The Republicans also differed with the Democrats on the question of internal improvements, supporting the view that Congress should undertake river and harbor improvements. The Republican platform denounced the Ostend Manifesto, a document secretly drawn up by three of the Pierce administration's ambassadors in Europe, that suggested the United States either buy or take Cuba from Spain. The Republicans termed the manifesto a "highwayman's plea, that 'might makes right.' "

Both parties advocated the building of a transcontinental transportation system, with the Republicans supporting the construction of a railroad.

Following are excerpts from the Republican platform of 1856:

Slavery. This Convention of Delegates, assembled in pursuance of a call addressed to the people of the United States, without regard to past political differences or divisions, who are opposed to the repeal of the Missouri Compromise; to the policy of the present Administration; to the extension of Slavery into Free Territory; in favor of the admission of Kansas as a Free State; of restoring the action of the Federal Government to the principles of Washington and Jefferson. . . .

That the Constitution confers upon Congress sovereign powers over the Territories of the United States for their government; and that in the exercise of this power, it is both the right and the imperative duty of Congress to prohibit in the Territories those twin relics of barbarism—Polygamy, and Slavery.

Cuba. That the highwayman's plea, that "might makes right," embodied in the Ostend Circular, was in every respect unworthy of American diplomacy, and would bring shame and dishonor upon any Government or people that gave it their sanction.

Transcontinental Railroad. That a railroad to the Pacific Ocean by the most central and practicable route is imperatively demanded by the interests of the whole country.

Internal Improvements. That appropriations by Congress for the improvement of rivers and harbors, of a national character, required for the accommodation and security of our existing commerce, are authorized by the Constitution, and justified by the obligation of the Government to protect the lives and property of its citizens.

AMERICAN (KNOW-NOTHINGS)

In addition to the Republicans, the American Party or Know-Nothings aspired to replace the Whigs as the nation's second major party. However, unlike the Republicans, the Know-Nothings were a national political organization, and the slavery issue that helped unite the Republicans divided the Know-Nothings. The main Know-Nothing concern was to place restrictions on the large number of European immigrants who arrived in the 1840s and 1850s.

The party held its first and only national convention in Philadelphia in February 1856. Several days before the convention began, the American Party's national council met and drew up the party platform. When the convention assembled, antislavery delegates objected to the platform, with its espousal of popular sovereignty, and called for the nomination of candidates who would outlaw slavery in the new territories. When their resolution was defeated, 141 to 59, these antislavery delegates—mainly from New England and Ohio—bolted the convention.

The remaining delegates nominated former president Millard Fillmore (1850–1853) of New York for president. Fillmore was popular in the South for his support of compromise slavery measures during his administration and was nominated on the second ballot. Andrew Jackson Donelson of Tennessee was chosen as the vice-presidential candidate.

In June 1856 several days before the Republican convention was scheduled to begin, the antislavery Know-Nothings assembled in New York and nominated Speaker of the House Nathaniel P. Banks of Massachusetts for the presidency and former governor William F. Johnston of Pennsylvania as his running mate. Banks, who actually favored Fremont's nomination, withdrew from the race when Fremont was chosen as the Re-

publican candidate. Johnston bowed out in favor of Fremont's running mate, William L. Dayton, later in the campaign.

The Know-Nothing convention that had met earlier in Philadelphia adopted a platform similar to that of the Democrats on the slavery question. The document advocated noninterference in the affairs of the states and the concept of popular sovereignty for deciding slavery in the territories. Although also calling for economy in government spending, the bulk of the Know-Nothing platform dealt with restricting immigrants. Among the nativistic planks were proposals that native-born citizens be given the first chance for all government offices, that the naturalization period for immigrants be extended to twenty-one years and that paupers and convicted criminals be kept from entering the United States.

Following are excerpts from the Know-Nothing platform of 1856:

Slavery, States' Rights. The unequalled recognition and maintenance of the reserved rights of the several states, and the cultivation of harmony and fraternal good-will between the citizens of the several states, and to this end, non-interference by Congress with questions appertaining solely to the individual states, and non-intervention by each state with the affairs of any other state.

The recognition of the right of the native-born and naturalized citizens of the United States, permanently residing in any territory thereof, to frame their constitutions and laws, and to regulate their domestic and social affairs in their own mode, subject only to the provisions of the federal Constitution, with the right of admission into the Union whenever they have the requisite population for one representative in Congress.

Nativism. *Americans must rule America;* and to this end, *native-*born citizens should be selected for all state, federal, or municipal offices of government employment, in preference to naturalized citizens. . . .

No person should be selected for political station (whether of native or foreign birth), who recognizes any alliance or obligation of any description to any foreign prince, potentate or power, who refuses to recognize the federal and state constitutions (each within its own sphere), as paramount to all other laws, as rules of particular [political] action.

A change in the laws of naturalization, making a continued residence of twenty-one years, of all not heretofore provided for, an indispensable requisite for citizenship hereafter, and excluding all paupers or persons convicted of crime from landing upon our shores.

DEMOCRATS

In June 1856 delegates from all thirty-one states gathered in Cincinnati, Ohio, for the party's seventh quadrennial convention. It was the first Democratic convention to be held outside Baltimore.

Roll-call votes were taken during the first two days on the establishment of a platform committee and on the method of ticket allocation for the galleries. The first close vote came on the credentials committee report concerning the seating of two contesting New York delegations. By a vote of 136 to 123, the convention agreed to a minority report seating both contending factions and splitting the state's vote between them.

Three men were in contention for the party's presidential nomination: President Franklin Pierce of New Hampshire, James

Buchanan of Pennsylvania, and Sen. Stephen A. Douglas of Illinois. All three had actively sought the nomination before. Ironically, Buchanan, who had spent the previous three years as ambassador to Great Britain, was in the most enviable position. Having been abroad, Buchanan had largely avoided the increasing slavery controversy that bedeviled his major rivals.

Buchanan led on the first ballot with 135½ votes with Pierce receiving 122½, and Douglas 33. As the balloting continued, Pierce lost strength, while both Buchanan and Douglas gained. After the fifteenth roll call, the vote stood: Buchanan, 168½, Douglas, 118½, and Pierce 3½. *(Table, p. 187.)*

While the two front-runners had substantial strength, neither of them was a sectional candidate. Both received votes from northern and southern delegations. With the possibility of a stalemate looming, Douglas withdrew after the sixteenth ballot. On the seventeenth roll call, Buchanan received all 296 votes, and the nomination.

On the first ballot for the vice presidency, eleven different individuals received votes. Rep. John A. Quitman of Mississippi led with 59 votes, followed by Rep. John C. Breckinridge of Kentucky, with 50. At the beginning of the second ballot, the New England delegations cast a nearly unanimous vote for Breckinridge, creating a bandwagon effect that resulted in the nomination of the Kentuckian. Ironically, before the vice-presidential balloting began, Breckinridge had asked that his name be withdrawn from consideration. Believing himself too young (he was thirty-five), Breckinridge stated that "promotion should follow seniority."

In spite of his earlier demurrer, Breckinridge was in the convention hall and announced his acceptance of the nomination. It marked one of the few times in American political history that a candidate was present for his or her nomination.

The party platform was considered in two segments, with the domestic and foreign policy sections debated separately. The theme of the domestic section, as in past platforms, was the Democrats' concept of a limited federal government. The unconstitutionality of a national bank, federal support for internal improvements, and distribution of proceeds from the sale of public land were again mentioned.

Nearly one-third of the entire platform was devoted to the slavery question, with support for the various congressional compromise measures stressed. The Democratic position was underscored in a passage that was capitalized in the convention *Proceedings:* "non-interference by Congress with slavery in state and territory, or in the District of Columbia."

In another domestic area, the Democrats denounced the Know-Nothings for being un-American. The convention approved the domestic policy section of the platform by a vote of 261 to 35, with only the New York delegation voting in opposition.

The foreign policy section expressed a nationalistic and expansionist spirit that was absent from previous Democratic platforms.

There were six different foreign policy planks, each voted on separately. The first plank, calling for free trade, passed 210 to 29. The second, favoring implementation of the Monroe Doctrine, passed 240 to 21. The third plank, backing westward continental expansion, was approved 203 to 56. The fourth plank, which expressed sympathy with the people of Central America, grew out of the U.S. dispute with Great Britain over control of that area. The plank was approved, 221 to 38. The fifth plank, calling for United States "ascendency in the Gulf of Mexico," passed 229 to 33. A final resolution, presented separately, called for the construction of roads to the Pacific Ocean. The resolution was at first tabled, 154 to 120, and a second vote to reconsider failed, 175 to 121. But when the resolution was raised a third time after the presidential nomination, it passed, 205 to 87.

Following are excerpts from the Democratic platform of 1856:

Slavery. That claiming fellowship with, and desiring the co-operation of all who regard the preservation of the Union under the Constitution as the paramount issue—and repudiating all sectional parties and platforms concerning domestic slavery, which seek to embroil the States and incite to treason and armed resistance to law in the Territories; and whose avowed purposes, if consummated, must end in civil war and disunion, the American Democracy recognize and adopt the principles contained in the organic laws establishing the Territories of Kansas and Nebraska as embodying the only sound and safe solution of the "slavery question" upon which the great national idea of the people of this whole country can repose in its determined conservatism of the Union—NON-INTERFERENCE BY CONGRESS WITH SLAVERY IN STATE AND TERRITORY, OR IN THE DISTRICT OF COLUMBIA.

Know-Nothings. [T]he liberal principles embodied in the Declaration of Independence . . . makes ours the land of liberty and the asylum of the oppressed . . . every attempt to abridge the privilege of becoming citizens . . . ought to be resisted.

Since the foregoing declaration was uniformly adopted by our predecessors in National Conventions, an adverse political and religious test has been secretly organized by a party claiming to be exclusively American, it is proper that the American Democracy should clearly define its relation thereto, and declare its determined opposition to all secret political societies, by whatever name they may be called.

Free Trade. That there are questions connected with the foreign policy of this country, which are inferior to no domestic question whatever. The time has come for the people of the United States to declare themselves in favor of free seas and progressive free trade.

Latin America. [W]e should hold as sacred the principles involved in the Monroe Doctrine: their bearing and import admit of no misconstruction; they should be applied with unbending rigidity.

Gulf of Mexico. That the Democratic party will expect of the next Administration that every proper effort be made to insure our ascendency in the Gulf of Mexico.

Transcontinental Roads. That the Democratic party recognizes the great importance, in a political and commercial point of view, of a safe and speedy communication, by military and postal roads, through our own territory, between the Atlantic and Pacific coasts.

WHIGS

On the verge of extinction, the Whig Party held its last national convention in September 1856. Delegates assembled in Baltimore from twenty-one states and endorsed the Know-Nothing ticket of Fillmore and Donelson.

However, the Whigs adopted their own platform. It avoided specific issues, instead calling for preservation of the Union. The platform criticized both the Democrats and Republicans for appealing to sectional passions and argued for the presidential candidacy of the former Whig, Millard Fillmore.

Following is an excerpt from the Whig platform of 1856:

Preserving the Union. That the Whigs of the United States are assembled here by reverence for the Constitution, and unalterable attachment to the National Union, and a fixed determination to do all in their power to preserve it for themselves and posterity. They have no new principles to announce—no new platform to establish, but are content broadly to rest where their fathers have rested upon the Constitution of the United States, wishing no safer guide, no higher law.

1860 Conventions

PRESIDENTIAL CANDIDATES

Stephen A. Douglas
Democrat

John C. Breckinridge
Southern Democrat

Abraham Lincoln
Republican

John Bell
Constitutional Union

DEMOCRATS

Rarely in U.S. history has there been a convention as tumultuous as the one that assembled in Charleston, S.C., in April 1860. The Democrats met at a time when their party was threatened by sectional division, caused by the explosive slavery question. The issue had grown increasingly inflammatory during the 1850s, and, because of rising emotions, the chances of a successful compromise solution decreased.

From the outset of the convention, there was little visible effort to obtain party unity. Parliamentary squabbling with frequent appeals to the chair marked the early sessions. Before the presidential balloting even began, twenty-seven separate roll calls on procedural and platform matters were taken.

A bitter dispute between northern and southern delegates over the wording of the platform's slavery plank precipitated a walkout by several dozen southern delegates. Both the majority and minority reports submitted to the convention called for a reaffirmation of the Democratic platform of 1856. In addition, however, the majority report (favored by the South) declared that no government—local, state, or federal—could outlaw slavery in the territories. The minority report took a more moderate position, stating that the decision on allowing slavery in the territories should be left to the Supreme Court.

After a day of debate, the convention agreed, by a vote of 152 to 151, to recommit both reports to the platform committee. Basically, the vote followed sectional lines, with southern delegates approving recommittal. However, the revised majority and mi-

nority reports subsequently presented to the convention were similar to the originals.

An amendment by Benjamin F. Butler of Massachusetts, to endorse the 1856 platform without any mention of slavery, was defeated, 198 to 105. After two procedural roll calls, the delegates voted, 165 to 138, to accept the minority report. The vote followed sectional lines, with the northern delegates victorious. (*Table, p. 188.*)

Unhappy with the platform and unwilling to accept it, forty-five delegates from nine states bolted the convention. The majority of six southern delegations withdrew (Alabama, Mississippi, Florida, Texas, South Carolina, and Louisiana), along with scattered delegates from three other states (Arkansas, Delaware, and North Carolina).

With the size of the convention reduced, chairman Caleb Cushing of Massachusetts made an important decision. He ruled that the two-thirds nominating majority would be based on the total votes allocated (303) rather than the number of delegates present and voting. Although Cushing's ruling was approved by a vote of 141 to 112, it countered precedents established at the 1840 and 1848 Democratic conventions, when the nominating majority was based on those present and voting.

Cushing's ruling made it nearly impossible for any candidate to amass the necessary two-thirds majority. Particularly affected was the front-runner, Sen. Stephen A. Douglas of Illinois, whose standing in the South had diminished with his continued support of popular sovereignty. Douglas moved into a big lead on the first ballot, receiving 145½ votes to 42 for Sen. Robert M. T. Hunter of Virginia and 35½ for James Guthrie of Kentucky. Despite his large lead over the rest of the field, Douglas was well short of the 202 votes needed for nomination and, with his limited sectional appeal, had little chance of gaining the needed delegates.

After three days of balloting and fifty-seven presidential roll calls, the standing of the three candidates had undergone little change. Douglas led with 151½ votes, followed by Guthrie with 65⅓, and Hunter with 16. The delegates, in session for ten days and wearied by the presidential deadlock, voted 194½ to 55½ to recess for six weeks and reconvene in Baltimore. This marked the first and only time that a major party adjourned its convention and moved it from one city to another.

Reconvening in Baltimore in June, the delegates were faced with another sticky question: whether or not to seat the delegates who had bolted the Charleston convention. The majority report presented by the credentials committee reviewed each case individually and recommended that the bolting southern delegates, except those from Alabama and Louisiana, be reseated. The minority report recommended that a larger majority of the withdrawing Charleston delegates be reseated. The minority report was defeated, 150 to 100½. Ten more roll calls followed on various aspects of the credentials dispute, but they did not change the result of the first vote. *(Table, p. 608.)*

The convention vote on credentials produced a new walkout, involving the majority of delegates from Virginia, North Carolina, Tennessee, Maryland, Kentucky, Missouri, Arkansas, California, and Oregon, and anti-Douglas delegates from Massachusetts. With the presidential balloting ready to resume, less than two-thirds of the original convention was present.

On the first ballot, Douglas received 173½ of the 190½ votes cast. On the second ballot, his total increased to 190½, but it was obviously impossible for him to gain two-thirds (202) of the votes allocated (303). After the second roll call, a delegate moved that Douglas, having obtained a two-thirds majority of the votes cast, be declared the Democratic presidential nominee. The motion passed unanimously on a voice vote. *(Table, p. 188.)*

The convention left the selection of the vice-presidential candidate to a caucus of the remaining southern delegates. They chose Sen. Benjamin Fitzpatrick of Alabama, who received all 198½ votes cast on the vice-presidential roll call.

Shortly after the convention adjourned, Fitzpatrick declined the nomination. For the first time in American history, a national committee filled a vacancy on the ticket. By a unanimous vote of committee members, the former governor of Georgia, Herschel V. Johnson, was chosen to be Douglas's running mate.

The Democratic platform, in addition to the controversial slavery plank, provided a reaffirmation of the 1856 platform, with its proposals for a limited federal government but an expansionist foreign policy. The 1860 platform added planks that continued the expansionist spirit, calling for the construction of a transcontinental railroad and acquisition of the island of Cuba.

Following are excerpts from the Democratic platform of 1860:

Slavery. Inasmuch as difference of opinion exists in the Democratic party as to the nature and extent of the powers of a territorial legislature, and as to the powers and duties of Congress, under the Constitution of the United States, over the institution of slavery within the Territories,

Resolved, That the Democratic party will abide by the decision of the Supreme Court of the United States upon these questions of Constitutional law.

Transcontinental Railroad. That one of the necessities of the age, in a military, commercial, and postal point of view, is speedy communication between the Atlantic and Pacific States; and the Democratic party pledge such Constitutional Government aid as will insure the construction of a Railroad to the Pacific coast, at the earliest practicable period.

Cuba. That the Democratic party are in favor of the acquisition of the Island of Cuba on such terms as shall be honorable to ourselves and just to Spain.

SOUTHERN DEMOCRATS (BRECKINRIDGE FACTION)

A small group of southern delegates that bolted the Charleston convention met in Richmond, Va., in early June. They decided to delay action until after the resumed Democratic convention had concluded. In late June they met in Baltimore with bolters from the regular Democratic convention. There were representatives from nineteen states among the more than 200 delegates attending, but most of the fifty-eight northern delegates were officeholders in the Buchanan administration. Vice President John C. Breckinridge of Kentucky won the presidential nomination, and Sen. Joseph Lane of Oregon was chosen as his running mate.

The platform adopted by the Southern Democrats was similar to the one approved by the Democratic convention at Charleston. The bolters reaffirmed the Democrats' 1856 platform, which called for the construction of a transcontinental railroad and acquisition of Cuba. But on the controversial slavery issue, the rump assemblage adopted the southerners' plank defeated at the Charleston convention. The failure to reach agreement on this one issue, the most disruptive sectional split in the history of American political parties, presaged the Civil War.

Following are excerpts from the platform adopted by the Southern (or Breckinridge faction) Democrats in 1860:

Resolved, that the platform adopted by the Democratic party at Cincinnati be affirmed, with the following explanatory resolutions:

1. That the Government of a Territory organized by an act of Congress is provisional and temporary, and during its existence all citizens of the United States have an equal right to settle with their property in the Territory, without their rights, either of person or property, being destroyed or impaired by Congressional or Territorial legislation.

2. That it is the duty of the Federal Government, in all its departments, to protect, when necessary, the rights of persons and property in the Territories, and wherever else its constitutional authority extends.

REPUBLICANS

With their major opposition split along sectional lines, the Republicans gathered for their convention in Chicago in a mood of optimism. The Democrats had already broken up at Charleston before the Republican delegates convened in May 1860.

The call for the convention was addressed not only to faithful party members but to other groups that shared the Republicans' dissatisfaction with the policies of the Buchanan administration. The call to the convention particularly emphasized the party's opposition to any extension of slavery into the territories.

Delegates from all the northern states and the territories of Kansas and Nebraska, the District of Columbia, and the slave states of Maryland, Delaware, Virginia, Kentucky, Missouri, and Texas assembled at Chicago's new 10,000-seat convention hall, known as the Wigwam. A carnival-like atmosphere enveloped Chicago, with bands marching through the streets and thousands of enthusiastic Republicans ringing the overcrowded convention hall.

Inside, the delegates' first debate concerned the credentials report. The question was raised whether the represented southern states should be allocated votes reflecting their electoral college strength, when there were few Republicans in these states. By a vote of 275½ to 171½, the convention recommitted the credentials report for the purpose of scaling down the vote allocation of the southern states.

A second debate arose over what constituted a nominating majority. The rules committee recommended that the nominating majority reflect the total electoral vote of all the states in the Union. The minority report argued that, since all the states were not represented, the nominating majority suggested by the rules committee would in fact require nearly a two-thirds majority. The minority report recommended instead that nominations be based on a simple majority of votes allocated for the states represented. The minority report passed, 349½ to 88½.

Sen. William H. Seward of New York was the front-runner for the presidential nomination and led on the first ballot. Seward received 173½ votes to lead runner-up Abraham Lincoln of Illinois, who had 102. Sen. Simon Cameron of Pennsylvania followed with 50½ votes, Salmon P. Chase of Ohio with 49, and Edward Bates of Missouri with 48. (Table, p. 189.)

With the packed galleries cheering their native son, Lincoln closed the gap on the second roll call. After two ballots, the voting stood: Seward, 184½; Lincoln, 181; Chase, 42½; Bates, 35. Lincoln, who had gained national prominence two years earlier as a result of his debates on slavery with Democrat Stephen A. Douglas in the 1858 campaign for the U.S. Senate, emerged as the candidate of the anti-Seward forces. On the third ballot, he won the nomination. When the third roll call was completed, Lincoln's vote total stood at 231½, 1½ votes short of a majority. But Ohio quickly shifted four votes to Lincoln, giving him the nomination. After changes by other states, the final vote was Lincoln, 340; Seward, 121½.

The primary contenders for the vice-presidential nomination were Sen. Hannibal Hamlin of Maine and Cassius M. Clay of Kentucky. Hamlin assumed a strong lead on the first ballot, receiving 194 votes to 100½ for Clay. On the second roll call, an increased vote for Hamlin from states in his native New England created a bandwagon for the Maine senator. Hamlin won the nomination on the second ballot with 367 votes, far outdistancing Clay, who received 86. After the roll call was completed, Hamlin's nomination was declared unanimous.

About half of the platform adopted by the Republican convention dealt with the slavery question. Unlike the Democrats, the Republicans clearly opposed the extension of slavery into the territories. However, the Republican platform also expressed support for states' rights, which served as a rebuke to radical abolitionism.

The Republican and Democratic platforms again were opposed on the question of internal improvements. The Republicans supported river and harbor improvements, while the Democrats, by reaffirming their 1856 platform, opposed any federal support for internal improvements. Both parties favored construction of a transcontinental railroad and opposed restrictions on immigration.

However, on two major issues, the Republicans went beyond the Democrats, advocating a protective tariff and homestead legislation.

Following are excerpts from the Republican platform of 1860:

Slavery. That the new dogma that the Constitution, of its own force, carries slavery into any or all of the territories of the United States, is a dangerous political heresy, at variance with the explicit provisions of that instrument itself, with contemporaneous exposition, and with legislative and judicial precedent; is revolutionary in its tendency, and subversive of the peace and harmony of the country.

That the normal condition of all the territory of the United States is that of freedom. . . . we deny the authority of Congress, of a territorial legislature, or of any individuals, to give legal existence to slavery in any territory of the United States.

States' Rights. That the maintenance inviolate of the rights of the states, and especially the right of each state to order and control its own domestic institutions according to its own judgment exclusively, is essential to that balance of powers on which the perfection and endurance of our political fabric depends; and we denounce the lawless invasion by armed force of the soil of any state or territory, no matter under what pretext, as among the gravest of crimes.

Tariff. That, while providing revenue for the support of the general government by duties upon imports, sound policy requires such an adjustment of these imports as to encourage the development of the industrial interests of the whole country.

Transcontinental Railroad. That a railroad to the Pacific Ocean is imperatively demanded by the interests of the whole country; that the federal government ought to render immediate and efficient aid in its construction; and that, as preliminary thereto, a daily overland mail should be promptly established.

CONSTITUTIONAL UNION

At the invitation of a group of southern Know-Nothing members of the House, the remnants of the 1856 Fillmore campaign, conservative Whigs and Know-Nothings, met in Baltimore in May 1860 to form the Constitutional Union Party.

The chief rivals for the presidential nomination were former senator John Bell of Tennessee and Gov. Sam Houston of Texas. Bell won on the second ballot, and Edward Everett of Massachusetts was selected as his running mate.

The Constitutional Union Party saw itself as a national unifying force in a time of crisis. The brief platform did not discuss issues, instead denouncing the sectionalism of the existing parties and calling for national unity.

Following are excerpts from the Constitutional Union platform of 1860:

Whereas, Experience has demonstrated that Platforms adopted by the partisan Conventions of the country have had the effect to mislead and deceive the people, and at the same time to widen the political divisions of the country, by the creation and encouragement of geographical and sectional parties; therefore

Resolved, that it is both the part of patriotism and of duty to *recognize* no political principle other than THE CONSTITUTION OF THE COUNTRY, THE UNION OF THE STATES, AND THE ENFORCEMENT OF THE LAWS.

1864 Conventions

PRESIDENTIAL CANDIDATES

Abraham Lincoln
Republican

George McClellan
Democrat

REPUBLICANS (UNION PARTY)

Although elements in the Republican Party were dissatisfied with the conduct of the Civil War, President Abraham Lincoln was in firm control of his party's convention, which met in Baltimore in June 1864. As with previous Republican conventions, the call was not limited to the party faithful. Democrats in support of the Lincoln war policy were encouraged to attend, and the name "Union Party" was used to describe the wartime coalition.

Delegates were present from all the Northern states, the territories, the District of Columbia, and the slave states of Arkansas, Florida, Louisiana, Tennessee, South Carolina, and Virginia. Credentials disputes occupied the early sessions. The credentials committee recommended that all the Southern states except South Carolina be admitted, but denied the right to vote. A minority report, advocating voting privileges for the Tennessee delegation, was passed, 310 to 151. A second minority report favoring voting privileges for Arkansas and Louisiana was approved, 307 to 167. However, the credentials committee recommendation that Florida and Virginia be denied voting rights, and South Carolina be excluded entirely, were accepted without a roll call.

Although dissatisfaction with the administration's war policy had spawned opposition to Lincoln, the boomlets for such presidential hopefuls as Treasury Secretary Salmon P. Chase petered out. The Lincoln forces controlled the convention, and the pres-

ident was easily renominated on the first ballot. Lincoln received 494 of the 516 votes cast, losing only Missouri's 22 votes, which were committed to Gen. Ulysses S. Grant. After the roll call, Missouri moved that the vote be made unanimous. *(Table, p. 190.)*

Lincoln did not publicly declare his preference for a vice-presidential running mate, leaving the selection to the convention. The main contenders included incumbent vice president, Hannibal Hamlin of Maine; former senator and military governor of Tennessee, Democrat Andrew Johnson; and former senator Daniel S. Dickinson of New York. Johnson led on the first ballot with 200 votes, followed by Hamlin with 150 and Dickinson with 108. After completion of the roll call, a switch to Johnson by the Kentucky delegation ignited a surge to the Tennessean that delivered him 492 votes and the nomination.

The Republican (Union) platform was approved without debate. Unlike the Democrats, who criticized the war effort and called for a quick, negotiated peace, the Republicans favored a vigorous prosecution of the war until the South surrendered unconditionally. The Republicans called for the eradication of slavery, with its elimination embodied in a constitutional amendment.

Although the Republican document focused on the Civil War, it also included planks encouraging immigration, urging the speedy construction of a transcontinental railroad and reaffirming the Monroe Doctrine.

Following are excerpts from the Republican (Union) platform of 1864:

Resolved, . . . we pledge ourselves, as Union men, animated by a common sentiment and aiming at a common object, to do everything in our power to aid the Government in quelling by force of arms the Rebellion now raging against its authority, and in bringing to the punishment due to their crimes the Rebels and traitors arrayed against it.

Resolved, That we approve the determination of the Government of the United States not to compromise with Rebels, or to offer them any terms of peace, except such as may be based upon an unconditional surrender of their hostility and a return to their just allegiance to the Constitution and laws of the United States, and that we call upon the Government to maintain this position and to prosecute the war with the utmost possible vigor to the complete suppression of the Rebellion, in full reliance upon the self-sacrificing patriotism, the heroic valor and the undying devotion of the American people to the country and its free institutions.

Resolved, That as slavery was the cause, and now constitutes the strength of this Rebellion, and as it must be, always and everywhere, hostile to the principles of Republican Government, justice and the National safety demand its utter and complete extirpation from the soil of the Republic . . . we are in favor, furthermore, of such an amendment to the Constitution, to be made by the people in conformity with its provisions, as shall terminate and forever prohibit the existence of Slavery within the limits of the jurisdiction of the United States.

Resolved, That the thanks of the American people are due to the soldiers and sailors of the Army and Navy, who have periled their lives in defense of the country and in vindication of the honor of its flag.

DEMOCRATS

The Democrats originally scheduled their convention for early summer but postponed it until late August to gauge the significance of military developments. The party, badly split during the 1860 campaign, no longer had the Southern faction with which to contend. But while there was no longer a regional split, new divisions arose over the continuing war. There was a large peace faction, known as the Copperheads, that favored a quick, negotiated peace with the South. Another faction supported the war but criticized its handling by the Lincoln administration. A third faction supported Lincoln's conduct of the war and defected to support the Republican president.

Although factionalized, the Democratic delegates who assembled in Chicago were optimistic about their party's chances. The war-weary nation, they thought, was ready to vote out the Lincoln administration if there was not a quick change in Northern military fortunes.

Although the border states were represented at the Democratic convention, the territories and seceded Southern states were not. In spite of the party's internal divisions, there was little opposition to the presidential candidacy of Gen. George B. McClellan of New Jersey. The former commander of the Union Army won on the first ballot, receiving 174 of the 226 votes cast. Former governor Thomas H. Seymour of Connecticut trailed with 38 votes. A switch to McClellan by several Ohio delegates prompted shifts by other delegations and brought his total to 202½. Clement Vallandigham, a leader of the Copperhead faction, moved that McClellan's nomination be made unanimous.

Eight candidates were placed in nomination for the vice presidency. James Guthrie of Kentucky led Rep. George H. Pendleton of Ohio, the favorite of the Copperheads, on the first ballot, 65½ to 55. However, shifts to Pendleton by Illinois, Kentucky, and New York after completion of the roll call created a bandwagon that led quickly to his unanimous nomination. In the convention hall at the time of his selection, Pendleton made a short speech of acceptance. *(Table, p. 190.)*

The platform adopted by the Democrats reflected the views of the Copperhead faction. The Lincoln administration's conduct of the Civil War was denounced, with particular criticism of the use of martial law and the abridgement of state and civil rights. The platform called for an immediate end to hostilities and a negotiated peace. The "sympathy" of the party was extended to soldiers and sailors involved in the war. Besides a criticism of the war and its conduct by the Lincoln administration, there were no other issues discussed in the platform.

Following are excerpts from the Democratic platform of 1864:

Resolved, That this convention does explicitly declare, as the sense of the American people, that after four years of failure to restore the Union by the experiment of war, during which, under the pretense of a military necessity of war-power higher than the Constitution, the Constitution itself has been disregarded in every part, and public liberty and private right alike trodden down, and the material prosperity of the country essentially impaired, justice, humanity, liberty, and the public welfare demand that immediate efforts be made for a cessation of hostilities, with a view of an ultimate convention of the States, or other peaceable means, to the end that, at the earliest practicable moment, peace may be restored on the basis of the Federal Union of the States.

Resolved, That the sympathy of the Democratic party is heartily and earnestly extended to the soldiery of our army and sailors of our navy, who are and have been in the field and on the sea under the flag of our country, and, in the events of its attaining power, they will receive all the care, protection, and regard that the brave soldiers and sailors of the republic have so nobly earned.

1868 Conventions

PRESIDENTIAL CANDIDATES

Ulysses S. Grant
Republican

Horatio Seymour
Democrat

REPUBLICANS

The "National Union Republican Party," as the political organization was termed in its platform, held its first postwar convention in Chicago in May 1868. Delegations from the states of the old Confederacy were accepted; several included African Americans.

The turbulent nature of postwar politics was evident in the fact that Gen. Ulysses S. Grant, the clear front-runner for the Republican nomination, had been considered a possible contender for the Democratic nomination barely a year earlier. Less than six months before the convention, the basically apolitical Grant had broken with Andrew Johnson, who had become president following the assassination of Abraham Lincoln in 1865.

Grant's was the only name placed in nomination, and on the ensuing roll call he received all 650 votes. *(Table, p. 191.)*

While the presidential race was cut and dried, the balloting for vice president was wide open, with eleven candidates receiving votes on the initial roll call. Sen. Benjamin F. Wade of Ohio led on the first ballot with 147 votes, followed by Gov. Reuben E. Fenton of New York with 126, Sen. Henry Wilson of Massachusetts with 119, and Speaker of the House Schuyler Colfax of Indiana with 115.

Over the next four ballots, Wade and Colfax were the front-runners, with Colfax finally moving ahead on the fifth ballot. His lead over Wade at this point was only 226 to 207, but numerous vote shifts after the roll call quickly pushed the Indiana representative over the top and gave him the nomination. After all the vote changes, Colfax's total stood at 541, followed by Fenton with 69 and Wade with 38.

Not surprisingly, the platform adopted by the Republicans differed sharply with the Democrats over reconstruction and Johnson's presidency. The Republican platform applauded the radical reconstruction program passed by Congress and denounced Johnson as "treacherous" and deserving of impeachment. The Republican platform approved of voting rights for black men in the South but determined that this was a subject for each state to decide in the rest of the nation.

The two parties also differed on their response to the currency question. While the Democrats favored a "soft money" policy, the Republicans supported a continued "hard money" approach, rejecting the Democratic proposal that the economic crisis could be eased by an increased supply of greenbacks.

Following are excerpts from the Republican platform of 1868:

Reconstruction. We congratulate the country on the assured success of the reconstruction policy of Congress, as evinced by the adoption, in the majority of the States lately in rebellion, of constitutions securing equal civil and political rights to all, and regard it as the duty of the Government to sustain those constitutions, and to prevent the people of such States from being remitted to a state of anarchy or military rule.

The guaranty by Congress of equal suffrage to all loyal men at the South was demanded by every consideration of public safety, of gratitude, and of justice, and must be maintained; while the question of suffrage in all the loyal States properly belongs to the people of those States.

President Andrew Johnson. We profoundly deplore the untimely and tragic death of Abraham Lincoln, and regret the accession of Andrew Johnson to the Presidency, who has acted treacherously to the people who elected him and the cause he was pledged to support; has usurped high legislative and judicial functions; has refused to execute the laws; has used his high office to induce other officers to ignore and violate the laws; has employed his executive powers to render insecure the property, the peace, the liberty, and life of the citizen; has abused the pardoning power; has denounced the National Legislature as unconstitutional; has persistently and corruptly resisted, by every means in his power, every proper attempt at the reconstruction of the States lately in rebellion; has perverted the public patronage into an engine of wholesale corruption; and has been justly impeached for high crimes and misdemeanors, and properly pronounced guilty thereof by the vote of thirty-five senators.

Currency. We denounce all forms of repudiation as a national crime; and national honor requires the payment of the public indebtedness in the utmost good faith to all creditors at home and abroad, not only according to the letter, but the spirit of the laws under which it was contracted.

DEMOCRATS

Reunited after the Civil War, the Democratic Party held its first postwar convention in New York's newly constructed Tammany Hall. It was no accident that convention proceedings began on July 4, 1868. The Democratic National Committee had set the date, and its chairman, August Belmont of New York, opened the first session with a harsh criticism of Republican reconstruction policy and the abridgement of civil rights.

Delegates from Southern states were voting members of the convention, but an effort to extend representation to the territories was defeated, 184 to 106.

Before the presidential balloting began, the convention chairman ruled that, as at the 1860 Charleston assembly, a nominating majority would be based on two-thirds of the total votes allocated (317) and not votes cast. On the opening ballot, the party's vice-presidential candidate four years earlier, George H. Pendleton of Ohio, took the lead. Pendleton, although popular in the economically depressed Midwest because of his plan to inflate the currency by printing more greenbacks, had little appeal in the eastern states. Nonetheless, he led on the first ballot with 105 votes. President Andrew Johnson was next, with 65 votes. Johnson's vote was largely complimentary and declined after the first roll call. Pendleton, however, showed increased strength, rising to a peak of 156½ votes on the eighth ballot. But Pendleton's total was well short of the 212 votes required to nominate, and his total steadily decreased after the eighth roll call. *(Table, p. 192.)*

The collapse of the Pendleton and Johnson candidacies produced a boom for Gen. Winfield Scott Hancock of Pennsylvania. Opponents of Hancock attempted to break his surge by calling for adjournment after the sixteenth ballot. Although the move for adjournment was defeated, 174½ to 14½, the Hancock boom began to lose momentum. The Civil War general peaked at 144½ votes on the eighteenth ballot, well short of a two-thirds majority.

With Hancock stymied, a new contender, Sen. Thomas A. Hendricks of Indiana, gained strength. Hendricks's vote rose to 132 on the twenty-first ballot, and the trend to the Indiana senator continued on the twenty-second ballot until the roll call reached Ohio. However, Ohio shifted its entire vote to Horatio Seymour, the permanent chairman of the convention and a former governor of New York. Seymour declined to be a candidate,

and so announced to the convention, but Ohio did not change its vote, and friends of Seymour hustled the reluctant candidate from the hall. The bandwagon had begun, and when the vote switches were completed, Seymour had received all 317 votes.

The vice-presidential nomination went to Gen. Francis P. Blair Jr. of Missouri, a former Republican, who was unanimously selected on the first ballot. The names of several other candidates were placed in nomination, but the announcement of Blair's candidacy created a bandwagon that led to the withdrawal of the others.

The Democratic platform was accepted by a voice vote without debate. The platform began by declaring the questions of slavery and secession to be permanently settled by the Civil War. Several planks criticized the Republican reconstruction program, passed by the party's Radical wing in Congress. The Radicals themselves were scathingly denounced for their "unparalleled oppression and tyranny." The Democratic platform expressed its support for Andrew Johnson's conduct as president and decried the attempts to impeach him.

For the first time, the question of the coinage and printing of money was discussed in the party platform. Two planks were included that could be generally interpreted as supporting Pendleton's inflationary greenback plan.

On the tariff issue, the Democrats called for a tariff that would primarily raise revenue but also protect American industry.

Following are excerpts from the Democratic platform of 1868:

Reconstruction. . . . [W]e arraign the Radical party for its disregard of right, and the unparalleled oppression and tyranny which have marked its career.

Instead of restoring the Union, it has, so far as in its power, dissolved it, and subjected ten States, in time of profound peace, to military despotism and negro supremacy.

President Andrew Johnson. That the President of the United States, Andrew Johnson, in exercising the power of his high office in resisting the aggressions of Congress upon the Constitutional rights of the States and the people, is entitled to the gratitude of the whole American people; and in behalf of the Democratic party, we tender him our thanks for his patriotic efforts in that regard.

Currency. . . . where the obligations of the government do not expressly state upon their face, or the law under which they were issued does not provide, that they shall be paid in coin, they ought, in right and in justice, to be paid in the lawful money of the United States. . . . One currency for the government and the people, the laborer and the officeholder, the pensioner and the soldier, the producer and the bond-holder.

1872 Conventions

PRESIDENTIAL CANDIDATES

Horace Greeley
Liberal Republican, Democrat

Ulysses S. Grant
Republican

LIBERAL REPUBLICANS

The short-lived Liberal Republican Party grew out of griev-ances that elements in the Republican Party had with the poli-cies of the Grant administration. There was particular dissatis-faction with the "carpetbag" governments in the South, support for extensive civil service reform and a general distaste for the corrupt administration of President Ulysses S. Grant. .

The idea for the Liberal Republican movement originated in Missouri, where, in the 1870 state elections, a coalition of reform Republicans and Democrats swept to victory. In January 1872 a state convention of this new coalition issued the call for a na-tional convention to be held that May in Cincinnati, Ohio.

Without a formal, nationwide organization, the delegate se-lection process was haphazard. Some of the delegates were self-appointed, but generally the size of each delegation reflected twice a state's electoral vote.

Three separate groups—reformers, anti-Grant politicians, and a coalition of four influential newspaper editors known as "the Quadrilateral"—vied for control of the convention. For the presidential nomination, the reformers favored either Charles Francis Adams of Massachusetts or Sen. Lyman Trumbull of Illinois. The professional politicians were inclined to Supreme Court justice David Davis of Illinois or Horace Greeley of New York. The newspaper editors opposed Davis.

On the first ballot, Adams led with 203 votes, followed by Greeley with 147, Trumbull with 110, Gov. B. Gratz Brown of Missouri with 95, and Davis with 92½. After the roll call, Brown announced his withdrawal from the race and his support for Greeley. For the next five ballots, Greeley and Adams battled for the lead. But on the sixth ballot, the professional politicians were able to ignite a stampede for Greeley that resulted in his nomination.

Many of the reform-minded delegates, disgusted with the se-lection of the New York editor, left the convention. The vice-presidential nomination went on the second ballot to a Greeley supporter, Governor Brown of Missouri.

The platform adopted by the Liberal Republicans differed with the one later accepted by the Republicans on three main points: Reconstruction, civil service reform, and the tariff.

The Liberal Republicans called for an end to Reconstruction with its "carpetbag" governments, a grant of universal amnesty to southern citizens, and a return to home rule in the South. The Liberal Republicans sharply criticized the corruption of civil service under the Grant administration and labeled its re-form one of the leading issues of the day. The civil service plank advocated a one-term limit on the presidency.

The presence of delegates supporting both protection and free trade led to a tariff plank that frankly stated the party's po-sition on the issue should be left to local determination.

Following are excerpts from the Liberal Republican platform of 1872:

Reconstruction. We demand the immediate and absolute removal of all disabilities imposed on account of the Rebellion, which was finally subdued seven years ago, believing that universal amnesty will result in complete pacification in all sections of the country.

Local self-government, with impartial suffrage, will guard the rights of all citizens more securely than any centralized power. The public welfare requires the supremacy of the civil over the military authority, and freedom of person under the protection of the *habeas corpus.*

Civil Rights. We recognize the equality of all men before the law, and hold that it is the duty of Government in its dealings with the peo-ple to mete out equal and exact justice to all of whatever nativity, race, color, or persuasion, religious or political.

Civil Service Reform. The Civil Service of the Government has become a mere instrument of partisan tyranny and personal ambition and an object of selfish greed. It is a scandal and reproach upon free institutions and breeds a demoralization dangerous to the perpetuity of republican government. We therefore regard such thorough reforms of the Civil Service as one of the most pressing necessities of the hour; that honesty, capacity, and fidelity constitute the only valid claim to public employment; that the offices of the Government cease to be a matter of arbitrary favoritism and patronage, and that public station become again a pest of honor. To this end it is imperatively required that no President shall be a candidate for reelection.

Tariff. . . . recognizing that there are in our midst honest but irreconcilable differences of opinion with regard to the respective systems of Protection and Free Trade, we remit the discussion of the subject to the people in their Congress Districts, and to the decision of Congress thereon, wholly free of Executive interference or dictation.

Homesteading. We are opposed to all further grants of lands to railroads or other corporations. The public domain should be held sacred to actual settlers.

DEMOCRATS

The Democratic convention that met in Baltimore in July 1872 was one of the most bizarre in American political history. In sessions totaling only six hours, the delegates endorsed the decisions on candidates and platform made at a convention one month earlier by the Liberal Republicans. The Democratic convention merely rubber-stamped the creation of a coalition of Liberal Republicans and the core of the Democratic Party. *(Table, p. 193.)*

This new coalition was established with little dissent. When it came time for the presidential balloting, nominating speeches were not allowed. On the subsequent roll call, Greeley, the nominee of the Liberal Republicans, received 686 of the allotted 732 votes. It was an ironic choice, because in earlier decades Greeley, as editor of the *New York Tribune,* had been a frequent critic of the Democratic Party. More than anything else, however, Greeley's selection underscored the lack of strong leadership in the post–Civil War Democratic Party.

In similar fashion, the convention endorsed the nomination of B. Gratz Brown for vice president. Brown, the governor of Missouri and the choice of the Liberal Republicans, was the early unanimous nominee of the Democrats, with 713 votes.

By a vote of 574 to 158, the delegates agreed to limit debate on the platform to one hour. Except for a brief introduction, the Democrats approved the same platform that had been adopted by the Liberal Republicans a month earlier. Key planks called for an end to Reconstruction and complete amnesty for Southern citizens, a return to a federal government with limited powers, civil service reform, and the halt of grants of public land to railroads and other corporations. Ironically, the platform also favored a hard-money policy, a reversal of the Democrats' soft-money stand in 1868. Although there was some objection to the point-by-point acceptance of the Liberal Republican platform, it was adopted by a vote of 671 to 62. *(For platform excerpts, see the Liberal Republicans section, p. 65.)*

REPUBLICANS

With the reform wing of the Republican Party already having bolted, the remaining elements of the party gathered in relative harmony in Philadelphia in June 1872. President Ulysses S. Grant was renominated without opposition, receiving all 752 votes cast. *(Table, p. 193.)*

The only contest at the convention centered around the vice-presidential nomination, with the incumbent, Schuyler Colfax of Indiana, and Sen. Henry Wilson of Massachusetts the two major rivals. Wilson took a slim plurality over Colfax on the first roll call, 364½ to 321½, but a vote shift by Virginia after completion of the roll gave Wilson the necessary majority with 399½ votes.

Without debate or opposition, the platform was adopted. It lauded the eleven years of Republican rule, noting the success of Reconstruction, the hard-money policy, and the homestead program. A tariff plank called for a duty on imports to raise revenue as well as to protect American business.

The platform also included several progressive planks, including a recommendation that the franking privilege be abolished, an extension of rights to women, and a call for federal and state legislation that would ensure equal rights for all races throughout the nation. The last plank was a significant change from the 1868 platform, which called for black suffrage in the South but left the decision on black voting rights to the individual states elsewhere.

Following are excerpts from the Republican platform of 1872:

Reconstruction. We hold that Congress and the President have only fulfilled an imperative duty in their measures for the suppression of violent and treasonable organizations in certain lately rebellious regions, and for the protection of the ballot-box, and therefore they are entitled to the thanks of the nation.

Civil Rights. Complete liberty and exact equality in the enjoyment of all civil, political, and public rights should be established and effectually maintained throughout the Union, by efficient and appropriate State and Federal legislation. Neither the law nor its administration should admit any discrimination in respect of citizens by reason of race, creed, color, or previous condition of servitude.

Civil Service Reform. Any system of the civil service under which the subordinate positions of the government are considered rewards for mere party zeal is fatally demoralizing, and we therefore favor a reform of the system by laws which shall abolish the evils of patronage, and make honesty, efficiency, and fidelity the essential qualifications for public positions, without practically creating a life-tenure of office.

Tariff. . . . [R]evenue . . . should be raised by duties upon importations, the details of which should be so adjusted as to aid in securing remunerative wages to labor, and to promote the industries, prosperity, and growth of the whole country.

Homesteading. We are opposed to further grants of the public lands to corporations and monopolies, and demand that the national domain be set apart for free homes for the people.

Women's Rights. The Republican party is mindful of its obligations to the loyal women of America for their noble devotion to the cause of freedom. Their admission to wider fields of usefulness is viewed with satisfaction, and the honest demand of any class of citizens for additional rights should be treated with respectful consideration.

1876 Conventions

PRESIDENTIAL CANDIDATES

Rutherford B. Hayes
Republican

Samuel J. Tilden
Democrat

REPUBLICANS

The Republican convention assembled in Cincinnati, Ohio, in mid-June 1876. The call to the convention extended the olive branch to the dissident Liberal Republicans, who in large measure had rejoined their original party.

One of the highlights of the early sessions was a speech by the prominent black leader Frederick Douglass, who lambasted the Republicans for freeing the slaves without providing means for their economic or physical security.

A dispute developed over the seating of two contesting Alabama delegations. It was a candidate-oriented dispute, with the majority report favoring a delegation strongly for House Speaker James G. Blaine of Maine. The minority report supported a delegation pledged to Sen. Oliver P. Morton of Indiana. In the subsequent roll call, the convention decided in favor of the Blaine delegation by a vote of 369 to 360.

The presidential race was contested by the champions of the three nearly equal wings of the party. The Radicals were led by senators Roscoe Conkling of New York and Morton; the Half-Breeds, by Blaine; and the reformers, by former Treasury secretary Benjamin H. Bristow of Kentucky.

A fiery nominating speech for Blaine, delivered by Col. Robert G. Ingersoll, referred to the House Speaker as the "plumed knight," an appellation that stuck with Blaine the rest of his political career. Although it was a compelling speech, its effect was reduced by a failure in the hall's lighting system, which forced an early adjournment.

Nonetheless, when balloting commenced the next morning, Blaine had a wide lead, receiving 285 votes on the first ballot, compared with 124 for Morton, 113 for Bristow, and 99 for Conkling. *(Table, p. 194.)*

In the middle of the second ballot, a procedural dispute arose over the legality of the unit rule. Three delegates in the Pennsylvania delegation wished to vote for another candidate and appealed to the chair. The chair ruled that their votes should be counted, even though Pennsylvania was bound by the state convention to vote as a unit. The ruling of the chair was upheld on a voice vote, but subsequent debate brought a roll call on reconsidering the decision. The motion to reconsider passed, 381 to 359. However, by a margin of 395 to 353, another roll call upheld the power of the convention chairman to abolish the unit rule.

Although the vote had long-range significance for future Republican conventions, in the short run it provided a slight boost for Blaine, who gained several delegates in Pennsylvania. On the next four ballots, Blaine retained his large lead but could not come close to the necessary 379 votes needed for nomination. The only candidate to show increased strength was Gov. Rutherford B. Hayes of Ohio, who jumped from 68 votes on the fourth roll call to 104 on the fifth.

On the sixth ballot, however, Blaine showed renewed strength, rising to 308 votes, while Hayes assumed second place with 113. The House Speaker continued to gain on the seventh ballot, but the anti-Blaine forces quickly and successfully united behind Hayes. The Ohio governor, a viable compromise choice who had not alienated any of the party factions, won the nomination with 384 votes to 351 for Blaine.

Five candidates were placed in nomination for the vice presidency. However, Rep. William A. Wheeler of New York was so far in the lead that the roll call was suspended after South Carolina voted, and Wheeler was declared the nominee by acclamation.

Platform debate centered on the party's immigration plank. A Massachusetts delegate proposed deletion of the plank, which called for a congressional investigation of oriental immigration. The delegate argued that the plank was inconsistent with the Republican principle that favored the equality of all races. However, by a vote of 518 to 229, the plank was retained as written.

The Republican platform included a scathing denunciation of the Democratic Party, but only on the issues of currency and tariff was it markedly different from the opposition. The Republicans, unlike the Democrats, favored complete payment of Civil

War bonds in hard money as quickly as possible. While the Democrats supported a tariff for revenue purposes only, the Republicans implied that the tariff should protect American industry as well as raise revenue.

As in past platforms, the Republicans called for the extension of civil rights, civil service reform, increased rights for women, the abolition of polygamy, and the distribution of public land to homesteaders. A new plank proposed that a constitutional amendment be passed forbidding the use of federal funds for non-public schools.

Following are excerpts from the Republican platform of 1876:

Currency. In the first act of congress, signed by President Grant, the national government . . . solemnly pledged its faith "to make provisions at the earliest practicable period, for the redemption of the United States notes in coin." Commercial prosperity, public morals, and the national credit demand that this promise be fulfilled by a continuous and steady progress to specie payment.

Tariff. The revenue necessary for current expenditures and the obligations of the public debt must be largely derived from duties upon importations, which, so far as possible, should be so adjusted as to promote the interests of American labor and advance the prosperity of the whole country.

Immigration. It is the immediate duty of congress fully to investigate the effects of the immigration and importation of Mongolians on the moral and material interests of the country.

Education. The public school system of the several states is the bulwark of the American republic; and, with a view to its security and permanence, we recommend an amendment to the constitution of the United States, forbidding the application of any public funds or property for the benefit of any school or institution under sectarian control.

Democratic Party. We therefore note with deep solicitude that the Democratic party counts, as its chief hope of success, upon the electoral vote of a united South, secured through the efforts of those who were recently arrayed against the nation; and we invoke the earnest attention of the country to the grave truth, that a success thus achieved would re-open sectional strife and imperil national honor and human rights.

We charge the Democratic party with being the same in character and spirit as when it sympathized with treason; with making its control of the house of representatives the triumph and opportunity of the nation's recent foes; with reasserting and applauding in the national capitol the sentiments of unrepentant rebellion; with sending Union soldiers to the rear, and promoting Confederate soldiers to the front; with deliberately proposing to repudiate the plighted faith of the government; with being equally false and imbecile upon the overshadowing financial question; with thwarting the ends of justice, by its partisan mismanagements and obstruction of investigation; with proving itself, through the period of its ascendancy in the lower house of Congress, utterly incompetent to administer the government;—and we warn the country against trusting a party thus alike unworthy, recreant, and incapable.

DEMOCRATS

America's rapid westward expansion was typified by the site of the Democratic Party's 1876 convention—St. Louis, Mo. It marked the first time that a national convention was held west of the Mississippi River.

The Democratic delegates assembled in late June. The one procedural matter debated was a proposal that the two-thirds rule be abolished at the 1880 convention and that the Democratic National Committee include such a recommendation in its next convention call. A move to table the proposal was defeated, 379 to 359. However, the national committee took no action on the proposal.

Two governors, Samuel J. Tilden of New York and Thomas A. Hendricks of Indiana, were the principal contenders for the presidential nomination, with Tilden having a substantial lead in delegates as the convention opened. Ironically, Tilden's most vocal opposition came from his New York delegation, where John Kelly of Tammany Hall spearheaded an effort to undermine Tilden's candidacy. Tilden's reform moves as governor had alienated Tammany Hall, and several times during the convention, Kelly took the floor to denounce Tilden.

Nonetheless, Tilden had a substantial lead on the first ballot, receiving 401½ votes to 140½ for Hendricks. Although short of the 492 votes needed to nominate, Tilden moved closer when Missouri switched its votes to him after the first roll call. The movement to Tilden continued on the second ballot, and he finished the roll call with 535 votes, more than enough to ensure his nomination. *(Table, p. 195.)*

Hendricks, the runner-up for the presidential nomination, was the nearly unanimous choice of the delegates for the vice presidency. Hendricks received 730 votes, with the other 8 votes not being cast.

The Democratic platform was an unusual one. Rather than being arranged in usual fashion with a series of numbered planks, it was written in paragraph form in language unusually powerful for a party platform. The theme of the document was the need for reform, and nearly half the paragraphs began with the phrase, "Reform is necessary. . . ."

Debate focused on the party's stand on the currency issue. The majority report proposed repeal of the Resumption Act of 1875, a hard-money measure that called for the payment of Civil War bonds in coin. A minority report sponsored by delegates from five eastern states proposing deletion of this position was defeated, 550 to 219. A second minority report, introduced by midwestern delegates, favored a more strongly worded opposition to the Resumption Act. It too was defeated, 505 to 229, with midwestern delegations providing the bulk of the minority vote. The platform as a whole was approved, 651 to 83, again with most of the dissenting votes coming from the Midwest.

Besides the currency proposal, the platform called for extensive civil service reform, a tariff for revenue purposes only, restrictions on Chinese immigration, and a new policy on the distribution of public land that would benefit the homesteaders and not the railroads. In addition to its reform theme, the platform was filled with sharp criticisms of Republican rule.

Following are excerpts from the Democratic platform of 1876:

Civil Service Reform. Reform is necessary in the civil service. Experience proves that efficient economical conduct of the government is not possible if its civil service be subject to change at every election, be a prize fought for at the ballot-box, be an approved reward of party zeal instead of posts of honor assigned for proved competency and held for fidelity in the public employ; that the dispensing of patronage should neither be a tax upon the time of our public men nor an instrument of their ambition. Here again, profession falsified in the performance attest that the party in power can work out no practical or salutary reform. Reform is necessary even more in the higher grades of the public service. President, Vice-President, judges, senators, representatives, cabinet officers—these and all others in authority are the people's servants. Their offices are not a private perquisite; they are a public trust. When the annals of this Republic show disgrace and censure of a Vice-President; a late Speaker of the House of Representatives marketing his rulings as a presiding officer; three Senators profiting secretly by their votes as law-makers; five chairmen of the leading committees of the late House of Representatives exposed in jobbery; a late Secretary of the Treasury forcing balances in the public accounts; a late Attorney-General misappropriating public funds; a Secretary of the Navy enriched and enriching friends by a percentage levied off the profits of contractors with his department; an Ambassador to England censured in a dishonorable speculation; the President's Private Secretary barely escaping conviction upon trial for guilty complicity in frauds upon the revenue; a Secretary of War impeached for high crimes and misdemeanors—the demonstration is complete, that the first step in reform must be the people's choice of honest men from another party, lest the disease of one political organization infect the body politic, and lest by making no change of men or parties, we get no change of measures and no real reform.

Currency. We denounce the improvidence which, in eleven years of peace, has taken from the people in Federal taxes thirteen times the whole amount of the legal-tender notes and squandered four times their sum in useless expense, without accumulating any reserve for their redemption. We denounce the financial imbecility and immorality of that party, which, during eleven years of peace, has made no advance toward resumption, no preparation for resumption, but instead has obstructed resumption by wasting our resources and exhausting all our surplus income, and while annually professing to intend a speedy return to specie payments, has annually enacted fresh hindrances thereto. As such hindrance we denounce the resumption clause of the act of 1875 and we here demand its repeal.

Tariff. We denounce the present tariff levied upon nearly four thousand articles as a masterpiece of injustice, inequality and false pretense, which yields a dwindling and not a yearly rising revenue, has impoverished many industries to subsidize a few. . . . We demand that all customhouse taxation shall be only for revenue.

Homesteading. Reform is necessary to put a stop to the profligate waste of public lands and their diversion from actual settlers by the party in power, which has squandered two hundred millions of acres upon railroads alone, and out of more than thrice that aggregate has disposed of less than a sixth directly to the tillers of the soil.

Immigration. . . . [W]e denounce the policy which thus discards the liberty-loving German and tolerates the revival of the coolie-trade in Mongolian women for immoral purposes, and Mongolian men held to perform servile labor contracts, and demand such modification of the treaty with the Chinese Empire, or such legislation within constitutional limitations, as shall prevent further importation or immigration of the Mongolian race.

1880 Conventions

PRESIDENTIAL CANDIDATES

James A. Garfield
Republican

James B. Weaver
Greenback

Winfield Hancock
Democrat

REPUBLICANS

The Republicans gathered in Chicago beginning June 2, 1880, for their seventh quadrennial nominating convention. For the first time, the convention call was addressed only to Republicans and not more broadly to others who sympathized with party principles.

The convention was divided into two factions. One, headed by Sen. Roscoe Conkling of New York, favored the nomination of former president Ulysses S. Grant for a third term. The anti-Grant faction, although not united around one candidate, included the eventual nominee, Rep. James A. Garfield of Ohio, among its leaders.

Preconvention skirmishing focused on the selection of a temporary chairman. The Grant forces desired one from their ranks who would uphold the unit rule—a rule important to Grant, because he had the support of a majority of delegates in several large states. However, the Grant strategy was blocked, and a temporary chairman neutral to both sides was chosen by the Republican National Committee, leaving the ultimate decision on the unit rule to the convention.

A test of strength between the two factions came early in the convention on an amended motion by Conkling directing the credentials committee to report to the convention prior to the rules committee. Conkling's amended motion was defeated, 406 to 318.

In spite of the defeat of the amended motion, much time was spent debating delegate credentials. More than fifty cases were presented in committee, and seven of them came to the floor for a vote. Five of the cases featured seating disputes among delegates selected in district caucuses and those chosen for the same seats in state conventions. In each case—involving delegates from the states of Illinois, Kansas, and West Virginia—the convention supported the claim of the delegates elected at the district level.

The Illinois credentials fight produced the only candidate-oriented division, with the Grant forces favoring the seating of the delegates selected at the state convention. But by a margin of 387 to 353, the convention voted to seat the delegates selected in the district caucuses. Three other votes were taken on disputed credentials from different Illinois districts, but all were decided in favor of the anti-Grant forces by a similar margin. *(Table, p. 196.)*

The majority report of the rules committee advocated that the controversial unit rule not be used. A motion by the Grant forces that the presidential nominations begin without passage of the rules committee report was defeated, 479 to 276. The vote was a key setback for the supporters of the former president, as the majority report was subsequently adopted by acclamation.

While the Grant forces suffered defeat on adoption of the unit rule, their candidate assumed the lead on the first ballot for president, with 304 votes. Sen. James G. Blaine of Maine followed closely with 284, and Treasury Secretary John Sherman of Ohio, the candidate nominated by Rep. Garfield, trailed with 93 votes.

Ballot after ballot was taken throughout the day, but after the twenty-eighth roll call, the last of the night, there was little change in the vote totals of the leading candidates. Grant led with 307 votes, Blaine stayed in second with 279, and Sherman had 91.

When balloting resumed the next morning, Sherman's vote total jumped to 116, the biggest gain among the contenders, but still well behind Grant and Blaine. Grant gained votes on the thirty-fourth ballot, rising to a new high of 312, but on the same roll call a boom for Garfield began, with the Ohio representative collecting 16 votes from Wisconsin. Garfield protested that he was not a candidate but was ruled out of order by the chairman.

The Ohio representative continued to gain on the thirty-fifth ballot, his vote total rising to 50. On the next ballot, Garfield won the nomination, receiving the votes of nearly all the anti-Grant delegates. At the end of the roll call, Garfield had 399 votes; Grant, 306, and Blaine, 42, with nine votes distributed among other candidates.

Four men were placed in nomination for the vice presidency, but Chester A. Arthur of New York was the easy winner on the first ballot. Arthur, the former collector of the port of New York, received 468 votes to 193 for former representative Elihu B. Washburne of Illinois. Most of Arthur's support came from delegates who had backed Grant.

The Republican platform was passed by a voice vote without debate. For the first time, the platform included planks that clearly called for the exercise of federal power, emphasizing that the Constitution was "a supreme law, and not a mere contract." This philosophy contrasted with the Democratic platform, which favored home rule and government decentralization.

The two parties also differed on the tariff issue. The Republicans favored a revenue tariff that would also protect American industry, while the Democrats explicitly called for a revenue tariff only.

In its original form, the Republican platform did not include a civil service plank. An amendment from the floor, however, calling for a "thorough, radical and complete" reform of the civil service, was passed by a voice vote.

Following are excerpts from the Republican platform of 1880:

Federal Power. The Constitution of the United States is a supreme law, and not a mere contract. Out of confederated States it made a sovereign nation. Some powers are denied to the Nation, while others are denied to the States; but the boundary between the powers delegated and those reserved is to be determined by the National and not by the State tribunal.

The work of popular education is one left to the care of the several States, but it is the duty of the National Government to aid that work to the extent of its constitutional power. The intelligence of the Nation is but the aggregate of the intelligence in the several States, and the destiny of the Nation must be guided, not by the genius of any one State, but by the aggregate genius of all.

Tariff. We affirm the belief, avowed in 1876, that the duties levied for the purpose of revenue should so discriminate as to favor American labor. . . .

Civil Service Reform. The Republican party, . . . adopts the declaration of President Hayes that the reform of the civil service should be thorough, radical and complete.

Chinese Immigration. . . . [T]he Republican party, regarding the unrestricted immigration of the Chinese as a matter of grave concernment . . . would limit and restrict that immigration by the enactment of such just, humane and reasonable laws and treaties as will produce that result.

GREENBACK PARTY

A coalition of farmer and labor groups met in Chicago beginning June 9, 1880, to hold the second national Greenback Party convention. The party's first convention was held four years earlier, but it was not until 1880 that the Greenback Party received more than 2 percent of the popular vote. The Greenbacks would hold their third and final convention four years later, but the party would receive under 2 percent in the 1884 election.

The 1880 convention attracted representatives of the various Greenback Party factions, as well as forty-four delegates from the Socialist Labor Party. Rep. James B. Weaver of Iowa was nominated for the presidency, and B. J. Chambers of Texas was chosen as his running mate.

The platform adopted was far broader than the one conceived by the Greenbacks at their first convention in 1876. That year they focused solely on the currency issue. For the agrarian interests, currency planks remained that called for the unlimited coinage of silver and gold and the issuance of currency by the federal government and not private banks. Also adopted for the farm elements were planks advocating increased public land for settlers, denouncing large monopolies and proposing that Congress control passenger and freight rates.

Included for the labor groups were proposals for an eight-hour day, the abolition of child labor, the improvement of working conditions and the curtailment of Chinese immigration.

The Greenback platform also included planks that favored a graduated income tax and women's suffrage.

Following are excerpts from the Greenback platform of 1880:

Currency. . . . All money, whether metallic or paper, should be issued and its volume controlled by the Government, and not by or through banking corporations, and when so issued should be a full legal-tender for all debts, public and private.

That the bonds of the United States should not be refunded, but paid as rapidly as practicable, according to contract. To enable the Government to meet these obligations, legal-tender currency should be substituted for the notes of the National banks, the National banking system abolished, and the unlimited coinage of silver, as well as gold, established by law.

Labor. That labor should be so protected by National and State authority as to equalize the burdens and insure a just distribution of its results; the eight-hour law of Congress should be enforced, the sanitary condition of industrial establishments placed under rigid control; the competition of contract labor abolished, a bureau of labor statistics established, factories, mines, and workshops inspected, the employment of children under fourteen years of age forbidden, and wages paid in cash.

Chinese Immigration. Slavery being simply cheap labor, and cheap labor being simple slavery, the importation and presence of Chinese serfs necessarily tends to brutalize and degrade American labor.

Homesteading. Railroad and land grants forfeited by reason of non-fulfillment of contract should be immediately reclaimed by the Government, and henceforth the public domain reserved exclusively as homes for actual settlers.

Regulation of Monopolies. It is the duty of Congress to regulate inter-state commerce. All lines of communication and transportation should be brought under such legislative control as shall secure moderate, fair and uniform rates for passenger and freight traffic.

We denounce as destructive to prosperity and dangerous to liberty, the action of the old parties in fostering and sustaining gigantic land, railroad, and money corporations and monopolies, invested with, and exercising powers belonging to the Government, and yet not responsible to it for the manner of their exercise.

Income Tax. All property should bear its just proportion of taxation, and we demand a graduated income tax.

Women's Suffrage. That every citizen of due age, sound mind, and not a felon, be fully enfranchised, and that this resolution be referred to the States, with recommendation for their favorable consideration.

DEMOCRATS

The Democrats held their thirteenth quadrennial nominating convention in Cincinnati, Ohio, in late June 1880. Credentials disputes enlivened the early sessions, with two competing New York delegations the focus of attention. The challenging group, controlled by Tammany Hall, requested 20 of New York's 70 votes. But by a margin of 457 to 205½, the convention refused the request.

Samuel J. Tilden, the Democratic standard-bearer in 1876 and the narrow loser in that controversial election, was not a candidate in 1880, although he did not officially notify his supporters of this fact until the presidential balloting had begun. Tilden's indecision, however, had long before opened the door for other prospective candidates.

On the first ballot, Gen. Winfield Scott Hancock of Pennsylvania, a candidate for the nomination in both 1868 and 1876, led with 171 votes, followed by Sen. Thomas F. Bayard of Delaware with 153½ and former representative Henry G. Payne of Ohio (who served as a stalking horse for the Tilden forces) with 81. (*Table, p. 197.*)

Tilden's declaration of noncandidacy was announced before the second ballot, and the Tilden forces shifted their strength to House Speaker Samuel J. Randall of Pennsylvania. Nonetheless, Hancock was the big gainer on the second ballot, his vote total jumping to 320. Randall followed with 128½, and Bayard slipped to third place with 112. Although Hancock was well short of the 492 votes needed for nomination, Wisconsin began a string of vote switches to Hancock that resulted in the military leader's selection. After all the changes, Hancock received 705 of the 738 votes cast.

The vice-presidential nomination went by acclamation to former representative William H. English of Indiana, the only candidate.

The platform was accepted without debate or opposition. Its style of short, sharp phrases contrasted with the 1876 platform, which was written in flowing sentences built around the theme of the necessity of reform.

The 1880 platform called for decentralization of the federal government with increased local government, currency based on hard money, a tariff for revenue only, civil service reform, and an end to Chinese immigration. The platform saved its harshest language to describe the party's reaction to the controversial election of 1876, which it labeled "the great fraud."

Following are excerpts from the Democratic platform of 1880:

Government Centralization. Opposition to centralization and to that dangerous spirit of encroachment which tends to consolidate the powers of all departments in one, and thus to create whatever be the form of government, a real despotism. No sumptuary laws; separation of Church and State, for the good of each; common schools fostered and protected.

Currency. Home rule; honest money, consisting of gold and silver, and paper convertible into coin on demand.

Tariff. [A] tariff for revenue only.

Civil Service Reform. We execrate the course of this administration in making places in the civil service a reward for political crime, and demand a reform by statute which shall make it forever impossible for a defeated candidate to bribe his way to the seat of the usurper by billeting villains upon the people.

Chinese Immigration. No more Chinese immigration, except for travel, education, and foreign commerce, and that even carefully guarded.

Election of 1876. The great fraud of 1876–1877, by which, upon a false count of the electoral voters of two States, the candidate defeated at the polls was declared to be President, and for the first time in American history, the will of the people was set aside under a threat of military violence, struck a deadly blow at our system of representative government. The Democratic party, to preserve the country from the horrors of a civil war, submitted for the time in firm and patriotic faith that the people would punish this crime in 1880. This issue precedes and dwarfs every other. It imposes a more sacred duty upon the people of the Union than ever addressed the conscience of a nation of free men.

1884 Conventions

PRESIDENTIAL CANDIDATES

James G. Blaine
Republican

Grover Cleveland
Democrat

REPUBLICANS

The Republicans gathered in Chicago in June 1884 for their convention. For the first time, the call to the convention prescribed how and when delegates should be selected, an effort to avoid the credentials disputes that had besieged the convention four years earlier.

The assassination of President James A. Garfield three years earlier had opened up the Republican presidential race, and the party warhorse, James G. Blaine of Maine, emerged as the front-runner for the nomination. However, there was strong opposition to Blaine from several candidates, including the incumbent president, Chester A. Arthur of New York.

The first test between the two sides was over the choice of a temporary chairman. The Blaine forces supported former senator Powell Clayton of Arkansas, while the anti-Blaine coalition favored a black delegate from Mississippi, John R. Lynch. Lynch won by a vote of 424 to 384. (*Table, p. 198.*)

A motion by the Blaine forces to adjourn after the presidential nominating speeches was also beaten, 412 to 391. But on the first ballot Blaine assumed the lead with 334½ votes, followed by President Arthur with 278 and Sen. George F. Edmunds of Vermont with 93. Most of Arthur's strength was in the South, where the administration's patronage power had great effect.

Blaine gained votes on the next two ballots, his total rising to 375 on the third ballot, while Arthur dropped slightly to 274. After this roll call, the anti-Blaine forces tried to force adjournment but were defeated, 458 to 356. On the fourth ballot, Blaine received the nomination, winning 541 votes to 207 for Arthur and 41 for Edmunds.

Sen. John A. Logan of Illinois was the only person placed in nomination for vice president. Logan, who earlier had been in contention for the presidential nomination, received 779 of the 820 votes in the convention for second place on the ticket.

The party platform was adopted without dissent, and on major issues was little different from the planks presented by the Democrats. The Republicans proposed a tariff that would both protect American industry and raise revenue, called for civil service reform, advocated restrictions on Chinese immigration, and favored increased availability of public lands for settlers. In addition, the Republicans adopted features of the Greenback Party platform, calling for government regulation of railroads and an eight-hour workday.

Following are excerpts from the Republican platform of 1884:

Tariff. We . . . demand that the imposition of duties on foreign imports shall be made, not "for revenue only," but that in raising the requisite revenues for the government, such duties shall be so levied as to afford security to our diversified industries and protection to the rights and wages of the laborer; to the end that active and intelligent labor, as well as capital, may have its just reward, and the laboring man his full share in the national prosperity.

Chinese Immigration. [W]e denounce the importation of contract labor, whether from Europe or Asia, as an offense against the spirit of American institutions; and we pledge ourselves to sustain the present law restricting Chinese immigration, and to provide such further legislation as is necessary to carry out its purposes.

Labor. We favor the establishment of a national bureau of labor; the enforcement of the eight hour law.

Regulation of Railroads. The principle of public regulation of railway corporations is a wise and salutary one for the protection of all classes of the people; and we favor legislation that shall prevent unjust discrimination and excessive charges for transportation, and that shall secure to the people, and the railways alike, the fair and equal protection of the laws.

DEMOCRATS

The 1884 Democratic convention was held in Chicago in July. For the first time, the party extended delegate voting rights to the territories and the District of Columbia.

A debate over the unit rule highlighted the first day of the convention. Delegates from Tammany Hall, a minority of the New York delegation, presented an amendment to the temporary rules designed to abolish the unit rule. All the New York delegates were bound by their state convention to vote as a unit. However, the national convention defeated the amendment by a vote of 463 to 332, thus limiting the power of the Tammany delegates.

A resolution was passed opening the position of party chairman to individuals who were not members of the Democratic National Committee. Another resolution, to eliminate the two-thirds rule at future conventions, was put to a vote, but the roll call was suspended when it became apparent the resolution would not pass.

Several peculiarities were evident during the presidential nominating speeches. Sen. Thomas A. Hendricks of Indiana, the favorite of the Hoosier delegation, nominated former senator Joseph E. McDonald as the state's favorite son in a speech listing attributes that easily could have described Hendricks. Two seconding speeches for Gov. Grover Cleveland of New York were delivered by Tammany delegates who actually used the time to denounce Cleveland.

In spite of the opposition within his delegation, Cleveland was the front-runner for the nomination and had a big lead on the first ballot. Cleveland received 392 votes, easily outdistancing Sen. Thomas F. Bayard of Delaware, who had 170. Former senator Allen G. Thurman of Ohio was next, with 88. Hendricks received one vote but protested to the convention that he was not a candidate.

A boom for Hendricks was undertaken on the second ballot, with the Indiana delegation shifting its support from McDonald to Hendricks. However, Cleveland also gained and continued to hold a large lead over the rest of the field. After two roll calls, these vote totals stood: Cleveland, 475; Bayard, 151½; Hendricks, 123½; Thurman, 60. With the New York governor holding a majority of the vote, North Carolina switched to Cleveland, and

this started a bandwagon that gave him the required two-thirds majority. After the shifts, Cleveland received 683 of the 820 votes in the convention. *(Table, p. 199.)*

Over the objections of the Indiana delegation, Hendricks was nominated for the vice presidency. The Indiana leaders were a bit upset that Hendricks did not receive the presidential nomination but did contribute to his nearly unanimous total for second place on the ticket. When the roll call was completed, Hendricks had received all but four votes.

The Democratic platform of 1884 was one of the longest documents adopted by the party in the nineteenth century. The platform was about 3,000 words long, with the first third devoted to a description of alleged Republican failures.

The platform straddled the increasingly important tariff issue. In 1880 the Democrats clearly favored a revenue tariff only, but the 1884 document called for both revenue and protection of American industry.

A minority report introduced by Benjamin F. Butler, former governor of Massachusetts, focused on the tariff issue. Butler advocated a duty on imports that would hit harder at luxury items and less on necessities than the tariff favored by the majority report and would ensure more protection for American labor. The minority report was defeated, 721½ to 96½.

Butler, a former Republican and, earlier in 1884, nominated for president by the Greenback and Anti-Monopoly parties, also introduced substitute planks on labor, monopoly, public corporations, currency, and civil service reform. These other planks were defeated by a voice vote, and the platform as written was adopted by acclamation.

Following are excerpts from the Democratic platform of 1884:

Tariff. Knowing full well, . . . that legislation affecting the operations of the people should be cautious and conservative in method, not in advance of public opinion, but responsive to its demands, the Democratic party is pledged to revise the tariff in a spirit of fairness to all interests.

But in making reduction in taxes, it is not proposed to injure any domestic industries, but rather to promote their healthy growth. From the foundation of this Government, taxes collected at the Custom House have been the chief source of Federal Revenue. Such they must continue to be. Moreover, many industries have come to rely upon legislation for successful continuance, so that any change of law must be at every step regardful of the labor and capital thus involved. The process of reform must be subject in the execution to this plain dictate of justice. . . .

Sufficient revenue to pay all the expenses of the Federal Government . . . can be got, under our present system of taxation, from the custom house taxes on fewer imported articles, bearing heaviest on articles of luxury, and bearing lightest on articles of necessity.

Civil Liberties—Civil Service Reform. We oppose sumptuary laws which vex the citizen and interfere with individual liberty; we favor honest Civil Service Reform, and the compensation of all United States officers by fixed salaries; the separation of Church and State; and the diffusion of free education by common schools, so that every child in the land may be taught the rights and duties of citizenship.

Chinese Immigration. [W]e . . . do not sanction the importation of foreign labor, or the admission of servile races, unfitted by habits, training, religion, or kindred, for absorption into the great body of our people, or for the citizenship which our laws confer. American civilization demands that against the immigration or importation of Mongolians to these shores our gates be closed.

1888 Conventions

PRESIDENTIAL CANDIDATES

Clinton B. Fisk
Prohibitionist

Grover Cleveland
Democrat

Benjamin Harrison
Republican

PROHIBITION

The Prohibition Party held its fifth national convention in Indianapolis in late May 1888. The party had held conventions since the 1872 campaign, but not until 1888 did the Prohibitionists receive at least 2 percent of the popular vote.

The 1888 convention selected Clinton B. Fisk of New Jersey for president and John A. Brooks of Missouri as his running mate. While the platform focused on the need for prohibition, planks were included that covered other issues. The Prohibition Party favored a tariff that would both protect American industry and raise revenue, supported the extension of voting rights, favored immigration restrictions, and proposed the abolition of polygamy.

Following are excerpts from the Prohibition Party platform of 1888:

Prohibition. That the manufacture, importation, exportation, transportation and sale of alcoholic beverages should be made public crimes, and prohibited as such.

Tariff. That an adequate public revenue being necessary, it may properly be raised by import duties; but import duties should be so reduced that no surplus shall be accumulated in the Treasury, and that the burdens of taxation shall be removed from foods, clothing and other comforts and necessaries of life, and imposed on such articles of import as will give protection both to the manufacturing employer and producing laborer against the competition of the world.

DEMOCRATS

When the Democratic convention assembled in St. Louis in early June 1888, the party, for the first time since the outset of the Civil War, was in control of the White House. There was no contest for the presidential nomination, with the incumbent, Grover Cleveland, renominated by acclamation. However, the death of Vice President Thomas A. Hendricks in 1885 left open the second place on the ticket.

Former senator Allen G. Thurman of Ohio was the favorite for the vice-presidential nomination and won easily on the first ballot with 684 votes. Gov. Isaac P. Gray of Indiana had 101 votes, and Gen. John C. Black of Illinois trailed with 36. After the nomination of the seventy-five-year-old Thurman, red bandannas were strung up around the hall. The bandanna was Thurman's political symbol, used extensively in his public habit of pinching snuff.

The platform was adopted by acclamation. It reaffirmed the Democratic platform written four years earlier, but in addition lauded the policies of President Cleveland and the achievements of Democratic rule, opposed the existing protective tariff and supported legislation to modify it and proposed a reformation of tax laws. A plank introduced from the floor favoring Irish home rule was included in the platform.

Following are excerpts from the Democratic platform of 1888:

Tariff. The Democratic party of the United States, in National Convention assembled, renews the pledge of its fidelity to Democratic faith and reaffirms the platform adopted by its representatives in the Convention of 1884, and indorses the views expressed by President Cleveland in his last annual message to Congress as the correct interpretation of that platform upon the question of Tariff reduction; and also indorses the efforts of our Democratic Representatives in Congress to secure a reduction of excessive taxation. . . .

Resolved, That this convention hereby indorses and recommends the early passage of the bill for the reduction of the revenue now pending in the House of Representatives.

Tax Reform. All unnecessary taxation is unjust taxation. . . . Every Democratic rule of governmental action is violated when through unnecessary taxation a vast sum of money, far beyond the needs of an economical administration, is drawn from the people and the channels of trade, and accumulated as a demoralizing surplus in the National Treasury. . . . The Democratic remedy is to enforce frugality in public expense and abolish needless taxation.

Federal Power. Chief among its principles of party faith are the maintenance of an indissoluble Union of free and indestructible States, now about to enter upon its second century of unexampled progress and renown; devotion to a plan of government regulated by a written

Constitution, strictly specifying every granted power and expressly re-serving to the States or people the entire ungranted residue of power.

REPUBLICANS

The Republicans assembled for their convention in Chicago in late June 1888. Not only was the party out of the White House for the first time since the Civil War, but a perennial contender for the presidential nomination, James G. Blaine, had taken himself out of the running. Although this encouraged a number of candidates to seek the nomination, none came near to mustering the needed majority as the balloting for president began.

The 832 convention votes were distributed among fourteen candidates, with Sen. John Sherman of Ohio leading the field with 229 votes. Circuit judge Walter Q. Gresham of Indiana followed with 107 votes, while four other candidates received more than 70 votes. During the rest of the day, two more ballots were taken, with little appreciable change in the strength of the candidates. After the third roll call, Sherman led with 244 votes, followed by Gresham with 123 and former governor Russell A. Alger of Michigan with 122.

The unexpected withdrawal from the race of Chauncey Depew of New York, the favorite of that state's delegation, prompted a call for adjournment after the third ballot. The motion passed, 531 to 287.

When balloting resumed the next morning, the biggest gainer was former senator Benjamin Harrison of Indiana. Although Sherman still held the lead with 235 votes on the fourth ballot, Harrison's vote total had leaped from 94 votes on the third to 216 on the fourth. There was little change on the fifth ballot, taken on a Saturday, and after the roll call the delegates approved, 492 to 320, a motion to adjourn until Monday. The motion was generally supported by delegates opposed to Harrison.

When the convention reconvened, both Sherman and Harrison showed small gains—Sherman rising to 244 votes and Harrison to 231. On the next roll call, the seventh, Harrison took the lead for the first time, thanks largely to a shift of votes from delegates previously holding out for Blaine. Harrison led, 279 to 230, and the trend to the Indianan accelerated to a bandwagon the next ballot. Harrison easily achieved a majority on the eighth roll call, winning 544 votes to 118 for Sherman. *(Table, p. 200.)*

Three individuals were placed in nomination for vice president, but former representative Levi P. Morton of New York was the runaway winner on the first ballot. Morton received 592 votes to easily outdistance Rep. William Walter Phelps of New Jersey, 119 votes, and William O. Bradley of Kentucky, 103.

The platform sharply differed from that of the Democrats on the important tariff issue, strongly supporting the protective tariff and opposing the legislation favored by the Democrats. Like the Democrats, the Republicans called for a reduction in taxes, specifically recommending repeal of taxes on tobacco and on alcohol used in the arts and for mechanical purposes. In other areas, the Republicans favored the use of both gold and silver as currency, strongly opposed the Mormon practice of polygamy, and called for veterans' pensions.

Following are excerpts from the Republican platform of 1888:

Tariff. We are uncompromisingly in favor of the American system of protection; we protest against its destruction as proposed by the President and his party. They serve the interests of Europe; we will support the interests of America. . . . The protective system must be maintained. Its abandonment has always been followed by general disaster to all interests, except those of the usurer and the sheriff. We denounce the Mills bill as destructive to the general business, the labor and the farming interests of the country, and we heartily indorse the consistent and patriotic action of the Republican Representatives in Congress in opposing its passage.

Tax Reform. The Republican party would effect all needed reduction of the National revenue by repealing the taxes upon tobacco, which are an annoyance and burden to agriculture, and the tax upon spirits used in the arts, and for mechanical purposes, and by such revision of the tariff laws as will tend to check imports of such articles as are produced by our people, the production of which gives employment to our labor, and releases from import duties those articles of foreign production (except luxuries), the like of which cannot be produced at home. If there shall remain a larger revenue than is requisite for the wants of the government we favor the entire repeal of internal taxes rather than the surrender of any part of our protective system at the joint behests of the whiskey trusts and the agents of foreign manufacturers.

Currency. The Republican party is in favor of the use of both gold and silver as money, and condemns the policy of the Democratic Administration in its efforts to demonetize silver.

Veterans' Benefits. The gratitude of the Nation to the defenders of the Union cannot be measured by laws. . . . We denounce the hostile spirit shown by President Cleveland in his numerous vetoes of measures for pension relief, and the action of the Democratic House of Representatives in refusing even a consideration of general pension legislation.

Polygamy. The political power of the Mormon Church in the Territories as exercised in the past is a menace to free institutions too dangerous to be longer suffered. Therefore we pledge the Republican party to appropriate legislation asserting the sovereignty of the Nation in all Territories where the same is questioned, and in furtherance of that end to place upon the statute books legislation stringent enough to divorce the political from the ecclesiastical power, and thus stamp out the attendant wickedness of polygamy.

1892 Conventions

PRESIDENTIAL CANDIDATES

Benjamin Harrison
Republican

Grover Cleveland
Democrat

James B. Weaver
Populist

REPUBLICANS

Although President Benjamin Harrison was unpopular with various elements in the Republican Party, administration forces were in control of the convention that assembled in early June 1892 in Minneapolis, Minn. A Harrison supporter, governor and former representative William McKinley of Ohio, was elected without opposition as the convention's permanent chairman.

A question concerning the credentials of six Alabama delegates resulted in a protracted debate on whether the six delegates in question could vote on their own case. The situation was resolved when the Alabama delegates voluntarily abstained from voting. The minority report, which proposed seating the six Alabama delegates on the original roll, was defeated, 463 to 423½, and the majority report was subsequently adopted, 476 to 365½. The two votes were candidate-oriented, with the winning side in each case composed largely of Harrison voters.

Harrison's chances of renomination were so strong that two other possibilities, James G. Blaine and McKinley, never publicly announced as candidates for the presidency. Harrison won easily on the first ballot, receiving 535⅙ votes to 182⅙ for Blaine and 182 for McKinley. McKinley was in the ironic position of presiding over the convention at the same time he was receiving votes on the presidential ballot. McKinley withdrew briefly as permanent chairman and moved that Harrison's nomination be made unanimous. The motion was withdrawn after objections but placed McKinley publicly on the Harrison bandwagon. (*Table, p. 201.*)

While the Republican Party had an incumbent vice president in Levi P. Morton, the New York delegation supported Whitelaw Reid, the former editor of the *New York Tribune* and ambassador to France. With Morton making little effort to retain his position, Reid was nominated by acclamation, the first time a Republican convention had dispensed with a roll call in choosing a member of its national ticket.

The platform was adopted by a voice vote, and on only two major issues did it differ from that of the Democrats. The Republicans supported a protective tariff, clearly diverging from the Democrats, who supported import duties for revenue only. The Republicans also included a plank that sympathized with the prohibition effort, while the Democrats announced their opposition "to all sumptuary laws."

Both parties favored a bimetallic currency, with gold and silver of equal value, and supported the construction of a canal across Nicaragua. In addition, the Republicans advocated an expansionist foreign policy.

Following are excerpts from the Republican platform of 1892:

Tariff. We reaffirm the American doctrine of protection. We call attention to its growth abroad. We maintain that the prosperous condition of our country is largely due to the wise revenue legislation of the Republican congress.

We believe that all articles which cannot be produced in the United States, except luxuries, should be admitted free of duty, and that on all imports coming into competition with the products of American labor, there should be levied duties equal to the difference between wages abroad and at home.

Currency. The American people, from tradition and interest, favor bi-metallism, and the Republican party demands the use of both gold and silver as standard money, with such restrictions and under such provisions, to be determined by legislation, as will secure the maintenance of the parity of values of the two metals so that the purchasing and debt-paying power of the dollar, whether of silver, gold, or paper, shall be at all times equal. The interests of the producers of the country, its farmers and its workingmen, demand that every dollar, paper or coin, issued by the government, shall be as good as any other.

Foreign Policy. We reaffirm our approval of the Monroe doctrine and believe in the achievement of the manifest destiny of the Republic in its broadest sense.

Central American Canal. The construction of the Nicaragua Canal is of the highest importance to the American people, both as a measure of National defense and to build up and maintain American commerce, and it should be controlled by the United States Government.

Prohibition. We sympathize with all wise and legitimate efforts to lessen and prevent the evils of intemperance and promote morality.

DEMOCRATS

One of the strangest conventions in party annals was held by the Democrats in Chicago in late June 1892. Much of the disturbance was due to stormy weather, with the accompanying noise and leaks in the roof frequently interrupting the proceedings. Inside the hall, the discomfort of the delegates was increased by the vocal opposition of 600 Tammany Hall workers to the renomination of former president Grover Cleveland of New York.

Although Cleveland was a solid favorite for renomination, he was opposed by his home state delegation. The Tammany forces engineered an early state convention that chose a delegation committed to Gov. David B. Hill. But in spite of the hostility of the New York delegation, Cleveland was able to win renomination on the first ballot, receiving 617⅓ votes to 114 for Hill and 103 for Gov. Horace Boles of Iowa. *(Table, p. 201.)*

Four individuals were placed in nomination for the vice presidency, with Adlai E. Stevenson of Illinois assuming the lead on the first ballot. Stevenson, a former representative and later assistant postmaster general during Cleveland's first administration, led former governor Isaac P. Gray of Indiana, 402 to 343. After the first roll call was completed, Iowa switched to Stevenson, starting a bandwagon that led quickly to his nomination. After all the switches had been tallied, Stevenson was the winner with 652 votes, followed by Gray with 185.

The platform debate centered around the tariff plank. The plank, as originally written, straddled the issue. But a sharply worded substitute proposed from the floor, calling for a tariff for revenue only, passed easily, 564 to 342. The currency section called for stable money, with the coinage of both gold and silver in equal amounts. The platform also included a plank that called for the construction of a canal through Nicaragua.

Following are excerpts from the Democratic platform of 1892:

Tariff. We denounce Republican protection as a fraud, a robbery of the great majority of the American people for the benefit of the few. We declare it to be a fundamental principle of the Democratic party that the Federal Government has no constitutional power to impose and collect tariff duties, except for the purpose of revenue only, and we demand that the collection of such taxes shall be limited to the necessities of the Government when honestly and economically administered.

Currency. We hold to the use of both gold and silver as the standard money of the country, and to the coinage of both gold and silver without discriminating against either metal or charge for mintage, but the dollar unit of coinage of both metals must be of equal intrinsic and exchangeable value, or be adjusted through international agreement or by such safeguards of legislation as shall insure the maintenance of the parity of the two metals and the equal power of every dollar at all times in the markets and in the payment of debts; and we demand that all paper currency shall be kept at par with and redeemable in such coin.

Central American Canal. For purposes of national defense and the promotion of commerce between the States, we recognize the early construction of the Nicaragua Canal and its protection against foreign control as of great importance to the United States.

Prohibition. We are opposed to all sumptuary laws, as an interference with the individual rights of the citizen.

Federal Power. [W]e solemnly declare that the need of a return to these fundamental principles of free popular government, based on home rule and individual liberty, was never more urgent than now, when the tendency to centralize all power at the Federal capital has become a menace to the reserved rights of the States that strikes at the very roots of our Government under the Constitution as framed by the fathers of the Republic.

PROHIBITION

The Prohibition Party's sixth convention was held in Cincinnati in late June 1892 and nominated John Bidwell of California for president and James B. Cranfill of Texas as his running mate. While the Prohibition Party continued to run a national ticket through the 1972 election, 1888 and 1892 marked the only years that the party received more than 2 percent of the popular vote.

Although beginning and ending with calls for prohibition, the 1892 platform as a whole was a reform-minded document, favoring women's suffrage and equal wages for women, an inflated currency and the nationalization of railroad, telegraph, and other public corporations.

Following are excerpts from the Prohibition platform of 1892:

Prohibition. . . . We declare anew for the entire suppression of the manufacture, sale, importation, exportation and transportation of alcoholic liquors as a beverage by Federal and State legislation, and the full powers of Government should be exerted to secure this result. Any party that fails to recognize the dominant nature of this issue in American politics is undeserving of the support of the people.

Women's Rights. No citizen should be denied the right to vote on account of sex, and equal labor should receive equal wages, without regard to sex.

Currency. The money of the country should consist of gold, silver, and paper, and be issued by the General Government only, and in sufficient quantity to meet the demands of business and give full opportunity for the employment of labor. To this end an increase in the volume of money is demanded, and no individual or corporation should be allowed to make any profit through its issue. It should be made a legal tender for the payment of all debts, public and private. Its volume should be fixed at a definite sum per capita and made to increase with our increase in population.

Tariff. Tariff should be levied only as a defense against foreign governments which levy tariff upon or bar out our products from their markets, revenue being incidental.

Government Nationalization. Railroad, telegraph, and other public corporations should be controlled by the Government in the interest of the people.

PEOPLE'S PARTY (POPULISTS)

The most successful of the nineteenth century farmer-labor coalitions was the People's Party, commonly known as the Populists, which formally organized as a political party at a convention in Cincinnati in May 1891. Further organization was accomplished at a convention in St. Louis the next February, from which emanated the call to the party's first national nominating convention, to be held that summer in Omaha, Neb. The election of 1892 was the only one in which the Populists received more than 2 percent of the national vote. Four years later the party endorsed the Democratic ticket, and from 1900 through 1908 the Populists ran separate tickets, but failed to receive 2 percent of the popular vote.

The call to the 1892 convention specified procedures for the selection of delegates and set the size of the convention at 1,776 delegates. In Omaha 1,300 to 1,400 delegates actually assembled for the Populist convention, which opened July 2. The field for the presidential nomination was reduced by the death early in 1892 of southern agrarian leader Leonidas L. Polk of North Carolina and the refusal of Judge Walter Q. Gresham of Indiana to seek the nomination. First place on the ticket went to former representative James B. Weaver of Iowa, who defeated Sen. James H. Kyle of South Dakota, 995 to 275.

James G. Field of Virginia won the vice-presidential nomination over Ben Terrell of Texas by a vote of 733 to 554. The ticket bridged any sectional division, pairing a former Union general (Weaver) with a former Confederate major (Field).

On July 4 the delegates enthusiastically adopted the platform. It contained few ideas that were not contained in the earlier platforms of other farmer-labor parties. But the document adopted by the Populists brought these proposals together into one forcefully written platform. More than half the platform was devoted to the preamble, which demanded widespread reform and sharply criticized the two major parties. It attacked the Democrats and Republicans for waging "a sham battle over the tariff," while ignoring more important issues.

The remainder of the platform was divided into three major parts that discussed finance, transportation, and land policy. The Populists proposed that the currency be inflated, with the unlimited coinage of silver and a substantial increase in the circulating medium to at least $50 per capita. The Populists' currency plank was sharply different from those of the two major parties, which favored a stable, bimetallic currency.

The Populists also went well beyond the two major parties in advocating the nationalization of the railroads and telegraph and telephone companies. Both the Populists and Democrats advocated land reform, although the proposals received greater emphasis in the Populist platform.

The Populists included a call for a graduated income tax and expanded government power.

Although not considered part of the platform, supplementary resolutions were passed that favored the initiative and referendum, a limit of one term for the president, the direct election of senators, the secret ballot and additional labor-oriented proposals that called for improvement in working conditions.

Following are excerpts from the Populist platform of 1892:

Preamble. The conditions which surround us best justify our co-operation; we meet in the midst of a nation brought to the verge of moral, political, and material ruin. Corruption dominates the ballot-box, the Legislatures, the Congress, and touches even the ermine of the bench. The people are demoralized; most of the states have been com-pelled to isolate the voters at the polling places to prevent universal intimidation and bribery. The newspapers are largely subsidized or muzzled, public opinion silenced, business prostrated, homes covered with mortgages, labor impoverished, and the land concentrating in the hands of capitalists. The urban workmen are denied the right to organize for self-protection; imported pauperized labor beats down their wages, a hireling standing army, unrecognized by our laws, is established to shoot them down, and they are rapidly degenerating into European conditions. The fruits of the toil of millions are boldly stolen to build up colossal fortunes for a few, unprecedented in the history of mankind; and the possessors of these, in turn despise the Republic and endanger liberty. From the same prolific womb of governmental injustice we breed the two great classes—tramps and millionaires . . .

We have witnessed for more than a quarter of a century the struggles of the two great political parties for power and plunder, while grievous wrongs have been inflicted upon the suffering people. We charge that the controlling influence dominating both these parties have permitted the existing dreadful conditions to develop without serious effort to prevent or restrain them. Neither do they now promise us any substantial reform. They have agreed together to ignore, in the coming campaign, every issue but one. They propose to drown the outcries of a plundered people with the uproar of a sham battle over the tariff, so that capitalists, corporations, national banks, rings, trusts, watered stock, the demonetization of silver and the oppressions of the usurers may all be lost sight of. They propose to sacrifice our homes, lives, and children on the altar of mammon; to destroy the multitude in order to secure corruption funds from the millionaires. . . .

We believe that the power of government—in other words, of the people—should be expanded (as in the case of the postal service) as rapidly and as far as the good sense of an intelligent people and the teachings of experience shall justify, to the end that oppression, injustice and poverty, shall eventually cease in the land.

While our sympathies as a party of reform are naturally upon the side of every proposition which will tend to make men intelligent, virtuous and temperate, we nevertheless regard these questions, important as they are, as secondary to the great issues now pressing for solution, and upon which not only our individual prosperity, but the very existence of free institutions depend; and we ask all men to first help us to determine whether we are to have a republic to administer, before we differ as to the conditions upon which it is to be administered, believing that the forces of reform this day organized will never cease to move forward, until every wrong is remedied, and equal rights and equal privileges securely established for all the men and women of this country.

Currency. We demand free and unlimited coinage of silver and gold at the present legal ratio of 16 to 1.

We demand that the amount of circulating medium be speedily increased to not less than $50 per capita.

We demand that postal savings banks be established by the government for the safe deposit of the earnings of the people and to facilitate exchange.

Transportation. Transportation being a means of exchange and a public necessity, the government should own and operate the railroads in the interest of the people. The telegraph and telephone, like the post office system, being a necessity for the transmission of news, should be owned and operated by the government in the interest of the people.

Land. The land, including all the natural sources of wealth, is the heritage of the people, and should not be monopolized for speculative purposes, and alien ownership of land should be prohibited. All land now held by railroad and other corporations in excess of their actual needs, and all lands now owned by aliens, should be reclaimed by the government and held for actual settlers only.

1896 Conventions

PRESIDENTIAL CANDIDATES

William McKinley
Republican

William J. Bryan
Democrat

REPUBLICANS

The currency issue, which spawned several third-party efforts in the late nineteenth century, emerged as the dominant issue of contention between the Republican and Democratic parties in the campaign of 1896. The forces in favor of the gold standard were firmly in control of the Republican convention that was held in St. Louis in early June 1896.

Actually, the convention was less a forum for the discussion of issues than a showcase for the political acumen of Mark Hanna of Ohio. Hanna, William McKinley's campaign manager, had been intensely courting delegates across the country, especially in the South, for more than a year before the convention. Before the rap of the opening gavel, Hanna had amassed a majority of the delegates for the popular Ohio governor.

The first evidence of McKinley strength came on a credentials question. A minority report was introduced claiming the credentials committee had held hearings on only two of 160 cases and proposing that the committee resume hearings. A maneuver to squelch the minority report was made when a delegate moved to cut off debate. With the McKinley forces providing most of the majority, the motion passed, 551½ to 359½.

Four other candidates in addition to McKinley were in contention for the presidential nomination, but McKinley was the runaway winner on the first ballot. He received 661½ votes to 84½ for the runner-up, House Speaker Thomas B. Reed of Maine. (Table, p. 202.)

There were two serious contenders for the vice-presidential nomination: Garret A. Hobart, a McKinley supporter and former state legislator from New Jersey, and Henry Clay Evans, a former candidate for governor of Tennessee. Hobart won, winning 523½ votes on the first ballot to 287½ for Evans.

As at the Democratic convention, the platform debate centered around the currency issue. The gold forces, firmly in control of the Republican convention, produced a majority report that called for maintenance of the gold standard until the time

when bimetallism could be effected by an international agreement. This plank did not satisfy the silver minority. Led by Sen. Henry M. Teller of Colorado, a minority plank was introduced favoring the unlimited coinage of silver and gold at the ratio of 16 to 1. Teller's plank, similar to the currency plank adopted later by the Democrats, was defeated, 818½ to 105½. A second roll call on adoption of the majority plank resulted in another decisive defeat for the silver forces. The majority plank carried, 812½ to 110½.

With the decisive defeat of the minority plank, Teller led a walkout by twenty-four silver delegates, including the entire Colorado and Idaho delegations and members of the Montana, South Dakota, and Utah delegations. The rest of the platform was adopted by a voice vote.

The currency plank that caused the commotion was buried deep in the middle of the Republican platform. The document began with a denunciation of Democratic rule and proceeded into a discussion of the merits of a protective tariff. A tariff for revenue purposes only was advocated in the Democratic platform, but the issue in the Republican document was clearly considered to be of secondary importance.

The Republican platform was also distinguishable from that of the Democrats in recommending a more expansionistic foreign policy, proposing stricter immigration restrictions and, for the first time, specifically denouncing the practice of lynching.

Following are excerpts from the Republican platform of 1896:

Currency. The Republican party is unreservedly for sound money. . . . We are unalterably opposed to every measure calculated to debase our currency or impair the credit of our country. We are therefore opposed to the free coinage of silver, except by international agreement with the leading commercial nations of the earth, which agreement we pledge ourselves to promote, and until such agreement can be obtained the existing gold standard must be maintained.

Tariff. We renew and emphasize our allegiance to the policy of protection, as the bulwark of American industrial independence, and the foundation of American development and prosperity. . . . Protection and Reciprocity are twin measures of American policy and go hand in hand. Democratic rule has recklessly struck down both, and both must be re-established. Protection for what we produce; free admission for the necessaries of life which we do not produce; reciprocal agreement of mutual interests, which gain open markets for us in return for our open markets for others. Protection builds up domestic industry and trade and secures our own market for ourselves; reciprocity builds up foreign trade and finds an outlet for our surplus.

Foreign Policy. Our foreign policy should be at all times firm, vigorous and dignified, and all our interests in the western hemisphere should be carefully watched and guarded.

The Hawaiian Islands should be controlled by the United States, and no foreign power should be permitted to interfere with them. The Nicaragua Canal should be built, owned and operated by the United States. And, by the purchase of the Danish Islands we should secure a much needed Naval station in the West Indies. . . . We therefore, favor the continued enlargement of the navy, and a complete system of harbor and sea-coast defenses.

Immigration. For the protection of the equality of our American citizenship and of the wages of our workingmen, against the fatal competition of low priced labor, we demand that the immigration laws be thoroughly enforced, and so extended as to exclude from entrance to the United States those who can neither read nor write.

Lynching. We proclaim our unqualified condemnation of the uncivilized and preposterous [barbarous] practice well known as lynching, and the killing of human beings suspected or charged with crime without process of law.

DEMOCRATS

The Democratic convention that assembled in Chicago in July 1896 was dominated by one issue—currency. Delegates' viewpoint on this single issue influenced their position on every vote taken. Generally, the party was split along regional lines, with eastern delegations favoring a hard-money policy with maintenance of the gold standard, and most southern and western delegations supporting a soft-money policy with the unlimited coinage of silver.

Division in the convention was apparent on the first day, when the silver forces challenged the national committee's selection of Gov. David B. Hill of New York as temporary chairman. The pro-silver delegates put up Sen. John W. Daniel of Virginia for the post, and Daniel won easily, 556 to 349. His victory indicated the dominance of the silver forces and presaged their ability to control the convention.

Two sets of credentials challenges were next on the agenda. By a voice vote, the convention agreed to seat a Nebraska delegation headed by a young silver supporter, William Jennings Bryan. By a vote of 558 to 368, the convention also defeated a recommendation to seat Michigan delegates supported by the hard-money-dominated national committee.

With their lack of strength apparent, the gold forces declined to run a candidate for president. However, the silver delegates could not initially coalesce behind one candidate, and fourteen individuals received votes on the first ballot. Rep. Richard P. "Silver Dick" Bland of Missouri was the pacesetter, with 235 votes, followed by Bryan, a former House member, with 137 and Robert E. Pattison, former Pennsylvania governor, with 97.

Bryan, thirty-six years old, earlier had electrified the convention during the platform debate on currency, with his memorable "Cross of Gold" speech, which had elevated him to the position of a major contender. (*Table, p. 203.*)

On the next two roll calls, both candidates showed gains. Bland's total climbed to 291 on the third ballot and Bryan's rose to 219. Bryan continued to gain on the next ballot and assumed the lead over Bland, 280 to 241. The movement to Bryan accelerated on the fifth ballot, and he won the nomination easily, receiving 652 of the 930 convention votes. Although Bryan was the nearly unanimous choice of the silver forces, 162 gold delegates indicated their dissatisfaction with the proceedings by refusing to vote.

With Bryan declining to indicate a preference for vice president, sixteen candidates received votes for the office on the first ballot. The Nebraska delegation, following Bryan's example, declined to participate in the vice-presidential balloting.

Former representative John C. Sibley of Pennsylvania took the lead on the first ballot with 163 votes, followed by Ohio editor and publisher John R. McLean with 111, and Maine shipbuilder Arthur Sewall with 100.

Bland spurted into the lead on the second ballot with 294 votes, followed by McLean and Sibley. After the roll call, Sibley withdrew, and on the third ballot the race between Bland and McLean tightened. The Missourian led, 255 to 210, but he too withdrew after the roll call. Sewall emerged as McLean's major competitor on the fourth ballot, and with the withdrawal of the Ohio journalist from the race, the nomination was Sewall's on the fifth ballot. Actually, Sewall's vote total of 602 on the final roll call was less than two-thirds of the convention vote, but with 251 disgruntled gold delegates refusing to vote, the required majority was reduced to only those voting.

Not surprisingly, the platform debate centered around the currency plank. The eastern delegations proposed that, until silver coinage could be arranged by international agreement, the gold standard should be maintained. The southern and western delegations countered by demanding that the unlimited coinage of silver should begin without requiring a delay to reach an international agreement. Bryan managed the platform debate for the silver forces and scheduled himself as the final speaker, an enviable position from which to make a deep impression on the emotion-packed convention.

Bryan made the most of his opportunity, ending his dramatic speech with the famous peroration: "You shall not press down upon the brow of labor this crown of thorns, you shall not crucify mankind upon a cross of gold." The gold plank was defeated, 626 to 303. Although the speech was a key factor in Bryan's nomination, it was not influential in defeating the gold plank, which was already doomed to defeat. (*Table, p. 203.*)

A resolution commending the Cleveland administration was also defeated, 564 to 357, and after several attempts to modify the currency plank were rejected by voice votes, the platform as a whole was adopted, 622 to 307.

Following are excerpts from the Democratic platform of 1896:

Currency. We demand the free and unlimited coinage of both silver and gold at the present legal ratio of 16 to 1 without waiting for the aid or consent of any other nation.

Railroads. The absorption of wealth by the few, the consolidation of our leading railroad systems, and the formation of trusts and pools require a stricter control by the Federal Government of those arteries of commerce. We demand the enlargement of the powers of the Interstate Commerce Commission and such restriction and guarantees in the control of railroads as will protect the people from robbery and oppression.

No Third Term. We declare it to be the unwritten law of this Republic, established by custom and usage of 100 years, and sanctioned by the examples of the greatest and wisest of those who founded and have maintained our Government that no man should be eligible for a third term of the Presidential office.

Federal Power. During all these years the Democratic Party has resisted the tendency of selfish interests to the centralization of governmental power, and steadfastly maintained the integrity of the dual scheme of government established by the founders of this Republic of republics.

Under its guidance and teachings the great principle of local self-government has found its best expression in the maintenance of the rights of the States and in its assertion of the necessity of confining the general government to the exercise of the powers granted by the Constitution of the United States.

1900 Conventions

PRESIDENTIAL CANDIDATES

William McKinley
Republican

William J. Bryan
Democrat

REPUBLICANS

Surface harmony was the hallmark of the Republican conclave held in Philadelphia in June 1900. The Colorado delegation, which had walked out of the 1896 convention, was honored by having one of its members, Sen. Edward O. Wolcott, chosen as temporary chairman.

There was no opposition to President William McKinley, and he won all 926 votes on the first roll call. However, the death of Vice President Garret A. Hobart in 1899 had left the second spot on the ticket open. McKinley did not have a preference and asked his campaign manager, Mark Hanna, not to influence the convention. McKinley's hands-off policy worked to the advantage of the popular governor of New York and hero of the Spanish-American War, Theodore Roosevelt, whom Hanna disliked. *(Table, p. 204.)*

Roosevelt's popularity, coupled with the desire of New York boss Thomas C. Platt to eliminate a powerful state rival, enabled the forty-one-year-old governor to clinch the nomination before balloting began. On the vice-presidential roll call, Roosevelt received all but one vote. The single uncast vote came from Roosevelt's New York delegation, which cast 71 of its 72 votes for Roosevelt.

The Republicans adopted a platform that applauded the four years of Republican rule and credited McKinley's policies with improving business conditions and winning the Spanish American War. The platform defended postwar expansionism and called for increased foreign trade and the creation of a Department of Commerce.

As in 1896, the Republican platform opposed the unlimited coinage of silver and supported maintenance of the gold standard. On the tariff issue, the Republicans continued to laud the protective duty on imports.

Following are excerpts from the Republican platform of 1900:

Foreign Trade, Panama Canal. We favor the construction, ownership, control and protection of an Isthmian Canal by the Government of the United States. New markets are necessary for the increasing surplus of our farm products. Every effort should be made to open and obtain new markets, especially in the Orient, and the Administration is warmly to be commended for its successful efforts to commit all trading and colonizing nations to the policy of the open door in China.

International Expansion. In accepting by the Treaty of Paris the just responsibility of our victories in the Spanish war, the President and the Senate won the undoubted approval of the American people. No other course was possible than to destroy Spain's sovereignty throughout the West Indies and in the Philippine Islands. That course created our responsibility before the world, and with the unorganized population whom our intervention had freed from Spain, to provide for the maintenance of law and order, and for the establishment of good government and for the performance of international obligations. Our authority could not be less than our responsibility; and whenever sovereign rights were extended it became the high duty of the Government to maintain its authority, to put down armed insurrection and to confer the blessings of liberty and civilization upon all the rescued peoples.

Antitrust. We recognize the necessity and propriety of the honest co-operation of capital to meet new business conditions and especially to extend our rapidly increasing foreign trade, but we condemn all conspiracies and combinations intended to restrict business, to create monopolies, to limit production, or to control prices; and favor such legislation as will effectively restrain and prevent all such abuses, protect and promote competition and secure the rights of producers, laborers, and all who are engaged in industry and commerce.

Currency. We renew our allegiance to the principle of the gold standard and declare our confidence in the wisdom of the legislation of the Fifty-sixth Congress, by which the parity of all our money and the stability of our currency upon a gold basis has been secured. . . .

We declare our steadfast opposition to the free and unlimited coinage of silver.

Tariff. We renew our faith in the policy of Protection to American labor. In that policy our industries have been established, diversified and maintained. By protecting the home market competition has been stimulated and production cheapened.

DEMOCRATS

The Democrats opened their 1900 convention in Kansas City, Mo., on July 4, and showed a degree of party harmony not evident at their convention four years earlier. After the party factionalism of 1896, the delegates made a conscious effort to display a unified front—an effort aided by the decline of the controversial silver issue. The discovery of new gold deposits in North America and the subsequent increase in currency had lessened the divisive impact of the silver issue.

William Jennings Bryan, the Democratic standard-bearer in 1896, was renominated without opposition, receiving all 936 votes. The harmony in the convention was evident when former New York senator David B. Hill, a leader of the gold forces four years earlier, gave a seconding speech for Bryan. *(Table, p. 204.)*

Seven names were placed in nomination for the vice presidency. However, two withdrew before the balloting began. Adlai E. Stevenson of Illinois, vice president under Grover Cleveland, led on the first roll call with 559½ votes, followed by Hill, who received 200 votes in spite of withdrawing from the race before the voting started. After completion of the ballot, a series of vote switches resulted in Stevenson's unanimous nomination.

The platform was adopted without floor debate. The major theme of the document was anti-imperialism, although an attack on trusts and a discussion of the currency question also were emphasized.

The anti-imperialism section was placed at the beginning of the platform and was labeled the most important issue of the campaign. The delegates enthusiastically accepted the plank, which forcefully criticized U.S. international expansion after the Spanish-American War. The platform asserted "that no nation can long endure half republic and half empire" and denounced increasing U.S. militarism. The Democratic position sharply differed from the one advocated by the Republicans, whose platform defended postwar expansionism.

After the anti-imperialism section was a sharp attack on monopolies, the most detailed antitrust section that had yet appeared in a Democratic platform. The plank called for more comprehensive antitrust legislation and more rigid enforcement of the laws already enacted. Although the Republicans also condemned monopolies, the issue received a mere one-sentence mention in their platform.

With the decline of the silver issue, the necessity of a prosilver plank was a matter of debate in the resolutions committee. However, Bryan threatened to withdraw his candidacy if the platform did not include a plank calling for the unlimited coinage of silver. By a majority of one vote, the resolutions committee included the silver plank, and it was accepted without dissent by the convention. The Democratic position set up another distinction with the Republicans, who, as four years earlier, favored maintenance of the gold standard.

In addition to the anti-imperialism, antitrust, and currency sections of the platform, the Democrats proposed the creation of a Department of Labor, favored the direct election of senators and, unlike the Republicans, supported the construction and ownership of a Nicaraguan canal. The Republican platform advocated construction and ownership of a canal across the Isthmus of Panama.

Following are excerpts from the Democratic platform of 1900:

Anti-imperialism. We hold that the Constitution follows the flag, and denounce the doctrine that an Executive or Congress deriving their existence and their powers from the Constitution can exercise lawful authority beyond it or in violation of it. We assert that no nation can long endure half republic and half empire, and we warn the American people that imperialism abroad will lead quickly and inevitably to despotism at home. . . .

We are not opposed to territorial expansion when it takes in desirable territory which can be erected into States in the Union, and whose people are willing and fit to become American citizens. We favor trade expansion by every peaceful and legitimate means. But we are unalterably opposed to seizing or purchasing distant islands to be governed outside the Constitution, and whose people can never become citizens. . . .

The importance of other questions, now pending before the American people is no wise diminished and the Democratic party takes no backward step from its position on them, but the burning issue of imperialism growing out of the Spanish war involves the very existence of the Republic and the destruction of our free institutions. We regard it as the paramount issue of the campaign. . . .

We oppose militarism. It means conquest abroad and intimidation and oppression at home. It means the strong arm which has ever been fatal to free institutions. . . . This republic has no place for a vast military establishment, a sure forerunner of compulsory military service and conscription. When the nation is in danger the volunteer soldier is his country's best defender.

Antitrust. We pledge the Democratic party to an unceasing warfare in nation, State and city against private monopoly in every form. Existing laws against trusts must be enforced and more stringent ones must be enacted. . . . Tariff laws should be amended by putting the products of trusts upon the free list, to prevent monopoly under the plea of protection.

Currency. We reaffirm and indorse the principles of the National Democratic Platform adopted at Chicago in 1896, and we reiterate the demand of that platform for an American financial system made by the American people for themselves, and which shall restore and maintain a bimetallic price-level, and as part of such system the immediate restoration of the free and unlimited coinage of silver and gold at the present legal ratio of 16 to 1, without waiting for the aid or consent of any other nation.

1904 Conventions

PRESIDENTIAL CANDIDATES

Eugene V. Debs
Socialist

Theodore Roosevelt
Republican

Alton B. Parker
Democrat

SOCIALISTS

The Socialist Party held its first national nominating convention in Chicago in early May 1904 and nominated Eugene V. Debs of Indiana for president and Benjamin Hanford of New York as his running mate. Debs ran in 1900 as the presidential candidate of two socialist groups, the Social Democratic Party and a moderate faction of the Socialist Labor Party.

The bulk of the platform was devoted to the philosophy of the international Socialist movement, with its belief in the eventual demise of capitalism and the ultimate achievement of a classless, worker-oriented society. To hasten the creation of a Socialist society, the platform favored many reforms advocated by the Populists and earlier agrarian-labor movements: the initiative, referendum, and recall; women's suffrage; tax reform, including the graduated income tax; the public ownership of transportation, communication, and exchange; and various labor benefits, including higher wages and shorter hours.

Following are excerpts from the Socialist platform of 1904:

To the end that the workers may seize every possible advantage that may strengthen them to gain complete control of the powers of government, and thereby the sooner establish the cooperative commonwealth, the Socialist Party pledges itself to watch and work, in both the economic and the political struggle, for each successive immediate interest of the working class; for shortened days of labor and increases of wages; for the insurance of the workers against accident, sickness and lack of employment; for pensions for aged and exhausted workers; for

the public ownership of the means of transportation, communication and exchange; for the graduated taxation of incomes, inheritances, franchises and land values, the proceeds to be applied to the public employment and improvement of the conditions of the workers; for the complete education of children, and their freedom from the workshop; for the prevention of the use of the military against labor in the settlement of strikes; for the free administration of justice; for popular government, including initiative, referendum, proportional representation, equal suffrage of men and women, municipal home rule, and the recall of officers by their constituents; and for every gain or advantage for the workers that may be wrested from the capitalist system, and that may relieve the suffering and strengthen the hands of labor. We lay upon every man elected to any executive or legislative office the first duty of striving to procure whatever is for the workers' most immediate interest, and for whatever will lessen the economic and political powers of the capitalist, and increase the like powers of the worker.

REPUBLICANS

President Theodore Roosevelt was totally in command of the Republican convention held in Chicago in June 1904. His most dangerous potential rival for the nomination, Sen. Mark Hanna of Ohio, had died in February, leaving the field clear for Roosevelt.

The rather trivial matter of most interest before the presidential balloting began was Hawaii's vote allocation. The rules committee recommended that the votes of the territory be reduced from six to two. A substitute amendment proposed that

Hawaii retain its six votes for the 1904 convention but that its vote allocation be reviewed by the national committee for future conventions. The substitute was accepted by the narrow margin of 495 to 490.

Roosevelt's nomination caused less commotion. On the first ballot, he received all 994 votes. The party leadership favored Sen. Charles W. Fairbanks of Indiana for the vice presidency. Although the Georgia, Illinois, Missouri, and Nebraska delegations noted that they preferred other candidates, Fairbanks was nominated by acclamation. (*Table, p. 206.*)

The party platform was adopted without dissent. In the document the Republicans charted little new ground, instead detailing the benefits of Republican rule and restating old positions. America's expansionistic foreign policy was praised, as was the protective tariff and the gold standard.

A display of Roosevelt theatrics followed the adoption of the platform. The convention chairman was instructed to read a message from the secretary of state to the American consul in Morocco: "We want either Perdicaris alive or Raisuli dead." The message referred to an alleged American citizen, Ion Perdicaris, who had been captured by the Moroccan chieftain, Raisuli. The American ultimatum read to the convention followed the dispatch of several ships to Morocco. The reading of the message roused the delegates, as it was no doubt intended to do.

Following are excerpts from the Republican platform in 1904:

Shipbuilding. We . . . favor legislation which will encourage and build up the American merchant marine, and we cordially approve the legislation of the last Congress which created the Merchant Marine Commission to investigate and report upon this subject.

Monopoly. Combinations of capital and of labor are the results of the economic movement of the age, but neither must be permitted to infringe upon the rights and interests of the people. Such combinations, when lawfully formed for lawful purposes, are alike entitled to the protection of the laws, but both are subject to the laws and neither can be permitted to break them.

DEMOCRATS

William Jennings Bryan, after two unsuccessful campaigns for the presidency, was not a candidate for the Democratic nomination in 1904. However, he was present at the party's convention in St. Louis that July and was a prominent factor in the proceedings.

Bryan's first appearance before the convention came during a credentials dispute, featuring a challenge by Bryan supporters in Illinois to the state delegation approved by the credentials committee. Bryan spoke in behalf of his supporters, but their minority report was beaten, 647 to 299.

Bryan appeared again to second the presidential nomination of Sen. Francis M. Cockrell of Missouri, one of eight candidates nominated. Much of his speech, however, was devoted to criticizing the conservative front-runner, Alton B. Parker, chief justice of the New York Court of Appeals, while boosting more progressive candidates. In spite of Bryan's opposition, Parker came within 9 votes of receiving the necessary two-thirds majority on the first ballot. Parker had 658 votes, followed by Rep. William Randolph Hearst of New York, with 200, and Cockrell, who trailed with 42. Although Hearst had progressive credentials, Bryan hesitated to support him and jeopardize his leadership of the progressive wing of the party.

With Parker so close to victory, Idaho shifted its votes to the New York judge, prompting enough switches by other states to give Parker 679 votes and the nomination. Hearst, with his strength in the Middle West and West, finished with 181 votes. (*Table, p. 205.*)

With the nomination in hand, Parker stunned the convention by sending a telegram to the New York delegation, announcing his support of the gold standard and advising the convention to select a new candidate if they found his position unacceptable. Parker supporters drafted a response stating that there was nothing to preclude his nomination, because the platform was silent on the currency issue.

Bryan, ill with a fever in his hotel but still a supporter of the silver cause, rose from his sickbed to join several southern leaders on the floor of the convention in denouncing Parker's telegram and the drafted response. Nonetheless, the response recommended by the Parker forces was approved, 794 to 191, with opposition principally from the Middle West and West.

For vice president, the convention chose former West Virginia senator Henry G. Davis. He nearly achieved a two-thirds majority on the first ballot, receiving 654 votes. With Davis's nomination so near, a motion to declare him the vice-presidential candidate was approved. Davis, at age eighty, was the oldest candidate ever put on a national ticket by a major party. He was a man of great wealth, and the Democrats hoped that he would give freely to their campaign.

Although the platform was accepted without debate by a voice vote, there was maneuvering behind the scenes to meet the objections of Bryan. The initial platform draft before the resolutions committee included a plank that declared that recent gold discoveries had removed the currency question as a political issue. Bryan found this plank objectionable and successfully fought in the resolutions committee for its deletion. Bryan was less successful in having an income tax plank included but was able to get a more strongly worded antitrust resolution.

Unlike the Democratic platform of 1900, which focused on anti-imperialism, antimonopoly, and currency, the 1904 platform covered about two dozen topics with nearly equal emphasis.

The Democrats and Republicans disagreed on one new issue: federal support for private shipping firms. The Democrats opposed government assistance; the Republicans favored it. But on other issues the platform of the Democrats, like that of the Republicans, broke little new ground, instead restating positions that had been included in earlier Democratic platforms. There was a continued attack on American imperialism and a call for a smaller army. There were planks that urged less international involvement and more emphasis on domestic improvements.

Following are excerpts from the Democratic platform of 1904:

Roosevelt Administration. The existing Republican administration has been spasmodic, erratic, sensational, spectacular and arbitrary. It has made itself a satire upon the Congress, courts, and upon the settled practices and usages of national and international law . . . the necessity of reform and the rescue of the administration of Government from the headstrong, arbitrary and spasmodic methods which distract business by uncertainty, and pervade the public mind with dread, distrust and perturbation.

Shipbuilding. We denounce the ship subsidy bill recently passed by the United States Senate as an iniquitous appropriation of public funds for private purposes and a wasteful, illogical and useless attempt to overcome by subsidy the obstructions raised by Republican legislation to the growth and development of American commerce on the sea.

We favor the upbuilding of a merchant marine without new or additional burdens upon the people and without bounties from the public treasury.

1908 Conventions

PRESIDENTIAL CANDIDATES

Eugene V. Debs
Socialist

William H. Taft
Republican

William J. Bryan
Democrat

SOCIALISTS

The Socialists met in Chicago in May 1908 and renominated the ticket that had represented the party four years earlier: Eugene V. Debs of Indiana for president and Benjamin Hanford of New York as his running mate.

The platform was divided into several major sections, including a discussion of principles, and topics entitled general demands, industrial demands, and political demands. The Socialists' goal was the creation of a classless society, and in pursuance of this goal the movement was identified as a party of the working class.

Among the general demands were proposals for public works programs to aid the unemployed and public ownership of land, means of transportation and communication, and monopolies.

Industrial demands included calls for reduced working hours, the abolition of child labor, and more effective inspections of working areas.

The section on political demands began with a restatement of earlier positions, with a call for tax reform; women's suffrage; and the initiative, referendum, and recall. However, the section also included more radical demands, such as the abolition of the Senate, the amendment of the Constitution by popular vote, the direct election of all judges and the removal of power from the Supreme Court to declare legislation passed by Congress unconstitutional.

Following are excerpts from the Socialist platform of 1908:

Public Works Projects. The immediate government relief for the unemployed workers by building schools, by reforesting of cutover and waste lands, by reclamation of arid tracts, and the building of canals, and by extending all other useful public works. All persons employed on such works shall be employed directly by the government under an eight hour work day and at the prevailing union wages. The government shall also loan money to states and municipalities without interest for the purpose of carrying on public works. It shall contribute to the funds of labor organizations for the purpose of assisting their unemployed members, and shall take such other measures within its power as will lessen the widespread misery of the workers caused by the misrule of the capitalist class.

Public Ownership. The collective ownership of railroads, telegraphs, telephones, steamship lines and all other means of social transportation and communication, and all land.

The collective ownership of all industries which are organized on a national scale and in which competition has virtually ceased to exist.

Labor. The improvement of the industrial condition of the workers.

(a) By shortening the workday in keeping with the increased productiveness of machinery.

(b) By securing to every worker a rest period of not less than a day and a half in each week.

(c) By securing a more effective inspection of workshops and factories.

(d) By forbidding the employment of children under sixteen years of age.

(e) By forbidding the interstate transportation of the products of child labor, of convict labor and of all uninspected factories.

(f) By abolishing official charity and substituting in its place compulsory insurance against unemployment, illness, accident, invalidism, old age and death.

Tax Reform. The extension of inheritance taxes, graduated in proportion to the amount of the bequests and the nearness of kin.

A graduated income tax.

Women's Suffrage. Unrestricted and equal suffrage for men and women. . . .

Senate. The abolition of the senate.

Constitutional and Judicial Reforms. The abolition of the power usurped by the supreme court of the United States to pass upon the constitutionality of legislation enacted by Congress. National laws to be repealed or abrogated only by act of Congress or by a referendum of the whole people.

That the constitution be made amendable by majority vote.

That all judges be elected by the people for short terms, and that the power to issue injunctions shall be curbed by immediate legislation.

REPUBLICANS

The Republicans held their convention in Chicago in June 1908. Although President Roosevelt declined to be a candidate for reelection, his choice for the presidency, Secretary of War William Howard Taft, was assured of nomination before the convention began.

Of the 980 seats at the convention, 223 were contested, but all the challenges were settled before the convention assembled. However, a dispute arose over the vote-allocation formula for the next convention. An amendment to the rules committee report proposed that the vote allocation be based on population rather than the electoral vote, as was currently in effect. Essentially, the amendment would have reduced the power of the southern delegations. But a combination of southern delegates and Taft supporters from other states defeated the amendment, 506 to 471. *(Table, p. 207.)*

Seven names were placed in nomination for the presidency, but Taft was a landslide winner on the first ballot, receiving 702 votes. Sen. Philander C. Knox of Pennsylvania was a distant runner-up with 68 votes.

For vice president, the convention selected Rep. James S. Sherman, a conservative New Yorker. Sherman won 816 votes on the first ballot, easily outdistancing former New Jersey governor Franklin Murphy, who had 77 votes.

The Wisconsin delegation, led by Sen. Robert M. La Follette, introduced a detailed minority report to the party platform. The Wisconsin proposals were considered in several separate sections. The first section included proposals for the establishment of a permanent tariff commission, the creation of a Department of Labor and the limitation of an eight-hour day for government workers. It was defeated, 952 to 28.

The second section recommended legislation to require the publication of campaign contributions. It was defeated, 880 to 94. Further sections of the minority report proposed the physical valuation of railroad property to help determine reasonable rates, and the direct election of senators. The railroad reform plank was beaten, 917 to 63, while the senatorial election plank

was rejected, 866 to 114. After these votes, the majority report on the platform was adopted by a voice vote.

The platform approved by the delegates applauded the benefits of Republican rule, noting that under the party's guidance the United States had become the wealthiest nation on Earth. The principle of a protective tariff was applauded, as was the gold standard, an expansionist foreign policy and support for America's merchant marine.

Following are excerpts from the Republican platform of 1908:

Party Differences. In history, the difference between Democracy and Republicanism is that the one stood for debased currency, the other for honest currency; the one for free silver, the other for sound money; the one for free trade, the other for protection; the one for the contraction of American influence, the other for its expansion; the one has been forced to abandon every position taken on the great issues before the people, the other has held and vindicated all.

The present tendencies of the two parties are even more marked by inherent differences. The trend of Democracy is toward socialism, while the Republican party stands for a wise and regulated individualism. . . . Ultimately Democracy would have the nation own the people, while Republicanism would have the people own the nation.

DEMOCRATS

The Democratic convention of 1908 was held in July in Denver, Colo.—the first convention held by a major party in a western state. The convention was dominated by the Bryan forces, who regained control of the party after the conservative Alton B. Parker's landslide defeat in 1904.

Bryan's strength was evident on the first roll-call vote, concerning a Pennsylvania credentials dispute. The majority report claimed there were voting irregularities in five Philadelphia districts and urged the seating of Bryan delegates in place of those elected. By a vote of 604½ to 386½, the convention defeated the minority report, which argued for the delegates initially elected in the primary. The majority report then passed by a voice vote.

Bryan's presidential nomination was never in doubt. He was an easy winner on the first ballot, receiving 888½ votes to 59½ for Judge George Gray of Delaware and 46 for Gov. John A. Johnson of Minnesota. *(Table, p. 206.)*

Bryan left the choice of his running mate to the delegates. Although four names were placed in nomination, former Indiana gubernatorial candidate John W. Kern was chosen by acclamation. The *New York Times* sarcastically described the consistency of the Bryan-Kern ticket: "For a man twice defeated for the Presidency was at the head of it, and a man twice defeated for governor of his state was at the tail of it."

The platform adopted by the convention was tailored to Bryan's liking and had as its theme, "Shall the people rule?" The first portion of the document criticized Republican rule, specifically denouncing government overspending, a growing Republican-oriented bureaucracy, and an unethical link between big business and the Republican Party characterized by large, unreported campaign contributions.

Meeting three weeks after the Republicans, the Democrats adopted most of the minority planks rejected earlier by the Republicans. Included in the Democratic platform were calls for the physical valuation of railroads, the creation of a Department of Labor, eight-hour workdays for government employees, the direct election of senators, and a prohibition against corporate campaign contributions and individual contributions over "a reasonable amount." The two parties continued to disagree on support of the American merchant marine, the nature of tariff revision, and the direction of foreign policy, particularly regarding the lands acquired after the Spanish-American War.

The Democratic platform restated the party's support of a lower tariff, more extensive antitrust legislation with more rigid enforcement, a graduated income tax, increased power for the Interstate Commerce Commission to regulate railroads, telephone and telegraph companies, and a recommendation of prompt independence for the Philippines.

The Democrats included a plank abhorring Roosevelt's attempt to create a "dynasty," a direct reference to the outgoing president's handpicking his war secretary, William Howard Taft, as the next Republican presidential candidate.

Following are excerpts from the Democratic platform of 1908:

Appeal to the Masses. The conscience of the nation is now aroused to free the Government from the grip of those who have made it a business asset of the favor-seeking corporations. It must become again a people's government, and be administered in all its departments according to the Jeffersonian maxim, "equal rights to all; special privileges to none."

"Shall the people rule?" is the overshadowing issue which manifests itself in all the questions now under discussion.

Campaign Contributions. We demand Federal legislation forever terminating the partnership which has existed between corporations of the country and the Republican party under the expressed or implied agreement that in return for the contribution of great sums of money wherewith to purchase elections, they should be allowed to continue substantially unmolested in their efforts to encroach upon the rights of the people. . . .

We pledge the Democratic party to the enactment of a law prohibiting any corporation from contributing to a campaign fund and any individual from contributing an amount above a reasonable maximum, and providing for the publication before election of all such contributions.

Labor. Questions of judicial practice have arisen especially in connection with industrial disputes. We deem that the parties to all judicial proceedings should be treated with rigid impartiality, and that injunctions should not be issued in any cases in which injunctions would not issue if no industrial dispute were involved. . . .

We favor the eight hour day on all Government work.

We pledge the Democratic party to the enactment of a law by Congress, as far as the Federal jurisdiction extends, for a general employer's liability act covering injury to body or loss of life of employees.

We pledge the Democratic party to the enactment of a law creating a Department of Labor, represented separately in the President's Cabinet, in which Department shall be included the subject of mines and mining.

1912 Conventions

PRESIDENTIAL CANDIDATES

Eugene V. Debs
Socialist

William H. Taft
Republican

Woodrow Wilson
Democrat

Theodore Roosevelt
Progressive

SOCIALISTS

Eugene V. Debs of Indiana was nominated by the Socialists in 1912 to make his fourth run for the presidency. The convention, which met in Indianapolis in May, chose Emil Seidel of Wisconsin as his running mate.

The platform adopted by the Socialists was similar to the one written four years earlier, with calls for increased worker benefits, public works jobs for the unemployed, public ownership of land and the means of transportation and communication, tax reform, widespread political reform, and a social insurance program.

The Socialists also added new proposals, advocating public ownership of the banking and currency system, the introduction of minimum wage scales, the elimination of the profit system in government contracts, an increase in corporation taxes, and the direct election of the president and vice president.

Following are excerpts from the Socialist platform of 1912:

Social Insurance. By abolishing official charity and substituting a non-contributory system of old age pensions, a general system of insurance by the State of all its members against unemployment and invalidism and a system of compulsory insurance by employers of their workers, without cost to the latter, against industrial diseases, accidents and death.

Government Contracts. By abolishing the profit system in government work and substituting either the direct hire of labor or the awarding of contracts to cooperative groups of workers.

Minimum Wage. By establishing minimum wage scales.

Tax Reform. The adoption of a graduated income tax, the increase of the rates of the present corporation tax and the extension of inheritance taxes, graduated in proportion to the value of the estate and to nearness of kin—the proceeds of these taxes to be employed in the socialization of industry.

Banking and Currency. The collective ownership and democratic management of the banking and currency system.

Direct Election of President. The election of the President and Vice-President by direct vote of the people.

REPUBLICANS

The 1912 Republican convention was one of the most tumultuous ever. It was held in Chicago in June and served as a fiery culmination to the bitter contest between President William Howard Taft and former president Theodore Roosevelt for the party's presidential nomination.

Roosevelt had overwhelmed Taft in the presidential primaries, but Roosevelt's popular strength was more than offset by Taft's control of the national committee and southern delegations. Taft supporters held thirty-seven of fifty-three seats on the national committee, an edge that the incumbent president's managers used to advantage in settling seating disputes. Of the 1,078 convention seats, 254 were contested before the national committee, and 235 were settled in favor of Taft delegates. Although a number of Roosevelt challenges were made with little justification, the dispensation of the challenges showed Taft's control of the convention organization.

With the conservative Republicans united behind Taft, Roosevelt faced the additional problem of sharing support from the progressive wing of the party with another candidate, Sen. Robert M. La Follette of Wisconsin. La Follette had only forty-one delegates; but, angered by Roosevelt's bid to control the progressive forces, refused to withdraw as a candidate.

The first skirmish at the convention was over the choice of a temporary chairman. The Taft forces favored Sen. Elihu Root of New York, while the Roosevelt delegates supported Gov. Francis E. McGovern of Wisconsin.

On a prolonged roll call, during which the vote of each delegate was taken individually, Root defeated McGovern, 558 to 501. *(Table, p. 208.)*

With the contest for the temporary chairmanship settled, the battle shifted to credentials. Virtually shut out in the settlement of credentials cases by the national committee, the Roosevelt forces brought seventy-two delegate challenges to the floor of the convention. Before consideration of the cases, the Roosevelt leaders moved that none of the challenged delegates (favorable to Taft) be allowed to vote on any of the credentials contests. However, a motion to table this proposal carried, 567 to 507, and the challenged delegates were allowed to vote on all cases except their own. Although the Taft forces were clearly in control of the convention, four credentials cases were presented for a vote, and all were decided in favor of the Taft delegates. The rest of the contests were settled by voice votes.

At this point, Roosevelt, who had dramatically come to Chicago to direct his forces, advised his delegates to abstain from voting but to remain in the convention as a silent protest to what he regarded as steamroller tactics. In the convention hall itself, the pro-Roosevelt galleries emphasized the feelings of their leader by rubbing sandpaper and blowing horns to imitate the sounds of a steamroller.

Only two names were placed in nomination for the presidency—Taft's and La Follette's. Taft was nominated by Warren G. Harding of Ohio, who himself would be president less than a decade later but at the time was merely a former lieutenant governor. With most of the Roosevelt delegates abstaining, Taft won easily on the first ballot with 556 votes. Roosevelt received 107 votes and La Follette 41, while 348 delegates were present and did not vote.

Vice President James S. Sherman was easily renominated, collecting 596 votes to 21 for the runner-up, Sen. William E. Borah of Idaho. However, 352 delegates were present but refused to vote, and 72 others were absent. In recognition of Sherman's failing health, the convention passed a resolution empowering the national committee to fill any vacancy on the ticket that might occur.

As in 1908, a progressive minority report to the platform was submitted. However, instead of taking individual votes on the various planks, the convention tabled the whole report by a voice vote. Subsequently, the majority report was accepted by a vote of 666 to 53, with 343 delegates present but not voting.

The platform lauded the accomplishments of the McKinley, Roosevelt, and Taft administrations but contained few major positions different from the Democrats' platform. The Republican platform included, however, new planks favoring judicial reform and legislation publicizing campaign contributions and outlawing corporate campaign donations.

Although the Roosevelt delegates had remained in the convention hall as a silent protest to the renomination of Taft and Sherman, the groundwork for the creation of a Roosevelt-led third party had begun as soon as the credentials contests were settled in favor of Taft. Before the Republican convention even began its presidential balloting, Roosevelt announced that he would accept the nomination of the "honestly elected majority" of the Republican convention or a new progressive party. The next day, June 22, after final adjournment of the Republican convention, many of the Roosevelt delegates assembled in a

Chicago auditorium to hear their leader announce his availability as a candidate of an honestly elected progressive convention. Gov. Hiram Johnson of California was named temporary chairman of the new party, and planning was begun to hold a national convention later in the summer.

Following are excerpts from the Republican platform of 1912:

Tariff. The protective tariff is so woven into the fabric of our industrial and agricultural life that to substitute for it a tariff for revenue only would destroy many industries and throw millions of our people out of employment. The products of the farm and of the mine should receive the same measure of protection as other products of American labor.

Campaign Contributions. We favor such additional legislation as may be necessary more effectually to prohibit corporations from contributing funds, directly or indirectly, to campaigns for the nomination or election of the President, the Vice-President, Senators, and Representatives in Congress.

We heartily approve the recent Act of Congress requiring the fullest publicity in regard to all campaign contributions, whether made in connection with primaries, conventions, or elections.

Judicial Reform. That the Courts, both Federal and State, may bear the heavy burden laid upon them to the complete satisfaction of public opinion, we favor legislation to prevent long delays and the tedious and costly appeals which have so often amounted to a denial of justice in civil cases and to a failure to protect the public at large in criminal cases.

DEMOCRATS

For the first time since 1872, the Democratic convention was held in Baltimore. The delegates, who assembled in the Maryland city in June, one week after the Republicans began their convention in Chicago, had a number of presidential candidates to choose from, although House Speaker Champ Clark of Missouri and Gov. Woodrow Wilson of New Jersey were the major contenders.

Once again, William Jennings Bryan had a major impact on the proceedings of a Democratic convention. His first appearance came in opposition to the national committee's selection of Judge Alton B. Parker of New York, the party's standard-bearer in 1904, as temporary chairman. Bryan nominated Sen. John W. Kern of Indiana for the post. In declining to be a candidate for temporary chairman, Kern recommended that Parker also withdraw as a candidate. But when Parker refused, Kern nominated Bryan for the post. Parker won on the roll call that followed, 579 to 508, with most of the Wilson delegates voting for Bryan, the Clark delegates splitting their support and delegates for other candidates favoring Parker. *(Table, p. 209.)*

The defeat of Bryan produced an avalanche of telegrams from across the country, with a contemporary estimate of more than 100,000 flooding the delegates in Baltimore. Most of the telegrams were written by progressives and served to weaken the candidacy of the more conservative Clark.

In an attempt to appease Bryan, Parker urged members of the platform committee to select the Nebraskan as their chairman. Bryan, however, refused this overture. Subsequently, the platform committee announced that, by a margin of 41 to 11, the committee had voted to delay presentation of the platform until after selection of the candidates.

The Wilson forces won their first key vote on a question involving the unit rule. The vote specifically concerned the Ohio delegation, where district delegates, elected for Wilson, were bound by the state convention to vote for Gov. Judson Harmon of Ohio. By a vote of 565½ to 491⅓, the convention approved the right of the district delegates to vote for Wilson.

The Wilson forces won another test on a credentials dispute concerning the South Dakota delegation. The credentials committee recommended seating a delegation pledged to Clark; but the convention, by a vote of 639½ to 437, supported the minority report, which called for seating delegates pledged to Wilson.

Bryan reappeared before the presidential balloting and introduced a resolution opposing the nomination of any candidate "who is the representative of or under obligation to J. Pierpont Morgan, Thomas F. Ryan, August Belmont, or any other member of the privilege-hunting and favor-seeking class." Bryan's resolution passed easily, 883 to 202½.

Six names were placed in nomination for the presidency. Clark led on the first ballot with 440½ votes, followed by Wilson with 324, Harmon with 148, and Rep. Oscar W. Underwood of Alabama with 117½. Under the two-thirds rule, 730 votes were needed to nominate. *(Table, p. 209.)*

For nine ballots, there was little change in the vote totals, but on the tenth roll call New York shifted its 90 votes from Harmon to Clark. Expecting a quick triumph, the Clark forces unleashed an hour-long demonstration. However, their celebration was premature. While Clark had 556 votes, a majority, his total was well short of the two-thirds majority required by the rules.

The tenth ballot proved to be the high-water mark for Clark. On succeeding roll calls, he slowly began to lose strength. During the fourteenth ballot, Bryan received permission to address the convention again, this time to explain his vote. "The Great Commoner" announced that he could not support a candidate endorsed by the Tammany-controlled New York delegation and, although bound earlier by state primary results to support Clark, was now switching his vote to Wilson. Most of the Nebraska delegation followed Bryan in voting for Wilson. After the fourteenth ballot, the vote totals stood: Clark, 553; Wilson, 361; Underwood, 111.

There were long intervals between other major vote switches. On the twentieth ballot, Kansas shifted 20 of its votes from Clark to Wilson. On the twenty-eighth ballot, after a weekend recess, Indiana's favorite son, Gov. Thomas R. Marshall, withdrew in favor of Wilson. The slow trend in favor of the New Jersey governor finally enabled Wilson to pass Clark on the thirtieth roll call, 450 to 455; Underwood remained a distant third with 121½ votes. *(Table, p. 209.)*

The convention adjourned for the evening after the forty-second ballot, but the Wilson momentum continued the next day. Illinois switched its 58 votes to Wilson on the forty-third ballot, giving him a simple majority with 602 votes. Clark continued to decline, slipping to 329 votes.

Wilson showed slight gains on the next two ballots, but the big break came on the forty-sixth roll call, when Underwood withdrew. This was followed by the withdrawal of Clark and the other remaining candidates. Wilson received 990 votes on the forty-sixth ballot, followed by Clark with 84.

Clark's failure to win the nomination marked the first occasion since 1844 that a candidate achieved a simple majority of the votes, without subsequently winning the necessary two-thirds majority. The forty-six roll calls also represented the highest number of presidential ballots taken at any convention, Republican or Democratic, since 1860.

Wilson preferred Underwood as his running mate, but the Alabama representative was not interested in second place on the ticket. On the vice-presidential roll call that followed, nine candidates received votes, led by Marshall with 389 votes and Gov. John Burke of North Dakota with 304⅗. Marshall lengthened his lead over Burke on the second ballot, 644½ to 386¼. After the roll call was completed, a New Jersey delegate moved that Marshall's nomination be made unanimous, and the motion passed.

The Democratic platform was approved without debate before selection of the vice-presidential candidate. The platform restated a number of positions included in earlier party documents. It blamed the high cost of living on the protective tariff and the existence of trusts, and it called for a lower, revenue-only tariff and the passage of stronger antitrust legislation. The tariff issue was one of the major areas on which there was a marked difference between the parties, as the Republicans continued to support a protective tariff.

As in 1908, planks were included favoring the publicizing of campaign contributions and calling for the prohibition of corporate contributions and a limit on individual contributions.

The Democrats' labor plank was also virtually a restatement of the party's position four years earlier, supporting creation of a Department of Labor, a more limited use of injunctions, the guaranteed right of workers to organize and passage of an employees' compensation law. In contrast to the Democrats' support of employers' liability, the Republicans advocated workmen's compensation legislation.

Unlike the Republicans, the Democrats called for federal legislation to regulate the rates of railroad, telegraph, telephone, and express companies based on valuation by the Interstate Commerce Commission. A plank was also included in the Democratic platform calling for the ratification of constitutional amendments establishing a graduated income tax and the direct election of senators—issues on which the Republican platform was silent. Imperialism was again denounced, as it had been in every Democratic platform since 1900.

New planks advocated a single-term presidency, the extension of presidential primaries to all states, reform of the judicial system to eliminate delays and cut expenses in court proceedings, and the strengthening of the government's pure food and public health agencies.

Following are excerpts from the Democratic platform of 1912:

Single-term Presidency. We favor a single Presidential term, and to that end urge the adoption of an amendment to the Constitution making the President of the United States ineligible to reelection, and we pledge the candidates of this Convention to this principle.

Presidential Primaries. The movement toward more popular government should be promoted through legislation in each State which will permit the expression of the preference of the electors for national candidates at presidential primaries.

Judicial Reform. We recognize the urgent need of reform in the administration of civil and criminal law in the United States, and we recommend the enactment of such legislation and the promotion of such measures as will rid the present legal system of the delays, expense, and uncertainties incident to the system as now administered.

States' Rights. Believing that the most efficient results under our system of government are to be attained by the full exercise by the States of their reserved sovereign powers, we denounce as usurpation the efforts of our opponents to deprive the States of any of the rights reserved to them, and to enlarge and magnify by indirection the powers of the Federal government.

PROGRESSIVES

Early in August 1912 the bolting Roosevelt forces assembled in Chicago and nominated their leader to guide a new party, the Progressives. More than 2,000 delegates, representing every state except South Carolina, gathered for the three-day convention. It was a diverse assembly that matched the Populists in crusading idealism and included, for the first time, women as well as men politicians and social workers as well as businessmen.

While the delegates enthusiastically sang "Onward, Christian Soldiers" and "The Battle Hymn of the Republic" and cheered the appearance of Roosevelt before the convention, there was some dissension caused by the party's racial policy.

During the campaign for the Republican presidential nomination, Taft had the support of party organizations in the South, which included African Americans. As a result, Roosevelt directed his appeal strictly to white leaders in the region. Describing southern black delegates as uneducated and purchasable, Roosevelt insisted that only "lily white" delegations from the South be seated at the Progressive convention, but he allowed blacks to be included in delegations from other states. Although there was no floor debate on this policy, a number of liberal delegates were dissatisfied with Roosevelt's decision.

Both Roosevelt and his handpicked choice for vice president, Gov. Hiram W. Johnson of California, were nominated by acclamation. Jane Addams, a Chicago social worker and leader in the women's rights movement, gave evidence of the role of women in the Progressive Party by delivering a seconding speech for Roosevelt.

Like the nominations of the Progressive standard-bearers, the party platform was adopted by acclamation. But the voice vote hid the dissatisfaction felt by midwestern and western Progressives over the antitrust plank. Most of the Progressives from these regions favored the busting of trusts through enforcement of the Sherman Antitrust Act. Roosevelt, however, favored government regulation rather than trust-busting.

The platform approved by the convention included the trust-busting position. However, Roosevelt and his close advisers deleted the section in the official report. While there was obvious disagreement in the party on this issue, there was no floor debate or roll-call vote on the subject.

With the theme "A Covenant with the People," the platform argued for increased democratization coupled with more people-oriented federal programs. The party favored nationwide presidential primaries; the direct election of senators; the initiative, referendum, and recall; and women's suffrage. Additionally, the Progressives proposed that state laws ruled unconstitutional be submitted to a vote of the state electorate.

The platform also advocated congressional reforms: the registration of lobbyists, the publicizing of committee hearings except in foreign affairs, and the recording of committee votes.

Like the Democrats, the Progressives favored creation of a Department of Labor and a more limited use of labor injunctions, but additionally the new party called for a prohibition of child labor and convict contract labor.

The Progressives went beyond both major parties in proposing the union of government health agencies into a single national health service and the creation of a social insurance system that would assist both the elderly and workers who were ill or unemployed. To help support their proposed federal programs, the Progressives recommended passage of the income tax amendment and establishment of a graduated inheritance tax.

Having adopted their platform and selected their candidates, the delegates to the Progressive convention adjourned by singing the "Doxology."

Following are excerpts from the Progressive platform of 1912:

Electoral Reform. In particular, the party declares for direct primaries of the nomination of State and National officers, for nationwide preferential primaries for candidates for the presidency; for the direct election of United States Senators by the people; and we urge on the States the policy of the short ballot, with responsibility to the people secured by the initiative, referendum and recall.

Women's Suffrage. The Progressive party, believing that no people can justly claim to be a true democracy which denies political rights on account of sex, pledges itself to the task of securing equal suffrage to men and women alike.

Judicial Reform. That when an Act, passed under the police power of the State, is held unconstitutional under the State Constitution, by the courts, the people, after an ample interval for deliberation, shall have an opportunity to vote on the question whether they desire the Act to become law, notwithstanding such decision.

Campaign Contributions. We pledge our party to legislation that will compel strict limitation of all campaign contributions and expenditures, and detailed publicity of both before as well as after primaries and elections.

Congressional Reform. We pledge our party to legislation compelling the registration of lobbyists; publicity of committee hearings except on foreign affairs, and recording of all votes in committee. . . .

National Health Service. We favor the union of all the existing agencies of the Federal Government dealing with the public health into a single national health service without discrimination against or for any one set of therapeutic methods, school of medicine, or school of healing with such additional powers as may be necessary to enable it to perform efficiently such duties in the protection of the public from preventable diseases as may be properly undertaken by the Federal authorities, including the executing of existing laws regarding pure food, quarantine and cognate subjects, the promotion of vital statistics and the extension of the registration area of such statistics, and cooperation with the health activities of the various States and cities of the Nation.

Social Insurance. The protection of home life against the hazards of sickness, irregular employment and old age through the adoption of a system of social insurance adapted to American use. . . .

Antitrust Action. We therefore demand a strong National regulation of inter-State corporations . . . we urge the establishment of a strong Federal administrative commission of high standing, which shall maintain permanent active supervision over industrial corporations engaged in inter-State commerce, or such of them as are of public importance, doing for them what the Government now does for the National banks, and what is now done for the railroads by the Inter-State Commerce Commission.

Income and Inheritance Taxes. We believe in a graduated inheritance tax as a National means of equalizing the obligations of holders of property to Government, and we hereby pledge our party to enact such a Federal law as will tax large inheritances, returning to the States an equitable percentage of all amounts collected.

We favor the ratification of the pending amendment to the Constitution giving the Government power to levy an income tax.

Tariff. We demand tariff revision because the present tariff is unjust to the people of the United States. Fair dealing toward the people requires an immediate downward revision of those schedules wherein duties are shown to be unjust or excessive. . . .

The Democratic party is committed to the destruction of the protective system through a tariff for revenue only—a policy which would inevitably produce widespread industrial and commercial disaster.

Republicans and Democrats. Political parties exist to secure responsible government and to execute the will of the people.

From these great tasks both of the old parties have turned aside. Instead of instruments to promote the general welfare, they have become the tools of corrupt interests which use them impartially to serve their selfish purposes. Behind the ostensible government sits enthroned an invisible government owing no allegiance and acknowledging no responsibility to the people.

To destroy this invisible government, to dissolve the unholy alliance between corrupt business and corrupt politics is the first task of the statesmanship of the day.

States' Rights. The extreme insistence on States' rights by the Democratic party in the Baltimore platform demonstrates anew its ability to understand the world into which it has survived or to administer the affairs of a union of States which have in all essential respects become one people.

1916 Conventions

PRESIDENTIAL CANDIDATES

Charles E. Hughes
Republican

Woodrow Wilson
Democrat

REPUBLICANS

The Republicans and Progressives both held their conventions in Chicago in early June 1916. Leaders of both parties were ready to negotiate to heal the split that had divided the Republican Party in 1912.

Before the convention began, the Republican National Committee already had effected reform in the vote-allocation formula. To meet the objection raised in 1912 that the South was overrepresented, the national committee adopted a new method of vote allocation that considered a state's Republican voting strength as well as its electoral vote. Under the new formula, the southern states lost seventy-eight delegate seats, or more than a third of their 1912 total.

But while the Republicans were willing to make some internal reforms, most party leaders were adamantly opposed to nominating the hero of the Progressives, Theodore Roosevelt. Before the presidential balloting began, the Republican convention approved by voice vote the selection of a five-man committee to meet jointly with representatives of the Progressive convention, with the hope of finding a course of action that would unify the two parties.

However, the Republican representatives reported back that the Progressives, while desiring unity with the Republicans, firmly favored the nomination of Roosevelt. The Republican convention chairman, Sen. Warren G. Harding of Ohio, instructed the conferees to continue negotiations but allowed the presidential balloting to begin.

Charles Evans Hughes, a Supreme Court justice and former governor of New York, was the front-runner for the Republican nomination. Hughes did not actively seek the nomination and remained on the Supreme Court during the preconvention period. But he was viewed by many party leaders as an ideal compromise candidate, because of his progressive credentials and lack of involvement in the divisive 1912 campaign.

However, some conservative party leaders felt Hughes was too progressive and sought other candidates. Seventeen men received votes on the first ballot, led by Hughes with 253½. Next were Sen. John W. Weeks of Massachusetts with 105 votes and former senator Elihu Root of New York with 103. Five of the other vote recipients had at least 65 votes each. The justice widened his lead on the second ballot, receiving 328½ votes to 98½ for Root. After the second roll call the convention voted 694½ to 286½ to recess for the evening. Most of the votes for adjournment came from delegates outside the Hughes column. *(Table, p. 630.)*

While the Republican convention was in recess, the joint committee of Republicans and Progressives continued to negotiate. The Republican members proposed Hughes as a compromise candidate, but in a message from his home in Oyster Bay, New York, Roosevelt stunned both parties by suggesting the name of Henry Cabot Lodge, a conservative senator from Massachusetts.

The Progressive delegates reacted defiantly to this recommendation by nominating Roosevelt by acclamation and selecting John M. Parker of Louisiana as his running mate. Roosevelt, however, immediately scotched the enthusiasm of the Progressive delegates by conditionally declining the nomination. Roosevelt informed the convention that he would support Hughes if the latter's positions on major issues were acceptable.

When the Republican convention reconvened the next day, the opposition to Hughes had evaporated. The New Yorker received 949½ of the 987 convention votes on the third ballot, and his nomination was subsequently declared unanimous.

Charles W. Fairbanks of Indiana, vice president under Roosevelt, was the convention's choice to fill out the Republican ticket. Fairbanks won on the first ballot by 863 votes to 108 for former Nebraska senator Elmer J. Burkett.

The Wisconsin delegation again presented its minority platform report, which included planks that denounced "dollar diplomacy" and called for women's suffrage, a referendum before any declaration of war, and constitutional amendments to establish the initiative, referendum, and recall. The minority report was defeated and the majority report was approved by voice votes.

The adopted platform harshly criticized the policies of the Wilson administration. In foreign policy, the Republicans denounced the Wilson government for "shifty expedients" and "phrase making" and promised "strict and honest neutrality." The platform condemned the administration for its intervention in Mexico and noninvolvement in the Philippines. The Republicans also called for a stronger national defense.

The two parties continued to disagree on the tariff issue, with the Republicans criticizing the lower (Democratic-passed) Underwood tariff and arguing for a higher, protective tariff. The Republican platform lauded the party's efforts in passing antitrust and transportation rate regulation, but it criticized the Democrats for harassing business.

Following are excerpts from the Republican platform of 1916:

Foreign Policy. We desire peace, the peace of justice and right, and believe in maintaining a strict and honest neutrality between the belligerents in the great war in Europe. We must perform all our duties and insist upon all our rights as neutrals without fear and without favor. We believe that peace and neutrality, as well as the dignity and influence of the United States, cannot be preserved by shifty expedients, by phrase making, by performances in language, or by attitudes ever changing in an effort to secure votes or voters.

National Defense. We must have a Navy so strong and so well proportioned and equipped, so thoroughly ready and prepared, that no enemy can gain command of the sea and effect a landing in force on either our Western or our Eastern coast. To secure these results we must have a coherent continuous policy of national defense, which even in these perilous days the Democratic party has utterly failed to develop, but which we promise to give to the country.

Merchant Marine. We are utterly opposed to the Government ownership of vessels as proposed by the Democratic party, because Government-owned ships, while effectively preventing the development of the American Merchant Marine by private capital, will be entirely unable to provide for the vast volume of American freights and will leave us more helpless than ever in the hard grip of foreign syndicates.

Tariff. The Republican party stands now, as always, in the fullest sense for the policy of tariff protection to American industries and American labor.

Business. The Republican party firmly believes that all who violate the laws in regulation of business, should be individually punished. But prosecution is very different from persecution, and business success, no matter how honestly attained, is apparently regarded by the Democratic party as in itself a crime. Such doctrines and beliefs choke enterprise and stifle prosperity. The Republican party believes in encouraging American business as it believes in and will seek to advance all American interests.

Women's Suffrage. The Republican party, reaffirming its faith in government of the people, by the people, for the people, as a measure of justice to one-half the adult people of this country, favors the extension of the suffrage to women, but recognizes the right of each state to settle this question for itself.

DEMOCRATS

The Democratic convention of 1916 was held in St. Louis in mid-June. The delegates were nearly unanimous in their support for President Woodrow Wilson, who was renominated by the vote of 1,092 to 1—the lone dissenting vote coming from an

Illinois delegate who disapproved of a motion to nominate Wilson by acclamation. With Wilson's approval, Vice President Thomas R. Marshall was renominated by acclamation.

For the first time in more than two decades, William Jennings Bryan was not a major convention force. Bryan was defeated in his bid to be a delegate-at-large from Nebraska and attended the convention as a reporter. He was invited to address the delegates and echoed the theme stressed by other speakers, that Wilson would keep the nation out of war.

Wilson was the recognized leader of the Democratic Party, but the pacifistic theme, emphasized by Bryan and other convention orators, struck a responsive chord among the delegates that was mildly alarming to Wilson and his managers. They initially had planned to accent the theme of Americanism and national unity.

The wording of the national unity plank was a matter of debate within the platform committee. The Democratic senators from Missouri warned that Wilson's strongly worded plank might offend German-American citizens. Nonetheless, the Wilson plank was retained and placed prominently near the beginning of the platform.

The only section of the platform brought to a floor vote was the plank on women's suffrage. The majority plank favored extending the vote to women, while a minority plank advocated leaving the matter to the individual states. The minority plank was defeated, 888½ to 181½. The rest of the platform was then adopted by a voice vote. The Democratic position on women's suffrage contrasted with that of the Republicans, who proposed leaving the matter up to the individual states. *(Table, p. 211.)*

The platform's inclusion of national unity and military preparedness planks was a contrast with earlier Democratic platforms around the turn of the century, which had consistently denounced imperialism and denied the need for a stronger military. Even though spurred by the war in Europe, the new planks were a notable change.

The rest of the platform focused on the progressive reforms of the Wilson administration, particularly in tariff, banking, labor, and agriculture. Wilson himself was lauded as "the greatest American of his generation."

Noticeably absent from the platform were two planks in the party's document four years earlier: a call for a single-term presidency and a defense of states' rights.

Following are excerpts from the Democratic platform of 1916:

National Unity. In this day of test, America must show itself not a nation of partisans but a nation of patriots. There is gathered here in America the best of the blood, the industry and the genius of the whole world, the elements of a great race and a magnificent society to be welded into a mighty and splendid Nation. Whoever, actuated by the purpose to promote the industry of a foreign power, in disregard of our own country's welfare or to injure this government in its foreign relations or cripple or destroy its industries at home, and whoever by arousing prejudices of a racial, religious or other nature creates discord and strife among our people so as to obstruct the wholesome process of unification, is faithless to the trust which the privileges of citizenship repose in him and is disloyal to his country.

Military Preparedness. We therefore favor the maintenance of an army fully adequate to the requirements of order, of safety, and of the protection of the nation's rights, the fullest development of modern methods of seacoast defence and the maintenance of an adequate reserve of citizens trained to arms and prepared to safeguard the people and territory of the United States against any danger of hostile action which may unexpectedly arise; and a fixed policy for the continuous development of a navy, worthy to support the great naval traditions of the United States and fully equal to the international tasks which this Nation hopes and expects to take a part in performing.

Tariff. We reaffirm our belief in the doctrine of a tariff for the purpose of providing sufficient revenue for the operation of the government economically administered, and unreservedly endorse the Underwood tariff law as truly exemplifying that doctrine.

Women's Suffrage. We recommend the extension of the franchise to the women of the country by the States upon the same terms as to men.

SOCIALISTS

The Socialists did not hold a convention in 1916 but did nominate candidates and adopt a platform. The candidates were chosen in a unique mail referendum. With Eugene V. Debs's refusal to run, the presidential nomination went to Allan L. Benson of New York. George R. Kirkpatrick of New Jersey was selected as his running mate.

More than half of the Socialist platform was devoted to criticizing the U.S. preparations for war. The Socialists opposed the war in Europe and viewed the American drive for preparedness as an effort by ruling capitalists to protect the system and their profits.

The Socialist platform specifically advocated no increase in military appropriations, a national referendum on any declaration of war, the shifting of the power to make foreign policy from the president to Congress, the abandonment of the Monroe Doctrine and immediate independence for the Philippines.

The rest of the platform was divided into sections entitled political demands, industrial demands, and collective ownership. The proposals in these sections paralleled earlier Socialist platforms, although there was a new plank, advocating lending by the federal government to local governments, which was an early expression of the concept of revenue-sharing.

Following are excerpts from the Socialist platform of 1916:

Militarism and Preparedness. The working class must recognize militarism as the greatest menace to all efforts toward industrial freedom, and regardless of political or industrial affiliations must present a united front in the fight against preparedness and militarism. . . . The war in Europe, which diminished and is still diminishing the remote possibility of European attack upon the United States, was nevertheless seized upon by capitalists and by unscrupulous politicians as a means of spreading fear throughout the country, to the end that, by false pretenses, great military establishments might be obtained. We denounce such "preparedness" as both false in principle, unnecessary in character and dangerous in its plain tendencies toward militarism.

Foreign Policy. We, therefore, demand that the power to fix foreign policies and conduct diplomatic negotiations shall be lodged in congress and shall be exercised publicly, the people reserving the right to order congress, at any time, to change its foreign policy.

Referendum on War. That no war shall be declared or waged by the United States without a referendum vote of the entire people, except for the purpose of repelling invasion.

Federal Loans to Local Governments. The government shall lend money on bonds to counties and municipalities at a nominal rate of interest for the purpose of taking over or establishing public utilities and for building or maintaining public roads or highways and public schools.

1920 Conventions

PRESIDENTIAL CANDIDATES

Eugene V. Debs
Socialist

Warren G. Harding
Republican

James M. Cox
Democrat

SOCIALISTS

The Socialists held their convention in New York in May and for the fifth time nominated Eugene V. Debs of Indiana for president. It was one of the strangest candidacies in American political history, because at the time Debs was serving a ten-year prison term in the Atlanta federal penitentiary for his outspoken opposition to the American war effort. Seymour Stedman of Ohio was chosen as his running mate.

The Socialist platform was again a distinctive document, going far beyond the platforms of the two major parties in the radical nature of the reforms proposed. The platform characterized the war policies and peace proposals of the Wilson administration as "despotism, reaction and oppression unsurpassed in the annals of the republic." It called for the replacement of the "mischievous" League of Nations with an international parliament. It favored recognition of both the newly established Irish Republic and the Soviet Union.

The Socialists continued to advocate extensive tax reform and included new calls for a tax on unused land and a progressive property tax on wartime profits that would help pay off government debts. The platform warned that the continuing militaristic mood of both major parties could lead to another war.

The Socialists continued to recommend extensive labor benefits, but for the first time they specifically mentioned migratory workers as needing government assistance.

Following are excerpts from the Socialist platform of 1920:

League of Nations. The Government of the United States should initiate a movement to dissolve the mischievous organization called the "League of Nations" and to create an international parliament, composed of democratically elected representatives of all nations of the world based upon the recognition of their equal rights, the principles of self determination, the right to national existence of colonies and other dependencies, freedom of international trade and trade routes by land and sea, and universal disarmament, and be charged with revising the Treaty of Peace on the principles of justice and conciliation.

Labor. Congress should enact effective laws to abolish child labor, to fix minimum wages, based on an ascertained cost of a decent standard of life, to protect migratory and unemployed workers from oppression, to abolish detective and strike-breaking agencies and to establish a shorter work-day in keeping with increased industrial productivity.

Blacks. Congress should enforce the provisions of the Thirteenth, Fourteenth and Fifteenth Amendments with reference to the Negroes, and effective federal legislation should be enacted to secure the Negroes full civil, political, industrial and educational rights.

REPUBLICANS

In mid-June, Republicans met for the fifth straight time in Chicago for their quadrennial convention. For the first time, women were on the floor in large numbers as delegates. With the constitutional amendment granting women the vote on the verge of passage, Republicans, especially in the Midwest and West, were quick to include women in their delegations.

The Republicans, as did the Democrats two weeks later, entered their convention with no clear front-runner for the presidential nomination. Three candidates were at the top of the list, but two of them, Maj. Gen. Leonard Wood of New Hampshire and Sen. Hiram Johnson of California, split the party's progressive wing, while the third entry, Gov. Frank Lowden of Illinois, ran poorly in the presidential primaries and was accused of campaign spending irregularities.

The names of eleven men were placed in nomination for the presidency, but none came close during the first day of balloting

to the 493 votes needed to nominate. Wood led on the initial roll call with 287½ votes, trailed by Lowden with 211½ and Johnson with 133½. Sen. Warren G. Harding of Ohio, who had not campaigned for the nomination as extensively as the three pacesetters, placed sixth with 65½ votes. Wood, Lowden, and Johnson all gained strength during the first three ballots. *(Table, p. 212.)*

After the third roll call, the Johnson delegates moved for adjournment but were defeated, 701½ to 275½. On the fourth ballot, Wood's vote total rose to 314½, well short of a majority but the highest mark attained yet by any candidate. At this point, Harding stood in fifth place with 61½ votes. Although a motion to adjourn had been soundly defeated after the previous roll call, the permanent chairman, Sen. Henry Cabot Lodge of Massachusetts, entertained a new motion to adjourn and declared it passed on a closely divided voice vote.

The adjournment gave Republican leaders a chance to confer and discuss the various presidential possibilities. Much is made in history books about Harding's selection that night in the legendary "smoke-filled room," when Harding was allegedly interviewed at two o'clock by Republican leaders and, answering their questions satisfactorily, was chosen as the nominee. The authenticity of the meeting has been questioned, as has the power of the politicians who made the designation. But, nonetheless, it was clear that Harding was a viable compromise choice who was both acceptable to the conservative party leadership and could be nominated by the delegates.

Harding's vote total rose slowly in the next day's balloting until the ninth ballot, when a large shift, primarily of Lowden delegates, boosted the Ohio senator's vote from 133 to 374½. This was the highest total for any candidate to this point and started a bandwagon that produced Harding's nomination on the tenth ballot. After the various switches, the final vote stood: Harding, 692½; Wood, 156, and Johnson, 80⅘, with the rest of the vote scattered.

Immediately after Harding's nomination, the vice-presidential balloting began. After the nomination of Sen. Irvine L. Lenroot of Wisconsin, a delegate from Oregon rose and, standing on his chair, nominated Gov. Calvin Coolidge of Massachusetts. An enthusiastic demonstration followed, showing the wide delegate support for Coolidge. The governor, who had risen to national prominence less than a year earlier with his handling of a Boston police strike, was a runaway winner on the one vice-presidential ballot. Coolidge received 674½ votes to Lenroot's 146½.

The Wisconsin delegation again presented a detailed minority report to the platform. It included planks that opposed entry into the League of Nations under the terms of the proposed treaty, objected to compulsory military service, called for the quick conclusion of peace negotiations and normalization of foreign relations and recommended a bonus for servicemen to match the wages of wartime civilian workers.

In domestic reforms, the Wisconsin report advocated the election of federal judges and the passage of a constitutional amendment that would establish the initiative, referendum, and recall. The entire minority report was rejected by a voice vote, and the platform as written was adopted in a similar manner.

The platform began by denouncing the Wilson administration for being completely unprepared for both war and peace. It went on to criticize Wilson for establishing an "executive autocracy" by arrogating to himself power that belonged to other branches of government.

The platform included a League of Nations plank that intentionally straddled the controversial issue, applauding the Republican-controlled Senate for defeating Wilson's League but pledging the party "to such agreements with the other nations of the world as shall meet the full duty of America to civilization and humanity."

To help cut federal spending, the Republicans favored consolidating some departments and bureaus and establishing an executive budget.

Both parties continued to differ on the tariff, with the Democrats reiterating their belief in a revenue tariff and the Republicans restating their support of a protective tariff.

Following are excerpts from the Republican platform of 1920:

League of Nations. The Republican party stands for agreement among the nations to preserve the peace of the world. . . .

The covenant signed by the President at Paris failed signally . . . and contains stipulations, not only intolerable for an independent people, but certain to produce the injustice, hostility and controversy among nations which it proposed to prevent.

[W]e pledge the coming Republican administration to such agreements with the other nations of the world as shall meet the full duty of America to civilization and humanity, in accordance with American ideals, and without surrendering the right of the American people to exercise its judgment and its power in favor of justice and peace.

DEMOCRATS

San Francisco was the host city for the 1920 Democratic convention, marking the first time a convention of one of the major parties was held west of the Rockies. Not only was the site a new one, but when the convention opened in late June, for the first time in a generation the Democratic Party had no recognized leader such as Cleveland, Bryan, or Wilson.

President Woodrow Wilson had some hope of a third nomination, but his failing health and skidding popularity made this an unrealistic prospect. But Wilson's refusal to endorse another candidate prevented the emergence of any presidential hopeful as a front-runner for the nomination. In all, twenty-four candidates received votes on the first presidential roll call, but none approached the 729 votes needed for nomination. William Gibbs McAdoo, Wilson's son-in-law and former Treasury secretary, led with 266 votes, in spite of having withdrawn from the race several days before the convention began. Attorney General A. Mitchell Palmer, famed for his efforts during the "Red Scare," followed closely with 254 votes. Two governors, Ohio's James M. Cox and New York's Alfred E. Smith, trailed with 134 and 109 votes respectively. *(Table, p. 213.)*

Another ballot was taken before evening adjournment, with the top four candidates retaining the same order and nearly the same vote.

During the next day's balloting, Cox gained steadily and passed both McAdoo and Palmer. When the majority of

McAdoo and Palmer delegates successfully carried a motion to recess after the sixteenth ballot, Cox held the lead with 454½ votes. McAdoo was next with 337 votes and Palmer trailed with 164½.

Six more ballots were taken during the evening session, and although Cox's lead narrowed, he still led McAdoo after the 22nd ballot, 430 to 372½. In the next day's balloting, McAdoo gradually gained ground until he finally passed Cox on the 30th ballot, 403½ to 400½. After completion of the roll call, the motion was made to eliminate the lowest candidate on each succeeding ballot until a nominee had been selected. This drastic proposal to shorten the convention was defeated, 812½ to 264.

Balloting continued without interruption through the 36th roll call. McAdoo still led with 399 votes, but his margin over Cox was reduced to 22 votes, and Palmer with 241 votes achieved his highest total since the 11th ballot.

A candidate was finally nominated during the evening session of the convention's third day of presidential balloting. The Palmer revival fizzled quickly, with most of his delegates going to either McAdoo or Cox. The Ohio governor regained the lead on the thirty-ninth ballot, when the majority of the Indiana delegation shifted from McAdoo to Cox. After this roll call, Cox led McAdoo, 468½ to 440, Palmer having slipped to 74. Cox continued to gain, and a last-ditch effort by McAdoo delegates to force an adjournment failed, 637 to 406. Cox's vote total reached 699½ votes on the forty-fourth ballot, and, with victory imminent, a motion was adopted to declare the Ohio governor the unanimous nominee of the convention. *(Table, p. 213.)*

Cox's choice for the vice-presidential nomination was Franklin D. Roosevelt of New York, the thirty-eight-year-old assistant secretary of the Navy. Roosevelt was nominated by acclamation.

William Jennings Bryan attended the convention and proposed five planks as amendments to the platform. Only his plank endorsing Prohibition, however, was submitted for a roll-call vote, and it was soundly beaten, 929½ to 155½. A counterproposal by a New York delegate, recognizing the legality of the Prohibition amendment to the Constitution but favoring the manufacture of beer and light wines for home use, was also defeated, 724½ to 356. The platform finally adopted did not discuss the Prohibition question.

Bryan's four other planks covered a wide range of issues. He favored establishing a national newspaper, reducing from two-thirds to a simple majority the vote needed to approve treaties in the Senate, expressed opposition to peacetime universal compulsory military training and recommended that interstate companies reveal the difference between the cost and selling price of their products. All four planks were defeated by voice votes.

One other amendment, calling for the recognition of Irish independence, came to the floor for a roll-call vote. It was beaten, 674 to 402½. Included instead was a milder plank sympathizing with the Irish struggle for independence. Subsequently, the delegates approved by voice vote the entire platform as it was first written.

Although the delegates were unwilling to renominate Wilson, the platform was largely devoted to praise of his leadership and legislation passed during his presidency. The platform reflected Wilson's thinking by placing the League of Nations plank prominently at the beginning and supporting the president's call for American membership. The plank did allow for reservations to the treaty, but none that would prevent American participation in the League.

Following are excerpts from the Democratic platform of 1920:

League of Nations. The Democratic Party favors the League of Nations as the surest, if not the only, practicable means of maintaining the permanent peace of the world and terminating the insufferable burden of great military and naval establishments. . . .

We commend the President for his courage and his high conception of good faith in steadfastly standing for the covenant agreed to by all the associated and allied nations at war with Germany, and we con-

demn the Republican Senate for its refusal to ratify the treaty merely because it was the product of Democratic statesmanship, thus interposing partisan envy and personal hatred in the way of the peace and renewed prosperity of the world. . . .

We advocate the immediate ratification of the treaty without reservations which would impair its essential integrity, but do not oppose the acceptance of any reservations making clearer or more specific the obligations of the United States to the league associates.

Irish Independence. The great principle of national self-determination has received constant reiteration as one of the chief objectives for which this country entered the war and victory established this principle.

Within the limitations of international comity and usage, this Convention repeats the several previous expressions of the sympathy of the Democratic Party of the United States for the aspirations of Ireland for self-government.

1924 Conventions

PRESIDENTIAL CANDIDATES

Calvin Coolidge
Republican

John W. Davis
Democrat

Robert M. La Follette
Progressive

REPUBLICANS

The Republicans gathered for their convention in Cleveland, Ohio, in June. For the first time, a convention was broadcast by radio. Also for the first time, Republican Party rules were changed to elect women to the national committee, with one man and one woman to be chosen from each state and territory.

Unlike the Democratic marathon that began two weeks later in New York, there was surface harmony at the Republican convention. President Calvin Coolidge's success in the spring primaries, and his ability to defuse the Teapot Dome corruption issue, eliminated any major opposition. Coolidge was easily nominated on the first ballot, receiving 1,065 votes. Sen. Robert M. La Follette of Wisconsin was a distant second with 34 votes, while Sen. Hiram W. Johnson of California collected the remaining 10. *(Table, p. 216.)*

The vice-presidential nomination was a confused matter. Eight candidates were nominated, and on the first ballot former Illinois governor Frank O. Lowden led with 222 votes. Although

Lowden publicly stated that he would not accept the nomination, he received a majority of the vote on the second roll call. A recess was taken to see if Lowden had changed his mind, but when it was certain that he had not the delegates resumed balloting.

On the third roll call, former budget bureau director Charles G. Dawes received 682½ votes to win nomination. Secretary of Commerce Herbert Hoover was second with 234½ votes.

As was its custom throughout the early twentieth century, the Wisconsin delegation proposed a detailed minority report to the platform. Proposals included government ownership of railroads and water power, an increased excess profits tax and reduced taxes on individuals with low incomes. The Wisconsin platform was rejected without a roll-call vote.

The platform that was adopted lauded the economy in government shown by the Republican administration and promised a reduction in taxes.

The Democrats and Republicans continued to differ on the tariff issue, with the Republicans again defending the protective tariff. The Ku Klux Klan was not mentioned in the Republican platform, nor was it discussed on the floor. The controversial organization was the subject of a divisive floor fight at the Democratic convention.

The Republican platform criticized the corruption found to exist in the Harding administration, but it also denounced efforts "to besmirch the names of the innocent and undermine the confidence of the people in the government under which they live."

In the area of foreign policy, the Republicans opposed membership in the League of Nations, although favoring participation in the World Court. While applauding the return of peace and reflecting the nation's increasing mood of isolationism, the Republicans opposed cutbacks in the Army and Navy.

Following are excerpts from the Republican platform of 1924:

Corruption. We demand the speedy, fearless and impartial prosecution of all wrong doers, without regard for political affiliations; but we declare no greater wrong can be committed against the people than the attempt to destroy their trust in the great body of their public servants. Admitting the deep humiliation which all good citizens share that our public life should have harbored some dishonest men, we assert that these undesirables do not represent the standard of our national integrity.

Taxes. We pledge ourselves to the progressive reduction of taxes of all the people as rapidly as may be done with due regard for the essential expenditures for the government administered with rigid economy and to place our tax system on a sound peace time basis.

League of Nations. This government has definitely refused membership in the league of nations or to assume any obligations under the covenant of the league. On this we stand.

Military. There must be no further weakening of our regular army and we advocate appropriations sufficient to provide for the training of all members of the national guard, the citizens' military training camps, the reserve officers' training camps and the reserves who may offer themselves for service. We pledge ourselves for service. We pledge ourselves to round out and maintain the navy to the full strength provided the United States by the letter and spirit of the limitation of armament conference.

War Profiteering. [S]hould the United States ever again be called upon to defend itself by arms the president be empowered to draft such material resources and such services as may be required, and to stabilize the prices of services and essential commodities, whether used in actual warfare or private activities.

Republican Philosophy. The prosperity of the American nation rests on the vigor of private initiative which has bred a spirit of independence and self-reliance. The republican party stands now, as always, against all attempts to put the government into business.

American industry should not be compelled to struggle against government competition. The right of the government to regulate, supervise and control public utilities and public interests, we believe, should be strengthened, but we are firmly opposed to the nationalization or government ownership of public utilities.

DEMOCRATS

The 1924 Democratic convention in New York's old Madison Square Garden was the longest in American history. From the opening gavel on June 24 through final adjournment on July 10, the convention spanned seventeen days. The reason for the convention's unprecedented length was an almost unbreakable deadlock between the party's rural and urban factions that extended the presidential balloting for a record 103 roll calls. *(Table, pp. 214–215.)*

Gov. Alfred E. Smith of New York was the candidate of the urban delegates, while William Gibbs McAdoo of California led the rural forces. But beyond any ideological differences between the two candidates was a bitter struggle between the urban and rural wings for control of the party. Smith, a Roman Catholic of Irish ancestry and an opponent of Prohibition and the Ku Klux Klan, embodied characteristics loathed by the rural leaders. McAdoo, a Protestant, a supporter of Prohibition and tolerant of the Ku Klux Klan, was equally unacceptable to the urban forces. Without a strong leader to unite the two factions, and with the two-thirds rule in effect, a long deadlock was inevitable.

Besides Smith and McAdoo, fourteen other candidates were nominated. The most memorable speech was delivered by Franklin D. Roosevelt, who, in nominating Smith, referred to him as "the happy warrior," a description that remained with Smith the rest of his career.

Presidential balloting commenced on Monday, June 30. McAdoo led on the first roll call with 431½ votes, followed by Smith with 241, with 733 votes needed for nomination. Through the week, 77 ballots were taken, but none of the candidates approached the required two-thirds majority. At the end of the week, after the seventy-seventh ballot, McAdoo led with 513 votes; Smith had 367; John W. Davis of New York, the eventual nominee, was a distant third with 76⅓, an improvement of 45½ votes over his first-ballot total. McAdoo had reached the highest total for any candidate, 530 votes, on the sixty-ninth ballot.

William Jennings Bryan, making his last appearance at a Democratic convention, as a delegate from Florida, was given permission to explain his opposition to Smith during the thirty-eighth ballot. But Bryan's final convention oration was lost in a chorus of boos from the urban forces who found his rural philosophy increasingly objectionable.

After the sixty-sixth ballot, the first of a series of proposals was introduced to break the deadlock. It was recommended that the convention meet in executive session and listen to each of the candidates. This received majority approval, 551 to 538, but a two-thirds majority was needed to change the rules. A second proposal, to invite Smith alone to address the convention, also fell short of the necessary two-thirds, although achieving a majority, 604½ to 473.

After the seventy-third ballot, it was recommended that the lowest vote-getter be dropped after each roll call until only five candidates remained, a proposal to be in effect for one day only. This recommendation was defeated, 589½ to 496. A more drastic motion, to adjourn after the seventy-fifth ballot and reconvene two weeks later in Kansas City, was decisively beaten, 1,007.3 to 82.7. The delegates did agree, however, to have representatives of each candidate hold a conference over the weekend.

Balloting resumed on Monday, July 7, with the seventy-eighth roll call. After the eighty-second ballot, a resolution was passed, 985 to 105, releasing all delegates from their commitments.

McAdoo's vote dropped sharply as the balloting progressed, and for the first time, on the eighty-sixth roll call, Smith passed him, 360 to 353½. A boom for Sen. Samuel M. Ralston of Indiana, which had begun on the eighty-fourth ballot, petered out on the ninety-third roll call when Ralston quit the race. At the time of his withdrawal, Ralston was in third place with 196¼ votes.

After the ballot, Roosevelt announced that Smith was willing to withdraw from the race if McAdoo would also. McAdoo rejected this suggestion. McAdoo did regain the lead from Smith on the ninety-fourth ballot, 395 to 364½, but with victory beyond reach, released his delegates after the ninety-ninth ballot.

Davis was the principal beneficiary of the McAdoo withdrawal, moving into second place on the 100th ballot and gaining the lead on the next roll call with 316 votes. Most of Smith's strength moved to Alabama's anti-Klan, anti-Prohibition senator, Oscar W. Underwood, who took second place on the 101st ballot with 229½ votes. Underwood, however, could not keep pace with Davis, who stretched his lead on the next two ballots. After the 103rd ballot, Davis's total stood at 575½ votes to 250½ for the Alabama senator.

Before the next ballot could begin, Iowa switched its vote to Davis, causing other shifts that brought Davis the nomination. After the changes had been recorded, Davis had 844 votes to 102½ for Underwood. The West Virginian's nomination was then declared unanimous.

The core of Davis's vote had come from the rural delegates; urban delegates gave him the necessary votes to win the nomination. After nine days of balloting, the Democrats had a presidential candidate.

The party leadership preferred Gov. Charles W. Bryan of Nebraska, William Jennings Bryan's younger brother, as Davis's running mate. Bryan trailed Tennessee labor leader George L. Berry on the first ballot, 263½ to 238, but vote switches begun by Illinois after the roll call brought Bryan the nomination. After the changes Bryan had 740 votes, barely beyond the two-thirds majority necessary.

The discord evident in the presidential and vice-presidential balloting had its roots in the spirited platform battle that preceded the nominations. The first subject of debate was the League of Nations, with the majority report recommending that American entry be determined by a national referendum. The minority plank argued that this was an unwieldy solution that would put the issue aside. Instead, the minority report favored entry into the League of Nations and World Court without reservation. The minority position was rejected, 742½ to 353½. Nonetheless, the Democrats differed markedly in their position from the Republicans, who flatly opposed membership in the League, although favoring participation in the World Court.

The League of Nations debate proved to be merely a warm-up for the controversial religious liberties plank. The focus of debate was the Ku Klux Klan, which was opposed by name in the minority report but was not mentioned in the majority report. In one of the closest votes in convention history, the minority plank was defeated, 543³⁄₂₀ to 543⁷⁄₂₀. The vote closely followed factional lines, with most rural delegates opposing condemnation of the Klan and urban delegates supporting the minority plank.

The rest of the platform stressed Democratic accomplishments during the Wilson presidency, in contrast to Republican corruption. Democratic links with the common man were emphasized, while the Republicans were denounced as the party of the rich. The Democratic platform advocated increased taxes on the wealthy in contrast to the Republicans, who promised a reduction in taxes.

The Democrats continued to advocate a low tariff that would encourage competition. A plank demanding states' rights appeared in the platform, but there were also calls for government regulation of the anthracite coal industry, federal support of the American merchant marine and legislation that would restrict and publicize individual campaign contributions.

There were planks favoring a cutback in the American military, a national referendum before any declaration of war (except outright aggression against the United States) and the drafting of resources as well as men during wartime. The anti-militaristic planks were a return to the position the party had held earlier in the twentieth century.

Following are excerpts from the Democratic platform of 1924:

Republican Corruption. Such are the exigencies of partisan politics that republican leaders are teaching the strange doctrine that public censure should be directed against those who expose crime rather than against criminals who have committed the offenses. If only three cabinet officers out of ten are disgraced, the country is asked to marvel at how many are free from taint. Long boastful that it was the only party "fit to govern," the republican party has proven its inability to govern even itself. It is at war with itself. As an agency of government it has ceased to function.

Income Tax. The income tax was intended as a tax upon wealth. It was not intended to take from the poor any part of the necessities of life. We hold that the fairest tax with which to raise revenue for the federal government is the income tax. We favor a graduated tax upon incomes, so adjusted as to lay the burdens of government upon the taxpayers in proportion to the benefits they enjoy and their ability to pay.

Campaign Contributions. We favor the prohibition of individual contributions, direct and indirect, to the campaign funds of congressmen, senators or presidential candidates, beyond a reasonable sum to be fixed in the law, for both individual contributions and total expenditures, with requirements for full publicity.

States' Rights. We demand that the states of the union shall be preserved in all their vigor and power. They constitute a bulwark against the centralizing and destructive tendencies of the republican party.

Anti-militarism. We demand a strict and sweeping reduction of armaments by land and sea, so that there shall be no competitive military program or naval building. Until international agreements to this end have been made we advocate an army and navy adequate for our national safety. . . .

War is a relic of barbarism and it is justifiable only as a measure defense.

War Profiteering. In the event of war in which the manpower the nation is drafted, all other resources should likewise be dra This will tend to discourage war by depriving it of its profits.

PROGRESSIVES

Under the sponsorship of the Conference of Political Action, representatives of various libe agrarian groups met in Cleveland on July 4 to launch the Progressive Party and ratify the ticket of Wisconsin senator Robert M. La Follette for president and Montana senator Burton K. Wheeler for vice president. The conference earlier had designated La Follette as its presidential nominee and had given him the power to choose his running mate. The national ticket of the Progressives crossed party lines, joining a Republican, La Follette, with a Democrat, Wheeler. The ticket was endorsed by the Socialists, who supported the Progressive candidates rather than run a separate national ticket.

In large part the Progressive platform advocated measures that had been proposed earlier by the Populists, Socialists, and Progressives before World War I. The key issue, as viewed by the La Follette Progressives, was "the control of government and industry by private monopoly." The platform favored the government ownership of railroads and water power, rigid federal control over natural resources, the outlawing of injunctions in labor disputes, a cutback in military spending, tax reform and political reform—including the direct election of the president, a national referendum before a declaration of war (except in cases of invasion), election of federal judges, and congressional power to override the Supreme Court.

Following are excerpts from the Progressive platform of 1924:

Anti-monopoly. The great issue before the American people today is the control of government and industry by private monopoly.

For a generation the people have struggled patiently, in the face of repeated betrayals by successive administrations, to free themselves from this intolerable power which has been undermining representative government.

Through control of government, monopoly has steadily extended its absolute dominion to every basic industry.

In violation of law, monopoly has crushed competition, stifled private initiative and independent enterprise. . . .

The equality of opportunity proclaimed by the Declaration of Independence and asserted and defended by Jefferson and Lincoln as the heritage of every American citizen has been displaced by special privilege for the few, wrested from the government of the many.

Tax Reform. We . . . favor a taxation policy providing for immediate reductions upon moderate incomes, large increases in the inheritance tax rates upon large estates to prevent the indefinite accumulation by inheritance of great fortunes in a few hands, taxes upon excess profits to penalize profiteering, and complete publicity, under proper safeguards, of all Federal tax returns.

Court Reform. We favor submitting to the people, for their considerate judgment, a constitutional amendment providing that Congress may by enacting a statute make it effective over a judicial vote.

We favor such amendment to the constitution as may be necessary to provide for the election of all Federal Judges, without party designation, for fixed terms not exceeding ten years, by direct vote of the people.

National Referendums. Over and above constitutions and statutes and greater than all is the supreme sovereignty of the people, and with them should rest the final decision of all great questions of national policy. We favor such amendments to the Federal Constitution as may be necessary to provide for the direct nomination and election of the President, to extend the initiative and referendum to the federal government, and to insure a popular referendum for or against war except in cases of actual invasion.

1928 Conventions

PRESIDENTIAL CANDIDATES

Alfred E. Smith
Democrat

typically brief statement: "I do not choose to run for President in 1928." While some business leaders hoped that Coolidge would be open to a draft, the taciturn incumbent made no effort to encourage them. The vacuum caused by Coolidge's absence was

in Kansas City, Mis-..., President Calvin ...o seek reelection with a

quickly filled by Commerce Secretary Herbert Hoover of California, whose success in the spring primaries solidified his position as the front-runner.

Hoover's strength was evident on the first roll call of the convention, a credentials challenge to eighteen Hoover delegates from Texas. In a vote that revealed candidate strength, the move to unseat the Hoover delegates was defeated, 659½ to 399½. In the presidential balloting that followed, he gained more votes to win the nomination easily on the first ballot. Hoover's vote total was swelled before the balloting began by the withdrawal of his principal opponent, former Illinois governor Frank O. Lowden, who declared in a letter that he could not accept the party platform's stand on agriculture. Six names were placed in nomination, but Hoover was a landslide winner, receiving 837 of the 1,089 convention votes. Lowden finished second with 74 votes. *(Table, p. 217.)*

Sen. Charles Curtis of Kansas was virtually unopposed for the vice-presidential nomination, receiving 1,052 votes. Curtis, whose maternal grandmother was half Kaw Indian, was the first member of a major party ticket with Native American heritage.

Although Wisconsin's prominent progressive leader, Robert M. La Follette, had died in 1925, his state's delegation again presented a minority platform. The report was presented by Sen. Robert M. La Follette Jr., who had taken over his father's Senate seat. Among the planks of the Wisconsin report were proposals favoring enactment of the McNary-Haugen farm bill, government operation of major water power projects, increased income taxes on the rich, and liberalization of Prohibition. No vote was taken on the Wisconsin proposals.

A resolution favoring repeal of Prohibition was tabled by a voice vote.

A separate agricultural resolution was proposed that advocated the basic provisions of the McNary-Haugen bill (twice vetoed by Coolidge), without mentioning the controversial bill by name. On a roll-call vote, the resolution was defeated, 807 to 277, with support centered in the farm states but with most Hoover delegates voting against it.

The platform as originally written was adopted by a voice vote. The platform promised continued prosperity and government economy. The belief in a protective tariff was reiterated. The document concluded with a plank entitled "home rule," which expressed the party's belief in self-reliance and strong local government.

Following are excerpts from the Republican platform of 1928:

Tariff. We reaffirm our belief in the protective tariff as a fundamental and essential principle of the economic life of this nation. . . . However, we realize that there are certain industries which cannot now successfully compete with foreign producers because of lower foreign wages and a lower cost of living abroad, and we pledge the next Republican Congress to an examination and where necessary a revision of these schedules to the end that American labor in these industries may again command the home market, may maintain its standard of living, and may count upon steady employment in its accustomed field.

Outlaw War. We endorse the proposal of the Secretary of State for a multilateral treaty proposed to the principal powers of the world and open to the signatures of all nations, to renounce war as an instrument of national policy and declaring in favor of pacific settlement of international disputes, the first step in outlawing war.

Agriculture. We promise every assistance in the reorganization of the market system on sounder and more economical lines and, where diversification is needed, Government financial assistance during the period of transition.

The Republican Party pledges itself to the enactment of legislation creating a Federal Farm Board clothed with the necessary powers to promote the establishment of a farm marketing system of farmer-owned and controlled stabilization corporations or associations to prevent and control surpluses through orderly distribution. . . .

We favor, without putting the Government into business, the establishment of a Federal system of organization for co-operative and orderly marketing of farm products.

Prohibition. The people through the method provided by the Constitution have written the Eighteenth Amendment into the Constitution. The Republican Party pledges itself and its nominees to the observance and vigorous enforcement of this provision of the Constitution.

Republican Philosophy. There is a real need of restoring the individual and local sense of responsibility and self-reliance; there is a real need for the people once more to grasp the fundamental fact that under our system of government they are expected to solve many problems themselves through their municipal and State governments, and to combat the tendency that is all too common to turn to the Federal Government as the easiest and least burdensome method of lightening their own responsibilities.

DEMOCRATS

The Democratic convention was held in late June in Houston, Texas, the first time since 1860 that the party's nominating convention had been conducted in a southern city. The rural and urban wings of the party, which had produced the fiasco in Madison Square Garden four years earlier, wanted no more bloodletting. This explained the acceptance of Houston as the convention site by the urban forces, whose presidential candidate, Gov. Alfred E. Smith of New York, was the front-runner for the nomination. Smith's path to the nomination was largely unobstructed, thanks to the decision of William Gibbs McAdoo not to run. McAdoo, the rural favorite in 1924, feared the possibility of another bitter deadlock that would destroy party unity.

The convention broke with tradition by bypassing politicians and selecting Claude G. Bowers of Indiana, a historian and an editorial writer for the *New York World,* as temporary chairman.

When it came time for the selection of a presidential candidate, Franklin D. Roosevelt once again placed Smith's name in nomination. On the roll call that followed, the New York governor came within 10 votes of the required two-thirds. Ohio quickly switched 44 of its votes to Smith, and the switch pushed "the happy warrior" over the top. When the vote switches were completed, Smith had received 849⅙ of the 1,100 convention votes. No other candidate's vote had totaled more than 100. Smith became the first Roman Catholic to head a major party presidential ticket. *(Table, p. 217.)*

Senate minority leader Joseph T. Robinson of Arkansas had little opposition for the vice presidency and was nominated on the first ballot with 914⅙ votes. Sen. Alben W. Barkley of Kentucky finished a distant second with 77 votes. After a vote switch, Robinson had 1,035⅙ votes. As a "dry" Protestant from the South, Robinson balanced the ticket. He was the first southerner to be nominated for national office by either major party since the Civil War.

For the first time since 1912, there were no roll-call votes on amendments to the Democratic platform. A minority plank was introduced calling for the party's complete support of Prohibition, but there was no effort to force a roll-call vote. The platform included a milder Prohibition plank that promised "an honest effort to enforce the eighteenth amendment (Prohibition)." On the surface there was little difference from the Republican plank, which pledged "vigorous enforcement" of Prohibition. But in a telegram read to the convention shortly before its final adjournment, Smith negated the effect of the milder plank by declaring there should be "fundamental changes in the present provisions for national Prohibition." Smith's statement was disappointing to many "dry" delegates and lessened whatever enthusiasm they felt for the New York governor. No other issues were discussed, and the platform as written was approved by a voice vote.

Agriculture, the most depressed part of the economy in the 1920s, received more space in the platform than any other issue. The Democrats opposed federal subsidies to farmers, but they advocated government loans to cooperatives and the creation of a federal farm board that would operate similarly to the Federal Reserve Board. While the Republican platform also favored creation of a farm board, as a whole it called for more initiative by the farmers themselves and less direct government help than did the Democratic platform.

Since the late nineteenth century, Democratic platforms had favored a low tariff. The 1928 tariff plank represented a change, expressing as much interest in ensuring competition and protecting the American wage-earner as in raising revenue. Instead of being consistently low, tariff rates were to be based on the difference between the cost of production in the United States and abroad. As a result of the Democrats' altered stand on the tariff, the positions of the two parties on this issue were the closest they had been in a generation.

The Democrats' 1928 platform did not mention the League of Nations, in contrast to the Republicans, who restated their opposition to the League. Both parties called for maintenance of American military strength until international disarmament agreements could be reached. A section of the Democratic foreign policy plank questioned the extent of presidential power in the area of international affairs. President Coolidge was specifically criticized for authorizing American military intervention in Nicaragua without congressional approval.

An unemployment plank was included in the Democratic platform that proposed the creation of public works jobs in times of economic hardship.

As was the case with most Democratic platforms since the early nineteenth century, there was a defense of states' rights and a plank that recognized education as an area of state responsibility. The Democrats made no mention of civil rights in contrast to the Republicans, who, as in 1920, proposed federal antilynching legislation.

Following are excerpts from the Democratic platform of 1928:

Prohibition. Speaking for the national Democracy, this convention pledges the party and its nominees to an honest effort to enforce the eighteenth amendment.

Agriculture. Farm relief must rest on the basis of an economic equality of agriculture with other industries. To give this equality a remedy must be found which will include among other things:

(a) Credit aid by loans to co-operatives on at least as favorable a basis as the government aid to the merchant marine.

(b) Creation of a federal farm board to assist the farmer and stock raiser in the marketing of their products, as the Federal Reserve Board has done for the banker and business man.

Presidential War Power. Abolition of the practice of the president of entering into and carrying out agreements with a foreign government, either de facto or de jure, for the protection of such government against revolution or foreign attack, or for the supervision of its internal affairs, when such agreements have not been advised and consented to by the Senate, as provided in the Constitution of the United States, and we condemn the administration for carrying out such an unratified agreement that requires us to use our armed forces in Nicaragua.

Tariff. Duties that will permit effective competition, insure against monopoly and at the same time produce a fair revenue for the support of government. Actual difference between the cost of production at home and abroad, with adequate safeguard for the wage of the American laborer must be the extreme measure of every tariff rate.

Unemployment and Public Works. We favor the adoption by the government, after a study of this subject, of a scientific plan whereby during periods of unemployment appropriations shall be made available for the construction of necessary public works and the lessening, as far as consistent with public interests, of government construction work when labor is generally and satisfactorily employed in private enterprise.

Education. We believe with Jefferson and other founders of the Republic that ignorance is the enemy of freedom and that each state, being responsible for the intellectual and moral qualifications of its citizens and for the expenditure of the moneys collected by taxation for the support of its schools, shall use its sovereign right in all matters pertaining to education.

1932 Conventions

PRESIDENTIAL CANDIDATES

Norman Thomas
Socialist

Herbert Hoover
Republican

Franklin D. Roosevelt
Democrat

SOCIALISTS

The Socialist Party held its convention in Milwaukee, Wis., in May and renominated the same ticket that had represented the party in 1928: Norman Thomas of New York for president and James H. Maurer of Pennsylvania for vice president. Aided by the deepening economic depression, the Socialists received more than 2 percent of the popular vote for the first time since 1920. The party continued to run a national ticket until 1956, but 1932 was the last election in which the Socialists received at least 2 percent of the vote.

By a vote of 117 to 64, the convention adopted a resolution supporting the efforts of the Soviet Union to create a Socialist society. An attempt to oust Morris Hillquit as national chairman of the party was beaten, 108 to 81.

The Socialist platform of 1932 contained a number of proposals that had been set forth in earlier party platforms, such as public ownership of natural resources and the means of transportation and communication, increased taxes on the wealthy, an end to the Supreme Court's power to rule congressional legislation unconstitutional, and a reduction in the size and expenditures of the military.

The platform also advocated United States recognition of the Soviet Union and American entry into the League of Nations. Repeal of Prohibition was recommended, as was the creation of a federal marketing system that would buy and market farm commodities.

To meet the hardship of the Depression, the Socialists listed a series of proposals, which included the expenditure of $10 billion for unemployment relief and public works projects.

Following are excerpts from the Socialist platform of 1932:

Unemployment Relief. 1. A Federal appropriation of $5,000,000,000 for immediate relief for those in need to supplement State and local appropriations.

2. A Federal appropriation of $5,000,000,000 for public works and roads, reforestation, slum clearance, and decent homes for the workers, by Federal Government, States and cities.

3. Legislation providing for the acquisition of land, buildings, and equipment necessary to put the unemployed to work producing food, fuel, and clothing and for the erection of houses for their own use.

4. The 6-hour day and the 5-day week without reduction of wages.

5. A comprehensive and efficient system of free public employment agencies.

6. A compulsory system of unemployment compensation with adequate benefits, based on contributions by the Government and by employers.

7. Old-age pensions for men and women 60 years of age and over.

8. Health and maternity insurance.

REPUBLICANS

As the party in power during the outset of the Great Depression, the Republicans bore the major political blame for the worsening economy. In a subdued mood, the party gathered in Chicago in June 1932 for its national convention.

Republican leaders did not view their electoral prospects optimistically for the fall election, but saw no realistic alternative to President Herbert Hoover.

Hoover was easily if unenthusiastically renominated, receiving 1,126½ of the 1,154 convention votes. The highlight of the presidential balloting was the attempt by former Maryland senator Joseph I. France, who ran in several spring primaries, to gain the rostrum and nominate former president Coolidge. France's dramatic plan, however, was foiled by convention managers, who refused him permission to speak and had him escorted from the hall. *(Table, p. 218.)*

Vice President Charles Curtis had stiff opposition in his bid for renomination. The incumbent was seriously challenged by Maj. Gen. James G. Harbord of New York and the national commander of the American Legion, Hanford MacNider of Iowa. Curtis was short of a majority after the first ballot, but Pennsylvania quickly shifted its 75 votes to the vice president and this pushed him over the top. With the vote standing at Curtis, 634¼; MacNider, 182¾, and Harbord, 161¾, Curtis's renomination was made unanimous.

The major platform controversy surrounded the Prohibition plank. The majority plank, supported by Hoover, was ambiguous. It called for the enforcement of Prohibition but advocated a national referendum that would permit each state to determine whether or not it wanted Prohibition. A more clear-cut minority plank favored repeal of Prohibition. The minority proposal was defeated, however, $690\frac{19}{36}$ to $460\frac{2}{9}$. Following this roll call, the rest of the platform was approved by a voice vote.

The document approved by the Republicans was the longest in the party's history—nearly 9,000 words. It blamed the nation's continued economic problems on a worldwide depression, but lauded Hoover's leadership in meeting the crisis. The Republicans saw reduced government spending and a balanced budget as keys to ending the Depression. The party platform viewed unemployment relief as a matter for private agencies and local governments to handle.

The Republicans continued their support of a protective tariff. On the agricultural issue, the party proposed acreage controls to help balance supply and demand.

The final plank of the Republican platform urged party members in Congress to demonstrate party loyalty by supporting the Republican program. The plank warned that the party's strength was jeopardized by internal dissent.

Following are excerpts from the Republican platform of 1932:

Unemployment Relief. The people themselves, by their own courage, their own patient and resolute effort in the readjustments of their own affairs, can and will work out the cure. It is our task as a party, by leadership and a wise determination of policy, to assist that recovery. . . .

True to American traditions and principles of government, the administration has regarded the relief problem as one of State and local responsibility. The work of local agencies, public and private has been coordinated and enlarged on a nation-wide scale under the leadership of the President.

Government Spending. We urge prompt and drastic reduction of public expenditure and resistance to every appropriation not demonstrably necessary to the performance of government, national or local.

Agriculture. The fundamental problem of American agriculture is the control of production to such volume as will balance supply with demand. In the solution of this problem the cooperative organization of farmers to plan production, and the tariff, to hold the home market for American farmers, are vital elements. A third element equally as vital is the control of the acreage of land under cultivation, as an aid to the efforts of the farmer to balance production.

Prohibition. We . . . believe that the people should have an opportunity to pass upon a proposed amendment the provision of which, while retaining in the Federal Government power to preserve the gains already made in dealing with the evils inherent in the liquor traffic, shall allow the States to deal with the problem as their citizens may determine, but subject always to the power of the Federal Government to protect those States where prohibition may exist and safeguard our citizens everywhere from the return of the saloon and attendant abuses.

DEMOCRATS

With the nation in the midst of the Depression, the Democratic Party had its best chance for victory since 1912. The delegates assembled in Chicago in late June 1932, confident that the convention's nominee would defeat President Hoover.

Gov. Franklin D. Roosevelt of New York entered the convention with a majority of the votes, but was well short of the two-thirds majority needed for nomination. Ironically, his principal opponent was the man he had nominated for the presidency three times, former New York governor Alfred E. Smith.

Roosevelt's strength was tested on several key roll calls before the presidential balloting began. Two of the votes involved credentials challenges to Roosevelt delegations from Louisiana and Minnesota. By a vote of $638\frac{3}{4}$ to $514\frac{1}{4}$, the delegates seated the Roosevelt forces from Louisiana, headed by Sen. Huey P. Long. By a wider margin of $658\frac{1}{4}$ to $492\frac{3}{4}$, the convention also seated the Roosevelt delegates from Minnesota. *(Table, p. 219.)*

After settlement of the credentials cases, the battleground shifted to the selection of the permanent convention chairman. The Roosevelt forces backed Sen. Thomas J. Walsh of Montana, who was recommended by the committee on permanent organization. The Smith and other anti-Roosevelt factions coalesced behind Jouett Shouse of Kansas, chairman of the executive committee of the Democratic National Committee, who was recommended for permanent chairman by the national committee. But by a vote of 626 to 528, the Roosevelt forces won again, and Walsh assumed the gavel as permanent chairman.

The Roosevelt managers considered challenging the two-thirds rule; but, realizing that a bruising fight could alienate some of their delegates, particularly in the South, they dropped the idea. Instead, the report of the rules committee recommended that a change in the two-thirds rule be delayed until the 1936 convention.

The presidential balloting began in the middle of an all-night session. After a motion to adjourn was defeated, $863\frac{1}{2}$ to $281\frac{1}{2}$, the first roll call began at 4:30 a.m. Roosevelt received a clear majority of $666\frac{1}{4}$ votes on the first ballot, compared with $201\frac{3}{4}$ for Smith and $90\frac{1}{4}$ for House Speaker John Nance Garner of Texas. The candidates needed 770 votes for the nomination. *(Table, p. 219.)*

Roosevelt gained slightly on the second ballot, advancing to $677\frac{3}{4}$ votes, while Smith dropped to $194\frac{1}{4}$ and Garner remained constant. Of side interest was the shift of Oklahoma's votes from its governor to Will Rogers, the state's famous humorist.

There were few changes on the next roll call, and at 9:15 a.m. the delegates agreed to adjourn. The vote totals after three ballots: Roosevelt, 682.79; Smith, $190\frac{1}{4}$; Garner, $101\frac{1}{4}$.

When balloting resumed the next evening, William Gibbs McAdoo of California quickly launched the bandwagon for Roosevelt by announcing that his state's 44 votes were switching from Garner to the New York governor. Other states followed California's lead, and when the fourth ballot was completed Roosevelt had 945 votes and the nomination. With the Smith vote holding at $190\frac{1}{2}$, no effort was made to make the nomination unanimous.

Although it is not clear whether there was a formal deal struck before the fourth ballot between the Garner and Roosevelt forces, the Texas representative was the unanimous choice of the convention for vice president. Forty states seconded his nomination, and no roll call was taken.

In an effort to break what he described as "absurd traditions," Roosevelt flew from Albany to Chicago to accept the presidential nomination personally. (Previously, a major party candidate would be formally notified of his nomination in a ceremony several weeks after the convention.) In his speech of acceptance, Roosevelt struck a liberal tone and issued his memorable pledge of "a new deal for the American people."

The platform adopted by the convention was not a blueprint for the New Deal to follow. It was fewer than 2,000 words long, the party's shortest platform since 1888, and less than one-fourth as long as the document adopted by the Republicans. It blamed the Depression on the "disastrous policies" practiced by the Republicans but made few new proposals, instead forcefully restating positions that had appeared in earlier party platforms.

The Democrats advocated a balanced budget with a cut of at least 25 percent in federal spending and called for removal of the federal government from competition with private enterprise in all areas except public works and natural resources.

The Democratic platform, unlike its Republican counterpart, advocated extensive unemployment relief and public works projects, regulation of holding companies and securities exchanges, "a competitive tariff for revenue," and the extension of farm cooperatives.

The plank that sparked the most enthusiasm among the delegates was the call for the repeal of Prohibition. A milder plank favored by "dry" delegates was resoundingly defeated, 934¾ to 213¾.

The only measure added from the floor of the convention favored "continuous responsibility of government for human welfare, especially for the protection of children." It was approved by a standing vote.

Following are excerpts from the Democratic platform of 1932:

Government Spending. We advocate an immediate and drastic reduction of governmental expenditures by abolishing useless commissions and offices, consolidating departments and bureaus, and eliminating extravagance to accomplish a saving of not less than twenty-five percent in the cost of the Federal Government. And we call upon the Democratic Party in the states to make a zealous effort to achieve a proportionate result.

We favor maintenance of the national credit by a federal budget annually balanced on the basis of accurate executive estimates within revenues, raised by a system of taxation levied on the principle of ability to pay.

Unemployment Relief, Public Works Projects. We advocate the extension of federal credit to the states to provide unemployment relief wherever the diminishing resources of the states makes it impossible for them to provide for the needy; expansion of the federal program of necessary and useful construction effected with a public interest, such as adequate flood control and waterways.

We advocate the spread of employment by a substantial reduction in the hours of labor, the encouragement of the shorter week by applying that principle in government service; we advocate advance planning of public works.

We advocate unemployment and old-age insurance under state laws.

Prohibition. We advocate the repeal of the Eighteenth Amendment. To effect such repeal we demand that the Congress immediately propose a Constitutional Amendment to truly represent [sic] the conventions in the states called to act solely on that proposal; we urge the enactment of such measures by the several states as will actually promote temperance, effectively prevent the return of the saloon, and bring the liquor traffic into the open under complete supervision and control by the states.

Agriculture. Extension and development of the Farm Cooperative movement and effective control of crop surpluses so that our farmers may have the full benefit of the domestic market.

The enactment of every constitutional measure that will aid the farmers to receive for their basic farm commodities prices in excess of cost.

1936 Conventions

PRESIDENTIAL CANDIDATES

Alfred M. Landon
Republican

Franklin D. Roosevelt
Democrat

William Lemke
Union

REPUBLICANS

The Republican convention, held in Cleveland in early June, was an unusually harmonious gathering for a party out of power. There were only two roll-call votes on the convention floor, for president and vice president, and both were one-sided.

The only matter of debate was the vote allocation for Alaska, Hawaii, and the District of Columbia. By a voice vote, the convention approved the minority report of the rules committee, which sliced the vote for these three from six to three votes apiece.

Former president Herbert Hoover received an enthusiastic reception when he spoke, but by that time Kansas governor Alfred M. Landon had the presidential nomination sewed up. Landon, one of the few Republican governors to be reelected during the Depression, received 984 votes on the first ballot, compared with 19 for Sen. William E. Borah of Idaho. *(Table, p. 220.)*

Before the balloting began, Landon had sent a telegram to the convention that expressed his agreement with the "word and spirit" of the party platform but elaborated his position on several points. The Kansan advocated the passage of a constitutional amendment to ensure women and children safe working conditions and to establish guidelines for wages and hours in the event that legislation passed by Congress was ruled unconstitutional. Landon's message also proposed extending the civil service to include all workers in federal departments and agencies below the rank of assistant secretary, and it defined "sound currency" as currency that could be exchanged for gold. Landon's pronouncements were met with thirty minutes of cheering.

For vice president, the convention selected Col. Frank Knox of Illinois, publisher of the *Chicago Daily News.* Knox, who earlier had campaigned energetically, if not successfully, for the presidential nomination, received all 1,003 votes on the first ballot.

The Republican platform, which began with the sentence, "America is in peril," focused on the alleged threat of New Deal policies to American constitutional government. The platform assailed the Roosevelt administration for "dishonoring American traditions" and promised to protect local self-government and the power of the Supreme Court.

The Republicans promised a balanced budget, reduced federal expenditures, a "sound currency," a more discriminating public works program, and the administration of unemployment relief by "non-political local agencies" that would be financed jointly by the various states and the federal government.

The Republicans shared with the Democrats the belief in an isolationist foreign policy and the concepts of social security, unemployment insurance, and crop control.

Following are excerpts from the Republican platform of 1936:

Roosevelt's "New Deal." America is in peril. The welfare of American men and women and the future of our youth are at stake. We dedicate ourselves to the preservation of their political liberty, their individual opportunity and their character as free citizens, which today for the first time are threatened by Government itself. . . .

The powers of Congress have been usurped by the President.

The integrity and authority of the Supreme Court have been flouted.

The rights and liberties of American citizens have been violated.

Regulated monopoly has displaced free enterprise.

The New Deal Administration constantly seeks to usurp the rights reserved to the States and to the people.

Unemployment Relief. The return of responsibility for relief administration to nonpolitical local agencies familiar with community problems. . . .

Undertaking of Federal public works only on their merits and separate from the administration of relief.

Government Spending, Currency. Balance the budget—not by increasing taxes but by cutting expenditures, drastically and immediately. . . .

We advocate a sound currency to be preserved at all hazards.

The first requisite to a sound and stable currency is a balanced budget.

Foreign Policy. We pledge ourselves to promote and maintain peace by all honorable means not leading to foreign alliances or political commitments.

Obedient to the traditional foreign policy of America and to the repeatedly expressed will of the American people, we pledge that America shall not become a member of the League of Nations nor of the World Court nor shall America take on any entangling alliances in foreign affairs.

DEMOCRATS

The 1936 Democratic convention, held in Philadelphia in late June, was one of the most harmonious in party history. There were no floor debates, and, for the first time since 1840, there were no roll-call votes.

The only matter that required discussion—elimination of the century-old two-thirds rule—was settled in the rules committee. There, by a vote of 36 to 13, the committee agreed to abrogate the rule, which had been a controversial part of Democratic conventions since 1832. To mollify the South, which was particularly threatened by elimination of the two-thirds rule, the rules committee added a provision that would include consideration of a state's Democratic voting strength in determining its future convention vote allocation. The rules committee report was approved by a voice vote.

Both President Franklin D. Roosevelt and Vice President John Nance Garner were renominated by acclamation, but more than a full day of oratory was expended in eulogizing the Democratic standard-bearers. Roosevelt was seconded by delegates from each of the states and territories—more than fifty separate speakers. Seventeen delegates spoke on behalf of Garner.

Both Roosevelt and Garner personally accepted their nominations in ceremonies at the University of Pennsylvania's Franklin Field. Before a crowd estimated as large as 100,000, Roosevelt electrified his listeners with a speech that blasted his adversaries among the rich as "economic royalists" and included the sentence: "This generation of Americans has a rendezvous with destiny."

As in 1932 the platform adopted by the Democrats was a short one, about 3,000 words. The document paid lip service to the concept of a balanced budget and reduced government spending, but it supported continuation of the extensive federal programs undertaken by the Roosevelt administration.

The platform did not, as many in past years had, mention states' rights; this reflected the party's changing view toward federal power. To counter what was viewed as obstructionism by the Supreme Court, the Democrats suggested the possibility of passing a "clarifying amendment" to the Constitution that would enable Congress and state legislatures to enact bills without the fear of an unfavorable decision from the Supreme Court.

The foreign policy plank recognized the isolationist mood of the period, calling for neutrality in foreign disputes and the avoidance of international commitments that would draw the United States into war.

Following are excerpts from the Democratic platform of 1936:

Federal Power. The Republican platform proposes to meet many pressing national problems solely by action of the separate States. We know that drought, dust storms, floods, minimum wages, maximum hours, child labor, and working conditions in industry, monopolistic and unfair business practices cannot be adequately handled exclusively by 48 separate State legislatures, 48 separate State administrations, and 48 separate State courts. Transactions and activities which inevitably overflow State boundaries call for both State and Federal treatment.

We have sought and will continue to seek to meet these problems through legislation within the Constitution.

If these problems cannot be effectively solved by legislation within the Constitution, we shall seek such clarifying amendment as will assure to the legislatures of the several States and to the Congress of the United States, each within its proper jurisdiction, the power to enact those laws which the State and Federal legislatures, within their respective spheres, shall find necessary, in order adequately to regulate commerce, protect public health and safety and safeguard economic security. Thus we propose to maintain the letter and spirit of the Constitution.

Government Spending. We are determined to reduce the expenses of government. We are being aided therein by the recession in unemployment. As the requirements of relief decline and national income advances, an increasing percentage of Federal expenditures can and will be met from current revenues, secured from taxes levied in accordance with ability to pay. Our retrenchment, tax and recovery programs thus reflect our firm determination to achieve a balanced budget and the reduction of the national debt at the earliest possible moment.

Foreign Policy. We reaffirm our opposition to war as an instrument of national policy, and declare that disputes between nations should be settled by peaceful means. We shall continue to observe a true neutrality in the disputes of others; to be prepared resolutely to resist aggression against ourselves; to work for peace and to take the profits out of war; to guard against being drawn, by political commitments, international banking or private trading, into any war which may develop anywhere.

UNION PARTY

With the support of Father Charles E. Coughlin and his National Union for Social Justice, on June 19, 1936, Rep. William Lemke of North Dakota, a Republican, declared his presidential candidacy on the newly formed Union Party ticket. Thomas O'Brien, a Boston railroad union lawyer, was announced as Lemke's running mate. The fledgling political organization had a brief existence, running a national ticket only in the 1936 election.

The Union Party was basically an extension of Coughlin's organization, and the Lemke-O'Brien ticket was endorsed at the National Union for Social Justice convention in August by a vote of 8,152 to 1.

The Union Party platform reportedly was written by Coughlin, Lemke, and O'Brien at the Roman Catholic priest's church in Royal Oak, Michigan. It was a brief document, fewer than 1,000 words, that contained fifteen points similar to the sixteen-point program favored by Coughlin's National Union. The primary distinctions between the Union Party and the two major parties were in currency expansion, civil service reform, and restrictions on wealth. The Union Party called for the creation of a central bank, regulated by Congress, that would issue currency to help pay off the federal debt and refinance agricultural and home mortgage indebtedness. The Union Party platform also proposed extending the civil service to all levels of the federal government and advocated placing restrictions on annual individual income coupled with a ceiling on gifts and inheritances. The new party differed from the Socialists by emphasizing that private property should not be confiscated.

Following are excerpts from the Union Party platform of 1936:

Currency Expansion. Congress and Congress alone shall coin and issue the currency and regulate the value of all money and credit in the United States through a central bank of issue.

Immediately following the establishment of the central bank of issue Congress shall provide for the retirement of all tax-exempt, interest-bearing bonds and certificates of indebtedness of the Federal Government and shall refinance all the present agricultural mortgage indebtedness for the farmer and all the home mortgage indebtedness for the farmer and all the home mortgage indebtedness for the city owner by the use of its money and credit which it now gives to the private bankers.

Civil Service Reform. Congress shall so legislate that all Federal offices and positions of every nature shall be distributed through civil-service qualifications and not through a system of party spoils and corrupt patronage.

Restrictions on Wealth. Congress shall set a limitation upon the net income of any individual in any one year and a limitation of the amount that such an individual may receive as a gift or as an inheritance, which limitation shall be executed through taxation.

Foreign Policy. Congress shall establish an adequate and perfect defense for our country from foreign aggression either by air, by land, or by sea, but with the understanding that our naval, air, and military forces must not be used under any consideration in foreign fields or in foreign waters either alone or in conjunction with any foreign power. If there must be conscription, there shall be a conscription of wealth as well as a conscription of men.

1940 Conventions

PRESIDENTIAL CANDIDATES

Wendell L. Willkie
Republican

Franklin D. Roosevelt
Democrat

REPUBLICANS

The Republican convention was held in Philadelphia in late June, and it culminated one of the most successful of all campaign blitzes. Wendell L. Willkie, an Indiana native who had never before run for public office, was nominated by the Republicans to run for president. A Democrat until 1938, Willkie had gained fame as a defender of private enterprise in opposition to Roosevelt's public power projects. Although Willkie had broad personal appeal, he and his well-financed group of political "amateurs" did not launch their presidential bid until late spring and missed the presidential primaries. Willkie's momentum came from his rapid rise in the Republican preference polls, as he soared from only 3 percent in early May to 29 percent six weeks later.

At the Republican convention, ten names were placed in nomination for the presidency. Willkie's principal rivals were Manhattan District Attorney Thomas E. Dewey, making his first presidential bid at age thirty-eight, and Sen. Robert A. Taft of

Ohio. On the first ballot, Dewey led with 360 votes, followed by Taft with 189, and Willkie with 105. For nomination 501 votes were needed. *(Table, p. 211.)*

After the first roll call, Dewey steadily lost strength, while Willkie and Taft gained. Willkie assumed the lead on the fourth ballot, passing both Dewey and Taft. Willkie's vote was 306, while Taft moved into second place with 254. Dewey dropped to third with 250.

On the fifth ballot, the contest narrowed to just Willkie and Taft, as both candidates continued to gain—Willkie jumping to 429 votes and Taft to 377. The shift of Michigan's votes to Willkie on the sixth ballot started a bandwagon for the Indianan that pushed him over the top. When the roll call was completed, Willkie was nominated with 655 votes, and a motion to make his nomination unanimous was adopted.

As his running mate, Willkie favored Senate minority leader Charles L. McNary of Oregon. McNary, a supporter of some New Deal measures, was opposed by Rep. Dewey Short of Missouri, a vocal anti–New Dealer. McNary, however, was able to win easily on a single ballot, receiving 890 votes to 108 for Short.

The Republican platform was adopted without debate, although an Illinois member of the platform committee commented that his state would have preferred a stronger antiwar plank. As it was, the Republican foreign policy plank sharply criticized the Roosevelt administration for not adequately preparing the nation's defense. However, the rest of the plank was similar to the one adopted three weeks later by the Democrats at the convention: opposing involvement in war but stressing national defense, and advocating aid to the Allies that would not be "inconsistent with the requirements of our own national defense."

In domestic affairs, the Republicans lambasted the extension of federal power under the New Deal and promised cuts in government spending and the reduction of federal competition with private enterprise. The Republican platform agreed with the concept of unemployment relief and Social Security initiated by the Roosevelt administration, but it proposed the administration of these programs by the states and not the federal government.

The Republicans attacked Roosevelt's monetary measures and advocated currency reforms that included congressional control.

The platform also proposed new amendments to the Constitution that would provide equal rights for men and women and would limit a president to two terms in office.

Following are excerpts from the Republican platform of 1940:

Foreign Policy. The Republican Party is firmly opposed to involving this Nation in foreign war. . . .

The Republican Party stands for Americanism, preparedness and peace. We accordingly fasten upon the New Deal full responsibility for our unpreparedness and for the consequent danger of involvement in war. . . .

Our sympathies have been profoundly stirred by invasion of unoffending countries and by disaster to nations whole [whose] ideals most closely resemble our own. We favor the extension to all peoples fighting for liberty, or whose liberty is threatened, of such aid as shall not be in violation of international law or inconsistent with the requirements of our own national defense.

Unemployment Relief. We shall remove waste, discrimination, and politics from relief-through administration by the States with federal grants-in-aid on a fair and nonpolitical basis, thus giving the man and woman on relief a larger share of the funds appropriated.

Currency. The Congress should reclaim its constitutional powers over money, and withdraw the President's arbitrary authority to manipulate the currency, establish bimetallism, issue irredeemable paper money, and debase the gold and silver coinage. We shall repeal the Thomas Inflation Amendment of 1933 and the (foreign) Silver Purchase Act of 1934, and take all possible steps to preserve the value of the Government's huge holdings of gold and reintroduce gold into circulation.

Women's Rights. We favor submission by Congress to the States of an amendment to the Constitution providing for equal rights for men and women.

No Third Term. To insure against the overthrow of our American system of government we favor an amendment to the Constitution providing that no person shall be President of the United States for more than two terms.

DEMOCRATS

At the time of both major party conventions in the summer of 1940, Hitler's forces were moving quickly and relentlessly across western Europe. International events assumed a major importance in political decisions. President Franklin D. Roosevelt, who gave evidence before 1940 that he would not seek a third term, became increasingly receptive to the idea of a draft as the Democratic convention drew nearer. The threat to American security caused by the awesomely successful Nazi military machine, coupled with Roosevelt's inability to find an adequate New Deal–style successor, seemed to spur the president's decision to accept renomination.

The Democratic convention was held in Chicago in mid-July. On the second night of the convention, a message from Roosevelt was read stating that he did not desire to run for re-election and urging the delegates to vote for any candidate they wished. Although worded in a negative way, the message did not shut the door on a draft. The delegates reacted, however, by sitting in stunned silence until a Chicago city official began shouting over the public address system, "We want Roosevelt." The cheerleading galvanized the delegates into an hour-long demonstration.

Presidential balloting was held the next day. Roosevelt won easily on the first roll call, although two members of his administration, Vice President John Nance Garner and Postmaster General James A. Farley of New York, ran against him. Roosevelt received 945$^{13}\!/_{30}$ of the 1,100 votes. Farley had 72⅞ and Garner had 61. *(Table, p. 220.)*

While the delegates were satisfied to have Roosevelt at the top of the ticket again, many balked at his choice for vice president, Agriculture Secretary Henry A. Wallace of Iowa. Wallace, a leading liberal in the administration and a former Republican, was particularly distasteful to conservative Democrats. Many delegates were expecting Roosevelt to leave the vice-presidential choice to the convention and were unhappy to have the candidate dictated to them.

It took a personal appearance at the convention by the president's wife, Eleanor Roosevelt, and a threat by the president that he would not accept the presidential nomination without his handpicked running mate, to steer the delegates toward Wallace. In spite of the pressure by the Roosevelt forces, the vote was scattered among thirteen candidates on the vice-presidential ballot. Wallace, though, was able to obtain a slim majority, 626$^{11}\!/_{30}$ votes to 329⅗ for the runner-up, House Speaker William B. Bankhead of Alabama. Because of the displeasure of many of the delegates, Wallace was asked not to address the convention.

The convention closed by hearing a radio address by Roosevelt, who stated that he had not wanted the nomination but accepted it because the existing world crisis called for personal sacrifice.

The party platform was adopted without a roll call, although there was an amendment presented by a Minnesota representative that opposed any violation of the two-term tradition. It was rejected by a voice vote. The platform as adopted was divided into three sections. The first discussed American military preparedness and foreign policy; the second detailed the New Deal's benefits for various segments of the economy (agriculture, labor, business); the third listed New Deal welfare measures, ranging from unemployment relief to low-cost housing.

As a concession to the party's isolationist wing, the first section contained the administration's promise not to participate in foreign wars or fight in foreign lands, except in case of an attack on the United States. The plank stressed the need of a strong national defense to discourage aggression, but also pledged to provide to free nations (such as Great Britain) material aid "not inconsistent with the interests of our own national self-defense."

An electric power plank was included in the second section of the platform as a direct result of the Republicans' selection of Wendell L. Willkie, a former utilities executive, as their presidential candidate. The Democrats argued in favor of the massive public power projects constructed during the New Deal and criticized private utilities such as the one formerly headed by Willkie.

The third section of the platform drew a sharp distinction from the Republicans on the issue of unemployment relief, opposing any efforts to turn the administration of relief over to the states or local governments.

Following are excerpts from the Democratic platform of 1940:

Democratic Achievements. Toward the modern fulfillment of the American ideal, the Democratic Party, during the last seven years, has labored successfully:

1. To strengthen democracy by defensive preparedness against aggression, whether by open attack or secret infiltration;

2. To strengthen democracy by increasing our economic efficiency; and

3. To strengthen democracy by improving the welfare of the people.

Foreign Policy. We will not participate in foreign wars, and we will not send our army, naval or air forces to fight in foreign lands outside of the Americas, except in case of attack. . . .

Weakness and unpreparedness invite aggression. We must be so strong that no possible combination of powers would dare to attack us. We propose to provide America with an invincible air force, a navy strong enough to protect all our seacoasts and our national interests, and a fully-equipped and mechanized army.

Unemployment Relief. We shall continue to recognize the obligation of Government to provide work for deserving workers who cannot be absorbed by private industry.

We are opposed to vesting in the states and local authorities the control of Federally-financed work relief. We believe that this Republican proposal is a thinly disguised plan to put the unemployed back on the dole.

Electric Power. The nomination of a utility executive by the Republican Party as its presidential candidate raises squarely the issue, whether the nation's water power shall be used for all the people or for the selfish interests of a few. We accept that issue.

1944 Conventions

PRESIDENTIAL CANDIDATES

Thomas E. Dewey
Republican

Franklin D. Roosevelt
Democrat

REPUBLICANS

For the first time since 1864, the nation was at war during a presidential election year. The Republicans held their convention first, meeting in Chicago in late June 1944. With a minimum of discord, the delegates selected a national ticket and adopted a platform. Gov. Thomas E. Dewey of New York, the front-runner for the presidential nomination, was the nearly unanimous selection when his last two rivals, Gov. John W. Bricker of Ohio and former Minnesota governor Harold E. Stassen, both withdrew from the race before the roll call. On the single ballot, Dewey received 1,056 of the 1,057 votes cast. The one dissenting vote was cast by a Wisconsin delegate for Gen. Douglas MacArthur. *(Table, p. 222.)*

As Dewey's running mate, the delegates unanimously selected Gov. Bricker, an isolationist and party regular, who received all 1,057 votes cast. During the nominating speeches, Rep. Charles A. Halleck of Indiana made the unusual move of recommending his state's first choice for vice president, William L. Hutcheson, for secretary of labor.

Dewey came to Chicago personally to accept the nomination, becoming the first Republican presidential candidate to break the tradition of waiting to accept the nomination in a formal notification ceremony. The thrust of Dewey's speech was an attack on the Roosevelt administration, which he referred to as "stubborn men grown old and tired and quarrelsome in office."

The platform was approved without dissent. The international section was written in a guarded tone. It favored "responsible participation by the United States in postwar cooperative organization" but declared that any agreement must be approved by a two-thirds vote of the Senate. The Republicans favored the establishment of a postwar Jewish state in Palestine.

The domestic section of the platform denounced the New Deal's centralization of power in the federal government, with its increased government spending and deficits. The Republicans proposed to stabilize the economy through the encouragement of private enterprise.

The platform restated several of the planks included four years earlier, among which were the call for an equal rights amendment, a two-term limitation on the president and the return of control over currency matters from the president to Congress.

The Republicans adopted a civil rights plank that called for a congressional investigation of the treatment of blacks in the military, passage of a constitutional amendment to eliminate the poll tax, and legislation that would outlaw lynching and permanently establish a Fair Employment Practice Commission.

Following are excerpts from the Republican platform of 1944:

Postwar International Organization. We favor responsible participation by the United States in post-war cooperative organization among sovereign nations to prevent military aggression and to attain permanent peace with organized justice in a free world.

Such organization should develop effective cooperative means to direct peace forces to prevent or repel military aggression. Pending this, we pledge continuing collaboration with the United Nations to assure these ultimate objectives. . . .

We shall sustain the Constitution of the United States in the attainment of our international aims; and pursuant to the Constitution of the United States any treaty or agreement to attain such aims made on behalf of the United States with any other nation or any association of nations, shall be made only by and with the advice and consent of the Senate of the United States provided two-thirds of the Senators present concur.

Israel. In order to give refuge to millions of distressed Jewish men, women and children driven from their homes by tyranny, we call for the opening of Palestine to their unrestricted immigration and land ownership, so that in accordance with the full intent and purpose of the Balfour Declaration of 1917 and the Resolution of a Republican Congress in 1922, Palestine may be constituted as a free and democratic Commonwealth. We condemn the failure of the President to insist that the mandatory of Palestine carry out the provision of the Balfour Declaration and of the mandate while he pretends to support them.

New Deal. Four more years of New Deal policy would centralize all power in the President, and would daily subject every act of every citizen to regulation by his henchmen; and this country could remain a Republic only in name. No problem exists which cannot be solved by American methods. We have no need of either the communistic or the fascist technique.

. . . The National Administration has become a sprawling, overlapping bureaucracy. It is undermined by executive abuse of power, confused lines of authority, duplication of effort, inadequate fiscal controls, loose personnel practices and an attitude of arrogance previously unknown in our history.

Economy. We reject the theory of restoring prosperity through government spending and deficit financing.

We shall promote the fullest stable employment through private enterprise.

Civil Rights. We pledge an immediate Congressional inquiry to ascertain the extent to which mistreatment, segregation and discrimination against Negroes who are in our armed forces are impairing morale and efficiency, and the adoption of corrective legislation.

We pledge the establishment by Federal legislation of a permanent Fair Employment Practice Commission.

The payment of any poll tax should not be a condition of voting in Federal elections and we favor immediate submission of a Constitutional amendment for its abolition.

We favor legislation against lynching and pledge our sincere efforts in behalf of its early enactment.

Agriculture. An American market price to the American farmer and the protection of such price by means of support prices, commodity loans, or a combination thereof, together with such other economic means as will assure an income to agriculture that is fair and equitable in comparison with labor, business and industry. We oppose subsidies as a substitute for fair markets.

Serious study of and search for a sound program of crop insurance with emphasis upon establishing a serf-supporting program.

DEMOCRATS

President Franklin D. Roosevelt, who four years earlier did not make a final decision about accepting a third nomination until the last moment, clearly stated his intention to run for a fourth term a week before the 1944 convention was to open in Chicago. In a message to Democratic National Chairman Robert E. Hannegan of Missouri released July 11, Roosevelt declared that while he did not desire to run, he would accept renomination reluctantly as a "good soldier."

The early sessions of the convention were highlighted by approval of the rules committee report and settlement of a credentials challenge. The rules committee mandated the national committee to revamp the convention's vote-allocation formula in a way that would take into account Democratic voting strength. This measure was adopted to appease southern delegates, who in 1936 were promised an increased proportion of the convention vote in return for elimination of the two-thirds rule. No action had been taken to implement the pledge in the intervening eight years.

The credentials dispute involved the Texas delegation, which was represented by two competing groups. By a voice vote, the convention agreed to seat both groups.

Vice President Henry A. Wallace enlivened the presidential nominations by appearing before the convention to urge

Roosevelt's renomination. Wallace termed the president the "greatest liberal in the history of the U.S." In the balloting that followed, Roosevelt easily defeated Sen. Harry F. Byrd of Virginia, who was supported by some conservative southern delegates unhappy with the domestic legislation favored by the New Deal. The final tally: Roosevelt, 1,086; Byrd, 89; former postmaster general James A. Farley, 1. *(Table, p. 222.)*

Roosevelt accepted the nomination in a radio address delivered from the San Diego Naval Base, where he had stopped off en route to a wartime conference.

The real drama of the convention, the selection of the vice-presidential nominee, came next. Roosevelt had been ambivalent about the choice of his running mate, encouraging several people to run but not publicly endorsing any of them. The president wrote an ambiguous letter to the convention chairman, which was read to the delegates. Roosevelt stated that if he were a delegate himself he would vote for Wallace's renomination, but that the ultimate choice was the convention's and it must consider the pros and cons of its selection.

In another message, written privately for National Chairman Hannegan, Roosevelt declared that he would be happy to run with either Missouri senator Harry S. Truman or Supreme Court justice William O. Douglas. Most of the party bosses preferred Truman to the more liberal alternatives, Wallace and Douglas. Truman originally was slated to nominate former South Carolina senator and Supreme Court justice James F. Byrnes for vice president. But, spurred by his political advisers, Roosevelt telephoned Truman in Chicago and urged him to accept the nomination. Truman reluctantly agreed.

Roosevelt's final preference for Truman was not publicly announced, and twelve names were placed before the convention. Wallace led on the first roll call with 429½ votes, followed by Truman with 319½. Favorite sons and other hopefuls shared the remaining votes cast.

Truman passed Wallace on the second ballot, 477½ to 473, and, immediately after completion of the roll call, Alabama began the bandwagon for the Missouri senator by switching its votes to him. When all the shifts had been made, Truman was an easy winner with 1,031 votes, while Wallace finished with 105.

The platform adopted by the convention was a short one, only 1,360 words. The first third of the platform lauded the accomplishments of Roosevelt's first three terms. The rest of the document outlined the party's proposals for the future. In foreign affairs, the Democrats advocated the creation of a postwar international organization that would have adequate forces available to prevent future wars. The party also called for U.S. membership in an international court of justice. The Democrats joined their Republican opponents in favoring the establishment of an independent Jewish state in Palestine.

The domestic section of the platform proposed a continuation of New Deal liberalism, with passage of an equal rights amendment for women, price guarantees and crop insurance for farmers, and the establishment of federal aid to education that would be administered by the states.

A minority report concerning foreign policy called for the establishment of an international air force to help keep peace. The proposal was rejected, however, when the platform committee chairman indicated that the existence of an air force was included in the majority report's call for "adequate forces" to be at the disposal of the proposed international organization.

Following are excerpts from the Democratic platform of 1944:

Postwar International Organizations. That the world may not again be drenched in blood by international outlaws and criminals, we pledge:

To join with the other United Nations in the establishment of an international organization based on the principle of the sovereign equality of all peace-loving states, open to membership by all such states, large and small, for the prevention of aggression and the maintenance of international peace and security.

To make all necessary and effective agreements and arrangements through which the nations would maintain adequate forces to meet the needs of preventing war and of making impossible the preparation for war and which would have such forces available for joint action when necessary.

Such organization must be endowed with power to employ armed forces when necessary to prevent aggression and preserve peace.

Israel. We favor the opening of Palestine to unrestricted Jewish immigration and colonization, and such a policy as to result in the establishment there of a free and democratic Jewish commonwealth.

Women's Rights. We favor legislation assuring equal pay for equal work, regardless of sex.

We recommend to Congress the submission of a Constitutional amendment on equal rights for women.

Education. We favor Federal aid to education administered by the states without interference by the Federal Government.

Agriculture. Price guarantees and crop insurance to farmers with all practical steps:

To keep agriculture on a parity with industry and labor.

To foster the success of the small independent farmer.

To aid the home ownership of family-sized farms.

To extend rural electrification and develop broader domestic and foreign markets for agricultural products.

Civil Rights. We believe that racial and religious minorities have the right to live, develop and vote equally with all citizens and share the rights that are guaranteed by our Constitution. Congress should exert its full constitutional powers to protect those rights.

1948 Conventions

PRESIDENTIAL CANDIDATES

Thomas E. Dewey
Republican

Harry S. Truman
Democrat

J. Strom Thurmond
States' Rights

Henry A. Wallace
Progressive

REPUBLICANS

The Republican convention was held in Philadelphia in late June. As in 1944, New York governor Thomas E. Dewey entered the convention as the front-runner for the nomination. But unlike four years earlier, when he was virtually handed the nomination, Dewey was contested by several candidates, including Sen. Robert A. Taft of Ohio and former Minnesota governor Harold E. Stassen.

In all, seven names were placed in nomination, with 548 votes needed to determine a winner. Dewey led on the first roll call with 434 votes, followed by Taft with 224 and Stassen with 157. Each of the other candidates received fewer than 100 votes. (*Table, p. 223.*)

On the second roll call, Dewey moved closer to the nomination, receiving 515 votes. Taft and Stassen continued to trail, with 274 and 149 votes respectively. At this point, the anti-Dewey forces requested a recess, which was agreed to by the confident Dewey organization.

Unable to form a coalition that could stop Dewey, all his opponents withdrew before the third ballot. On the subsequent roll call, the New York governor was the unanimous choice of the convention, receiving all 1,094 votes.

Dewey's choice for vice president was California governor Earl Warren, who was nominated by acclamation. Warren had been a favorite-son candidate for the presidency and agreed to take second place on the ticket only after receiving assurances that the responsibilities of the vice presidency would be increased if Dewey were elected.

The Republican platform was adopted without dissent. The wording of the platform was unusually positive for a party out of the White House. The failures of the Truman administration were dismissed in a short paragraph, with the rest of the document praising the accomplishments of the Republican 80th Congress and detailing the party's proposals for the future.

One of the major issues of the 1948 campaign was the controversial Taft-Hartley labor law, a measure supported by the Republicans, but which most Democratic leaders felt should be repealed. The Republicans were silent on national health insurance, and the party's housing position stressed private initiative rather than federal legislation. As in 1944 the Republicans opposed the poll tax and segregation in the military and favored legislation to outlaw lynching.

The Republican platform accepted the concept of a bipartisan foreign policy. Paragraphs were inserted that supported the Marshall Plan for European recovery, the United Nations and recognition of Israel.

Following are excerpts from the Republican platform of 1948:

Civil Rights. This right of equal opportunity to work and to advance in life should never be limited in any individual because of race, religion, color, or country of origin. We favor the enactment and just enforcement of such Federal legislation as may be necessary to maintain this right at all times in every part of this Republic. . . .

Lynching or any other form of mob violence anywhere is a disgrace to any civilized state, and we favor the prompt enactment of legislation to end this infamy. . . .

We favor the abolition of the poll tax as a requisite to voting.

We are opposed to the idea of racial segregation in the armed services of the United States.

Housing. Housing can best be supplied and financed by private enterprise; but government can and should encourage the building of better homes at less cost. We recommend Federal aid to the States for local slum clearance and low-rental housing programs only where there is a need that cannot be met either by private enterprise or by the States and localities.

Labor. Here are some of the accomplishments of this Republican Congress: a sensible reform of the labor law, protecting all rights of Labor while safeguarding the entire community, against those breakdowns in essential industries which endanger the health and livelihood of all. . . .

We pledge continuing study to improve labor-management legislation in the light of experience and changing conditions. . . .

We favor equal pay for equal work regardless of sex.

Internal Security. We pledge a vigorous enforcement of existing laws against Communists and enactment of such new legislation as may be necessary to expose the treasonable activities of Communists and defeat their objective of establishing here a godless dictatorship controlled from abroad.

Foreign Policy. We are proud of the part that Republicans have taken in those limited areas of foreign policy in which they have been permitted to participate. We shall invite the Minority Party to join us under the next Republican Administration in stopping partisan politics at the water's edge.

United Nations. We believe in collective security against aggression and in behalf of justice and freedom. We shall support the United Nations as the world's best hope in this direction, striving to strengthen it and promote its effective evolution and use. The United Nations should progressively establish international law, be freed of any veto in the peaceful settlement of international disputes, and be provided with the armed forces contemplated by the Charter.

Israel. We welcome Israel into the family of nations and take pride in the fact that the Republican Party was the first to call for the establishment of a free and independent Jewish Commonwealth.

DEMOCRATS

The Democratic delegates were in a melancholy mood when they gathered in Philadelphia in mid-July 1948. Franklin D. Roosevelt was dead; the Republicans had regained control of Congress in 1947; Roosevelt's successor, Harry S. Truman, appeared unable to stem massive defections of liberals and southern conservatives from the New Deal coalition.

The dissatisfaction of southern delegates with policies of the national party was a prominent feature of the 1948 convention. Although the national committee had been mandated by the 1944 convention to devise a new vote-allocation procedure that would appease the South, the redistribution of votes for the 1948 convention merely added two votes to each of the thirty-six states that backed Roosevelt in the 1944 election. This did not appreciably bolster southern strength.

As the convention progressed, southern displeasure focused on the civil rights issue. The Mississippi delegation included in its credentials resolutions against civil rights that bound the delegation to bolt the convention if a states' rights plank was not included in the platform. The Mississippi resolutions also denied the power of the national convention to require the Democratic Party of Mississippi to support any candidate who favored President Truman's civil rights program or any candidate who failed to denounce that program.

A minority report was introduced that recommended the Mississippi delegation not be seated. This proposal was defeated by a voice vote, and, in the interest of party harmony, no roll-call vote was taken. However, in an unusual move, several delegations, including those of California and New York, asked that they be recorded in favor of the minority report.

Joined by several other southern states, Texas presented a minority proposal to the rules committee report, which favored reestablishment of the two-thirds rule. The minority proposal, however, was beaten by a voice vote.

When the presidential balloting began, the entire Mississippi delegation and thirteen members of the Alabama delegation withdrew in opposition to the convention's stand on civil rights. However, their withdrawal in no way jeopardized the nomination of Truman. Some party leaders had earlier flirted with the possibility of drafting Gen. Dwight D. Eisenhower or even Supreme Court justice William O. Douglas. But the lack of interest of these two men in the Democratic nomination left the field clear for Truman.

The incumbent won a clear majority on the first ballot, receiving 926 votes to 266 for Georgia senator Richard B. Russell, who received the votes of more than 90 percent of the remaining southern delegates. Among the states of the Old Confederacy, Truman received only 13 votes, all from North Carolina. After several small vote switches, the final tally stood: Truman, 947½; Russell, 263. (*Table, p. 224.*)

Veteran Kentucky senator Alben W. Barkley, the convention's keynoter, was nominated by acclamation for vice president.

Truman appeared before the convention to accept the nomination and aroused the dispirited delegates with a lively speech attacking the Republican Congress. Referring to it as the "worst 80th Congress," Truman announced that he would call a special session so that the Republicans could pass the legislation they said they favored in their platform.

The Democratic platform was adopted by a voice vote, after a heated discussion of the civil rights section. As presented to the convention by the platform committee, the plank favored equal rights for all citizens but was couched in generalities such as those in the 1944 plank. Southern delegates wanted a weaker commitment to civil rights, and various southern delegations offered three different amendments.

One, presented by former governor Dan Moody of Texas and signed by fifteen members of the platform committee, was a broadly worded statement that emphasized the power of the states. A second amendment, sponsored by two Tennessee members of the platform committee, was a brief, emphatic statement declaring the rights of the states. The third amendment, introduced by the Mississippi delegation as a substitute for the Moody amendment, specifically listed the powers of the states to maintain segregation. The Moody amendment was beaten, 924 to 310, with nearly all the support limited to the South. The other two amendments were rejected by voice vote. (*Table, p. 224.*)

Northern liberals countered by proposing to strengthen the civil rights plank. Introduced by former representative Andrew J. Biemiller of Wisconsin and championed by Mayor Hubert H. Humphrey of Minneapolis, the amendment commended Truman's civil rights program and called for congressional action to guarantee equal rights in voting participation, employment opportunity, personal security, and military service. The Biemiller amendment was passed, 651½ to 582½, with delegations from the larger northern states supporting it. Delegations from the South were in solid opposition and were joined by delegates from border and small northern states. (*Table, p. 224.*)

The rest of the platform lauded Truman's legislative program and blamed the Republican Congress for obstructing beneficial legislation. In the New Deal tradition, the platform advocated the extension of Social Security, raising of the minimum wage, establishment of national health insurance, and the creation of a permanent flexible price support system for farmers. Congress was blamed for obstructing passage of federal aid to education, comprehensive housing legislation, and funding for the Marshall Plan to help rebuild Europe. The Republicans were also criticized for crippling reciprocal trade agreements, passage of the Taft-Hartley Act, and even the rising rate of inflation.

The development of the cold war with the communist world produced a new issue, internal security, on which the two major parties differed sharply. While the Republican position stressed the pursuit of subversives, the Democrats placed more emphasis on the protection of individual rights.

In foreign affairs, the Democratic platform called for the establishment of a United Nations military force, international control of the atomic bomb, and recognition of the state of Israel.

Following are excerpts from the Democratic platform of 1948:

Civil Rights. We highly commend President Harry S Truman for his courageous stand on the issue of civil rights.

We call upon the Congress to support our President in guaranteeing these basic and fundamental American Principles: (1) the right of full and equal political participation; (2) the right to equal opportunity of employment; (3) the right of security of person; (4) and the right of equal treatment in the service and defense of our nation.

Housing. We shall enact comprehensive housing legislation, including provisions for slum clearance and low-rent housing projects initiated by local agencies. This nation is shamed by the failure of the Republican 80th Congress to pass the vitally needed general housing legislation as recommended by the President. Adequate housing will end the need for rent control. Until then, it must be continued.

Social Security, Health Insurance. We favor the extension of the Social Security program established under Democratic leadership, to provide additional protection against the hazards of old age, disability, disease or death. We believe that this program should include:

Increases in old-age and survivors' insurance benefits by at least 50 percent, and reduction of the eligibility age for women from 65 to 60 years; extension of old-age and survivors' and unemployment insurance to all workers not now covered; insurance against loss of earnings on account of illness or disability; improved public assistance for the needy.

Labor. We advocate the repeal of the Taft-Hartley Act. It was enacted by the Republican 80th Congress over the President's veto. . . .

We favor the extension of the coverage of the Fair Labor Standards Act as recommended by President Truman, and the adoption of a minimum wage of at least 75 cents an hour in place of the present obsolete and inadequate minimum of 40 cents an hour.

We favor legislation assuring that the workers of our nation receive equal pay for equal work, regardless of sex.

United Nations. We will continue to lead the way toward curtailment of the use of the veto. We shall favor such amendments and modifications of the charter as experience may justify. We will continue our efforts toward the establishment of an international armed force to aid its authority. We advocate the grant of a loan to the United Nations recommended by the President, but denied by the Republican Congress, for the construction of the United Nations headquarters in this country.

Disarmament. We advocate the effective international control of weapons of mass destruction, including the atomic bomb, and we approve continued and vigorous efforts within the United Nations to

bring about the successful consummation of the proposals which our Government has advanced.

Israel. We pledge full recognition to the State of Israel. We affirm our pride that the United States under the leadership of President Truman played a leading role in the adoption of the resolution of November 29, 1947, by the United Nations General Assembly for the creation of a Jewish State.

Internal Security. We shall continue vigorously to enforce the laws against subversive activities, observing at all times the constitutional guarantees which protect free speech, the free press and honest political activity. We shall strengthen our laws against subversion to the full extent necessary, protecting at all times our traditional individual freedoms.

STATES' RIGHTS (DIXIECRATS)

Provoked by the Democratic convention's adoption of a strong civil rights plank, Gov. Fielding L. Wright of Mississippi invited other southern Democrats to meet in Birmingham, Ala., on July 17 to select a regional ticket that would reflect southern views.

It was a disgruntled group that gathered in Birmingham, just three days after the close of the Democratic convention. Placards on the floor of the convention hall identified thirteen states, yet there were no delegates from Georgia, Kentucky, or North Carolina, and Virginia was represented by four University of Virginia students and an Alexandria woman who was returning home from a trip south. Most major southern politicians shied away from the bolters, fearing that involvement would jeopardize their standing with the national party and their seniority in Congress.

Former Alabama governor Frank M. Dixon with a keynote address vocalized the mood of the convention by charging that Truman's civil rights program would "reduce us to the status of a mongrel, inferior race, mixed in blood, our Anglo-Saxon heritage a mockery."

As its standard-bearers, the convention chose Gov. J. Strom Thurmond of South Carolina for president and Gov. Wright for vice president. Thurmond's acceptance speech touched on another grievance of bolting southern Democrats: their decreasing power within the Democratic Party. Thurmond warned: "If the South should vote for Truman this year, we might just as well petition the Government to give us a colonial status."

The platform adopted by the Dixiecrats was barely 1,000 words long, but it forcefully presented the case for states' rights. The platform warned that the tendency toward greater federal power ultimately would establish a totalitarian police state.

The Dixiecrats saved their most vitriolic passages to describe the civil rights plank adopted by the Democratic convention. They declared their support for segregation and charged that the plank adopted by the Democrats was meant "to embarrass and humiliate the South."

The platform also charged the national Democratic Party with ingratitude, claiming that the South had supported the Democratic ticket with "clock-like regularity" for nearly 100 years, but that now the national party was being dominated by states controlled by the Republicans.

Following are excerpts from the States' Rights platform of 1948:

States' Rights. We believe that the protection of the American people against the onward march of totalitarian government requires a faithful observance of Article X of the American Bill of Rights which provides that: "The powers not delegated to the United States by the Constitution, nor prohibited by it to the states, are reserved to the states respectively, or to the people."

Civil Rights. We stand for the segregation of the races and the racial integrity of each race; the constitutional right to choose one's associates; to accept private employment without governmental interference, and to earn one's living in any lawful way. We oppose the elimination of segregation employment by Federal bureaucrats called for by the misnamed civil rights program. We favor home rule, local self-government, and a minimum interference with individual rights.

We oppose and condemn the action of the Democratic convention in sponsoring a civil rights program calling for the elimination of segregation, social equality by Federal fiat, regulation of private employment practices, voting and local law enforcement.

We affirm that the effective enforcement of such a program would be utterly destructive of the social, economic and political life of the Southern people, and of other localities in which there may be differences in race, creed or national origin in appreciable numbers.

PROGRESSIVES

On December 29, 1947, former vice president Henry A. Wallace announced his presidential candidacy at the head of a new liberal party. Officially named the Progressive Party at its convention in Philadelphia in late July 1948, the new party was composed of some liberal Democrats as well as more radical groups and individuals that included some communists.

Nearly 3,200 delegates nominated Wallace for the presidency and Democratic senator Glen H. Taylor of Idaho as his running mate. The colorful Taylor and his family regaled the delegates with their rendition of "When You Were Sweet Sixteen."

On the final night of the convention, 32,000 spectators assembled to hear Wallace deliver his acceptance speech at Shibe Park. The Progressive standard-bearer expressed his belief in "progressive capitalism," which would place "human rights above property rights," and envisioned "a new frontier. . . . across the wilderness of poverty and sickness."

Former Roosevelt associate Rexford G. Tugwell chaired the seventy-four-member platform committee that drafted a detailed platform, about 9,000 words in length, that was adopted by the convention. The platform denounced the two major parties as champions of big business and claimed the new party to be the true "political heirs of Jefferson, Jackson and Lincoln." However, many political observers and opponents of the Progressives dismissed the new party as a Communist-front organization.

Although numerous positions taken by the Progressives in 1948 were considered radical, many were later adopted or seriously considered by the major parties.

The foreign policy plank advocated negotiations between the United States and the Soviet Union ultimately leading to a peace agreement, and it sharply criticized the "anti-Soviet hysteria" of the period. The platform called for repeal of the draft, repudiation of the Marshall Plan, worldwide disarmament featuring abolition of the atomic bomb, amnesty for conscientious objectors imprisoned in World War II, recognition and aid to Israel, extension of United Nations humanitarian programs, and the establishment of a world legislature.

In the domestic area, the Progressives opposed internal security legislation, advocated the eighteen-year-old vote, favored the creation of a Department of Culture, called for food stamp and school hot lunch programs, and proposed a federal housing plan that would build 25 million homes in ten years and subsidize low-income housing.

The Progressives also reiterated the proposals of earlier third parties by favoring the direct election of the president and vice president, extensive tax reform, stricter control of monopolies, and the nationalization of the principal means of communication, transportation, and finance.

The Progressives joined the Democrats and Republicans in proposing strong civil rights legislation and an equal rights amendment for women.

Following are excerpts from the Progressive platform of 1948:

Soviet Union. The Progressive Party . . . demands negotiation and discussion with the Soviet Union to find areas of agreement to win the peace.

Disarmament. The Progressive Party will work through the United Nations for a world disarmament agreement to outlaw the atomic bomb, bacteriological warfare, and all other instruments of mass destruction; to destroy existing stockpiles of atomic bombs and to establish United Nations controls, including inspection, over the production of atomic energy; and to reduce conventional armaments drastically in accordance with resolutions already passed by the United Nations General Assembly.

World Legislation. The only ultimate alternative to war is the abandonment of the principle of the coercion of sovereignties by sovereignties and the adoption of the principle of the just enforcement upon individuals of world federal law, enacted by a world federal legislature with limited but adequate powers to safeguard the common defense and the general welfare of all mankind.

Draft. The Progressive Party calls for the repeal of the peacetime draft and the rejection of Universal Military Training.

Amnesty. We demand amnesty for conscientious objectors imprisoned in World War II.

Internal Security. We denounce anti-Soviet hysteria as a mask for monopoly, militarism, and reaction. . . .

The Progressive Party will fight for the constitutional rights of Communists and all other political groups to express their views as the first line in the defense of the liberties of a democratic people.

Civil Rights. The Progressive Party condemns segregation and discrimination in all its forms and in all places. . . .

We call for a Presidential proclamation ending segregation and all forms of discrimination in the armed services and Federal employment.

We demand Federal anti-lynch, anti-discrimination, and fair-employment-practices legislation, and legislation abolishing segregation in interstate travel.

We call for immediate passage of anti–poll tax legislation, enactment of a universal suffrage law to permit all citizens to vote in Federal elections, and the full use of Federal enforcement powers to assure free exercise of the right to franchise.

Food Stamps, School Lunches. We also call for assistance to low-income consumers through such programs as the food stamp plan and the school hot-lunch program.

Housing. We pledge an attack on the chronic housing shortage and the slums through a long-range program to build 25 million new homes during the next ten years. This program will include public subsidized housing for low-income families.

Nationalization. As a first step, the largest banks, the railroads, the merchant marine, the electric power and gas industry, and industries primarily dependent on government funds or government purchases such as the aircraft, the synthetic rubber and synthetic oil industries must be placed under public ownership.

Youth Vote. We call for the right to vote at eighteen.

1952 Conventions

PRESIDENTIAL CANDIDATES

Dwight D. Eisenhower
Republican

Adlai E. Stevenson
Democrat

REPUBLICANS

For the third straight time, both major parties held their conventions in the same city. In 1952 the site was Chicago; the Republicans met there in early July two weeks before the Democrats. The battle for the presidential nomination pitted the hero of the party's conservative wing, Sen. Robert A. Taft of Ohio, against the favorite of most moderate and liberal Republicans, Gen. Dwight D. Eisenhower. The general, a Texas native, had resigned as supreme commander of the North Atlantic Treaty Organization (NATO) less than six weeks before the convention to pursue the nomination actively.

As in 1912, when Taft's father had engaged in a bitter struggle with Theodore Roosevelt for the nomination, the outcome of the presidential race was determined in preliminary battles over convention rules and credentials.

The first confrontation came on the issue of the voting rights of challenged delegates. The Taft forces proposed adoption of the 1948 rules, which would have allowed contested delegates to vote on all credentials challenges except their own. The Eisenhower forces countered by proposing what they called a "fair play amendment," which would seat only those contested delegates who were approved by at least a two-thirds vote of the national committee. At stake were a total of sixty-eight delegates from Georgia, Louisiana, and Texas, with the large majority of the challenged delegates in favor of Taft. The Taft forces introduced a substitute to the "fair play amendment," designed to

exempt seven delegates from Louisiana. On the first test of strength between the two candidates, the Eisenhower forces were victorious, as the substitute amendment was defeated, 658 to 548. The "fair play amendment" was subsequently approved by a voice vote. (*Table, p. 225.*)

The second confrontation developed with the report of the credentials committee. The Eisenhower forces presented a minority report concerning the contested Georgia, Louisiana, and Texas seats. After a bitter debate, a roll-call vote was taken on the Georgia challenge, with the Eisenhower forces winning again, 607 to 531.

The Louisiana and Texas challenges were settled in favor of the Eisenhower forces without a roll-call vote. The favorable settlement of the credentials challenges increased the momentum behind the Eisenhower candidacy.

Before the presidential balloting began, a nonpartisan debate was held on a proposal to add state chairmen to the national committee from states recording Republican electoral majorities and to remove the requirement that women hold one of each state's seats on the national committee. The proposal was primarily intended to decrease southern influence on the national committee. But the major opposition was raised by a number of women delegates who objected to the rule change; however, their effort to defeat it was rejected by voice vote.

Five men were nominated for the presidency, but on completion of the first roll call Eisenhower had 595 votes and was within nine votes of victory. Taft was a strong second with 500 votes. However, before a second ballot could begin, Minnesota switched 19 votes from favorite son Harold E. Stassen to Eisenhower, giving the latter the nomination. After a series of vote changes, the final tally stood: Eisenhower, 845; Taft, 280; other candidates, 81. The general's nomination was subsequently made unanimous.

Eisenhower's choice as a running mate, thirty-nine-year-old senator Richard Nixon of California, was nominated by acclamation. Eisenhower promised in his acceptance speech to lead a "crusade" against "a party too long in power."

The 6,000-word platform was adopted by a voice vote. The document included a sharp attack on the Democrats, charging the Roosevelt and Truman administrations with "violating our liberties . . . by seizing powers never granted," "shielding traitors" and attempting to establish "national socialism." The foreign policy section, written by John Foster Dulles, supported the concept of collective security but denounced the Truman policy of containment and blamed the administration for the communist takeover of China. The Republican platform advocated increased national preparedness.

As well as castigating the Democrats for an incompetent foreign policy, the Republicans denounced their opposition for laxness in maintaining internal security. A plank asserted: "There are no Communists in the Republican Party."

On most domestic issues the platform advocated a reduction in federal power. The civil rights plank proposed federal action to outlaw lynching, poll taxes, and discriminatory employment practices. However, unlike the plank four years earlier, the Republican position included a paragraph that declared the individual states had primary responsibility for their domestic institutions. On a related issue of states' rights, the Republicans, as in 1948, favored state control of tideland resources.

Following are excerpts from the Republican platform of 1952:

Democratic Failures. We charge that they have arrogantly deprived our citizens of precious liberties by seizing powers never granted.

We charge that they work unceasingly to achieve their goal of national socialism. . . .

We charge that they have shielded traitors to the Nation in high places, and that they have created enemies abroad where we should have friends.

We charge that they have violated our liberties by turning loose upon the country a swarm of arrogant bureaucrats and their agents who meddle intolerably in the lives and occupations of our citizens.

We charge that there has been corruption in high places, and that examples of dishonesty and dishonor have shamed the moral standards of the American people.

We charge that they have plunged us into war in Korea without the consent of our citizens through their authorized representatives in the Congress, and have carried on the war without will to victory. . . .

Tehran, Yalta and Potsdam were the scenes of those tragic blunders with others to follow. The leaders of the Administration in power acted without the knowledge or consent of Congress or of the American people. They traded our overwhelming victory for a new enemy and for new oppressions and new wars which were quick to come.

. . . And finally they denied the military aid that had been authorized by Congress and which was crucially needed if China were to be saved. Thus they substituted on our Pacific flank a murderous enemy for an ally and friend.

Internal Security. By the Administration's appeasement of Communism at home and abroad it has permitted Communists and their fellow travelers to serve in many key agencies and to infiltrate our American life. . . .

There are no Communists in the Republican Party. We have always recognized Communism to be a world conspiracy against freedom and religion. We never compromised with Communism and we have fought to expose it and to eliminate it in government and American life.

Civil Rights. We believe that it is the primary responsibility of each State to order and control its own domestic institutions, and this power, reserved to the states, is essential to the maintenance of our Federal Republic. However, we believe that the Federal Government should take supplemental action within its constitutional jurisdiction to oppose discrimination against race, religion or national origin.

We will prove our good faith by:

Appointing qualified persons, without distinction of race, religion or national origin, to responsible positions in the Government.

Federal action toward the elimination of lynching.

Federal action toward the elimination of poll taxes as a prerequisite to voting.

Appropriate action to end segregation in the District of Columbia.

Enacting Federal legislation to further just and equitable treatment in the area of discriminatory employment practices. Federal action should not duplicate state efforts to end such practices; should not set up another huge bureaucracy.

Labor. We favor the retention of the Taft-Hartley Act.

. . . We urge the adoption of such amendments to the Taft-Hartley Act as time and experience show to be desirable, and which further protect the rights of labor, management and the public.

DEMOCRATS

The Democrats held their 1952 convention in Chicago in late July. The convention lasted six days, the longest by either party in the post–World War II years. The proceedings were enlivened by disputes over credentials and a party loyalty pledge and a wide-open race for the presidential nomination.

The legitimately selected Texas delegation, dominated by the Dixiecrat wing of the state party, was challenged by a delegation loyal to the national party, but chosen in a rump assembly. Without a roll-call vote, the convention approved the credentials of the Dixiecrat-oriented delegates, although their seating was protested by Northern liberals.

The Dixiecrat bolt of 1948 resulted in the introduction of a party loyalty pledge at the 1952 convention. The resolution, introduced by Sen. Blair Moody of Michigan, proposed that no delegates be seated who would not assure the credentials committee that they would work to have the Democratic national ticket placed on the ballot in their state under the party's name. This resolution was aimed at several southern states that had listed the Thurmond-Wright ticket under the Democratic Party label on their state ballots in 1948.

Sen. Spessard L. Holland of Florida introduced a substitute resolution that simply declared it would be "honorable" for each delegate to adhere to the decisions reached in the convention. Holland's resolution, however, was defeated and Moody's was approved, both by voice votes.

The report of the credentials committee listed three southern states—Louisiana, South Carolina, and Virginia—that declined to abide by the Moody resolution. The question of their seating rights came to a head during the roll call for presidential nominations, when Virginia questioned its own status in the convention. A motion to seat the Virginia delegation in spite of its nonobservance of the resolution was presented for a vote. Although not agreeing to the pledge, the chairman of the Virginia delegation indicated that the problem prompting the Moody resolution was covered by state law. After a long, confusing roll call, interrupted frequently by demands to poll individual delegates, the motion to seat the Virginia delegation passed, 650½ to 518. (*Table, p. 226.*)

After efforts to adjourn were defeated, the Louisiana and South Carolina delegations offered assurances similar to those presented by Virginia and were seated by a voice vote.

Eleven names were placed in nomination for the presidency, although the favorite of most party leaders, Illinois governor Adlai E. Stevenson, was a reluctant candidate. Stevenson expressed interest only in running for reelection as governor, but a draft-Stevenson movement developed and gained strength quickly as the convention proceeded.

Sen. Estes Kefauver of Tennessee, a powerful vote-getter in the primaries, was the leader on the first ballot, with 340 votes. He was followed by Stevenson with 273; Sen. Richard B. Russell of Georgia, the southern favorite, with 268; and W. Averell Harriman of New York with 123½.

The second ballot saw gains by the three front-runners, with Kefauver's vote rising to 362½, Stevenson's to 324½, and Russell's to 294. A recess was taken during which Harriman and Massachusetts' favorite son, Gov. Paul A. Dever, both withdrew in favor of Stevenson.

The Illinois governor won a narrow majority on the third ballot, receiving 617½ of the 1,230 convention votes. Kefauver finished with 275½ and Russell with 261. The selection of Stevenson represented the first success for a presidential draft movement of a reluctant candidate since the nomination of James A. Garfield by the Republicans in 1880. (*Table, p. 226.*)

For vice president, Stevenson chose Sen. John J. Sparkman of Alabama, who was nominated by acclamation.

Although a reluctant candidate, Stevenson promised the delegates a fighting campaign but warned: "Better we lose the election than mislead the people; and better we lose than misgovern the people."

The Democratic platform was adopted without the rancor that had accompanied consideration of the party platform four years earlier. The document was approved by a voice vote, although both the Georgia and Mississippi delegations asked that they be recorded in opposition.

The platform promised extension and improvement of New Deal and Fair Deal policies that had been proposed and enacted over the previous twenty years. The party's foremost goal was stated to be "peace with honor," which could be achieved by support for a strengthened United Nations, coupled with the policy of collective security in the form of American assistance for allies around the world. The peaceful use of atomic energy was pledged, as were efforts to establish an international control system. However, the platform also promised the use of atomic weapons, if needed, for national defense.

The civil rights plank was nearly identical to the one that appeared in the 1948 platform. Federal legislation was called for to guarantee equal rights in voting participation, employment opportunity, and personal security.

The platform called for extending and changing the Social Security system. A plank favored elimination of the work clause so that the elderly could collect benefits and still work.

Political reform was recommended that would require the disclosure of campaign expenses in federal elections.

The Democrats and Republicans took different stands on several major domestic issues. The Democrats favored repeal of the Taft-Hartley Act; the Republicans proposed to retain the act but make modifications where necessary. The Democrats advocated closing tax loopholes and, after defense needs were met, reducing taxes. The Republicans called for tax reduction based on a cut in government spending. In education, the Democrats favored federal assistance to state and local units; the Republicans viewed education solely as the responsibility of local and state governments.

The Democrats favored continuation of federal power projects, while the Republicans opposed "all-powerful federal socialistic valley authorities."

Both parties favored a parity price program for farmers. The Democrats advocated a mandatory price support program for basic agricultural products at not less than 90 percent of parity, and the Republicans proposing a program that would establish "full parity prices for all farm products."

Following are excerpts from the Democratic platform of 1952:

Atomic Energy. In the field of atomic energy, we pledge ourselves:

(1) to maintain vigorous and non-partisan civilian administrations, with adequate security safeguards;

(2) to promote the development of nuclear energy for peaceful purposes in the interests of America and mankind;

(3) to build all the atomic and hydrogen firepower needed to defend our country, deter aggression, and promote world peace;

(4) to exert every effort to bring about bona fide international control and inspection of all atomic weapons.

Civil Rights. We will continue our efforts to eradicate discrimination based on race, religion or national origin. . . .

We are proud of the progress that has been made in securing equality of treatment and opportunity in the Nation's armed forces and the civil service and all areas under Federal jurisdiction. . . .

At the same time, we favor Federal legislation effectively to secure these rights to everyone:

(1) the right to equal opportunity for employment;

(2) the right to security of persons;

(3) the right to full and equal participation in the Nation's political life, free from arbitrary restraints.

Agriculture. We will continue to protect the producers of basic agricultural commodities under the terms of a mandatory price support program at not less than ninety percent of parity. We continue to advocate practical methods for extending price supports to other storables and to the producers of perishable commodities, which account for three-fourths of all farm income.

Campaign Finance. We advocate new legislation to provide effective regulation and full disclosure of campaign expenditures in elections to Federal office, including political advertising from any source.

Labor. We strongly advocate the repeal of the Taft-Hartley Act.

Tax Reform. We believe in fair and equitable taxation. We oppose a Federal general sales tax. We adhere to the principle of ability to pay. We have enacted an emergency excess profits tax to prevent profiteering from the defense program and have vigorously attacked special tax privileges. . . . As rapidly as defense requirements permit, we favor reducing taxes, especially for people with lower incomes. . . .

Justice requires the elimination of tax loopholes which favor special groups. We pledge continued efforts to the elimination of remaining loopholes.

Social Security. We favor the complete elimination of the work clause for the reason that those contributing to the Social Security program should be permitted to draw benefits, upon reaching the age of eligibility, and still continue to work.

Education. Local, State and Federal governments have shared responsibility to contribute appropriately to the pressing needs of our educational system. We urge that Federal contributions be made available to State and local units which adhere to basic minimum standards.

The Federal Government should not dictate nor control educational policy.

1956 Conventions

PRESIDENTIAL CANDIDATES

Adlai E. Stevenson
Democrat

Dwight D. Eisenhower
Republican

DEMOCRATS

Both parties held their conventions in August, the latest date ever for the Republicans and the latest for the Democrats since the wartime convention of 1864. For the first time since 1888 the date of the Democratic convention preceded that of the Republicans. The Democrats met in mid-August in Chicago with an allotment of 1,372 votes, the largest in party history. The increased allotment was the result of a new distribution formula, which for the first time rewarded states for electing Democratic governors and senators in addition to supporting the party's presidential candidate.

A provision of the convention call handled the party loyalty question, a thorny issue at the 1952 convention, by assuming that, in the absence of a challenge, any delegate would be understood to have the best interests of the party at heart. Another provision of the call threatened any national committeeman who did not support the party's national ticket with removal from the Democratic National Committee.

In an unusual occurrence, nominating speeches were delivered by a past and a future president for men who would not attain the office themselves. Sen. John F. Kennedy of Massachusetts placed Adlai E. Stevenson's name in nomination, while former president Harry S. Truman seconded the nomination of New York governor W. Averell Harriman. Truman criticized Stevenson as a "defeatist" but was countered by Eleanor Roosevelt, who appeared before the convention in support of the former Illinois governor.

In spite of the oratorical byplay, Stevenson was in good position to win the nomination before the convention even began, having eliminated his principal rival, Sen. Estes Kefauver of Tennessee, in the primaries. Stevenson won a majority on the first ballot, receiving 905½ votes to easily defeat Harriman, who had 210. Sen. Lyndon B. Johnson of Texas finished third, with 80 votes. Upon completion of the roll call, a motion was approved to make Stevenson's nomination unanimous. *(Table, p. 227.)*

In an unusual move, Stevenson announced that he would not personally select his running mate but would leave the choice to the convention. Stevenson's desire for an open selection was designed to contrast with the expected cut-and-dried nature of the upcoming Republican convention. But the unusual move caught both delegates and prospective candidates off guard.

Numerous delegations passed on the first ballot, and upon completion of the roll call votes were scattered among thirteen different candidates. When the vote totals were announced at the end of the roll call, Kefauver led with 483½ votes, followed by Kennedy with 304, Sen. Albert A. Gore of Tennessee with 178, Mayor Robert F. Wagner of New York City with 162½, and Sen. Hubert H. Humphrey of Minnesota with 134½. A total of 687 votes were needed to nominate.

With a coalition that included most of the southern and eastern delegates, Kennedy drew into the lead on the second ballot. After the roll call but before the chair recognized vote changes, the totals stood: Kennedy, 618; Kefauver, 551½; Gore, 110½. Kentucky, the first state to be recognized, shifted its 30 votes to Kennedy, leaving the thirty-nine-year-old senator fewer than 40 votes short of the nomination.

But Gore was recognized next and began a bandwagon for Kefauver by withdrawing in favor of his Tennessee colleague. Other states followed Gore's lead, and at the conclusion of the vote shifts Kefauver had a clear majority. The final tally was Kefauver, 755½ and Kennedy, 589. Kennedy moved that his opponent's nomination be made unanimous.

Ironically, Kefauver won a majority of the votes in only two states in his home region, Tennessee and Florida. His strength lay in midwestern and western delegations.

As in 1948 platform debate focused on the civil rights issue. A Minnesota member of the platform committee introduced a minority report that advocated a civil rights plank stronger than that in the majority report. The plank presented by the platform committee pledged to carry out Supreme Court decisions on desegregation, but not through the use of force. The party promised to continue to work for equal rights in voting, employment, personal security, and education. The Minnesota substitute was more specific, as it favored federal legislation to achieve equal voting rights and employment opportunities and to guarantee personal safety. The minority plank also favored more rigid enforcement of civil rights legislation. Although several states clamored for a roll-call vote, the chair took a voice vote, which went against the Minnesota substitute.

The entire platform was the longest yet approved by a Democratic convention, about 12,000 words. The document was divided into eleven sections, the first dealing with defense and foreign policy and the remainder with domestic issues.

The platform described President Eisenhower as a "political amateur . . . dominated . . . by special privilege." It applauded the legislative accomplishments of the Democratic Congress elected in 1954 and proposed a continuation of the social and economic legislation begun during the New Deal.

The foreign policy of the Eisenhower administration was criticized in a plank that accused the Republicans of cutting funds for the military in an attempt to balance the budget. The Democrats declared that the United States must have the strongest military in the world to discourage aggression by America's enemies. The foreign policy plank also pledged to strengthen the United Nations as a peacekeeping organization and promised to work diligently for worldwide disarmament.

The platform blamed the Republicans for allowing big business to dominate the economy and promised tax relief and other government assistance to help small business. The Democrats advocated repeal of the Taft-Hartley Act, as the party had done in every platform since 1948, and favored an increase in the minimum wage. Tax reductions were proposed for lower-income taxpayers, and an increase of at least $200 in the personal tax exemption was recommended.

For farmers, the Democrats proposed price supports at 90 percent of parity on basic crops, as opposed to the Republican program of flexible price supports.

For the first time since the beginning of the New Deal, the Democratic platform mentioned the importance of states' rights. The party also reiterated its position on education, which advocated federal assistance, but stated that ultimate control of the schools lay in the hands of state and local governments.

In political reform the platform proposed restrictions on government secrecy and repeated the party's call for the passage of an equal rights amendment.

Following are excerpts from the Democratic platform of 1956:

Foreign Policy. *The Failure at Home.* Political considerations of budget balancing and tax reduction now come before the wants of our national security and the needs of our Allies. The Republicans have slashed our own armed strength, weakened our capacity to deal with military threats, stifled our air force, starved our army and weakened our capacity to deal with aggression of any sort save by retreat or by the alternatives, "massive retaliation" and global atomic war. Yet, while our troubles mount, they tell us our prestige was never higher, they tell us we were never more secure.

Disarmament. To eliminate the danger of atomic war, a universal, effective and enforced disarmament system must be the goal of responsible men and women everywhere. So long as we lack enforceable international control of weapons, we must maintain armed strength to avoid war. But technological advances in the field of nuclear weapons make disarmament an ever more urgent problem. Time and distance can never again protect any nation of the world.

Labor. We unequivocally advocate repeal of the Taft-Hartley Act. The Act must be repealed because State "right-to-work" laws have their genesis in its discriminatory anti-labor provisions. . . .

The Taft-Hartley Act has been proven to be inadequate, unworkable and unfair. It interferes in an arbitrary manner with collective bargaining, causing imbalance in the relationship between management and labor.

Agriculture. Undertake immediately by appropriate action to endeavor to regain the full 100 percent of parity the farmers received under the Democratic Administrations. We will achieve this by means of supports on basic commodities at 90 percent of parity and by means of commodity loans, direct purchases, direct payments to producers, marketing agreements and orders, production adjustments, or a combination of these, including legislation, to bring order and stability into the relationship between the producer, the processor and the consumer.

Education. We are now faced with shortages of educational facilities that threaten national security, economic prosperity and human well-being. The resources of our States and localities are already strained to the limit. Federal aid and action should be provided, within the traditional framework of State and local control.

Tax Reform. We favor realistic tax adjustments, giving first consideration to small independent business and the small individual taxpayer. Lower-income families need tax relief; only a Democratic victory will assure this. We favor an increase in the present personal tax exemption of $600 to a minimum of at least $800.

Government Secrecy. *Freedom of Information.* During recent years there has developed a practice on the part of Federal agencies to delay and withhold information which is needed by Congress and the general public to make important decisions affecting their lives and destinies. We believe that this trend toward secrecy in Government should be reversed and that the Federal Government should return to its basic tradition of exchanging and promoting the freest flow of information possible in those unclassified areas where secrets involving weapons development and bona fide national security are not involved.

States' Rights. While we recognize the existence of honest differences of opinion as to the true location of a Constitutional line of demarcation between the Federal Government and the States, the Democratic Party expressly recognizes the vital importance of the respective States in our Federal Union. The Party of Jefferson and Jackson pledges itself to continued support of those sound principles of local government which will best serve the welfare of our people and the safety of our democratic rights.

Civil Rights. We are proud of the record of the Democratic Party in securing equality of treatment and opportunity in the nation's armed forces, the Civil Service, and in all areas under Federal jurisdiction. The Democratic Party pledges itself to continue its efforts to eliminate illegal discriminations of all kinds, in relation to (1) full rights to vote, (2) full rights to engage in gainful occupations, (3) full rights to enjoy security of the person, and (4) full rights to education in all publicly supported institutions.

Recent decisions of the Supreme Court of the United States relating to segregation in publicly supported schools and elsewhere have brought consequences of vast importance to our Nation as a whole and especially to communities directly affected. We reject all proposals for the use of force to interfere with the orderly determination of these matters by the courts.

REPUBLICANS

The Republicans opened their convention in San Francisco three days after the close of the Democratic convention in Chicago. In contrast to the turbulent convention of their adversaries, the Republicans' renomination of Dwight D. Eisenhower and Richard Nixon was a formality. The only possible obstacle to Eisenhower's candidacy was his health, but by August 1956 his recovery from a heart attack and an ileitis operation was complete enough to allow him to seek a second term. On the convention's single roll call for president, Eisenhower received all 1,323 votes. *(Table, p. 227.)*

What drama occurred at the Republican convention surrounded the vice-presidential nomination. Several weeks before the opening of the convention, former Minnesota governor Harold Stassen, the disarmament adviser to Eisenhower, had begun a movement to replace Vice President Nixon with Massachusetts governor Christian A. Herter. However, with lack of interest from party leaders, this movement petered out. At the convention both Herter and Stassen gave nominating speeches for Nixon. During the roll call, a commotion was caused by a Nebraska delegate, who attempted to nominate "Joe Smith." Af-

ter some discussion, it was determined that "Joe Smith" was a fictitious individual, and the offending delegate was escorted from the hall. On the one ballot for vice president, a unanimous vote was recorded for Nixon.

While no opposition to the platform was expressed on the floor of the convention, several southern delegates were unhappy with the civil rights plank and withdrew from the convention. The plank in question listed advances in desegregation under the Republican administration, voiced acceptance of the Supreme Court ruling on school desegregation, and pledged to enforce existing civil rights statutes.

The platform as a whole was slightly longer than the Democratic document and was dedicated to Eisenhower and "the youth of America." Unlike the Democratic platform, which began with a discussion of foreign policy and national defense, the first issue pursued by the Republicans was the economy.

The Eisenhower administration was praised for balancing the budget, reducing taxes, and halting inflation. The platform promised continued balanced budgets, gradual reduction of the national debt, and cuts in government spending consistent with the maintenance of a strong military. Two measures favored by the Democrats, tax relief for small businesses and tax reductions for low-income and middle-income families, were both mentioned as secondary economic goals in the Republican platform.

The labor plank advocated revision but not repeal of the Taft-Hartley Act. The agricultural section favored elimination of price-depressing surpluses and continuation of the flexible price-support program. As they had for the past quarter century, the Republicans joined the Democrats in recommending passage of an equal rights amendment.

The foreign policy section of the Republican platform praised the Eisenhower administration for ending the Korean War, stemming the worldwide advance of communism and entering new collective security agreements. The plank also emphasized the necessity of a bipartisan foreign policy. The "preservation" of Israel was viewed as an "important tenet of American foreign policy," a notable difference from the Democratic platform, which took a more even-handed approach toward both Israel and the Arab states.

The national defense section emphasized the nation's possession of "the strongest striking force in the world," a rebuttal to Democratic charges that the Republicans had jeopardized the efficiency of the armed forces in an effort to balance the budget.

Following are excerpts from the Republican platform of 1956:

Economy. We pledge to pursue the following objectives:

Further reductions in Government spending as recommended in the Hoover Commission Report, without weakening the support of a superior defense program or depreciating the quality of essential services of government to our people.

Continued balancing of the budget, to assure the financial strength of the country which is so vital to the struggle of the free world in its battle against Communism; and to maintain the purchasing power of a sound dollar, and the value of savings, pensions and insurance.

Gradual reduction of the national debt.

Then, insofar as consistent with a balanced budget, we pledge to work toward these additional objectives:

Further reductions in taxes with particular consideration for low and middle income families.

Initiation of a sound policy of tax reductions which will encourage small independent businesses to modernize and progress.

Labor. Revise and improve the Taft-Hartley Act so as to protect more effectively the rights of labor unions, management, the individual worker, and the public. The protection of the right of workers to organize into unions and to bargain collectively is the firm and permanent policy of the Eisenhower Administration.

Agriculture. This program must be versatile and flexible to meet effectively the impact of rapidly changing conditions. It does not envision making farmers dependent upon direct governmental payments for their incomes. Our objective is markets which return full parity to our farm and ranch people when they sell their products.

Civil Rights. The Republican Party accepts the decision of the U.S. Supreme Court that racial discrimination in publicly supported schools must be progressively eliminated. We concur in the conclusion of the Supreme Court that its decision directing school desegregation should be accomplished with "all deliberate speed" locally through Federal District Courts. The implementation order of the Supreme Court recognizes the complex and acutely emotional problems created by its decision in certain sections of our country where racial patterns have been developed in accordance with prior and long-standing decisions of the same tribunal.

We believe that true progress can be attained through intelligent study, understanding, education and good will. Use of force or violence by any group or agency will tend only to worsen the many problems inherent in the situation. This progress must be encouraged and the work of the courts supported in every legal manner by all branches of the Federal Government to the end that the constitutional ideal of equality before the law, regardless of race, creed or color, will be steadily achieved.

Foreign Policy. The advance of Communism has been checked, and, at key points, thrown back. The once-monolithic structure of International Communism, denied the stimulant of successive conquests, has shown hesitancy both internally and abroad.

National Defense. We *have* the strongest striking force in the world—in the air—on the sea—and a magnificent supporting land force in our Army and Marine Corps.

Israel. We regard the preservation of Israel as an important tenet of American foreign policy. We are determined that the integrity of an independent Jewish State shall be maintained. We shall support the independence of Israel against armed aggression. The best hope for peace in the Middle East lies in the United Nations. We pledge our continued efforts to eliminate the obstacles to a lasting peace in this area.

1960 Conventions

PRESIDENTIAL CANDIDATES

John F. Kennedy
Democrat

Richard M. Nixon
Republican

DEMOCRATS

For the first time, a national political convention was held in Los Angeles. More than 4,000 delegates and alternates converged on the California metropolis in July to select the Democratic standard-bearers for 1960. The delegate-allocation method had been changed since 1956 by the Democratic National Committee, from a formula that included Democratic voting strength to a system that emphasized population only. No states lost seats, but the new formula tended to strengthen populous northern states.

The early sessions of the convention dealt with rules and credentials. The convention rules, approved without debate, included the compromise loyalty pledge adopted by the 1956 convention. The only credentials dispute involved two contesting delegations from the Commonwealth of Puerto Rico. By a voice vote, the convention agreed to seat both delegations while splitting the vote of the Commonwealth.

The front-runner for the presidential nomination was Massachusetts senator John F. Kennedy, whose success in the primaries and support from many of the party's urban leaders put him on the verge of a nominating majority. His principal rival was Senate majority leader Lyndon B. Johnson of Texas, although the favorite of the convention galleries was Adlai E. Stevenson, the party's unsuccessful standard-bearer in 1952 and 1956. Johnson challenged Kennedy to a debate, which was held before a joint gathering of the Massachusetts and Texas delegations. Coming the day before the balloting, the debate had little effect on the ultimate outcome.

Nine men were nominated, but Kennedy received a clear majority on the first ballot. At the end of the roll call, the Massachusetts senator had 806 votes, to easily outdistance Johnson, who received 409. Sen. Stuart Symington of Missouri was a distant third with 86 votes, and Stevenson followed with 79½. A motion to make Kennedy's nomination unanimous was approved by a voice vote. Kennedy's selection marked the first time since 1920 that a senator had been nominated for the presidency by Democrats or Republicans and the first time since 1928 that a Roman Catholic had been represented on a national ticket of one of the two major parties. (Table, p. 228.)

Kennedy surprised some supporters and political observers by choosing his erstwhile adversary, Johnson, as his running mate. A motion to nominate Johnson by acclamation was approved by a voice vote.

Kennedy delivered his acceptance speech to 80,000 spectators at the Los Angeles Coliseum. He envisioned the United States as "on the edge of a new frontier—the frontier of the 1960s—a frontier of unknown opportunities and perils—a frontier of unfulfilled hopes and threats," adding that this "new frontier . . . is not a set of promises—it is a set of challenges."

The Democratic platform was easily the longest yet written by the party, about 20,000 words. The platform itself was approved by a voice vote, although the civil rights and fiscal responsibility planks were debated on the convention floor, and roll-call votes had been taken in committee.

Regional hearings had been held by subcommittees of the 108-member platform committee in the spring, but votes on controversial issues were not taken by the full committee until the convention. A plank that urged elimination of the immigration quota system was approved, 66 to 28, with opposition led by Sen. James O. Eastland of Mississippi. An agricultural plank recommending price supports at 90 percent of parity was passed, 66 to 22, with opponents claiming that it was a restatement of the liberal program proposed by the National Farmers Union. A motion to reconsider the plank was defeated, 38 to 32. An Eastland motion to delete condemnation of "right-to-work" laws was defeated without a recorded vote.

The civil rights plank caused the greatest controversy. Sen. Sam J. Ervin Jr. of North Carolina introduced motions to delete portions that proposed establishing a Fair Employment Practices Commission, continuing the Civil Rights Commission as a permanent agency, granting the attorney general the power to file civil injunction suits to prevent discrimination, and setting 1963 as the deadline for the initiation of school desegregation plans. Ervin's motions were defeated by a voice vote, and the entire plank was approved, 66 to 24.

Delegates from nine southern states signed a statement that repudiated the civil rights plank. Led by Georgia Democratic Chairman James H. Gray and Ervin, these nine states introduced a minority report on the convention floor calling for elimination of the platform's civil rights plank. After an hour's debate, the minority report was rejected by a voice vote.

As approved by the convention, the platform began with a discussion of foreign policy. The Democrats blamed the Republican administration for allowing the United States' military strength to deteriorate. The national defense plank declared there was a "missile gap, space gap, and limited-war gap," and promised to improve America's military position so that it would be second to none. The Democrats recommended creation of "a national peace agency for disarmament planning and research." The money saved by international disarmament, the plank stated, could be used to attack world poverty.

Foreign military aid was viewed as a short-range necessity that should be replaced by economic aid "as rapidly as security considerations permit." At the same time, the platform proposed that development programs be placed on a "long-term basis to permit more effective planning."

The Democrats' economic plank called for an average national growth rate of 5 percent annually. Economic growth at this rate would create needed tax revenue, the Democrats believed, which—coupled with cuts in government waste, closing of tax loopholes and more extensive efforts to catch tax evaders—would help balance the budget. The Democrats promised to use measures such as public works projects and temporary tax cuts to combat recessions or depressions.

The platform promised an increase in the minimum wage to $1.25 an hour and pledged to extend coverage to include more workers. There was a pledge to amend the Social Security program so the elderly could continue working without sacrificing basic benefits.

Equal rights legislation was favored, although the platform did not call for passage of a constitutional amendment of 1960.

Following are excerpts from the Democratic platform of 1960:

National Defense. Our military position today is measured in terms of gaps—missile gap, space gap, limited-war gap. . . .

This is the strength that must be erected:

1. Deterrent military power such that the Soviet and Chinese leaders will have no doubt that an attack on the United States would surely be followed by their own destruction.

2. Balanced conventional military forces which will permit a response graded to the intensity of any threats of aggressive force.

3. Continuous modernization of these forces through intensified research and development, including essential programs now slowed down, terminated, suspended or neglected for lack of budgetary support.

Disarmament. This requires a national peace agency for disarmament planning and research to muster the scientific ingenuity, coordination, continuity, and seriousness of purpose which are now lacking in our arms control efforts. . . .

As world-wide disarmament proceeds, it will free vast resources for a new international attack on the problem of world poverty.

Immigration. The national-origins quota system of limiting immigration contradicts the founding principles of this nation. It is inconsistent with our belief in the rights of man. This system was instituted after World War I as a policy of deliberate discrimination by a Republican Administration and Congress.

Foreign Aid. Where military assistance remains essential for the common defense, we shall see that the requirements are fully met. But as rapidly as security considerations permit, we will replace tanks with tractors, bombers with bulldozers, and tacticians with technicians.

Civil Rights. We believe that every school district affected by the Supreme Court's school desegregation decision should submit a plan providing for at least first-step compliance by 1963, the 100th anniversary of the Emancipation Proclamation.

For this and for the protection of all other Constitutional rights of Americans, the Attorney General should be empowered and directed to file civil injunction suits in Federal courts to prevent the denial of any civil right on grounds of race, creed or color.

Economy. We Democrats believe that our economy can and must grow at an average rate of 5 percent annually, almost twice as fast as our average annual rate since 1953. We pledge ourselves to policies that will achieve this goal without inflation. . . .

The policies of a Democratic Administration to restore economic growth will reduce current unemployment to a minimum.

Tax Reform. We shall close the loopholes in the tax laws by which certain privileged groups legally escape their fair share of taxation.

Labor. We pledge to raise the minimum wage to $1.25 an hour and to extend coverage to several million workers not now protected.

Agriculture. The Democratic Administration will work to bring about full parity income for farmers in all segments of agriculture by helping them to balance farm production with the expanding needs of the nation and the world.

Measures to this end include production and marketing quotas measured in terms of barrels, bushels and bales, loans on basic commodities at not less than 90 percent of parity, production payments, commodity purchases, and marketing orders and agreements.

Government Spending. The Democratic Party believes that state and local governments are strengthened—not weakened—by financial assistance from the Federal Government. We will extend such aid without impairing local administration through unnecessary Federal interference or red tape.

REPUBLICANS

On July 25, ten days after the close of the Democratic convention, the Republican convention opened in Chicago. Although Vice President Richard Nixon had a lock on the presidential nomination, the party's two major figures four years later, Arizona senator Barry Goldwater and New York governor Nelson A. Rockefeller, both had major roles in convention activities.

Both Goldwater and Rockefeller announced that they did not want their names placed in nomination, but the Arizona delegation disregarded Goldwater's request and nominated him anyway. In a convention speech, the Arizona senator withdrew his name and went on to advise conservative Republicans to work within the party: "Let's grow up conservatives. . . . If we want to take this party back—and I think we can someday—let's get to work."

On the roll call that followed, Nixon was a nearly unanimous choice, receiving 1,321 votes to 10 for Goldwater (all from

Louisiana). On a voice vote, Nixon's nomination was made unanimous. *(Table, p. 228.)*

Nixon reportedly wanted Rockefeller as his running mate but was unable to persuade the New Yorker to join the ticket. The Republican standard-bearer subsequently turned to United Nations Ambassador Henry Cabot Lodge Jr., a former senator from Massachusetts who had been beaten for reelection by Kennedy in 1952. On the vice-presidential ballot, Lodge received all but one vote. The lone dissenter, a Texas delegate, initially abstained but switched his vote to Lodge at the end of the roll call.

In his acceptance speech, Nixon promised to campaign in all fifty states and rebutted a theme in Kennedy's acceptance speech. "Our primary aim must be not to help government, but to help people—to help people attain the life they deserve," said Nixon.

Much of the drama of the 1960 Republican convention surrounded the party platform. The highlight of the platform maneuvering was a late-night meeting involving Nixon and Rockefeller, held at Rockefeller's New York City apartment two days before the opening of the convention. The meeting, a secret to most of Nixon's closest aides, resulted in a fourteen-point agreement between the two Republican leaders on major issues contained in the platform. The agreement, informally dubbed the "compact of Fifth Avenue," was issued by Rockefeller, who declared that the meeting was held at Nixon's insistence.

Half of the fourteen points dealt with national security and foreign policy. The other half discussed domestic issues, including government reorganization, civil rights, agriculture, economic growth, and medical care for the elderly. Although not markedly different in wording from the draft of the platform committee, the "compact" expressed a tone of urgency that was not evident in the draft.

The Nixon-Rockefeller agreement was made with the knowledge of the platform committee chairman, Charles H. Percy of Illinois, but was greeted with hostility by many members of the committee and by party conservatives. Goldwater termed the "compact" a "surrender" and the "Munich of the Republican Party" that would ensure the party's defeat that fall.

The two issues of greatest controversy were civil rights and national defense. The original civil rights plank, drafted by the platform committee, did not express support for civil rights demonstrations or promise federal efforts to gain job equality for blacks. The Nixon-Rockefeller agreement did both. Nixon threatened to wage a floor fight if the stronger civil rights plank was not inserted in the platform. By a vote of 50 to 35, the platform committee agreed to reconsider the original civil rights plank; by a margin of 56 to 28, the stronger plank was approved.

With the approval of both Rockefeller and President Dwight D. Eisenhower, several changes were made in the national security plank that emphasized the necessity of quickly upgrading America's armed forces. The platform committee approved reconsideration of the original defense plank by a voice vote, and the whole platform was adopted unanimously.

With disagreements resolved in the committee, there were neither minority reports nor floor fights. The convention approved the platform by a voice vote.

In its final form, the Republican platform was shorter than its Democratic counterpart, although still nearly 15,000 words in length. The foreign policy section asserted that the nation's greatest task was "to nullify the Soviet conspiracy." The platform claimed that America's military strength was second to none but, in line with the Nixon-Rockefeller "compact," indicated that improvements were needed in some parts of the armed forces.

The Republicans joined their Democratic opposition in favoring a workable disarmament program but did not advocate a phaseout of foreign military aid, as did the Democrats. However, the Republicans proposed a change in the funding of foreign aid that emphasized "the increasing use of private capital and government loans, rather than outright grants."

The Republicans agreed with the Democrats that the nation should experience more rapid economic growth but did not adopt the 5 percent annual growth rate favored by the Democrats. The Republicans stressed the virtues of a balanced budget and regarded free enterprise, rather than massive government programs, as the key to economic growth.

As in 1956, the two parties differed on farm price supports. The Republicans supported a program of flexible support payments, while the Democrats recommended setting price supports at 90 percent of parity.

Both parties proposed allowing individuals to work beyond their mandatory retirement age, although the Democrats tied their proposal to amendment of the Social Security program.

The Republicans did not urge elimination of the immigration quota system, as did their opponents, but they favored overhaul of the system to allow an increase in immigration.

On the issue of equal rights, the Republicans continued to favor passage of a constitutional amendment. The Democrats had backed away from this position, which they had held in earlier platforms, instead proposing the passage of equal rights legislation in Congress.

As they had since the beginning of the New Deal, the Republican and Democratic platforms differed noticeably as to the extent and desirability of federal spending. The Democrats viewed federal assistance to state and local governments as beneficial. The Republicans believed the federal government could help meet the problems of urban growth, but that state and local governments should administer all the programs they could best handle.

Following are excerpts from the Republican platform of 1960:

National Defense. The future of freedom depends heavily upon America's military might and that of her allies. Under the Eisenhower-Nixon Administration, our military might has been forged into a power second to none. . . .

The strategic imperatives of our national defense policy are these:

A second-strike capability, that is, a nuclear retaliatory power that can survive surprise attack, strike back, and destroy any possible enemy.

Highly mobile and versatile forces, including forces deployed, to deter or check local aggressions and "brush fire wars" which might bring on all-out nuclear war.

Disarmament. We are similarly ready to negotiate and to institute realistic methods and safeguards for disarmament, and for the suspension of nuclear tests. We advocate an early agreement by all nations to forego nuclear tests in the atmosphere, and the suspension of other tests as verification techniques permit.

Immigration. The annual number of immigrants we accept be at least doubled.

Obsolete immigration laws be amended by abandoning the outdated 1920 census data as a base and substituting the 1960 census.

The guidelines of our immigration policy be based upon judgment of the individual merit of each applicant for admission and citizenship.

Foreign Aid. Agreeable to the developing nations, we would join with them in inviting countries with advanced economies to share with us a proportionate part of the capital and technical aid required. We would emphasize the increasing use of private capital and government loans, rather than outright grants, as a means of fostering independence and mutual respect.

Civil Rights. *Voting.* We pledge:

Continued vigorous enforcement of the civil rights laws to guarantee the right to vote to all citizens in all areas of the country. . . .

Public Schools. We pledge:

The Department of Justice will continue its vigorous support of court orders for school desegregation . . .

We oppose the pretense of fixing a target date 3 years from now for the mere submission of plans for school desegregation. Slow-moving school districts would construe it as a three-year moratorium during which progress would cease, postponing until 1963 the legal process to enforce compliance. We believe that each of the pending court actions should proceed as the Supreme Court has directed and that in no district should there be any such delay.

Employment. We pledge:

Continued support for legislation to establish a Commission on Equal Job Opportunity to make permanent and to expand with legislative backing the excellent work being performed by the President's Committee on Government Contracts. . . .

Housing. We pledge:

Action to prohibit discrimination in housing constructed with the aid of federal subsidies.

Economy. We reject the concept of artificial growth forced by massive new federal spending and loose money policies. The only effective way to accelerate economic growth is to increase the traditional strengths of our free economy—initiative and investment, productivity and efficiency.

Agriculture. Use of price supports at levels best fitted to specific commodities, in order to widen markets, ease production controls, and help achieve increased farm family income.

Government Reorganization. The President must continue to be able to reorganize and streamline executive operations to keep the executive branch capable of responding effectively to rapidly changing conditions in both foreign and domestic fields. . . .

Government Spending. Vigorous state and local governments are a vital part of our federal union. The federal government should leave to state and local governments those programs and problems which they can best handle and tax sources adequate to finance them. We must continue to improve liaison between federal, state and local governments. We believe that the federal government, when appropriate, should render significant assistance in dealing with our urgent problems of urban growth and change. No vast new bureaucracy is needed to achieve this objective.

1964 Conventions

PRESIDENTIAL CANDIDATES

Barry Goldwater
Republican

Lyndon B. Johnson
Democrat

REPUBLICANS

Division between the party's conservative and moderate wings, muted during the Eisenhower administration, exploded at the Republicans' July 13–16 convention in San Francisco. Although Sen. Barry Goldwater of Arizona, the hero of Republican conservatives, had a commanding lead as the convention opened, he was vigorously challenged by Pennsylvania governor William W. Scranton, the belated leader of the moderate forces. Two days before the presidential balloting, a letter in Scranton's name was sent to Goldwater. It charged the Goldwater organization with regarding the delegates as "little more than a flock of chickens whose necks will be wrung at will." The message continued, describing Goldwater's political philosophy as a "crazy-quilt collection of absurd and dangerous positions." The letter concluded by challenging the Arizona senator to a debate before the convention. Although the message was written by Scranton's staff without his knowledge, the Pennsylvania governor supported the substance of the letter. Goldwater declined the invitation to debate.

Although seven names were placed in nomination for the presidency, the outcome was a foregone conclusion. Goldwater was an easy winner on the first ballot, receiving 883 of the 1,308 votes. Scranton was a distant second with 214 votes; New York governor Nelson A. Rockefeller followed with 114. Scranton moved that Goldwater's nomination be made unanimous, and his motion was approved by a voice vote. Support for the major moderate candidates, Scranton and Rockefeller, was centered in the Northeast. Goldwater had an overwhelming majority of the delegates from other regions. *(Table, p. 229.)*

As his running mate, Goldwater selected the Republican national chairman, Rep. William E. Miller of New York. On disclosing his choice of Miller, Goldwater stated that "one of the reasons I chose Miller is that he drives Johnson nuts." On the vice-presidential roll call, the conservative New York representative received 1,305 votes, with three delegates from Tennessee ab-

staining. A Roman Catholic, Miller became the first member of that faith ever to run on a Republican Party national ticket.

Goldwater's acceptance speech was uncompromising and did not attempt to dilute his conservatism in an effort to gain votes: "Anyone who joins us in all sincerity we welcome. Those who do not care for our cause, we don't expect to enter our ranks in any case. And let our Republicanism so focused and so dedicated not be made fuzzy and futile by unthinking and stupid labels. I would remind you that extremism in the defense of liberty is no vice. And let me remind you also that moderation in the pursuit of justice is no virtue."

By a voice vote, the convention adopted the party platform, but not before the moderate forces waged floor fights on three issues—extremism, civil rights, and control of nuclear weapons. Within the platform committee, 70 to 80 different amendments were presented, but when the platform reached the floor the moderates concentrated on these three specific issues.

Extremism was the first issue considered, with Sen. Hugh Scott of Pennsylvania introducing an amendment that specifically denounced efforts of the John Birch Society, the Ku Klux Klan, and the Communist Party to infiltrate the Republican Party. Rockefeller spoke on behalf of the amendment but was booed throughout his speech. Rockefeller argued that a "radical, high-financed, disciplined minority" was trying to take over the Republican Party, a minority "wholly alien to the middle course . . . the mainstream." The amendment was rejected on a standing vote, by a margin estimated at two to one.

A second amendment on extremism, proposed by Michigan governor George W. Romney, condemned extremist groups but not by name. The Romney amendment was similarly rejected on a standing vote by about the same margin. Scott introduced a civil rights amendment adding additional pledges to the existing plank, including more manpower for the Justice Department's Civil Rights Division; a statement of pride in Republican support of the 1964 Civil Rights Act; requirements for first-step compliance with school desegregation by all school districts in one year; voting guarantees to state as well as federal elections, and promises to eliminate job bias. The platform's brief plank on civil rights called for "full implementation and faithful execution" of the 1964 act, but it also stated that "the elimination of any such discrimination is a matter of heart, conscience and education as well as of equal rights under law." On a roll-call vote, the Scott amendment was defeated, 897 to 409. The pattern of the vote closely followed the presidential ballot, with support for the amendment centered in the Northeast. *(Table, p. 229.)*

Romney offered a brief, alternative civil rights plank that pledged action at the state, local, and private levels to eliminate discrimination in all fields. It was defeated by a voice vote.

Scott proposed another amendment, declaring the president to have sole authority to control the use of nuclear weapons. This contrasted with Goldwater's position advocating that North Atlantic Treaty Organization (NATO) commanders be given greater authority in the use of tactical nuclear weapons. The Scott amendment was rejected on a standing vote.

In its final form, the Republican platform was barely half as long as its Democratic counterpart. The Republican platform was divided into four sections, the first two enumerating Democratic failures in foreign policy and domestic affairs. The last two sections detailed Republican proposals.

The Republicans were suspicious of any détente with the communist world, instead calling for "a dynamic strategy of victory . . . for freedom." The platform contended that American military strength was deteriorating and promised the establishment of a military force superior to that of the nation's enemies. The Republicans expressed distrust of the 1963 nuclear test ban treaty and vowed to "never unilaterally disarm America." The platform promised to revitalize NATO, which was viewed as a keystone of Republican foreign policy.

Coupled with the anticommunism of the foreign policy sections was the central theme of the domestic sections—the need to trim the power of the federal government and to relocate it in state and local governments. This conservative philosophy was evident in various domestic planks. The Republicans promised a reduction of at least $5 billion in federal spending and pledged to end budget deficits.

The "one person, one vote" ruling of the Supreme Court brought the recommendation by the Republicans that a constitutional amendment be passed to allow states with bicameral legislatures to use a measurement other than population.

Following are excerpts from the Republican platform of 1964:

Peace. This Administration has sought accommodations with Communism without adequate safeguards and compensating gains for freedom. It has alienated proven allies by opening a "hot line" first with a sworn enemy rather than with a proven friend, and in general pursued a risky path such as began at Munich a quarter century ago. . . .

The supreme challenge to this policy is an atheistic imperialism—Communism. . . .

National Defense. This Administration has adopted policies which will lead to a potentially fatal parity of power with Communism instead of continued military superiority for the United States.

It has permitted disarmament negotiations to proceed without adequate consideration of military judgment. . . . It has failed to take minimum safeguards against possible consequences of the limited nuclear test ban treaty, including advanced underground tests where permissible and full readiness to test elsewhere should the need arise. . . .

We will maintain a superior, not merely equal, military capability as long as the Communist drive for world domination continues. It will be a capability of balanced force, superior in all its arms, maintaining flexibility for effective performance in the rapidly changing science of war.

Republicans will never unilaterally disarm America.

Berlin. We will demand that the Berlin Wall be taken down prior to the resumption of any negotiations with the Soviet Union on the status of forces in, or treaties affecting, Germany.

Cuba. We Republicans will recognize a Cuban government in exile; we will support its efforts to regain the independence of its homeland; we will assist Cuban freedom fighters in carrying on guerrilla warfare against the Communist regime; we will work for an economic boycott by all nations of the free world in trade with Cuba. . . .

Vietnam. We will move decisively to assure victory in South Vietnam. While confining the conflict as closely as possible, America must move to end the fighting in a reasonable time and provide guarantees against further aggression. We must make it clear to the Communist world that, when conflict is forced with America, it will end only in victory for freedom.

Federal Power. Humanity is tormented once again by an age-old issue—is man to live in dignity and freedom under God or to be enslaved—are men in government to serve, or are they to master, their fellow men? . . .

1. Every person has the right to govern himself, to fix his own goals, and to make his own way with a minimum of governmental interference.

2. It is for government to foster and maintain an environment of freedom encouraging every individual to develop to the fullest his God-given powers of mind, heart and body; and, beyond this, government should undertake only needful things, rightly of public concern, which the citizen cannot himself accomplish.

We Republicans hold that these two principles must regain their primacy in our government's relations, not only with the American people, but also with nations and peoples everywhere in the world.

Economy. In furtherance of our faith in the individual, we also pledge prudent, responsible management of the government's fiscal affairs to protect the individual against the evils of spendthrift government—protecting most of all the needy and fixed-income families against the cruelest tax, inflation—and protecting every citizen against the high taxes forced by excessive spending, in order that each individual may keep more of his earning for his own and his family's use.

Tax Reform. In furtherance of our faith in limited, frugal and efficient government we also pledge: credit against Federal taxes for specified State and local taxes paid, and a transfer to the States of excise and other Federal tax sources. . . .

Civil Rights. Full implementation and faithful execution of the Civil Rights Act of 1964, and all other civil rights statutes, to assure equal rights and opportunities guaranteed by the Constitution to every citizen; . . . continued opposition to discrimination based on race, creed, national origin or sex. We recognize that the elimination of any such discrimination is a matter of heart, conscience, and education, as well as of equal rights under law.

Education. To continue the advancement of education on all levels, through such programs as selective aid to higher education, strengthened State and local tax resources, including tax credits for college education, while resisting the Democratic efforts which endanger local control of schools. . . .

School Prayer. Support of a Constitutional amendment permitting those individuals and groups who choose to do so to exercise their religion freely in public places, provided religious exercises are not prepared or prescribed by the state or political subdivision thereof and no person's participation therein is coerced, thus preserving the traditional separation of church and state. . . .

Obscenity. Enactment of legislation, despite Democratic opposition, to curb the flow through the mails of obscene materials which has flourished into a multimillion dollar obscenity racket. . . .

Medical Care for Elderly. Full coverage of all medical and hospital costs for the needy elderly people, financed by general revenues through broader implementation of Federal-State plans. . . .

Reapportionment. Support of a Constitutional amendment, as well as legislation, enabling States having bicameral legislatures to apportion one House on bases of their choosing, including factors other than population. . . .

DEMOCRATS

In late August in Atlantic City, N.J., the Democratic convention nominated President Lyndon B. Johnson for a full term in the White House. The proceedings were stage-managed by the president and were met with little visible dissent on the convention floor. The four-day event August 24–27 was a political triumph for the veteran politician from Texas, who less than a year earlier had been the assassinated John F. Kennedy's vice president.

The Democratic convention was larger than any previous convention of an American political party, with 5,260 delegates and alternates. A new vote-allocation formula was in effect that combined consideration of a state's electoral vote with its support for the Kennedy-Johnson ticket in 1960. While no states lost votes from four years earlier, many of the larger states gained significantly. As a result, there were 2,316 votes at the 1964 convention, compared with 1,521 in 1960.

With no controversy surrounding either the party nominee or platform, attention focused on the credentials challenge brought by the integrated Mississippi Freedom Democratic Party against the all-white delegation sent by the regular state party. By a voice vote, the convention approved a compromise negotiated by Minnesota senator Hubert H. Humphrey. The settlement called for seating of the Mississippi regulars, provided they signed a written pledge to back the national ticket and urged the state's presidential electors to do likewise. It also proposed the seating of Democrats as delegates at large, and the remainder of the delegation as honored guests; and it stipulated that at future conventions delegations would be barred from states that allowed racial discrimination in voting. Although the convention approved this solution, the Freedom Democrats rejected the compromise, and all but four members of the regular Mississippi delegation refused to sign the pledge and left the convention.

The convention also approved a recommendation requiring the Alabama delegation to sign a personal loyalty oath, the result of the state party's placing "unpledged" (anti-Johnson)

electors on the Alabama ballot. Eleven Alabama members signed the loyalty oath; the remaining forty-two delegates and alternates withdrew from the convention.

The roll-call vote for president was dispensed with, and Johnson was nominated by acclamation. Immediately after his selection, Johnson made the unprecedented move of appearing before the delegates to announce his choice for vice president, Humphrey. Johnson had tried to make his selection as suspenseful and dramatic as possible. Although most observers felt Humphrey would be the choice, earlier that day Johnson had called both the Minnesota senator and Connecticut senator Thomas J. Dodd to the White House. However, at this meeting Johnson invited Humphrey to be on the ticket, and later that night the delegates nominated Humphrey by acclamation. (The 1964 Democratic convention was only the second in party history in which there were no roll-call votes—the other time was 1936.)

On the final day of the convention, the two nominees delivered their acceptance speeches. Humphrey frequently referred to the Republican candidate, Senator Goldwater, as "the temporary Republican spokesman," and listed major legislation supported by a majority of both parties in the Senate, "but not Senator Goldwater."

The emotional highlight of the convention was the appearance of Attorney General Robert F. Kennedy, who introduced a film about the presidency of his late brother.

By a voice vote, the convention approved the party platform. Following the trend toward longer and longer documents, the platform was 22,000 words in length. Although the document was adopted without debate on the convention floor, several roll-call votes were taken in the platform committee. By a vote of 53 to 16, the committee rejected a proposal by Senator Joseph S. Clark of Pennsylvania to strengthen the disarmament plank. Clark's proposal called for further disarmament "under world law," wording that the committee majority did not want to include.

By a margin of 39 to 38, the platform committee pledged to support a constitutional amendment giving the District of Columbia representation in Congress. On another roll-call vote (52 to 19), the committee promised to repeal the Taft-Hartley Act provision permitting state right-to-work laws.

Without a recorded vote, the committee adopted another provision by Senator Clark proposing revision of congressional rules and procedures to "assure majority rule after reasonable debate and to guarantee that major legislative proposals of the President can be brought to a vote after reasonable consideration in committee." The proposal was a reference to the Senate cloture rule, requiring a two-thirds vote to cut off debate, and to the power of the House Rules Committee to keep legislation from the floor.

The entire platform was a wide-ranging document designed to appeal to as many segments of the electorate as possible. Self-described as a "covenant of unity," the platform was written in a moderate tone to contrast with the unqualified conservatism expressed in the Republican platform.

The latter three-quarters of the Democratic platform was a section entitled "An Accounting of Stewardship, 1961–1964," which described the accomplishments of the Kennedy-Johnson administration in thirty-eight areas of public policy. The first quarter of the platform discussed the party's position on major issues of the day, from peace and national defense to civil rights, the economy, agriculture, natural resources, urban affairs, federal power and government reform, and extremism.

In view of the militant anticommunism of Senator Goldwater and the Republican platform, the Democrats viewed peace and national defense as winning issues with a majority of the electorate. The Democrats claimed that the world was closer to peace than in 1960, due in part to the overwhelming U.S. nuclear superiority and internal splits in the communist world, as well as the success of international negotiations such as those resulting in the nuclear test ban treaty. But, in an allusion to Goldwater's stance, the platform warned that recklessness by a president in foreign policy could result in nuclear disaster. The Democratic platform included a provision rejected by the Republicans, insisting that control of nuclear weapons must be kept in the hands of the president.

While peace and national defense were stressed by the Democrats, the Republican platform concentrated on the need to limit the power of the federal government. On this issue, the Democratic platform contained a recommendation to help state and local governments develop new revenue sources. But the Democratic plank also included an assertion that contradicted the Republicans' criticism of expanding federal power: "No government at any level can properly complain of violation of its power, if it fails to meet its responsibilities."

Neither party had a civil rights plank containing specifics. The difference was wording, with the Democrats promising "fair, effective enforcement" of the 1964 Civil Rights Act, but precluding the use of quotas in combating racial discrimination. The Republicans pledged "full implementation and faithful execution" of civil rights laws.

Without dissent, the Democratic platform included a provision that condemned extremism of the right and left, especially the Communist Party, the Ku Klux Klan, and the John Birch Society.

The two parties differed in their opinion of the health of the economy. The Republicans blamed their opposition for inflation and continuing unemployment and promised a reduction of at least $5 billion in federal spending. The Democrats countered by claiming the Kennedy-Johnson administration had engineered "the longest and strongest peacetime prosperity in modern history."

Following are excerpts from the Democratic platform of 1964:

Peace. At the start of the third decade of the nuclear age, the preservation of peace requires the strength to wage war and the wisdom to avoid it. The search for peace requires the utmost intelligence, the clearest vision, and a strong sense of reality. . . . Battered by economic failures, challenged by recent American achievements in space, torn by the Chinese-Russian rift, and faced with American strength and courage—international Communism has lost its unity and momentum.

National Defense. Specifically, we must and we will:
—Continue the overwhelming supremacy of our Strategic Nuclear Forces.
—Strengthen further our forces for discouraging limited wars and fighting subversion.
—Maintain the world's largest research and development effort, which has initiated more than 200 new programs since 1961, to ensure continued American leadership in weapons systems and equipment. . . .

Control of the use of nuclear weapons must remain solely with the highest elected official in the country—the President of the United States. . . .

The complications and dangers in our restless, constantly changing world require of us consummate understanding and experience. One rash act, one thoughtless decision, one unchecked reaction—and cities could become smouldering ruins and farms parched wasteland.

Civil Rights. The Civil Rights Act of 1964 deserves and requires full observance by every American and fair, effective enforcement if there is any default. . . .

Extremism. We condemn extremism, whether from the Right or Left, including the extreme tactics of such organizations as the Communist Party, the Ku Klux Klan and the John Birch Society.

Federal Power. The Democratic Party holds to the belief that government in the United States—local, state and federal—was created in order to serve the people. Each level of government has appropriate powers and each has specific responsibilities. The first responsibility of government at every level is to protect the basic freedoms of the people. No government at any level can properly complain of violation of its power, if it fails to meet its responsibilities.

The federal government exists not to grow larger, but to enlarge the individual potential and achievement of the people.

The federal government exists not to subordinate the states, but to support them.

Economy. In 42 months of uninterrupted expansion under Presidents Kennedy and Johnson, we have achieved the longest and strongest peacetime prosperity in modern history. . . .

It is the national purpose, and our commitment, that every man or woman who is willing and able to work is entitled to a job and to a fair wage for doing it.

1968 Conventions

PRESIDENTIAL CANDIDATES

Richard M. Nixon
Republican

Hubert H. Humphrey
Democrat

George C. Wallace
American Independent

REPUBLICANS

The Republican convention, held August 5–8 in Miami Beach, Fla., had a surface tranquility that the later Democratic convention lacked. Only two roll-call votes were taken to nominate presidential and vice-presidential candidates.

The credentials committee considered only one serious challenge, and that involved a single delegate. By a 32–32 vote, the committee defeated an unexpectedly strong attempt to overturn the preconvention decision to seat Rep. H. R. Gross of Iowa rather than a Des Moines housewife. The full convention approved the credentials committee report without a roll-call vote.

Delegates approved the rules committee report without comment. It contained recommendations to prohibit discrimination in the selection of future convention delegates and to add the Republican state chairmen as members of the Republican National Committee.

Twelve names were placed in nomination for the presidency, although the contest was clearly among three candidates: the front-runner, former vice president Richard Nixon, and two governors, Nelson A. Rockefeller of New York and Ronald Reagan of California. The ideological gulf between the more liberal Rockefeller and the more conservative Reagan made it difficult for them to agree on a common strategy to stop Nixon, even when Reagan abandoned his favorite-son status for active candidacy two days before the balloting.

To head off the defection to Reagan of his more conservative supporters, Nixon seemed to take a sharp tack to the right the day before the balloting. He told southern delegations he would not run an administration that would "ram anything down your throats," that he opposed school busing, that he would appoint "strict constitutionalists" to the Supreme Court, and that he was critical of federal intervention in local school board affairs.

Nixon won the nomination on the first ballot, receiving 692 votes (25 more than necessary) to easily outdistance Rockefeller, who had 277, and Reagan, who had 182. After vote switches, the final totals were Nixon, 1,238, Rockefeller, 93, and Reagan, 2. In a brief speech, Reagan moved that Nixon's nomination be made unanimous, but his motion was never put to a vote. (Table, p. 230.)

In his selection of a running mate, Nixon surprised many observers by tapping Gov. Spiro T. Agnew of Maryland. Agnew, who had delivered the major nominating speech for Nixon, had, ironically, been one of Rockefeller's earliest and strongest supporters. But Agnew ceased his active support of Rockefeller in March, irked by the New York governor's indecision about entering the race, and, at the beginning of convention week, announced his support for Nixon.

The name of Michigan governor George Romney also was placed in nomination for vice president. Agnew was an easy winner, receiving 1,119 votes to 186 for Romney, who made no effort to withdraw his name. After completion of the roll call, a Romney motion to make Agnew's nomination unanimous was approved.

The delegates approved without debate the 1968 Republican platform, which steered a careful middle course between conservatives and liberals on domestic policy and between "doves" and "hawks" on the touchy Vietnam issue. The 11,500-word document was somewhat more liberal in tone than that of 1960 and was far removed from the militantly conservative tone of the 1964 document.

A major floor fight on the platform was averted when platform committee members, led by Senate minority leader Everett McKinley Dirksen of Illinois, substituted for the original hard-line war plank new language stressing the need for de-Americanization of both the military and civilian efforts in Vietnam. "Doves" and "hawks" alike went along with the revised version.

As originally written, the plank criticized the Johnson administration for not leaving key Vietnam decisions to the military and for the administration's policy of military gradualism. Both Nixon and Rockefeller backers opposed the strong language, and a compromise Vietnam plank was accepted. As well as advocating the de-Americanization of the war, it proposed concentrating on protection of the South Vietnamese population rather than on capturing territory, and on efforts to strengthen local forces and responsibility. Although the adopted platform endorsed continued negotiations with Hanoi, it remained silent on the important issues of a bombing pause and of a possible Saigon coalition that would include the communists.

In its discussion of national defense, the platform criticized the administration for failure to develop superior new weaponry. The document indicated that, when the Vietnam War was over, a reduced defense budget might make possible increased federal spending on social welfare programs. But it neither suggested how much more spending nor recommended any substantial increases in the near future.

The platform treated rioting and crime in militant fashion: "We will not tolerate violence!" The crime plank criticized the Johnson administration for not taking effective action against crime and pledged "an all-out federal-state-local crusade."

In its youth plank, the Republicans urged the states to lower the voting age to eighteen but did not endorse proposals for a constitutional amendment to lower the federal voting age. The plank also advocated action to shorten the period in which young men were eligible for the draft and proposed to develop eventually a voluntary force.

Following are excerpts from the Republican platform of 1968:

Vietnam. The Administration's Vietnam policy has failed—militarily, politically, diplomatically, and with relation to our own people.

We condemn the Administration's breach of faith with the American people respecting our heavy involvement in Vietnam. Every citizen bitterly recalls the Democrat campaign oratory of 1964: "We are not about to send American boys 9–10,000 miles away from home to do what Asian boys ought to be doing for themselves."

The entire nation has been profoundly concerned by hastily-extemporized, undeclared land wars which embroil massive U.S. Army forces thousands of miles from our shores. It is time to realize that not every international conflict is susceptible of solution by American ground forces. . . .

We pledge to adopt a strategy relevant to the real problems of the war, concentrating on the security of the population, on developing a greater sense of nationhood, and on strengthening the local forces. It will be a strategy permitting a progressive de-Americanization of the war, both military and civilian. . . .

National Defense. Grave errors, many now irretrievable, have characterized the direction of our nation's defense.

A singular notion—that salvation for America lies in standing still—has pervaded the entire effort. Not retention of American superiority but parity with the Soviet Union has been made the controlling doctrine in many critical areas. We have frittered away superior military capabilities, enabling the Soviets to narrow their defense gap, in some areas to outstrip us, and to move to cancel our lead entirely by the early Seventies.

China. Improved relations with Communist nations can come only when they cease to endanger other states by force or threat. Under existing conditions, we cannot favor recognition of Communist China or its admission to the United Nations.

Crime. Fire and looting, causing millions of dollars of property damage, have brought great suffering to home owners and small businessmen, particularly in black communities least able to absorb catastrophic losses. The Republican Party strongly advocates measures to alleviate and remove the frustrations that contribute to riots. We simultaneously support decisive action to quell civil disorder, relying primarily on state and local governments to deal with these conditions.

America has adequate peaceful and lawful means for achieving even fundamental social change if the people wish it. *We will not tolerate violence!*

For the future, we pledge an all-out, federal-state-local crusade against crime, including:

—Leadership by an Attorney General who will restore stature and respect to that office. . . .

—Enactment of legislation to control indiscriminate availability of firearms, safeguarding the right of responsible citizens to collect, own and use firearms for legitimate purposes, retaining primary responsibility at the state level, with such federal laws as necessary to better enable the states to meet their responsibilities.

DEMOCRATS

While violence flared in the streets and thousands of police and guards imposed security precautions unprecedented at presidential nominating conventions, the 1968 Democratic convention met August 26–29 in Chicago to nominate Hubert H. Humphrey of Minnesota for the presidency and to endorse the controversial Vietnam policies of the Johnson-Humphrey administration.

Twin themes—physical force to keep order and political force to overrule minority sentiment in the Democratic Party—were apparent throughout the convention.

The physical force, supplied by 11,900 Chicago police, 7,500 army regulars, 7,500 Illinois National Guardsmen, and 1,000 FBI and Secret Service agents, was exerted to keep vociferous Vietnam War critics away from the convention headquarters hotels and the International Amphitheatre where official sessions were held. A security ring several blocks wide guarded the Amphitheatre, itself surrounded by a barbed wire fence and multiple security checkpoints for entering delegates, reporters, and guests. No violence erupted in the Amphitheatre area, but near the downtown hotels there were days of bitter demonstrations that ended with repeated police use of tear gas. At the end of convention week, the Chicago police announced that 589 persons had been arrested, with more than 119 police and 100 demonstrators injured.

The political force was exerted by the Johnson administration organization backing Vice President Humphrey, whose supporters enjoyed clear control of convention proceedings from start to end. In a distinct minority were the antiwar factions that rallied around the candidacies of Sens. Eugene J. McCarthy of Minnesota and George McGovern of South Dakota. The McCarthy forces mounted a series of challenges to the Humphrey faction—on credentials, rules, the platform, and finally the nomination itself.

In the first business of the convention, the Humphrey and McCarthy forces joined to ban the 136-year-old unit rule, which enabled the majority of a split delegation to cast the delegation's entire vote for the candidate favored by the majority. Delegates rejected by voice vote a motion by the Texas delegation to retain the rule through the 1968 convention. However, as expected, the brief moments of unity ended when the convention moved on to consider credentials challenges.

The credentials committee had considered an unprecedented number of challenges, involving delegates from fifteen states. Although McCarthy supported almost all the challenges, his candidacy was not always the paramount issue. In the case of the disputed southern delegations, racial imbalance, the party loyalty issue, or a combination of both, were more important. Of the seventeen different challenges, McCarthy supported all but one (in Wisconsin); McGovern backed all the southern challenges; Humphrey supported only the Mississippi challenge publicly.

In a historic move, the convention by a voice vote seated a new loyalist Democratic faction from Mississippi and unseated the delegation of the traditionally segregationist, conservative regular party. The credentials committee decided all other challenges in favor of the regular delegations, but minority reports were filed for the Alabama, Georgia, North Carolina, and Texas challengers. The North Carolina case was decided by a voice vote supporting the regular delegation, but the other three cases were settled by roll-call votes.

The first state to be considered was Texas, and, by a vote of 1,368¼ to 956¾, the convention approved the seating of the regular delegation led by Gov. John B. Connally. The rival McCarthy-supported Texas faction was led by Sen. Ralph Yarborough. (*Table, p. 231.*)

The Georgia case was considered next, with the credentials committee recommending that both rival delegations be seated and the Georgia vote split evenly between them. However, both delegations found this to be an unsatisfactory solution and presented reports to have their entire delegation seated alone. A minority report to seat the challenging Loyal National Democrats, led by black state representative Julian Bond, was defeated 1,415.45 to 1,043.55. A minority report to seat the regular delegation, handpicked by Gov. Lester G. Maddox and Democratic state chairman James H. Gray, was rejected by a voice vote. The solution recommended by the credentials committee was subsequently approved by a voice vote.

The Alabama case involved three competing factions: the regulars, the largely black National Democratic Party of Alabama (NDPA), and the integrated Alabama Independent Democratic Party (AIDP), created solely to run a slate of presidential electors loyal to the national party against the third-party candidacy of the state's former governor, George C. Wallace. The credentials committee proposed seating all members of the regular delegation who would sign a loyalty pledge and replacing those who would not sign with loyal members of the AIDP delegation. However, the McCarthy-backed NDPA introduced a minority report to seat its entire delegation. By a vote of 1,607 to 880¾, the convention rejected this minority report and by a voice vote approved the recommendation of the credentials committee.

The remainder of the credentials committee report was approved, including a resolution instructing the Democratic National Committee to include, in the call for the 1972 convention, encouragement to state parties to ensure that all Democrats in each state have a "meaningful and timely" opportunity to participate in delegate selection.

McCarthy, McGovern, and other liberal factions won their greatest breakthrough on convention rules, obtaining by a vote of 1,351¼ to 1,209 elimination of the unit rule at every level of party activity leading up to and including the 1972 convention. Many Humphrey-pledged delegates also backed the unit rule change. Also a part of this successful minority report was the requirement that the delegate-selection process in 1972 be public and held within the calendar year of the convention.

On Wednesday night, on the third day of the convention, while nominations and balloting for president took place at the Amphitheatre, the worst violence of the convention broke out downtown, and television screens carried pictures of phalanxes of Chicago police advancing on demonstrators. At the same time, hundreds of Chicago mayor Richard J. Daley's workers were brought into the galleries with apparent improper credentials. Some delegates, apparently refusing to show their credentials to the omnipresent security guards, were physically ejected from the convention floor. The McCarthy and McGovern forces charged "atrocities" and tried to adjourn the convention for two weeks. House majority leader Carl Albert of Oklahoma, the convention chairman, refused to accept their motions.

In addition to Humphrey, McCarthy, and McGovern, only two other candidates were placed in nomination—the Rev. Channing E. Phillips of the District of Columbia, who became the first black ever nominated for the presidency at a national convention, and North Carolina governor Dan K. Moore.

The emotional highlight of the session was provided by McGovern's nominator, Connecticut senator Abraham A. Ribicoff, who charged that "with George McGovern as president of the United States we wouldn't have to have Gestapo tactics in the streets of Chicago."

Humphrey was an easy winner on the first ballot, receiving 1,759¼ votes to 601 for McCarthy, 146½ for McGovern, and 67½ for Phillips. Humphrey's winning majority included the bulk of party moderates, big-city organizations of the North (including Daley's), and southern conservatives. In a tumultuous ending to one of the wildest nights in American politics, Chairman Albert gaveled through a motion to make the nomination unanimous (despite major opposition on the floor) and adjourned the session. (*Table, p. 231.*)

As his running mate, Humphrey chose Maine senator Edmund S. Muskie. Julian Bond's name also was placed in nomination, but Bond, then twenty-eight, withdrew, explaining that he was under the "legal age" to be president (the constitutional minimum is thirty-five). Before the end of the first ballot, Albert recognized Mayor Daley, who moved that Muskie be declared the vice-presidential nominee by acclamation. With the convention in a particularly unruly state, the Daley motion was quickly adopted. At the time the roll call was suspended, Muskie already had received 1,942½ votes, a majority. Bond was a distant second with 48¼.

The 18,000-word platform, adopted by a voice vote, was a document that met the demands of the Democratic Party's liberals word for word in almost every section except that which dealt with U.S. policy in Vietnam. At one point during the platform-writing sessions, it appeared that Humphrey might assent to a plank calling for a halt in U.S. bombing of North Vietnam. But President Johnson reportedly sent personal instructions that the plank should support administration policy.

The administration plank, approved 62–35 in the platform committee, supported a bombing halt only when it "would not endanger the lives of our troops in the field," did not call for a reduction in search-and-destroy missions or a withdrawal of troops until the end of the war, and advocated a new government in Saigon only after the war had ended. The minority plank, drafted by McCarthy and McGovern, called for an immediate halt to the bombing, reduction of offensive operations in the South Vietnamese countryside, a negotiated troop withdrawal, and encouragement of the South Vietnamese government to negotiate with communist insurgents.

Following nearly three hours of debate the minority plank was defeated, 1,567¾ to 1,041¼. After the result was announced, members of the New York delegation and others slipped on black armbands and sang "We Shall Overcome." *(Table, p. 231.)*

Unlike the Republican platform, which called for decreased United States involvement in Vietnam, Democrats adopted a plan that called for a continued strong American war effort. Although the Democrats agreed with Republicans that the South Vietnamese eventually should take over their nation's defense, they gave no indication that an expanded Vietnamese role could lead to U.S. troop reductions in the near future.

Following are excerpts from the Democratic platform of 1968:

Vietnam. Recognizing that events in Vietnam and the negotiations in Paris may affect the timing and the actions we recommend we would support our Government in the following steps:

Bombing—Stop all bombing of North Vietnam when this action would not endanger the lives of our troops in the field; this action should take into account the response from Hanoi.

Troop Withdrawal—Negotiate with Hanoi an immediate end or limitation of hostilities and the withdrawal from South Vietnam of all foreign forces—both United States and allied forces, and forces infiltrated from North Vietnam. . . .

National Defense. We must and will maintain a strong and balanced defense establishment adequate to the task of security and peace. There must be no doubt about our strategic nuclear capacity, our capacity to meet limited challenges, and our willingness to act when our vital interests are threatened. . . .

We face difficult and trying times in Asia and in Europe. We have responsibilities and commitments we cannot escape with honor.

China. The immediate prospects that China will emerge from its self-imposed isolation are dim. But both Asians and Americans will have to coexist with the 750 million Chinese on the mainland. We shall continue to make it clear that we are prepared to cooperate with China whenever it is ready to become a responsible member of the international community. We would actively encourage economic, social and cultural exchange with mainland China as a means of freeing that nation and her people from their narrow isolation.

Crime. In fighting crime we must not foster injustice. Lawlessness cannot be ended by curtailing the hard-won liberties of all Americans. The right of privacy must be safeguarded. Court procedures must be expedited. Justice delayed is justice denied.

A respect for civil peace requires also a proper respect for the legitimate means of expressing dissent. A democratic society welcomes criticism within the limits of the law. Freedom of speech, press, assembly and association, together with free exercise of the franchise, are among the legitimate means to achieve change in a democratic society. But when the dissenter resorts to violence, he erodes the institutions and values which are the underpinnings of our democratic society. We must not and will not tolerate violence.

Electoral Reform. We fully recognize the principle of one man, one vote in all elections. We urge that due consideration be given to the question of Presidential primaries throughout the nation. We urge reform of the electoral college and election procedures to assure that the votes of the people are fully reflected.

AMERICAN INDEPENDENT PARTY

Former Alabama governor George C. Wallace declared his third-party presidential candidacy on February 8, 1968. The vehicle for his candidacy was his personally created American Independent Party. No convention was held by the party to ratify his selection. (A descendant of the 1968 Wallace campaign, the American Party ran a national ticket in 1972 but received less than 2 percent of the vote.)

On February 14 Wallace announced the choice of former Georgia governor Marvin Griffin as his "interim" vice-presidential running mate, but he made clear that an official candidate would be chosen later in the campaign. Griffin's tentative candidacy was necessary to allow the American Independent Party to get on the ballot in several states. On October 3 Wallace announced his choice of retired air force general Curtis E. LeMay, an Ohio native, as his official running mate.

Ten days later, Wallace released the text of his party's platform. The document generally took a harder line toward domestic and international problems than did the Democratic and Republican platforms. Wallace favored termination of the Vietnam War through negotiations but added that, if negotiations failed, the United States should seek a military solution.

As expected, the emphasis of the platform on domestic issues centered on returning control of local affairs to the states and communities, with the federal government serving in an assisting role rather than an authoritarian manner.

Following are excerpts from the American Independent Party platform of 1968:

Vietnam. We earnestly desire that the conflict be terminated through peaceful negotiations and we will lend all aid, support, effort, sincerity and prayer to the efforts of our negotiators. Negotiation will be given every reasonable and logical chance for success and we will be patient to an extreme in seeking an end to the war through this means. If it becomes evident that the enemy does not desire to negotiate in good faith, that our hopes of termination of hostilities are not being realized and that the lives and safety of our committed troops are being further endangered, we must seek a military conclusion.

Crime. Lawlessness has become commonplace in our present society. The permissive attitude of the executive and judiciary at the national level sets the tone for this moral decay. The criminal and anarchist who preys on the decent law abiding citizen is rewarded for his misconduct through never ending justification and platitudes from those in high places who seem to have lost their concern for that vast segment of America that so strongly believes in law and order. . . .

We will appoint as Attorney General a person interested in the enforcement rather than the disruption of legal processes and restore that office to the dignity and stature it deserves and requires.

Federal Power. The Federal Government, in derogation and flagrant violation of this Article [X] of the Bill of Rights, has in the past three decades seized and usurped many powers not delegated to it, such as, among others: the operation and control of the public school system of the several states; the power to prescribe the eligibility and qualifications of those who would vote in our state and local elections; the power to intrude upon and control the farmer in the operation of his farm; the power to tell the property owner to whom he can and cannot sell or rent his property; and, many other rights and privileges of the individual citizen, which are properly subject to state or local control, as distinguished from federal control. The Federal Government has forced the states to reapportion their legislatures, a prerogative of the states alone. The Federal Government has attempted to take over and control the seniority and apprenticeship lists of the labor unions; the Federal Government has adopted so-called "Civil Rights Acts," particularly the one adopted in 1964, which have set race against race and class against class, all of which we condemn.

The Judiciary. In the period of the past three decades, we have seen the Federal judiciary, primarily the Supreme Court, transgress repeatedly upon the prerogatives of the Congress and exceed its authority by enacting judicial legislation, in the form of decisions based upon political and sociological considerations, which would never have been enacted by the Congress. We have seen them, in their solicitude for the criminal and lawless element of our society, shackle the police and other law enforcement agencies; and, as a result, they have made it increasingly difficult to protect the law-abiding citizen from crime and criminals. This is one of the principal reasons for the turmoil and the near revolutionary conditions which prevail in our country today, and particularly in our national capital. The Federal judiciary, feeling secure in their knowledge that their appointment is for life, have far exceeded their constitutional authority, which is limited to interpreting or construing the law.

It shall be our policy and our purpose, at the earliest possible time, to propose and advocate and urge the adoption of an amendment to the United States Constitution whereby members of the Federal judiciary at District level be required to face the electorate on his record at periodical intervals; and, in the event he receives a negative vote upon such election, his office shall thereupon become vacant, and a successor shall be appointed to succeed him.

With respect to the Supreme Court and the Courts of Appeals I [George Wallace] would propose that this amendment require reconfirmation of the office holder by the United States Senate at reasonable intervals.

1972 Conventions

PRESIDENTIAL CANDIDATES

George McGovern
Democrat

Richard M. Nixon
Republican

DEMOCRATS

Massive reforms in convention rules and delegate-selection procedures made the 1972 Democratic convention, held in Miami Beach, Florida, July 10–13, significantly different from the violence-plagued assembly in Chicago four years earlier.

Two special commissions created by the 1968 convention drafted the reforms. The Commission on Rules, chaired by Rep. James G. O'Hara of Michigan, composed the first set of rules ever written on Democratic convention procedure. Among the reforms that the Democratic National Committee adopted were:

• A new vote-allocation formula based nearly equally on electoral college strength and the Democratic vote in recent presidential elections.

• An expansion of the convention rules, platform, and credentials committees so that their make-up would reflect state population differences rather than the previous method of allocating two seats to each state.

• The assurance that women and men be equally represented on committees and among convention officers.

• The requirement that the meetings and votes of all convention committees be open to the public.

• The requirement that the reports and minority views of all the committees be released at specified dates before the opening of the convention.

• The banning of floor demonstrations for candidates.

• The arrangement of the states and territories for roll calls in random sequence determined by lot rather than in the traditional alphabetical order.

The Commission on Party Structure and Delegate Selection, first chaired by Sen. George McGovern of South Dakota and later by Rep. Donald M. Fraser of Minnesota, formulated eighteen guidelines to be met by the states in the delegate-selection process. With the approval of these guidelines by the Democratic National Committee, they became part of the 1972 convention call, thus requiring the states to be in full compliance with the guidelines before they would be seated.

Among the important features of the eighteen guidelines were the elimination of the unit rule; the restriction that no more than 10 percent of a state's delegation be named by its state committee; the requirement that all steps in the delegate-selection process be publicly advertised and held in easily accessible public places within the calendar year of the convention; the requirement that women, youth, and minority groups be included in delegations "in reasonable relationship" to their presence in the state's population; and the establishment of a detailed, public method of hearing delegate challenges.

The reforms encouraged an unprecedented number of challenges. The credentials committee opened hearings in Washington, D.C., two weeks before the start of the convention, faced with eighty-two challenges from thirty states and one territory. A total of 1,289 delegates were challenged, representing more than 40 percent of the convention delegates. More than four-fifths of the challenges were filed on grounds of noncompliance with reform commission guidelines regarding adequate representation of women, youth, and minorities.

The most controversial challenges involved the California delegation and the part of the Illinois delegation controlled by Mayor Richard J. Daley of Chicago. The credentials committee, in a move that surprised supporters of McGovern, a candidate for the presidential nomination, upheld a challenge of California's winner-take-all primary law, stripping McGovern of 151 of the 271 delegate votes he had won in the primary.

The committee voted 72 to 66 to award the 151 convention seats to Sen. Hubert H. Humphrey of Minnesota and seven other candidates in proportion to their share of the popular ballots cast in the state's June primary. Although McGovern was clearly the front-runner for the nomination, the decision, if not overturned by the full convention, threatened his chances of being selected.

In a tense and dramatic balloting session the next day, the committee voted 71 to 61 to unseat fifty-nine Chicago delegates, including Daley, on grounds that the procedures under which they had been selected violated five of the party's reform guidelines. Most of the Illinois delegates challenging Daley supported McGovern.

The emotional credentials challenges were considered on the first night of the convention. Twenty-three challenges from fif-teen states were brought to the convention floor, but the spotlight was on the California and Illinois cases. A key preliminary vote took place on a challenge to the South Carolina delegation brought by the National Women's Political Caucus. The challenge, seeking to increase the number of women in the state delegation, was rejected by a vote of 1,555.75 to 1,429.05. *(Table, p. 232.)*

The outcome of the vote could have set an important precedent on what constituted a majority on subsequent challenges. Anti-McGovern forces had hoped to get a ruling from the chair allowing an absolute majority of 1,509 delegates to prevail rather than a simple majority of delegates actually voting.

Convention chairman Lawrence F. O'Brien (also chairman of the Democratic National Committee) had announced earlier that a majority would consist of one-half plus one of the number of eligible voters. The rules provided that no delegates could vote on their own credentials challenges.

Because the winning total on the South Carolina vote exceeded by a wide margin both the eligible majority and the absolute majority of the convention's 3,016 votes, the anti-McGovern coalition was unable to force a test of what constituted a majority. Thus the vote, although it rejected the position of South Carolina challengers favorable to McGovern, set the stage for returning the 151 California delegates to McGovern. The McGovern forces subsequently won the crucial California challenge, 1,618.28 to 1,238.22. *(Table, p. 232.)*

Following the defeat of a compromise in the Chicago case, a minority report asking for seating of the Daley delegates alone, was defeated 1,486.04 to 1,371.56. The vote seated a group, a majority of which supported McGovern, headed by Chicago alderman William Singer and black activist Jesse L. Jackson. *(Table, p. 232.)*

No other roll-call votes were needed to resolve the remaining credentials challenges. After the settlement of all the delegate contests, the convention had a composition unlike that of any previous major party convention. The 1972 Democratic assembly was the largest in major party history, with 3,203 delegates casting 3,016 votes. Unlike the situation in 1968, most delegates were chosen in state primary elections rather than in state conventions or caucuses. Nearly two-thirds of the delegates to the 1972 convention were selected in primaries, while only 41 percent had been elected by the primary system four years earlier, when Humphrey won the Democratic nomination without entering any primaries.

There were also large increases in the number of women, youth, and racial minorities at the 1972 convention. The proportion of women delegates rose from 13 percent in 1968 to 40 percent in 1972; the number of youth delegates (age thirty and under) dramatically jumped from 2.6 percent in 1968 to 21 percent four years later; and black delegates made up 15 percent of the 1972 convention, compared with 5.5 percent in 1968. But while women, youth, and blacks were better represented than at earlier conventions, there was a lower level of participation by elected party officials. Only thirty of the 255 Democratic U.S. House members were present in Miami Beach.

The report of the rules committee was approved on the second day of the convention by a voice vote. The report proposed the abolition of winner-take-all primaries in 1976; the abolition of cross-over voting by Republicans in future Democratic presidential primaries; the selection of a woman as chairman of the 1976 convention, with the job rotating between the sexes thereafter; the creation of a special fund in the Democratic National Committee to subsidize the expenses of poor delegates at future national conventions and other party councils, and the appointment of a commission to make "appropriate revisions" in the reform guidelines.

Although the delegates overwhelmingly accepted these reforms, they balked at approving the party charter drafted by the rules committee. The new charter, the first ever written for a major party, was intended to free the national party of four-year presidential election cycles and to broaden public involvement in major national policy questions. But the charter was opposed by some party leaders, particularly members of Congress, who viewed the document as shifting power from elected politicians to the grass-roots level. By a vote of 2,408.45 to 195.10, the convention approved a compromise resolution to delay consideration of the charter until a proposed midterm policy conference in 1974. The compromise also enlarged the Democratic National Committee and revised its membership to reflect Democratic strength in the various states.

The settlement of the California challenge on the opening night of the convention in favor of the McGovern forces effectively locked up the presidential nomination for the South Dakota senator. The next day, two of his major rivals in the primaries, Senators Humphrey and Muskie, withdrew from the race. In the balloting on the third day of the convention, McGovern was an easy winner on the first roll call. Before switches, McGovern had received 1,728.35 votes to 525 for Sen. Henry M. Jackson of Washington, 381.7 for Gov. George C. Wallace of Alabama, and 151.95 for Rep. Shirley Chisholm of New York. After vote changes, McGovern's vote total rose to 1,864.95, but no attempt was made to make his nomination unanimous. *(Table, p. 232.)*

With McGovern's first choice for vice president, Sen. Edward M. Kennedy of Massachusetts, rebuffing all overtures, McGovern selected Sen. Thomas F. Eagleton of Missouri. The vice-presidential balloting was prolonged by the nomination of six other candidates, and, by the time the roll call was suspended, votes were distributed among more than seventy different "candidates." Eagleton received 1,741.81 votes, a majority. On the motion of Frances T. "Sissy" Farenthold, the runner-up, the roll call was suspended and Eagleton was nominated by acclamation.

Because of the long vice-presidential roll call, it was nearly 3 a.m. before McGovern was able to deliver his acceptance speech, costing him the prime-time television audience. In the speech, he stressed the antiwar theme that was a basic part of his campaign and implored the nation to "come home" to its founding ideals.

Barely ten days after selection of the Democratic ticket, on July 25, Eagleton disclosed that he voluntarily had hospitalized himself three times between 1960 and 1966 for "nervous exhaustion and fatigue." McGovern strongly supported his running mate at the time, but in the following days, his support for the Missouri senator began to wane. After meeting with McGovern on July 31, Eagleton withdrew from the ticket. It marked the first time since 1860 that a major party candidate had withdrawn from a national ticket after the convention had adjourned.

On August 5 McGovern announced that his choice to replace Eagleton was R. Sargent Shriver of Maryland, U.S. ambassador to France and the former director of the Peace Corps and the Office of Economic Opportunity. The newly enlarged Democratic National Committee formally nominated Shriver in an August 8 meeting in Washington.

The 1972 Democratic platform was probably the most liberal and the longest (about 25,000 words) ever offered by a major political party. The platform was more a collection of independent reform proposals than a unified plan of action. Its recommendations, largely written by separate subject-area task forces, did not translate into a compact program for Congress to consider or for a president to propose. But the platform's common themes reflected the changes in the party since 1968 and set it off from all other Democratic platforms of the previous generation.

The National Welfare Rights Organization sponsored a measure requiring the federal government to guarantee every family of four an annual income of $6,500. It lost, 1,852.86 to 999.34. *(Table, p. 232.)*

The platform's position on the Vietnam War was blunt and unequivocal. As "the first order of business" of a Democratic administration, the platform pledged "immediate and complete withdrawal of all U.S. forces in Indochina." The plank also promised an end to military aid to the Saigon regime but pledged economic assistance to Vietnam to help the nation emerge from the war. Amnesty for war resisters was recommended after the return of American prisoners of war.

Following are excerpts from the Democratic platform of 1972:

Vietnam. We believe that war is a waste of human life. We are determined to end forthwith a war which has cost 50,000 American lives, $150 billion of our resources, that has divided us from each other, drained our national will and inflicted incalculable damage to countless people. We will end that war by a simple plan that need not be kept secret: The immediate total withdrawal of all Americans from Southeast Asia.

Vietnam Amnesty. To those who for reasons of conscience refused to serve in this war and were prosecuted or sought refuge abroad, we state our firm intention to declare an amnesty, on an appropriate basis, when the fighting has ceased and our troops and prisoners of war have returned.

Poverty. The next Democratic Administration must end the present welfare system and replace it with an income security program which places cash assistance in an appropriate context with all of the measures outlined above, adding up to an earned income approach to ensure each family an income substantially more than the poverty level defined in the area. Federal income assistance will supplement the income of working poor people and assure an adequate income for those unable to work.

Crime. There must be laws to control the improper use of hand guns. Four years ago a candidate for the presidency was slain by a hand gun. Two months ago, another candidate for that office was gravely wounded. Three out of four police officers killed in the line of duty are slain with hand guns. Effective legislation must include a ban on sale of hand guns known as Saturday night specials which are unsuitable for sporting purposes.

Free Expression and Privacy. The new Democratic Administration should bring an end to the pattern of political persecution and investigation, the use of high office as a pulpit for unfair attack and intimidation and the blatant efforts to control the poor and to keep them from acquiring additional economic security or political power.

The epidemic of wiretapping and electronic surveillance engaged in by the Nixon Administration and the use of grand juries for purposes of political intimidation must be ended. The rule of law and the supremacy of the Constitution, as these concepts have traditionally been understood, must be restored.

Rights of Women. Women historically have been denied a full voice in the evolution of the political and social institutions of this country and are therefore allied with all underrepresented groups in a common desire to form a more humane and compassionate society. The Democratic Party pledges the following:
- A priority effort to ratify the Equal Rights Amendment. . . .
- Appointment of women to positions of top responsibilities in all branches of the federal government, to achieve an equitable ratio of women and men.

Presidential Elections. We favor a Constitutional change to abolish the Electoral College and to give every voter a direct and equal voice in Presidential elections. The amendment should provide for a runoff election, if no candidate received more than 40 percent of the popular vote.

REPUBLICANS

Six weeks after the Democratic convention, the Republicans gathered in the same Miami Beach convention hall. The August 21–23 convention, precisely programmed to make the most of free prime time, was a gigantic television spectacular from start to finish. The main business of the convention, the nomination of President Richard Nixon and Vice President Spiro T. Agnew to a second term, was a carefully planned ritual.

The selection of Miami Beach as the convention city provided as much drama as the convention itself. Initially the Republicans had chosen San Diego, Calif., as the host city, but the reluctance of that city to provide necessary facilities on schedule, coupled with the revelation that the International Telephone and Telegraph Corp. had pledged as much as $400,000 in local contributions, led the Republican National Committee to move the convention to Miami Beach.

Despite the preliminary organizational problems, the atmosphere of the convention itself was almost euphoric, and the sessions proceeded with dispatch. The five sessions lasted only sixteen hours and fifty-nine minutes, compared with the thirty hours and eighteen minutes of the Democratic convention.

The one debate, which lasted only an hour, occurred over the adoption of new procedures for selecting national convention delegates. The Republican National Committee's preconvention rules committee approved a 1976 delegate-allocation plan initiated by Sen. John G. Tower of Texas and Rep. Jack F. Kemp of New York. The plan emphasized a state's Republican presidential vote in awarding bonus delegates. It was viewed as especially beneficial to small southern and western states. The convention

rules committee amended the Tower-Kemp plan to make it more palatable to larger states by adding some bonus delegates for states electing Republican governors and members of Congress.

However, Rep. William A. Steiger of Wisconsin introduced a different plan, weighted more toward states electing Republican governors and members of Congress—a plan that would work to the advantage of the larger states. The debate on the contrasting plans focused on the question of whether states should be rewarded chiefly for delivering their electoral votes to a Republican presidential candidate or whether the bonus should be based to some extent on gubernatorial and congressional contests.

The dispute was in part a battle between liberals and conservatives. Final victory for the conservatives was achieved on a 910 to 434 roll-call vote that defeated the Steiger amendment. The reallocation formula adopted by the delegates would expand the 1976 convention to more than 2,000 delegates, compared with the 1,348 who went to Miami Beach in 1972.

The struggle over the delegate-allocation formula was the only sign of party division at the convention. Nixon was renominated on the third night, receiving 1,347 of the 1,348 votes. The only opposing vote was cast reluctantly by a delegate from New Mexico for Rep. Paul N. McCloskey Jr. of California, whose antiwar challenge of the president had fizzled after the year's first primary in New Hampshire. (*Table, p. 234.*)

One measure of the unity that surrounded the festive proceedings was the appearance of Gov. Nelson A. Rockefeller of New York to deliver Nixon's nominating speech. Rockefeller had become a loyal supporter of the president after having been his chief rival for the Republican nomination in 1960 and 1968.

Agnew was nominated the next night with 1,345 votes. There were two abstentions and one waggish vote for newscaster David Brinkley.

In his acceptance speech, Nixon combined a review of his first four years with promises for the next four and indirect but highly partisan attacks on his Democratic opponent, George McGovern. Nixon stressed that the choice in the upcoming election was "not between radical change and no change, the choice . . . is between change that works and change that won't work."

The Republican platform provoked little discussion and was approved by a voice vote. Two amendments were offered. The first, which would have pledged a prohibition on deficit federal spending, was defeated by voice vote. The second, advocating self-determination for American Indians, was approved by voice vote with the consent of the platform committee chairman, Rep. John J. Rhodes of Arizona.

The document, approximately 20,000 words long, was generally moderate in its proposals and conservative in language, in contrast to the Democrats' liberal platform.

The actual drafting of the Republican platform was heavily influenced by the White House, and platform committee sessions were held behind closed doors. In contrast, the Democrats held ten regional hearings around the country, drafted their platform in public, and were required by party rules to produce a final version at least ten days before the convention opened.

Following are excerpts from the Republican platform of 1972:

Vietnam. We will continue to seek a settlement of the Vietnam War which will permit the people of Southeast Asia to live in peace under political arrangements of their own choosing. We take specific note of the remaining major obstacle to settlement—Hanoi's demand that the United States overthrow the Saigon government and impose a Communist-dominated government on the South Vietnamese. We stand unequivocally at the side of the President in his effort to negotiate honorable terms, and in his refusal to accept terms which would dishonor this country.

Vietnam Amnesty. We are proud of the men and women who wear our country's uniform, especially of those who have borne the burden of fighting a difficult and unpopular war. Here and now we reject all proposals to grant amnesty to those who have broken the law by evading military service. We reject the claim that those who fled are more deserving, or obeyed a higher morality, than those next in line who served in their places.

Tax Reform. We reject the deceitful tax "reform" cynically represented as one that would soak the rich, but in fact one that would sharply raise the taxes of millions of families in middle-income brackets as well. We reject as well the lavish spending promised by the opposition Party which would more than double the present budget of the United States Government. This, too, would cause runaway inflation or force heavy increases in personal taxes.

Gun Control. [We pledge to] safeguard the right of responsible citizens to collect, own and use firearms for legitimate purposes, including hunting, target shooting and self-defense. We will strongly support efforts of all law enforcement agencies to apprehend and prosecute to the limit of the law all those who use firearms in the commission of crimes.

Women's Rights. Continued . . . support of the Equal Rights Amendment to the Constitution, our Party being the first national party to back this Amendment.

School Prayer. We reaffirm our view that voluntary prayer should be freely permitted in public places—particularly, by school children while attending public schools—provided that such prayers are not prepared or prescribed by the state or any of its political subdivisions and that no person's participation is coerced, thus preserving the traditional separation of church and state.

Health. To assure access to basic medical care for all our people, we support a program financed by employers, employees and the Federal Government to provide comprehensive health insurance coverage, including insurance against the cost of long-term and catastrophic illnesses and accidents and renal failure which necessitates dialysis, at a cost which all Americans can afford. . . .

We oppose nationalized compulsory health insurance. This approach would at least triple in taxes the amount the average citizen now pays for health and would deny families the right to choose the kind of care they prefer. Ultimately it would lower the overall quality of health care for all Americans.

1976 Conventions

PRESIDENTIAL CANDIDATES

Jimmy Carter
Democrat

Gerald R. Ford
Republican

DEMOCRATS

Jimmy Carter, whose presidential primary campaign flouted Democratic Party regulars, brought the party's diverse elements together July 12–15 in a show of unaccustomed unity. The four-day 1976 convention in New York City was the party's most harmonious in twelve years and a stark contrast to the bitter and divisive conventions of 1968 and 1972.

The spirit of harmony was evident in the committee reports. No credentials challenges were carried to the convention floor and just one minority plank to the platform was offered. Only the rules committee report sparked much debate, and it was muted compared with the emotional struggles in the previous two conventions.

The lack of a spirited competition for the presidential nomination was an important factor in the absence of credentials challenges. However, the groundwork for the harmonious atmosphere had been established months earlier, when the Democratic National Committee adopted new delegate-selection and convention rules.

The delegate-selection rules abolished the implicit quota system that had been the basis of most challenges in 1972. The only basis for a challenge in 1976 was the violation of a state's delegate-selection or affirmative action plan to ensure the fair representation of minorities. Because all states had their plans approved by the national committee's Compliance Review Commission, the credentials committee was not weighing the fairness of the plan but merely whether the state party had implemented it. In reverse of the 1972 system, the burden of proof was on the challenging individual or group, not on the state parties.

The task of challengers was further impeded by the action of the national committee in October 1975, raising the petition requirement for convention minority reports from 10 percent to 25 percent of credentials committee members.

The stringent new rules had an effect on the demographic composition of the convention. A postconvention survey by the national committee indicated that 36 percent of the delegates in 1976 were women, compared with 38 percent in 1972; 7 percent were black compared with 15 percent four years earlier, and 14 percent were youths, compared with 21 percent in 1972.

The first roll call of the convention came on a rules committee minority report that would have permitted extended debate on the platform. The measure was promoted by party liberals, who complained that the restrictive convention rules cut off their chance for full debate. They urged platform debate on a maximum of three issues for a total of one hour, if at least three hundred delegates from ten states signed a petition for such issues. The proposal called for debate only; no votes would have been taken.

Carter delegates, though, were nearly unanimous in their opposition, fearing that adoption of the minority report would unduly lengthen the proceedings. The convention rejected the minority report by a vote of 735 to 1,957½.

Liberals had better luck when the rules relating to future conventions were considered. By voice votes, they won approval of majority reports to establish the party's new Judicial Council as an arbiter of party rules and to eliminate the controversial loophole primary.

A loophole primary permitted election of delegates on a winner-take-all basis at the congressional district level. Carter and Democratic National Chairman Robert S. Strauss both favored the minority report, which called simply for review of the loophole primary by the newly established Commission on the Role and Future of Presidential Primaries, headed by Michigan state chairman Morley Winograd.

Liberals argued that this was not enough. They claimed that the loophole primary violated the party charter, which required proportional representation. Their position prevailed in the rules committee by a razor-thin margin of 58½ to 58¼. Although Carter managers were unhappy with the majority report, they did not press for a roll call and the convention approved it by voice vote.

But the convention rejected on roll-call votes liberal amendments to mandate the size and agenda of the party's 1978 midterm conference and to lower the minority report requirement at future conventions. The minority report on the 1978

conference would have required a prescribed agenda that included the discussion of policy matters. It also would have mandated a conference of at least 2,000 delegates, two-thirds of them elected at the congressional district level. On the roll call the proposal ran ahead 1,240 to 1,128, but it failed because of convention rules requiring a constitutional majority of 1,505 votes.

Another roll call came on the unsuccessful attempt by liberal delegates to have the minority report requirement at future conventions lowered from 25 percent to 15 percent of convention committee members. It was rejected, 1,249 to 1,354½.

Potentially the most explosive of the rules issues, regarding a "female quota" at future conventions, was settled in behind-the-scenes meetings between Carter and representatives of the women's caucus. At a rules committee meeting in Washington, D.C., in late June, the women's caucus had demanded equal representation with men in state delegations at future conventions. The Carter forces balked at this. Carter's views prevailed in the rules committee, which urged each state to promote equal division between the sexes but left the implementation of the rule to each state party. The women's caucus filed a minority report.

Both sides expressed a willingness to compromise, and in New York City on July 11 and 12 Carter met with representatives of the women's caucus. They reached a compromise that encouraged—but did not require—equal representation for women at the party's midterm conference and at future conventions. Language was inserted calling for the national committee to "encourage and assist" state parties in achieving equal division.

The compromise also included agreements between Carter and the women on other questions. Carter promised to establish an independent women's division in the party outside the realm of the chairman and pledged full party representation for women. The candidate promised to work for the ratification of the Equal Rights Amendment and pledged high government positions for women. With acceptance of this compromise by the women's caucus, the minority report was withdrawn and the compromise language on equal division was worked into the majority report.

Balloting for president came on July 14, the third day of the convention, but it was merely a formality. Carter had locked up the nomination more than a month earlier when he won the June 8 Ohio primary, a victory that prompted a cascade of endorsements and stymied his remaining opposition. Besides Carter, three other names were placed in nomination: Rep. Morris K. Udall of Arizona, Carter's most persistent primary challenger; Gov. Edmund G. "Jerry" Brown Jr. of California; and antiabortion crusader Ellen McCormack. The proceedings, though, turned into a love-feast as Udall before the balloting and Brown afterwards appeared at the convention to declare their support for Carter.

On the presidential roll call, Carter received 2,238½ of the convention's 3,008 votes, topping the needed majority little more than halfway through the balloting with the vote from Ohio. Udall finished second with 329½ votes, followed by Brown with 300½, Gov. George C. Wallace of Alabama with 57, and McCormack with 22. The rest of the vote was scattered. After completion of the roll call—and vote switches in California,

Rhode Island, and Louisiana—a motion to make the nomination unanimous was approved by voice vote. *(Table, p. 235.)*

The following morning Carter announced that his choice for vice president was Sen. Walter F. Mondale of Minnesota. Carter noted that it was a difficult decision, admitting that he had changed his mind three times in the previous thirty days.

In explaining his choice, Carter cited Mondale's experience and political philosophy, his concept of the presidency, and the preparation Mondale had made for his interview with Carter. Most of all, Carter emphasized compatibility, saying, "It's a very sure feeling that I have."

Mondale was one of seven prospective running mates Carter had personally interviewed. At his home in Plains, Georgia, Carter had interviewed, besides Mondale, Sens. Edmund S. Muskie (Maine) and John Glenn (Ohio). At the New York convention he interviewed Sens. Henry M. Jackson (Washington), Frank Church (Idaho), and Adlai E. Stevenson III (Illinois), and Rep. Peter W. Rodino Jr. (New Jersey). Rodino withdrew his name from consideration shortly after his interview.

Like the presidential roll call the previous night, the balloting for vice president on July 15 was a formality. Mondale had only one declared opponent, Gary Benoit, a Massachusetts college student and a Wallace delegate. Two others were nominated but withdrew—Rep. Ronald V. Dellums of California and Vietnam War resister Fritz Efaw of Oklahoma. Dellums, an African American from Oakland, appeared personally to withdraw his name and used the opportunity to plead with Carter to pay attention to the needs of minorities at home and to Third World aspirations abroad.

On the roll call, Mondale swamped his rivals, receiving 2,817 votes, more than 90 percent of the convention total. Retiring House Speaker Carl Albert (Oklahoma) finished a distant second with 36 votes, all cast as a complimentary gesture by his home state delegation. Rep. Barbara C. Jordan (Texas), an African American from Houston, followed with 28 votes, an apparent tribute to her dramatic keynote address.

Following the balloting, Mondale delivered his acceptance speech and succeeded in arousing the delegates with a partisan oratorical style reminiscent of his Minnesota mentor, Sen. Hubert H. Humphrey.

"We have just lived through the worst scandal in American history," Mondale declared, "and are now led by a president who pardoned the person who did it." His reference to the Watergate affair and to the Nixon pardon brought the delegates to their feet.

Carter's acceptance speech, unlike Mondale's, was not a rousing one in the traditional sense. But Carter was able to begin his address before 11 p.m., in the prime television slot that Strauss had promised as a contrast to George McGovern's nearly unheard 3 a.m. acceptance speech in 1972.

The 1976 platform had been carefully constructed by the Carter forces at platform committee meetings in Washington, D.C., in June. The ninety-page document was something of a throwback to earlier years—a broad statement of party goals rather than a list of legislative programs and controversial stands on issues. The platform and the care with which it was

written reflected the Democrats' determination to avoid the platform fights and issues that proved costly to the party in the previous two elections.

Unlike 1972, when there was sharp, divisive debate on twenty minority planks, only one minority plank—on revising the 1939 Hatch Act to allow federal employees to run for political office and participate in partisan campaigns—was presented to the delegates in Madison Square Garden. It was approved by the Carter forces and was adopted by a voice vote after minimal debate.

Following are excerpts from the Democratic platform of 1976:

Economy. To meet our goals we must set annual targets for employment, production and price stability; the Federal Reserve must be made a full partner in national economic decisions and become responsive to the economic goals of Congress and the President. . . .

Full Employment. We have met the goals of full employment with stable prices in the past and can do it again. The Democratic Party is committed to the right of all adult Americans willing, able and seeking work to have opportunities for useful jobs at living wages. To make that commitment meaningful, we pledge ourselves to the support of legislation that will make every responsible effort to reduce adult unemployment to 3 percent within 4 years. . . .

Government Reform. The Democratic Party is committed to the adoption of reforms such as zero-based budgeting, mandatory reorganization timetables, and sunset laws which do not jeopardize the implementation of basic human and political rights.

An Office of Citizen Advocacy should be established as part of the executive branch, independent of any agency, with full access to agency records and with both the power and the responsibility to investigate complaints.

We support the revision of the Hatch Act so as to extend to federal workers the same political rights enjoyed by other Americans as a birthright, while still protecting the Civil Service from political abuse.

We call for legislative action to provide for partial public financing on a matching basis of the congressional elections, and the exploration of further reforms to insure the integrity of the electoral process.

Health. We need a comprehensive national health insurance system with universal and mandatory coverage. Such a national health insurance system should be financed by a combination of employer-employee shared payroll taxes and general tax revenues. Consideration should be given to developing a means of support for national health insurance that taxes all forms of economic income.

Welfare Reform. We should move toward replacement of our existing inadequate and wasteful system with a simplified system of income maintenance, substantially financed by the federal government, which includes a requirement that those able to work be provided with appropriate available jobs or job training opportunities. Those persons who are physically able to work (other than mothers with dependent children) should be required to accept appropriate available jobs or job training.

As an interim step, and as a means of providing immediate federal fiscal relief to state and local governments, local governments should no longer be required to bear the burden of welfare costs. Further, there should be a phased reduction in the states' share of welfare costs.

Civil Rights and Liberties. We pledge effective and vigorous action to protect citizens' privacy from bureaucratic and technological intrusions, such as wiretapping and bugging without judicial scrutiny and supervision; and a full and complete pardon for those who are in legal or financial jeopardy because of their peaceful opposition to the Vietnam War, with deserters to be considered on a case-by-case basis.

We fully recognize the religious and ethical nature of the concerns which many Americans have on the subject of abortion. We feel, however, that it is undesirable to attempt to amend the U.S. Constitution to overturn the Supreme Court decision in this area.

Gun Control. Handguns simplify and intensify violent crime. Ways must be found to curtail the availability of these weapons. The Democratic Party must provide the leadership for a coordinated federal and state effort to strengthen the presently inadequate controls over the manufacture, assembly, distribution and possession of handguns and to ban Saturday night specials.

Furthermore, since people and not guns commit crimes, we support mandatory sentencing for individuals convicted of committing a felony with a gun.

The Democratic Party, however, affirms the right of sportsmen to possess guns for purely hunting and target-shooting purposes.

Energy. The Democratic energy platform begins with a recognition that the federal government has an important role to play in insuring the nation's energy future, and that it must be given the tools it needs to protect the economy and the nation's consumers from arbitrary and excessive energy price increases and help the nation embark on a massive domestic energy program focusing on conservation, coal conversion, exploration and development of new technologies to insure an adequate short-term and long-term supply of energy for the nation's needs. . . .

The huge reserves of oil, gas and coal on federal territory, including the outer continental shelf, belong to all the people. The Republicans have pursued leasing policies which give the public treasury the least benefit and the energy industry the most benefit from these public resources. Consistent with environmentally sound practices, new leasing procedures must be adopted to correct these policies, as well as insure the timely development of existing leases. . . .

We also support the legal prohibition against corporate ownership of competing types of energy, such as oil and coal. We believe such "horizontal" concentration of economic power to be dangerous both to the national interest and to the functioning of the competitive system.

Environment. The Democratic Party's strong commitment to environmental quality is based on its conviction that environmental protection is not simply an aesthetic goal, but is necessary to achieve a more just society. Cleaning up air and water supplies and controlling the proliferation of dangerous chemicals is a necessary part of a successful national health program. Protecting the worker from workplace hazards is a key element of our full employment program. . . .

Latin America. We must make clear our revulsion at the systematic violations of basic human rights that have occurred under some Latin American military regimes.

We pledge support for a new Panama Canal treaty, which insures the interests of the United States in that waterway, recognizes the principles already agreed upon, takes into account the interests of the Canal work force, and which will have wide hemispheric support.

REPUBLICANS

After four boisterous, raucous, and sometimes tearful days, Republicans ended their 1976 national convention on a positive note absent during most of a gathering characterized by strident attacks on the Democrats and the Congress they controlled. Delegates arrived in Kansas City, Mo., for the August 16–19 convention more evenly split than they had been since 1952, when Dwight D. Eisenhower edged Sen. Robert A. Taft of Ohio (1939–

1953) for the GOP nomination. Both major rivals for the nomination, President Gerald R. Ford (breaking with tradition) and former California governor Ronald Reagan, arrived in town three days before the balloting to continue their pursuit of delegates.

Ford, relying heavily on the prestige of the presidency that sometimes had failed to produce results during the seven-month campaign, invited a number of wavering delegates to his hotel suite in the new Crown Center Hotel while Reagan also courted delegates personally.

By a margin of 111 votes on August 17, the Reagan forces lost the first and probably the most important roll call of the convention. The vote came on a Reagan-sponsored amendment to the rules committee report that would have required all presidential candidates to name their running mates before the presidential balloting the next night.

The idea of a test vote on the vice-presidential question was sprung by Reagan's campaign manager, John Sears, barely a week before the convention, when on August 9 he appeared before the rules committee and urged that the proposal be included as Section C of Rule 16. The amendment was clearly aimed at throwing Ford on the defensive, because Reagan had designated Sen. Richard S. Schweiker of Pennsylvania as his running mate on July 26. Under the proposal, failure of a candidate to comply would have freed all delegates from any commitments to vote for him.

The convention debate and vote on Rule 16C was the focal point of the August 17 session. Supporters characterized the proposal as a "right-to-know" amendment. "A presidential candidate must tell us who's on his team before we are expected to join him," argued former Missouri representative Thomas B. Curtis, the sponsor of the amendment. "The delegates have the right to be consulted for a day of decision that will have an impact for years to come."

Speakers against the amendment countered that it was solely a maneuver of the Reagan forces and that any vice-presidential selection reform should be deliberately considered on its merits.

The final court stood at 1,069 in favor of the amendment and 1,180 against, with ten abstentions. The vote was the first tangible evidence of Ford strength at the convention and paved the way for his nomination. (*Table, p. 236.*)

On the presidential roll call August 18, the final vote was 1,187 for Ford, 1,070 for Reagan, one vote from the New York delegation for Commerce Secretary Elliot L. Richardson, and one abstention. (*Table, p. 236.*) On a voice vote the convention made the nomination unanimous.

Ford added to the partisan style of the Republican ticket the next day by selecting Sen. Robert J. "Bob" Dole of Kansas as his running mate after Reagan ruled out his acceptance of the second spot. While little mentioned during speculation about Ford's vice-presidential choice, Dole, a former chairman of the Republican National Committee, was seen as an effective gut fighter who would allow Ford to keep his campaign style presidential in the battle against Carter.

Vice President Nelson A. Rockefeller nominated his potential successor, telling the crowd that the Kansas senator not only could stand the heat of political battle, but also could "really dole it out." Rockefeller, unpopular with conservatives, had not sought to continue in the job he had gained through appointment in 1974.

On the vice-presidential roll call, Dole received 1,921 of the convention's 2,259 votes. Sen. Jesse A. Helms of North Carolina, a hero of the conservatives, finished a distant second with 103 votes. The remaining votes were scattered among twenty-nine other "candidates."

Ford's acceptance speech concentrated on his record since taking office in mid-1974. The president took credit for cutting inflation in half, increasing employment to a record level, and bringing the country to peace.

Ford diverged from his prepared text to issue a direct challenge to Carter. "I'm ready, eager to go before the American people and debate the real issues face to face with Jimmy Carter," the president said. "The American people have the right to know first-hand exactly where both of us stand." No major party presidential nominees had debated since the Kennedy-Nixon debates in 1960.

By the time the convention got around to debating the platform the night of August 17, an expected bitter struggle between Ford and Reagan forces had been deflated by the earlier vote on rules. The arena, which had been packed two hours earlier, held a somewhat smaller crowd after midnight. Many Ford delegates in particular, confident that they had won the main event, left while members of the platform committee presented the sixty-five-page document.

Two minority planks were offered, in accordance with platform committee rules that required petitions signed by 25 percent of the members. The first, sponsored by Ann F. Peckham of Wisconsin, called for deleting all platform references to abortion. The committee-approved section supported a constitutional amendment "to restore protection of the right to life of unborn children." After a twelve-minute debate, the minority plank was defeated by voice vote and the abortion language stayed in.

The second minority report, a six-paragraph addition to the foreign policy section, was sponsored by thirty-four Reagan supporters on the platform committee. Without mentioning names, it criticized President Ford and Secretary of State Henry A. Kissinger for losing public confidence, making secret international agreements, and discouraging the hope of freedom for those who did not have it—presumably captive nations.

Many of Ford's supporters, including Rep. John B. Anderson of Illinois and Senate minority leader Hugh Scott of Pennsylvania, earlier had expressed strong opposition to the "morality in foreign policy" plank, as it came to be called. Ford's floor leader, Sen. Robert P. Griffin of Michigan, and Rep. David C. Treen of Louisiana sought compromise language in informal negotiations on the floor. But the Reagan forces, led by Senator Helms, were adamant.

Not wishing to offend the Reagan contingent further, Ford's supporters decided not to fight. Sen. Roman L. Hruska of Nebraska, chairman of the foreign policy subcommittee, announced from the podium that there would be no organized opposition to the plank. It was passed by voice vote. The convention then approved the platform.

The document reflected the nearly equal influence of President Ford and Ronald Reagan at the convention. It was a traditional Republican blueprint for limited government—a clear contrast with the Democratic platform.

Ordinarily, the platform of the party holding the White House heaps praise on the incumbent president and boasts of the way he has led the nation. This Republican platform did not. With Ford embroiled in a contest for the nomination, the platform writers chose to mention him by name only a few times. Richard Nixon was never mentioned. There were only vague references to Watergate.

Following are excerpts from the Republican Party platform of 1976:

Economy. We believe it is of paramount importance that the American people understand that the number one destroyer of jobs is inflation.

Republicans hope every American realizes that if we are to permanently eliminate high unemployment, it is essential to protect the integrity of our money. That means putting an end to deficit spending.

Wage and price controls are not the solution to inflation. They attempt to treat only the symptom—rising prices—not the cause. Historically, controls have always been a dismal failure, and in the end they create only shortages, black markets and higher prices. For these reasons the Republican Party strongly opposes any reimposition of such controls, on a standby basis or otherwise. . . .

Government Reform. There must be functional realignment of government, instead of the current arrangement by subject areas or constituencies.

Revenue Sharing is an effort to reverse the trend toward centralization. Revenue Sharing must continue without unwarranted federal strictures and regulations.

Block grant programs should be extended to replace many existing categorical health, education, child nutrition and social programs.

While we oppose a uniform national primary, we encourage the concept of regional presidential primaries, which would group those states which voluntarily agree to have presidential primaries in a geographical area on a common date.

Criminal Justice. Each state should have the power to decide whether it wishes to impose the death penalty for certain crimes. All localities are urged to tighten their bail practices and to review their sentencing and parole procedures.

Gun Control. We support the right of citizens to keep and bear arms. We oppose federal registration of firearms. Mandatory sentences for crimes committed with a lethal weapon are the only effective solution to this problem.

Civil Rights and Liberties. The Republican Party reaffirms its support for ratification of the Equal Rights Amendment. Our Party was the first national party to endorse the E.R.A. in 1940. We continue to believe its ratification is essential to insure equal rights for all Americans.

The Republican Party favors a continuance of the public dialogue on abortion and supports the efforts of those who seek enactment of a constitutional amendment to restore protection of the right to life for unborn children.

Welfare Reform. We oppose federalizing the welfare system; local levels of government are most aware of the needs of their communities.

We also oppose the guaranteed annual income concept or any programs that reduce the incentive to work.

Those features of the present law, particularly the food stamp program, that draw into assistance programs people who are capable of paying for their own needs should be corrected. The humanitarian purpose of such programs must not be corrupted by eligibility loopholes.

Health. We support extension of catastrophic illness protection to all who cannot obtain it. We should utilize our private health insurance system to assure adequate protection for those who do not have it. Such an approach will eliminate the red tape and high bureaucratic costs inevitable in a comprehensive national program.

The Republican Party opposes compulsory national health insurance.

Energy. One fact should now be clear: We must reduce sharply our dependence on other nations for energy and strive to achieve energy independence at the earliest possible date. We cannot allow the economic destiny and international policy of the United States to be dictated by the sovereign powers that control major portions of the world's petroleum supplies. . . .

Foreign Policy. We recognize and commend that great beacon of human courage and morality, Alexander Solzhenitsyn, for his compelling message that we must face the world with no illusions about the nature of tyranny. Ours will be a foreign policy that keeps this ever in mind.

Ours will be a foreign policy which recognizes that in international negotiations we must make no undue concessions; that in pursuing détente we must not grant unilateral favors with only the hope of getting future favors in return.

Agreements that are negotiated, such as the one signed in Helsinki, must not take from those who do not have freedom the hope of one day gaining it.

Finally, we are firmly committed to a foreign policy in which secret agreements, hidden from our people, will have no part.

Latin America. By continuing its policies of exporting subversion and violence, Cuba remains outside the Inter-American family of nations. We condemn attempts by the Cuban dictatorship to intervene in the affairs of other nations; and, as long as such conduct continues, it shall remain ineligible for admission to the Organization of American States.

The United States intends that the Panama Canal be preserved as an international waterway for the ships of all nations. . . . In any talks with Panama, however, the United States negotiators should in no way cede, dilute, forfeit, negotiate or transfer any rights, power, authority, jurisdiction, territory or property that are necessary for the protection and security of the United States and the entire Western Hemisphere.

1980 Conventions

PRESIDENTIAL CANDIDATES

Jimmy Carter
Democrat

Ronald Reagan
Republican

John B. Anderson
Independent

REPUBLICANS

Ronald Reagan, the sixty-nine-year-old former California governor, was installed as the Republican presidential nominee at the party's national convention, but his moment of glory nearly was overshadowed by an unusual flap over the number-two spot. The choosing of Reagan's running mate provided the only suspense at the GOP convention, held July 14–17 in Detroit's Joe Louis Arena.

Who would fill the number-one spot had been determined long before when Reagan won twenty-eight of the thirty-four Republican presidential primaries and eliminated all of his major rivals. The last to withdraw—George Bush—was tapped by

Reagan July 16 as his ticket mate in a dramatic postmidnight appearance before the delegates.

For most of the evening of July 16, it looked as though Gerald R. Ford would occupy the second spot on the ticket, which would have made him the first former president to run for vice president. A number of Republicans had described the combination as a "dream ticket." Groups of Reagan and Ford supporters had met four times to "discuss" the possibility of forging a Reagan-Ford ticket.

The discussions reportedly centered around providing a role for Ford somewhat akin to the White House chief of staff's. Ford further fed the speculation, offering a simple solution to the temporary problem that would have been posed by the Twelfth Amendment to the Constitution. The amendment would have had the effect of prohibiting the members of the electoral college from California from voting for both Reagan and Ford because both were California residents. The amendment says that the electors from any state must vote for at least one person who is not from that state. Ford said Reagan's lawyers had researched the residency question and determined that legally there would be no problem if the former president changed his residence to Michigan, which he represented in the House for twenty-five years, or to Colorado, where he owned a home.

As the evening of July 16 wore on, the speculation heightened. About 9:15 p.m. Reagan telephoned Ford to ask him to make up his mind whether he wanted the vice president's job. Meanwhile, convention officials proceeded to call the roll of the states, and Reagan received enough votes to become the official nominee.

But at about 11:15 p.m. the Reagan-Ford arrangement fell apart. Ford went to Reagan's suite in the Detroit Plaza Hotel and the two men agreed that it would be better for Ford to campaign for the GOP ticket rather than be a member of it. "His [Ford's] instinct told him it was not the thing to do," Reagan said later.

When it became apparent that efforts to persuade Ford to join the ticket had failed, Reagan turned to Bush, a moderate with proven vote-getting ability. The Reagan camp refused to acknowledge that Bush had been the second choice, even though it was widely perceived that way. "There was everybody else and then the Ford option," Edwin Meese, Reagan's chief of staff, said later.

Bush had been Reagan's most persistent competitor through the long primary season, but he won only six primaries—Michigan, Massachusetts, Connecticut, Pennsylvania, the District of Columbia, and Puerto Rico. Bush was one of the vice-presidential possibilities favored by those in the party who believed that Reagan had to reach outside the GOP's conservative wing if he were to have broad appeal in November.

Bush supporters said that his Texas residency would balance the ticket geographically and that his extensive government service would overcome criticism that Reagan did not have any Washington experience. Bush served from 1967 to 1971 in the U.S. House and had been ambassador to the United Nations, head of the U.S. liaison office in Peking, and director of the Central Intelligence Agency.

The Republican Party's 1980 platform was more a blueprint for victory in November than a definitive statement of party views. Rather than slug it out over specifics, the party's moderate and conservative wings agreed to blur their differences to appear united, to broaden the party's appeal and to smooth Reagan's way to the White House.

Overwhelmingly, platform committee members agreed the document should be consistent with Reagan's positions. Thus, though one media poll found delegates overwhelmingly in favor of resuming a peacetime draft, the platform bowed to the view of its nominee and stated its opposition to a renewal of the draft "at this time." In the same manner, the party's platform took no position on ratification of the Equal Rights Amendment (ERA)

to the Constitution. Since 1940 Republican platforms had supported an ERA amendment. Reagan, however, opposed ratification, and ERA opponents far outnumbered the amendment's supporters on the platform committee. Yet Reagan, in a gesture to moderates, suggested that the platform not take a position on the issue, and the committee agreed.

Most of the platform document consisted of policy statements on which most Republicans agreed. There were calls for tax cuts, pleas for less government regulation, and harsh criticisms of the Carter administration. In two areas, however, the platform took a particularly hard-line position. The platform supported a constitutional amendment that would outlaw abortion and called on a Reagan administration to appoint federal judges who opposed abortion. On defense, platform writers took an already hard-line plank that had been drafted by party staff and moved it sharply to the right. The platform called for massive increases in defense spending and scoffed at the Carter administration's proposed Strategic Arms Limitation Treaty (SALT II).

On the other hand, to pick up votes from organized labor, blacks, and the poor, the platform made some new overtures to those traditionally non-Republican groups. It pledged to strengthen enforcement of the civil rights laws, made overtures to U.S. workers put out of their jobs by competition from foreign imports, and promised to save America's inner cities.

The platform was adopted by the convention July 15 without change, but not before an unsuccessful attempt was made to reopen on the floor one of its more controversial sections: the section suggesting that Reagan appoint federal judges who oppose abortion. Sen. Charles H. Percy of Illinois called it "the worst plank I have ever seen in any platform by the Republican Party." The moderates sought to round up support for reopening the platform on the floor, but their efforts failed.

Ronald Reagan received the Republican nomination on the first ballot. (Table, p. 237.)

In his acceptance speech, Reagan combined sharp jabs at the alleged shortcomings of the Carter administration with a reaffirmation of his conservative credo. Reagan cited three grave threats to the nation's existence—"a disintegrating economy, a weakened defense, and an energy policy based on the sharing of scarcity." The culprits, Reagan contended, were President Carter and the Democratic Congress. He said they had preached that the American people needed to tighten their belts. "I utterly reject that view," he declared.

Following are excerpts from the Republican Party platform of 1980:

Taxes. . . . [W]e believe it is essential to cut personal tax rates out of fairness to the individual. . . .

Therefore, the Republican Party supports across-the-board reductions in personal income tax rates, phased in over three years, which will reduce tax rates from the range of 14 to 70 percent to a range of from 10 to 50 percent.

. . . Republicans will move to end tax bracket creep caused by inflation. We support tax indexing to protect taxpayers from the automatic tax increases caused when cost-of-living wage increases move them into higher tax brackets.

Black Americans. During the next four years we are committed to policies that will:

• encourage local governments to designate specific enterprise zones within depressed areas that will promote new jobs, new and expanded businesses and new economic vitality;

• open new opportunities for black men and women to begin small businesses of their own by, among other steps, removing excessive regulations, disincentives for venture capital and other barriers erected by the government;

• bring strong, effective enforcement of federal civil rights statutes, especially those dealing with threats to physical safety and security which have recently been increasing; and

• ensure that the federal government follows a nondiscriminatory system of appointments . . . with a careful eye for qualified minority aspirants.

Women's Rights. We acknowledge the legitimate efforts of those who support or oppose ratification of the Equal Rights Amendment.

We reaffirm our Party's historic commitment to equal rights and equality for women.

We support equal rights and equal opportunities for women, without taking away traditional rights of women such as exemption from the military draft. We support the enforcement of all equal opportunity laws and urge the elimination of discrimination against women.

We reaffirm our belief in the traditional role and values of the family in our society. . . . The importance of support for the mother and homemaker in maintaining the values of this country cannot be overemphasized.

Abortion. While we recognize differing views on this question among Americans in general—and in our own Party—we affirm our support of a constitutional amendment to restore protection of the right to life for unborn children. We also support the Congressional efforts to restrict the use of taxpayers' dollars for abortion.

Education. . . . [T]he Republican Party supports deregulation by the federal government of public education, and encourages the elimination of the federal Department of Education.

We support Republican initiatives in the Congress to restore the right of individuals to participate in voluntary, non-denominational prayer in schools and other public facilities. . . .

Crime. We believe that the death penalty serves as an effective deterrent to capital crime and should be applied by the federal government and by states which approve it as an appropriate penalty for certain major crimes.

We believe the right of citizens to keep and bear arms must be preserved. Accordingly, we oppose federal registration of firearms. Mandatory sentences for commission of armed felonies are the most effective means to deter abuse of this right.

Foreign Competition. The Republican Party recognizes the need to provide workers who have lost their jobs because of technological obsolescence or imports the opportunity to adjust to changing economic conditions. In particular, we will seek ways to assist workers threatened by foreign competition.

The Republican Party believes that protectionist tariffs and quotas are detrimental to our economic well-being. Nevertheless, we insist that our trading partners offer our nation the same level of equity, access, and fairness that we have shown them.

Big Government. The Republican Party reaffirms its belief in the decentralization of the federal government and in the traditional American principle that the best government is the one closest to the people. There, it is less costly, more accountable, and more responsive to people's needs. . . .

Energy. We are committed to . . . a strategy of aggressively boosting the nation's energy supplies; stimulating new energy technology and more efficient energy use; restoring maximum feasible choice and freedom in the marketplace for energy consumers and producers alike; and eliminating energy shortages and disruptions. . . .

Balanced Budget. If federal spending is reduced as tax cuts are phased in, there will be sufficient budget surpluses to fund the tax cuts, and allow for reasonable growth in necessary program spending.

. . . We believe a Republican President and a Republican Congress can balance the budget and reduce spending through legislative actions, eliminating the necessity for a Constitutional amendment to compel it. However, if necessary, the Republican Party will seek to adopt a Constitutional amendment to limit federal spending and balance the budget, except in time of national emergency as determined by a two-thirds vote of Congress.

National Security. Republicans commit themselves to an immediate increase in defense spending to be applied judiciously to critically needed programs. We will build toward a sustained defense expenditure sufficient to close the gap with the Soviets. Republicans approve and endorse a national strategy of peace through strength. . . .

Nuclear Forces. . . . We reject the mutual-assured-destruction (MAD) strategy of the Carter Administration. . . . We propose, instead, a credible strategy which will deter a Soviet attack by the clear capability of our forces to survive and ultimately to destroy Soviet military targets.

A Republican Administration will strive for early modernization of our theater nuclear forces so that a seamless web of deterrence can be maintained against all levels of attack, and our credibility with our European allies is restored.

Defense Manpower and the Draft. The Republican Party is not prepared to accept a peacetime draft at this time. . . . We will not consider a peacetime draft unless a well-managed, Congressionally-funded, full-scale effort to improve the all-volunteer force does not meet expectations.

The Americas. We deplore the Marxist Sandinista takeover of Nicaragua and the Marxist attempts to destabilize El Salvador, Guatemala, and Honduras. We do not support United States assistance to any Marxist government in this hemisphere and we oppose the Carter Administration aid program for the government of Nicaragua. However, we will support the efforts of the Nicaraguan people to establish a free and independent government.

DEMOCRATS

President Jimmy Carter emerged victorious from a deeply divided Democratic National Convention unsure whether his plea for unity to supporters of rival Sen. Edward M. Kennedy of Massachusetts had succeeded. Kennedy had been Carter's main opponent in his quest for renomination throughout the spring primary season. When it became apparent that Kennedy had not won in the primaries and caucuses the delegate support he needed, he turned his efforts to prying the nomination away from the president at the convention.

Kennedy's presence was strong throughout the convention week and expressions of support for the senator sometimes upstaged those for the incumbent president. Chants of "We want Ted" rocked off the walls of New York's Madison Square Garden during the convention's four days, August 11–14. Their echo faintly followed the president as he left the podium following his acceptance speech.

Kennedy's efforts to wrest the nomination from Carter centered around a proposed new convention rule that bound delegates to vote on the first ballot for the candidates under whose banner they were elected. When the convention opened, Carter could count 315 more votes than he needed for the nomination—votes that he had won in nominating caucuses and presidential primaries. As a result, Kennedy's only chance to gain the nomination was to defeat the binding rule.

Opponents of the binding rule argued that political conditions had changed since the delegates were elected months earlier and that to bind them would break with a century and a half of Democratic tradition.

But most Carter supporters scoffed at that contention, stressing that delegates were free to vote their conscience on all roll calls but the first one for president. Passage of the rule was simply fair play, they added. It had been adopted in 1978 without opposition by the party's most recent rules-review commission and the Democratic National Committee. Only when it was apparent that Carter was winning, claimed Atlanta mayor Maynard Jackson, did the Kennedy camp want to change the rules to allow a "fifth ball, a fourth out, or a tenth inning."

When the measure finally came to a vote, Carter forces turned back the attempt to overturn the proposed rule. The vote was 1,936.418 to 1,390.580 against Kennedy's position. *(Table, p. 238.)*

Shortly after the vote, Kennedy ended his nine-month challenge to the president by announcing that his name would not be placed in nomination August 13. Passage of the binding rule ensured Carter's renomination.

Despite the loss on the binding rule, the Kennedy camp succeeded in molding the party platform more to their liking. The final document was filled with so many concessions to the Kennedy forces that it won only a half-hearted endorsement from the president. The platform battle, one of the longest in party history, filled seventeen hours of debate and roll calls that stretched over two days, August 12 and 13.

Most of Carter's concessions and outright defeats came on the economic and human needs sections of the 40,000-word document. It was these revisions that Carter rejected—as diplomatically as possible—in a statement issued several hours after the debate wound to a close.

The marathon platform debate reached its high point on Tuesday evening, August 12, when Kennedy addressed the delegates in behalf of his minority report on the economic chapter. Kennedy's speech provided the Democratic convention with its most exciting moments. The address, which sparked a forty-minute emotional demonstration when it was over, called for Democratic unity and laced into the Republican nominee, Ronald Reagan.

Kennedy defended his liberal ideology, supporting national health insurance and federal spending to restore deteriorated urban areas. He lashed out at Reagan's proposal for a massive tax cut, labeling it as beneficial only to the wealthy. Buoyed by the Kennedy oratory, the convention went on to pass by voice vote three liberal Kennedy platform planks on the economy, thereby rejecting the more moderate versions favored by Carter.

The first of the Kennedy-sponsored planks was a statement pledging that fairness would be the overriding principle of the Democrats' economic policy and that no actions would be taken that would "significantly increase" unemployment. The convention next approved a Kennedy plank seeking a $12 billion anti-recession jobs program, a $1 billion rail renewal plan, and an expanded housing program for low- and moderate-income families. The final Kennedy economic plank was a statement of opposition to fighting inflation through a policy of high interest rates and unemployment. Carter had agreed to this plank the day before the convention opened.

Carter floor managers realized that it would be difficult to block passage of the Kennedy economic proposals. After the senator's emotion-filled speech, Carter advisers—realizing their position could not prevail—quickly sought to change from a roll call to a voice vote on the economic planks.

During the floor demonstration that followed Kennedy's speech, a series of telephone calls ricocheted between the podium and the senator's campaign trailer located off the convention floor. The negotiations involved how many elements of the Kennedy program would be accepted by voice vote. In the end, Carter prevailed on only one of Kennedy's economic minority reports, the call for an immediate wage and price freeze followed by controls.

Shortly after Carter's renomination August 13, Kennedy issued a statement endorsing the platform and pledging his support for Carter. In the final moments before adjournment, Kennedy made a stiff and brief appearance on the platform with Carter, Vice President Walter F. Mondale, and a host of Democratic officeholders. But the coolness of his appearance—accompanied by the warmest reception of the night—left questionable the commitment of the senator and his supporters to work strenuously for Carter's reelection.

Carter won the Democratic nomination with 2,123 votes compared with Kennedy's 1,150.5. Other candidates split 54.5 votes. *(Table, p. 238.)*

In his acceptance speech, Carter alluded to the convention's divisions. He led off with praise for Kennedy's tough campaign, thanks for his concessions during the convention, and an appeal for future help. "Ted, your party needs—and I need—you, and your idealism and dedication working for us." Carter spent much of the speech characterizing Reagan's programs as a disastrous "fantasy world" of easy answers. He avoided detailed comments on the economic issues over which he and Kennedy had split, confining himself to statements that he wanted jobs for all who needed them.

As expected, Mondale was renominated for vice president. The vice president's acceptance speech set delegates chanting "Not Ronald Reagan" as Mondale reeled off a list of liberal values and programs that, he said, most Americans agreed with. Mondale was one of the few speakers to unequivocally praise Carter's record, which he did at some length. The speech ended with a warning not to "let anyone make us less than what we can be."

Following are excerpts from the Democratic Party platform of 1980:

Employment. We specifically reaffirm our commitment to achieve all the goals of the Humphrey-Hawkins Full Employment Act within the currently prescribed dates in the Act, especially those relating to a joint reduction in unemployment and inflation. Full employment is important to the achievement of a rising standard of living, to the pursuit of sound justice, and to the strength and vitality of America.

Antirecession Assistance. A Democratic antirecession program must recognize that Blacks, Hispanics, other minorities, women, and older workers bear the brunt of recession. We pledge a $12 billion antirecession jobs program, providing at least 800,000 additional jobs, including full funding of the counter-cyclical assistance program for the cities, a major expansion of the youth employment and training program to give young people in our inner cities new hope, expanded training programs for women and displaced homemakers to give these workers a fair chance in the workplace, and new opportunities for the elderly to contribute their talents and skills.

Tax Reductions. We commit ourselves to targeted tax reductions designed to stimulate production and combat recession as soon as it appears so that tax reductions will not have a disproportionately inflationary effect. We must avoid untargeted tax cuts which would increase inflation.

Federal Spending. Spending restraint must be sensitive to those who look to the federal government for aid and assistance, especially to our nation's workers in times of high unemployment. At the same time, as long as inflationary pressures remain strong, fiscal prudence is essential to avoid destroying the progress made to date in reducing the inflation rate.

Fiscal policy must remain a flexible economic tool. We oppose a Constitutional amendment requiring a balanced budget.

Interest Rates. . . . [W]e must continue to pursue a tough anti-inflationary policy which will lead to an across-the-board reduction in interest rates on loans.

In using monetary policy to fight inflation, the government should be sensitive to the special needs of areas of our economy most affected by high interest rates.

Worker Protection. The Democratic Party will not pursue a policy of high interest rates and unemployment as the means to fight inflation. We will take no action whose effect will be a significant increase in unemployment, no fiscal action, no monetary action, no budgetary action. The Democratic Party remains committed to policies that will not produce high interest rates or high unemployment.

OSHA protections should be properly administered, with the concern of the worker being the highest priority; legislative or administrative efforts to weaken OSHA's basic worker protection responsibilities are unacceptable.

We will continue to oppose a sub-minimum wage for youth and other workers and to support increases in the minimum wage so as to ensure an adequate income for all workers.

Human Needs. While we recognize the need for fiscal restraint . . . we pledge as Democrats that for the sole and primary purpose of fiscal restraint alone, we will *not* support reductions in the funding of any program whose purpose is to serve the basic human needs of the most needy in our society—programs such as unemployment, income maintenance, food stamps, and efforts to enhance the educational, nutritional or health needs of children.

Education. . . . [W]e will continue to support the Department of Education and assist in its all-important educational enterprise. . . .

. . .The federal government and the states should be encouraged to equalize or take over educational expenses, relieving the overburdened . . . taxpayer. . . . The Democratic Party continues to support programs aimed at achieving communities integrated both in terms of race and economic class. . . .

Equal Rights Amendment. . . . [T]he Democratic Party must ensure that ERA at last becomes the 27 Amendment to the Constitution. We oppose efforts to rescind ERA in states which have already ratified the amendment, and we shall insist that past rescissions are invalid.

Abortion. The Democratic Party recognizes reproductive freedom as a fundamental human right. We therefore oppose government interference in the reproductive decisions of Americans, especially those government programs or legislative restrictions that deny poor Americans their right to privacy by funding or advocating one or a limited number of reproductive choices only. Specifically, the Democratic Party opposes . . . restrictions on funding for health services for the poor that deny poor women especially the right to exercise a constitutionally-guaranteed right to privacy.

Gun Control. The Democratic Party affirms the right of sportsmen to possess guns for purely hunting and target-shooting purposes. However, handguns simplify and intensify violent crime. . . . The Democratic Party supports enactment of federal legislation to strengthen the presently inadequate regulations over the manufacture, assembly, distribution, and possession of handguns and to ban "Saturday night specials."

Energy. We must make energy conservation our highest priority, not only to reduce our dependence on foreign oil, but also to guarantee that our children and grandchildren have an adequate supply of energy. . . .

National Security. Our fourth major objective is to strengthen the military security of the United States and our Allies at a time when trends in the military balance have become increasingly adverse. America is now, and will continue to be, the strongest power on earth. It was the Democratic Party's greatest hope that we could, in fact, reduce our military effort. But realities of the world situation, including the unremitting buildup of Soviet military forces, required that we begin early to reverse the decade-long decline in American defense efforts.

NATIONAL UNITY CAMPAIGN

Rep. John B. Anderson of Illinois, a Republican, declared himself an independent candidate for the presidency April 24, 1980, after it became clear that he could not obtain his party's presidential nomination. Anderson created the National Unity Campaign as the vehicle for his third-party candidacy. No party convention was held to select Anderson or to ratify the selection.

On August 25 Anderson announced he had tapped former Wisconsin governor Patrick J. Lucey, a Democrat, to be his running mate. The selection of Lucey was seen as a move by Anderson to attract liberal Democrats disgruntled by President Jimmy Carter's renomination. Anderson's choice of a running mate and the August 30 release of a National Unity Campaign platform helped establish him as a genuine contender in the presidential race.

The 317-page platform put forth specific proposals on a variety of national issues, emphasizing domestic questions. The positions taken generally were fiscally conservative and socially liberal, remaining true to Anderson's "wallet on the right, heart on the left" philosophy.

The platform made clear that Anderson's primary goal was to restore the nation's economic health by adopting fiscal and tax policies that would "generate a substantial pool of investment capital," which then would be used to increase productivity and create jobs. Anderson proposed countercyclical revenue sharing to direct federal funds to areas hardest hit by the election year recession. He rejected mandatory wage and price controls as a cure for inflation, proposing instead a program under which the government would encourage labor and management to work toward agreement on proper levels for wages and prices and use tax incentives to encourage compliance with the standards set. In contrast to both Carter and Reagan, Anderson opposed tax cuts for individuals. He also criticized constitutional amendments to balance the federal budget, saying that while the budget should be balanced "in ordinary times," it could be expected to run a deficit in times of "economic difficulty."

Anderson's energy policy made reducing oil imports the top priority. His platform proposed a 50-cent-a-gallon excise tax on gasoline to discourage consumption, with the revenue to be used to cut Social Security taxes. Anderson favored the decontrol of oil prices begun under Carter and proposed a 40-mile-per-gallon fuel economy standard for new autos.

For American cities, Anderson proposed using about 90 percent of alcohol and tobacco taxes to help build mass transit systems and fight deterioration of public facilities. He also favored offering tax incentives to encourage businesses to locate in blighted urban areas.

Following are excerpts from the National Unity Campaign platform of 1980:

Economy. We will construct a Wage-Price Incentives Program. Our administration will invite labor and management leaders to agree upon fair and realistic guidelines and to determine appropriate tax-based incentives to encourage compliance. . . .

In the absence of sharp and prolonged increases in the rate of inflation, we will oppose mandatory wage and price standards.

Gasoline Tax. We would couple decontrol of oil and gas prices with an excise tax of 50 cents per gallon on gasoline, the full revenues of that tax being returned to individuals through reductions in payroll taxes and increased Social Security benefits. . . . We will employ tax credits and other incentives to promote substitution of nonpetroleum energy for oil, adoption of energy-efficient systems in industry and elsewhere,

improvements in transportation and energy production technologies, and development of less wasteful structures for home and commerce.

Cities. . . . [A]n Anderson-Lucey Administration will propose an Urban Reinvestment Trust Fund. Funded through . . . revenues from the Federal alcohol and tobacco excise taxes and phased in over three years, it will disburse approximately $3.9 billion annually. It will be used for upgrading, repair and replacement of [urban] capital plant and equipment.

Within our distressed older cities, there are zones of devastation, blighted by crime, arson and population flight. . . . We favor legislation that would create "enterprise zones" in these areas, by lowering corporate, capital gains, payroll and property taxes and by furnishing new tax incentives. . . .

Social Issues. We are committed to ratification of the Equal Rights Amendment. We oppose government intrusion in the most intimate of family decisions-the right to bear or not to bear children-and will fight against any constitutional amendment prohibiting abortion. We support public funding of family planning services and other efforts to enable women to find . . . alternatives to abortion.

National Defense and Arms Control. In strategic forces, we will maintain a stable balance by preserving essential equivalence with the Soviet Union. To meet an evolving threat to our deterrent, we will modernize and diversify our strategic arsenal.

The growing concern over the threat to fixed, land-based missiles poses an urgent problem to both the United States and the Soviet Union. Economically, environmentally and strategically, the . . . cure proposed by the Carter Administration-the MX system-is unsound. . . .

We favor . . . a short-term . . . nuclear test ban treaty between the United States, the Soviet Union and the United Kingdom. . . .

For a more effective defense, we will rely heavily on collective security arrangements with our principal allies in NATO and Japan. We will work to reinforce and enhance our historic partnership with our Western European allies.

We will propose to Moscow supplementary measures that could make possible the ratification of the SALT II Treaty and the start of SALT III negotiations. These proposals will respond to concerns expressed in the U.S. Senate regarding such issues as verification and future force reductions.

1984 Conventions

PRESIDENTIAL CANDIDATES

Walter F. Mondale
Democrat

Ronald Reagan
Republican

DEMOCRATS

Ending a long and difficult nomination campaign with a display of party unity and a historic vice-presidential choice, Walter F. Mondale used the 1984 Democratic convention to sound the opening themes of his challenge to President Ronald Reagan: family, fairness, the flag, and the future.

Accepting their nominations July 19 before cheering, flag-waving delegates at the San Francisco convention, the presidential candidate and his running mate, Rep. Geraldine A. Ferraro of New York, served notice that they would hold Reagan to account for his policies in their uphill battle to capture the White House. "Here is the truth about the [nation's] future," Mondale told the Democrats as they wrapped up their four-day convention. "We are living on borrowed money and borrowed time."

The spectacle of Mondale and Ferraro, with their families, celebrating with delegates in the jammed Moscone Center capped a week in which the Democrats came together to choose their ticket and shore up party unity. Toward that end, the convention succeeded to a greater degree than had seemed possible when the former vice president was battling Sen. Gary Hart of Colorado and Jesse L. Jackson in the primaries and caucuses. There was little acrimony over consideration of the party platform. And, once Mondale was nominated, the three rivals seemed to put aside their most visible differences.

The fifty-six-year-old Minnesotan had been the apparent winner since the final round of primaries on June 5, when he took New Jersey, which gave him the 1,967 pledged delegates needed to take the nomination. Mondale finished the convention balloting with nearly a thousand votes more than Hart, his closest competitor, yet he was by no means an overwhelming choice. He polled 2,191 votes—about 56 percent of a possible 3,933. Jackson received 465.5 votes. (Table, p. 240.)

The Democratic unity displayed in San Francisco—so different from the 1980 convention, when the struggle between President Jimmy Carter and Sen. Edward M. Kennedy of Massachu-

setts left the party torn and battered—was largely because of delegates' deeply felt antipathy to the policies of the Reagan administration. The unusual harmony, at least in part, was also because of Gov. Mario M. Cuomo of New York, who electrified delegates with his keynote address on the opening night, July 16. In an eloquent appeal for family values and compassion for the poor, he set the tone for the rest of the convention. His speech was rivaled in intensity only by Ferraro's nomination by acclamation July 19 and an impassioned speech given by Jackson on July 17.

Speaking forcefully but without dramatic oratorical flourishes, and repeatedly interrupted by emotional applause, Cuomo combined an appeal to Democratic traditions with specific attacks on the domestic and foreign policies of the Reagan administration. Noting Reagan's reference to America as "a shining city on a hill," Cuomo said that "the hard truth is that not everyone is sharing in this city's splendor and glory. There is despair, Mr. President, in the faces that you don't see, in the places that you don't visit in your shining city."

Pledging a government of "new realism" that would combine strong but conciliatory foreign policies with tough economic initiatives, Mondale vowed in his acceptance speech to squeeze the budget and raise taxes to reduce soaring deficits, then approaching $200 billion a year. "Let's tell the truth. . . . Mr. Reagan will raise taxes, and so will I," Mondale said. "He won't tell you. I just did."

To Ferraro, the first woman put on the national ticket by a major party, her nomination by acclamation was a special honor. Quoting the late Rev. Martin Luther King Jr., she said that " 'Occasionally in life there are moments which cannot be completely explained in words. Their meaning can only be articulated by the inaudible language of the heart.' Tonight is such a moment for me. My heart is filled with pride."

The 45,000-word platform adopted at the convention created few divisions in the party, but few candidates were enthusiastic about using it in their fall campaigns. Adopted in an emphatic but seldom angry four-hour debate July 17, the platform drew heavily from Mondale's campaign themes. It also contained significant contributions from Hart and Jackson.

The debate on five minority planks offered by Hart and Jackson was lackluster compared with the heated platform struggles between Carter and Kennedy at the 1980 convention. The first sign that Mondale would surmount the Jackson challenges came on the plank pledging "no first use" of nuclear weapons. After a brief debate, it was defeated, with 1,405.7 delegates voting for it and 2,216.3 against. *(Table, p. 240.)*

Jackson supporters said it was "morally and militarily insane" even to consider using nuclear weapons, but Mondale's backers said the platform's arms control language was strong enough in promising movement toward a "no-first-use" stance.

In contrast to the opposition to Jackson's national security planks, Hart's "peace plank" was readily accepted by Mondale. Delegates adopted it, 3,271.8 to 351.2. The plank said a Democratic president would not "hazard American lives or engage in unilateral military involvement" in areas such as the Persian Gulf or Central America unless American objectives were clear and diplomatic efforts had been exhausted. *(Table, p. 240.)*

Jackson's two other minority reports dealt with issues of special interest to his black constituency: runoff primaries in the South and affirmative action. His call to abolish runoff primaries was defeated, but a compromise version of the affirmative action plank was accepted.

Ten southern states used runoff primaries when no candidate received a majority in the fast primary. Jackson claimed these second elections diluted minority voting strength because white voters often reverted to racial loyalty when a runoff choice was between a white and a black candidate. Supporters of second primaries argued that they prevented the nomination of fringe candidates who could receive a plurality in first-round primaries when more credible candidates split the vote. The dual primaries plank was defeated 2,500.8 to 1,253.2. *(Table, p. 240.)*

The other dispute was whether the platform should reject the use of quotas to overturn discrimination in employment and education. As adopted in June, the platform specifically rejected quotas but called for affirmative action goals and timetables to end discrimination in hiring, promotions, and education.

Following are excerpts from the Democratic platform of 1984:

Budget Deficits. . . . The Democratic Party is pledged to reducing these intolerable deficits. We will reassess defense expenditures; create a tax system that is both adequate and fair; control skyrocketing health costs without sacrificing quality of care; and eliminate other unnecessary expenditures.

We oppose the artificial and rigid Constitutional restraint of a balanced budget amendment. Further we oppose efforts to call a federal constitutional convention for this purpose.

Tax Reform. We will cap the effect of the Reagan tax cuts for wealthy Americans and enhance the progressivity of our personal income tax code, limiting the benefits of the third year of the Reagan tax cuts to the level of those with incomes of less than $60,000. We will partially defer indexation while protecting average Americans. We will close loopholes, eliminate the preferences and write-offs, exemptions,

and deductions which skew the code toward the rich and toward unproductive tax shelters. Given the fact that there has been a veritable hemorrhage of capital out of the federal budget, reflected in part by the huge budget deficit, there must be a return to a fair tax on corporate income. . . .

Controlling Domestic Spending. Social Security is one of the most important and successful initiatives in the history of our country, and it is an essential element of the social compact that binds us together as a community. There is no excuse—as the Reagan Administration has repeatedly suggested—for slashing Social Security to pay for excesses in other areas of the budget. We will steadfastly oppose such efforts, now and in the future.

It is rather in the area of health care costs that reform is urgently needed. By 1988, Medicare costs will rise to $106 billion; by the turn of the century, the debt of the trust fund may be as great as $1 trillion. In the Republican view, the problem is the level of benefits which senior citizens and the needy receive. As Democrats, we will protect the interests of health care beneficiaries. The real problem is the growing cost of health care services. . . .

Affirmative Action. The Democratic Party firmly commits itself to protect the civil rights of every citizen and to pursue justice and equal treatment under the law for all citizens. The Party reaffirms its longstanding commitment to the eradication of discrimination in all aspects of American life through the use of affirmative action goals, timetables, and other verifiable measurements to overturn historic patterns and historic burdens of discrimination in hiring, training, promotions, contract procurement, education, and the administration of all Federal programs. . . .

Equal Rights for Women. A top priority of a Democratic Administration will be ratification of the unamended Equal Rights Amendment. . . . The Democratic Party defines nondiscrimination to encompass both equal pay for equal work and equal pay for work of comparable worth, and we pledge to take every step, including enforcement of current law and amending the Constitution to include the unamended ERA, to close the wage gap.

Abortion. . . . The Democratic Party recognizes reproductive freedom as a fundamental human right. We therefore oppose government interference in the reproductive decisions of Americans, especially government interference which denies poor Americans their right to privacy by funding or advocating one or a limited number of reproductive choices only. . . .

Voting Rights Act. A Democratic President and Administration pledge to eliminate any and all discriminatory barriers to full voting rights, whether they be at-large requirements, second-primaries, gerrymandering, annexation, dual registration, dual voting or other practices. Whatever law, practice, or regulation discriminates against the voting rights of minority citizens, a Democratic President and Administration will move to strike it down. . . .

Homosexual Rights. . . . All groups must be protected from discrimination based on race, color, sex, religion, national origin, language, age, or sexual orientation. We will support legislation to prohibit discrimination in the workplace based on sexual orientation. We will assure that sexual orientation per se does not serve as a bar to participation in the military. . . .

Gun Control. We support tough restraints on the manufacture, transportation, and sale of snubnosed handguns, which have no legitimate sporting use and are used in a high proportion of violent crimes.

Arms Control. . . . A Democratic President will propose an early summit with regular, annual summits to follow, with the Soviet leaders, and meetings between senior civilian and military officials, in order to reduce tensions and explore possible formal agreements. . . . A new Democratic Administration will implement a strategy for peace which makes arms control an integral part of our national security policy. We must move the world back from the brink of nuclear holocaust and set a new direction toward an enduring peace, in which lower levels of military spending will be possible. Our ultimate aim must be to abolish all nuclear weapons in a world safe for peace and freedom. . . .

These steps should lead promptly to the negotiation of a comprehensive, mutual and verifiable freeze on the testing, production, and deployment of all nuclear weapons. Building on this initiative, the Democratic President will update and resubmit the SALT II Treaty to the Senate for its advice and consent. . . .

Defense Policy. The Reagan Administration measures military might by dollars spent. The Democratic Party seeks prudent defense based on sound planning and a realistic assessment of threats. . . .

A Democratic President will be prepared to apply military force when vital American interests are threatened, particularly in the event of an attack upon the United States or its immediate allies. But he or she will not hazard American lives or engage in unilateral military involvement:

- Where our objectives are not clear;
- Until all instruments of diplomacy and non-military leverage, as appropriate, have been exhausted;
- Where our objectives threaten unacceptable costs or unreasonable levels of military force;
- Where the local forces supported are not working to resolve the causes of conflict;
- Where multilateral or allied options for the resolution of conflict are available. . . .

The Middle East. . . . The Democratic Party opposes any consideration of negotiations with the PLO, unless the PLO abandons terrorism, recognizes the state of Israel, and adheres to U.N. Resolutions 242 and 338.

Jerusalem should remain forever undivided with free access to the holy places for people of all faiths. As stated in the 1976 and 1980 platforms, the Democratic Party recognizes and supports the established status of Jerusalem as the capital of Israel. As a symbol of this stand, the U.S. Embassy should be moved from Tel Aviv to Jerusalem.

Central America. . . . We must terminate our support for the contras and other paramilitary groups fighting in Nicaragua. We must halt those U.S. military exercises in the region which are being conducted for no other real purpose than to intimidate or provoke the Nicaraguan government or which may be used as a pretext for deeper U.S. military involvement in the area.

REPUBLICANS

A jubilant Republican Party wound up its August 20–23 convention in Dallas, Texas, confident that President Ronald Reagan and Vice President George Bush would be the winning team in November. With the ticket's renomination certain beforehand, the convention was more a celebration than a business meeting of GOP activists. Behind the cheering and display of party unity, however, ran a current of dissent: moderates, who were greatly outnumbered, voiced unhappiness with the party's direction and its platform.

During convention week, speaker after speaker criticized the Democrats, saying they represented a legacy of "malaise" from Jimmy Carter's administration and promised only a future of fear. Reagan, too, emphasized that theme in his fifty-five-minute acceptance speech. To repeated interruptions of applause and cheers, he drew sharp differences between Republicans and Democrats and between himself and the Democratic presidential nominee, Walter F. Mondale. "The choices this year are not just between two different personalities or between two political parties," Reagan said. "They are between two different visions of the future, two fundamentally different ways of governing—their government of pessimism, fear and limits . . . or ours of hope, confidence and growth."

In his acceptance speech, Bush vigorously touted the Reagan administration's record. "Under this president, more lands have been acquired for parks, more for wilderness," he said. "The quality of life is better—and that's a fact." In foreign affairs, Bush said, " . . . there is new confidence in the U.S. leadership around the world. . . . Because our president stood firm in defense of freedom, America has regained respect throughout the world. . . ."

Speakers in previous sessions had sought to make the same points. They tried to link former vice president Mondale to the policies and problems of the administration in which he had served. "Carter-Mondale" became their shorthand for a list of evils: inflation, high interest rates, foreign policy failures, and sagging national spirit.

GOP leaders also were eager to portray the Democratic ticket and the party's leadership as out of step with most Democrats. They gave the spotlight to Democrats-turned-Republicans and issued one of their warmest welcomes to Jeane J. Kirkpatrick, the U.S. representative to the United Nations, whom one party leader referred to as an "enlightened Democrat." Kirkpatrick delivered a foreign policy speech during the opening session.

Yet the convention was clearly a Republican event, with the administration firmly in control and many of its members on hand. The party's leaders also made clear they were making a pitch for women voters, in response to the candidacy of Rep. Geraldine A. Ferraro, D-N.Y., Mondale's running mate.

The delegates moved to renominate Reagan and Bush. Although the outcome came as no surprise, there was an unusual joint roll call on the nominations, with Reagan receiving 2,233 votes and Bush, 2,235. *(Table, p. 239.)*

Earlier, after spirited debate, the 106-member platform committee adopted a 1984 campaign document that conformed in virtually all respects to the themes Reagan had sounded during his first term in office. The convention itself ratified the 30,000-word platform with no debate August 21. On almost every aspect of public policy, the document stood in stark contrast to the platform the Democrats had adopted in San Francisco.

However, in its strong stand against tax increases and its criticism of the independent Federal Reserve Board, the Republican platform went further than the White House wanted. Administration representatives led by former transportation secretary Drew Lewis sought to soften the tax plank, but, while they succeeded in modifying some of the language, they were unable to alter it substantially. The tax section of the Republican platform pledged that the party would continue efforts to lower tax rates and would support tax reform that "will lead to a fair and simple tax system." The platform said the party believed that a "modified flat tax—with specific exemptions for such items as mortgage interest—is a most promising approach."

Taxes had mushroomed as an election issue when Mondale said in his acceptance speech at the Democratic National Convention that, regardless of who won in November, tax increases would be necessary in 1985 to combat record federal budget deficits. Mondale also accused Reagan of having a secret plan to raise taxes.

Despite an hour-long debate, the GOP platform committee had refused to endorse the proposed Equal Rights Amendment (ERA)—which Reagan opposed—or compromise language stating that the Republicans respected those who supported the amendment. The committee also turned aside challenges by party moderates to language endorsing voluntary prayer in public schools and opposing federal financing for abortions under any circumstances.

Following are excerpts from the Republican platform of 1984:

Economic Policy. Our most important economic goal is to expand and continue the economic recovery and move the nation to full employment without inflation. We therefore oppose any attempts to increase taxes, which would harm the recovery and reverse the trend to restoring control of the economy to individual Americans. We favor reducing deficits by continuing and expanding the strong economic recovery brought about by the policies of this Administration and by eliminating wasteful and unnecessary government spending. . . .

Tax Policy. The Republican Party pledges to continue our efforts to lower tax rates, change and modernize the tax system, and eliminate the incentive-destroying effects of graduated tax rates. We therefore support tax reform that will lead to a fair and simple tax system and believe a modified flat tax—with specific exemptions for such items as mortgage interest—is a most promising approach.

Balancing the Budget. The congressional budget process is bankrupt. Its implementation has not brought spending under control, and it must be thoroughly reformed. We will work for the constitutional amendment requiring a balanced federal budget passed by the Republican Senate but blocked by the Democrat-controlled House and denounced by the Democrat Platform. If Congress fails to act on this issue, a constitutional convention should be convened to address only this issue in order to bring deficit spending under control.

The President is denied proper control over the federal budget. To remedy this, we support enhanced authority to prevent wasteful spending, including a line-item veto. . . .

Monetary Policy. Just as our tax policy has only laid the groundwork for a new era of prosperity, reducing inflation is only the first step in restoring a stable currency. A dollar now should be worth a dollar in the future. This allows real economic growth without inflation and is the primary goal of our monetary policy.

The Federal Reserve Board's destabilizing actions must therefore stop. We need coordination between fiscal and monetary policy, timely information about Fed decisions, and an end to the uncertainties people face in obtaining money and credit. The Gold Standard may be a useful mechanism for realizing the Federal Reserve's determination to adopt monetary policies needed to sustain price stability.

Energy. We will complete America's energy agenda. Natural gas should be responsibly decontrolled as rapidly as possible so that fami-

lies and businesses can enjoy the full benefits of lower prices and greater production, as with decontrolled oil. We are committed to the repeal of the confiscatory windfall profits tax, which has forced the American consumer to pay more for less and left us vulnerable to the energy and economic stranglehold of foreign producers. . . .

We are committed to the termination of the Department of Energy. President Reagan has succeeded in abolishing that part which was telling Americans what to buy, where to buy it, and at what price—the regulatory part of DOE. Then he reduced the number of bureaucrats by 25 percent. Now is the time to complete the job.

Education. We believe that education is a local function, a State responsibility, and a federal concern. The federal role in education should be limited. It includes helping parents and local authorities ensure high standards, protecting civil rights, and ensuring family rights. . . .

We have enacted legislation to guarantee equal access to school facilities by student religious groups. Mindful of our religious diversity, we reaffirm our commitment to the freedoms of religion and speech guaranteed by the Constitution of the United States and firmly support the rights of students to openly practice the same, including the right to engage in voluntary prayer in schools. . . .

Crime and Gun Control. . . . Republicans will continue to defend the constitutional right to keep and bear arms. When this right is abused and armed felonies are committed, we believe in stiff, mandatory sentencing. . . .

Abortion. The unborn child has a fundamental individual right to life which cannot be infringed. We therefore reaffirm our support for a human life amendment to the Constitution, and we endorse legislation to make clear that the Fourteenth Amendment's protections apply to unborn children. We oppose the use of public revenues for abortion and will eliminate funding for organizations which advocate or support abortions. . . .

We applaud President Reagan's fine record of judicial appointments, and we reaffirm our support for the appointment of judges at all levels of the judiciary who respect traditional family values and the sanctity of innocent human life. . . .

Central America. Today, democracy is under assault throughout [Central America]. Marxist Nicaragua threatens not only Costa Rica and Honduras, but also El Salvador and Guatemala. The Sandinista regime is building the largest military force in Central America, importing Soviet equipment, Eastern bloc and PLO advisers, and thousands of Cuban mercenaries. The Sandinista government has been increasingly brazen in its embrace of Marxism-Leninism. The Sandinistas have systematically persecuted free institutions, including synagogue and church, schools, the private sector, the free press, minorities, and families and tribes throughout Nicaragua. We support continued assistance to the democratic freedom fighters in Nicaragua. Nicaragua cannot be allowed to remain a Communist sanctuary, exporting terror and arms throughout the region. . . .

The Soviet Union. Stable and peaceful relations with the Soviet Union are possible and desirable, but they depend upon the credibility of American strength and determination. . . . Our policy of peace through strength encourages freedom-loving people everywhere and provides hope for those who look forward one day to enjoying the fruits of self-government. . . .

1988 Conventions

PRESIDENTIAL CANDIDATES

Michael S. Dukakis
Democrat

George Bush
Republican

DEMOCRATS

After years of internal warfare, the Democrats staged a remarkable show of unity at their 1988 national convention, held July 18–21 in Atlanta, Ga. For once, the issue-oriented activists who dominated the Democratic nominating process for nearly two decades subordinated their agendas to the goal of party victory, avoiding the self-inflicted wounds that had marred so many conventions since the 1968 Chicago debacle.

Massachusetts governor Michael S. Dukakis arrived at the convention with enough delegate support to ensure his nomination as the Democratic presidential candidate. Earlier, on July 12, he had announced his choice of running mate, Sen. Lloyd Bentsen of Texas.

The only risk of serious political conflict at the convention came from Jesse L. Jackson, who finished second in the delegate race. The convention approached with some of Jackson's hard-core supporters threatening boycotts, protest marches, and walkouts. Some saw Dukakis's selection of Bentsen as a snub to Jackson. A breakthrough, however, came at a three-hour morning meeting July 18 of Dukakis, Jackson, and Bentsen. Afterward, Jackson said he was committed to helping elect the ticket, although he would still allow his name to be placed in nomination. In answer to a reporter's question, he said he no longer sought the vice presidency.

With the Dukakis-Jackson agreement reached, the atmosphere inside Atlanta's Omni Coliseum on opening night was remarkably fraternal. Democratic National Committee Chairman Paul G. Kirk Jr. persistently underlined the theme of unity, pointing to the fact that the credentials and rules reports—sources of numerous battles and test votes at past conventions—had been previously ratified by the Dukakis and Jackson campaigns. Both were adopted without discussion. Texas state treasurer Ann Richards delivered a folksy keynote address that included one of the more memorable quips in convention oratory. "Poor George," she said. "He can't help it. He was born with a silver foot in his mouth."

In the afternoon of the second day of the convention, the candidates' campaigns eliminated their last major grounds for argument—the minority planks of the Democratic platform—with a minimum of rancor.

In the debate on what the Jackson campaign called the "fair tax" plank, Manhattan Borough president David Dinkins said that "the rich and the corporations" received the bulk of the Reagan administration tax cuts, which he blamed for the large federal deficits. But Denver mayor Federico Pena warned that passage of the plank would be campaign fodder for Republicans, who persistently portrayed the Democrats as the "tax-and-spend" party. Delegates defeated it 1,091.5 to 2,499. *(Table, p. 242.)*

More emotion was expressed over the nuclear-strategy plank, with Jackson supporters waving placards and changing, "No first use!" Supporters said the plank would show Democratic commitment to world peace. But Dukakis supporters, while expressing solidarity with the cause of nuclear disarmament, said the defense strategy that called for use of nuclear weapons in the event of an invasion of western Europe was a bedrock of the NATO alliance. They also said that, should Dukakis be elected president, the plank could deprive him of an effective tool to force the Soviets to the bargaining table. The minority plank was defeated, 1,220.59 to 2,474.13. *(Table, p. 242.)*

Without debate the delegates adopted a compromise package of nine other amendments pressed by the Jackson camp and accepted by Dukakis. These embodied much of the spirit and some of the specifics that Jackson had tried to insert into the platform all along—a denunciation of aid to "irregular" forces in Central America, a national health program, sharply higher spending for education, and a moratorium on missile flight testing.

Notwithstanding the concessions to Jackson, the platform drafted by the Dukakis forces remained a general statement of party themes, rather than a series of promises to constituency groups. At 4,500 words, the platform was one-tenth the length of its 1984 counterpart.

Rousing speeches by Sen. Edward M. Kennedy and Jackson topped the evening schedule. Kennedy, introduced by his nephew John F. Kennedy Jr., accused Bush of "burying his head in his hands and hiding from the record of Reagan-Bush mistakes." Kennedy then listed a series of issues—Iran-contra, the Noriega drug connection, domestic budget cuts, civil rights—on which he said the Reagan administration had made wrong choices, following each example with the refrain, "Where was George?" The delegates spontaneously picked up the slogan as a chant.

In his fifty-five-minute speech, Jackson invoked the heroes of the civil rights movement, including Martin Luther King Jr., and briefly shared the stage with Rosa Parks, heroine of the 1955 Montgomery, Alabama, bus boycott. He said that his campaign was a historic culmination of earlier black struggles. The speech was climaxed by Jackson's call for Americans to "never surrender" to poverty, drugs, malnutrition, inequality, disease, or physical handicaps. "Keep hope alive," he concluded. "Keep hope alive."

Arkansas governor Bill Clinton nominated Dukakis the evening of July 20 with a thirty-five-minute speech that will be remembered more for its duration than its content. Clinton praised Dukakis as "a man with vision, a shining vision for this country."

The roll call, marked by the usual "Great State of . . ." boosterism, went as predetermined by the primary-and-caucus process. The one surprise came from Minnesota, where three antiabortion delegates registered support for Rep. Richard H. Stallings of Idaho, who shared their opposition to abortion. Four other candidates received one or two votes each.

The only apparent suspense was which state would put Dukakis over the 2,082-vote total he needed to clinch the nomination. But the Dukakis campaign—cognizant of California's importance in November—had even taken care of that detail. They arranged for several delegations to pass on the first call to ensure that California would have the honor. The final tally was Dukakis 2,876.25 delegate votes; Jackson, 1,218.5. *(Table, p. 242.)*

For his acceptance speech on the final night of the convention, Dukakis was introduced by his cousin, Olympia Dukakis, an Oscar-winning actress and New Jersey delegate. Dukakis described himself as a product of the American dream. He paid tribute to his immigrant parents, and tears welled in his eyes when he talked about how proud his father would have been of his son, and of his adopted country. He cited individuals who represented America's cultural diversity, including Jackson.

Following are excerpts from the Democratic platform of 1988:

Economy. . . . We believe that all Americans have a fundamental right to economic justice in a stronger, surer national economy, an economy that must grow steadily without inflation, that can generate a rising standard of living for all and fulfill the desire of all to work in dignity up to their full potential in good health with good jobs at good wages, an economy that is prosperous in every region, from coast to coast, including our rural towns and our older industrial communities, our mining towns, our energy producing areas and the urban areas that have been neglected for the past seven years.

Education. . . . [T]he education of our citizens, from Head Start to institutions of higher learning, deserves our highest priority. . . . We pledge to better balance our national priorities by significantly increasing federal funding for education. . . .

Drugs. . . . [I]llegal drugs pose a direct threat to the security of our nation from coast to coast. . . . [E]very arm and agency of government at every federal, state and local level—including every useful diplomatic, military, educational, medical and law enforcement effort necessary—should at long last be mobilized and coordinated with private efforts under the direction of a National Drug "Czar" to halt both the international supply and the domestic demand for illegal drugs now ravaging our country; and that the legalization of illicit drugs would represent a tragic surrender in a war we intend to win. . . .

Criminal Justice. . . . [T]he federal government should provide increased assistance to local criminal justice agencies, enforce a ban on "cop killer" bullets that have no purpose other than the killing and maiming of law enforcement officers, reinforce our commitment to help crime victims, and assume a leadership role in securing the safety of our neighborhoods and homes.

Individual Rights. . . . [W]e must work for the adoption of the Equal Rights Amendment to the Constitution; that the fundamental right of reproductive choice should be guaranteed regardless of ability to pay; that our machinery for civil rights enforcement and legal services to the poor should be rebuilt and vigorously utilized; and that our immigration policy should be reformed to promote fairness, nondiscrimination and family reunification and to reflect our constitutional freedoms of speech, association and travel. We further believe that the voting rights of all minorities should be protected, the recent surge in hate violence and negative stereotyping combatted, the discriminatory English-only pressure groups resisted, our treaty commitments with Native Americans enforced by culturally sensitive officials, and the lingering effects of past discrimination eliminated by affirmative action, including goals, timetables, and procurement set-asides.

Health Care. . . . We believe that all Americans should enjoy access to affordable, comprehensive health services for both the physically and mentally ill, from prenatal care for pregnant women at risk to more adequate care for our Vietnam and other veterans, from well-baby care to childhood immunization to Medicare; that a national health program providing federal coordination and leadership is necessary to restrain health care costs while assuring quality care and advanced medical research; that quality, affordable, long-term home and health care should be available to all senior and disabled citizens, allowing them to live with dignity in the most appropriate setting; that an important first step toward comprehensive health services is to ensure that every family should have the security of basic health insurance; and that the HIV/AIDS epidemic is an unprecedented public health emergency requiring increased support for accelerated research on, and expedited FDA approval of, treatments and vaccines. . . .

Voting Rights. . . . [T]his country's democratic processes must be revitalized: by securing universal, same day and mail-in voter registration as well as registration on the premises of appropriate government agencies; by preventing the misuse of at-large elections, the abuse of election day challenges and registration roll purges, any undercounting in the national census, and any dilution of the one-person, one-vote principle; by ending discrimination against public employees who are denied the right to full political participation; by supporting statehood for the District of Columbia; by treating the offshore territories under our flag equitably and sensitively under federal policies, assisting their economic and social development and respecting their right to decide their future in their relationship with the United States; by empowering the commonwealth of Puerto Rico with greater autonomy within its relationship with the United States to achieve the economic, social and political goals of its people, and by giving it just and fair participation in federal programs; by assuring and pledging the full and equal access of women and minorities to elective office and party endorsement; and by minimizing the domination and distortion of our elections by moneyed interests. . . .

Defense. We believe that our national strength has been sapped by a defense establishment wasting money on duplicative and dubious new weapons instead of investing more in readiness and mobility; that our national strength will be enhanced by more stable defense budgets and by a commitment from our allies to assume a greater share of the costs and responsibilities required to maintain peace and liberty. . . .

Arms Control. We believe in following up the INF [intermediate-range nuclear force] Treaty, a commendable first step, with mutual, verifiable and enforceable agreements that will make significant reductions in strategic weapons in a way that diminishes the risk of nuclear attack by either superpower; reduce conventional forces to lower and equivalent levels in Europe, requiring deeper cuts on the Warsaw Pact side; ban chemical and space weapons in their entirety; promptly initiate a mutual moratorium on missile flight testing and halt all nuclear weapons testing while strengthening our efforts to prevent the spread of these weapons to other nations before the nightmare of nuclear terrorism engulfs us all.

International Relations. . . . [W]e believe that this country, maintaining the special relationship with Israel founded upon mutually shared values and strategic interests, should provide new leadership to deliver the promise of peace and security through negotiations that has been held out to Israel and its neighbors by the Camp David Accords. . . . We further believe that the United States must fully support the Arias Peace Plan, which calls for an end to the fighting, national reconciliation, guarantees of justice, freedom, human rights and democracy, an end to support for irregular forces, and a commitment by the Central American governments to prevent the use of their territory to destabilize others in the region. . . .

REPUBLICANS

On the opening day of the Republican national convention, held August 15–18 in New Orleans's Louisiana Superdome, the delegates hailed Ronald Reagan's valedictory, a swan song from a politician who had carried GOP conservatives to unprecedented levels of power. The delegates greeted Reagan as a conquering hero, and they cheered enthusiastically at many of his applause lines. But the mood was tempered by the poignancy of the moment—a realization that Reagan was making his last convention speech as leader of his party and his country, and that the future for Republicans was uncertain.

For his part, Reagan was firm if slightly subdued in his farewell speech. He offered again his optimistic vision of America and took some predictable jabs at his Democratic critics. But the most pertinent symbol of Reagan's role in the 1988 campaign was his strong praise of Vice President George Bush, saying "George played a major role in everything that we have accomplished in these eight years." Reagan responded to the Democrats' "Where was George?" chant by intoning, "George was there." Reagan's promise of campaign assistance and his call for Bush to "win one for the Gipper" was a lift for Bush supporters, who had been disturbed by Reagan's previously pallid endorsement of their candidate.

The Republicans had plenty of theater scheduled for August 16, with an agenda that included New Jersey governor Thomas H. Kean's keynote address and speeches by evangelist and former GOP presidential candidate Pat Robertson, former United Nations representative Jeane J. Kirkpatrick, and former president Gerald R. Ford. But Bush himself stole the show with his midafternoon announcement that he had selected dark-horse prospect Sen. Dan Quayle of Indiana as his running mate.

Bush made the choice public at a welcoming ceremony on the New Orleans riverfront. He praised Quayle, who was a generation younger than Bush, as "a man of the future." News reporters, meanwhile, had little to distract them from their rounds on the vice-presidential rumor circuit as the reports of the credentials, rules, and platform committees were approved without debate in the morning session.

But there was no press "honeymoon" for the prospective vice-presidential nominee. A series of tough questions asked at an August 17 news conference with Bush made the afternoon difficult for Quayle—and, by extension, for Bush. The most potentially explosive issue raised was whether Quayle, a member of Indiana's Pulliam publishing family, had used family influence to gain enlistment in the Indiana National Guard in 1969 to avoid service in the Vietnam War. Quayle first referred to the question as "a cheap shot." Then he dismissed it, saying his thoughts at the time centered on plans for law school, marriage, and family. The controversy, however, did not subdue the enthusiasm of convention delegates—for their soon-to-be presidential nominee George Bush or his choice of vice president. In the evening session, after a lengthy roll call, George W. Bush announced the Texas delegation votes that put his father over the top unopposed. *(Table, p. 243.)*

The Indiana senator was nominated by acclamation. A new party rule had eliminated the necessity of a roll call and made it difficult for dissident delegates to call for one had there been opposition to Bush's choice.

Early on in his acceptance speech Quayle confronted the National Guard issue briefly and with a somewhat defiant tone. After expressing pride in his congressional service, he said, "As a young man, I served six years in the National Guard, and like the millions of Americans who have served in the Guard . . . I am proud of it."

With Bush trailing his Democratic opponent, Michael S. Dukakis, in public opinion polls, media commentators and Bush supporters alike said he had to make the "speech of his life" in accepting the presidential nomination on the night of August 18. Bush did not waste the opportunity.

He hit on the conservative hot-button issues—the Pledge of Allegiance (Dukakis had vetoed, on constitutional grounds, a bill requiring Massachusetts public school students to recite the pledge), the death penalty, voluntary school prayer, gun ownership, opposition to abortion, prison furloughs—that had been raised by speaker after speaker during the convention.

Restating his promise not to raise taxes, which he said Dukakis would not rule out, Bush said he would tell persistent tax proponents to "Read my lips. 'No new taxes.'" Bush finished his speech by leading the convention in the Pledge of Allegiance, ending a week in which a record may have been set for mentions of the pledge.

Following are excerpts from the Republican platform of 1988:

Jobs. . . . The Republican Party puts the creation of jobs and opportunity first. . . . We will use new technologies, such as computer data bases and telecommunications, to strengthen and streamline job banks matching people who want work with available jobs.

We advocate incentives for educating, training, and retraining workers for new and better jobs—through programs like the Job Training Partnership Act, which provides for a public/private partnership. . . .

With its message of economic growth and opportunity, the GOP is the natural champion of blacks, minorities, women and ethnic Americans. . . . We are the party of real social progress. Republicans welcome the millions of forward-looking Americans who want an "opportunity society," not a welfare state. . . .

Taxes. *We oppose any attempts to increase taxes.* Tax increases harm the economic expansion and reverse the trend to restoring control of the economy to individual Americans.

We reject calls for higher taxes from all quarters—including "bipartisan commissions." The decisions of our government should not be left to a body of unelected officials. . . .

Health. Republicans believe in reduced government control of health care while maintaining an unequivocal commitment to quality health care. . . .

AIDS. We will vigorously fight against AIDS. . . . Continued research on the virus is vital. We will continue as well to provide experimental drugs that may prolong life. We will establish within the Food and Drug Administration a process for expedited review of drugs which may benefit AIDS patients. We will allow supervised usage of experimental treatments.

We must not only marshal our scientific resources against AIDS, but must also protect those who do not have the disease. In this regard, education plays a critical role. AIDS education should emphasize that abstinence from drug abuse and sexual activity outside of marriage is the safest way to avoid infection with the AIDS virus. . . .

Social Security. We pledge to preserve the integrity of the Social Security trust funds. We encourage public officials at all levels to safeguard the integrity of public and private pension funds against raiding. . . .

Equal Rights, Religious Rights, Abortion. "Deep in our hearts, we do believe":

• That bigotry has no place in American life. We denounce those persons, organizations, publications and movements which practice or promote racism, anti-Semitism or religious intolerance.

• That the Pledge of Allegiance should be recited daily in schools in all States. . . .

• In defending religious freedom. Mindful of our religious diversity, we firmly support the right of students to engage in voluntary prayer in schools. We call for full enforcement of the Republican legislation that now guarantees equal access to school facilities by student religious groups.

• That the unborn child has a fundamental right to life which cannot be infringed. We therefore reaffirm our support for a human life amendment to the Constitution, and we endorse legislation to make clear that the Fourteenth Amendment's protections apply to unborn children. We oppose the use of public revenues for abortion and will eliminate funding for organizations which advocate or support abortion. . . .

Disabled. We support efforts to provide disabled voters full access to the polls and opportunity to participate in all aspects of the political process. . . .

Gun Ownership. Republicans defend the constitutional right to keep and bear arms. . . .

Workers' Rights. We affirm the right of all freely to form, join or assist labor organizations to bargain collectively, consistent with state laws. . . . We renew our longstanding support for the right of states to enact "Right-to-Work" laws. To protect the political rights of every worker, we oppose the use of compulsory dues or fees for partisan purposes. . . .

Crime. We will forge ahead with the Republican anti-crime agenda:

• Republicans oppose furloughs for those criminals convicted of first degree murder and others who are serving a life sentence without possibility of parole. We believe that victims' rights should not be accorded less importance than those of convicted felons.

• We will re-establish the federal death penalty. . . .

Drugs. The Republican Party is committed to a drug-free America. Our policy is strict accountability, for users of illegal drugs as well as for those who profit by that usage. . . .

• The Republican Party unequivocally opposes legalizing or decriminalizing any illicit drug.

• We support strong penalties, including the death penalty for major drug traffickers. . . .

Oil. We will set an energy policy for the United States to maintain a viable core industry and to ensure greater energy self sufficiency through private initiatives. We will adopt forceful initiatives to reverse the decline of our domestic oil production. Republicans support:

• Repeal of the counterproductive Windfall Profits Tax.

• Maintenance of our schedule for filling the Strategic Petroleum Reserve to reach 750 million barrels by 1993 and encouragement of our allies to maintain similar reserves. . . .

Environment. Republicans propose the following program for the environment in the 1990s:

• We will work for further reductions in air and water pollution and effective actions against the threats posed by acid rain. . . .

• A top priority of our country must be the continued improvement of our National Parks and wildlife areas. . . .

The Americas. The Republican party reaffirms its strong support of the Monroe Doctrine as the foundation for our policy throughout the Hemisphere, and pledges to conduct foreign policy in accord with its principles. . . .

Republicans will continue to oppose any normalization of relations with the government of Cuba as long as Fidel Castro continues to oppress the Cuban people at home and to support international terrorism and drug trafficking abroad. We will vigorously continue our support for establishment of a genuinely representative government directly elected by the Cuban people. We reiterate our support of Radio Marti and urge the creation of TV Marti to better reach the oppressed people of Cuba. . . .

Soviet Union. Steady American leadership is needed now more than ever to deal with the challenges posed by a rapidly changing Soviet Union. Americans cannot afford a future administration which eagerly attempts to embrace perceived, but as yet unproven, changes in Soviet policy. Nor can we indulge naive inexperience or an overly enthusiastic endorsement of current Soviet rhetoric. . . .

Republicans proudly reaffirm the Reagan Doctrine: America's commitment to aid freedom-fighters against the communist oppression which destroys freedom and the human spirit. . . .

The Middle East. The foundation of our policy in the Middle East has been and must remain the promotion of a stable and lasting peace, recognizing our moral and strategic relationship with Israel. . . .

We will continue to maintain Israel's qualitative advantage over any adversary or coalition of adversaries.

We will continue to solidify our strategic relationship with Israel. . . .

We oppose the creation of an independent Palestinian state; its establishment is inimical to the security interests of Israel, Jordan and the U.S. . . .

Strategic Defense Initiative (SDI). We are committed to rapid and certain deployment of SDI as technologies permit, and we will deter-mine the exact architecture of the system as technologies are tested and proven. . . .

Arms Control. Arms reduction can be an important aspect of our national policy only when agreements enhance the security of the United States and its allies. [T]rue arms reductions as a means to improve U.S. security, not just the perception of East-West détente. . . .

• We will consistently undertake necessary improvements in our forces to maintain the effectiveness of our deterrent.

• We will not negotiate in areas which jeopardize our security. In particular, we will not compromise plans for the research, testing, or the rapid and certain deployment of SDI. . . .

1992 Conventions

PRESIDENTIAL CANDIDATES

Bill Clinton
Democrat

George Bush
Republican

Ross Perot
Independent

DEMOCRATS

The Democrats, meeting July 13–16 at Madison Square Garden in New York, nominated a national ticket of party moderates and adopted a 1992 platform heavily influenced by the centrist ideas of the Democratic Leadership Council (DLC) and its think tank, the Progressive Policy Institute.

The convention stressed the themes Democrats planned to push in the fall campaign: redefining the party in the centrist vein, emphasizing youth, traditional family values, and mainstream policy views—as desired by its nominee, Arkansas governor and DLC leader, Bill Clinton. Every bit as unsubtle were the efforts to redefine the nominee's personal image. In appealing to youth, as in much else, Clinton, forty-five, was assisted by his running mate, Sen. Albert "Al" Gore Jr., forty-four, of Tennessee, making their ticket the youngest in the twentieth century.

Despite the refusal of former California governor Edmund G. "Jerry" Brown Jr. to hop on the bandwagon or the stunning July 16 announcement from independent presidential candidate Ross Perot that he was bowing out (a decision he later reversed), Clinton controlled the focus and direction of the convention. He declined to yield to the tough tactics of black activist and former presidential candidate Jesse L. Jackson, demonstrating a tough-mindedness of his own.

The convention was marked by relatively few fractional disputes. Controversy involved primarily the question of whether Brown would be allowed to address the convention from the podium. Brown arrived with more than 600 delegates, enough to cause some disturbance. For most of the first session, they milled in the well beneath the main stage, heckling speakers and waving signs. Some covered their mouths with labels or duct tape.

In the end, Brown was allowed to give his seconding speech on July 15. But that meant he spoke at shortly after 8 p.m. (5 p.m. in California), well before the commercial broadcast networks had switched from their regular programming to convention coverage. Gradually, the Brown delegates softened their protest and ended any serious attempt to disrupt the convention.

A large section of the opening program was designed to give exposure to six of the Democrats' leading female Senate candidates, all of whom spoke briefly from the convention floor. Dianne Feinstein of California, the last to speak, dismissed Republicans who referred to the wave of female candidates as "just gender politics." "It's not just about gender. It's about an agenda, an agenda of change," Feinstein said.

Heralding the "Year of the Woman," Democratic women played a major role at the convention, and issues women had highlighted—abortion rights, women's health care, and the Clarence Thomas–Anita F. Hill hearings—were discussed from the podium, always to loud cheers from the floor.

Instead of the usual keynote speaker, the Democrats opted for three: Sen. Bill Bradley of New Jersey, Gov. Zell Miller of Georgia, and former Texas representative Barbara Jordan. They stressed that the party had changed, blasted the Bush administration for economic policies that favored the rich, and portrayed Clinton as a candidate from modest roots who was in touch with the people.

The Democrats later solidified their move to the center by adopting a platform devoid of many of the liberal planks and slogans that characterized previous documents. The debate over the party's manifesto was brief and uninspired. Clinton's overwhelming delegate strength and Democrats' frustration with three straight presidential losses helped mute any complaints over the centrist platform that clearly reflected the Clinton view of how the Democratic Party should present itself to voters.

The platform emphasized the need for economic growth and pledged efforts to uphold law and order, use of military force overseas where necessary, a cutoff in welfare benefits after two years, and support for the right of states to enact death penalty statutes. The platform did include more traditional Democratic viewpoints, such as protecting abortion rights, providing civil rights for homosexuals, and taxing wealthy people at higher rates.

By earlier agreement, delegates pledged to former senator Paul E. Tsongas of Massachusetts were allowed to offer and debate four minority planks. Three of the planks ultimately were rejected by voice vote. One called for investment-related tax breaks. Another, on the deficit, called for limits on government spending, including Medicare and other politically sensitive entitlements. A third proposed increasing the gasoline tax by five cents per gallon to benefit new spending on roads and bridges. A roll-call vote was held on the fourth plank, which said that a middle-class tax cut and a tax credit for families with children ought to be delayed until the deficit was under control. This had a been a key difference between Tsongas and Clinton during the campaign. Delegates defeated the plank, 953 to 2,287. *(Table, p. 244.)*

New York governor Mario M. Cuomo formally nominated Clinton, saluting him as the "comeback kid." The final roll-call tally was Clinton, 3,372; Brown, 596; and Tsongas, 209, and subsequently the nomination was approved by acclamation. After the vote, Clinton paid a surprise "thank you" visit to the convention, as John F. Kennedy had done in 1960.

The next day, in his fifty-four-minute acceptance speech, some twenty minutes longer than the seemingly interminable nominating speech he gave in 1988, Clinton described himself as "a product of the American middle class" who would accept the nomination "in the name of all the people who do the work, pay the taxes, raise the kids, and play by the rules. . . . " Pledging a "government that is leaner, not meaner," he called for "a New Covenant, based not simply on what each of us can take, but on what all of us must give to our nation." Clinton and Gore paid respect to the intensity of women's political feeling. They en-

dorsed abortion rights and equal rights in the workplace; both lavished praise on their wives, receiving roars of approval from the audience; and when Clinton talked of a notional child "somewhere at this very moment . . . born in America," he deliberately used female pronouns to refer to her.

Clinton often referred to himself as "the comeback kid." He claimed the title after rebounding from loss of the New Hampshire primary (to Tsongas) and damaging stories about his alleged relationship with a singer and about the means by which he avoided the Vietnam War draft.

Following are excerpts from the Democratic platform of 1992:

Economic Opportunity. Our party's first priority is opportunity-broad-based, non-inflationary economic growth and the opportunity that flows from it. Democrats in 1992 hold nothing more important for America than an economy that offers growth and jobs for all. . . . We reject both the do-nothing government of the last 12 years and the big government theory that says we can hamstring business and tax and spend our way to prosperity. . . .

The Deficit. Addressing the deficit requires fair and shared sacrifice of all Americans for the common good. . . . In place of the Republican supply side disaster, the Democratic investment, economic conversion and growth strategy will generate more revenues from a growing economy. We must also tackle spending by putting everything on the table. . . .

Education. A competitive American economy requires the global market's best-educated, best-trained, most flexible work force. It's not enough to spend more on our schools; we must insist on results. We oppose the Bush administration's efforts to bankrupt the public school system—the bedrock of democracy—through private school vouchers. . . .

Health Care. All Americans should have universal access to quality, affordable health care-not as a privilege but as a right. That requires tough controls on health costs, which are rising at two to three times the rate of inflation, terrorizing American families and businesses and depriving millions of the care they need. We will enact a uniquely American reform of the health-care system. . . . We must be united in declaring war on AIDS and HIV disease, implement the recommendations of the National Commission on AIDS and fully fund the Ryan White Care Act; provide targeted and honest prevention campaigns; combat HIV-related discrimination; make drug treatment available for all addicts who seek it; guarantee access to quality care; expand clinical trials for treatments and vaccines; and speed up the FDA [Food and Drug Administration] drug approval process.

Energy. We reject the Republican myth that energy efficiency and environmental protection are enemies of economic growth. We will make our economy more efficient, using less energy, reducing our dependence on foreign oil, and producing less solid and toxic waste. . . .

Civil and Equal Rights. We don't have an American to waste. Democrats will continue to lead the fight to ensure that no Americans suffer discrimination or deprivation of rights on the basis of race, gender, language, national origin, religion, age, disability, sexual orientation or other characteristics irrelevant to ability. We support ratification of the Equal Rights Amendment, affirmative action, stronger protection of voting rights for racial and ethnic minorities, including language access to voting, and continued resistance to discriminatory English-only pressure groups. . . . provide civil rights protection for gay men and lesbians and an end to Defense Department discrimination; respect Native American culture and our treaty commitments; require the

United States government to recognize its trustee obligations to the inhabitants of Hawaii generally and to Native Hawaiians in particular; and fully enforce the Americans with Disability Act to enable people with disabilities to achieve independence and function at their highest possible level.

Welfare Reform. Welfare should be a second chance, not a way of life. We want to break the cycle of welfare by adhering to two simple principles: No one who is able to work can stay on welfare forever, and no one who works should live in poverty. . . . We will give them the help they need to make the transition from welfare to work, and require people who can work to go to work within two years in available jobs either in the private sector or in community service to meet unmet needs. That will restore the covenant that welfare was meant to be: A promise of temporary help for people who have fallen on hard times.

Abortion. Democrats stand behind the right of every woman to choose, consistent with *Roe v. Wade*, regardless of ability to pay, and support a national law to protect that right. . . .

Environment . . . We will oppose Republican efforts to gut the Clean Air Act in the guise of competitiveness. We will reduce the volume of solid waste and encourage the use of recycled materials while discouraging excess packaging. To avoid the mistakes of the past, we will actively support energy efficiency, recycling and pollution-prevention strategies.

Government Reform. Democrats in 1992 intend to lead a revolution in government, challenging it to act responsibly and be accountable, starting with the hardest and most urgent problems of the deficit and economic growth. . . .

Crime and Drugs. To empower America's communities, Democrats pledge to restore government as upholder of basic law and order for crime-ravaged communities. The simplest and most direct way to restore order in our cities is to put more police on the streets. . . . We support a reasonable waiting period to permit background checks for purchases of handguns, as well as assault weapons controls to ban the possession, sale, importation and manufacture of the most deadly assault weapons. . . .

Defense. . . . The United States must be prepared to use military force decisively when necessary to defend our vital interests. The burdens of collective security in a new era must be shared fairly, and we should encourage multilateral peacekeeping through the United Nations and other international efforts.

Middle East Peace. Support for the peace process now under way in the Middle East, rooted in the tradition of the Camp David accords. Direct negotiations between Israel, her Arab neighbors and Palestinians, with no imposed solutions, are the only way to achieve enduring security for Israel and full peace for all parties in the region. . . .

Human Rights. Standing everywhere for the rights of individuals and respect for ethnic minorities against the repressive acts of governments-against torture, political imprisonment and all attacks on civilized standards of human freedom. This is a proud tradition of the Democratic Party, which has stood for freedom in South Africa and continues to resist oppression in Cuba. Our nation should once again promote the principle of sanctuary for politically oppressed people everywhere, be they Haitian refugees, Soviet Jews seeking U.S. help in their successful absorption into Israeli society or Vietnamese fleeing communism. Forcible return of anyone fleeing political repression is a betrayal of American values.

REPUBLICANS

Five weeks after the Democratic convention, the Republicans convened in Houston August 17–20 and did their best to per-

suade voters to remember the past and trust in experience. From the rousing opening night performance of former president Ronald Reagan to the repeated calls to honor traditional family values, the Republican National Convention looked backward as much as it looked ahead.

There were frequent references to having defeated communism and having won the Persian Gulf War. Voters were asked to ignore the Democrats' attempt to remake themselves in a more moderate image and to remember instead what life was like under Jimmy Carter, the most recent Democratic president.

There was little moderation evident in the party platform adopted for George Bush's second term. The GOP approved a hard-line approach opposing abortion rights and any attempt to increase taxes. On the social issues front, there were planks favoring school choice, school prayer, and family unity.

Finally, the delegates needed little prompting to vent their frustrations at the "liberal media" for praising Democratic nominee Clinton, dwelling on dissension over the GOP's antiabortion stance, and overemphasizing the weak economy. Bush sought to link Clinton to the Democratic Congress, which he blamed for the nation's problems—a refrain that would be played over and over throughout the week.

This was a homecoming of sorts for Bush. A New Englander by birth who went to Texas to work in the oil business, he retained his residency at a Houston hotel.

Party activists also sought a fresh start for Dan Quayle, widely perceived as being bumbling, gaffe-prone, and ineffective. But many conservatives still viewed the vice president as a hero, and because Quayle survived attempts to dump him from the ticket during the weeks leading up to the convention, GOP strategists looked forward to remaking his image as a thoughtful, middle-class American fighting for family values.

When the convention opened it already had become clear that efforts to force a debate on abortion had fallen short. A majority in six delegations was required to challenge the platform's call for a constitutional ban on all abortions, but abortion rights supporters said they could muster majorities in only four delegations—Maine, Massachusetts, New Mexico, and the Virgin Islands. The reason, they said, was that delegates felt it was more important to avoid embarrassing Bush than to force an open debate. In the end the platform was approved by voice vote. There were cries of "no!" when the document was put to delegates, but no public challenge.

In his speech conservative columnist Patrick J. Buchanan, who had unsuccessfully challenged Bush in the primaries, appealed to his supporters to throw their support to the president. He acknowledged the disagreements that led him to challenge Bush but said the convention marked the time to unite.

Buchanan's remarks were enthusiastically received in the hall, but the biggest response came for President Reagan, who described his speech as the "last chapter" in his political career. At eighty-one, the grand patriarch of the Republican Party showed all the oratorical skills and political spirit that had made him the hero of GOP conservatives.

"We stood tall and proclaimed that communism was destined for the ash heap of history," he said. "We never heard so much ridicule from our liberal friends. But we knew then what the liberal Democrat leaders just couldn't figure out: The sky would not fall if America restored her strength and resolve. The sky would not fall if an American president spoke the truth. The only thing that would fall was the Berlin Wall."

The nomination roll call was arranged so that Texas, the convention's host state and technically Bush's home, put him over the top. The final tally was 2,166 votes for Bush, 18 for Buchanan, and 3 for others, before the nomination was approved by acclamation. New Hampshire never cast its 23 votes. *(Table, p. 245.)*

In their acceptance speeches, Bush and Quayle sought to offset negative publicity against them while hurling their negativity at the Democrats. Speaking first, Quayle defiantly answered his legion of detractors. "I know my critics wish I were not standing here tonight," he said. "They don't like our values. They look down on our beliefs. They're afraid of our ideas. And they know the American people stand on our side."

Bush came out fighting against the Democratic-controlled Congress and Clinton. Responding to the concerns of delegates still angry over his broken "no-new-taxes" pledge, Bush admitted that it had been a mistake but posed a question to the electorate. "Who do you trust in this election—the candidate who has raised taxes one time and regrets it, or the other candidate who raised taxes and fees 128 times and enjoyed it every time?"

Trust was again the issue as Bush highlighted his role as commander in chief in winning the Persian Gulf War against Iraq. His success and the remaining threats to peace allowed Bush to raise questions about what his opponent would have done.

Following are excerpts from the Republican platform of 1992:

Family Values. Our greatness starts at home—literally. So Republicans believe government should strengthen families, not replace them. Today, more than ever, the traditional family is under assault. We believe our laws should reflect what makes our nation prosperous and wholesome: faith in God, hard work, service to others and limited government. . . . [W]e want to expand the Young Child Tax Credit to $500 per child and make it available to all families with children under the age of 10. . . .

Education. The Republican strategy is based on sound principle. Parents have the right to choose the best school for their children. Schools should teach right from wrong. Schools should reinforce parental authority, not replace it. . . .

[W]e support the right of students to engage in voluntary prayer in schools and the right of the community to do so at commencements or other occasions. We will strongly enforce the law guaranteeing equal access to school facilities. We also advocate recitation of the Pledge of Allegiance in schools as a reminder of the principles that sustain us as one nation under God. . . .

AIDS. We are committed to ensure that our nation's response to AIDS is shaped by compassion, not fear or ignorance and will oppose, as a matter of decency and honor, any discrimination against Americans who are its victims. . . . Above all, a cure must be found. We have committed enormous resources—$4.2 billion over the past four years for research alone, more than for any disease except cancer. . . .

Social Security. We reaffirm our commitment to a strong Social Security system. To stop penalizing grandparents and other seniors who care for children, we pledge to continue the Republican crusade to end the earnings limitation for Social Security recipients. . .

Cultural Values. We oppose any legislation or law that legally recognizes same-sex marriages and allows such couples to adopt children or provide foster care. . . .

Welfare Reform. Today's welfare system is anti-work and anti-marriage. It taxes families to subsidize illegitimacy. It rewards unethical behavior and penalizes initiative. It cannot be merely tinkered with by Congress; it must be re-created by states and localities. Republican governors and legislators in several states have already launched dramatic reforms, especially with workfare and learnfare. Welfare can no longer be a check in the mail with no responsibility. . . .

Individual Rights. The protection of individual rights is the foundation for opportunity and security. . . .

We believe the unborn child has a fundamental individual right to life that cannot be infringed. We therefore reaffirm our support for a human life amendment to the Constitution, and we endorse legislation to make clear that the 14th Amendment's protections apply to unborn children. We oppose using public revenues for abortion and will not fund organizations that advocate it. . . .

Republicans defend the constitutional right to keep and bear arms. We call for stiff mandatory sentences for those who use firearms in a crime. . . .

Taxes. We will oppose any effort to increase taxes. . . . We believe the tax increases of 1990 should ultimately be repealed. . . . As the deficit comes under control, we aspire to further tax rate cuts, strengthening incentives to work, save, invest and innovate. We also support President Bush's efforts to reduce federal spending and to cap the growth of non-Social Security entitlements. . . . We support further tax simplification. . . .

Government Reform. We reaffirm our support for a constitutional amendment to limit the number of terms House members and senators may serve. . . .

Congress must stop exempting itself from laws such as the minimum wage and the civil rights statutes, as well as laws that apply to the executive branch. The Independent Counsel Act is a case in point. . . . If that act is reauthorized, it must be extended to Congress as well. Safety and health regulations, civil rights and minimum wage laws are further examples of areas where Congress has set itself apart from the people. This practice must end. . . .

Budget Reform. Republicans vigorously support a balanced budget, a balanced-budget constitutional amendment and a line-item veto for the president.

Republicans believe this balancing of the budget should be achieved, not by increasing taxes to match spending, but by cutting spending to current levels of revenue. We prefer a balanced-budget amendment that contains a supermajority requirement to raise taxes. . . .

Campaign Reform. We will require congressional candidates to raise most of their funds from individuals within their home constituencies. This will limit outside special-interest money and result in less expensive campaigns, with less padding for incumbents. To the same end, we will strengthen the role of political parties to remove pressure on candidates to spend so much time soliciting funds. We will eliminate political action committees supported by corporations, unions or trade associations, and restrict the practice of bundling.

Energy. We will. . . . [allow] access, under environmental safeguards, to the coastal plain of the Arctic National Wildlife Refuge, possibly one of the largest petroleum reserves in our country, and to selected areas of the outer continental shelf (OCS). . . .

Public Lands. The millions of acres that constitute this nation's public lands must continue to provide for a number of uses. We are committed to the multiple use of our public lands. We believe that recreation, forestry, ranching, mining, oil and gas exploration, and production on our public lands can be conducted in a way compatible with their conservation. . . .

Transportation. To keep America on the move, we assert the same principle that guides us in all other sectors of the economy: consumers benefit through competition within the private sector. That is why we will complete the job of trucking deregulation. We will also abolish the Interstate Commerce Commission, finally freeing shippers and consumers from horse-and-buggy regulation. . . .

Middle East Peace. The basis for negotiations must be U.N. Security Council Resolutions 242 and 338. Peace must come from direct negotiations.

A meaningful peace must assure Israel's security while recognizing the legitimate rights of the Palestinian people. We oppose the creation of an independent Palestinian state. Nor will we support the creation of any political entity that would jeopardize Israel's security. . . .

Disarmament. We will banish the threat of nuclear annihilation from the face of the earth-not by savaging our military, as some Democrats might insist but by building on the historic diplomatic achievements of Presidents Bush and Reagan.

This means ensuring stable command and control of the former Soviet arsenal, complete acceptance and verified implementation of all treaty obligations by the successor states to the Soviet Union, and achieving the additional 50 percent reduction in strategic forces now agreed upon. . . .

Defense. Republicans call for a controlled defense drawdown, not a free fall. That is why President Bush proposes to carefully reduce defense spending over the next four years by an additional $34 billion, including $18 billion in outlays, with a 25 percent reduction in personnel. He has already eliminated over 100 weapon systems. Around the world, American forces are coming home from the frontiers of the Cold War. More than 550 overseas bases are being closed or realigned. Yet U.S. forces retain the ability to meet the challenge of another Desert Storm with equal success. . . .

We applaud the president's efforts to assist all individuals and communities adversely affected by the ongoing defense build-down, with more than 30 defense adjustment programs already in place and more than $7 billion committed to the effort in just the next two years. . . .

INDEPENDENT PEROT

The 1992 independent candidacy of Texas billionaire H. Ross Perot began with a call-in television show rather than with a nominating convention. Undeclared at first, the Perot candidacy began February 20 with his appearance on CNN's *Larry King Live* when Perot expressed a willingness to run for president. Under King's prodding, Perot said that if the people "register me

in fifty states" he would use his own money for a "world-class campaign."

Perot, a Naval Academy graduate who founded his computer company after leaving IBM, had been in the public eye for years, financing expeditions to help find American prisoners in Vietnam and rescue his employees in Iran, reforming the Texas school system, trying to shake up General Motors' management, and appearing on radio and TV talk shows to warn about the mounting federal deficit.

Tens of thousands of volunteers responded to Perot's challenge and began circulating petitions to place his name on the ballot in states from coast to coast. Meanwhile, Perot began forming a campaign organization. Polls in early spring showed him leading both President Bush and challenger Clinton. In June he hired as strategists Hamilton Jordan, manager of Carter's 1976 and 1980 campaigns, and Edward J. Rollins, manager of Reagan's 1984 reelection campaign.

But Perot's standing in the polls began to fall as the media spotlight produced a spate of negative publicity about his quirky personality and fitness to operate within the political system he pledged to reform. On July 16 Perot abruptly announced he was dropping out of the race and closing down his operation.

Perot gave several reasons for his decision. He said he "didn't have any drive to be president" and that he was concerned the election would be thrown to the House of Representatives if he took enough votes from Bush and Clinton to deny both the required electoral vote majority. Earlier he had complained that Republican dirty tricks were undermining his campaign.

By this time Perot had qualified for the ballot in twenty-four states and was well on his way to the goal of qualifying in all fifty states. His disappointed followers felt betrayed by the sudden withdrawal.

But just as suddenly, Perot was back in the race. On October 16 he said he was returning because the major parties had failed to address the problems he had been highlighting in his speeches, both as a private citizen and a political candidate. "We gave them a chance," he said, "They didn't do it."

With the campaign revived, volunteers succeeded in getting Perot on the ballot in every state. Because some states required that he have a running mate, Perot chose retired admiral and former Vietnam War prisoner James B. Stockdale of California. The campaign, which Perot called United We Stand America, later became the Reform Party, which nominated Perot for president in 1996. The organization had no formal platform in 1992 or 1996.

1996 Conventions

PRESIDENTIAL CANDIDATES

Bill Clinton
Democrat

Bob Dole
Republican

Ross Perot
Reform

REPUBLICANS

The Republican Party on August 12–15 showcased GOP presidential nominee Robert J. "Bob" Dole, the former Senate majority leader from Kansas, and his vice-presidential selection, former New York representative Jack F. Kemp, at the party's nominating convention in San Diego, Calif. Seeking to energize loyalists while also expanding its base, the convention's carefully orchestrated moments melded the twin themes of compassion and conservatism.

Organizers succeeded in banishing any hint of controversy and leaving the delegates with little to do but wave their colorful Dole-Kemp placards and present a picture of enthusiastic party unity for the network television cameras. The paucity of controversy cheered Republicans, who still remembered the 1992 convention in Houston that was marked by strident speeches on abortion and other hot-button social issues. In contrast, San Diego conventioneers were treated to speech after speech that stressed inclusion and moderation.

The Republican platform—as rigidly conservative as any in recent memory—was the designated forum for the party's sharper ideological right wing. Party moderates were kept happy during convention week with prime-time speaking slots. The social conservatives—who were at least a plurality in the ranks of the delegates—were rarely on stage during prime time.

On Monday, August 17, the delegates formally adopted the 1996 party platform by voice vote at the convention's sparsely attended opening morning session. The smooth and swift approval belied the fierce, prolonged struggle over the plank calling for a constitutional amendment to ban abortion. During platform deliberations the week before the convention, social conservatives who dominated the platform-writing process soundly defeated multiple amendments to soften the abortion plank or acknowledge differing views of the issue within the party. At the urging of the Dole campaign, however, the platform committee agreed to add the texts of defeated amendments as an appendix headed "Minority Views." Thereafter, also

at the urging of the Dole camp, abortion rights advocates dropped their planned protest on the convention floor.

Even most of the delegates pledged to conservative commentator Patrick J. Buchanan seemed to approve of the deal. Although Buchanan was denied a podium speech and his delegates were not allowed to place his name in nomination, his supporters said they appreciated the tone of unity and found plenty of reasons to rally around the Dole-Kemp ticket.

A highlight of the first evening came when Nancy Reagan delivered a tribute to her husband, former president Ronald Reagan, who, suffering from Alzheimer's disease, did not attend the GOP convention for the first time in more than three decades. The audience barely had a chance to collect its emotions before retired Army general Colin L. Powell marched to the podium and confirmed his status as a rising GOP star. Sounding the theme of the evening—and indeed the convention itself—Powell said the GOP "must always be the party of inclusion." In a rare acknowledgment of the party's tensions over social issues that lurked out of sight of the cameras, Powell declared his support for abortion rights and affirmative action.

Reflecting the party's new emphasis on diversity, female and minority speakers dominated the podium, even though their numbers were disproportionately low among the 1,990 delegates. The selection of New York representative Susan Molinari, an abortion rights supporter, as keynote speaker was another signal to moderates that they were welcome in the party. However, Molinari avoided mentioning abortion in her speech.

In the convention's most intriguing role reversal, House Speaker and convention chair Newt Gingrich, who rose to power and to controversy as a partisan firebrand, used his one short speaking slot Tuesday to praise volunteer efforts—presenting a softer, warmer side of the Republican Party. Wednesday, August 14, was highlighted by an unconventional appearance by Elizabeth Hanford Dole, the nominee's wife, who took a hand-held microphone to the convention floor to praise her husband's personal and political qualities.

The delegates formally made Bob Dole their presidential candidate following a nominating speech by Sen. John McCain of Arizona. The roll call of the states proved anticlimactic. It lasted about an hour and a half, yet the balloting was not unanimous. Dole ended up with 1,928 of the 1,990 delegate votes; Buchanan received 43 votes. *(Table, p. 246.)*

On the final evening, Dole and Kemp delivered acceptance speeches that laid the basis for their campaign against President Bill Clinton. Kemp, a fervent and enthusiastic promoter of the GOP as the party of opportunity, promised that Republican policies—including tax cuts and reduced regulation—would unleash a burst of economic activity benefiting all Americans.

In his speech, Dole prominently mentioned his proposed across-the-board, 15 percent income tax cut that had become the centerpiece of his campaign. But he also prescribed racial and ethnic tolerance as a dictum for the party. "If there is anyone who has mistakenly attached himself to our party in the belief that we are not open to citizens of every race and religion, then let me remind you," Dole said sternly, "tonight this hall belongs to the party of Lincoln, and the exits, which are clearly marked, are for you to walk out of as I stand this ground without compromise."

Yet, no matter how well Dole and the Republicans papered over differences at the convention, the party remained split between its traditional base of fiscal conservatives and its new base of social-issue activists who wanted to see their positions turned into policy.

Following are excerpts from the Republican platform of 1996:

Tax Relief. American families are suffering from the twin burdens of stagnant incomes and near-record taxes. . . . American families deserve better. They should be allowed to keep more of their hard-earned money so they can spend on their priorities. . . .

In response to this unprecedented burden confronting America, we support an across-the-board, 15-percent tax cut to marginal tax rates. . . . To remove impediments to job creation and economic growth, we support reducing the top tax rate on capital gains by 50 percent. . . . The income tax on Social Security benefits . . . must be repealed. . . .

To protect the American people from those who would undo their forthcoming victory over big government, we support legislation requiring a super-majority vote in both houses of Congress to raise taxes. . . .

Balancing the Budget. . . . Republicans support a Balanced Budget Amendment to the Constitution, phased in over a short period and with appropriate safeguards for national emergencies. . . .

Homeownership. . . . We support transforming public housing into private housing, converting low-income families into proud homeowners. Resident management of public housing is a first step toward that goal, which includes eliminating the Department of Housing and Urban Development (HUD). HUD's core functions will be turned over to the states. . . .

Changing Washington from the Ground Up. . . . We support elimination of the Departments of Commerce, Housing and Urban Development, Education, and Energy, and the elimination, defunding or privatization of agencies which are obsolete, redundant, of limited value, or too regional in focus. Examples of agencies. . . . are the National Endowment for the Arts, the National Endowment for the Humanities, the Corporation for Public Broadcasting and the Legal Services Corporation. . . .

Government Reform. . . . True reform is indeed needed: ending taxpayer subsidies for campaigns, strengthening party structures to guard against rogue operations, requiring full and immediate disclosure of all contributions, and cracking down on the indirect support, or "soft money," by which special interest groups underwrite their favored candidates. . . .

Regulatory Reform. . . . A Republican administration will require periodic review of existing regulations to ensure they are effective and do away with obsolete and conflicting rules. We will encourage civil servants to find ways to reduce regulatory burdens on the public and will require federal agencies to disclose the costs of new regulations on individuals and small businesses. . . . We will require agencies to conduct cost-benefit analyses of their regulations. . . .

Restoring Justice to the Courts. . . . The federal judiciary, including the U.S. Supreme Court, has overstepped its authority under the Constitution. It has usurped the right of citizen legislators and popularly elected executives to make law by declaring duly enacted laws to be "unconstitutional" through the misapplication of the principle of judicial review. . . . A Republican president will ensure that a process is established to select for the federal judiciary nominees who understand that their task is first and foremost to be faithful to the Constitution and to the intent of those who framed it. . . .

The Nation's Capital. . . . We reaffirm the constitutional status of the District of Columbia as the seat of government of the United States and reject calls for statehood for the District. . . . We call for structural reform of the city's government and its education system. . . .

Upholding the Rights of All. . . . We oppose discrimination based on sex, race, age, creed, or national origin and will vigorously enforce anti–discrimination statutes. We reject the distortion of those laws to cover sexual preference, and we endorse the Defense of Marriage Act to prevent states from being forced to recognize same-sex unions. Because we believe rights inhere in individuals, not in groups, we will attain our nation's goal of equal rights without quotas or other forms of preferential treatment. . . .

The unborn child has a fundamental individual right to life which cannot be infringed. We support a human life amendment to the Constitution and we endorse legislation to make clear that the Fourteenth Amendment's protections apply to unborn children. Our purpose is to have legislative and judicial protection of that right against those who perform abortions. . . .

We applaud Bob Dole's commitment to revoke the Clinton executive orders concerning abortion and to sign into law an end to partial-birth abortions. . . .

We defend the constitutional right to keep and bear arms. . . .

A Sensible Immigration Policy. . . . Illegal aliens should not receive public benefits other than emergency aid, and those who become parents while illegally in the United States should not be qualified to claim benefits for their offspring. Legal immigrants should depend for assistance on their sponsors, who are legally responsible for their financial well-being, not the American taxpayers. . . .

From Many, One. . . . While we benefit from our differences, we must also strengthen the ties that bind us to one another. Foremost among those is the flag. Its deliberate desecration is not "free speech," but an assault against our history and our hopes. We support a constitutional amendment that will restore to the people, through their elected representatives, their right to safeguard Old Glory. . . .

We support the official recognition of English as the nation's common language. . . .

Improving Education. . . . The federal government has no constitutional authority to be involved in school curricula or to control jobs in the workplace. That is why we will abolish the Department of Education, end federal meddling in our schools and promote family choice at all levels of learning. . . .

We will continue to work for the return of voluntary prayer to our schools. . . .

Health Care. Our goal is to maintain the quality of America's health care—the best in the world, bar none—while making health care and health insurance more accessible and more affordable. . . .

We reaffirm our determination to protect Medicare. We will ensure a significant annual expansion in Medicare. That isn't "cutting Medicare." It's a projected average annual rate of growth of 7.1 percent a year—more than twice the rate of inflation—to ensure coverage for those who need it now and those who will need it in the future . . .

The Middle East. . . . We applaud the Republican Congress for enacting legislation to recognize Jerusalem as the undivided capital of Israel. A Republican administration will ensure that the U.S. Embassy is moved to Jerusalem by May 1999. . . .

The Men and Women of Defense. . . . We affirm that homosexuality is incompatible with military service. . . . We reaffirm our support for the exemption of women from ground combat units and are concerned about the current policy of involuntarily assigning women to combat or near-combat units. . . .

REFORM PARTY

Founded in fall 1995 by Texas billionaire and presidential aspirant H. Ross Perot, the Reform Party conducted its first presidential nominating convention in an unusual two-stage process. The first session convened in Long Beach, Calif., on August 11, 1996, and the second session met one week later across the country at Valley Forge, Pa., on August 18. During the intervening week, ballots were sent to 1.3 million Reform Party members who voted in a "national primary" for the candidate of their choice by mail, electronic mail, or phone—an array of methods that party officials clearly saw as the election system of the future.

Perot had spent an estimated $6 million of his own money in bankrolling the party. After winning 19 percent of the popular vote in his unsuccessful independent bid against Democrat Clinton and Republican President George Bush in the 1992 presidential election, Perot had formed the nonpartisan education organization, United We Stand America (UWSA), to promote his ideas on the national agenda. In 1995 Perot and UWSA supporters spun off the Reform Party as a full-fledged political party.

The California session drew roughly 2,000 members—a fairly homogeneous group demographically, overwhelmingly white, and predominantly middle-aged or older. In the main, they tended to be politically disenchanted, strong proponents of the military, and strong supporters of reform in the mechanics of government and electoral politics.

Speeches by the party's two presidential candidates—Perot and former Democratic governor Richard D. Lamm of Colorado—highlighted the first session, which was televised nationally on C-SPAN and CNN. Lamm took a number of swipes

at the Democrats and Republicans, saying "They do not enjoy a right of perpetual existence." But he also made it clear he was an alternative to Perot. "The torch must pass," said Lamm. "The Reform Party is larger than any one individual."

Lamm echoed Perot in urging the party to build on the need for campaign reform, fiscal responsibility, and increased immigration controls. The latter issue, in particular, struck a chord with the Long Beach audience, which responded with cheers when Lamm declared that "the Statue of Liberty stands for liberty, not unlimited immigration."

But if Lamm spoke politely, like an invited guest, Perot played the garrulous host. Perot had every reason to be optimistic. He led Lamm by a ratio of more than 2-to-1 in the first round of nomination balloting that determined the party's primary finalists. "I want to be your president," Perot declared, trying to dispel memories of 1992, when he abruptly quit the presidential race in July, only to reenter in October.

During the following week, Lamm criticized the ground rules of the party's nominating process, which were devised by Perot operatives. "I don't think it has been a fair playing field or party-building endeavor as I was promised," he said.

The modern balloting system had its snags, too. Some participants complained that they did not receive ballots in time to vote. Even Lamm had trouble obtaining a ballot for himself. In the final tally, only 5 percent of the party's declared membership voted. On August 17, national coordinator Russell Verney announced that Perot had won the nomination by taking 65 percent of the primary vote to Lamm's 35 percent.

In his acceptance speech the following day at the Valley Forge convention center, Perot stressed the issues he was known for—reduced federal debt, lobbying reform, and higher ethical standards for elected officials. Perot especially ripped both parties for not following through on promising to form a task force to reform campaign finance. Despite his earlier criticism of public financing—Perot had spent more than $60 million to self-finance his 1992 campaign—he announced that he would accept federal matching funds in 1996. But in accepting the nearly $30 million in public matching funds for which he qualified, Perot had to limit his personal funding to $50,000. At the end of his speech, Perot urged supporters to contribute to his campaign, as a telephone number flashed on screens behind him. Perot then hastened from the stage for an appearance on CNN's *Larry King Live*, the program on which he made many of his campaign announcements in 1992 and 1996.

The Reform Party did not have a formal 1996 platform.

DEMOCRATS

Meeting in Chicago for the eleventh time in the party's history, the Democratic Party on August 26–29 jubilantly renominated President Clinton and Vice President Albert "Al" Gore Jr. Democratic officials produced a convention designed to stir the viewing public's emotions. Speakers and videos highlighted the party's racial and ethnic diversity while drawing attention to Clinton's efforts to ease the burdens on middle-class families. Taking advantage of meeting two weeks after the Republicans nominated Dole, Democrats repeatedly hammered away at Dole's offer to be "a bridge to the past" as proof that the GOP wanted to turn back the clock on economic, social, and cultural change.

Despite the apparent unity, the convention exposed the unresolved philosophical divisions between the party's liberal and centrist wings. Members of centrist Democratic Party groups such as the Blue Dogs, a group of House deficit hawks, and the Democratic Leadership Council insisted that their blueprint for smaller government was gradually becoming the party's dominant position. They pointed to the 1996 platform, adopted without dissent August 27, which was generally more conservative than past documents. "Our platform calls for a balanced budget," said Rep. Charles W. Stenholm of Texas. "That's a first."

Some veteran liberals, such as Rep. Charles B. Rangel of New York, acknowledged the party's move to the center. "America has shifted on us," Rangel said. "Americans should be prepared to raise the taxes, invest in productivity, and create the jobs. But they can't support that. They'd rather cut taxes, invest in defense, and build jails."

The high point of the first evening was the appearance of a pair of lifelong Republicans: former Ronald Reagan press secretary James S. Brady, and his wife, Sarah. In a reference to the Republican convention, Sarah Brady said, "Jim, we must have made a wrong turn. This isn't San Diego." The Bradys, who had become gun control proponents after James Brady was partially paralyzed from being shot during the 1981 attempt to assassinate President Reagan, called for increased efforts to reduce gun violence. They praised Clinton for enacting the Brady bill, which imposed a seven-day waiting period for handgun purchases.

Actor Christopher Reeve, paralyzed from a horse-riding accident in 1995, capped the evening's speeches with a plea for compassion and assistance to Americans with disabilities. Reeve, speaking from a wheelchair, held the hushed audience's attention as he called for increased research funding for multiple sclerosis, Parkinson's disease, spinal cord injuries, and AIDS.

On the second night former New York governor Mario M. Cuomo and civil rights leader Jesse L. Jackson from the liberal wing of the party spoke to the convention—although before the late-night portion of the broadcast by the three major television networks. While the two men agreed to disagree with the president over welfare reform, they launched some of the harshest partisan attacks of the convention. Cuomo proclaimed a need to elect a Democratic majority to Congress to fend off the Republicans' conservative agenda. "They are the real threat," he said. Jackson focused on the need to improve conditions in economically deprived sections of the United States. His repeated plea to "keep that faith" with poor and struggling Americans became a chant echoed by the rapt audience.

Following the keynote speech by Gov. Evan Bayh of Indiana, the evening's theme was "Families First." Speakers included an opponent of abortion, Rep. Tony P. Hall of Ohio. "Many of us have felt left out [in the past]," Hall said. "This year it's different." In 1992 Pennsylvania's antiabortion governor, Robert P. Casey, had not been permitted to speak at the Democratic convention. The final speaker, first lady Hillary Rodham Clinton, closed out the evening with a passionate explanation of her view of family values.

The next night Gore's speech broke tradition by being scheduled the day before the president's acceptance speech. Gore rallied the convention with sharp jabs at the Republican nominee. "In his speech from San Diego, Senator Dole offered himself as a bridge to the past," said Gore. "Tonight, Bill Clinton and I offer ourselves as a bridge to the future."

But the most memorable part of his speech was a deeply personal glimpse at a family tragedy. Seeking to underscore the dangers of underage smoking, Gore recounted the final, painful days and hours of his sister who began smoking at age thirteen and ultimately died of lung cancer.

The nomination of Clinton followed, with Sen. Christopher J. Dodd of Connecticut, the DNC general chairman, hailing the president for leading the nation into an era of prosperity, while courageously taking on powerful special interests such as the gun lobby and the tobacco industry. The formality of the presidential roll call culminated the evening. The final tally was announced as a unanimous 4,289 votes for Clinton, although there appeared to be roughly a dozen votes that were not cast during the roll call. (*Table, p. 247.*)

President Clinton capped the Democratic convention with a sixty-six-minute policy address that chronicled his administration's accomplishments. The president's speech was designed to burnish his centrist image and lay the foundation for a second term. In his address, the president resolved to "build a bridge to the twenty-first century, to meet our values and protect our values."

Clinton promised to balance the budget without threatening Medicare and Medicaid, education programs, or environmental protection. He also proposed a series of modest initiatives including deploying of 30,000 reading specialists to help enlist 1 million volunteer reading tutors, expanding controls on handgun sales, providing targeted tax cuts such as tax credits and deductions for college tuition and tax breaks for first-time home buyers, and increasing funding for cleaning up superfund toxic waste sites.

Following are excerpts from the Democratic platform of 1996:

Balancing the Budget. . . . In 1992, we promised to cut the deficit in half over four years. We did. Our 1993 economic plan cut spending by over a quarter trillion dollars in five years. . . . Now the Democratic Party is determined to finish the job and balance the budget. President Clinton has put forward a plan to balance the budget by 2002 while living up to our commitments to our elderly and our children and maintaining strong economic growth. . . . Today's Democratic Party believes we have a duty to care for our parents, so they can live their lives in dignity. That duty includes securing Medicare and Medicaid, finding savings without reducing quality or benefits, and protecting Social Security for future generations. . . .

Tax Relief. . . . Today's Democratic Party is committed to targeted tax cuts that help working Americans invest in their future, and we insist that any tax cuts are completely paid for, because we are determined to balance the budget. . . .

Foreign Trade. We believe that if we want the American economy to continue strong growth, we must continue to expand trade, and not retreat from the world. . . . We must continue to work to lower foreign trade barriers. . . .

Education. . . . In the next four years, we must do even more to make sure America has the best public schools on earth. . . . We must hold students, teachers, and schools to the highest standards. Every child should be able to read by the end of the third grade. Students should be required to demonstrate competency and achievement for promotion or graduation. Teachers should be required to meet high standards for professional performance and be rewarded for the good jobs they do—and there should be a fair, timely, cost-effective process to remove those who do not measure up. . . . We should expand public school choice, but we should not take American tax dollars from public schools and give them to private schools. We should promote public charter schools that are held to the highest standards of accountability and access. . . .

Health Care. The Democratic Party is committed to ensuring that Americans have access to affordable, high-quality health care. . . . In the next four years, we must take further steps to ensure that Americans have access to quality, affordable health care. We should start by making sure that people get help paying premiums so they do not lose health care while they're looking for a new job. We support expanded coverage of home care, hospice, and community-based services, so the elderly and people with disabilities of all ages can live in their own communities and as independently as possible. We . . . believe health insurance coverage for mental health care is vitally important and we support parity for mental health care.

Retirement. . . . We want . . . to make sure people can carry their pensions with them when they change jobs, protect pensions even further, and expand the number of workers with pension coverage. Democrats created Social Security, we oppose efforts to dismantle it, and we will fight to save it. We must ensure that it is on firm financial footing well into the next century. . . .

Fighting Crime. . . . President Clinton beat back fierce Republican opposition. . . . to answer the call of America's police officers and pass the toughest Crime Bill in history. . . . And it is making a difference. In city after city and town after town, crime rates are finally coming down. . . . Any attempt to repeal the Brady Bill or assault weapons ban will be met with a veto. We must do everything we can to stand behind our police officers, and the first thing we should do is pass a ban on cop-killer bullets. . . .

Immigration. . . . We support a legal immigration policy that is pro-family, pro-work, pro-responsibility, and pro-citizenship, and we deplore those who blame immigrants for economic and social problems. . . . We cannot tolerate illegal immigration and we must stop it. . . .

We deplore those who use the need to stop illegal immigration as a pretext for discrimination. And we applaud the wisdom of Republicans . . . who oppose the mean-spirited and shortsighted effort of Republicans in Congress to bar the children of illegal immigrants from schools. . . .

Welfare Reform. . . . Over the past four years, President Clinton has dramatically transformed the welfare system. . . . Welfare rolls are finally coming down—there are 1.3 million fewer people on welfare today than there were when President Clinton took office in January 1993.

. . . Thanks to President Clinton and the Democrats, the new welfare bill includes the health care and child care people need so they can go to work confident their children will be cared for. Thanks to President Clinton and the Democrats, the new welfare bill imposes time limits and real work requirements. . . . Thanks to President Clinton and the Democrats, the new welfare bill cracks down on deadbeat parents and requires minor mothers to live at home with their parents or with another responsible adult. . . .

We know the new bill passed by Congress is far from perfect—parts of it should be fixed because they go too far and have nothing to do with welfare reform. . . .

Abortion. The Democratic Party stands behind the right of every woman to choose, consistent with *Roe v. Wade,* and regardless of ability to pay. President Clinton took executive action to make sure that the right to make such decisions is protected for all Americans. Over the last four years, we have taken action to end the gag rule and ensure safety at family planning and women's health clinics. We believe it is a fundamental constitutional liberty that individual Americans—not government—can best take responsibility for making the most difficult and intensely personal decisions regarding reproduction. . . .

Political Reform. . . . The President and the Democratic Party support the bipartisan McCain-Feingold campaign finance reform bill. It will limit campaign spending, curb the influence of PACs and lobbyists, and end the soft money system. Perhaps most important of all, this bill provides free TV time for candidates, so they can talk directly to citizens about real issues and real ideas. . . . It is time to take the reins of democracy away from big money and put them back in the hands of the American people, where they belong. We applaud efforts by broadcasters and private citizens alike, to increase candidates' direct access to voters through free TV. . . .

The Middle East. . . . Jerusalem is the capital of Israel and should remain an undivided city accessible to people of all faiths. We are also committed to working with our Arab partners for peace to build a brighter, more secure and prosperous future for all the people of the Middle East. . . .

Protecting Our Environment. . . . We are committed to protecting the majestic legacy of our National Parks. . . . We will be good stewards of our old-growth forests, oppose new offshore oil drilling and mineral exploration and production in our nation's many environmentally critical areas, and protect our oceans from oil spills and the dumping of toxic and radioactive waste. . . .

Fighting Discrimination. Today's Democratic Party knows we must renew our efforts to stamp out discrimination and hatred of every kind, wherever and whenever we see it. . . . We believe everyone in America should learn English so they can fully share in our daily life, but we strongly oppose divisive efforts like English-only legislation. . . .

Religious Freedom. Today's Democratic Party understands that all Americans have a right to express their faith. . . . Americans have a right to express their love of God in public, and we applaud the President's work to ensure that children are not denied private religious expression in school. . . .

2000 Conventions

PRESIDENTIAL CANDIDATES

George W. Bush
Republican

Al Gore
Democrat

Ralph Nader
Green

REPUBLICANS

Meeting July 31–August 3 in Philadelphia, the Republican Party made history by naming George W. Bush, the son of a president, as the GOP standard-bearer for 2000. The proud father, former president George Bush, was among the many family members applauding the party's choice.

Delegates hoped a victory by Texas governor Bush would give the nation its second father-son presidential pair. The first was Federalist John Adams (1797–1801) and Democratic-Republican John Quincy Adams (1825–1829). Both were one-term presidents, as was the senior Bush, who lost to Democrat Bill Clinton in 1992.

In another historical irony, the nomination pitted Bush against Vice President Albert "Al" Gore Jr., who with Clinton halted twelve years of Republican control of the White House and who hoped to extend the Democrats' eight-year administration, just as George Bush had done for the GOP on Ronald Reagan's retirement in 1988.

The overriding difference between the two situations, as the Clinton-Gore strategists put it back then, was "the economy, stupid." Where Bush was washed out of office in a sea of red ink, Gore was riding a crest of unprecedented prosperity and federal budget surpluses. The year 2000 was a time of plenty that both parties sought to exploit.

In their acceptance speeches Bush and his running mate, former defense secretary Richard B. Cheney, assailed the Democrats for overlooking the opportunities of an overflowing treasury. "For eight years the Clinton-Gore administration has coasted through prosperity," Bush said. "So much promise to no great purpose. Instead of seizing this moment, the . . . administration has squandered it." Similarly the party's 32,000-word platform was replete with references to prosperity and ways to use it, chiefly through tax cuts, which Bush said would benefit all taxpayers and not just the rich.

Bush's nomination at Philadelphia's First Union Center was strictly a formality. He, like Gore, had secured the nomination months earlier through primary victories that won him enough delegates to eliminate the competition. The next strongest primary candidate, Sen. John McCain of Arizona, endorsed Bush and released his delegates to him. For the vote, the convention planners used a novel "rolling roll call" that took several days. Bush and Cheney won the votes of all 2,066 delegates. (Table, p. 248.)

In keeping with the convention's themes of unity and inclusion, there were no floor fights on rules or on platform planks. Averting one such fight, the rules committee rejected, 66–33, the so-called Delaware plan to limit the GOP presidential primary schedule to four months, with smaller states voting first. The Republican National Committee approved the plan, but big states objected that it would weaken their strength in the delegate-selection process.

A floor fight was also avoided over the issue of abortion. Moderates tried unsuccessfully to remove platform language supporting a constitutional ban on abortion, fearing that it would hurt GOP candidates, especially among women voters. Bush told the delegates that as president he would sign a ban on partial-birth abortions if Congress sent him one.

Although only 4 percent of the delegates were African Americans, the convention gave prominent roles to minorities. African American retired general Colin L. Powell gave the keynote address. Among other speakers were the nominee's wife, Laura, as well as Hispanics and a gay House member, Jim Kolbe of Arizona. As Kolbe spoke several Texas delegates removed their cowboy hats and bowed heads to show, as one put it, that they were not "condoning perversion."

The platform reaffirmed the party's opposition to homosexuality in the military, but in other ways it reflected Bush's self-described "compassionate conservatism." Missing were past GOP calls for eliminating the Education and Energy departments and federal agencies supporting the arts and humanities. Added was a new women's health section supporting more research on diseases that disproportionately affect women. The document also welcomed "New Americans" in a softened stance on immigration.

Following are excerpts from the Republican platform of 2000:

Taxes and Budget. . . . When the average American family has to work more than four months out of every year to fund all levels of government, it's time to change the tax system, to make it simpler, flatter, and fairer for everyone. It's time for an economics of inclusion that will let people keep more of what they earn and accelerate movement up the opportunity ladder.

We therefore enthusiastically endorse the principles of Governor Bush's Tax Cut with a Purpose:

• Replace the five current tax brackets with four lower ones, ensuring all taxpayers significant tax relief while targeting it especially toward low-income workers.

• Help families by doubling the child tax credit to $1,000, making it available to more families, and eliminating the marriage penalty.

• Encourage entrepreneurship and growth by capping the top marginal rate, ending the death tax, and making permanent the Research and Development credit.

• Promote charitable giving and education. Foster capital investment and savings to boost today's dangerously low personal savings rate. . . .

Family Matters. We support the traditional definition of "marriage" as the legal union of one man and one woman, and we believe that federal judges and bureaucrats should not force states to recognize other living arrangements as marriages. . . . We do not believe sexual preference should be given special legal protection or standing in law.

Education. . . . Raise academic standards through increased local control and accountability to parents, shrinking a multitude of federal programs into five flexible grants in exchange for real, measured progress in student achievement.

Assist states in closing the achievement gap and empower needy families to escape persistently failing schools by allowing federal dollars to follow their children to the school of their choice.

. . . We recognize that. . . . the role of the federal government must be progressively limited as we return control to parents, teachers, and local school boards. . . . The Republican Congress rightly opposed attempts by the Department of Education to establish federal testing that would set the stage for a national curriculum. We believe it's time to test the Department, and each of its programs, instead. . . .

Abortion. . . . The Supreme Court's recent decision, prohibiting states from banning partial-birth abortions—a procedure denounced by a committee of the American Medical Association and rightly branded as four-fifths infanticide—shocks the conscience of the nation. As a country, we must keep our pledge to the first guarantee of the Declaration of Independence. That is why we say the unborn child has a fundamental individual right to life which cannot be infringed. We support a human life amendment to the Constitution and we endorse legislation to make clear that the Fourteenth Amendment's protections apply to unborn children. . . .

Gun Laws. . . . We defend the constitutional right to keep and bear arms, and we affirm the individual responsibility to safely use and store firearms. . . . Although we support background checks to ensure that guns do not fall into the hands of criminals, we oppose federal licensing of law-abiding gun owners and national gun registration as a violation of the Second Amendment and an invasion of privacy of honest citizens. . . .

New Americans. . . . Our country's ethnic diversity within a shared national culture is unique in all the world. We benefit from our differences, but we must also strengthen the ties that bind us to one another.

Foremost among those is the flag. Its deliberate desecration is not "free speech" but an assault against both our proud history and our greatest hopes. We therefore support a constitutional amendment that will restore to the people, through their elected representatives, their right to safeguard Old Glory.

Another sign of our unity is the role of English as our common language. . . . For newcomers, it has always been the fastest route to the mainstream of American life. English empowers. That is why fluency in English must be the goal of bilingual education programs. We support the recognition of English as the nation's common language. At the same time, mastery of other languages is important for America's competitiveness in the world market. . . .

As a nation of immigrants, we welcome all new Americans who have entered lawfully and are prepared to follow our laws and provide for themselves and their families. In their search for a better life, they strengthen our economy, enrich our culture, and defend the nation in war and in peace. To ensure fairness for those wishing to reside in this country, and to meet the manpower needs of our expanding economy, a total overhaul of the immigration system is sorely needed. . . .

Saving Social Security. . . . Anyone currently receiving Social Security, or close to being eligible for it, will not be impacted by any changes. Key changes should merit bipartisan agreement so any reforms will be a win for the American people rather than a political victory for any one party. . . .

Personal savings accounts must be the cornerstone of restructuring. Each of today's workers should be free to direct a portion of their payroll taxes to personal investments for their retirement future. . . . Today's financial markets offer a variety of investment options, including some that guarantee a rate of return higher than the current Social Security system with no risk to the investor. . . .

Health Care. . . . Medicare, at age 35, needs a new lease on life. It's time to bring this program, so critical for 39 million seniors and individuals with disabilities, into the Twenty-first Century. It's time to modernize the benefit package to match current medical science, improve the program's financial stability, and cut back the bureaucratic jungle that is smothering it. It's time to give older Americans access to the same health insurance plan the Congress has created for itself, so that seniors will have the same choices and security as Members of Congress, including elimination of all current limitations and restrictions that prevent the establishment of medical savings accounts. . . .

We intend to save this beleaguered system with a vision of health care adapted to the changing demands of a new century. It is as simple, and yet as profound, as this: All Americans should have access to high-quality and affordable health care. . . . In achieving that goal, we will promote a health care system that supports, not supplants, the private sector; that promotes personal responsibility in health care decision-making; and that ensures the least intrusive role for the federal government. . . .

Women's Health. . . . Across this country, and at all levels of government, Republicans are at the forefront in aggressively developing health care initiatives targeted specifically at the needs of women. The enormous increases in the NIH [National Institutes of Health] budget brought about by the Republican Congress will make possible aggressive new research and clinical trials into diseases and health issues that disproportionately affect women as well as into conditions that affect the elderly, the majority of whom are women. And we are leading efforts to reach out to underserved and minority female populations, where disparities persist in life expectancy, infant mortality and death rates from cancer, heart disease, and diabetes. . . .

Energy. . . . By any reasonable standard, the Department of Energy has utterly failed in its mission to safeguard America's energy security.

The Federal Energy Regulatory Commission has been no better, and the Environmental Protection Agency (EPA) has been shutting off America's energy pipeline with a regulatory blitz that has only just begun. In fact, 36 oil refineries have closed in just the last eight years, while not a single new refinery has been built in this country in the last quarter-century. EPA's patchwork of regulations has driven fuel prices higher in some areas than in others. . . .

A Military for the Twenty-First Century. . . . Over the past seven years, a shrunken American military has been run ragged by a deployment tempo that has eroded its military readiness. Many units have seen their operational requirements increased four-fold, wearing out both people and equipment. Only last fall the Army certified two of its premier combat divisions as unready for war because of underfunding, mismanagement, and over commitment to peacekeeping missions around the globe. More Army units and the other armed services report similar problems. It is a national scandal that almost one quarter of our Army's active combat strength is unfit for wartime duty. . . .

The new Republican government will renew the bond of trust between the Commander-in-Chief, the American military, and the American people. The military is not a civilian police force or a political referee. We believe the military must no longer be the object of social experiments. We affirm traditional military culture. We affirm that homosexuality is incompatible with military service. . . .

The Middle East and Persian Gulf. . . . It is important for the United States to support and honor Israel, the only true democracy in the Middle East. We will ensure that Israel maintains a qualitative edge in defensive technology over any potential adversaries. We will not pick sides in Israeli elections. The United States has a moral and legal obligation to maintain its Embassy and Ambassador in Jerusalem. Immediately upon taking office, the next Republican president will begin the process of moving the U. S. Embassy from Tel Aviv to Israel's capital, Jerusalem. . . .

DEMOCRATS

Declaring himself "my own man," Vice President Gore stepped from the shadow of President Clinton and accepted the Democratic Party's nomination for president on the final night of the party's August 14–17 convention at Los Angeles's Staples Center. Reinforcing the independence he sought to portray, Gore earlier had taken a gamble unprecedented in American politics. He chose as his running mate Sen. Joseph I. Lieberman of Connecticut, making him the first person of Jewish descent to run on a major party's national ticket. Besides being of a religious minority, Lieberman had at times broken with his party on economic issues and had sternly deplored Clinton's sexual affair with Monica Lewinsky.

But the convention delegates enthusiastically accepted Gore's choice of Lieberman as his partner against Bush and Cheney, the Republican ticket named two weeks earlier in Philadelphia. Like Bush and Cheney, Gore and Lieberman won the unanimous approval of their respective delegates. Gore had locked up the presidential nomination by defeating former senator Bill Bradley in the Democratic primaries. In a convention speech, Bradley urged Gore's election.

Most public opinion polls showed Gore trailing Bush before the conventions. Afterward both nominees received a "bounce" from their convention performances, but Gore's choice of running mate and his "my own man" ploy appeared to have been somewhat more popular than Bush's effort. Polls after the Democratic convention showed Gore leading Bush slightly.

Although Gore had been in the public eye for much of his life—as a House member, senator, and eight years as vice president—he devoted much of his acceptance speech to telling the delegates and television audience "who I truly am." He told of growing up in Carthage, Tennessee, and paid tribute to his recently deceased father, former senator Albert A. Gore, and his mother, one of the first woman graduates of Vanderbilt University Law School.

He praised Clinton as "a leader who moved us out of the valley of recession and into the longest period of prosperity in American history." But he also distanced himself from the moral behavior in office that led to Clinton's impeachment and Senate trial. "If you entrust me with the presidency, I know I won't always be the most exciting politician," Gore said, adding, "I will never let you down."

Even Clinton seemed to recognize Gore's need to shake loose the moral baggage of the president he had served for eight years. In his farewell speech to the convention, Clinton praised Gore's character as an adviser, leader, and champion of ordinary Americans. Choosing Gore as his partner, Clinton said, was "one of the very best decisions of my life."

Gore's speech and the party platform stressed the prosperity and budget surpluses achieved during Clinton's two terms. Gore pledged to continue balancing the budget while delivering "the right kind of tax cuts." The Bush kind, he said, would benefit the wealthy and leave little to pay down the national debt or meet the needs of poor and working families. "They're for the powerful," Gore said. "We're for the people."

Although Lieberman voted against conviction of Clinton after earlier criticizing him from the Senate floor, he had been an advocate of moral decency long before the Lewinsky affair came to light. Gore's wife, Tipper, had a similar background as a critic of explicit rock music in the 1980s. And, despite Hollywood's importance as a revenue source for the Democrats, the party platform contained a plank calling on the entertainment industry to assume more responsibility in protecting children from violence and cruelty.

Gore's film actor friend and Harvard roommate Tommy Lee Jones nominated Gore. Tipper Gore introduced her husband to the 4,339 delegates. One of Gore's daughters, Karenna Gore Schiff, also spoke to the convention. No other names were placed in nomination, and there were no floor fights over the party rules or platform. (*Table, p. 249.*)

Following are excerpts from the Democratic platform of 2000:

Fiscal Discipline. . . . Today, for most families, the federal tax burden is the lowest it has been in twenty years. The Bush tax slash takes a different course. It is bigger than any cut Newt Gingrich ever dreamed of. It would let the richest one percent of Americans afford a new sports car and middle class Americans afford a warm soda. It is so out-of-step with reality that the Republican Congress refused to enact it. It would undermine the American economy and undercut our prosperity. . . . Democrats seek the right kind of tax relief—tax cuts that are specifically targeted to help those who need them the most.

These tax cuts would let families live their values by helping them save for college, invest in their job skills and lifelong learning, pay for health insurance, afford child care, eliminate the marriage penalty for working families, care for elderly or disabled loved ones, invest in clean cars and clean homes, and build additional security for their retirement.

Retirement Security. . . . The choice for Americans on this vital part of our national heritage has never been more clear: Democrats believe in using our prosperity to save Social Security; the Republicans' tax cut would prevent America from ensuring our senior citizens have a secure retirement. We owe it to America's children and their children to make the strength and solvency of Social Security a major national priority.

That's why Al Gore is committed to making Social Security safe and secure for more than half a century by using the savings from our current unprecedented prosperity to strengthen the Social Security Trust Fund in preparation for the retirement of the Baby Boom generation. . . .

To build on the success of Social Security, Al Gore has proposed the creation of Retirement Savings Plus—voluntary, tax-free, personally-controlled, privately-managed savings accounts with a government match that would help couples build a nest egg of up to $400,000. . . .

Education. . . . George W. Bush and the Republican Party offer neither real accountability nor reasonable investment [in education]. . . . Their version of accountability relies on private school vouchers that would offer too few dollars to too few children to escape their failing schools. These vouchers would pass the buck on accountability while pulling bucks out of the schools that need them most. . . .

By the end of the next presidential term, we should have a fully qualified, well trained teacher in every classroom in every school in every part of this country and every teacher should pass a rigorous test to get there.

By the end of the next presidential term, every failing school in America should be turned around—or shut down and reopened under new public leadership.

By the end of the next presidential term, we should ensure that no high school student graduates unless they have mastered the basics of reading and math—so that the diploma they receive really means something.

By the end of the next presidential term, parents across the nation ought to be able to choose the best public school for their children. . . .

We should make a college education as universal as high school is today. Al Gore has proposed a new National Tuition Savings program to tie together state tuition savings programs in more than 30 states so that parents can save for college tax-free and inflation-free. We propose a tax cut for tuition and fees for post-high school education and training that allows families to choose either a $10,000 a year tax deduction or a $2,800 tax credit. . . .

Fighting Crime. . . . Strong and Sensible Gun Laws. . . . Democrats believe that we should fight gun crime on all fronts—with stronger laws and stronger enforcement. That's why Democrats fought and passed the Brady Law and the Assault Weapons Ban. We increased federal, state, and local gun crime prosecution by 22 percent since 1992. Now gun crime is down by 35 percent.

Now we must do even more. We need mandatory child safety locks, to protect our children. We should require a photo license I.D., a full background check, and a gun safety test to buy a new handgun in America. We support more federal gun prosecutors, ATF agents and inspectors, and giving states and communities another 10,000 prosecutors to fight gun crime.

Hate Crimes. . . . Hate crimes are more than assaults on people, they are assaults on the very idea of America. They should be punished with extra force. Protections should include hate violence based on gender, disability or sexual orientation. And the Republican Congress should stop standing in the way of this pro-civil rights, anti-crime legislation. . . .

Valuing Families. . . . Responsible Entertainment. . . . Parents and the entertainment industry must accept more responsibility. Many parents are not aware of the resources available to them, such as the V-chip technology in television sets and Internet filtering devices, that can help them shield children from violent entertainment. The entertainment industry must accept more responsibility and exercise more self-restraint, by strictly enforcing movie ratings, by taking a close look at violence in its own advertising, and by determining whether the ratings systems are allowing too many children to be exposed to too much violence and cruelty.

Health Care. Universal Health Coverage. There is much more left to do. We must redouble our efforts to bring the uninsured into coverage step-by-step and as soon as possible. We should guarantee access to affordable health care for every child in America. We should expand coverage to working families, including more Medicaid assistance to help with the transition from welfare to work. . . . In addition, Americans aged 55 to 65—the fastest growing group of uninsured—should be allowed to buy into the Medicare program to get the coverage they need. By taking these steps, we can move our nation closer to the goal of providing universal health coverage for all Americans.

. . . A Real Patients' Bill of Rights. Medical decisions should be made by patients and their doctors and nurses, not accountants and bureaucrats at the end of a phone line a thousand miles away. . . . Americans need a real, enforceable Patients' Bill of Rights with the right to see a specialist, the right to appeal decisions to an outside board, guaranteed coverage of emergency room care, and the right to sue when they are unfairly denied coverage. . . .

Protecting and Strengthening Medicare. It is time we ended the tragedy of elderly Americans being forced to choose between meals and medication. It is time we modernized Medicare with a new prescription drug benefit. This is an essential step in making sure that the best new cures and therapies are available to our seniors and disabled Americans. We cannot afford to permit our seniors to receive only part of the medical care they need. . . .

Abortion. Choice. The Democratic Party stands behind the right of every woman to choose, consistent with *Roe v. Wade,* and regardless of ability to pay. We believe it is a fundamental constitutional liberty that individual Americans—not government—can best take responsibility for making the most difficult and intensely personal decisions regarding reproduction. This year's Supreme Court rulings show to us all that eliminating a woman's right to choose is only one justice away. That's why the stakes in this election are as high as ever. . . .

Campaign Finance Reform. . . . The big-time lobbyists and special interest were so eager [in 2000] to invest in George W. Bush and deliver campaign cash to him hand-over-fist that he became the first major party nominee to pull out of the primary election financing structure and refuse to abide by campaign spending limits.

In this year's presidential primaries it became clear that the Republican establishment is violently opposed to John McCain's call for reforming our democracy. Al Gore supports John McCain's campaign for political reform. In fact, the McCain-Feingold bill is the very first piece of legislation that a President Al Gore will submit to Congress—and he will fight for it until it becomes the law of the land.

Then he will go even further—much further. He will insist on tough new lobbying reform, publicly-guaranteed TV time for debates and advocacy by candidates, and a crackdown on special interest issue ads. . . .

Transforming the Military. . . . The Democratic Party understands that, good as they are, the armed forces must continue to evolve. They must not only remain prepared for conventional military action, but must sharpen their ability to deal with new missions and new kinds of threats. They must become more agile, more versatile, and must more completely incorporate the revolutionary implications and advantages of American supremacy in information technology.

. . . A high-tech fighting force must recruit, train, and retain a professional all-volunteer force of the highest caliber. . . . While the number of soldiers and families on food stamps is down by two-thirds over the past decade, it is unacceptable that any member of our armed forces should have to rely on food stamps. Al Gore is committed to equal treatment of all service members and believes all patriotic Americans be allowed to serve their country without discrimination, persecution, and violence. . . .

Middle East. . . . Jerusalem is the capital of Israel and should remain an undivided city accessible to people of all faiths. In view of the government of Israel's courageous decision to withdraw from Lebanon, we believe special responsibility now resides with Syria to make a contribution toward peace. The recently-held Camp David summit, while failing to bridge all the gaps between Israel and the Palestinians, demonstrated President Clinton's resolve to do all the United States could do to bring an end to that long conflict. Al Gore, as president, will demonstrate the same resolve. . . .

GREENS

Building on the modest success of his token candidacy four years earlier, consumer advocate Ralph Nader emerged in 2000 as a full-fledged presidential candidate. He accepted the Green Party nomination at its June 25 convention in Denver with a broad-brush attack on the institutions of power in the United States.

Pledging "government of, by, and for the people—not monied interests," Nader called for a collective understanding of the "inequalities afflicting so many of our citizens. . . . What is so normalized now must be defined as intolerable and unworthy of this great country of ours."

Delegates from thirty-nine state Green parties nominated Nader by a 295–21 vote. They also renominated Native American Winona LaDuke, Nader's 1996 running mate, and ratified a lengthy platform setting forth the party's "key values."

In contrast to 1996, when he won 0.7 percent of the presidential vote as the Greens' nominal candidate in fewer than half the states, with no serious campaigning and only a $5,000 budget, Nader was already an active candidate before the Denver convention. He had barnstormed in all fifty states and had raised $1 million of a projected $5 million war chest. His goal was to win at least 5 percent of the vote, which would entitle the Greens to federal matching campaign funds in 2004.

At age sixty-six, Nader had received widespread respect for his forty-two years of public service in areas of consumer safety,

the environment, and economic justice. But his candidacy against Republican Bush and Democrat Gore soured many in his normal constituency, particularly liberals who feared it would hurt Gore. The *New York Times,* in a June 30 editorial entitled "Mr. Nader's Misguided Crusade," said Nader was engaging in a "self-indulgent exercise" that would distract voters from the clear-cut choices offered by Bush and Gore.

Nader, however, denied being a "spoiler" of Gore's chances. He told reporters, "I'm worried about Gore taking votes away from me."

The candidate devoted much of his nearly two-hour acceptance speech to attacks on "corporate welfare," the "Bush and Gore duopoly," the International Monetary Fund and the World Trade Organization, and "corporatization" that he said is "fast going global" and undermining "our legitimate local state and national sovereignties." He called for universal health insurance, a higher minimum wage, and banning or sharply limiting PACs (political action committees) and "soft money" given to parties.

Nader assailed the Commission on Presidential Debates for excluding third-party candidates from the planned debates between the major party nominees. The shutout, he said, limits "the competitive democratic process on which the American electoral system is supposed to be built."

Following are excerpts from the Green Party platform of 2000:

Democracy. A growing and grave imbalance between the often-converging power of Big Business, Big Government and the citizens of this country has seriously damaged our democracy. . . . It's time to end "corporate welfare" as we know it. . . .

Political Reform. We propose comprehensive campaign finance reform, including caps on spending and contributions, at the national and state level, and/or full public financing of elections to remove undue influence in political campaigns. We will work to ban or greatly limit political action committees and restrict soft money contributions. . . .

We believe in majority rule. Accordingly, we call for the use of instant runoff voting in chief executive races (mayor, governor, president, etc.) where voters can rank their favorite candidates (1, 2, 3, etc.) to guarantee that the winner has majority support and that voters aren't relegated to choosing between the "lesser of two evils."

The Electoral College is an eighteenth century anachronism. We call for a constitutional amendment abolishing the Electoral College and providing for the direct election of the president by Instant Runoff Voting. Until that time, we call for a proportional allocation of delegates in state primaries.

Foreign Policy. . . . Greens believe the more than $300 billion defense budget must be cut. The Green Party calls for military spending to be cut by 50 percent over the next 10 years, with increases in spending for social programs. . . .

It is our belief that the massive debt owed by the Third World is causing immense misery and environmental destruction. foreign aid must be addressed in the context of retiring this debt and not forcing "structural adjustments" via the International Monetary Fund (IMF) and World Bank on the economies of the underdeveloped world. . . .

Health Care. . . . Alongside the many Americans calling for action that makes health care a right, not a privilege, the Green Party states with a clear voice its strong support for universal health care. . . . We call for passage of legislation at the national and state level that guarantees comprehensive benefits for all Americans. A single-insurer system funded by the federal government and administered at the state and local levels remains viable and is an essential barometer of our national health and well-being. . . .

We believe the right of a woman to control her own body is inalienable. It is essential that the option of a safe, legal abortion remains available. . . .

Social Security. . . . The Green Party opposes the "privatization" of Social Security. The Social Security trust fund, contrary to claims being made by Republican and Democrat candidates, is not about to "go broke" and does not need to be "fixed" by Wall Street. . . . Considering that the bottom 20 percent of American senior citizens get roughly 80 percent of their income from Social Security, and that without Social Security nearly 70 percent of black elderly and 60 percent of Latino elderly households would be in poverty, it is critical that the public protections of Social Security are not privatized and subjected to increased risk based on misleading projections of shortfalls.

Criminal Justice. . . . We support the 'Brady Bill' and thoughtful, carefully considered gun control.

. . . . We do not support, as a matter of conscience, the death penalty.

Civil and Equal Rights. . . . We call for an end to official support for any remaining badges and indicia of slavery and specifically call for the immediate removal of the Confederate battle flag from any and all government buildings because we recognize that, to many, this remains a painful reminder of second-class status on the basis of race. . . .

We affirm the right to openly embrace sexual orientation in the intimate choice of who we love. . . . We support the rights of gay, lesbian, bisexual and transgendered people in housing, jobs, civil marriage and benefits, child custody—and in all areas of life, the right to be treated equally with all other people. . . .

We will resist discriminatory English-only pressure groups. We call for a national language policy that would encourage all citizens to be fluent in at least two languages.

Native Americans. . . . As Greens we feel a special affinity to the respect for community and the Earth that many Native peoples have at their roots. . . . We recognize that Native American land and treaty rights often stand at the front-line against government and multinational corporate attempts to plunder energy, mineral, timber, fish, and game resources, polluting water, air, and land in the service of the military, economic expansion, and the consumption of natural resources. Therefore, we support legal, political, and grassroots efforts by and on behalf of Native Americans to protect their traditions, rights, livelihoods, and their sacred spaces.

Energy Policy. . . . If we do not alter our energy use soon—and drastically—the ecological crisis may be exacerbated past a point where it can be resolved. A comprehensive energy policy must be a critical element of our environmental thinking. Investing in energy efficiency and renewable energy is key to sustainability. . . . Extensive conservation measures will bring huge resource savings for both the economy and the environment. Conservation, along with energy efficiency and renewables, is an essential part of an effective energy policy. The Greens call for pervasive efforts on the energy conservation front . . .

Nuclear Issues. . . . The Green Party recognizes that there is no such thing as nuclear waste "disposal." All six of the "low-level" nuclear waste dumps in the United States have leaked. There are no technological quick fixes which can effectively isolate nuclear waste from the biosphere for the duration of its hazardous life. Therefore, it is essential that generation of additional nuclear wastes be stopped. . . .

The Green Party calls for the early retirement of nuclear power reactors as soon as possible (in no more than five years) and for a phaseout of other technologies that use or produce nuclear waste. . . .

Fossil Fuels. . . . We call for transition energy strategies, including the use of relatively clean-burning natural gas, as a way to reorder our energy priorities and over-reliance on traditional fuels. . . . We call for a gradual phase-out of gasoline and other fossil fuels.

Emissions Reduction. . . . With only 4 percent of the earth's people, the United States produces more than 20 percent of emissions. From 1990 to 1996, total U.S. emissions grew by an amount equal to what Brazil and Indonesia produce every year. Per capita, the United States emits 85 percent more than Germany, twice as much as England and Japan, and currently nearly ten times as much as China. The Green Party urges the U.S. Congress to act immediately to address the critical global warming and climate change issues. . . .

Trade. . . . We reject trade agreements negotiated in secret and unduly influenced by corporate attorneys and representatives. In particular, we oppose the North American Free Trade Agreement (NAFTA), the General Agreement On Tariffs And Trade (GATT), and its progeny, the World Trade Organization (WTO). . . . We demand that these agreements be updated to include more specific environmental, worker, health and safety standards in the text itself, not as "side agreements."

National Debt. . . . . During the 1980s, our national debt grew from approximately $1 trillion to over $5 trillion. During that time, we refused to fund Social Security, food stamps, public housing, higher education, public transportation, etc., etc. In effect when you neglect the economic well-being of the society and refuse to protect the environment, the result can hardly be described as a surplus. . . . To help make up for our nation's neglect, we support tax increases on megacorporate and wealthy interests; defense budget reductions. . . . and entitlement reductions to those who can afford reductions most. Entitlement spending is over one-half of the federal budget. One way to reduce entitlement costs substantially would be by "means testing," i.e., by scaling back payments to the six million citizens in families with incomes over $50,000 annually.

2004 Conventions

PRESIDENTIAL CANDIDATES

John F. Kerry
Democrat

George W. Bush
Republican

DEMOCRATS

The 2004 Democratic and Republican conventions, the first after the terrorist attacks of 2001, convened under an umbrella of unprecedented security. The federal government alone allocated up to $50 million for protection at each meeting. In late July, the Democrats gathered at the FleetCenter in Boston—the first time either major party had met in that city. By chance it was also the home town of the party's presidential nominee, John F. Kerry.

The Democrats, as has become the norm for recent conventions, put on a unified display throughout the four-day event as the 4,964 delegates and alternates were hopeful of unseating incumbent president George W. Bush. Many convention attendees were angry at the Bush administration for its rationale, later discredited, for going to war with Iraq, for its inadequate preparation for the war's aftermath, and for the mounting toil in U.S. casualties and deaths. Some Democrats still refused to accept the legitimacy of Bush's presidency after the bitterly controversial 2000 election.

One of the first speakers on July 26 was former president Jimmy Carter, who said that "recent policies have cost our nation its reputation as the world's most admired champion of freedom and justice. What a difference these few months of extremism have made. . . . With our allies disunited, the world resenting us, and the Middle East ablaze, we need John Kerry to restore life to the global war against terrorism."

Also speaking on the first night was former president Bill Clinton and his wife, Sen. Hillary Clinton of New York. In his remarks the former president, who received a draft deferment during the Vietnam War, contrasted Kerry with himself, President Bush, and Vice President Richard B. Cheney. Clinton said that "many young men, including the current president, the vice president, and me, could have gone to Vietnam and didn't. John Kerry came from a privileged background. He could have avoided going too, but instead, he said: Send me." Now it was

time, Clinton said, "to say to him what he has always said to America: Send me."

One surprising speaker for the Democrats on the first night was a Reagan, Ron Reagan, son of former Republican president Ronald Reagan, who had recently died. Reagan spoke in support of medical research using embryonic stem cells to help find cures for spinal cord injuries and diseases such as Alzheimer's, which had afflicted his father after he left the presidency. His mother, Nancy Reagan, also had publicly opposed the Bush administration's strict limitations on funding for stem cell research. The Democratic platform supported limited research.

On July 27 Senate candidate Barack Obama of Illinois, the son of an African American farmer from Kenya, gave the convention's keynote speech. The self-described "skinny kid with a funny name," said, "The audacity of hope! That is God's greatest gift to us, the bedrock of this nation, the belief in things not seen, the belief that there are better days ahead." Obama's electrifying speech prompted television network commentators to predict a bright future for the forty-three-year-old keynoter, including possibly an eventual presidential candidacy.

The word "hope" also was threaded through John Edwards's vice-presidential acceptance speech on July 28. The North Carolina senator urged the delegates to say "hope is on the way" to people at home who are despondent for a number of reasons, such as having a loved one fighting in Iraq. The presidential nomination roll call of the states was a foregone conclusion as most of Kerry's primary opponents, including Edwards, had released their delegates before the convention, giving the nominee a near unanimous tally. (Table, p. 251.)

On the convention's final night Kerry, saluting crisply at the beginning of his acceptance speech, said that he was "reporting for duty" as the party's candidate to unseat President Bush. Kerry's words touched off an immense cheer as the delegates seemed ready to support Kerry in challenging the adage that "you don't switch horses in midstream," especially in wartime.

The Massachusetts senator sought to counter Republican criticism that he might be weak on defense in light of his opposition to the Vietnam War after serving in it as a patrol boat commander. "I defended this country as a young man and I will defend it as president," he said. "Let there be no mistake: I will never hesitate to use force when it is required. Any attack will be met with a swift and certain response. I will never give any nation or international institution a veto over our national security. And I will build a stronger American military. I will fight a smarter, more effective war on terror."

Kerry was joined on the platform by what he called "my band of brothers," men who served with him in Vietnam and were now supporting his candidacy. Among them was Jim Rassman, who credited Kerry with saving his life by pulling him from the river after he fell off the patrol boat. Former Georgia senator Max Cleland, who lost both legs and an arm in Vietnam, introduced Kerry.

The Democratic platform ran about 18,000 words and focused on national security and policies that benefited the middle class. Besides stem cell research, the platform also voiced support for preserving Social Security, maintaining abortion rights, and leaving the issue of same-sex marriage up to the states.

Following are excerpts from the Democratic platform of 2004:

Defeating Terrorism. . . . Today, the Bush Administration is waging a war against a global terrorist movement committed to our destruction with insufficient understanding of our enemy or effort to address the underlying factors that can give rise to new recruits. This war isn't just a manhunt. We cannot rest until Osama bin Laden is captured or killed, but that day will mark only a victory in the war on terror, not its end. Terrorists like al Qaeda and its affiliates are unlike any adversary our nation has ever known. We face a global terrorist movement of many groups, funded from different sources with separate agendas, but all committed to assaulting the United States and free and open societies around the globe. Despite his tough talk, President Bush's actions against terrorism have fallen far short. He still has no comprehensive strategy for victory. After allowing bin Laden to escape from our grasp at Tora Bora, he diverted crucial resources from the effort to destroy al Qaeda in Afghanistan. His doctrine of unilateral preemption has driven away our allies and cost us the support of other nations.

We must put in place a strategy to win—an approach that recognizes and addresses the many facets of this mortal challenge, from the terrorists themselves to the root causes that give rise to new recruits, and uses all the tools at our disposal. Agents of terrorism work in the shadows of more than 60 nations, on every continent. The only possible path to victory will be found in the company of others, not walking alone. With John Kerry as Commander-in-Chief, we will never wait for a green light from abroad when our safety is at stake, but we must enlist those whose support we need for ultimate victory.

Iraq. . . . More than a year ago, President Bush stood on an aircraft carrier under a banner that proclaimed "mission accomplished." But today we know that the mission is not finished, hostilities have not ended, and our men and women in uniform fight almost alone with the target squarely on their backs.

People of good will disagree about whether America should have gone to war in Iraq, but this much is clear: this Administration badly exaggerated its case, particularly with respect to weapons of mass destruction and the connection between Saddam's government and al Qaeda. This Administration did not build a true international coali-

tion. This Administration disdained the United Nations weapons inspection process and rushed to war without exhausting diplomatic alternatives. Ignoring the advice of military leaders, this Administration did not send sufficient forces into Iraq to accomplish the mission. And this Administration went into Iraq without a plan to win the peace.

Now this Administration has been forced to change course in order to correct this fundamental mistake. They are now taking up the suggestions that many Democrats have been making for over a year. And they must—because having gone to war, we cannot afford to fail at peace. We cannot allow a failed state in Iraq that inevitably would become a haven for terrorists and a destabilizing force in the Middle East. And we must secure more help from an international community that shares a huge stake in helping Iraq become a responsible member of that community, not a breeding ground for terror and intolerance.

Strengthening Military. . . . The Bush Administration was right to call for the "transformation" of the military. But their version of transformation neglected to consider that the dangers we face have also been transformed. The Administration was concerned with fighting classic conventional wars, instead of the asymmetrical threats we now face in Iraq, Afghanistan, and the war against al Qaeda. To rise to those challenges, we must strengthen our military, including our Special Forces, improve our technology, and task our National Guard with homeland security. . . .

We will add 40,000 new soldiers—not to increase the number of soldiers in Iraq, but to sustain our overseas deployments and prevent and prepare for other possible conflicts. This will help relieve the strain on our troops and bring back more of our soldiers, guardsmen and reservists. We are dedicated to keeping our military operating on a volunteer basis. We are committed to management reform both to ensure that our defense funding is spent effectively and to help pay for these new forces. . . .

Homeland Security. The first and foremost responsibility of government is to protect its citizens from harm. Unfortunately, Washington today is not doing enough to make America safe.

We have made some progress since the terrible attacks of September 11th. We have taken steps to secure our airports. After resisting Democratic efforts for months, the Administration finally agreed to create the Department of Homeland Security.

But we have not done nearly enough. Our intelligence services remain fragmented and lack coordination. Millions of massive shipping containers arrive at American ports every year without being searched and without even a reliable list of their contents. Our borders are full of holes. Our chemical plants are vulnerable to attack. Across America, police officers, firefighters, and other first responders still lack the information, protective gear, and communications equipment to do their jobs safely and successfully. . . .

Protecting Retirement Security. . . . We are absolutely committed to preserving Social Security. It is a compact across the generations that has helped tens of millions of Americans live their retirement years in dignity instead of poverty. Democrats believe in the progressive, guaranteed benefit that has ensured that seniors and people with disabilities receive a benefit not subject to the whims of the market or the economy. We oppose privatizing Social Security or raising the retirement age. We oppose reducing the benefits earned by workers just because they have also earned a benefit from certain public retirement plans. We will repeal discriminatory laws that penalize some retired workers and their families while allowing others to receive full benefits. Because the massive deficits under the Bush Administration have raided hundreds of billions of dollars from Social Security, the most important step we can take to strengthen Social Security is to restore fiscal responsibility. Social Security matters to all Americans, Democrats and Republicans, and strengthening Social Security should be a common cause.

Standing Up for Middle Class. . . . President Bush and the Republicans in Congress have ignored the middle class since day one of this Administration. They have catered to the wealth of the richest instead of honoring the work of the rest of us. They have promised almost everything and paid for almost nothing. And the middle class is shouldering more taxes, earning less money, and bearing higher costs. The bottom line for the middle class under President Bush and the Republican Party is this: Instead of working hard to get ahead, the middle class is working hard just to get by. . . .

First, we must restore our values to our tax code. We want a tax code that rewards work and creates wealth for more people, not a tax code that hoards wealth for those who already have it. With the middle class under assault like never before, we simply cannot afford the massive Bush tax cuts for the very wealthiest. We should set taxes for families making more than $200,000 a year at the same level as in the late 1990s, a period of great prosperity when the wealthiest Americans thrived without special treatment. We will cut taxes for 98 percent of Americans and help families meet the economic challenges of their everyday lives. And we will oppose tax increases on middle class families, including those living abroad.

Reforming Health Care. . . . We oppose privatizing Medicare. We will not allow Republicans to destroy a commitment that has done so much good for so many seniors and people with disabilities over the past 39 years. Instead, we want to strengthen Medicare and make it more efficient.

We will ensure that seniors across the country, particularly in small-town and rural America, no longer suffer from geographic discrimination.

We will end the disgrace of seniors being forced to choose between meals and medication. Today, our seniors are paying too much for prescription drugs, while options abroad are far cheaper and just as safe. We will allow the safe reimportation of drugs from other countries.

Stem Cell Research. President Bush has rejected the calls from Nancy Reagan, Christopher Reeve and Americans across the land for assistance with embryonic stem cell research. We will reverse his wrongheaded policy. Stem cell therapy offers hope to more than 100 million Americans who have serious illnesses—from Alzheimer's to heart disease to juvenile diabetes to Parkinson's. We will pursue this research under the strictest ethical guidelines, but we will not walk away from the chance to save lives and reduce human suffering.

Voting Rights. Voting is the foundation of democracy, a central act of civic engagement, and an expression of equal citizenship. Voting rights are important precisely because they are protective of all other rights. We will call for legislative action that will fully protect and enforce the fundamental Constitutional right of every American to vote—to ensure that the Constitution's promise is fully realized and that, in disputed elections, every vote is counted fully and fairly.

To advance these goals, and to guarantee the integrity of our elections and to increase voter confidence, we will seek action to ensure that voting systems are accessible, independently auditable, accurate, and secure. We will support the full funding of programs to realize this goal. Finally, it is the priority of the Democratic Party to fulfill the promise of election reform, reauthorize the expiring provisions of the Voting Rights Act, and vigorously enforce all our voting rights laws.

A Strong American Community. We will extend the promise of citizenship to those still struggling for freedom. Today's immigration laws do not reflect our values or serve our security, and we will work for real reform. The solution is not to establish a massive new status of second-class workers; that betrays our values and hurts all working people. Undocumented immigrants within our borders who clear a background check, work hard and pay taxes should have a path to earn full participation in America. We will hasten family reunification for parents and children, husbands and wives, and offer more English-language and civic education classes so immigrants can assume all the rights and responsibilities of citizenship. As we undertake these steps, we will work with our neighbors to strengthen our security so we are safer from those who would come here to harm us. We are a nation of immigrants, and from Arab-Americans in California to Latinos in Florida, we share the dream of a better life in the country we love.

We will defend the dignity of all Americans against those who would undermine it. Because we believe in the privacy and equality of women, we stand proudly for a woman's right to choose, consistent with Roe v. Wade, and regardless of her ability to pay. We stand firmly against Republican efforts to undermine that right. At the same time, we strongly support family planning and adoption incentives. Abortion should be safe, legal, and rare.

We support full inclusion of gay and lesbian families in the life of our nation and seek equal responsibilities, benefits, and protections for these families. In our country, marriage has been defined at the state level for 200 years, and we believe it should continue to be defined there. We repudiate President Bush's divisive effort to politicize the Constitution by pursuing a "Federal Marriage Amendment." Our goal is to bring Americans together, not drive them apart. . . .

Diversity. . . . We pledge to stand up for our beliefs and rally Americans to our cause. But we recognize that disagreements will remain, and we believe disagreement should not mean disrespect. Members of our party have deeply held and differing views on some matters of conscience and faith. We view diversity of views as a source of strength, and we welcome into our ranks all Americans who seek to build a stronger America. We are committed to resolving our differences in a spirit of civility, hope and mutual respect.

That's the America we believe in.

REPUBLICANS

For their convention held August 30 to September 2, the Republicans strategically chose New York, the city that lost the most lives and property in the 2001 terrorist attacks on the United States. The heavily secured convention site's proximity to lower Manhattan, where the World Trade Center towers fell, provided the delegates a constant reminder of President Bush's finest hour: his calming leadership when the nation needed it most.

Even the Democratic nominee Kerry had given grudging praise to the president in his nomination acceptance speech in Boston a month earlier. "I am proud that after September 11th all our people rallied to President Bush's call for unity to meet the danger," Kerry said. "There were no Democrats. There were no Republicans. There were only Americans. How we wish it had stayed that way."

Clearly, the Republicans, in choosing New York City as their convention site for the first time, hoped to recapture the post–September 11 spirit and show that the feeling of unity had indeed "stayed that way." They wanted the public to remember it was a Republican president who had taken the nation safely past that dreadful day. They also sought to show that their party was best suited to protect Americans from future attacks.

One of the first speakers to address the Madison Square Garden convention in television prime time was former New York

City mayor Rudolph Giuliani, who himself had won widespread praise for the city's response to the terrorist attack. He noted that shortly after September 11, 2001, the president had gone before Congress and "announced the Bush doctrine when he said: 'Our war on terror begins with Al Qaeda, but it doesn't end there. It will not end until every terrorist group of global reach has been found, stopped and defeated. Either you are with us or you are with the terrorists.' "

Another speaker on opening night was Sen. John McCain of Arizona, who had sought the party's presidential nomination in 2000. Defending his former rival's decision to invade Iraq, he said the choice "wasn't between a benign status quo and the bloodshed of war. It was between war and a graver threat." McCain singled out Michael Moore as a "disingenuous filmmaker" who had opposed that decision. Moore, sitting in the press section, had made *Fahrenheit 9/11,* a documentary sharply critical of the Iraq war. At the mention of Moore, the delegates booed and chanted, "Four More Years!"

Many of the 2,509 delegates and 2,344 alternates wore on their faces Band-Aids depicting the Purple Heart medal. They were mocking Kerry's three Purple Hearts for being wounded in Vietnam War action. After the Democratic convention in July, a group called Swift Boat Veterans for Truth began airing television ads accusing Kerry of lying to obtain medals for what they claimed were superficial wounds. McCain denounced the ads as "dishonest and dishonorable."

Addressing the convention on August 31, film actor and California governor Arnold Schwarzenegger told of listening to presidential candidates Richard Nixon and Hubert H. Humphrey, shortly after his arrival from Austria in 1968. Impressed with Nixon's views, he asked a friend who was translating for him whether Nixon was Republican or Democrat. When the friend replied "Republican," Schwarzenegger said, " 'Then I'm a Republican,' and I've been one ever since. And, trust me, in my wife's family that is no small achievement." The delegates laughed, knowing his wife is Maria Shriver, a member of the Kennedy family of stalwart Democrats.

The Republicans scored a victory when they signed up conservative Democratic senator Zell Miller of Georgia to give the keynote address on September 1. "Motivated more by partisan politics than by national security, today's Democratic leaders see America as an occupier, not a liberator. Nothing makes this Marine madder than someone calling American troops invaders rather than liberators," Miller said. Angry with his party, he fumed that the "nation is being torn apart and made weaker because of the Democrats' manic obsession to bring down our commander in chief." Miller, a keynoter at the 1992 Democratic convention, was leaving the Senate in 2005.

Conspicuously missing from the speakers' rostrum was Nancy Reagan, widow of former president Ronald Reagan, who died two months earlier. She reportedly had declined several invitations to speak because she objected to the party's use of her husband's quotes and images. She also disagreed with the administration's limits on funding for embryonic stem cell research to find cures for diseases such as Alzheimer's, which afflicted her husband.

As they did in 2000, the Republicans used a "rolling roll call" of the state delegations spanning three days for the formal renomination of President Bush. In the final tally Bush received 2,508 votes with one abstention. Vice President Cheney was renominated by acclamation. *(Table, p. 250.)*

In his acceptance speech on September 1, Cheney praised Bush's steady, determined leadership in time of war and doubted whether Kerry was up to the task. He pointed to the various defense measures that Kerry had opposed during his lengthy Senate career as a weakness in the critical area of national security. "A senator can be wrong for 20 years, without consequence to the nation. But a president—a president—always casts the deciding vote. And in this time of challenge, America needs—and America has—a president we can count on to get it right."

On September 2 President Bush delivered his nomination acceptance speech to enthusiastic convention crowd. He defended the administration's decision to invade Iraq: "We must, and we will, confront threats to America before it is too late. In Saddam Hussein, we saw a threat." According to Bush, the decision to go to war was in keeping with what he called "the most solemn duty of the American president . . . to protect the American people." For his domestic agenda, he promised to promote "an ownership society," where citizens "own their health care plans, and have the confidence of owning a piece of their retirement."

The Republican platform ran 42,000 words long and focused greatly on national security. The word "terror" or a variant, such as "terrorist," appeared almost 200 times. The platform also supported the tax cuts initiated during the president's first term, advocated drilling in the Arctic National Wildlife Refuge, and opposed abortion rights and same-sex marriage.

Following are excerpts from the Republican platform of 2004:

Iraq. As Republicans, we do not equivocate, as others have done, about whether America should have gone to war in Iraq. The best intelligence available at the time indicated that Saddam Hussein was a threat. On that point, President Bush, members of both parties in Congress, and the United Nations agreed. While the stockpiles of weapons of mass destruction we expected to find in Iraq have not yet materialized, we have confirmed that Saddam Hussein had the capability to reconstitute his weapons programs and the desire to do so. Our nation did the right thing, and the American people are now safer because we and our allies ended the brutal dictatorship of Saddam Hussein, halting his decades-long pursuit of chemical, biological, and nuclear weapons. President Bush had a choice to make: Trust a madman or defend America. He chose defending America.

War on Terror. We applaud President Bush for his success in mobilizing such international cooperation in the War on Terror, which the 9/11 Commission judges to be "on a vastly enlarged scale" and to have expanded dramatically since September 11, 2001. We also question the credibility of our opponents, who claim to support global alliances while nominating a candidate who has insulted our allies by calling the nations fighting in Iraq "window-dressing" and referring to them as a "coalition of the coerced and the bribed." Directing ugly rhetoric at America's allies in a time of war is irresponsible. It does not represent the gratitude and respect the vast majority of Americans have for the men and women from other nations who are risking their lives to make the world safer.

Private Retirement Accounts. Individual ownership of voluntary personal retirement accounts for today's workers will make Social Security more equitable, but, just as importantly, will put the system on sure financial footing. Fifty years ago there were 16 workers to support every one beneficiary of Social Security. Today there are just 3.3 workers for each beneficiary. By the time young men and women who are entering the workforce today turn 65, there will be only two workers for each beneficiary. Doing nothing is not an option. We must keep faith with both the past and the future by strengthening and enhancing Social Security. . . .

An Ownership Era. Ownership gives citizens a vital stake in their communities and their country. By expanding ownership, we will help turn economic growth into lasting prosperity. As Republicans, we trust people to make decisions about how to spend, save, and invest their own money. We want individuals to own and control their income. We want people to have a tangible asset that they can build and rely on, making their own choices and directing their own future. Ownership should not be the preserve of the wealthy or the privileged. As Republicans who believe in the power of ownership to create better lives, we want more people to own a home. We want more people to own and build small businesses. We want more people to own and control their health care. We want more people to own personal retirement accounts. . . .

Lower Taxes and Economic Growth. In 2001, President Bush and the Republican Congress worked together to pass the most sweeping tax relief in a generation. By letting families, workers, and small business owners keep more of the money they earn, they helped bring America from recession to a steadily expanding economy. Despite enduring the after-effects of the stock market's irrational exuberance in the late 1990s, terrorist attacks on our nation, and corporate scandals that bubbled to the surface after years of inattention, the U.S. economy has now grown for 33 straight months. And unlike four years ago, there are no signs of an end to the current economic growth.

Fiscal Discipline and Government Reform. It is important to view the size of the [federal] deficit in relation to the size of the nation's economy. By that measure, today's deficit, although unwelcome, is well within historical ranges. A deficit that is 3.8 percent of GDP [gross domestic product], as is now projected for this year, would be smaller than the deficits in nine of the last 25 years, and far below the peak deficit figure of 6 percent of GDP reached in 1983. This deficit is also in line with what other industrialized nations are facing today. The U.S. deficit matches the average deficit within the Organization for Economic Cooperation and Development, and is below the levels of France, Germany, and Japan.

Much more importantly, because the President and Congress enacted pro-growth economic policies, the deficit is headed strongly in the right direction. Next year's projected deficit, at 2.7 percent of GDP, would be smaller than those in 14 of the last 25 years. As Republicans in Congress work with the President to restrain spending and strengthen economic growth, the federal deficit will fall to 1.5 percent of the nation's economic output in 2009—well below the 2.2 percent average of the last 40 years.

Corporate Responsibility. After fraudulent corporate practices rooted in the irrational exuberance of the late 1990s began to surface in the closing months of 2001, President Bush worked with the Congress to take decisive action to restore honesty and integrity to America's corporate boardrooms. In July 2002, President Bush signed the Sarbanes-Oxley Act, the most far-reaching reform of American business practices since the 1940s. Under this new law, CEOs and Chief Financial Officers are required to personally vouch for the truth and fairness of their companies' disclosures; for the first time, an independent board has been es-

tablished to oversee the accounting profession; investigators have been given new tools to root out corporate fraud; and enhanced penalties are ensuring that dishonest corporate officials do hard time.

Reforming the Litigation System. America's litigation system is broken. Junk and frivolous lawsuits are driving up the cost of doing business in America by forcing companies to pay excessive legal expenses to fight off or settle often baseless lawsuits. Those costs are being paid by small business owners, manufacturers, their employees, and consumers. A typical small business with $10 million in annual revenue pays about $150,000 a year in tort liability costs. That is money that could be used to invest and hire new employees. Inefficiency and waste in the legal system is costing the average American family of four $1,800 every year, equivalent to an extra 3 percent tax on wages. And the bulk of jury awards to plaintiffs don't even go to the people who deserve it. Injured persons on average collect less than 50 cents of every dollar that the legal system costs. Trial lawyers get rich from the misfortune of others. If small business is America's economic engine, trial lawyers are the brakes: They cost hundreds of thousands of good jobs, drive honest employers out of business, deprive women of critical medical care—then skip out with fat wallets and nary a thought for the economic havoc and human misery they leave in their wake.

Developing U.S. Oil Resources. Using the most sophisticated technologies, we can explore and develop oil resources here at home with minimal environmental impact. Our Party continues to support energy development in the coastal plain of the Arctic National Wildlife Refuge (ANWR), which, according to the U.S. Geological Survey, holds as much as 16 billion barrels of oil—enough to replace oil imports from Saudi Arabia for nearly 20 years. The drilling footprint can be confined to just 2,000 acres (the entire refuge contains 19 million acres), about the size of Washington's Dulles Airport, on ice roads that melt away in the summer, leaving little trace of human intervention. We have already wasted precious time. If the previous Administration had not vetoed the ANWR proposal passed by the Republican Congress in 1995, at this moment ANWR would be producing up to one million barrels of oil a day.

Reforming the Medical Liability System. The medical liability system is harming our medical delivery system. Doctors are afraid to practice medicine. Frequent, unwarranted, lawsuits force doctors out of certain specialty areas and geographic regions. The most dangerous result of this is the declining availability of emergency trauma care and women's health services. In many cases, costs are so prohibitive that many obstetrics/gynecology practices are scaling back service or choosing not to practice altogether. Junk lawsuits add at least $60 billion to health care costs in America because doctors are forced to practice defensive medicine, ordering extensive, unnecessary, and expensive tests and procedures to keep trial lawyers at bay.

The President has proposed, and the Republican House of Representatives has passed, reforms that would speed compensation to injured patients, reduce health care costs, and improve Americans' access to quality health care. Shamefully driven by the powerful trial lawyer lobby, Democrat Senators have repeatedly thwarted the efforts of the Republican majority to deliver meaningful medical liability reform. They have employed their obstructionist tactics three times in the current Congress alone. The Republican Party reaffirms its commitment to putting patients and doctors ahead of trial lawyers. We will continue to battle for litigation reforms that help keep doctors in practice, adopt reasonable caps on non-economic awards in medical malpractice suits, and ensure that Americans have access to quality affordable health care.

Faith-Based and Community Services. We applaud President Bush's efforts to promote the generous and compassionate work of

America's faith-based and neighborhood charities. The President established the Office of Faith-Based and Community Initiatives in the White House to coordinate federal, state, and local efforts to tear down barriers that have prevented religiously affiliated groups from applying for government grants on an equal footing with secular organizations. While the federal government must not promote religious activity, advocate on behalf of any religion, or fund any organization that discriminates on the basis of religion when providing taxpayer-funded services, no organization should be disqualified from receiving federal funds simply because it displays religious symbols, has a statement of faith in its mission statement, or has a religious leader on its board.

Voting Rights. The foundation of our democratic republic is our commitment to conducting free and fair elections. Unfortunately, in November 2000, too many people believed they were denied the right to vote. Many African Americans, Hispanics, and others fear they may lose the right to vote because of inaccurate or insecure technology or because of a rolling back in the gains made by the passage of civil rights legislation. Our national commitment to a voting process that has integrity was underscored in 2002 when the Congress passed and the President signed the Help America Vote Act (HAVA). We will continue to do all we can to ensure that every lawful vote counts for all Americans.

Judiciary. In the federal courts, scores of judges with activist backgrounds in the hard-left now have lifetime tenure. Recent events have made it clear that these judges threaten America's dearest institutions and our very way of life. In some states, activist judges are redefining the institution of marriage. The Pledge of Allegiance has already been invalidated by the courts once, and the Supreme Court's ruling has left the Pledge in danger of being struck down again—not because the American people have rejected it and the values that it embodies, but because a handful of activist judges threaten to overturn commonsense and tradition. And while the vast majority of Americans support a ban on partial birth abortion, this brutal and violent practice will likely continue by judicial fiat. We believe that the self-proclaimed supremacy of these judicial activists is antithetical to the democratic ideals on which our nation was founded. President Bush has established a solid record of nominating only judges who have demonstrated respect for the Constitution and the democratic processes of

our republic, and Republicans in the Senate have strongly supported those nominees. We call upon obstructionist Democrats in the Senate to abandon their unprecedented and highly irresponsible filibuster of President Bush's highly qualified judicial nominees, and to allow the Republican Party to restore respect for the law to America's courts.

Protecting Marriage. After more than two centuries of American jurisprudence, and millennia of human experience, a few judges and local authorities are presuming to change the most fundamental institution of civilization, the union of a man and a woman in marriage. Attempts to redefine marriage in a single state or city could have serious consequences throughout the country, and anything less than a Constitutional amendment, passed by the Congress and ratified by the states, is vulnerable to being overturned by activist judges. On a matter of such importance, the voice of the people must be heard. The Constitutional amendment process guarantees that the final decision will rest with the American people and their elected representatives. President Bush will also vigorously defend the Defense of Marriage Act, which was supported by both parties and passed by 85 votes in the Senate. This common sense law reaffirms the right of states not to recognize same-sex marriages licensed in other states.

Defense of Life. We praise the President for his bold leadership in defense of life. We praise him for signing the Born Alive Infants Protection Act. This important legislation ensures that every infant born alive—including an infant who survives an abortion procedure—is considered a person under federal law.

We praise Republicans in Congress for passing, with strong bipartisan support, a ban on the inhumane procedure known as partial birth abortion. And we applaud President Bush for signing legislation outlawing partial birth abortion and for vigorously defending it in the courts.

In signing the partial birth abortion ban, President Bush reminded us that "the most basic duty of government is to defend the life of the innocent. Every person, however frail or vulnerable, has a place and a purpose in this world." We affirm the inherent dignity and worth of all people. We oppose the non-consensual withholding of care or treatment because of disability, age, or infirmity, just as we oppose euthanasia and assisted suicide, which especially endanger the poor and those on the margins of society.

CHAPTER 5

Key Convention Ballots

THIS SECTION PRESENTS the results of important balloting from the presidential nominating conventions of three major American political parties (Whigs, Democrats, and Republicans) from 1835 to 2004. The balloting results are arranged in chronological order by convention year. Major contenders for the respective party nominations appear in the tables by last name only. Full names and other detailed descriptions of each convention can be found in Chapter 4, Convention Chronology. Each table contains a reference indicating the page where this information appears.

The source for the balloting results for the 1835–1972 conventions is Richard C. Bain and Judith H. Parris, *Convention Decisions and Voting Records* (Washington, D.C.: Brookings Institution, 1973). Permission to use this material was granted by the Brookings Institution, which holds the copyright. The sources for the 1976 to 2004 vote totals are *The Official Proceedings of the Democratic National Convention* and the Republican National Committee. *Convention Decisions and Voting Records* contains ballots for three major parties in American history—the Democrats, the Whigs, and modern Republicans. This section includes ballots from conventions of these three parties alone.

In selecting ballots to include here, Congressional Quarterly followed several criteria:

• To include nominating ballots and selected other critical presidential ballots. The Democratic Party conventions of 1832, 1840, 1888, 1916, 1936, and 1964 nominated presidential candidates by acclamation without balloting.

• To include key ballots on important procedural issues, credentials contests, and platform disputes.

• To exclude all ballots for vice-presidential candidates.

VOTE TOTAL DISCREPANCIES

Bain and Parris note frequent discrepancies between totals given in the published proceedings of the party conventions and the totals reached by adding up the state-by-state delegation votes. They state: "Wherever the discrepancy was obvious and the correct figure could be clearly derived, the record has been printed in corrected form. When the added totals of detailed figures listed differ from the sums printed in the proceedings, both totals are given."

Congressional Quarterly has followed this same procedure. For example, on page 185, the forty-ninth presidential ballot of the 1852 Democratic Party convention appears. Franklin Pierce is listed as receiving 279 votes, the sum of the column. A footnote, however, indicates that the convention proceedings recorded Pierce as receiving 283 votes.

1835 Democratic

(Narrative, p. 45)

Delegation	Total Votes	First Pres. Ballot Van Buren
Connecticut	8	8
Delaware	3	3
Georgia	11	11
Indiana	9	9
Kentucky	15	15
Louisiana	5	5
Maine	10	10
Maryland	10	10
Massachusetts	14	14
Mississippi	4	4
Missouri	4	4
New Hampshire	7	7
New Jersey	8	8
New York	42	42
North Carolina	15	15
Ohio	21	21
Pennsylvania	30	30
Rhode Island	4	4
Tennessee	15	15
Vermont	7	7
Virginia	23	23
Total	265	265

1844 Democratic

(Narrative, p. 49)

Delegation	Total Votes	Amendment Ratifying Two-Thirds Rule Yea	Nay	First Pres. Ballot[1] Van Buren	Cass	Fifth Pres. Ballot[2] Van Buren	Cass	Ninth Pres. Ballot (Before shift)[3] Polk	Cass	Ninth Pres. Ballot (After shift) Polk
Alabama	9	9	—	1	8	1	8	9	—	9
Arkansas	3	3	—	—	—	—	—	3	—	3
Connecticut	6	3	3	6	—	—	—	6	—	6
Delaware	3	3	—	—	3	—	3	3	—	3
Georgia	10	10	—	—	9	—	9	9	—	10
Illinois	9	9	—	5	2	2	4	9	—	9
Indiana	12	12	—	3	9	1	11	12	—	12
Kentucky	12	12	—	—	—	—	—	12	—	12
Louisiana	6	6	—	—	—	—	—	6	—	6
Maine	9	—	9	8	—	8	1	7	1	9
Maryland	8	6	2	2	4	2	6	7	1	8
Massachusetts	12	5	7	8	1	7	3	10	2	12
Michigan	5	5	—	1	4	—	5	—	5	5
Mississippi	6	6	—	—	6	—	6	6	—	6
Missouri	7	—	7	7	—	7	—	7	—	7
New Hampshire	6	—	6	6	—	2	—	6	—	6
New Jersey	7	7	—	3	2	—	4	2	5	7
New York	36	—	36	36	—	36	—	35	—	36
North Carolina	11	5	5	2	4	—	7	11	—	11
Ohio	23	—	23	23	—	20	3	18	2	23
Pennsylvania	26	12	13	26	—	16	—	19	7	26
Rhode Island	4	2	2	4	—	1	1	4	—	4
Tennessee	13	13	—	—	13	—	13	13	—	13
Vermont	6	3	3	5	1	—	6	—	6	6
Virginia	17	17	—	—	17	—	17	17	—	17
Total	266	148	118	146	83	103	107	231	29	266

1. Other candidates: Richard M. Johnson, 24; John C. Calhoun, 6; James Buchanan, 4; Levi Woodbury, 2; Commodore Stewart, 1.
2. Other candidates: Johnson, 29; Buchanan, 26; not voting, 1.
3. Not voting, 6.

1844 Whig

(Narrative, p. 48)

Delegation	Total Votes	First Pres. Ballot Clay	Delegation	Total Votes	First Pres. Ballot Clay
Alabama	9	9	Missouri	7	7
Arkansas	3	3	New Hampshire	6	6
Connecticut	6	6	New Jersey	7	7
Delaware	3	3	New York	36	36
Georgia	10	10	North Carolina	11	11
Illinois	9	9	Ohio	23	23
Indiana	12	12	Pennsylvania	26	26
Kentucky	12	12	Rhode Island	4	4
Louisiana	6	6	South Carolina	9	9
Maine	9	9	Tennessee	13	13
Maryland	8	8	Vermont	6	6
Massachusetts	12	12	Virginia	17	17
Michigan	5	5			
Mississippi	6	6	Total	275	275

1848 Democratic

(Narrative, p. 50)

Delegation	Total Votes	Adoption of Two-Thirds Rule Yea	Nay	Not Voting	Amendment on N.Y. Credentials Yea	Nay	Not Voting	First Pres. Ballot[1] Cass	Buchanan	Woodbury	Fourth Pres. Ballot[2] Cass	Buchanan	Woodbury
Alabama	9	9	—	—	—	9	—	—	4	5	—	4	5
Arkansas	3	3	—	—	—	3	—	3	—	—	3	—	—
Connecticut	6	6	—	—	6	—	—	—	—	6	—	—	6
Delaware	3	2	1	—	1	2	—	3	—	—	3	—	—
Florida	3	3	—	—	—	3	—	—	—	—	—	—	3
Georgia	10	10	—	—	—	10	—	—	2	5	10	—	—
Illinois	9	9	—	—	9	—	—	9	—	—	9	—	—
Indiana	12	3	9	—	7	5	—	12	—	—	12	—	—
Iowa	4	4	—	—	4	—	—	1	3	—	4	—	—
Kentucky	12	12	—	—	10	2	—	7	1	1	8	1	1
Louisiana	6	6	—	—	—	6	—	6	—	—	6	—	—
Maine	9	9	—	—	9	—	—	—	—	9	—	—	9
Maryland	8	7	1	—	2	5	1	6	—	2	6	—	2
Massachusetts	12	10	2	—	11	1	—	—	—	12	8	—	4
Michigan	5	5	—	—	—	5	—	5	—	—	5	—	—
Mississippi	6	6	—	—	—	6	—	6	—	—	6	—	—
Missouri	7	1	6	—	1	4	2	7	—	—	7	—	—
New Hampshire	6	6	—	—	6	—	—	—	—	6	—	—	6
New Jersey	7	7	—	—	7	—	—	—	7	—	7	—	—
New York	36	—	—	36	—	—	36	—	—	—	—	—	—
North Carolina	11	11	—	—	—	11	—	—	10	1	11	—	—
Ohio	23	—	23	—	14	9	—	23	—	—	23	—	—
Pennsylvania	26	—	26	—	19	7	—	—	26	—	—	26	—
Rhode Island	4	3	1	—	2	2	—	1	—	3	4	—	—
South Carolina	9	9	—	—	—	9	—	—	—	—	9	—	—
Tennessee	13	13	—	—	9	4	—	7	2	1	7	2	2
Texas	4	4	—	—	4	—	—	4	—	—	4	—	—
Vermont	6	1	5	—	5	1	—	4	—	2	6	—	—
Virginia	17	17	—	—	—	17	—	17	—	—	17	—	—
Wisconsin	4	—	4	—	—	4	—	4	—	—	4	—	—
Total	290	176	78	36	126	125	39	125	55	53	179	33	38

1. Other candidates: John C. Calhoun, 9; W. J. Worth, 6; George M. Dallas, 3; not voting, 39.
2. Other candidates: William O. Butler, 4; Worth, 1; not voting, 35.

1848 Whig

(Narrative, p. 51)

Delegation	Total Votes	First Pres. Ballot[1]			Fourth Pres. Ballot[2]		
		Taylor	Clay	Scott	Taylor	Clay	Scott
Alabama	7	6	1	—	6	1	—
Arkansas	3	3	—	—	3	—	—
Connecticut	6	—	6	—	3	3	—
Delaware	3	—	—	—	2	—	1
Florida	3	3	—	—	3	—	—
Georgia	10	10	—	—	10	—	—
Illinois	8	4	3	1	8	—	—
Indiana	12	1	2	9	7	1	4
Iowa	4	2	1	—	4	—	—
Kentucky	12	7	5	—	11	1	—
Louisiana	6	5	1	—	6	—	—
Maine	9	5	1	—	5	—	3
Maryland	8	—	8	—	8	—	—
Massachusetts	12	—	—	—	1	—	2
Michigan	5	—	3	2	2	—	3
Mississippi	6	6	—	—	6	—	—
Missouri	7	6	—	—	7	—	—
New Hampshire	6	—	—	—	2	—	—
New Jersey	7	3	4	—	4	3	—
New York	36	—	29	5	6	13	17
North Carolina	11	6	5	—	10	1	17
Ohio	23	1	1	20	1	1	21
Pennsylvania	26	8	12	6	12	4	10
Rhode Island	4	—	4	—	4	—	—
South Carolina	2	1	1	—	1	1	—
Tennessee	13	13	—	—	13	—	—
Texas	4	4	—	—	4	—	—
Vermont	6	1	5	—	2	2	2
Virginia	17	15	2	—	16	1	—
Wisconsin	4	1	3	—	4	—	—
Total	280	111	97	43	171	32	63

1. Other candidates: Daniel Webster, 22; John McLean, 2; John M. Clayton, 4.
2. Other candidate: Webster, 14.

1852 Democratic

(Narrative, p. 52)

Delegation	Total Votes	First Pres. Ballot[1]		Twentieth Pres. Ballot[2]			Thirtieth Pres. Ballot[3]			Thirty-Fifth Pres. Ballot[4]				Forty-Eighth Pres. Ballot[5]				Forty-ninth Pres. Ballot[6]
		Cass	Buchanan	Buchanan	Cass	Douglas	Douglas	Buchanan	Cass	Cass	Douglas	Marcy	Buchanan	Marcy	Cass	Pierce	Douglas	Pierce
Alabama	9	—	9	9	—	—	—	9	—	—	—	—	9	9	—	—	—	9
Arkansas	4	—	4	—	—	4	4	—	—	—	4	—	—	—	—	—	4	4
California	4	—	—	1	—	3	3	1	—	2	1	—	1	—	4	—	—	4
Connecticut	6	2	2	2	2	1	6	—	—	3	3	—	—	6	—	—	—	6
Delaware	3	3	—	—	3	—	—	—	—	3	—	—	—	—	3	—	—	3
Florida	3	—	—	—	—	2	2	—	—	—	2	—	—	—	—	—	2	3
Georgia	10	—	10	10	—	—	—	10	—	—	10	—	—	10	—	—	—	10
Illinois	11	—	—	—	—	11	11	—	—	—	11	—	—	—	—	—	11	11
Indiana	13	—	—	—	—	—	—	—	—	13	—	—	—	—	13	—	—	13
Iowa	4	2	—	—	1	3	4	—	—	2	2	—	—	—	2	—	2	4
Kentucky	12	12	—	—	12	—	—	—	—	12	—	—	—	—	—	12	—	12
Louisiana	6	6	—	—	6	—	6	—	—	6	—	—	—	—	6	—	—	6
Maine	8	5	3	1	4	3	5	2	—	2	5	—	1	—	—	8	—	8
Maryland	8	8	—	—	8	—	—	—	8	8	—	—	—	1	1	5	—	5
Massachusetts	13	9	—	—	1	7	7	—	1	7	1	5	—	6	—	6	1	13
Michigan	6	6	—	—	6	—	—	—	6	6	—	—	—	—	6	—	—	6
Mississippi	7	—	7	7	—	—	—	7	—	—	—	7	—	7	—	—	—	7
Missouri	9	9	—	—	—	9	9	—	—	9	—	—	—	—	9	—	—	9
New Hampshire	5	4	—	—	5	—	—	2	—	5	—	—	—	—	—	5	—	5
New Jersey	7	7	—	7	—	—	—	7	—	7	—	—	—	7	—	—	—	7
New York	35	11	—	—	12	—	1	—	11	12	1	22	—	24	10	—	1	35
North Carolina	10	—	10	9	—	1	4	6	—	—	—	10	—	10	—	—	—	10
Ohio	23	16	—	—	13	6	9	—	7	18	3	—	—	—	15	—	4	17
Pennsylvania	27	—	27	27	—	—	—	27	—	—	—	—	27	—	—	—	—	27
Rhode Island	4	3	—	—	—	4	4	—	—	4	—	—	—	—	—	4	—	4
Tennessee	12	6	6	4	5	3	7	5	—	9	2	—	1	9	—	—	1	12
Texas	4	—	—	—	—	—	—	—	—	—	—	—	—	—	—	—	—	4
Vermont	5	5	—	—	—	5	5	—	—	—	5	—	—	—	—	—	5	5
Virginia	15	—	15	15	—	—	—	15	—	—	—	—	—	—	—	15	—	15
Wisconsin	5	2	—	—	3	2	5	—	—	3	2	—	—	—	3	—	2	5
Total	288	116	93	92	81	64	92	91	33	131	52	44	39	89	72	55	33	279[a]

1. Other candidates: William L. Marcy, 27; Stephen A. Douglas, 20; Joseph Lane, 13; Samuel Houston, 8; J. B. Weller, 4; Henry Dodge, 3; William O. Butler, 2; Daniel S. Dickinson, 1; not voting, 1.

2. Other candidates: Marcy, 26; Lane, 13; Houston, 10; Butler, 1; Dickinson, 1.

3. Other candidates: Marcy, 26; Butler, 20; Lane, 13; Houston, 12; Dickinson, 1.

4. Other candidates: Franklin Pierce, 15; Houston, 5; Butler, 1; Dickinson, 1.

5. Other candidates: Buchanan, 28; Houston, 6; Linn Boyd, 2; Butler, 1; R. J. Ingersoll, 1; Dickinson, 1.

6. Other candidates: Cass, 2; Douglas, 2; Butler, 1; Houston, 1; not voting, 3.

a. Sum of column; proceedings record 283.

1852 Whig

(Narrative, p. 53)

Delegation	Total Votes	First Pres. Ballot			50th Pres. Ballot			52nd Pres. Ballot			53rd Pres. Ballot		
		Scott	Fillmore	Webster	Scott	Fillmore	Webster	Scott	Fillmore	Webster	Scott	Fillmore	Webster
Alabama	9	—	9	—	—	9	—	—	9	—	—	9	—
Arkansas	4	—	4	—	—	4	—	—	4	—	—	4	—
California	4	2	1	1	3	1	—	3	—	1	3	—	1
Connecticut	6	2	1	3	2	1	3	2	1	3	2	1	3
Delaware	3	3	—	—	3	—	—	3	—	—	3	—	—
Florida	3	—	3	—	—	3	—	—	3	—	—	3	—
Georgia	10	—	10	—	—	10	—	—	10	—	—	10	—
Illinois	11	11	—	—	11	—	—	11	—	—	11	—	—
Indiana	13	13	—	—	13	—	—	13	—	—	13	—	—
Iowa	4	—	4	—	1	3	—	1	3	—	1	3	—
Kentucky	12	—	12	—	—	12	—	—	12	—	—	11	—
Louisiana	6	—	6	—	—	6	—	—	6	—	—	6	—
Maine	8	8	—	—	8	—	—	8	—	—	8	—	—
Maryland	8	—	8	—	—	8	—	—	8	—	—	8	—
Massachusetts	13	2	—	11	2	—	11	2	—	11	2	—	11
Michigan	6	6	—	—	6	—	—	6	—	—	6	—	—
Mississippi	7	—	7	—	—	7	—	—	7	—	—	7	—
Missouri	9	—	9	—	3	6	—	1	6	—	3	6	—
New Hampshire	5	1	—	4	1	—	4	1	—	4	5	—	—
New Jersey	7	7	—	—	7	—	—	7	—	—	7	—	—
New York	35	24	7	2	25	7	1	25	7	1	25	7	1
North Carolina	10	—	10	—	—	10	—	—	10	—	—	10	—
Ohio	23	22	1	—	23	—	—	23	—	—	23	—	—
Pennsylvania	27	26	1	—	26	1	—	27	—	—	27	—	—
Rhode Island	4	1	1	2	2	—	2	2	—	2	3	—	1
South Carolina	8	—	8	—	—	8	—	—	8	—	—	8	—
Tennessee	12	—	12	—	—	12	—	4	8	—	3	9	—
Texas	4	—	4	—	—	4	—	—	4	—	—	4	—
Vermont	5	1	1	3	2	—	3	2	2	1	5	—	—
Virginia	15	1	13	—	3	10	—	3	10	—	8	6	—
Wisconsin	5	1	1	3	1	1	3	2	—	2	1	—	4
Total	296	132[a]	133	29	142	122[a]	27	148[a]	118	25	159	112	21

a. The sum of the column for Scott on the first ballot is 131 votes, for Fillmore on the 50th ballot 123 votes and for Scott on the 52nd ballot is 146 votes. The source for these discrepancies is the *Baltimore Sun* for June 19, 1852, and June 22, 1852. The *Sun* reported June 19, 1852, total votes for Scott on the first ballot as 132 votes; however, the column of figures for the state-by-state ballots reported in the *Sun* add up to 131 votes. Similarly, on June 22, 1852, the *Sun* reported 122 votes for Fillmore on the 50th ballot and 148 for Scott on the 52nd ballot, but the state-by-state ballots reported in the *Sun* add up to 123 votes and 146 votes, respectively. Bain's *Convention Decisions and Voting Records* used the *Baltimore Sun* as its source for the 1852 Whig convention ballots.

1856 Republican

(Narrative, p. 55)

Delegation	Total Votes	Informal Pres. Ballot[1] Fremont	McLean	Formal Pres. Ballot[2] Fremont	Delegation	Total Votes	Informal Pres. Ballot[1] Fremont	McLean	Formal Pres. Ballot[2] Fremont
California	12	12	—	12	Minnesota	2	—	—	—
Connecticut	18	18	—	18	New Hampshire	15	15	—	15
Delaware	9	—	9	9	New Jersey	21	7	14	21
Illinois	34	14	19	33	New York	105	93	3	105
Indiana	39	18	21	39	Ohio	69	30	39	55
Iowa	12	12	—	12	Pennsylvania	81	10	71	57
Kansas	10	9	—	9	Rhode Island	12	12	—	12
Kentucky	5	5	—	5	Vermont	15	15	—	15
Maine	24	13	11	24	Wisconsin	15	15	—	15
Maryland	9	4	3	7	District of Columbia	3	—	—	—
Massachusetts	39	39	—	39					
Michigan	18	18	—	18	Total	567	359	190	520

1. Other candidates: Nathaniel Banks, 1; Charles Sumner, 2; William Seward, 1; absent or not voting, 14.
2. Other candidates: John McLean, 37; Seward, 1; absent or not voting, 9.

1856 Democratic

(Narrative, p. 56)

Delegation	Total Votes	First Pres. Ballot Buchanan	Pierce	Douglas	Other	Tenth Pres. Ballot Buchanan	Pierce	Douglas	Other	Fifteenth Pres. Ballot Buchanan	Douglas	Other	17th Pres. Ballot Buchanan
Alabama	9	—	9	—	—	—	9	—	—	—	9	—	9
Arkansas	4	—	4	—	—	—	—	4	—	—	4	—	4
California	4	—	—	—	4	—	—	—	4	—	—	4	4
Connecticut	3	6	—	—	—	6	—	—	—	6	—	—	6
Delaware	3	3	—	—	—	3	—	—	—	3	—	—	3
Florida	3	—	3	—	—	—	3	—	—	—	3	—	3
Georgia	10	—	10	—	—	3	—	7	—	3	7	—	10
Illinois	11	—	—	11	—	—	—	11	—	—	11	—	11
Indiana	13	13	—	—	—	13	—	—	—	13	—	—	13
Iowa	4	—	—	4	—	2	—	2	—	2	2	—	4
Kentucky	12	4	5	3	—	4½	—	7½	—	4	7	1	12
Louisiana	6	6	—	—	—	6	—	—	—	6	—	—	6
Maine	8	5	3	—	—	6	2	—	—	7	—	1	8
Maryland	8	6	2	—	—	7	1	—	—	8	—	—	8
Massachusetts	13	4	9	—	—	6	7	—	—	10	3	—	13
Michigan	6	6	—	—	—	6	—	—	—	6	—	—	6
Mississippi	7	—	7	—	—	—	7	—	—	—	7	—	7
Missouri	9	—	—	9	—	—	—	9	—	—	9	—	9
New Hampshire	5	—	5	—	—	—	5	—	—	—	5	—	5
New Jersey	7	7	—	—	—	7	—	—	—	7	—	—	7
New York	35	17	18	—	—	18	17	—	—	17	18	—	35
North Carolina	10	—	10	—	—	—	10	—	—	—	10	—	10
Ohio	23	13½	4½	4	1	13	3½	5	1½	13½	6½	3	23
Pennsylvania	27	27	—	—	—	27	—	—	—	27	—	—	27
Rhode Island	4	—	4	—	—	—	4	—	—	4	—	—	4
South Carolina	8	—	8	—	—	—	8	—	—	—	8	—	8
Tennessee	12	—	12	—	—	—	—	12	—	12	—	—	12
Texas	4	—	4	—	—	—	4	—	—	—	4	—	4
Vermont	5	—	5	—	—	—	—	5	—	—	5	—	5
Virginia	15	15	—	—	—	15	—	—	—	15	—	—	15
Wisconsin	5	3	—	2	—	5	—	—	—	5	—	—	5
Total	296	135½	122½	33	5[1]	147½	80½	62½	5½[2]	168½	118½	9[3]	296

1. Other candidate: Lewis Cass, 5.
2. Other candidate: Cass, 5½.
3. Other candidates: Cass, 4½; Franklin Pierce, 3½; not voting, 1.

1860 Democratic

(Narrative, p. 58)

Charleston Convention   Baltimore Convention

Delegation	Total Votes	Butler Amend. on 1856 platform Yea	Nay	Minority Report on platform Yea	Nay	First Pres. Ballot[1] Douglas	Hunter	Guthrie	57th Pres. Ballot[2] Douglas	Guthrie	Minority Report on Credentials Yea	Nay	Not Voting	Reconsider Louisiana Credentials Yea	Nay	Not Voting	First Pres. Ballot[3] Douglas	Second Pres. Ballot[4] Douglas
Alabama	9	—	9	—	9	—	—	—	—	—	—	—	9	—	—	9	9	9
Arkansas	4	—	4	—	4	—	1	—	—	—	½	½	3	½	½	3	1	1½
California	4	—	4	—	4	—	—	—	—	—	4	—	—	—	4	—	—	—
Connecticut	6	2½	3½	6	—	3½	—	—	3½	2½	2½	3½	—	3½	2½	—	3½	3½
Delaware	3	3	—	—	3	—	2	—	—	—	2	—	1	—	2	1	—	—
Florida	3	—	3	—	3	—	—	—	—	—	—	—	3	—	—	3	—	—
Georgia	10	10	—	—	10	—	—	—	—	—	—	—	10	—	—	10	—	—
Illinois	11	—	11	11	—	11	—	—	11	—	—	11	—	11	—	—	11	11
Indiana	13	—	13	13	—	13	—	—	13	—	—	13	—	13	—	—	13	13
Iowa	4	—	4	4	—	4	—	—	4	—	—	4	—	4	—	—	4	4
Kentucky	12	9	3	2½	9½	—	—	12	—	12	10	2	—	2	10	—	—	3
Louisiana	6	—	6	—	6	—	—	—	—	—	—	—	6	—	—	6	6	6
Maine	8	3	5	8	—	5	—	3	5	3	2½	5½	—	5½	2½	—	5½	7
Maryland	8	5½	2½	3½	4½	2	5	—	4	4	5½	2	½	2	6	—	2½	2½
Massachusetts	13	8	5	7	6	5½	6	—	6	6	8	5	—	5	8	—	10	10
Michigan	6	—	6	6	—	6	—	—	6	—	—	6	—	6	—	—	6	6
Minnesota	4	1½	2½	4	—	4	—	—	3	—	1½	2½	—	2½	1½	—	2½	4
Mississippi	7	—	7	—	7	—	—	—	—	—	—	—	7	—	—	7	—	—
Missouri	9	4½	4½	4	5	4½	—	4½	4½	4½	5	4	—	4½	4½	—	4½	4½
New Hampshire	5	—	5	5	—	5	—	—	5	—	½	4½	—	4½	½	—	5	5
New Jersey	7	5	2	5	2	—	—	7	2	5	4	3	—	2½	4½	—	2½	2½
New York	35	—	35	35	—	35	—	—	35	—	—	35	—	35	—	—	35	35
North Carolina	10	10	—	—	10	1	9	—	1	—	9	1	—	1	8½	½	1	1
Ohio	23	—	23	23	—	23	—	—	23	—	—	23	—	23	—	—	23	23
Oregon	3	3	—	—	3	—	—	—	—	—	3	—	—	—	3	—	—	—
Pennsylvania	27	16½	10½	12	15	9	3	9	9½	17½	17	10	—	10	17	—	10	19
Rhode Island	4	—	4	4	—	4	—	—	4	—	—	4	—	4	—	—	4	4
South Carolina	8	—	8	—	8	—	1	—	—	—	—	—	8	—	—	8	—	—
Tennessee	12	11	1	1	11	—	—	—	1	11	10	1	1	2	10	—	3	3
Texas	4	—	4	—	4	—	—	—	—	—	—	—	4	—	—	4	—	—
Vermont	5	—	5	5	—	5	—	—	5	—	1½	3½	—	4½	½	—	5	5
Virginia	15	12½	12½	1	14	—	15	—	1	—	14	1	—	—	15	—	1½	3
Wisconsin	5	—	5	5	—	5	—	—	5	—	—	5	—	—	5	—	5	5
Total	303	105	198	165	138	145½	42	35½[a]	151½	65½	100½	150	52½	151[b]	100½[c]	51½	173½	190½[d]

1. Other candidates: Andrew Johnson, 12; Daniel S. Dickinson, 7; Joseph Lane, 6; Isaac Toucey, 2½; Jefferson Davis, 1½; James A. Pearce, 1; not voting, 50.

2. Other candidates: Robert M. T. Hunter, 16; Lane, 14; Dickinson, 4; Davis, 1; not voting 51.

3. Other candidates: James Guthrie, 9; John C. Breckinridge, 5; Thomas S. Bocock, 1; Horatio Seymour, 1; Henry A. Wise, ½; Dickinson, ½; not voting, 112½.

4. Other candidates: Breckinridge, 7½; Guthrie, 5½; not voting, 99½.

a. Sum of column; proceedings record 35.

b. Sum of column; proceedings record 150½.

c. Sum of column; proceedings record 99.

d. Sum of column; proceedings record 181½.

1860 Republican

(Narrative, p. 59)

Delegation	Total Votes	First Pres. Ballot[1]					Second Pres. Ballot[2]		Third Pres. Ballot[3] (Before shift)		Third Pres. Ballot[4] (After shift)	
		Seward	Lincoln	Cameron	Bates	Chase	Seward	Lincoln	Seward	Lincoln	Seward	Lincoln
California	8	8	½	—	—	—	8	—	8	—	3	5
Connecticut	12	—	2	—	7	2	—	4	1	4	1	8
Delaware	6	—	—	—	6	—	—	6	—	6	—	6
Illinois	22	—	22	—	—	—	—	22	—	22	—	22
Indiana	26	—	26	—	—	—	—	26	—	26	—	26
Iowa	8	2	2	1	1	1	2	5	2	5½	—	8
Kansas	6	6	—	—	—	—	6	—	6	—	—	6
Kentucky	23	5	6	—	—	8	7	9	6	13	—	23
Maine	16	10	6	—	—	—	10	6	10	6	—	16
Maryland	11	13	—	—	8	—	3	—	2	9	2	9
Massachusetts	26	21	4	—	—	—	22	4	18	8	18	8
Michigan	12	12	—	—	—	—	12	—	12	—	12	—
Minnesota	8	8	—	—	—	—	8	—	8	—	—	8
Missouri	18	—	—	—	18	—	—	—	—	—	—	18
Nebraska	6	2	1	1	—	2	3	1	3	1	—	6
New Hampshire	10	—	—	—	—	1	1	9	1	9	—	10
New Jersey	14	1	7	—	—	—	4	—	5	8	5	8
New York	70	70	—	—	—	—	70	—	70	—	70	—
Ohio	46	—	8	—	—	34	—	14	—	29	—	46
Oregon	5	—	—	—	5	—	—	—	1	4	—	5
Pennsylvania	54	1½	4	47½	—	—	2½	48	—	52	½	53
Rhode Island	8	—	—	—	1	1	—	3	1	5	—	8
Texas	6	4	—	—	2	—	6	—	6	—	—	6
Vermont	10	—	—	—	—	—	—	10	—	10	—	10
Virginia	23	8	14	1	—	—	8	14	8	14	—	23
Wisconsin	10	10	—	—	—	—	10	—	10	—	10	—
District of Columbia	2	2	—	—	—	—	2	—	2	—	—	2
Total	466	173½	102	50½	48	49	184½	181	180	231½	121½	340[a]

1. Other candidates: Benjamin F. Wade, 3; John McLean, 12; John M. Reed, 1; William L. Dayton, 14; Charles Sumner, 1; John C. Fremont, 1; Jacob Collamer, 10; absent and not voting, 1.

2. Other candidates: Edward Bates, 35; Simon Cameron, 2; McLean, 8; Salmon P. Chase, 42½; Dayton, 10; Cassius M. Clay, 2; absent and not voting 1.

3. Other candidates: Edward Bates, 22; Chase, 24½; McLean, 5; Dayton, 1; Clay, 1; absent and not voting, 1.

4. Other candidates: Chase, 2; Dayton, 1; Clay, 1; McLean, ½.

a. Sum of column; proceedings record 364.

1864 Republican

(Narrative, p. 61)

Delegation	Total Votes	First Pres. Ballot[1]	
		Lincoln	Grant
Arkansas	10	10	—
California	10	7	—
Colorado	6	6	—
Connecticut	12	12	—
Delaware	6	6	—
Illinois	32	32	—
Indiana	26	26	—
Iowa	16	16	—
Kansas	6	6	—
Kentucky	22	22	—
Louisiana	14	14	—
Maine	14	14	—
Maryland	14	14	—
Massachusetts	24	24	—
Michigan	16	16	—
Minnesota	8	8	—
Missouri	22	—	22
Nebraska	6	6	—
Nevada	6	6	—
New Hampshire	10	10	—
New Jersey	14	14	—
New York	66	66	—
Ohio	42	42	—
Oregon	6	6	—
Pennsylvania	52	52	—
Rhode Island	8	8	—
Tennessee	15	15	—
Vermont	10	10	—
West Virginia	10	10	—
Wisconsin	16	16	—
Total	519	494[a]	22

1. Not voting, 3.
a. Sum of column; proceedings record 484.

1864 Democratic

(Narrative, p. 62)

Delegation	Total Votes	First Pres. Ballot[1]		First Pres. Ballot	
		McClellan	Seymour	McClellan	Seymour
		(Before shift)		(After shift)	
California	5	2½	2½	5	—
Connecticut	6	5½	—	6	—
Delaware	3	—	3	—	3
Illinois	16	16	—	16	—
Indiana	13	9½	3½	9½	3½
Iowa	8	3	—	8	—
Kansas	3	3	—	3	—
Kentucky	11	5½	5½	11	—
Maine	7	4	3	7	—
Maryland	7	—	7	—	7
Massachusetts	12	11½	—	12	—
Michigan	8	6½	—	8	—
Minnesota	4	4	—	4	—
Missouri	11	6½	—	7	4
New Hampshire	5	5	—	5	—
New Jersey	7	7	—	7	—
New York	33	33	—	33	—
Ohio	21	8½	10½	15	6
Oregon	3	2	1	3	—
Pennsylvania	26	26	—	26	—
Rhode Island	4	4	—	4	—
Vermont	5	4	1	5	—
Wisconsin	8	7	1	8	—
Total	226	174	38	202½	23½[a]

1. Other candidates: Horatio Seymour, 12 (votes on table are for Thomas H. Seymour); Charles O'Connor, ½; blank, 1½.
a. Sum of column; proceedings record 28½.

1868 Republican

(Narrative, p. 63)

Delegation	Total Votes	First Pres. Ballot Grant
Alabama	18	18
Arkansas	10	10
California	10	10
Colorado	6	6
Connecticut	12	12
Delaware	6	6
Florida	6	6
Georgia	18	18
Idaho	2	2
Illinois	32	32
Indiana	26	26
Iowa	16	16
Kansas	6	6
Kentucky	22	22
Louisiana	14	14
Maine	14	14
Maryland	14	14
Massachusetts	24	24
Michigan	16	16
Minnesota	8	8
Mississippi	14	14
Missouri	22	22
Montana	2	2
Nebraska	6	6
Nevada	6	6
New Hampshire	10	10
New Jersey	14	14
New York	66	66
North Carolina	18	18
Dakota[a]	2	2
Ohio	42	42
Oregon	6	6
Pennsylvania	52	52
Rhode Island	8	8
South Carolina	12	12
Tennessee	20	20
Texas	12	12
Vermont	10	10
Virginia	20	20
West Virginia	10	10
Wisconsin	16	16
District of Columbia	2	2
Total	650	650

a. Dakota Territory, includes North and South Dakota.

1868 Democratic

(Narrative, p. 64)

Delegation	Total Votes	First Pres. Ballot[1]				22nd Pres. Ballot[2] (Before shift)		22nd Pres. Ballot (After shift)
		Pendleton	Hancock	Church	Johnson	Hancock	Hendricks	Seymour
Alabama	8	—	—	—	8	8	—	8
Arkansas	5	—	—	—	—	—	5	5
California	5	2	—	—	—	—	5	5
Connecticut	6	—	—	—	—	—	—	6
Delaware	3	3	—	—	—	3	—	3
Florida	3	—	—	—	3	—	3	3
Georgia	9	—	—	—	9	9	—	9
Illinois	16	16	—	—	—	—	16	16
Indiana	13	13	—	—	—	—	13	13
Iowa	8	8	—	—	—	—	8	8
Kansas	3	2	—	—	—	1	2	3
Kentucky	11	11	—	—	—	—	—	11
Louisiana	7	—	7	—	—	7	—	7
Maine	7	1½	4½	—	1	4½	2½	7
Maryland	7	4½	—	—	2½	6	1	7
Massachusetts	12	1	11	—	—	—	—	12
Michigan	8	—	—	—	—	—	8	8
Minnesota	4	4	—	—	—	—	4	4
Mississippi	7	—	7	—	—	7	—	7
Missouri	11	5	2	1	½	2	8	11
Nebraska	3	3	—	—	—	—	3	3
Nevada	3	—	—	—	—	—	3	3
New Hampshire	5	2	2	—	—	4½	½	5
New Jersey	7	—	—	—	—	—	7	7
New York	33	—	—	33	—	—	33	33
North Carolina	9	—	—	—	9	—	9	9
Ohio	21	21	—	—	—	—	—	21
Oregon	3	3	—	—	—	—	3	3
Pennsylvania	26	—	—	—	—	26	—	26
Rhode Island	4	—	—	—	—	—	—	4
South Carolina	6	—	—	—	6	6	—	6
Tennessee	10	—	—	—	10	3½	1½	10
Texas	6	—	—	—	6	6	—	6
Vermont	5	—	—	—	—	—	5	5
Virginia	10	—	—	—	10	10	—	10
West Virginia	5	5	—	—	—	—	5	5
Wisconsin	8	—	—	—	—	—	—	—
Total	317	105	33½	34	65	103½	145½	317

1. Other candidates: James E. English, 16; Joel Parker, 13; Asa Packer, 26; James R. Doolittle, 13; Thomas A. Hendricks, 2½; Frank P. Blair, ½; Reverdy Johnson, 8½.

2. Other candidates: Horatio Seymour, 22; English, 7; Doolittle, 4; Johnson, 4; not voting, 31.

1872 Democratic

(Narrative, p. 66)

Delegation	Total Votes	First Pres. Ballot[1] Greeley
Alabama	20	20
Arkansas	12	12
California	12	12
Connecticut	12	12
Delaware	6	—
Florida	8	6
Georgia	22	18
Illinois	42	42
Indiana	30	30
Iowa	22	22
Kansas	10	10
Kentucky	24	24
Louisiana	16	16
Maine	14	14
Maryland	16	16
Massachusetts	26	26
Michigan	22	22
Minnesota	10	10
Mississippi	16	16
Missouri	30	30
Nebraska	6	6
Nevada	6	6
New Hampshire	10	10
New Jersey	18	9
New York	70	70
North Carolina	20	20
Ohio	44	44
Oregon	6	6
Pennsylvania	58	58
Rhode Island	8	8
South Carolina	14	14
Tennessee	24	24
Texas	16	16
Vermont	10	10
Virginia	22	22
West Virginia	10	8
Wisconsin	20	20
Total	732	686

1. Other candidates: Thomas F. Bayard, 15; Jeremiah S. Black, 21; William S. Groesbeck, 2; blank, 8.

1872 Republican

(Narrative, p. 66)

Delegation	Total Votes	First Pres. Ballot[1] Grant
Alabama	20	20
Arizona	2	2
Arkansas	12	12
California	12	12
Colorado	2	2
Connecticut	12	12
Delaware	6	6
Florida	8	8
Georgia	22	22
Idaho	2	2
Illinois	42	42
Indiana	30	30
Iowa	22	22
Kansas	10	10
Kentucky	24	24
Louisiana	16	16
Maine	14	14
Maryland	16	16
Massachusetts	26	26
Michigan	22	22
Minnesota	10	10
Mississippi	16	16
Missouri	30	30
Montana	2	2
Nebraska	6	6
Nevada	6	6
New Hampshire	10	10
New Jersey	18	18
New Mexico	2	2
New York	70	70
North Carolina	20	20
Dakota[a]	2	2
Ohio	44	44
Oregon	6	6
Pennsylvania	58	58
Rhode Island	8	8
South Carolina	14	14
Tennessee	24	24
Texas	16	16
Utah	2	2
Vermont	10	10
Virginia	22	22
Washington	2	2
West Virginia	10	10
Wisconsin	20	20
Wyoming	2	2
District of Columbia	2	2
Total	752	752

a. Dakota Territory, includes North and South Dakota.

1876 Republican

(Narrative, p. 67)

Delegation	Total Votes	First Pres. Ballot[1]				Abolish Unit Rule			Fifth Pres. Ballot[2]					Sixth Pres. Ballot[3]					Seventh Pres. Ballot[4]	
		Blaine	Morton	Conkling	Bristow	Yea	Nay	Not Voting	Blaine	Bristow	Conkling	Hayes	Morton	Blaine	Morton	Conkling	Bristow	Hayes	Blaine	Hayes
Ala.	20	10	—	—	7	20	—	—	16	4	—	—	—	15	—	—	4	1	17	—
Ariz.	2	2	—	—	—	2	—	—	2	—	—	—	—	2	—	—	—	—	2	—
Ark.	12	—	12	—	—	4	8	—	1	—	—	—	11	1	11	—	—	—	11	—
Calif.	12	9	—	1	2	11	1	—	6	—	3	3	—	6	—	2	—	4	6	6
Colo.	6	6	—	—	—	6	—	—	6	—	—	—	—	6	—	—	—	—	6	1
Conn.	12	—	—	—	2	3	9	—	2	8	—	2	—	2	—	—	7	3	2	3
Del.	6	6	—	—	—	5	1	—	6	—	—	—	—	6	—	—	—	—	6	—
Fla.	8	1	4	3	—	4	4	—	2	—	—	—	3	4	4	—	—	—	8	—
Ga.	22	5	6	8	3	9	13	—	8	2	6	—	5	9	4	6	2	—	14	7
Idaho	2	2	—	—	—	2	—	—	2	—	—	—	—	2	—	—	—	—	2	—
Ill.	42	38	—	—	3	38	4	—	33	5	—	3	—	32	—	—	5	3	35	2
Ind.	30	—	30	—	—	1	29	—	—	—	—	—	30	—	30	—	—	—	—	25
Iowa	22	22	—	—	—	22	—	—	21	—	1	—	—	21	—	—	—	1	22	—
Kan.	10	10	—	—	—	10	—	—	10	—	—	—	—	10	—	—	—	—	10	—
Ky.	24	—	—	—	24	1	23	—	—	24	—	—	—	—	—	—	24	—	—	24
La.	16	2	14	—	—	6	10	—	5	—	—	—	11	6	10	—	—	—	14	2
Maine	14	14	—	—	—	14	—	—	14	—	—	—	—	14	—	—	—	—	14	—
Md.	16	16	—	—	—	16	—	—	16	—	—	—	—	16	—	—	—	—	16	—
Mass.	26	6	—	—	17	15	7	4	5	19	—	—	—	5	—	—	19	—	5	21
Mich.	22	8	—	1	9	3	19	—	—	—	—	22	—	—	—	—	—	22	—	22
Minn.	10	10	—	—	—	7	3	—	9	—	—	—	—	9	—	—	—	—	9	1
Miss.	16	—	11	1	3	9	6	1	—	8	2	2	4	1	5	2	4	4	—	16
Mo.	30	14	12	1	2	25	5	—	20	3	—	2	5	18	7	—	3	2	20	10
Mont.	2	2	—	—	—	2	—	—	1	—	—	1	—	1	—	—	—	1	—	2
Neb.	6	6	—	—	—	6	—	—	6	—	—	—	—	6	—	—	—	—	6	—
Nev.	6	—	—	2	3	—	6	—	—	1	2	1	—	—	—	2	2	1	—	6
N.H.	10	7	—	—	3	10	—	—	7	3	—	—	—	7	—	—	3	—	7	3
N.J.	18	13	—	—	—	15	3	—	12	—	—	6	—	12	—	—	—	6	12	6
N.M.	2	2	—	—	—	2	—	—	2	—	—	—	—	2	—	—	—	1	2	—
N.Y.	70	—	—	69	1	15	54	1	—	2	68	—	—	—	—	68	2	—	9	61
N.C.	20	9	2	7	1	6	13	1	—	—	12	—	1	12	—	—	—	1	—	20
Dak.[a]	2	2	—	—	—	2	—	—	2	—	—	—	—	2	—	—	—	—	2	—
Ohio	44	—	—	—	—	14	30	—	—	—	—	44	—	—	—	—	—	44	—	44
Ore.	6	6	—	—	—	6	—	—	6	—	—	—	—	6	—	—	—	—	6	—
Pa.	58	—	—	—	—	1	57	—	5	—	—	—	—	14	—	—	—	—	30	28
R.I.	8	2	—	—	6	1	7	—	2	6	—	—	—	2	—	—	6	—	2	6
S.C.	14	—	13	—	1	2	12	—	5	3	—	1	5	10	2	—	1	1	7	7
Tenn.	24	4	10	—	10	19	5	—	7	10	—	—	7	7	1	—	12	4	6	18
Texas	16	2	5	3	6	4	12	—	3	3	—	1	8	2	4	1	1	7	1	15
Utah	2	2	—	—	—	2	—	—	2	—	—	—	—	2	—	—	—	—	2	—
Vt.	10	1	—	—	8	5	5	—	—	8	—	2	—	—	—	—	8	2	—	10
Va.	22	16	3	3	—	19	2	1	16	—	—	—	3	13	4	—	3	2	14	8
Wash.	2	2	—	—	—	2	—	—	2	—	—	—	—	2	—	—	—	—	2	—
W.Va.	10	8	—	—	—	10	—	—	7	—	—	2	—	6	—	—	—	4	6	4
Wis.	20	20	—	—	—	17	3	—	16	3	—	—	1	16	1	—	3	—	16	4
Wyo.	2	—	—	—	2	—	2	—	—	2	—	—	—	—	—	—	2	—	—	2
D.C.	2	—	2	—	—	2	—	—	1	—	—	—	1	1	1	—	—	—	2	—
Total	756	285	124	99	113	395	353	8	286	114	82	104	95	308	85	81	111	113	351	384

1. Other candidates: Rutherford B. Hayes, 61; John F. Hartranft, 58; Marshall Jewell, 11; William A. Wheeler, 3; not voting, 2.

2. Other candidates: Hartranft, 69; Elihu B. Washburne, 3; Wheeler, 2; not voting, 2.

3. Other candidates: Hartranft, 50; Washburne, 4; Wheeler, 2; not voting, 2.

4. Other candidates: Benjamin H. Bristow, 21.

a. Dakota Territory, includes North and South Dakota.

1876 Democratic

(Narrative, p. 68)

Delegation	Total Votes	First Pres. Ballot[1]			Second Pres. Ballot[2]	
		Tilden	Hendricks	Hancock	Tilden	
Alabama	20	13	5	2	20	—
Arkansas	12	12	—	—	12	—
California	12	12	—	—	12	—
Colorado	6	—	6	—	6	—
Connecticut	12	12	—	—	12	—
Delaware	6	—	—	—	6	—
Florida	8	8	—	—	8	—
Georgia	22	5	—	1	22	—
Illinois	42	19	23	—	26	16
Indiana	30	—	30	—	—	30
Iowa	22	14	6	2	22	—
Kansas	10	—	10	—	2	8
Kentucky	24	24	—	—	24	—
Louisiana	16	9	—	5	16	—
Maine	14	14	—	—	14	—
Maryland	16	11	3	—	14	2
Massachusetts	26	26	—	—	26	—
Michigan	22	14	8	—	19	3
Minnesota	10	10	—	—	10	—
Mississippi	16	16	—	—	16	—
Missouri	30	—	14	—	30	—
Nebraska	6	6	—	—	6	—
Nevada	6	3	3	—	4	—
New Hampshire	10	10	—	—	10	—
New Jersey	18	—	—	—	18	—
New York	70	70	—	—	70	—
North Carolina	20	9	4	5	20	—
Ohio	44	—	—	—	—	—
Oregon	6	6	—	—	6	—
Pennsylvania	58	—	—	58	—	—
Rhode Island	8	8	—	—	8	—
South Carolina	14	14	—	—	14	—
Tennessee	24	—	24	—	—	24
Texas	16	10½	2½	2	16	—
Vermont	10	10	—	—	10	—
Virginia	22	17	1	—	17	1
West Virginia	10	—	—	—	—	—
Wisconsin	20	19	1	—	19	1
Total	738	401½[a]	140½	75	535	85

1. Other candidates: William Allen, 54; Allen G. Thurman, 3; Thomas F. Bayard, 33; Joel Parker, 18; James O. Broadhead, 16.
2. Other candidates: Allen, 54; Bayard, 4; Winfield Scott Hancock, 58; Thurman, 2.
a. Sum of column; proceedings record 404½.

1880 Republican

(Narrative, p. 69)

Delegation	Total Votes	Minority Report Illinois 1st Dist.			First Pres. Ballot[1]				34th Pres. Ballot[2]				35th Pres. Ballot[3]					36th Pres. Ballot[4]			
		Yea	Nay	Not Voting	Grant	Blaine	Sherman	Other	Grant	Blaine	Sherman	Other	Grant	Blaine	Sherman	Garfield	Other	Grant	Blaine	Garfield	Other
Ala.	20	16	4	—	16	1	3	—	16	4	—	—	16	4	—	—	—	16	4	—	—
Ariz.	2	—	2	—	—	2	—	—	—	2	—	—	—	2	—	—	—	—	2	—	—
Ark.	12	12	—	—	12	—	—	—	12	—	—	—	12	—	—	—	—	12	—	—	—
Calif.	12	—	12	—	—	12	—	—	—	12	—	—	—	12	—	—	—	—	12	—	—
Colo.	6	6	—	—	6	—	—	—	6	—	—	—	6	—	—	—	6	—	—	—	—
Conn.	12	—	10	2	—	3	—	9	—	3	—	9	—	3	—	—	9	—	1	11	—
Del.	6	—	6	—	—	6	—	—	—	6	—	—	—	6	—	—	—	1	6	—	—
Fla.	8	8	—	—	8	—	—	—	8	—	—	—	8	—	—	—	—	8	—	—	—
Ga.	22	6	16	—	6	8	8	—	8	9	5	—	8	9	5	—	—	8	10	1	3
Idaho	2	—	2	—	—	2	—	—	—	2	—	—	—	2	—	—	—	—	2	—	—
Ill.	42	40	—	2	24	10	—	8	24	10	—	8	24	10	—	—	8	24	6	7	5
Ind.	30	5	25	—	1	26	2	1	2	20	2	6	1	2	—	27	—	1	—	29	—
Iowa	22	—	22	—	—	22	—	—	—	22	—	—	—	22	—	—	—	—	22	—	—
Kan.	10	—	—	10	4	6	—	—	4	6	—	—	4	6	—	—	—	4	—	6	—
Ky.	24	21	3	—	20	1	3	—	20	1	3	—	20	1	3	—	—	20	1	3	—
La.	16	8	8	—	8	2	6	—	8	4	4	—	8	4	4	—	—	8	—	8	—
Maine	14	—	14	—	—	14	—	—	—	14	—	—	—	14	—	—	—	—	14	—	—
Md.	16	8	8	—	7	7	2	—	7	2	7	—	7	3	2	4	—	6	—	10	—
Mass.	26	4	22	—	3	—	2	21	4	—	21	1	4	—	21	—	1	4	—	22	—
Mich.	22	1	21	—	1	21	—	—	1	21	—	—	1	21	—	—	—	1	—	21	—
Minn.	10	4	6	—	—	—	—	10	—	6	—	4	1	6	—	—	3	2	—	8	—
Miss.	16	11	5	—	6	4	6	—	8	4	3	1	8	4	3	1	—	7	—	9	—
Mo.	30	29	1	—	29	—	—	1	29	—	—	1	29	—	—	—	1	29	—	1	—
Mont.	2	—	2	—	—	2	—	—	—	2	—	—	—	2	—	—	—	—	—	2	—
Neb.	6	—	6	—	—	6	—	—	—	6	—	—	—	6	—	—	—	—	—	6	—
Nev.	6	—	6	—	—	6	—	—	—	6	—	—	—	6	—	—	—	2	1	3	—
N.H.	10	—	10	—	—	10	—	—	—	10	—	—	—	10	—	—	—	—	—	10	—
N.J.	18	—	18	—	—	16	—	2	—	14	2	2	—	14	2	—	2	—	—	18	—
N.M.	2	—	2	—	—	2	—	—	—	2	—	—	—	2	—	—	—	—	—	2	—
N.Y.	70	47	22	1	51	17	2	—	50	18	2	—	50	18	2	—	—	50	—	20	—
N.C.	20	19	1	—	6	—	14	—	6	—	14	—	6	—	13	1	—	5	—	15	—
Dak.[a]	2	1	1	—	1	1	—	—	1	1	—	—	1	1	—	—	—	—	—	2	—
Ohio	44	16	28	—	—	9	34	1	—	9	34	1	—	9	34	—	1	—	—	43	1
Ore.	6	—	6	—	—	6	—	—	—	6	—	—	—	6	—	—	—	—	—	6	—
Pa.	58	34	24	—	32	23	3	—	35	22	—	1	36	20	—	1	1	37	—	21	—
R.I.	8	—	8	—	—	8	—	—	—	8	—	—	—	8	—	—	—	—	—	8	—
S.C.	14	10	4	—	13	—	1	—	11	1	2	—	11	1	2	—	—	8	—	6	—
Tenn.	24	16	8	—	16	6	1	1	17	4	3	—	17	4	3	—	—	15	1	8	—
Texas	16	11	4	1	11	2	2	1	13	1	1	1	13	1	1	—	—	13	—	3	—
Utah	2	—	2	—	1	1	—	—	1	1	—	—	1	1	—	—	—	—	—	2	—
Vt.	10	4	6	—	—	—	—	10	—	—	—	10	—	—	—	—	10	—	—	10	—
Va.	22	13	9	—	18	3	1	—	16	3	3	—	16	3	3	—	—	19	—	3	—
Wash.	2	—	2	—	—	2	—	—	—	2	—	—	—	2	—	—	—	—	—	2	—
W.Va.	10	—	10	—	1	8	—	1	1	8	1	—	1	8	1	—	—	1	—	9	—
Wis.	20	1	19	—	1	7	3	9	2	1	—	17	2	2	—	16	—	—	—	20	—
Wyo.	2	1	1	—	1	1	—	—	1	1	—	—	1	1	—	—	—	—	—	2	—
D.C.	2	1	1	—	1	1	—	—	1	1	—	—	1	1	—	—	—	—	—	2	—
Total	756	353	387	16	304	284	93	75	312	275	107	62	313	257	99	50	37	306	42	399	9

1. Other candidates: George F. Edmunds, 34; Elihu B. Washburne, 30; William Windom, 10; not voting 1.
2. Other candidates: Washburne, 30; James A. Garfield, 17; Edmunds, 11; Windom, 4.
3. Other candidates: Washburne, 23; Edmunds, 11; Windom, 3.
4. Other candidates: Washburne, 5; John Sherman, 3; not voting, 1.
a. Dakota Territory, includes North and South Dakota.

1880 Democratic

(Narrative, p. 71)

Delegation	Total Votes	First Pres. Ballot[1]			Second Pres. Ballot[2] (Before shift)			Second Pres. Ballot[3] (After shift)
		Bayard	Hancock	Payne	Hancock	Bayard	Randall	Hancock
Alabama	20	7	7	—	11	5	—	20
Arkansas	12	—	—	—	—	—	—	12
California	12	—	—	—	5	—	—	12
Colorado	6	—	—	—	—	—	—	6
Connecticut	12	4	—	2	—	1	—	12
Delaware	6	6	—	—	—	6	—	6
Florida	8	8	—	—	—	8	—	8
Georgia	22	5	8	—	7	5	—	22
Illinois	42	—	—	—	—	42	—	42
Indiana	30	—	—	—	—	—	—	—
Iowa	22	3	7	2	9	1	12	21
Kansas	10	—	—	—	10	—	—	10
Kentucky	24	6	1	—	8	7	—	24
Louisiana	16	—	16	—	16	—	—	16
Maine	14	—	14	—	14	—	—	14
Maryland	16	16	—	—	—	16	—	14
Massachusetts	26	11½	6	—	11	7	3½	26
Michigan	22	2	5	1	14	4	1	22
Minnesota	10	—	10	—	10	—	—	10
Mississippi	16	8	5	—	6	8	—	16
Missouri	30	4	12	—	28	2	—	30
Nebraska	6	—	—	6	—	—	6	6
Nevada	6	—	—	—	—	—	1	6
New Hampshire	10	3	4	—	5	—	5	10
New Jersey	18	10	—	—	7	4	4	18
New York	70	—	—	70	—	—	70	70
North Carolina	20	7	9	—	20	—	—	20
Ohio	44	—	—	—	—	—	—	44
Oregon	6	—	—	—	—	—	—	6
Pennsylvania	58	7	28	—	32	—	25	58
Rhode Island	8	2	2	—	6	—	1	8
South Carolina	14	14	—	—	—	14	—	14
Tennessee	24	9	11	—	14	8	—	24
Texas	16	5	9	—	11	5	—	16
Vermont	10	—	10	—	10	—	—	10
Virginia	22	10	3	—	7	8	—	22
West Virginia	10	—	3	—	7	1	—	10
Wisconsin	20	6	1	—	10	2	—	20
Total	738	153½	171	81	320	112	128½	705

1. Other candidates: Allen G. Thurman, 68½; Stephen J. Field, 65; William R. Morrison, 62; Thomas A. Hendricks, 49½; Samuel J. Tilden, 38; Horatio Seymour, 8; W. A. H. Loveland, 5; Samuel J. Randall, 6; Thomas Ewing, 10; Joseph E. McDonald, 3; George B. McClellan, 2; Joel Parker, 1; Jeremiah Black, 1; Hugh J. Jewett, 1; James E. English, 1; Lothrop, 1; not voting, 10½.

2. Other candidates: Hendricks, 31; English, 19; Tilden, 6; Thurman, 50; Parker, 2; Field, 65½; Jewett, 1; not voting, 3.

3. Other candidates: Hendricks, 30; Bayard, 2; Tilden, 1.

1884 Republican

(Narrative, p. 72)

Delegation	Total Votes	Temporary Chairman[1] Lynch	Temporary Chairman[1] Clayton	First Pres. Ballot[2] Arthur	First Pres. Ballot[2] Blaine	First Pres. Ballot[2] Edmunds	Third Pres. Ballot[3] Arthur	Third Pres. Ballot[3] Blaine	Fourth Pres. Ballot[4] Arthur	Fourth Pres. Ballot[4] Blaine
Alabama	20	19	1	17	1	—	17	2	12	8
Arizona	2	—	2	—	2	—	—	2	—	2
Arkansas	14	1	13	4	8	2	3	11	3	11
California	16	—	16	—	16	—	—	16	—	16
Colorado	6	—	6	—	6	—	—	6	—	6
Connecticut	12	6	6	—	—	—	—	—	—	—
Delaware	6	1	5	1	5	—	1	5	1	5
Florida	8	7	1	7	1	—	7	1	5	3
Georgia	24	24	—	24	—	—	24	—	24	—
Idaho	2	2	—	2	—	—	1	1	—	2
Illinois	44	16	28	1	3	—	1	3	3	34
Indiana	30	10	20	9	18	1	10	18	—	30
Iowa	26	3	23	—	26	—	—	26	2	24
Kansas	18	4	14	4	12	—	—	15	—	18
Kentucky	26	20	6	16	5½	—	16	6	15	9
Louisiana	16	11	4	10	2	—	9	4	7	9
Maine	12	—	12	—	12	—	—	12	—	12
Maryland	16	6	10	6	10	—	4	12	1	15
Massachusetts	28	24	4	2	1	25	3	1	7	3
Michigan	26	12	14	2	15	7	4	18	—	26
Minnesota	14	6	8	1	7	6	2	7	—	14
Mississippi	18	16	2	17	1	—	16	1	16	2
Missouri	32	14	16	10	5	6	11	12	—	32
Montana	2	1	1	—	1	1	—	1	—	2
Nebraska	10	2	8	2	8	—	—	10	—	10
Nevada	6	—	6	—	6	—	—	6	—	6
New Hampshire	8	8	—	4	—	4	5	—	2	3
New Jersey	18	9	9	—	9	6	1	11	—	17
New Mexico	2	2	—	2	—	—	2	—	2	—
New York	72	46	26	31	28	12	32	28	30	29
North Carolina	22	17	3	19	2	—	18	4	12	8
Dakota[a]	2	—	2	—	2	—	—	2	—	2
Ohio	46	22	23	—	21	—	—	25	—	46
Oregon	6	—	6	—	6	—	—	6	—	6
Pennsylvania	60	13	45	11	47	1	8	50	8	51
Rhode Island	8	8	—	—	—	8	—	—	1	7
South Carolina	18	18	—	17	1	—	16	2	15	2
Tennessee	24	21	2	16	7	—	17	7	12	11
Texas	26	12	12	11	13	—	11	14	8	15
Utah	2	—	2	2	—	—	2	—	—	2
Vermont	8	8	—	—	—	8	—	—	—	—
Virginia	24	20	4	21	2	—	20	4	20	4
Washington	2	1	1	—	2	—	—	2	—	2
West Virginia	12	—	12	—	12	—	—	12	—	12
Wisconsin	22	11	10	6	10	6	10	11	—	22
Wyoming	2	2	—	2	—	—	2	—	—	2
District of Columbia	2	1	1	1	1	—	1	1	1	1
Total	820	424	384	278	334½	93	274	375	207	541

1. Not voting, 12.
2. Other candidates: John A. Logan, 63½; John Sherman, 30; Joseph R. Hawley, 13; Robert T. Lincoln, 4; William T. Sherman, 2; not voting, 2.
3. Other candidates: George F. Edmunds, 69; Logan, 53; John Sherman, 25; Hawley 13; Lincoln, 8; William T. Sherman, 3; not voting 9, 1.
4. Other candidates: Edmunds, 41; Hawley, 15; Logan, 7; Lincoln, 2; not voting, 7.
a. Dakota Territory, includes North and South Dakota.

1884 Democratic

(Narrative, p. 73)

Delegation	Total Votes	Unit Rule: Amendment to Permit Polling of Delegates			First Pres. Ballot[1]			Second Pres. Ballot[2] (Before shift)			Second Pres. Ballot[3] (After shift)	
		Yea	Nay	Not Voting	Cleveland	Bayard	Thurman	Cleveland	Bayard	Hendricks	Cleveland	Bayard
Alabama	20	15	5	—	4	14	1	5	14	—	5	14
Arizona	2	—	—	2	2	—	—	2	—	—	2	—
Arkansas	14	—	14	—	14	—	—	14	—	—	14	—
California	16	16	—	—	—	—	16	—	—	—	16	—
Colorado	6	4	2	—	—	—	1	6	—	—	6	—
Connecticut	12	2	10	—	12	—	—	12	—	—	12	—
Delaware	6	6	—	—	—	6	—	—	6	—	—	6
Florida	8	2	6	—	8	—	—	6	2	—	8	—
Georgia	24	12	12	—	10	12	—	14	10	—	22	2
Idaho	2	—	—	2	2	—	—	2	—	—	2	—
Illinois	44	22	22	—	28	2	1	38	3	1	43	—
Indiana	30	30	—	—	—	—	—	—	—	30	30	—
Iowa	26	6	20	—	23	1	1	22	—	4	26	—
Kansas	18	3	15	—	11	5	2	12	4	—	17	1
Kentucky	26	20	6	—	—	—	—	3	7	15	4	21
Louisiana	16	—	16	—	13	1	1	15	—	—	15	—
Maine	12	2	10	—	12	—	—	12	—	—	12	—
Maryland	16	—	16	—	6	10	—	10	6	—	16	—
Massachusetts	28	21	7	—	5	21	2	8	7½	12½	8	7½
Michigan	26	12	12	2	14	1	11	13	—	13	23	—
Minnesota	14	—	14	—	14	—	—	14	—	—	14	—
Mississippi	18	18	—	—	1	15	1	2	14	2	2	14
Missouri	32	8	24	—	15	10	3	21	5	6	32	—
Montana	2	—	—	2	2	—	—	2	—	—	2	—
Nebraska	10	5	5	—	8	1	1	9	1	—	9	1
Nevada	6	6	—	—	—	—	6	—	—	5	—	—
New Hampshire	8	—	8	—	8	—	—	8	—	—	8	—
New Jersey	18	14	4	—	4	3	—	5	2	11	5	2
New Mexico	2	—	—	2	2	—	—	1	—	—	2	—
New York	72	—	72	—	72	—	—	72	—	—	72	—
North Carolina	22	10	12	—	—	22	—	—	22	—	22	—
Dakota[a]	2	—	—	2	2	—	—	2	—	—	2	—
Ohio	46	25	21	—	21	—	23	21	—	1	46	—
Oregon	6	—	6	—	2	4	—	2	2	2	6	—
Pennsylvania	60	21	39	—	5	—	—	42	2	11	42	2
Rhode Island	8	—	8	—	6	2	—	6	2	—	7	1
South Carolina	18	3	14	1	8	10	—	8	9	1	10	8
Tennessee	24	17	7	—	2	8	9	2	10	1	24	—
Texas	26	12	10	4	11	10	4	12	12	1	26	—
Utah	2	—	—	2	—	—	—	1	—	1	2	—
Vermont	8	—	8	—	8	—	—	8	—	—	8	—
Virginia	24	6	18	—	13	9	1	13	8	2	23	—
Washington	2	—	—	2	1	—	—	2	—	—	2	—
West Virginia	12	9	3	—	7	2	2	6	3	—	10	2
Wisconsin	22	5	17	—	12	1	2	20	—	2	22	—
Wyoming	2	—	—	2	2	—	—	2	—	—	2	—
District of Columbia	2	—	—	2	2	—	—	—	—	2	2	—
Total	820	332	463	25	392	170	88	475	151½	123½	683	81½

1. Other candidates: Joseph E. McDonald, 56; Samuel J. Randall, 78; John G. Carlisle, 27; George Hoadly, 3; Thomas A. Hendricks, 1; Samuel J. Tilden, 1; Roswell P. Flower, 4.

2. Other candidates: Allen G. Thurman, 60; Randall, 5; McDonald, 2; Tilden, 2; not voting, 1.

3. Other candidates: Hendricks, 45½; Thurman, 4; Randall, 4; McDonald, 2.

a. Dakota Territory, includes North and South Dakota.

1888 Republican

(Narrative, p. 75)

Delega-tion	Total Votes	First Pres. Ballot[1] Alger	Allison	Depew	Gresham	Harrison	Sherman	Sixth Pres. Ballot[2] Alger	Allison	Gresham	Harrison	Sherman	Seventh Pres. Ballot[3] Alger	Allison	Gresham	Harrison	Sherman	Eighth Pres. Ballot[4] Alger	Gresham	Harrison	Sherman
Ala.	20	6	—	1	—	1	12	6	—	—	1	12	6	—	—	12	—	10	—	3	5
Ariz.	2	2	—	—	—	—	—	2	—	—	—	—	2	—	—	—	—	—	—	2	—
Ark.	14	—	—	—	1	1	2	14	—	—	—	—	14	—	—	—	—	14	—	—	—
Calif.	16	—	—	—	—	—	—	—	—	—	—	—	1	—	—	15	—	—	—	15	—
Colo.	6	—	1	—	3	2	—	—	—	—	5	—	—	6	—	—	—	—	—	6	—
Conn.	12	—	—	—	—	—	—	2	4	—	—	6	2	—	—	4	5	—	—	12	—
Del.	6	—	—	—	6	—	—	—	—	1	5	—	—	1	—	5	—	—	—	6	—
Fla.	8	—	—	—	—	1	4	5	—	—	1	1	3	—	—	4	1	4	—	2	2
Ga.	24	—	—	—	1	2	19	—	—	1	2	19	1	—	1	3	17	3	1	10	9
Idaho	2	—	1	—	1	—	—	—	—	2	—	—	—	2	—	—	—	—	—	2	—
Ill.	44	—	—	44	—	—	—	—	—	41	3	—	1	—	40	3	—	—	40	4	—
Ind.	30	—	—	—	1	29	—	—	—	1	29	—	—	—	1	29	—	—	1	29	—
Iowa	26	—	26	—	—	—	—	—	26	—	—	—	—	26	—	—	—	1	3	22	—
Kan.	18	—	—	—	—	—	—	2	3	3	6	1	1	3	—	12	1	1	—	16	—
Ky.	26	4	—	1	5	4	12	6	—	2	7	9	3	—	2	10	9	1	2	15	7
La.	16	2	3	1	1	—	9	3	2	2	—	9	3	2	2	—	9	4	—	9	3
Maine	12	3	2	3	1	2	1	2	1	2	1	3	1	2	2	2	1	—	1	5	3
Md.	16	—	2	1	1	5	5	—	1	—	6	6	—	—	—	9	6	—	—	11	4
Mass.	28	6	2	1	2	4	9	8	2	1	5	11	2	3	1	9	11	1	—	25	2
Mich.	26	26	—	—	—	—	—	26	—	—	—	—	26	—	—	—	—	26	—	—	—
Minn.	14	1	—	2	11	—	—	3	—	5	6	—	2	—	4	8	—	1	—	13	—
Miss.	18	—	—	1	3	—	14	—	—	3	—	14	—	—	3	—	14	—	3	4	11
Mo.	32	6	3	2	11	3	6	15	1	11	2	2	14	1	12	3	2	15	8	7	2
Mont.	2	—	1	—	1	—	—	—	1	1	—	—	—	1	1	—	—	—	—	2	—
Neb.	10	2	3	—	1	—	3	2	5	—	—	3	2	5	—	2	1	1	—	9	—
Nev.	6	3	3	—	—	—	—	5	—	—	—	—	—	6	—	—	—	2	—	4	—
N.H.	8	—	—	4	—	4	—	—	1	—	6	1	—	—	—	8	—	—	—	8	—
N.J.	18	—	—	—	—	—	—	—	—	1	14	—	1	—	1	10	1	—	—	18	—
N.M.	2	1	—	—	—	—	—	1	—	—	—	1	1	—	—	—	1	—	—	2	—
N.Y.	72	—	—	71	—	—	1	—	—	—	72	—	—	—	—	72	—	—	—	72	—
N.C.	22	2	—	1	2	1	15	9	—	—	2	11	7	—	—	3	12	3	—	8	11
Dak.[a]	10	1	1	2	1	1	1	—	—	—	10	—	—	—	—	10	—	—	—	10	—
Ohio	46	—	—	—	—	—	46	—	—	—	1	45	—	—	—	1	45	—	—	1	45
Ore.	6	—	—	—	4	1	—	—	5	—	—	—	—	6	—	—	—	—	—	6	—
Pa.	60	1	—	5	—	—	29	—	—	—	6	54	—	—	—	9	51	—	—	59	1
R.I.	8	—	8	—	—	—	—	—	8	—	—	—	—	6	—	2	—	—	—	8	—
S.C.	18	3	—	1	—	—	11	11	—	—	1	6	11	—	—	1	6	10	—	4	4
Tenn.	24	9	1	2	1	1	7	6	1	—	1	8	9	1	—	3	5	3	—	20	—
Texas	26	2	7	—	5	1	7	3	8	3	1	7	2	8	1	3	7	—	—	26	—
Utah	2	—	2	—	—	—	—	—	2	—	—	—	—	2	—	—	—	—	—	2	—
Vt.	8	—	—	—	8	—	—	—	—	—	8	—	—	—	—	8	—	—	—	8	—
Va.	24	3	3	—	1	5	11	3	5	—	6	10	3	5	—	6	10	—	—	15	9
Wash.	6	—	1	—	3	1	—	1	—	4	1	—	1	—	4	1	—	—	—	6	—
W.Va.	12	1	—	—	2	2	5	1	—	1	2	5	—	—	5	3	1	—	—	12	—
Wis.	22	—	—	—	—	—	—	—	—	1	21	—	—	—	2	20	—	—	—	22	—
Wyo.	2	—	2	—	—	—	—	—	2	—	—	—	—	2	—	—	—	—	—	2	—
D.C.	2	—	—	—	—	—	—	1	—	—	—	—	1	—	—	—	—	—	—	2	—
Totals	832	84	72	99	107	85	229	137	73	91	231	244	120	76	91	279	230	100	59	544	118

1. Other candidates: James G. Blaine, 35; John J. Ingalls, 28; William W. Phelps, 25; Jeremiah M. Rusk, 25; Edwin H. Fitler, 24; Joseph R. Hawley, 13; Robert T. Lincoln, 3; William McKinley, 2; no voting, 1.

2. Other candidates: Blaine, 40; McKinley, 12; Joseph B. Foraker, 1; Frederick D. Grant, 1; not voting, 2.

3. Other candidates: McKinley, 16; Blaine, 15; Lincoln, 2; Foraker, 1; Creed Haymond, 1; not voting, 1.

4. Other candidates: Blaine, 5; McKinley, 4; not voting, 2.

a. Dakota Territory, includes North and South Dakota.

1892 Republican

(Narrative, p. 76)

First Pres. Ballot[1]

Delegation	Total Votes	Harrison	Blaine	McKinley
Alabama	22	15	—	7
Arizona	2	1	1	—
Arkansas	16	15	—	1
California	18	8	9	1
Colorado	8	—	8	—
Connecticut	12	4	—	8
Delaware	6	4	1	1
Florida	8	8	—	—
Georgia	26	26	—	—
Idaho	6	—	6	—
Illinois	48	34	14	—
Indiana	30	30	—	—
Iowa	26	20	5	1
Kansas	20	11	—	9
Kentucky	26	22	2	1
Louisiana	16	8	8	—
Maine	12	—	12	—
Maryland	16	14	—	2
Massachusetts	30	18	1	11
Michigan	28	7	2	19
Minnesota	18	8	9	1
Mississippi	18	13½	4½	—
Missouri	34	28	4	2
Montana	6	5	1	—
Nebraska	16	15	—	1
Nevada	6	—	6	—
New Hampshire	8	4	2	—
New Jersey	20	18	2	—
New Mexico	6	6	—	—
New York	72	27	35	10
North Carolina	22	17⅔	2⅔	1
North Dakota	6	2	4	—
Ohio	46	1	—	45
Oklahoma	2	2	—	—
Oregon	8	1	—	7
Pennsylvania	64	19	3	42
Rhode Island	8	5	1	1
South Carolina	18	13	3	2
South Dakota	8	8	—	—
Tennessee	24	17	4	3
Texas	30	22	6	—
Utah	2	2	—	—
Vermont	8	8	—	—
Virginia	24	9	13	2
Washington	8	1	6	1
West Virginia	12	12	—	—
Wisconsin	24	19	2	3
Wyoming	6	4	2	—
Alaska	2	2	—	—
District of Columbia	2	—	2	—
Indian Territory	2	1	1	—
Total	906	535⅙	182⅙	182

1. Other candidates: Thomas B. Reed, 4; Robert T. Lincoln, 1; not voting, 1⅔.

* Source: Official Proceeding, 10th Republican Convention.

1892 Democratic

(Narrative, p. 77)

First Pres. Ballot[1]

Delegation	Total Votes	Cleveland	Boies	Hill
Alabama	22	14	1	2
Arizona	6	5	—	—
Arkansas	16	16	—	—
California	18	18	—	—
Colorado	8	—	5	3
Connecticut	12	12	—	—
Delaware	6	6	—	—
Florida	8	5	—	—
Georgia	26	17	—	5
Idaho	6	—	6	—
Illinois	48	48	—	—
Indiana	30	30	—	—
Iowa	26	—	26	—
Kansas	20	20	—	—
Kentucky	26	18	2	—
Louisiana	16	3	11	1
Maine	12	9	—	1
Maryland	16	6	—	—
Massachusetts	30	24	1	4
Michigan	28	28	—	—
Minnesota	18	18	—	—
Mississippi	18	8	3	3
Missouri	34	34	—	—
Montana	6	—	6	—
Nebraska	16	15	—	—
Nevada	6	—	4	—
New Hampshire	8	8	—	—
New Jersey	20	20	—	—
New Mexico	6	4	1	1
New York	72	—	—	72
North Carolina	22	3⅓	1	—
North Dakota	6	6	—	—
Ohio	46	14	16	6
Oklahoma[a]	4	4	—	—
Oregon	8	8	—	—
Pennsylvania	64	64	—	—
Rhode Island	8	8	—	—
South Carolina	18	2	13	3
South Dakota	8	7	1	—
Tennessee	24	24	—	—
Texas	30	23	6	1
Utah	2	2	—	—
Vermont	8	8	—	—
Virginia	24	12	—	11
Washington	8	8	—	—
West Virginia	12	7	—	1
Wisconsin	24	24	—	—
Wyoming	6	3	—	—
Alaska	2	2	—	—
District of Columbia	2	2	—	—
Total	910	617⅓	103	114

1. Other candidates: Arthur P. Gorman, 36½; John G. Carlisle, 14; Adlai E. Stevenson, 16⅔; James E. Campbell, 2: William R. Morrison, 3; William E. Russell, 1; William C. Whitney, 1; Robert E. Pattison, 1; not voting, ½.

a. Including Indian Territory, 2 votes.

1896 Republican

(Narrative, p. 79)

Delegation	Total Votes	First Pres. Ballot[1] McKinley	Reed	Morton	Allison	Quay
Alabama	22	19	2	1	—	—
Arizona	6	6	—	—	—	—
Arkansas	16	16	—	—	—	—
California	18	18	—	—	—	—
Colorado	8	—	—	—	—	—
Connecticut	12	7	5	—	—	—
Delaware	6	6	—	—	—	—
Florida	8	6	—	2	—	—
Georgia	26	22	2	—	—	2
Idaho	6	—	—	—	—	—
Illinois	48	46	2	—	—	—
Indiana	30	30	—	—	—	—
Iowa	26	—	—	—	26	—
Kansas	20	20	—	—	—	—
Kentucky	26	26	—	—	—	—
Louisiana	16	11	4	—	½	½
Maine	12	—	12	—	—	—
Maryland	16	15	1	—	—	—
Massachusetts	30	1	29	—	—	—
Michigan	28	28	—	—	—	—
Minnesota	18	18	—	—	—	—
Mississippi	18	17	—	—	—	1
Missouri	34	34	—	—	—	—
Montana	6	1	—	—	—	—
Nebraska	16	16	—	—	—	—
Nevada	6	3	—	—	—	—
New Hampshire	8	—	8	—	—	—
New Jersey	20	19	1	—	—	—
New Mexico	6	5	—	—	1	—
New York	72	17	—	55	—	—
North Carolina	22	19½	2½	—	—	—
North Dakota	6	6	—	—	—	—
Ohio	46	46	—	—	—	—
Oklahoma[a]	12	10	1	—	1	—
Oregon	8	8	—	—	—	—
Pennsylvania	64	6	—	—	—	58
Rhode Island	8	—	8	—	—	—
South Carolina	18	18	—	—	—	—
South Dakota	8	8	—	—	—	—
Tennessee	24	24	—	—	—	—
Texas	30	21	5	—	3	—
Utah	6	3	—	—	3	—
Vermont	8	8	—	—	—	—
Virginia	24	23	1	—	—	—
Washington	8	8	—	—	—	—
West Virginia	12	12	—	—	—	—
Wisconsin	24	24	—	—	—	—
Wyoming	6	6	—	—	—	—
Alaska	4	4	—	—	—	—
District of Columbia	2	—	1	—	1	—
Total	924	661½	84½	58	35½	61½

1. Other candidates: J. Donald Cameron, 1; not voting, 22.
a. Including Indian Territory, 6 votes.

1896 Democratic

(Narrative, p. 80)

Delegation	Total Votes	Minority Gold Standard Plank			First Pres. Ballot[1]			Fourth Pres. Ballot[2]			Fifth Pres. Ballot[3]	
		Yea	Nay	Not Voting	Bryan	Bland	Pattison	Bryan	Bland	Pattison	Bryan	Pattison
Alabama	22	—	22	—	—	—	—	22	—	—	22	—
Arizona	6	—	6	—	—	6	—	—	6	—	6	—
Arkansas	16	—	16	—	—	16	—	—	16	—	16	—
California	18	—	18	—	4	—	—	12	2	—	18	—
Colorado	8	—	8	—	—	—	—	8	—	—	8	—
Connecticut	12	12	—	—	—	—	—	—	—	2	—	2
Delaware	6	5	1	—	1	—	3	1	—	3	1	3
Florida	8	3	5	—	1	2	1	5	—	—	8	—
Georgia	26	—	26	—	26	—	—	26	—	—	26	—
Idaho	6	—	6	—	—	6	—	6	—	—	6	—
Illinois	48	—	48	—	—	48	—	—	48	—	48	—
Indiana	30	—	30	—	—	—	—	—	—	—	30	—
Iowa	26	—	26	—	—	—	—	—	—	—	26	—
Kansas	20	—	20	—	—	20	—	20	—	—	20	—
Kentucky	26	—	26	—	—	—	—	—	—	—	26	—
Louisiana	16	—	16	—	16	—	—	16	—	—	16	—
Maine	12	10	2	—	2	2	5	2	2	5	4	4
Maryland	16	12	4	—	4	—	11	5	—	10	5	10
Massachusetts	30	27	3	—	1	2	3	1	2	3	6	3
Michigan	28	—	28	—	9	4	—	28	—	—	28	—
Minnesota	18	11	6	1	2	—	2	10	1	—	11	—
Mississippi	18	—	18	—	18	—	—	18	—	—	18	—
Missouri	34	—	34	—	—	34	—	—	34	—	34	—
Montana	6	—	6	—	—	4	—	—	6	—	6	—
Nebraska	16	—	16	—	16	—	—	16	—	—	16	—
Nevada	6	—	6	—	—	—	—	6	—	—	6	—
New Hampshire	8	8	—	—	—	—	1	—	—	1	—	1
New Jersey	20	20	—	—	—	—	—	—	—	2	—	2
New Mexico	6	—	6	—	—	6	—	—	6	—	6	—
New York	72	72	—	—	—	—	—	—	—	—	—	—
North Carolina	22	—	22	—	22	—	—	22	—	—	22	—
North Dakota	6	—	6	—	—	—	—	—	—	—	4	—
Ohio	46	—	46	—	—	—	—	—	—	—	46	—
Oklahoma[a]	12	—	12	—	—	12	—	—	12	—	12	—
Oregon	8	—	8	—	—	—	—	8	—	—	8	—
Pennsylvania	64	64	—	—	—	—	64	—	—	64	—	64
Rhode Island	8	8	—	—	—	—	6	—	—	6	—	6
South Carolina	18	—	18	—	—	—	—	18	—	—	18	—
South Dakota	8	8	—	—	6	—	1	7	—	1	8	—
Tennessee	24	—	24	—	—	24	—	—	24	—	24	—
Texas	30	—	30	—	—	30	—	—	30	—	30	—
Utah	6	—	6	—	—	6	—	—	6	—	6	—
Vermont	8	8	—	—	4	—	—	4	—	—	4	—
Virginia	24	—	24	—	—	—	—	—	24	—	24	—
Washington	8	3	5	—	1	7	—	2	6	—	4	—
West Virginia	12	—	12	—	—	—	—	1	10	—	2	—
Wisconsin	24	24	—	—	4	—	—	5	—	—	5	—
Wyoming	6	—	6	—	—	—	—	6	—	—	6	—
Alaska	6	6	—	—	—	6	—	—	6	—	6	—
District of Columbia	6	2	4	—	—	—	—	5	—	—	6	—
Total	930	303	626	1	137	235	97	280	241	97	652	95

1. Other candidates: Horace Boies, 67; Claude Matthews, 37; John R. McLean, 54; Joseph C. S. Blackburn, 82; Adlai E. Stevenson, 6; Henry M. Teller, 8; William E. Russell, 2; Benjamin R. Tillman, 17; James E. Campbell, 1; Sylvester Pennoyer, 8; David B. Hill, 1; not voting, 178.

2. Other candidates: Boies, 33; Mathews, 36; Blackburn, 27; McLean, 46; Stevenson, 8; Hill, 1; not voting, 161.

3. Other candidates: Richard P. Bland, 11; Stevenson, 8; Hill, 1; David Turpie, 1; not voting, 162.

a. Including Indian Territory, 6 votes.

1900 Republican

(Narrative, p. 81)

Delegation	Total Votes	First Pres. Ballot McKinley
Alabama	22	22
Arizona	6	6
Arkansas	16	16
California	18	18
Colorado	8	8
Connecticut	12	12
Delaware	6	6
Florida	8	8
Georgia	26	26
Idaho	6	6
Illinois	48	48
Indiana	30	30
Iowa	26	26
Kansas	20	20
Kentucky	26	26
Louisiana	16	16
Maine	12	12
Maryland	16	16
Massachusetts	30	30
Michigan	28	28
Minnesota	18	18
Mississippi	18	18
Missouri	34	34
Montana	6	6
Nebraska	16	16
Nevada	6	6
New Hampshire	8	8
New Jersey	20	20
New Mexico	6	6
New York	72	72
North Carolina	22	22
North Dakota	6	6
Ohio	46	46
Oklahoma[a]	12	12
Oregon	8	8
Pennsylvania	64	64
Rhode Island	8	8
South Carolina	18	18
South Dakota	8	8
Tennessee	24	24
Texas	30	30
Utah	6	6
Vermont	8	8
Virginia	24	24
Washington	8	8
West Virginia	12	12
Wisconsin	24	24
Wyoming	6	6
Alaska	4	4
District of Columbia	2	2
Hawaii	2	2
Total	926	926

a. Including Indian Territory, 6 votes.

1900 Democratic

(Narrative, p. 82)

Delegation	Total Votes	First Pres. Ballot Bryan
Alabama	22	22
Arizona	6	6
Arkansas	16	16
California	18	18
Colorado	8	8
Connecticut	12	12
Delaware	6	6
Florida	8	8
Georgia	26	26
Idaho	6	6
Illinois	48	48
Indiana	30	30
Iowa	26	26
Kansas	20	20
Kentucky	26	26
Louisiana	16	16
Maine	12	12
Maryland	16	16
Massachusetts	30	30
Michigan	28	28
Minnesota	18	18
Mississippi	18	18
Missouri	34	34
Montana	6	6
Nebraska	16	16
Nevada	6	6
New Hampshire	8	8
New Jersey	20	20
New Mexico	6	6
New York	72	72
North Carolina	22	22
North Dakota	6	6
Ohio	46	46
Oklahoma[a]	12	12
Oregon	8	8
Pennsylvania	64	64
Rhode Island	8	8
South Carolina	18	18
South Dakota	8	8
Tennessee	24	24
Texas	30	30
Utah	6	6
Vermont	8	8
Virginia	24	24
Washington	8	8
West Virginia	12	12
Wisconsin	24	24
Wyoming	6	6
Alaska	6	6
District of Columbia	6	6
Hawaii	6	6
Total	936	936

a. Including Indian Territory, 6 votes.

1904 Democratic

(Narrative, p. 84)

Delegation	Total Votes	First Pres. Ballot[1] (Before shift) Parker	First Pres. Ballot[1] (Before shift) Hearst	First Pres. Ballot[2] (After shift) Parker	First Pres. Ballot[2] (After shift) Hearst	Sending Telegram to Parker Yea	Sending Telegram to Parker Nay	Sending Telegram to Parker Not Voting
Alabama	22	22	—	22	—	22	—	—
Arizona	6	—	6	—	6	—	6	—
Arkansas	18	18	—	18	—	18	—	—
California	20	—	20	—	20	16	4	—
Colorado	10	4	5	4	5	4	6	—
Connecticut	14	14	—	14	—	14	—	—
Delaware	6	—	—	—	—	6	—	—
Florida	10	6	4	6	4	6	4	—
Georgia	26	26	—	26	—	26	—	—
Idaho	6	—	6	6	—	—	6	—
Illinois	54	—	54	—	54	54	—	—
Indiana	30	30	—	30	—	30	—	—
Iowa	26	—	26	—	26	—	26	—
Kansas	20	7	10	7	10	—	20	—
Kentucky	26	26	—	26	—	26	—	—
Louisiana	18	18	—	18	—	18	—	—
Maine	12	7	1	7	1	7	2	3
Maryland	16	16	—	16	—	16	—	—
Massachusetts	32	—	—	—	—	32	—	—
Michigan	28	28	—	28	—	28	—	—
Minnesota	22	9	9	9	9	9	13	—
Mississippi	20	20	—	20	—	20	—	—
Missouri	36	—	—	—	—	—	36	—
Montana	6	6	—	6	—	—	6	—
Nebraska	16	—	4	—	4	—	16	—
Nevada	6	—	6	2	4	2	4	—
New Hampshire	8	8	—	8	—	8	—	—
New Jersey	24	24	—	24	—	24	—	—
New Mexico	6	—	6	—	6	6	—	—
New York	78	78	—	78	—	78	—	—
North Carolina	24	24	—	24	—	24	—	—
North Dakota	8	—	—	—	—	—	8	—
Ohio	46	46	—	46	—	31	6	9
Oklahoma[a]	12	7	3	7	3	7	5	—
Oregon	8	4	2	4	2	4	4	—
Pennsylvania	68	68	—	68	—	68	—	—
Rhode Island	8	2	6	2	6	2	5	1
South Carolina	18	18	—	18	—	18	—	—
South Dakota	8	—	8	—	8	—	8	—
Tennessee	24	24	—	24	—	24	—	—
Texas	36	36	—	36	—	36	—	—
Utah	6	6	—	6	—	6	—	—
Vermont	8	8	—	8	—	8	—	—
Virginia	24	24	—	24	—	24	—	—
Washington	10	—	10	10	—	10	—	—
West Virginia	14	10	2	13	1	14	—	—
Wisconsin	26	—	—	—	—	26	—	—
Wyoming	6	—	6	—	6	2	2	2
Alaska	6	6	—	6	—	6	—	—
District of Columbia	6	6	—	6	—	6	—	—
Hawaii	6	—	6	—	6	2	4	—
Puerto Rico	6	2	—	2	—	6	—	—
Total	1000	658	200	679	181	794	191	15

1. Other candidates: George Gray, 12; Nelson A. Miles, 3; Francis M. Cockrell, 42; Richard Olney, 38; Edward C. Wall, 27; George B. McClellan, 3; Charles A. Towne, 2; Robert E. Pattison, 4; John S. Williams, 8; Bird S. Coler, 1; Arthur P. Gorman, 2.

2. Other candidates: Gray, 12; Miles, 3; Cockrell, 42; Olney, 38; Wall, 27; McClellan, 3; Towne, 2; Pattison, 4; Williams, 8; Coler, 1.

a. Including Indian Territory, 6 votes.

1904 Republican

(Narrative, p. 83)

Delegation	Total Votes	First Pres. Ballot Roosevelt
Alabama	22	22
Arizona	6	6
Arkansas	18	18
California	20	20
Colorado	10	10
Connecticut	14	14
Delaware	6	6
Florida	10	10
Georgia	26	26
Idaho	6	6
Illinois	54	54
Indiana	30	30
Iowa	26	26
Kansas	20	20
Kentucky	26	26
Louisiana	18	18
Maine	12	12
Maryland	16	16
Massachusetts	32	32
Michigan	28	28
Minnesota	22	22
Mississippi	20	20
Missouri	36	36
Montana	6	6
Nebraska	16	16
Nevada	6	6
New Hampshire	8	8
New Jersey	24	24
New Mexico	6	6
New York	78	78
North Carolina	24	24
North Dakota	8	8
Ohio	46	46
Oklahoma[a]	12	12
Oregon	8	8
Pennsylvania	68	68
Rhode Island	8	8
South Carolina	18	18
South Dakota	8	8
Tennessee	24	24
Texas	36	36
Utah	6	6
Vermont	8	8
Virginia	24	24
Washington	10	10
West Virginia	14	14
Wisconsin	26	26
Wyoming	6	6
Alaska	6	6
District of Columbia	2	2
Hawaii	6	6
Philippine Islands	2	2
Puerto Rico	2	2
Total	994	994

a. Including Indian Territory, 6 votes.

1908 Democratic

(Narrative, p. 86)

Delegation	Total Votes	First Pres. Ballot[1] Bryan
Alabama	22	22
Arizona	6	6
Arkansas	18	18
California	20	20
Colorado	10	10
Connecticut	14	9
Delaware	6	—
Florida	10	10
Georgia	26	4
Idaho	6	6
Illinois	54	54
Indiana	30	30
Iowa	26	26
Kansas	20	20
Kentucky	26	26
Louisiana	18	18
Maine	12	10
Maryland	16	7
Massachusetts	32	32
Michigan	28	28
Minnesota	22	—
Mississippi	20	20
Missouri	36	36
Montana	6	6
Nebraska	16	16
Nevada	6	6
New Hampshire	8	7
New Jersey	24	—
New Mexico	6	6
New York	78	78
North Carolina	24	24
North Dakota	8	8
Ohio	46	46
Oklahoma	14	14
Oregon	8	8
Pennsylvania	68	49½
Rhode Island	8	5
South Carolina	18	18
South Dakota	8	8
Tennessee	24	24
Texas	36	36
Utah	6	6
Vermont	8	7
Virginia	24	24
Washington	10	10
West Virginia	14	14
Wisconsin	26	26
Wyoming	6	6
Alaska	6	6
District of Columbia	6	6
Hawaii	6	6
Puerto Rico	6	6
Total	1002	888½

1. Other candidates: John A. Johnson, 46; George Gray, 59½; not voting, 8.

1908 Republican

(Narrative, p. 86)

Delegation	Total Votes	Minority Report on Changing Delegate Apportionment Formula			Minority Plank for Direct Election of Senators		First Pres. Ballot[1]
		Yea	Nay	Not Voting	Yea	Nay	Taft
Alabama	22	—	22	—	—	22	22
Arizona	2	—	2	—	—	2	2
Arkansas	18	—	18	—	—	18	18
California	20	—	20	—	—	20	20
Colorado	10	10	—	—	—	10	10
Connecticut	14	14	—	—	—	14	14
Delaware	6	—	6	—	—	6	6
Florida	10	—	10	—	—	10	10
Georgia	26	—	26	—	—	26	17
Idaho	6	—	6	—	3	3	6
Illinois	54	54	—	—	1	53	3
Indiana	30	30	—	—	11	19	—
Iowa	26	6	20	—	1	25	26
Kansas	20	—	20	—	—	20	20
Kentucky	26	1	25	—	2	24	24
Louisiana	18	—	18	—	—	18	18
Maine	12	12	—	—	—	12	12
Maryland	16	—	16	—	1	15	16
Massachusetts	32	32	—	—	—	32	32
Michigan	28	18	10	—	5	23	27
Minnesota	22	10	11	1	—	22	22
Mississippi	20	—	20	—	—	20	20
Missouri	36	12	24	—	4	32	36
Montana	6	—	6	—	—	6	6
Nebraska	16	7	9	—	16	—	16
Nevada	6	—	6	—	—	6	6
New Hampshire	8	8	—	—	—	8	5
New Jersey	24	23	1	—	—	24	15
New Mexico	2	—	—	2	—	2	2
New York	78	78	—	—	—	78	10
North Carolina	24	—	24	—	—	24	24
North Dakota	8	—	8	—	—	8	8
Ohio	46	8	38	—	2	44	42
Oklahoma	14	—	14	—	14	—	14
Oregon	8	3	5	—	—	8	8
Pennsylvania	68	68	—	—	13	55	1
Rhode Island	8	8	—	—	—	8	8
South Carolina	18	—	18	—	—	18	13
South Dakota	8	8	—	—	8	—	8
Tennessee	24	—	24	—	—	24	24
Texas	36	—	36	—	—	36	36
Utah	6	6	—	—	2	4	6
Vermont	8	8	—	—	—	8	8
Virginia	24	—	24	—	—	24	21
Washington	10	4	6	—	—	10	10
West Virginia	14	14	—	—	5	9	14
Wisconsin	26	26	—	—	25	1	1
Wyoming	6	—	6	—	—	6	6
Alaska	2	2	—	—	—	2	2
District of Columbia	2	1	1	—	—	2	1
Hawaii	2	—	2	—	1	1	2
Philippine Islands	2	—	2	—	—	2	2
Puerto Rico	2	—	2	—	—	2	2
Total	980	471	506	3	114	866	702

1. Other candidates: Philander C. Knox, 68; Charles E. Hughes, 67; Joseph G. Cannon, 58; Charles W. Fairbanks, 40; Robert M. La Follette, 25; Joseph B. Foraker, 16; Theodore Roosevelt, 3; not voting, 1.

1912 Republican

(Narrative, p. 88)

Delegation	Total Votes	Temporary Chairman[1]		Table Motion Prohibiting Challenged Taft Delegates from Voting			First Pres. Ballot[2]		
		Root	McGovern	Yea	Nay	Not Voting	Taft	Roosevelt	Present, Not Voting
Alabama	24	22	2	22	2	—	22	—	2
Arizona	6	6	—	6	—	—	6	—	—
Arkansas	18	17	1	17	1	—	17	—	1
California	26	2	24	2	24	—	2	—	24
Colorado	12	12	—	12	—	—	12	—	—
Connecticut	14	14	—	14	—	—	14	—	—
Delaware	6	6	—	6	—	—	6	—	—
Florida	12	12	—	12	—	—	12	—	—
Georgia	28	22	6	24	4	—	28	—	—
Idaho	8	—	8	—	8	—	1	—	—
Illinois	58	9	49	7	51	—	2	53	1
Indiana	30	20	10	20	9	1	20	3	7
Iowa	26	16	10	16	10	—	16	—	—
Kansas	20	2	18	2	18	—	2	—	18
Kentucky	26	23	3	24	2	—	24	2	—
Louisiana	20	20	—	20	—	—	20	—	—
Maine	12	—	12	—	12	—	—	—	12
Maryland	16	8	8	9	7	—	1	9	5
Massachusetts	36	18	18	18	18	—	15	—	21
Michigan	30	19	10	20	10	—	20	9	1
Minnesota	24	—	24	—	24	—	—	—	24
Mississippi	20	16	4	16	4	—	17	—	3
Missouri	36	16	20	16	20	—	16	—	20
Montana	8	8	—	8	—	—	8	—	—
Nebraska	16	—	16	—	16	—	—	2	14
Nevada	6	6	—	6	—	—	6	—	—
New Hampshire	8	8	—	8	—	—	8	—	—
New Jersey	28	—	28	—	28	—	—	2	26
New Mexico	8	6	2	7	1	—	7	1	—
New York	90	76	13	75	15	—	76	8	6
North Carolina	24	3	21	2	22	—	1	1	22
North Dakota	10	—	9	2	8	—	—	—	—
Ohio	48	14	34	14	34	—	14	—	34
Oklahoma	20	4	16	4	16	—	4	1	15
Oregon	10	3	6	5	5	—	—	8	2
Pennsylvania	76	12	64	12	64	—	9	2	62
Rhode Island	10	10	—	10	—	—	10	—	—
South Carolina	18	11	7	11	6	1	16	—	1
South Dakota	10	—	10	—	10	—	—	5	—
Tennessee	24	23	1	23	1	—	23	1	—
Texas	40	31	8	29	9	2	31	—	8
Utah	8	7	1	7	1	—	8	—	—
Vermont	8	6	2	6	2	—	6	—	2
Virginia	24	22	2	21	3	—	22	—	1
Washington	14	14	—	14	—	—	14	—	—
West Virginia	16	—	16	—	16	—	—	—	16
Wisconsin	26	—	12	—	26	—	—	—	—
Wyoming	6	6	—	6	—	—	6	—	—
Alaska	2	2	—	2	—	—	2	—	—
District of Columbia	2	2	—	2	—	—	2	—	—
Hawaii	6	—	6	6	—	—	6	—	—
Philippine Islands	2	2	—	2	—	—	2	—	—
Puerto Rico	2	2	—	2	—	—	2	—	—
Total	1078	558	501	567	507	4	556[a]	107	348[b]

1. Other candidates: W.S. Lauder, 12; Asle J. Gronna, 1; not voting, 6.
2. Other candidates: Robert M. La Follette, 41; Albert B. Cummins, 17; Charles E. Hughes, 2; absent and not voting, 7.
a. Sum of column; proceedings record 561.
b. Sum of column; proceedings record 349.

1912 Democratic

(Narrative, p. 89)

Delegation	Total Votes	Temporary Chairman[1] Bryan	Temporary Chairman[1] Parker	First Pres. Ballot[2] Clark	First Pres. Ballot[2] Wilson	First Pres. Ballot[2] Harmon	First Pres. Ballot[2] Underwood	Tenth Pres. Ballot[3] Clark	Tenth Pres. Ballot[3] Wilson	Tenth Pres. Ballot[3] Underwood	Thirtieth Pres. Ballot[4] Clark	Thirtieth Pres. Ballot[4] Wilson	Thirtieth Pres. Ballot[4] Underwood	43rd Pres. Ballot[5] Clark	43rd Pres. Ballot[5] Wilson	45th Pres. Ballot[6] Clark	45th Pres. Ballot[6] Wilson	46th Pres. Ballot[7] Wilson
Ala.	24	1½	22½	—	—	—	24	—	—	24	—	—	24	—	—	—	—	24
Ariz.	6	4	2	6	—	—	—	6	—	—	4	2	—	3	2	3	3	6
Ark.	18	—	18	18	—	—	—	18	—	—	18	—	—	18	—	18	—	18
Calif.	26	7	18	26	—	—	—	26	—	—	26	—	—	26	—	26	—	2
Colo.	12	6	6	12	—	—	—	12	—	—	12	—	—	11	1	2	10	12
Conn.	14	2	12	—	—	—	—	7	—	7	7	3	4	1	5	2	5	14
Del.	6	6	—	—	6	—	—	—	6	—	—	6	—	—	6	—	6	6
Fla.	12	1	11	—	—	—	12	—	—	12	—	—	12	—	2	—	3	7
Ga.	28	—	28	—	—	—	28	—	—	28	—	—	28	—	—	—	—	28
Idaho	8	8	—	8	—	—	—	8	—	—	2½	5½	—	1	7	1½	6½	8
Ill.	58	—	58	58	—	—	—	58	—	—	58	—	—	—	58	—	58	58
Ind.	30	8	21	—	—	—	—	—	—	—	1	28	—	1	28	—	30	30
Iowa	26	13	13	26	—	—	—	26	—	—	12	14	—	11½	14½	9	17	26
Kan.	20	20	—	20	—	—	—	20	—	—	—	20	—	—	20	—	20	20
Ky.	26	7½	17½	26	—	—	—	26	—	—	26	—	—	26	—	26	—	26
La.	20	10	10	11	9	—	—	10	10	—	7	12	—	6	14	5	15	18
Maine	12	1	11	1	9	—	2	1	11	—	1	9	2	1	11	1	11	12
Md.	16	1½	14½	16	—	—	—	16	—	—	11	4½	—	9	5½	8½	7	16
Mass.	36	18	15	36	—	—	—	33	1	2	—	7	—	—	9	—	9	36
Mich.	30	9	21	12	10	7	—	18	9	—	18	12	—	2	28	2	28	30
Minn.	24	24	—	—	24	—	—	—	24	—	—	24	—	—	24	—	24	24
Miss.	20	—	20	—	—	—	20	—	—	20	—	—	20	—	—	—	—	20
Mo.	36	14	22	36	—	—	—	36	—	—	36	—	—	36	—	36	—	—
Mont.	8	7	1	8	—	—	—	8	—	—	2	6	—	1	7	1	7	8
Neb.	16	13	3	12	—	4	—	13	3	—	3	13	—	3	13	3	13	16
Nev.	6	6	—	6	—	—	—	6	—	—	6	—	—	6	—	6	—	—
N.H.	8	5	3	8	—	—	—	5	3	—	3	5	—	3	5	3	5	8
N.J.	28	24	4	2	24	—	2	4	24	—	4	24	—	4	24	4	24	24
N.M.	8	8	—	8	—	—	—	8	—	—	8	—	—	8	—	8	—	8
N.Y.	90	—	90	—	—	90	—	90	—	—	90	—	—	90	—	90	—	90
N.C.	24	9	15	—	16½	½	7	—	18	6	—	17½	6½	—	22	—	22	24
N.D.	10	10	—	—	10	—	—	—	10	—	—	10	—	—	10	—	10	10
Ohio	48	19	29	1	10	35	—	6	11	—	—	19	10	—	20	—	23	23
Okla.	20	20	—	10	10	—	—	10	10	—	10	10	—	10	10	10	10	20
Ore.	10	9	1	—	10	—	—	—	10	—	—	10	—	—	10	—	10	10
Pa.	76	67	9	—	71	5	—	5	71	—	4	72	—	2	74	—	76	76
R.I.	10	—	10	10	—	—	—	10	—	—	10	—	—	10	—	10	—	10
S.C.	18	18	—	—	18	—	—	—	18	—	—	18	—	—	18	—	18	18
S.D.	10	10	—	—	10	—	—	—	10	—	—	10	—	—	10	—	10	10
Tenn.	24	7	17	6	6	6	6	13	7½	3½	13½	8	2½	10	8	8	10	24
Texas	40	40	—	—	40	—	—	—	40	—	—	40	—	—	40	—	40	40
Utah	8	4	4	1½	6	½	—	1½	6½	—	1½	6½	—	1½	6½	—	8	8
Vt.	8	—	8	—	—	—	—	—	8	—	—	8	—	—	8	—	8	8
Va.	24	10	14	—	9½	—	14½	—	9½	14	3	9½	11½	—	24	—	24	24
Wash.	14	14	—	14	—	—	—	14	—	—	14	—	—	14	—	14	—	14
W.Va.	16	4½	10½	16	—	—	—	16	—	—	16	—	—	—	16	—	16	16
Wis.	26	26	—	6	19	—	—	6	20	—	6	19	—	4	22	—	26	26
Wyo.	6	6	—	6	—	—	—	6	—	—	6	—	—	—	6	—	6	6
Alaska	6	2	4	4	—	—	—	3	3	—	6	—	—	1	5	—	6	6
D.C.	6	—	6	6	—	—	—	6	—	—	6	—	—	6	—	6	—	—
Hawaii	6	2	4	2	3	—	1	2	3	1	2	3	1	2	4	2	4	6
Phil. Is.	6	2	4	—	—	—	—	—	—	—	—	—	—	—	—	—	—	—
P.R.	6	4	2	2	3	—	1	2	4	—	1½	4½	—	1	4½	1	4½	6
Total	1094	508	579	440½	324	148	117½	556	350½	117½	455	460	121½	329	602	306	633	990

1. Other candidates: James A. O'Gorman, 4; John W. Kern, 1; not voting, 2.
2. Other candidates: Simeon E. Baldwin, 22; Thomas R. Marshall, 31; William J. Bryan, 1; William Sulzer, 2; not voting, 8.
3. Other candidates: Judson Harmon, 31; Marshall, 31; Kern, 1; Bryan, 1; not voting, 6.
4. Other candidates: Eugene N. Foss, 30; Harmon, 19; Kern, 2; not voting, ½.
5. Other candidates: Oscar W. Underwood, 98½; Harmon, 28; Foss, 27; Bryan, 1; Kern, 1; not voting, 7½.
6. Other candidates: Underwood, 97; Foss, 27; Harmon, 25; not voting, 6.
7. Other candidates: Champ Clark, 84; Harmon, 12; not voting, 8.

1916 Republican

(Narrative, p. 92)

Delegation	Total Votes	First Pres. Ballot[1]			Second Pres. Ballot[2]		Third Pres. Ballot[3]
		Hughes	Root	Weeks	Hughes	Root	Hughes
Alabama	16	8	—	3	9	—	16
Arizona	6	4	—	—	4	—	6
Arkansas	15	1	3	3	—	2	15
California	26	9	8	3	11	12	26
Colorado	12	—	5	—	—	5	12
Connecticut	14	5	5	1	5	7	14
Delaware	6	—	—	—	—	—	6
Florida	8	8	—	—	8	—	8
Georgia	17	5	—	6	6	—	17
Idaho	8	4	—	—	4	1	8
Illinois	58	—	—	—	—	—	58
Indiana	30	—	—	—	—	—	30
Iowa	26	—	—	—	—	—	26
Kansas	20	10	2	3	10	2	20
Kentucky	26	10	—	—	11	—	26
Louisiana	12	4	1	3	6	1	12
Maine	12	6	1	3	8	1	12
Maryland	16	7	1	5	7	1	15
Massachusetts	36	4	—	28	12	—	32
Michigan	30	—	—	—	28	—	30
Minnesota	24	—	—	—	—	—	24
Mississippi	12	4	—	1½	4	—	8½
Missouri	36	18	—	8	22	—	34
Montana	8	—	—	—	—	—	7
Nebraska	16	—	—	—	2	—	16
Nevada	6	4	2	—	4	2	6
New Hampshire	8	—	—	8	3	3	8
New Jersey	28	12	12	1	16	3	27
New Mexico	6	2	—	2	2	—	5
New York	87	42	43	—	43	42	87
North Carolina	21	6	2	3	6	2	14
North Dakota	10	—	—	—	—	—	10
Ohio	48	—	—	—	—	—	48
Oklahoma	20	5	1	6	5	1	19
Oregon	10	10	—	—	10	—	10
Pennsylvania	76	2	—	—	8	1	72
Rhode Island	10	10	—	—	10	—	10
South Carolina	11	2	1	3	4	—	6
South Dakota	10	—	—	—	—	—	10
Tennessee	21	9	—	3½	8	½	18
Texas	26	1	1	1	3	3	26
Utah	8	4	3	—	5	2	7
Vermont	8	8	—	—	8	—	8
Virginia	15	5½	3	3	8½	5	15
Washington	14	5	8	—	5	—	14
West Virginia	16	1	—	5	4	1	16
Wisconsin	26	11	—	—	11	—	23
Wyoming	6	6	—	—	6	—	6
Alaska	2	1	—	1	1	—	2
Hawaii	2	—	—	1	1	—	2
Philippine Islands	2	—	1	—	—	1	2
Total	987	253½	103	105	328½	98½	949½

1. Other candidates: Albert B. Cummins, 85; Theodore E. Burton, 77½; Charles W. Fairbanks, 74½; Lawrence Y. Sherman, 66; Theodore Roosevelt, 65; Philander C. Knox, 36; Henry Ford, 32; Martin G. Brumbaugh, 29; Robert M. La Follette, 25; William H. Taft, 14; Coleman du Pont, 12; Frank B. Willis, 4; William E. Borah, 2; Samuel W. McCall, 1; not voting, 2½.

2. Other candidates: Fairbanks, 88½; Cummins, 85; Roosevelt, 81; John W. Weeks, 79; Burton, 76½; Sherman, 65; Knox, 36; La Follette, 25; du Pont, 13; John Wanamaker, 5; Willis, 1; Leonard Wood, 1; Warren G. Harding, 1; McCall, 1; not voting, 2.

3. Other candidates: Roosevelt, 18½; La Follette, 3; du Pont, 5; Henry Cabot Lodge, 7; Weeks, 3; not voting, 1.

1916 Democratic

(Narrative, p. 93)

Delegation	Total Votes	Minority Plank on Women's Suffrage		
		Yea	Nay	Not Voting
Alabama	24	1	23	—
Arizona	6	—	6	—
Arkansas	18	—	18	—
California	26	—	26	—
Colorado	12	—	12	—
Connecticut	14	1	13	—
Delaware	6	—	6	—
Florida	12	4	8	—
Georgia	28	23½	4½	—
Idaho	8	—	8	—
Illinois	58	1	57	—
Indiana	30	24	6	—
Iowa	26	—	26	—
Kansas	20	—	20	—
Kentucky	26	—	26	—
Louisiana	20	8	12	—
Maine	12	—	6	6
Maryland	16	16	—	—
Massachusetts	36	6	30	—
Michigan	30	—	30	—
Minnesota	24	9	15	—
Mississippi	20	—	20	—
Missouri	36	4	24	8
Montana	8	—	8	—
Nebraska	16	—	16	—
Nevada	6	—	6	—
New Hampshire	8	1	7	—
New Jersey	28	10	11	7
New Mexico	6	—	6	—
New York	90	—	90	—
North Carolina	24	11	13	—
North Dakota	10	—	10	—
Ohio	48	20	28	—
Oklahoma	20	—	20	—
Oregon	10	—	10	—
Pennsylvania	76	—	76	—
Rhode Island	10	1	9	—
South Carolina	18	—	18	—
South Dakota	10	—	10	—
Tennessee	24	—	24	—
Texas	40	32	8	—
Utah	8	—	8	—
Vermont	8	—	8	—
Virginia	24	—	24	—
Washington	14	—	14	—
West Virginia	16	8	8	—
Wisconsin	26	—	26	—
Wyoming	6	—	6	—
Alaska	6	—	6	—
District of Columbia	6	—	6	—
Hawaii	6	—	6	—
Philippine Islands	6	1	4	1
Puerto Rico	6	—	6	—
Total	1092	181½	888½	22

1920 Republican

(Narrative, p. 95)

Delegation	Total Votes	First Pres. Ballot[1] Wood	Lowden	Johnson	Fourth Pres. Ballot[2] Wood	Lowden	Johnson	Eighth Pres. Ballot[3] Wood	Lowden	Harding	Ninth Pres. Ballot[4] Wood	Lowden	Harding	Tenth Pres. Ballot[5] (Before shift) Wood	Harding	Tenth Pres. Ballot[6] (After shift) Wood	Harding
Alabama	14	4	6	3	4	6	4	4	6	4	4	6	4	3	8	3	8
Arizona	6	6	—	—	6	—	—	6	—	—	6	—	—	6	—	—	6
Arkansas	13	6	6	—	2½	10½	—	1½	11½	—	1½	10½	1	—	13	—	13
California	26	—	—	26	—	—	26	—	—	—	—	—	—	—	—	—	—
Colorado	12	9	2	—	9	2	—	6	3	3	6	1	5	6	5	—	12
Connecticut	14	—	14	—	—	13	1	1	11	—	—	—	13	—	13	—	13
Delaware	6	—	—	—	—	2	—	—	—	3	—	—	3	—	6	—	6
Florida	8	4½	2½	—	6½	1½	—	7	1	—	1	—	7	½	7½	½	7½
Georgia	17	8	9	—	8	9	—	8	9	—	8	8	1	7	10	7	10
Idaho	8	5	—	1	5	1	1	4	2	1	5	1	1	3	2	3	2
Illinois	58	14	41	3	—	41	17	—	41	—	—	41	—	—	22.2	—	38.2
Indiana	30	22	—	8	18	3	6	15	4	11	15	4	11	8	20	9	21
Iowa	26	—	26	—	—	26	—	—	26	—	—	26	—	—	26	—	26
Kansas	20	14	6	—	14	6	—	10	6	4	—	—	20	1	18	1	18
Kentucky	26	—	20	1	—	26	—	—	26	—	—	26	—	—	26	—	26
Louisiana	12	3	3	1	3	6	—	3	7	2	—	—	12	—	12	—	12
Maine	12	11	—	—	11	—	—	12	—	—	12	—	—	12	—	12	—
Maryland	16	16	—	—	16	—	—	16	—	—	16	—	—	10	5	10	5
Massachusetts	35	7	—	—	16	—	—	11	—	—	11	1	1	17	17	17	17
Michigan	30	—	—	30	—	—	30	13	7	—	15	6	1	1	25	1	25
Minnesota	24	19	3	2	17	5	2	16	5	—	17	5	—	21	2	21	2
Mississippi	12	4½	2	2	7½	2½	—	8½	1½	2	7½	—	4½	2½	9½	—	12
Missouri	36	4½	18	3	8½	19	1	2½	15½	17	—	—	36	—	36	—	36
Montana	8	—	—	8	—	—	8	—	—	—	—	—	—	—	—	—	—
Nebraska	16	3	—	13	6	—	10	14	—	—	16	—	—	5	4	5	4
Nevada	6	2	1½	2	2½	2	1½	1½	—	3½	1½	—	3½	—	3½	—	3½
New Hampshire	8	8	—	—	8	—	—	8	—	—	8	—	—	8	—	8	—
New Jersey	28	17	—	11	17	—	11	16	—	2	15	—	4	15	5	15	5
New Mexico	6	6	—	—	6	—	—	6	—	—	6	—	—	6	—	—	6
New York	88	10	2	—	20	32	5	23	45	8	5	4	66	6	68	6	68
North Carolina	22	—	—	1	3	15	2	2	16	4	3	—	18	2	20	2	20
North Dakota	10	2	—	8	3	1	6	3	4	—	3	4	—	1	9	—	10
Ohio	48	9	—	—	9	—	—	9	—	39	9	—	39	—	48	—	48
Oklahoma	20	1½	18½	—	2	18	—	2	18	—	½	—	18	½	18	½	18
Oregon	10	1	—	9	5	—	5	4	—	1	4	—	1	3	2	3	2
Pennsylvania	76													14	60	14	60
Rhode Island	10	10	—	—	10	—	—	10	—	—	10	—	—	—	10	—	10
South Carolina	11	—	8	—	—	11	—	—	11	—	—	—	11	—	11	—	11
South Dakota	10	10	—	—	10	—	—	10	—	—	10	—	—	6	4	6	4
Tennessee	20	20	—	—	19	1	—	10	7	3	6	1	13	—	20	—	20
Texas	23	8½	5	1½	8	9½	1	5	8½	8½	1	1	19½	—	23	—	23
Utah	8	5	2	—	5	2	—	4	2	2	2	2	4	1	5	1	5
Vermont	8	8	—	—	8	—	—	8	—	—	8	—	—	8	—	8	—
Virginia	15	3	12	—	3	12	—	3	10	2	4	—	11	1	14	1	14
Washington	14	—	—	—	—	—	—	—	—	—	—	—	—	5	6	—	14
West Virginia	16	—	—	—	8	—	1	9	—	7	8	—	7	—	16	—	16
Wisconsin	26	1	—	—	1	—	2	1	—	—	1	—	—	—	1	—	1
Wyoming	6	—	3	—	3	3	—	—	—	6	—	—	6	—	6	—	6
Alaska	2	—	—	—	1	—	—	1	—	—	1	—	1	—	2	—	2
District of Columbia	2	2	—	—	2	—	—	2	—	—	—	—	2	—	2	—	2
Hawaii	2	—	—	—	—	2	—	—	2	—	—	—	2	—	2	—	2
Philippine Islands	2	2	—	—	2	—	—	2	—	—	2	—	—	2	—	2	—
Puerto Rico	2	1	1	—	1	1	—	1	1	—	—	—	2	—	2	—	2
Total	984	287½	211½	133½	314½	289	140½	299	307	133[a]	249	121½	374½	181½	644.7	156	692.2

1. Other candidates: Warren G. Harding, 65½; William C. Sproul, 84; Calvin Coolidge, 34; Herbert Hoover, 5½; Coleman du Pont, 7; Jeter C. Pritchard, 21; Robert M. La Follette, 24; Howard Sutherland, 17; William E. Borah, 2; Charles B. Warren, 1; Miles Poindexter, 20; Nicholas M. Butler, 69½; not voting, 1.

2. Other candidates: Harding, 61½; Sproul, 79½; Coolidge, 25; Hoover, 5; du Pont, 2; La Follette, 22; Sutherland, 3; Borah, 1; Poindexter, 15; Butler, 20; James E. Watson, 4; Knox, 2.

3. Other candidates: Hiram W. Johnson, 87; Coolidge, 30; du Pont, 3; Frank B. Kellogg, 1; La Follette, 24; Poindexter, 15; Irvine L. Lenroot, 1; Hoover, 5; Butler, 2; Knox, 1; Sproul, 76.

4. Other candidates: Johnson, 82; Sproul, 78; Coolidge, 28; Hoover, 6; Lenroot, 1; Butler, 2; Knox, 1; La Follette, 24; Poindexter, 14; Will H. Hays, 1; H. F. MacGregor, 1; not voting, 1.

5. Other candidates: Frank Lowden, 28; Johnson, 80⅘; Hoover, 10½; Coolidge, 5; Butler, 2; Lenroot, 1; Hays, 1; Knox, 1; La Follette, 24; Poindexter, 2; not voting, 2½.

6. Other candidates: Lowden, 11; Johnson, 80⅘; Hoover, 9½; Coolidge, 5; Butler, 2; Lenroot, 1; Hays, 1; Knox, 1; La Follette, 24; not voting, ½.

a. Sum of column; proceedings record 133½.

1920 Democratic

(Narrative, p. 96)

Delegation	Total Votes	First Pres. Ballot[1] McAdoo	Cox	Palmer	Smith	Thirtieth Pres. Ballot[2] McAdoo	Cox	Palmer	39th Pres. Ballot[3] McAdoo	Cox	44th Pres. Ballot[4] McAdoo	Cox
Alabama	24	9	3	6	2	12	7	—	8	—	8	13
Arizona	6	4	1	—	—	3	2	—	4	2	2½	3½
Arkansas	18	3	7	2	—	3	14	1	4	14	—	18
California	26	10	4	3	1	10	13	1	14	12	13	13
Colorado	12	3	—	8	—	5	6	—	4	7	3	9
Connecticut	14	—	—	—	—	1	6	4	3	10	2	12
Delaware	6	4	—	—	—	4	2	—	4	2	3	3
Florida	12	1	—	8	—	3	9	—	3	9	—	12
Georgia	28	—	—	28	—	—	—	28	28	—	—	28
Idaho	8	8	—	—	—	8	—	—	8	—	8	—
Illinois	58	9	9	35	5	21	36	1	18	38	13	44
Indiana	30	—	—	—	—	29	—	—	11	19	—	30
Iowa	26	—	—	—	—	—	26	—	—	26	—	26
Kansas	20	20	—	—	—	20	—	—	20	—	20	—
Kentucky	26	3	23	—	—	5	20	—	5	20	—	26
Louisiana	20	5	2	2	—	4	14	—	7	12	—	20
Maine	12	5	—	5	—	7	—	5	12	—	5	5
Maryland	16	5½	5½	—	—	5½	8½	—	5½	8½	—	13½
Massachusetts	36	4	4	17	7	2	15	16	1	33	—	35
Michigan	30	15	—	12	—	15	6	9	14	12	—	—
Minnesota	24	10	2	7	—	14	4	4	16	7	15	8
Mississippi	20	—	—	—	—	—	20	—	—	20	—	20
Missouri	36	15½	2½	10	—	18	6	5	20½	11½	17	18
Montana	8	1	—	—	—	8	—	—	8	—	2	6
Nebraska	16	—	—	—	—	7	—	—	7	—	2	5
Nevada	6	—	6	—	—	—	6	—	—	6	—	6
New Hampshire	8	4	—	1	—	5	2	1	5	2	6	2
New Jersey	28	—	—	—	—	—	28	—	—	28	—	28
New Mexico	6	2	—	1	—	6	—	—	6	—	6	—
New York	90	—	—	—	90	20	70	—	20	70	20	70
North Carolina	24	—	—	—	—	24	—	—	24	—	24	—
North Dakota	10	6	1	2	—	8	2	—	9	1	4	2
Ohio	48	—	48	—	—	—	48	—	—	48	—	48
Oklahoma	20	—	—	—	—	—	—	—	—	—	—	—
Oregon	10	10	—	—	—	10	—	—	10	—	10	—
Pennsylvania	76	2	—	73	—	2	1	73	2	1	4	68
Rhode Island	10	2	—	5	2	3	4	3	1	7	1	9
South Carolina	18	18	—	—	—	18	—	—	18	—	18	—
South Dakota	10	—	—	—	—	6	4	—	6	3	3	5
Tennessee	24	2	8	9	—	—	—	—	—	—	—	—
Texas	40	40	—	—	—	40	—	—	40	—	40	—
Utah	8	8	—	—	—	8	—	—	8	—	7	1
Vermont	8	4	2	1	1	1	6	1	4	4	—	8
Virginia	24	—	—	—	—	—	—	—	10	11	2½	18½
Washington	14	10	—	—	—	14	—	—	11	2½	—	13
West Virginia	16	—	—	—	—	—	—	—	—	—	—	—
Wisconsin	26	11	5	3	1	19	7	—	19	7	3	23
Wyoming	6	6	—	—	—	6	—	—	6	—	3	3
Alaska	6	2	1	3	—	2	1	3	4	2	—	6
Canal Zone	2	1	—	1	—	1	—	1	2	—	2	—
District of Columbia	6	—	—	6	—	—	—	6	—	6	—	6
Hawaii	6	2	—	4	—	1	5	—	1	5	—	6
Philippine Islands	6	—	—	—	—	3	2	1	3	2	2	4
Puerto Rico	6	1	—	2	—	2	—	2	6	—	1	5
Total	1094	266	134	254a	109	403½	400½	165	440	468½	270	699½

1. Other candidates: Homer S. Cummings, 25; James W. Gerard, 21; Robert L. Owen, 33; Gilbert M. Hitchcock, 18; Edwin T. Meredith, 27; Edward I. Edwards, 42; John W. Davis, 32; Carter Glass, 26½; Furnifold M. Simmons, 24; Francis B. Harrison, 6; John S. Williams, 20; Thomas R. Marshall, 37; Champ Clark, 9; Oscar W. Underwood, ½; William R. Hearst, 1; William J. Bryan, 1; Bainbridge Colby, 1; Josephus Daniels, 1; Wood, 4.
2. Other candidates: Cummings, 4; Owen, 33; Davis, 58; Glass, 24; Clark, 2; Underwood, 2; not voting, 2.
3. Other candidates: A. Mitchell Palmer, 74; Davis, 71½; Owen, 32; Cummings, 2; Clark, 2; Colby, 1; not voting, 3.
4. Other candidates: Palmer, 1; Davis, 52; Owen, 34; Glass, 1½; Colby, 1; not voting, 36.
a. Sum of column; proceedings record 256.

1924 Democratic

(Narrative, p. 98)

Delegation	Total Votes	Minority Report on League of Nations			Minority Report on Ku Klux Klan			First Pres. Ballot[1]		Fiftieth Pres. Ballot[2]		Ninetieth Pres. Ballot[3]		
		Yea	Nay	Not Voting	Yea	Nay	Not Voting	McAdoo	Smith	McAdoo	Smith	McAdoo	Smith	Ralston
Alabama	24	12½	11½	—	24	—	—	—	—	—	—	—	—	—
Arizona	6	1½	4½	—	1	5	—	4½	—	3½	—	3½	—	—
Arkansas	18	3	15	—	—	18	—	—	—	—	—	—	—	—
California	26	4	22	—	7	19	—	26	—	26	—	26	—	—
Colorado	12	9½	2½	—	6	6	—	—	—	4	3	1	3	½
Connecticut	14	5	9	—	13	1	—	—	6	4	10	2	12	—
Delaware	6	6	—	—	6	—	—	—	—	—	—	—	—	—
Florida	12	5	7	—	1	11	—	12	—	10	1	9	—	3
Georgia	28	—	28	—	1	19½	7½	28	—	28	—	28	—	—
Idaho	8	8	—	—	—	8	—	8	—	8	—	8	—	—
Illinois	58	10	48	—	45	13	—	12	15	13	20	12	36	6
Indiana	30	—	30	—	5	25	—	—	—	—	—	—	—	30
Iowa	26	—	26	—	13½	12½	—	26	—	26	—	—	—	—
Kansas	20	—	20	—	—	20	—	—	—	20	—	—	—	—
Kentucky	26	9½	16½	—	9½	16½	—	26	—	26	—	26	—	—
Louisiana	20	—	20	—	—	20	—	—	—	—	—	—	—	—
Maine	12	11	1	—	8	4	—	2	3½	2½	4½	1½	4½	—
Maryland	16	—	16	—	16	—	—	—	—	—	—	—	—	—
Massachusetts	36	8	28	—	35½	½	—	1½	33	2½	33½	2½	33½	—
Michigan	30	6	24	—	12½	16½	1	—	—	15	15	—	10	20
Minnesota	24	10	14	—	17	7	—	5	10	6	15	6	15	—
Mississippi	20	—	20	—	—	20	—	—	—	—	—	—	—	20
Missouri	36	2	34	—	10½	25½	—	36	—	36	—	—	—	36
Montana	8	—	8	—	1	7	—	7	1	7	—	7	1	—
Nebraska	16	—	16	—	3	13	—	1	—	13	3	1	—	—
Nevada	6	—	6	—	—	6	—	6	—	6	—	—	—	6
New Hampshire	8	8	—	—	2½	5½	—	—	—	4½	3½	3	3½	—
New Jersey	28	—	28	—	28	—	—	—	—	—	28	—	28	—
New Mexico	6	—	6	—	1	5	—	6	—	6	—	6	—	—
New York	90	35	55	—	90	—	—	—	90	2	88	2	88	—
North Carolina	24	6	18	—	3 17/20	20 3/20	—	24	—	17	—	3	—	—
North Dakota	10	1	9	—	10	—	—	10	—	5	5	5	5	—
Ohio	48	48	—	—	32½	15½	—	—	—	—	—	—	20½	17
Oklahoma	20	—	20	—	—	20	—	20	—	—	—	—	—	20
Oregon	10	1	9	—	—	10	—	10	—	10	—	10	—	—
Pennsylvania	76	52	22	2	49½	24½	2	25½	35½	25½	38½	25½	39½	—
Rhode Island	10	—	10	—	10	—	—	—	10	—	10	—	10	—
South Carolina	18	18	—	—	—	18	—	18	—	18	—	18	—	—
South Dakota	10	—	10	—	6	4	—	10	—	9	—	9	—	—
Tennessee	24	15	9	—	3	21	—	24	—	24	—	24	—	—
Texas	40	—	40	—	—	40	—	40	—	40	—	40	—	—
Utah	8	5½	2½	—	4	4	—	8	—	8	—	8	—	—
Vermont	8	2	6	—	8	—	—	1	7	1	7	—	8	—
Virginia	24	24	—	—	2½	21½	—	—	—	—	—	—	—	—
Washington	14	—	14	—	—	14	—	14	—	14	—	14	—	—
West Virginia	16	16	—	—	7	9	—	—	—	—	—	—	—	1
Wisconsin	26	4	22	—	25	1	—	3	23	3	23	1	23	—
Wyoming	6	3	3	—	2	4	—	—	—	1	4½	—	3	—
Alaska	6	—	5	—	6	—	—	1	3	1	3	—	5	—
Canal Zone	6	—	6	—	2	4	—	6	—	6	—	3	3	—
District of Columbia	6	—	6	—	6	—	—	6	—	6	—	6	—	—
Hawaii	6	—	6	—	4	2	—	1	1	1	1	1	—	—
Philippine Islands	6	2	4	—	2	2	2	3	3	3	3	2	2	—
Puerto Rico	6	1	5	—	2	4	—	—	—	—	—	—	1	—
Virgin Islands	—	—	—	—	—	—	—	—	—	—	—	—	—	—
Total	1098	353½	742½	2	542 7/20	543 3/20	12½	431½	241	461½	320½	314	354½	159½

1. Other candidates: Oscar W. Underwood, 42½; Joseph T. Robinson, 21; Willard Saulsbury, 7; Samuel M. Ralston, 30; Jonathan M. Davis, 20; Albert C. Ritchie, 22½; Woodbridge N. Ferris, 30; James M. Cox, 59; Charles W. Bryan, 18; Fred H. Brown, 17; George S. Silzer, 38; Carter Glass, 25; John W. Davis, 31; William E. Sweet, 12; Patrick Harrison, 43½; Houston Thompson, 1; John B. Kendrick, 6.

2. Other candidates: John W. Davis, 64; Ralston, 58; Underwood, 42½; Robinson, 44; Glass, 24; Cox, 54; Ritchie, 16½; Saulsbury, 6; Thomas J. Walsh, 1; Jonathan M. Davis, 2; Owen, 4.

3. Other candidates: Underwood, 42½; Robinson, 20; John W. Davis, 65½; Glass, 30½; Ritchie, 16½; Saulsbury, 6; Walsh, 5; Bryan, 15; Jonathan M. Davis, 22; Josephus Daniels, 19; Edwin T. Meredith, 26; not voting, 2.

1924 Democratic

(Narrative, p. 98)

Delegation	100th Pres. Ballot[4] McAdoo	Smith	Davis	101st Pres. Ballot[5] Underwood	Smith	Davis	Meredith	102nd Pres. Ballot[6] Underwood	Davis	Walsh	103rd Pres. Ballot[7] (Before shift) Underwood	Davis	103rd Pres. Ballot[8] (After shift) Underwood	Davis
Alabama	—	—	—	24	—	—	—	24	—	—	24	—	—	24
Arizona	3	—	—	3	—	—	—	3	—	—	3	—	3	—
Arkansas	—	—	—	—	—	—	—	—	—	—	—	—	—	—
California	16½	—	—	—	1	—	3	—	—	26	2	2	—	26
Colorado	½	3½	1½	1	3	2½	1	6½	1½	—	5	3	5	3
Connecticut	2	12	—	11	—	1	—	11	—	3	11	—	—	14
Delaware	—	—	—	—	—	6	—	—	—	—	6	—	6	—
Florida	9	—	3	—	—	3	—	—	5	4	—	6	—	6
Georgia	28	—	—	—	—	5	12	1	13	—	—	27	—	27
Idaho	—	—	—	—	—	—	—	—	—	8	—	8	—	8
Illinois	—	35	6	20	—	4	13	20	3	13	19	19	—	58
Indiana	—	—	14	3	—	10	6	10	10	—	5	25	5	25
Iowa	—	—	—	—	—	—	26	—	—	—	—	—	—	26
Kansas	—	—	20	—	—	20	—	—	20	—	—	20	—	20
Kentucky	12	—	8½	1	1	9	½	1	9	6½	1	22½	—	26
Louisiana	—	—	20	—	—	20	—	—	20	—	—	20	—	20
Maine	1	2	8	5	—	6	—	8	4	—	10	2	10	2
Maryland	—	—	—	—	—	16	—	—	16	—	—	16	—	16
Massachusetts	2½	33½	—	—	33	—	—	8	½	2	23½	2	23½	2
Michigan	—	10	15	10	—	12	1	14	16	—	—	29½	—	29½
Minnesota	6	15	1	—	15	1	—	14	2	1	16	3	16	3
Mississippi	—	—	—	—	—	20	—	—	20	—	—	20	—	20
Missouri	—	—	36	—	—	36	—	—	36	—	—	36	—	36
Montana	1	—	—	—	—	—	—	—	—	8	—	—	—	—
Nebraska	—	2	—	—	—	1	11	2	—	4	2	1	2	1
Nevada	—	6	—	—	—	—	—	—	—	6	—	6	—	6
New Hampshire	—	1	2	—	1	1	1½	—	3½	4½	—	3½	—	3½
New Jersey	—	28	—	16	—	—	—	16	2	—	16	1	16	1
New Mexico	6	—	—	—	1½	1	1	—	2½	—	—	2	—	2
New York	2	88	—	86½	—	—	—	84	1	1	44	4	—	60
North Carolina	—	—	—	1	—	20	1	—	23	—	5½	18½	—	24
North Dakota	3	5	—	—	5	—	1	5	—	5	—	—	—	—
Ohio	—	15	23	5	10	23	5	7	25	—	4	41	1	46
Oklahoma	—	—	—	—	—	—	—	—	20	—	—	20	—	20
Oregon	10	—	—	1	—	2	1	1	2	—	1	5	1	5
Pennsylvania	17½	39½	9	6	36½	19½	1	32½	29½	4	31½	37½	—	76
Rhode Island	—	10	—	10	—	—	—	10	—	—	—	10	—	10
South Carolina	18	—	—	—	—	18	—	—	18	—	—	18	—	18
South Dakota	—	—	—	—	—	—	—	2	—	—	2	—	2	—
Tennessee	6	—	8	1	—	15	—	—	19	—	—	19	—	19
Texas	40	—	—	—	—	—	40	—	40	—	—	40	—	40
Utah	—	—	4	—	—	—	—	—	4	4	—	8	—	8
Vermont	—	8	—	4	—	4	—	4	4	—	—	8	—	8
Virginia	—	—	—	—	—	12	—	—	12	—	—	12	—	24
Washington	—	—	—	—	—	—	—	—	—	14	—	14	—	14
West Virginia	—	—	16	—	—	16	—	—	16	—	—	16	—	16
Wisconsin	—	22	—	8	9	—	1	11	—	9	8	1	1	22
Wyoming	—	3	½	—	3	3	—	—	6	—	—	6	—	6
Alaska	—	6	—	6	—	—	—	6	—	—	2	4	2	4
Canal Zone	3	3	—	—	—	1	3	3	3	—	—	6	—	6
District of Columbia	—	—	—	—	—	—	—	6	—	—	6	—	6	—
Hawaii	1	1	3	1	1	4	—	1	4	—	1	4	1	4
Philippine Islands	2	2	—	5	—	—	1	5	—	—	1	4	1	4
Puerto Rico	—	1	5	1	—	5	—	1	5	—	1	5	1	5
Virgin Islands	—	—	—	—	—	—	—	—	—	—	—	—	—	—
Total	190	351½	203½	229½	121	316	130	317	415½	123	250½	575½	102½	844

4. Other candidates: Underwood, 41½; Robinson, 46; Bryan, 2; Saulsbury, 6; Walsh, 52½; Owen, 20; Ritchie, 17½; Meredith 75½; David F. Houston, 9; Glass, 35; Daniels, 24; Newton D. Baker, 4; George L. Berry, 1; James W. Gerard, 19; not voting, 9.

5. Other candidates: Robinson, 22½; William G. McAdoo, 52; Walsh, 98; Ritchie, ½; Berry, 1; A. A. Murphree, 4; Houston, 9; Owen, 23; Cummings, 9; Glass, 59; Gerard, 16; Baker, 1; Daniels, 24; Cordell Hull, 2; not voting, 3½.

6. Other candidates: Robinson, 21; McAdoo, 21; Alfred E. Smith, 44; Thompson, 1; Ritchie, ½; Bryan, 1; Gerard, 7; Glass, 67; Cordell Daniels, 2; Berry, 1½; Meredith, 66½; Henry T. Allen, 1; Hull, 1; not voting, 8.

7. Other candidates: McAdoo, 14½; Robinson, 21; Meredith, 42½; Glass, 79; Hull, 1; Smith, 10½; Daniels, 1; Gerard, 8; Thompson, 1; Walsh, 84½, not voting, 9.

8. Other candidates: Robinson, 20; McAdoo, 11½; Smith, 7½; Walsh, 58; Meredith, 15½; Glass, 23; Gerard, 7; Hull, 1; not voting, 8.

1924 Republican

(Narrative, p. 97)

Delegation	Total Votes	First Pres. Ballot[1] Coolidge
Alabama	16	16
Arizona	9	9
Arkansas	14	14
California	29	29
Colorado	15	15
Connecticut	17	17
Delaware	9	9
Florida	10	10
Georgia	18	18
Idaho	11	11
Illinois	61	61
Indiana	33	33
Iowa	29	29
Kansas	23	23
Kentucky	26	26
Louisiana	13	13
Maine	15	15
Maryland	19	19
Massachusetts	39	39
Michigan	33	33
Minnesota	27	27
Mississippi	12	12
Missouri	39	39
Montana	11	11
Nebraska	19	19
Nevada	9	9
New Hampshire	11	11
New Jersey	31	31
New Mexico	9	9
New York	91	91
North Carolina	22	22
North Dakota	13	7
Ohio	51	51
Oklahoma	23	23
Oregon	13	13
Pennsylvania	79	79
Rhode Island	13	13
South Carolina	11	11
South Dakota	13	3
Tennessee	27	27
Texas	23	23
Utah	11	11
Vermont	11	11
Virginia	17	17
Washington	17	17
West Virginia	19	19
Wisconsin	29	1
Wyoming	9	9
Alaska	2	2
District of Columbia	2	2
Hawaii	2	2
Philippine Islands	2	2
Puerto Rico	2	2
Total	1109	1065

1. Other candidates: Robert M. La Follette, 34; Hiram W. Johnson, 10.

1928 Republican

(Narrative, p. 100)

Delegation	Total Votes	First Pres. Ballot[1] Hoover
Alabama	15	15
Arizona	9	9
Arkansas	11	11
California	29	29
Colorado	15	15
Connecticut	17	17
Delaware	9	9
Florida	10	9
Georgia	16	15
Idaho	11	11
Illinois	61	24
Indiana	33	—
Iowa	29	7
Kansas	23	—
Kentucky	29	29
Louisiana	12	11
Maine	15	15
Maryland	19	19
Massachusetts	39	39
Michigan	33	33
Minnesota	27	11
Mississippi	12	12
Missouri	39	28
Montana	11	10
Nebraska	19	11
Nevada	9	9
New Hampshire	11	11
New Jersey	31	31
New Mexico	9	7
New York	90	90
North Carolina	20	17
North Dakota	13	4
Ohio	51	36
Oklahoma	20	—
Oregon	13	13
Pennsylvania	79	79
Rhode Island	13	12
South Carolina	11	11
South Dakota	13	2
Tennessee	19	19
Texas	26	26
Utah	11	9
Vermont	11	11
Virginia	15	15
Washington	17	17
West Virginia	19	1
Wisconsin	26	9
Wyoming	9	9
Alaska	2	2
District of Columbia	2	2
Hawaii	2	2
Philippine Islands	2	2
Puerto Rico	2	2
Total	1089	837

1. Other candidates: Frank O. Lowden, 74; Charles Curtis, 64; James E. Watson, 45; George W. Norris, 24; Guy D. Goff, 18; Calvin Coolidge, 17; Charles G. Dawes, 4; Charles E. Hughes, 1; not voting, 5.

1928 Democratic

(Narrative, p. 101)

Delegation	Total Votes	First Pres. Ballot[1] (Before shift) Smith	First Pres. Ballot[2] (After shift) Smith
Alabama	24	1	1
Arizona	6	6	6
Arkansas	17	17	17
California	26	26	26
Colorado	12	12	12
Connecticut	14	14	14
Delaware	6	6	6
Florida	12	—	—
Georgia	28	—	—
Idaho	8	8	8
Illinois	58	56	56
Indiana	30	—	25
Iowa	26	26	26
Kansas	20	—	11½
Kentucky	26	26	26
Louisiana	20	20	20
Maine	12	12	12
Maryland	16	16	16
Massachusetts	36	36	36
Michigan	30	30	30
Minnesota	24	24	24
Mississippi	20	—	9½
Missouri	36	—	—
Montana	8	8	8
Nebraska	16	—	12
Nevada	6	6	6
New Hampshire	8	8	8
New Jersey	28	28	28
New Mexico	6	6	6
New York	90	90	90
North Carolina	24	4⅔	4⅔
North Dakota	10	10	10
Ohio	48	1	45
Oklahoma	20	10	10
Oregon	10	10	10
Pennsylvania	76	70½	70½
Rhode Island	10	10	10
South Carolina	18	—	—
South Dakota	10	10	10
Tennessee	24	—	23
Texas	40	—	—
Utah	8	8	8
Vermont	8	8	8
Virginia	24	6	6
Washington	14	14	14
West Virginia	16	10½	10½
Wisconsin	26	26	26
Wyoming	6	6	6
Alaska	6	6	6
Canal Zone	6	6	6
District of Columbia	6	6	6
Hawaii	6	6	6
Philippine Islands	6	6	6
Puerto Rico	6	6	6
Virgin Islands	2	2	2
Total	1100	724⅔	849⅙

1. Other candidates: Cordell Hull, 71⅚; Walter F. George, 52½; James A. Reed, 48; Atlee Pomerene, 47; Jesse H. Jones, 43; Evans Woollen, 32; Patrick Harrison, 20; William A. Ayres, 20; Richard C. Watts, 18; Gilbert M. Hitchcock, 16; Vic Donahey, 5; Houston Thompson, 2.

2. Other candidates: George, 52½; Reed, 52; Hull, 50⅚; Jones, 43; Watts, 18; Harrison, 8½; Woollen, 7; Donahey, 5; Ayres, 3; Pomerene, 3; Hitchcock, 2; Thompson, 2; Theodore G. Bilbo, 1; not voting, 2½.

1932 Republican

(Narrative, p. 103)

Delegation	Total Votes	Repeal of Prohibition Plank		First Pres. Ballot[1]
		Yea	Nay	Hoover
Alabama	19	—	19	19
Arizona	9	9	—	9
Arkansas	15	—	15	15
California	47	6	41	47
Colorado	15	1	14	15
Connecticut	19	19	—	19
Delaware	9	—	9	9
Florida	16	—	16	16
Georgia	16	2	14	16
Idaho	11	—	11	11
Illinois	61	45	15½	54½
Indiana	31	28	3	31
Iowa	25	3	22	25
Kansas	21	4	17	21
Kentucky	25	15	10	25
Louisiana	12	—	12	12
Maine	13	5	8	13
Maryland	19	—	19	19
Massachusetts	34	16	17	34
Michigan	41	25½	15½	41
Minnesota	25	—	25	25
Mississippi	11	11	—	11
Missouri	33	8½	23¾	33
Montana	11	—	11	11
Nebraska	17	1	16	17
Nevada	9	8	1	9
New Hampshire	11	—	11	11
New Jersey	35	35	—	35
New Mexico	9	2	7	8
New York	97	76	21	97
North Carolina	28	3	25	28
North Dakota	11	—	11	9
Ohio	55	12²⁄₉	42²⁄₉	55
Oklahoma	25	—	25	25
Oregon	13	3	10	9
Pennsylvania	75	51	23	73
Rhode Island	8	8	—	8
South Carolina	10	—	10	10
South Dakota	11	3	8	11
Tennessee	24	1	23	24
Texas	49	—	49	49
Utah	11	1	10	11
Vermont	9	9	—	9
Virginia	25	—	25	25
Washington	19	11	8	19
West Virginia	19	4	15	19
Wisconsin	27	22	5	15
Wyoming	9	9	—	9
Alaska	2	—	2	2
District of Columbia	2	—	2	2
Hawaii	2	2	—	2
Philippine Islands	2	1	1	2
Puerto Rico	2	—	2	2
Total	1154	460²⁄₉	690¹⁹⁄₃₆	1126½

1. Other candidates: John J. Blaine, 13; Calvin Coolidge, 4½; Joseph I. France, 4; Charles G. Dawes, 1; James W. Wadsworth, 1; not voting, 4.

1932 Democratic

(Narrative, p. 104)

Delega-tion	Total Votes	Louisiana Credentials Yea	Nay	Not Voting	Minnesota Credentials Yea	Nay	Not Voting	Permanent Organization Yea	Nay	First Pres. Ballot[1] Roosevelt	Smith	Second Pres. Ballot[2] Roosevelt	Smith	Third Pres. Ballot[3] Roosevelt	Smith	Fourth Pres. Ballot[4] Roosevelt	Smith
Ala.	24	—	24	—	—	24	—	4½	19½	24	—	24	—	24	—	24	—
Ariz.	6	—	6	—	—	6	—	—	6	6	—	6	—	6	—	6	—
Ark.	18	—	18	—	—	18	—	—	18	18	—	18	—	18	—	18	—
Calif.	44	44	—	—	44	—	—	44	—	—	—	—	—	—	—	44	—
Colo.	12	—	12	—	—	12	—	—	12	12	—	12	—	12	—	12	—
Conn.	16	9½	6½	—	9¼	6¾	—	9½	6½	—	16	—	16	—	16	—	16
Del.	6	1	5	—	—	6	—	1	5	6	—	6	—	6	—	6	—
Fla.	14	3	11	—	—	14	—	—	14	14	—	14	—	14	—	14	—
Ga.	28	—	28	—	—	28	—	—	28	28	—	28	—	28	—	28	—
Idaho	8	—	8	—	—	8	—	—	8	8	—	8	—	8	—	8	—
Ill.	58	50¼	7¾	—	48	10	—	42	16	15¼	2¼	15¼	2¼	15¼	2¼	58	—
Ind.	30	30	—	—	30	—	—	30	—	14	2	16	2	16	2	30	—
Iowa	26	13	13	—	—	26	—	10	16	26	—	26	—	26	—	26	—
Kan.	20	—	20	—	—	20	—	6½	13½	20	—	20	—	20	—	20	—
Ky.	26	—	26	—	—	26	—	—	26	26	—	26	—	26	—	26	—
La.	20	—	20	—	—	20	—	—	20	20	—	20	—	20	—	20	—
Maine	12	6	6	—	6	6	—	7	5	12	—	12	—	12	—	12	—
Md.	16	16	—	—	16	—	—	16	—	—	—	—	—	—	—	16	—
Mass.	36	36	—	—	36	—	—	36	—	—	36	—	36	—	36	—	36
Mich.	38	—	38	—	—	38	—	—	38	38	—	38	—	38	—	38	—
Minn.	24	1	23	—	1	23	—	3	21	24	—	24	—	24	—	24	—
Miss.	20	—	20	—	—	20	—	—	20	20	—	20	—	20	—	20	—
Mo.	36	19½	19½	—	16½	19½	—	16½	10½	12	—	18	—	20½	—	36	—
Mont.	8	—	8	—	—	8	—	—	8	8	—	8	—	8	—	8	—
Neb.	16	—	16	—	—	16	—	1	15	16	—	16	—	16	—	16	—
Nev.	6	—	6	—	—	6	—	—	6	6	—	6	—	6	—	6	—
N.H.	8	—	8	—	—	8	—	—	8	8	—	8	—	8	—	8	—
N.J.	32	32	—	—	32	—	—	32	—	—	32	—	32	—	32	—	32
N.M.	6	—	6	—	—	6	—	3	3	6	—	6	—	6	—	6	—
N.Y.	94	65	29	—	65	29	—	67	27	28½	65½	29½	64½	31	63	31	63
N.C.	26	20½	5½	—	—	26	—	4	22	26	—	26	—	25⁴⁄₁₀₀	—	26	—
N.D.	10	—	10	—	2½	7½	—	1	9	9	—	10	—	9	—	10	—
Ohio	52	40	11	1	48½	2½	1	49½	2½	—	—	½	—	2½	—	29	17
Okla.	22	22	—	—	22	—	—	22	—	—	—	—	—	—	—	22	—
Ore.	10	—	10	—	—	10	—	1	9	10	—	10	—	10	—	10	—
Pa.	76	20½	55½	—	25	49	2	27½	48½	44½	30	44½	23½	45½	21	49	14½
R.I.	10	10	—	—	10	—	—	10	—	—	10	—	10	—	10	—	10
S.C.	18	—	18	—	—	18	—	—	18	18	—	18	—	18	—	18	—
S.D.	10	—	10	—	—	10	—	—	10	10	—	10	—	10	—	10	—
Tenn.	24	—	24	—	—	24	—	—	24	24	—	24	—	24	—	24	—
Texas	46	46	—	—	46	—	—	46	—	—	—	—	—	—	—	46	—
Utah	8	—	8	—	—	8	—	—	8	8	—	8	—	8	—	8	—
Vt.	8	—	8	—	—	8	—	—	8	8	—	8	—	8	—	8	—
Va.	24	24	—	—	24	—	—	24	—	—	—	—	—	—	—	24	—
Wash.	16	—	16	—	—	16	—	—	16	16	—	16	—	16	—	16	—
W.Va.	16	—	16	—	3	13	—	—	16	16	—	16	—	16	—	16	—
Wis.	26	2	24	—	2	24	—	2	24	24	2	24	2	24	2	24	2
Wyo.	6	—	6	—	—	6	—	—	6	6	—	6	—	6	—	6	—
Alaska	6	—	6	—	—	6	—	6	—	5	—	6	—	6	—	6	—
Canal Z.	6	—	6	—	—	6	—	—	6	6	—	6	—	6	—	6	—
D.C.	6	—	6	—	—	6	—	—	6	6	—	6	—	6	—	6	—
Hawaii	6	—	6	—	—	6	—	—	6	6	—	6	—	6	—	6	—
Phil. Is.	6	6	—	—	6	—	—	6	—	—	6	—	6	—	6	—	6
P.R.	6	—	6	—	—	6	—	—	6	6	—	6	—	6	—	6	—
Vir. Is.	2	—	2	—	—	2	—	—	2	2	—	2	—	2	—	2	—
Total	1154	514¼	638¾	1	492¾	658¼	3	528	626	666¼	201¾	677¾	194¼	682⁷⁹⁄₁₀₀	190¼	945	190½

1. Other candidates: John N. Garner, 90¼; Harry F. Byrd, 25; Melvin A. Traylor, 42¼; Albert C. Ritchie, 21; James A. Reed, 24; George White, 52; William H. Murray, 23; Newton D. Baker, 8½.

2. Other candidates: Garner, 90¼; Byrd, 24; Traylor, 40¼; Ritchie, 23½; Reed, 18; White, 50½; Baker, 8; Will Rogers, 22; not voting, 5½.

3. Other candidates: Garner, 101¼; Byrd, 24⁹⁶⁄₁₀₀; Traylor, 40¼; Richie, 23½; Reed, 27½; White, 52½; Baker, 8½; not voting, 2½.

4. Other candidates: Ritchie, 3½; White, 3; Baker, 5½; James M. Cox, 1; not voting, 5½.

1936 Republican

(Narrative, p. 106)

Delegation	Total Votes	First Pres. Ballot[1] Landon
Alabama	13	13
Arizona	6	6
Arkansas	11	11
California	44	44
Colorado	12	12
Connecticut	19	19
Delaware	9	9
Florida	12	12
Georgia	14	14
Idaho	8	8
Illinois	57	57
Indiana	28	28
Iowa	22	22
Kansas	18	18
Kentucky	22	22
Louisiana	12	12
Maine	13	13
Maryland	16	16
Massachusetts	33	33
Michigan	38	38
Minnesota	22	22
Mississippi	11	11
Missouri	30	30
Montana	8	8
Nebraska	14	14
Nevada	6	6
New Hampshire	11	11
New Jersey	32	32
New Mexico	6	6
New York	90	90
North Carolina	23	23
North Dakota	8	8
Ohio	52	52
Oklahoma	21	21
Oregon	10	10
Pennsylvania	75	75
Rhode Island	8	8
South Carolina	10	10
South Dakota	8	8
Tennessee	17	17
Texas	25	25
Utah	8	8
Vermont	9	9
Virginia	17	17
Washington	16	16
West Virginia	16	15
Wisconsin	24	6
Wyoming	6	6
Alaska	3	3
District of Columbia	3	3
Hawaii	3	3
Philippine Islands	2	2
Puerto Rico	2	2
Total	1003	984

1. Other candidates: William E. Borah, 19.

1940 Democratic

(Narrative, p. 109)

Delegation	Total Votes	First Pres. Ballot[1] Roosevelt
Alabama	22	20
Arizona	6	6
Arkansas	18	18
California	44	43
Colorado	12	12
Connecticut	16	16
Delaware	6	6
Florida	14	12½
Georgia	24	24
Idaho	8	8
Illinois	58	58
Indiana	28	28
Iowa	22	22
Kansas	18	18
Kentucky	22	22
Louisiana	20	20
Maine	10	10
Maryland	16	7½
Massachusetts	34	21½
Michigan	38	38
Minnesota	22	22
Mississippi	18	18
Missouri	30	26½
Montana	8	8
Nebraska	14	13
Nevada	6	2
New Hampshire	8	8
New Jersey	32	32
New Mexico	6	6
New York	94	64½
North Carolina	26	26
North Dakota	8	8
Ohio	52	52
Oklahoma	22	22
Oregon	10	10
Pennsylvania	72	72
Rhode Island	8	8
South Carolina	16	16
South Dakota	8	3
Tennessee	22	22
Texas	46	—
Utah	8	8
Vermont	6	6
Virginia	22	5¹⁴⁄₁₅
Washington	16	15
West Virginia	16	12
Wisconsin	24	21
Wyoming	6	6
Alaska	6	—
Canal Zone	6	—
District of Columbia	6	6
Hawaii	6	6
Philippine Islands	6	6
Puerto Rico	6	3
Virgin Islands	2	2
Total	1100	946¹³⁄₃₀

1. Other candidates: James A. Farley, 72⁹⁄₁₀; John N. Garner; 61; Millard E. Tydings, 9½; Cordell Hull, 5⅔; not voting, 4½.

1940 Republican

(Narrative, p. 108)

Delegation	Total Votes	First Pres. Ballot[1] Dewey	Taft	Willkie	Fourth Pres. Ballot[2] Dewey	Taft	Willkie	Fifth Pres. Ballot[3] Taft	Willkie	Sixth (before shift)[4] Taft	Willkie	Sixth (after shift)[5] Willkie
Alabama	13	7	6	—	7	5	1	7	5	7	6	13
Arizona	6	—	—	—	—	—	6	—	6	—	6	6
Arkansas	12	2	7	2	3	7	2	10	2	10	2	12
California	44	7	7	7	9	11	10	12	9	22	17	44
Colorado	12	1	4	3	1	4	3	4	4	6	5	12
Connecticut	16	—	—	16	—	—	16	—	16	—	16	16
Delaware	6	—	1	3	—	—	6	—	6	—	6	6
Florida	12	6	1	—	9	2	—	3	7	2	10	12
Georgia	14	7	3	—	6	3	2	7	6	7	6	14
Idaho	8	8	—	—	8	—	—	7	—	6	2	8
Illinois	58	52	2	4	17	27	10	30	17	33	24	58
Indiana	28	7	7	9	5	6	15	7	20	5	23	28
Iowa	22	—	—	—	2	—	—	13	7	15	7	22
Kansas	18	—	—	—	11	2	5	—	18	—	18	18
Kentucky	22	12	8	—	9	13	—	22	—	22	—	22
Louisiana	12	5	5	—	6	6	—	12	—	12	—	12
Maine	13	—	—	—	2	2	9	—	13	—	13	13
Maryland	16	16	—	—	—	—	14	1	14	1	15	16
Massachusetts	34	—	—	1	—	2	28	2	28	2	30	34
Michigan	38	—	—	—	2	—	—	—	—	2	35	38
Minnesota	22	3	4	6	2	9	9	12	9	11	10	22
Mississippi	11	3	8	—	2	9	—	11	—	9	2	11
Missouri	30	10	3	6	4	3	18	7	21	4	26	30
Montana	8	8	—	—	3	3	2	4	4	4	4	8
Nebraska	14	14	—	—	2	5	5	9	5	6	8	14
Nevada	6	—	2	2	—	1	4	2	4	2	4	6
New Hampshire	8	—	—	—	—	—	4	2	6	2	6	8
New Jersey	32	20	—	12	6	1	23	1	26	—	32	32
New Mexico	6	3	1	2	1	1	4	2	4	1	5	6
New York	92	61	—	8	48	5	35	10	75	7	78	92
North Carolina	23	9	7	2	6	6	9	11	12	8	15	23
North Dakota	8	2	1	1	2	1	3	4	4	4	4	8
Ohio	52	—	52	—	—	52	—	52	—	52	—	52
Oklahoma	22	22	—	—	10	6	3	18	4	5	17	22
Oregon	10	—	—	—	1	—	1	—	1	3	7	10
Pennsylvania	72	1	—	1	—	—	19	—	21	—	72	72
Rhode Island	8	1	3	3	—	4	4	4	4	3	5	8
South Carolina	10	10	—	—	8	—	2	—	9	—	10	10
South Dakota	8	—	—	—	4	1	—	7	1	2	6	8
Tennessee	18	8	3	2	5	6	5	9	6	5	10	17
Texas	26	—	26	—	—	26	—	26	—	26	—	26
Utah	8	2	2	1	2	2	1	3	5	1	7	8
Vermont	9	1	3	3	1	3	5	3	6	2	7	9
Virginia	18	2	9	5	—	7	11	7	11	2	16	18
Washington	16	13	3	—	12	3	—	16	—	4	10	16
West Virginia	16	8	5	3	6	3	7	9	6	—	15	15
Wisconsin	24	24	—	—	24	—	—	—	—	2	20	24
Wyoming	6	1	1	2	3	2	1	3	3	—	6	6
Alaska	3	1	2	—	—	2	1	3	—	1	2	3
District of Columbia	3	2	1	—	—	1	2	1	2	—	3	3
Hawaii	3	—	—	—	—	—	—	1	1	—	3	3
Philippine Islands	2	—	1	1	—	1	1	1	1	—	2	2
Puerto Rico	2	1	1	—	1	1	—	2	—	—	2	2
Total	1000	360	189	105	250	254	306	377	429	318	655	998

1. Other candidate: Arthur H. Vandenberg, 76; Arthur H. James, 74; Joseph W. Martin, 44; Hanford MacNider, 34; Frank E. Gannett, 33; H. Styles Bridges, 28; Arthur Capper, 18; Herbert Hoover, 17; Charles L. McNary, 13; Harlan J. Bushfield, 9.

2. Other candidates: Vandenberg, 61; James, 56; Hoover, 31; MacNider, 26; McNary, 8; Gannett, 4; Bridges, 1; not voting, 3.

3. Other candidates: James, 59; Thomas E. Dewey, 57; Vandenberg, 42; Hoover, 20; McNary, 9; MacNider, 4; Gannett, 1; not voting, 2.

4. Other candidates: Dewey, 11; Hoover, 10; Gannett, 1; McNary, 1; not voting, 4.

5. Not voting, 2.

1944 Republican

(Narrative, p. 110)

Delegation	Total Votes	First Pres. Ballot[1] Dewey
Alabama	14	14
Arizona	8	8
Arkansas	12	12
California	50	50
Colorado	15	15
Connecticut	16	16
Delaware	9	9
Florida	15	15
Georgia	14	14
Idaho	11	11
Illinois	59	59
Indiana	29	29
Iowa	23	23
Kansas	19	19
Kentucky	22	22
Louisiana	13	13
Maine	13	13
Maryland	16	16
Massachusetts	35	35
Michigan	41	41
Minnesota	25	25
Mississippi	6	6
Missouri	30	30
Montana	8	8
Nebraska	15	15
Nevada	6	6
New Hampshire	11	11
New Jersey	35	35
New Mexico	8	8
New York	93	93
North Carolina	25	25
North Dakota	11	11
Ohio	50	50
Oklahoma	23	23
Oregon	15	15
Pennsylvania	70	70
Rhode Island	8	8
South Carolina	4	4
South Dakota	11	11
Tennessee	19	19
Texas	33	33
Utah	8	8
Vermont	9	9
Virginia	19	19
Washington	16	16
West Virginia	19	19
Wisconsin	24	23
Wyoming	9	9
Alaska	3	3
District of Columbia	3	3
Hawaii	5	5
Philippine Islands	2	—
Puerto Rico	2	2
Total	**1059**	**1056**

1. Other candidates: Douglas MacArthur, 1; absent, 2.

1944 Democratic

(Narrative, p. 111)

Delegation	Total Votes	First Pres. Ballot[1] Roosevelt
Alabama	24	22
Arizona	10	10
Arkansas	20	20
California	52	52
Colorado	12	12
Connecticut	18	18
Delaware	8	8
Florida	18	14
Georgia	26	26
Idaho	10	10
Illinois	58	58
Indiana	26	26
Iowa	20	20
Kansas	16	16
Kentucky	24	24
Louisiana	22	—
Maine	10	10
Maryland	18	18
Massachusetts	34	34
Michigan	38	38
Minnesota	24	24
Mississippi	20	—
Missouri	32	32
Montana	10	10
Nebraska	12	12
Nevada	8	8
New Hampshire	10	10
New Jersey	34	34
New Mexico	10	10
New York	96	94½
North Carolina	30	30
North Dakota	8	8
Ohio	52	52
Oklahoma	22	22
Oregon	14	14
Pennsylvania	72	72
Rhode Island	10	10
South Carolina	18	14½
South Dakota	8	8
Tennessee	26	26
Texas	48	36
Utah	10	10
Vermont	6	6
Virginia	24	—
Washington	18	18
West Virginia	18	17
Wisconsin	26	26
Wyoming	8	8
Alaska	6	6
Canal Zone	6	6
District of Columbia	6	6
Hawaii	6	6
Philippine Islands	6	6
Puerto Rico	6	6
Virgin Islands	2	2
Total	**1176**	**1086**

1. Other candidates: Harry F. Byrd, 89; James A. Farley, 1.

1948 Republican

(Narrative, p. 113)

Delegation	Total Votes	First Pres. Ballot[1]			Second Pres. Ballot[2]			Third Pres. Ballot
		Dewey	Stassen	Taft	Dewey	Stassen	Taft	Dewey
Alabama	14	9	—	5	9	—	5	14
Arizona	8	3	2	3	4	2	2	8
Arkansas	14	3	4	7	3	4	7	14
California	53	—	—	—	—	—	—	53
Colorado	15	3	5	7	3	8	4	15
Connecticut	19	—	—	—	—	—	—	19
Delaware	9	5	1	2	6	1	2	9
Florida	16	6	4	6	6	4	6	16
Georgia	16	12	1	—	13	1	—	16
Idaho	11	11	—	—	11	—	—	11
Illinois	56	—	—	—	5	—	50	56
Indiana	29	29	—	—	29	—	—	29
Iowa	23	3	13	5	13	7	2	23
Kansas	19	12	1	2	14	1	2	19
Kentucky	25	10	1	11	11	1	11	25
Louisiana	13	6	—	7	6	—	7	13
Maine	13	5	4	1	5	7	—	13
Maryland	16	8	3	5	13	—	3	16
Massachusetts	35	17	1	2	18	1	3	35
Michigan	41	—	—	—	—	—	—	41
Minnesota	25	—	25	—	—	25	—	25
Mississippi	8	—	—	8	—	—	8	8
Missouri	33	17	6	8	18	6	7	33
Montana	11	5	3	3	6	2	3	11
Nebraska	15	2	13	—	6	9	—	15
Nevada	9	6	1	2	6	1	2	9
New Hampshire	8	6	2	—	6	2	—	8
New Jersey	35	—	—	—	24	6	2	35
New Mexico	8	3	2	3	3	2	3	8
New York	97	96	—	1	96	—	1	97
North Carolina	26	16	2	5	17	2	4	26
North Dakota	11	—	11	—	—	11	—	11
Ohio	53	—	9	44	1	8	44	53
Oklahoma	20	18	—	1	19	—	1	20
Oregon	12	12	—	—	12	—	—	12
Pennsylvania	73	41	1	28	40	1	29	73
Rhode Island	8	1	—	1	4	—	2	8
South Carolina	6	—	—	6	—	—	6	6
South Dakota	11	3	8	—	7	4	—	11
Tennessee	22	6	—	—	8	—	13	22
Texas	33	2	1	30	2	2	29	33
Utah	11	5	2	4	6	2	3	11
Vermont	9	7	2	—	7	2	—	9
Virginia	21	10	—	10	13	—	7	21
Washington	19	14	2	1	14	2	3	19
West Virginia	16	11	5	—	13	3	—	16
Wisconsin	27	—	19	—	2	19	—	27
Wyoming	9	4	3	2	6	3	—	9
Alaska	3	2	—	1	3	—	—	3
District of Columbia	3	2	—	—	3	—	—	3
Hawaii	5	3	—	1	3	—	2	5
Puerto Rico	2	—	—	2	1	—	1	2
Total	1094	434	157	224	515	149	274	1094

1. Other candidates: Arthur H. Vandenberg, 62; Earl Warren, 59; Dwight H. Green, 56; Alfred E. Driscoll, 35; Raymond E. Baldwin, 19; Joseph W. Martin, 18; B. Carroll Reece, 15; Douglas MacArthur, 11; Everett M. Dirksen, 1; not voting, 3.
2. Other candidates: Vandenberg, 62; Warren, 57; Baldwin, 19; Martin, 10; MacArthur, 7; Reece, 1.

1948 Democratic

(Narrative, p. 114)

Delegation	Total Votes	Pro-Southern Amendment to Civil Rights Plank		Plank Endorsing Truman's Civil Rights Policy		First Pres. Ballot[1] (Before shift)		First Pres. Ballot[2] (After shift)	
		Yea	Nay	Yea	Nay	Truman	Russell	Truman	Russell
Alabama	26	26	—	—	26	—	26	—	26
Arizona	12	—	12	—	12	12	—	12	—
Arkansas	22	22	—	—	22	—	22	—	22
California	54	1½	52½	53	1	53½	—	54	—
Colorado	12	3	9	10	2	12	—	12	—
Connecticut	20	—	20	20	—	20	—	20	—
Delaware	10	—	10	—	10	10	—	10	—
Florida	20	20	—	—	20	—	19	—	20
Georgia	28	28	—	—	28	—	28	—	28
Idaho	12	—	12	—	12	12	—	12	—
Illinois	60	—	60	60	—	60	—	60	—
Indiana	26	—	26	17	9	25	—	26	—
Iowa	20	—	20	18	2	20	—	20	—
Kansas	16	—	16	16	—	16	—	16	—
Kentucky	26	—	26	—	26	26	—	26	—
Louisiana	24	24	—	—	24	—	24	—	24
Maine	10	—	10	3	7	10	—	10	—
Maryland	20	—	20	—	20	20	—	20	—
Massachusetts	36	—	36	36	—	36	—	36	—
Michigan	42	—	42	42	—	42	—	42	—
Minnesota	26	—	26	26	—	26	—	26	—
Mississippi	22	22	—	—	22	—	—	—	—
Missouri	34	—	34	—	34	34	—	34	—
Montana	12	—	12	1½	10½	12	—	12	—
Nebraska	12	—	12	3	9	12	—	12	—
Nevada	10	—	10	—	10	10	—	10	—
New Hampshire	12	—	12	1	11	11	—	11	—
New Jersey	36	—	36	36	—	36	—	36	—
New Mexico	12	—	12	—	12	12	—	12	—
New York	98	—	98	98	—	83	—	98	—
North Carolina	32	32	—	—	32	13	19	13	19
North Dakota	8	—	8	—	8	8	—	8	—
Ohio	50	—	50	39	11	50	—	50	—
Oklahoma	24	—	24	—	24	24	—	24	—
Oregon	16	3	13	7	9	16	—	16	—
Pennsylvania	74	—	74	74	—	74	—	74	—
Rhode Island	12	—	12	—	12	12	—	12	—
South Carolina	20	20	—	—	20	—	20	—	20
South Dakota	8	—	8	8	—	8	—	8	—
Tennessee	28	28	—	—	28	—	28	—	28
Texas	50	50	—	—	50	—	50	—	50
Utah	12	—	12	—	12	12	—	12	—
Vermont	6	—	6	6	—	5½	—	5½	—
Virginia	26	26	—	—	26	—	26	—	26
Washington	20	—	20	20	—	20	—	20	—
West Virginia	20	—	20	7	13	15	4	20	—
Wisconsin	24	—	24	24	—	24	—	24	—
Wyoming	6	1½	4½	4	2	6	—	6	—
Alaska	6	3	3	2	4	6	—	6	—
Canal Zone	2	—	2	—	2	2	—	2	—
District of Columbia	6	—	6	6	—	6	—	6	—
Hawaii	6	—	6	6	—	6	—	6	—
Puerto Rico	6	—	6	6	—	6	—	6	—
Virgin Islands	2	—	2	2	—	2	—	2	—
Total	1234	310[a]	924[b]	651½	582½	926	266	947½	263

1. Other candidates: Paul V. McNutt, 2½; James A. Roe, 15; Alben W. Barkley, 1; not voting, 23½.
2. Other candidates: McNutt, ½; not voting, 23.
a. Sum of column; proceedings record 309.
b. Sum of column; proceedings record 925.

1952 Republican

(Narrative, p. 117)

Delegation	Total Votes	Pro-Taft Amendment on Louisiana Delegates		Pro-Eisenhower Report on Georgia Delegates		First Pres. Ballot[1] (Before shift)		First Pres. Ballot[2] (After shift)	
		Yea	Nay	Yea	Nay	Eisenhower	Taft	Eisenhower	Taft
Alabama	14	9	5	5	9	5	9	14	—
Arizona	14	12	2	3	11	4	10	4	10
Arkansas	11	11	—	3	8	4	6	11	—
California	70	—	70	62	8	—	—	—	—
Colorado	18	1	17	17	1	15	2	17	1
Connecticut	22	2	20	21	1	21	1	22	—
Delaware	12	5	7	8	4	7	5	12	—
Florida	18	15	3	5	13	6	12	18	—
Georgia	17	17	—	—	—	14	2	16	1
Idaho	14	14	—	—	14	—	14	14	—
Illinois	60	58	2	1	59	1	59	1	59
Indiana	32	31	1	3	29	2	30	2	30
Iowa	26	11	15	16	10	16	10	20	6
Kansas	22	2	20	20	2	20	2	22	—
Kentucky	20	18	2	2	18	1	19	13	7
Louisiana	15	13	2	—	2	13	2	15	—
Maine	16	5	11	11	5	11	5	15	1
Maryland	24	5	19	15	9	16	8	24	—
Massachusetts	38	5	33	33	5	34	4	38	—
Michigan	46	1	45	32	14	35	11	35	11
Minnesota	28	—	28	28	—	9	—	28	—
Mississippi	5	5	—	—	5	—	5	5	—
Missouri	26	4	22	21	5	21	5	26	—
Montana	8	7	1	1	7	1	7	1	7
Nebraska	18	13	5	7	11	4	13	7	11
Nevada	12	7	5	2	10	5	7	10	2
New Hampshire	14	—	14	14	—	14	—	14	—
New Jersey	38	5	33	32	6	33	5	38	—
New Mexico	14	8	6	5	9	6	8	6	8
New York	96	1	95	92	4	92	4	95	1
North Carolina	26	14	12	10	16	12	14	26	—
North Dakota	14	11	3	3	11	4	8	5	8
Ohio	56	56	—	—	56	—	56	—	56
Oklahoma	16	10	6	4	12	4	7	8	4
Oregon	18	—	18	18	—	18	—	18	—
Pennsylvania	70	13	57	52	18	53	15	70	—
Rhode Island	8	2	6	6	2	6	1	8	—
South Carolina	6	5	1	1	5	2	4	6	—
South Dakota	14	14	—	—	14	—	14	7	7
Tennessee	20	20	—	—	20	—	20	20	—
Texas	38	22	16	—	—	33	5	38	—
Utah	14	14	—	—	14	—	14	14	—
Vermont	12	—	12	12	—	12	—	12	—
Virginia	23	13	10	7	16	9	14	19	4
Washington	24	4	20	19	5	20	4	21	3
West Virginia	16	15	1	1	15	1	14	3	13
Wisconsin	30	24	6	6	24	—	24	—	24
Wyoming	12	8	4	4	8	6	6	12	—
Alaska	3	3	—	—	3	1	2	3	—
Canal Zone	—	—	—	—	—	—	—	—	—
District of Columbia	6	6	—	—	6	—	6	6	—
Hawaii	8	7	1	3	5	3	4	4	4
Puerto Rico	3	2	1	1	2	—	3	1	2
Virgin Islands	1	—	1	1	—	1	—	1	—
Total	1206	548	658	607	531	595	500	845	280

1. Other candidates: Earl Warren, 81; Harold E. Stassen, 20; Douglas MacArthur, 10.
2. Other candidates: Warren, 77; MacArthur, 4.

1952 Democratic

(Narrative, p. 118)

Delegation	Total Votes	Seating Virginia Delegation			Table Motion to Adjourn			First Pres. Ballot[1]				Second Pres. Ballot[2]				Third Pres. Ballot[3]		
		Yea	Nay	Not Voting	Yea	Nay	Not Voting	Harriman	Kefauver	Russell	Stevenson	Harriman	Kefauver	Russell	Stevenson	Kefauver	Russell	Stevenson
Alabama	22	22	—	—	13½	8½	—	—	8	13	—	—	7½	14	½	7½	14	½
Arizona	12	12	—	—	12	—	—	—	—	—	—	—	—	12	—	—	12	—
Arkansas	22	22	—	—	19	3	—	—	—	—	—	1	1½	18	1½	1½	—	20½
California	68	4	61	3	—	68	—	—	68	—	—	—	68	—	—	68	—	—
Colorado	16	4½	11½	—	4	12	—	5	2	8½	½	5	5	2½	3½	4	3½	8½
Connecticut	16	—	16	—	16	—	—	—	—	—	16	—	—	—	16	—	—	16
Delaware	6	6	—	—	6	—	—	—	—	—	6	—	—	—	6	—	—	6
Florida	24	24	—	—	19	5	—	—	5	19	—	—	5	19	—	5	19	—
Georgia	28	28	—	—	28	—	—	—	—	28	—	—	—	28	—	—	28	—
Idaho	12	12	—	—	—	12	—	3½	3	1	1½	—	—	—	12	—	—	12
Illinois	60	52	8	—	53	7	—	1	3	—	53	—	3	—	54	3	—	54
Indiana	25	14½	6½	5	25	1	—	—	1	—	25	—	1	—	25	1	—	25
Iowa	24	17	7	—	8	15	1	½	8	2	8	½	8½	3	9½	8	3	10
Kansas	16	—	16	—	16	—	—	—	—	—	16	—	—	—	16	—	—	16
Kentucky	26	26	—	—	26	—	—	—	—	—	—	—	—	—	—	—	—	—
Louisiana	20	20	—	—	20	—	—	—	—	20	—	—	—	20	—	—	20	—
Maine	10	2½	7½	—	4½	5½	—	1½	1½	2½	3½	1	1	2½	4½	½	2½	7
Maryland	18	18	—	—	18	—	—	—	18	—	—	—	15½	2	—	8½	2½	6
Massachusetts	36	16	19	1	30	4½	1½	—	—	—	—	—	2½	—	—	5	1	25
Michigan	40	—	40	—	—	40	—	—	40	—	—	—	40	—	—	—	—	40
Minnesota	26	—	26	—	—	26	—	—	—	—	—	1½	17	—	7½	13	—	13
Mississippi	18	18	—	—	18	—	—	—	—	18	—	—	—	18	—	—	18	—
Missouri	34	34	—	—	29	5	—	1½	2	—	18	1½	2	—	19½	2	—	22
Montana	12	—	12	—	12	—	—	—	—	—	—	3	3	3	—	—	—	12
Nebraska	12	8	3	1	—	12	—	—	5	1	2	—	5	1	2	3	1	8
Nevada	10	10	—	—	9½	½	—	—	½	8	1	—	½	7½	2	½	7½	2
New Hampshire	8	1	7	—	—	8	—	—	8	—	—	—	8	—	—	8	—	—
New Jersey	32	—	32	—	24	8	—	1	3	—	28	—	4	—	28	4	—	28
New Mexico	12	12	—	—	12	—	—	1	1½	4	1	—	1½	6	4½	1½	3½	7
New York	94	7	87	—	5	89	—	83½	1	—	6½	84½	—	1	6½	4	—	86½
North Carolina	32	32	—	—	32	—	—	—	—	26	5½	—	—	24	7	—	24	7½
North Dakota	8	8	—	—	8	—	—	—	2	2	2	—	—	—	—	—	—	8
Ohio	54	33½	14½	6	26	28	—	1	29½	7	13	1	27½	8	17½	27	1	26
Oklahoma	24	24	—	—	24	—	—	—	—	—	—	—	—	—	—	—	—	—
Oregon	12	4	8	—	—	12	—	—	12	—	—	—	12	—	—	11	—	1
Pennsylvania	70	57	13	—	35	35	—	4½	22½	—	36	2½	21½	—	40	—	—	70
Rhode Island	12	10	2	—	10	2	—	1½	3½	—	5½	—	4	—	8	—	—	12
South Carolina	16	—	—	16	—	—	16	—	16	—	—	—	—	16	—	—	16	—
South Dakota	8	—	8	—	—	8	—	—	8	—	—	—	8	—	—	8	—	—
Tennessee	28	—	28	—	—	28	—	—	28	—	—	—	28	—	—	28	—	—
Texas	52	52	—	—	52	—	—	—	—	52	—	—	—	52	—	—	52	—
Utah	12	3	9	—	—	12	—	6½	½	2	½	9	1½	—	½	—	—	12
Vermont	6	—	6	—	6	—	—	—	½	—	5	—	½	½	5	—	½	5½
Virginia	28	—	—	28	28	—	—	—	—	28	—	—	—	28	—	—	28	—
Washington	22	12½	9½	—	3	10	—	—	12	½	6	2	12½	½	6	11	½	10½
West Virginia	20	13½	5	1½	10	9	1	—	5½	7	1	—	7½	6½	5½	7½	3½	9
Wisconsin	28	1	27	—	—	28	—	—	28	—	—	—	28	—	—	28	—	—
Wyoming	10	5½	4½	—	2½	7½	—	3½	1½	½	3	2½	3	—	4½	—	—	10
Alaska	6	—	6	—	—	6	—	—	6	—	—	—	6	—	—	6	—	—
Canal Zone	2	2	—	—	2	—	—	—	—	2	—	—	—	2	—	—	—	2
D.C.	6	—	6	—	—	6	—	6	—	—	—	6	—	—	—	—	—	6
Hawaii	6	—	6	—	4	2	—	1	1	—	2	—	1	—	5	1	—	5
Puerto Rico	6	2	4	—	1	5	—	—	—	—	6	—	—	—	6	—	—	6
Virgin Islands	2	—	2	—	—	2	—	—	1	—	1	—	1	—	1	—	—	2
Total	1230	650½	518	61½	671	539½ᵃ	19½	123½	340	268	273	121	362½	294	324½	275½	261	617½

1. Other candidates: Alben W. Barkley, 48½; Robert S. Kerr, 65; J. William Fulbright, 22; Paul H. Douglas, 3; Oscar R. Ewing, 4; Paul A. Dever, 37½; Hubert H. Humphrey, 26; James E. Murray, 12; Harry S. Truman, 6; William O. Douglas, ½; not voting, 1.

2. Other candidates: Barkley, 78½; Paul H. Douglas, 3; Kerr, 5½; Ewing, 3; Dever, 30½; Truman, 6; not voting, 1½.

3. Other candidates: Barkley, 67½; Paul H. Douglas, 3; Dever, ½; Ewing, 3; not voting, 2.

a. Sum of column; proceedings record 534.

1956 Democratic

(Narrative, p. 120)

	Total Votes	First Pres. Ballot[1]		
Delegation		Stevenson	Harriman	Other
Alabama	26	15½	—	10½
Arizona	16	16	—	—
Arkansas	26	26	—	—
California	68	68	—	—
Colorado	20	13½	6	½
Connecticut	20	20	—	—
Delaware	10	10	—	—
Florida	28	25	—	3
Georgia	32	—	—	32
Idaho	12	12	—	—
Illinois	64	53½	8½	2
Indiana	26	21½	3	1½
Iowa	24	16½	7	½
Kansas	16	16	—	—
Kentucky	30	—	—	30
Louisiana	24	24	—	—
Maine	14	10½	3½	—
Maryland	18	18	—	—
Massachusetts	40	32	7½	½
Michigan	44	39	5	—
Minnesota	30	19	11	—
Mississippi	22	—	—	22
Missouri	38	—	—	38
Montana	16	10	6	—
Nebraska	12	12	—	—
Nevada	14	5½	7	1½
New Hampshire	8	5½	1½	1
New Jersey	36	36	—	—
New Mexico	16	12	3½	½
New York	98	5½	92½	—
North Carolina	36	34½	1	½
North Dakota	8	8	—	—
Ohio	58	52	½	5½
Oklahoma	28	—	28	—
Oregon	16	16	—	—
Pennsylvania	74	67	7	—
Rhode Island	16	16	—	—
South Carolina	20	2	—	18
South Dakota	8	8	—	—
Tennessee	32	32	—	—
Texas	56	—	—	56
Utah	12	12	—	—
Vermont	6	5½	½	—
Virginia	32	—	—	32
Washington	26	19½	6	½
West Virginia	24	24	—	—
Wisconsin	28	22½	5	½
Wyoming	14	14	—	—
Alaska	6	6	—	—
Canal Zone	3	3	—	—
District of Columbia	6	6	—	—
Hawaii	6	6	—	—
Puerto Rico	6	6	—	—
Virgin Islands	3	3	—	—
Total	1372	905½	210	256½

1. Other candidates: Lyndon B. Johnson, 80; James C. Davis, 33; Albert B. Chandler, 36½; John S. Battle, 32½; George B. Timmerman, 23½; W. Stuart Symington, 45½; Frank Lausche, 5½.

1956 Republican

(Narrative, p. 122)

Delegation	Total Votes	First Pres. Ballot Eisenhower
Alabama	21	21
Arizona	14	14
Arkansas	16	16
California	70	70
Colorado	18	18
Connecticut	22	22
Delaware	12	12
Florida	26	26
Georgia	23	23
Idaho	14	14
Illinois	60	60
Indiana	32	32
Iowa	26	26
Kansas	22	22
Kentucky	26	26
Louisiana	20	20
Maine	16	16
Maryland	24	24
Massachusetts	38	38
Michigan	46	46
Minnesota	28	28
Mississippi	15	15
Missouri	32	32
Montana	14	14
Nebraska	18	18
Nevada	12	12
New Hampshire	14	14
New Jersey	38	38
New Mexico	14	14
New York	96	96
North Carolina	28	28
North Dakota	14	14
Ohio	56	56
Oklahoma	22	22
Oregon	18	18
Pennsylvania	70	70
Rhode Island	14	14
South Carolina	16	16
South Dakota	14	14
Tennessee	28	28
Texas	54	54
Utah	14	14
Vermont	12	12
Virginia	30	30
Washington	24	24
West Virginia	16	16
Wisconsin	30	30
Wyoming	12	12
Alaska	4	4
District of Columbia	6	6
Hawaii	10	10
Puerto Rico	3	3
Virgin Islands	1	1
Total	1323	1323

1960 Democratic

(Narrative, p. 123)

First Pres. Ballot[1]

Delegation	Total Votes	Kennedy	Johnson	Stevenson	Symington
Alabama	29	3	20	1/2	3 1/2
Alaska	9	9	—	—	—
Arizona	17	17	—	—	—
Arkansas	27	—	27	—	—
California	81	33 1/2	7 1/2	31 1/2	8
Colorado	21	13 1/2	—	5 1/2	2
Connecticut	21	21	—	—	—
Delaware	11	—	11	—	—
Florida	29	—	—	—	—
Georgia	33	—	33	—	—
Hawaii	9	1 1/2	3	3 1/2	1
Idaho	13	6	4 1/2	1/2	2
Illinois	69	61 1/2	—	2	5 1/2
Indiana	34	34	—	—	—
Iowa	26	21 1/2	1/2	2	1/2
Kansas	21	21	—	—	—
Kentucky	31	3 1/2	25 1/2	1 1/2	1/2
Louisiana	26	—	26	—	—
Maine	15	15	—	—	—
Maryland	24	24	—	—	—
Massachusetts	41	41	—	—	—
Michigan	51	42 1/2	—	2 1/2	6
Minnesota	31	—	—	—	—
Mississippi	23	—	—	—	—
Missouri	39	—	—	—	39
Montana	17	10	2	2 1/2	2 1/2
Nebraska	16	11	1/2	—	4
Nevada	15	5 1/2	6 1/2	2 1/2	1/2
New Hampshire	11	11	—	—	—
New Jersey	41	—	—	—	—
New Mexico	17	4	13	—	—
New York	114	104 1/2	3 1/2	3 1/2	2 1/2
North Carolina	37	6	27 1/2	3	—
North Dakota	11	11	—	—	—
Ohio	64	64	—	—	—
Oklahoma	29	—	29	—	—
Oregon	17	16 1/2	—	1/2	—
Pennsylvania	81	68	4	7 1/2	—
Rhode Island	17	17	—	—	—
South Carolina	21	—	21	—	—
South Dakota	11	4	2	1	2 1/2
Tennessee	33	—	33	—	—
Texas	61	—	61	—	—
Utah	13	8	3	—	1 1/2
Vermont	9	9	—	—	—
Virginia	33	—	33	—	—
Washington	27	14 1/2	2 1/2	6 1/2	3
West Virginia	25	15	5 1/2	3	1 1/2
Wisconsin	31	23	—	—	—
Wyoming	15	15	—	—	—
Canal Zone	4	—	4	—	—
District of Columbia	9	9	—	—	—
Puerto Rico	7	7	—	—	—
Virgin Islands	4	4	—	—	—
Total	1521	806	409	79 1/2	86

1. Other candidates: Ross R. Barnett, 23 (Mississippi); George A. Smathers, 30 (29 in Florida, 1/2 in Alabama, 1/2 in North Carolina); Hubert H. Humphrey, 42 1/2 (31 in Minnesota, 8 in Wisconsin, 1 1/2 in South Dakota, 1/2 in Nebraska, 1/2 in Utah); Robert B. Meyner, 43 (41 in New Jersey, 1 1/2 in Pennsylvania, 1/2 in Alabama); Herschel C. Loveless, 1 1/2 (Iowa); Orval E. Faubus, 1/2 (Alabama); Edmund G. Brown, 1/2 (California); Albert D. Rosellini, 1/2 (Washington).

1960 Republican

(Narrative, p. 125)

First Pres. Ballot

Delegation	Total Votes	Nixon	Goldwater
Alabama	22	22	—
Alaska	6	6	—
Arizona	14	14	—
Arkansas	16	16	—
California	70	70	—
Colorado	18	18	—
Connecticut	22	22	—
Delaware	12	12	—
Florida	26	26	—
Georgia	24	24	—
Hawaii	12	12	—
Idaho	14	14	—
Illinois	60	60	—
Indiana	32	32	—
Iowa	26	26	—
Kansas	22	22	—
Kentucky	26	26	—
Louisiana	26	16	10
Maine	16	16	—
Maryland	24	24	—
Massachusetts	38	38	—
Michigan	46	46	—
Minnesota	28	28	—
Mississippi	12	12	—
Missouri	26	26	—
Montana	14	14	—
Nebraska	18	18	—
Nevada	12	12	—
New Hampshire	14	14	—
New Jersey	38	38	—
New Mexico	14	14	—
New York	96	96	—
North Carolina	28	28	—
North Dakota	14	14	—
Ohio	56	56	—
Oklahoma	22	22	—
Oregon	18	18	—
Pennsylvania	70	70	—
Rhode Island	14	14	—
South Carolina	13	13	—
South Dakota	14	14	—
Tennessee	28	28	—
Texas	54	54	—
Utah	14	14	—
Vermont	12	12	—
Virginia	30	30	—
Washington	24	24	—
West Virginia	22	22	—
Wisconsin	30	30	—
Wyoming	12	12	—
District of Columbia	8	8	—
Puerto Rico	3	3	—
Virgin Islands	1	1	—
Total	1331	1321	10

1964 Republican

(Narrative, p. 127)

Delegation	Total Votes	Minority Amendment on Civil Rights[1]		First Pres. Ballot[2] (Before shift)			First Pres. Ballot[3] (After shift)		
		Yea	Nay	Goldwater	Rockefeller	Scranton	Goldwater	Rockefeller	Scranton
Alabama	20	—	20	20	—	—	20	—	—
Alaska	12	12	—	—	—	8	—	—	8
Arizona	16	—	16	16	—	—	16	—	—
Arkansas	12	—	12	9	1	2	12	—	—
California	86	—	86	86	—	—	86	—	—
Colorado	18	—	18	15	—	3	18	—	—
Connecticut	16	11	5	4	—	12	16	—	—
Delaware	12	11	1	7	—	5	10	—	2
Florida	34	—	34	34	—	2	34	—	—
Georgia	24	—	24	22	—	2	24	—	—
Hawaii	8	4	4	4	—	—	8	—	—
Idaho	14	—	14	14	—	—	14	—	—
Illinois	58	4	54	56	2	—	56	2	—
Indiana	32	—	32	32	—	—	32	—	—
Iowa	24	2	22	14	—	10	24	—	—
Kansas	20	2	18	18	—	1	18	—	1
Kentucky	24	1	23	21	—	3	22	—	2
Louisiana	20	—	20	20	—	—	20	—	—
Maine	14	11	3	—	—	—	—	—	—
Maryland	20	17	3	6	1	13	7	1	12
Massachusetts	34	27	7	5	—	26	34	—	—
Michigan	48	37	9	8	—	—	48	—	—
Minnesota	26	17	9	8	—	—	26	—	—
Mississippi	13	—	13	13	—	—	13	—	—
Missouri	24	1	23	23	—	1	24	—	—
Montana	14	—	14	14	—	—	14	—	—
Nebraska	16	—	16	16	—	—	16	—	—
Nevada	6	—	6	6	—	—	6	—	—
New Hampshire	14	14	—	—	—	14	—	—	14
New Jersey	40	40	—	20	—	20	38	—	2
New Mexico	14	—	14	14	—	—	14	—	—
New York	92	86	6	5	87	—	87	—	—
North Carolina	26	—	26	26	—	—	26	—	—
North Dakota	14	1	13	7	1	—	14	—	—
Ohio	58	—	58	57	—	—	58	—	—
Oklahoma	22	—	22	22	—	—	22	—	—
Oregon	18	10	8	—	18	—	16	—	—
Pennsylvania	64	62	2	4	—	60	64	—	—
Rhode Island	14	11	3	3	—	11	14	—	—
South Carolina	16	—	16	16	—	—	16	—	—
South Dakota	14	—	14	12	—	2	14	—	—
Tennessee	28	—	28	28	—	—	28	—	—
Texas	56	—	56	56	—	—	56	—	—
Utah	14	—	14	14	—	—	14	—	—
Vermont	12	8	4	3	2	2	3	2	2
Virginia	30	—	30	29	—	1	30	—	—
Washington	24	1	23	22	—	1	22	—	1
West Virginia	14	4	10	10	2	2	12	1	1
Wisconsin	30	—	30	30	—	—	30	—	—
Wyoming	12	—	12	12	—	—	12	—	—
District of Columbia	9	7	2	4	—	5	4	—	5
Puerto Rico	5	5	—	—	—	5	5	—	—
Virgin Islands	3	3	—	—	—	3	3	—	—
Total	1308	409	897	883	114	214	1220	6	50

1. Not voting, 2.

2. Other candidates: George Romney, 41 (40 in Michigan, 1 in Kansas); Margaret C. Smith, 27 (14 in Maine, 5 in Vermont, 3 in North Dakota, 2 in Alaska, 1 in Massachusetts, 1 in Ohio, 1 in Washington); Walter H. Judd, 22 (18 in Minnesota, 3 in North Dakota, 1 in Alaska); Hiram L. Fong, 5 (4 in Hawaii, 1 in Alaska); Henry C. Lodge, 2 (Massachusetts).

3. Other candidates: Smith, 22 (14 in Maine, 5 in Vermont, 2 in Alaska, 1 in Washington); Fong, 1 (Alaska); Judd, 1 (Alaska); Romney, 1 (Kansas); not voting, 7 (5 in New York, 2 in Oregon).

1968 Republican

(Narrative, p. 131)

Delegation	Total Votes	First Pres. Ballot[1] (Before shift)			First Pres. Ballot (After shift)		
		Nixon	Rockefeller	Reagan	Nixon	Rockefeller	Reagan
Alabama	26	14	—	12	26	—	—
Alaska	12	11	1	—	12	—	—
Arizona	16	16	—	—	16	—	—
Arkansas	18	—	—	—	18	—	—
California	86	—	—	86	86	—	—
Colorado	18	14	3	1	18	—	—
Connecticut	16	4	12	—	16	—	—
Delaware	12	9	3	—	12	—	—
Florida	34	32	1	1	34	—	—
Georgia	30	21	2	7	30	—	—
Hawaii	14	—	—	—	14	—	—
Idaho	14	9	—	5	14	—	—
Illinois	58	50	5	3	58	—	—
Indiana	26	26	—	—	26	—	—
Iowa	24	13	8	3	24	—	—
Kansas	20	—	—	—	19	1	—
Kentucky	24	22	2	—	24	—	—
Louisiana	26	19	—	7	26	—	—
Maine	14	7	7	—	14	—	—
Maryland	26	18	8	—	26	—	—
Massachusetts	34	—	34	—	34	—	—
Michigan	48	4	—	—	48	—	—
Minnesota	26	9	15	—	26	—	—
Mississippi	20	20	—	—	20	—	—
Missouri	24	16	5	3	24	—	—
Montana	14	11	—	3	14	—	—
Nebraska	16	16	—	—	16	—	—
Nevada	12	9	3	—	12	—	—
New Hampshire	8	8	—	—	8	—	—
New Jersey	40	18	—	—	40	—	—
New Mexico	14	8	1	5	14	—	—
New York	92	4	88	—	4	88	—
North Carolina	26	9	1	16	26	—	—
North Dakota	8	5	2	1	8	—	—
Ohio	58	2	—	—	58	—	—
Oklahoma	22	14	1	7	22	—	—
Oregon	18	18	—	—	18	—	—
Pennsylvania	64	22	41	1	64	—	—
Rhode Island	14	—	14	—	14	—	—
South Carolina	22	22	—	—	22	—	—
South Dakota	14	14	—	—	14	—	—
Tennessee	28	28	—	—	28	—	—
Texas	56	41	—	15	54	—	2
Utah	8	2	—	—	8	—	—
Vermont	12	9	3	—	12	—	—
Virginia	24	22	2	—	24	—	—
Washington	24	15	3	6	24	—	—
West Virginia	14	11	3	—	13	1	—
Wisconsin	30	30	—	—	30	—	—
Wyoming	12	12	—	—	12	—	—
District of Columbia	9	6	3	—	6	3	—
Puerto Rico	5	—	5	—	5	—	—
Virgin Islands	3	2	1	—	3	—	—
Total	1333	692	277	182	1238	93	2

1. Other candidates: James A. Rhodes, 55 (Ohio); George Romney, 50 (44 in Michigan, 6 in Utah); Clifford P. Case, 22 (New Jersey); Frank Carlson, 20 (Kansas); Winthrop Rockefeller, 18 (Arkansas); Hiram L. Fong, 14 (Hawaii); Harold Stassen, 2 (1 in Minnesota, 1 in Ohio); John V. Lindsay, 1 (Minnesota).

1968 Democratic

(Narrative, p. 132)

Delega-tion	Total Votes	Texas Credentials[1]		Georgia Credentials[2]		Alabama Credentials[3]		End Unit Rule[4]		Report on Vietnam[5]		First Pres. Ballot[6]			
		Yea	Nay	Yea	Nay	Yea	Nay	Yea	Nay	Yea	Nay	Humprey	McCarthy	McGovern	Phillips
Ala.	32	32	—	10	22	—	—	5½	24½	1½	30½	23	—	—	—
Alaska	22	17	5	5	17	14	8	22	—	10	12	17	2	3	—
Ariz.	19	1¼	17	17	2	7½	11½	—	19	6½	12½	14½	2½	2	—
Ark.	33	33	—	3	29	8	23	—	32	7	25	30	2	—	—
Calif.	174	1	173	173	1	173	1	173	1	166	6	14	91	51	17
Colo.	35	—	35	30	5	34	1	35	—	21	14	16½	10	5½	3
Conn.	44	30	12	13	27	21	21	9	30	13	30	35	8	—	1
Del.	22	21	—	3	18	2	19	—	21	—	21	21	—	—	—
Fla.	63	58	4	9	54	6	57	11	52	7	56	58	5	—	—
Ga.	43	—	—	—	—	25	17½	39	4	19½	23½	19½	13½	1	3
Hawaii	26	26	—	4	22	—	26	3	23	—	26	26	—	—	—
Idaho	25	22½	2½	4½	20½	2	23	1	24	10	15	21	3½	½	—
Ill.	118	114	4	12	83	18	100	3	115	13	105	112	3	3	—
Ind.	63	34	10	25	38	13	41½	63	—	15	47½	49	11	2	1
Iowa	46	37½	8½	32	12	24½	21½	46	—	36	10	18½	19½	5	—
Kan.	38	38	—	3½	34½	5½	31½	6	20	4½	33½	34	1	3	—
Ky.	46	40½	5½	6	40	6½	39½	6½	39½	7	39	41	5	—	—
La.	36	32	4	7	29	—	36	—	36	2½	33½	35	—	—	—
Maine	27	25	1	5	22	—	26	27	—	4½	22½	23	4	—	—
Md.	49	46	3	3	46	2	47	49	—	12	37	45	2	2	—
Mass.	72	16	47	39	24	29	29	37	31	56	16	2	70	—	—
Mich.	96	70	23	35	58	26	67	43½	44½	52	44	72½	9½	7½	6½
Minn.	52	34½	14½	16	33	23½	28½	16	33½	16½	34½	38	11½	—	2½
Miss.	24	2	18½	18	2	12½	8½	21½	½	19½	2½	9½	6½	4	—
Mo.	60	48	12	12	48	8	52	60	—	10	50	56	3½	—	½
Mont.	26	20	4	2½	21½	3½	22½	12½	12	6	20	23½	2½	—	—
Neb.	30	12	16	11	18	13	15	26	2	19	11	15	6	9	—
Nev.	22	13	7	14	8	12½	9½	22	—	3½	18½	18½	2½	1	—
N.H.	26	6	20	23	2	25	—	23	3	23	3	6	20	—	—
N.J.	82	43	25	22	51	21	61	21	61	24	57	62	19	—	1
N.M.	26	13	13	11	15	11	15	11	15	11½	14½	15	11	—	—
N.Y.	190	—	190	190	—	80e	82e	190	—	148	42	96½	87	1½	2
N.C.	59	54½	4½	3½	55½	1	58	2	57	7	51	44½	2	½	—
N.D.	25	17	5	5	17	7	18	17	5	6	19	18	7	—	—
Ohio	115	37½	27	21	80	30½	65	23	92	48	67	94	18	2	—
Okla.	41	40	1	1	40	6½	34	6	35	4	37	37½	2½	½	½
Ore.	35	10	23	32	—	31	3	31	—	29	6	—	35	—	—
Pa.	130	80½	42½	31½	90½	22¼	100½	39¾	79½	35¼	92¼	103¾	21½	2½	1½
R.I.	27	24½	2½	12	11	2½	24½	3½	23½	5	22	23½	2½	—	—
S.C.	28	28	—	4	22	—	28	4½	23½	1	27	28	—	—	—
S.D.	26	1	25	26	—	24	2	26	—	26	—	2	—	24	—
Tenn.	51	48½	1	—	51	½	49½	2½	46½	2	49	49½	½	1	—
Texas	104	—	—	2.55	101.45	—	104	5	99	—	104	100½	2½	—	1
Utah	26	18	8	7	19	5	21	26	—	6	20	23	2	—	1
Vt.	22	5	13	17	4	14	7	22	—	17	5	8	6	7	—
Va.	54	21½	22½	8½	35½	1	53	9½	43½	—	46	42½	5½	—	2
Wash.	47	31½	15½	18	29	16	28	21½	25½	15½	31½	32½	8½	6	—
W.Va.	38	19	12	8	22	9	29	38	—	8	30	34	3	—	—
Wis.	59	5	54	52	7	54	4	58	1	52	7	8	49	1	1
Wyo.	22	18½	3½	2	20	6½	15½	3	19	3½	18½	18½	3½	—	—
Canal Z.	5	4	—	2	3	—	4	1	4	1½	3½	4	—	1	—
D. C.	23	—	22	22	—	23	—	23	—	21	2	2	—	—	21
Guam	5	4½	½	—	5	—	5	½	4½	½	4½	5	—	—	—
P.R.	8	8	—	7½	—	—	8	1	7	—	8	8	—	—	—
Vir. Is.	5	5	—	2½	—	—	5	5	—	—	5	5	—	—	—
Total	2622	1368¼a	956¾b	1043.55c	1415.45d	880¾f	1607g	1351¼h	1209i	1041¼	1567¾	1759¼j	601	146½	67½

1. Not voting, 297.
2. Not voting, 163.
3. Not voting, 134½.
4. Not voting, 61¾.
5. Not voting, 13.
6. Other candidates: Dan K. Moore. 17½ (12 in North Carolina, 3 in Virginia, 2 in Georgia, ½ in Alabama); Edward M. Kennedy, 12¾ (proceedings record, 12½) (3½ in Alabama, 3 in Iowa, 3 in New York, 1 in Ohio, 1 in West Virginia, ¾ in Pennsylvania; ½ in Georgia); Bryant, 1½ (Alabama); George C. Wallace, ½ (Alabama); James H. Gray, ½ (Georgia); not voting, 15 (3 in Alabama, 3 in Georgia, 2 in Mississippi, 1 in Arkansas, 1 in California, 1 in Delaware, 1 in Louisiana, 1 in Rhode Island, 1 in Vermont, 1 in Virginia).

a. Sum of column; proceedings record, 1368.
b. Sum of column; proceedings record, 955.
c. Sum of column; proceedings record, 1041½.
d. Sum of column; proceedings record, 1413.
e. New York vote announced after outcome of roll call.
f. Sum of column; proceedings record (without New York vote), 801½.
g. Sum of column; proceedings record (without New York), 1525.
h. Sum of column; proceedings record,1350.
i. Sum of column; proceedings record, 1206.
j. Sum of column; proceedings record, 1761¾ .

1972 Democratic

(Narrative, p. 135)

Delegation[1]	Total Votes	Minority Report South Carolina Credentials			Minority Report California Credentials			Minority Report Illinois Credentials		
		Yea	Nay	Not Voting	Yea	Nay	Not Voting	Yea	Nay	Not Voting
California	271	120	151	—	120	—	151	84	136	51
South Carolina	32	—	9	23	3	29	—	31	1	—
Ohio	153	63	87	3	75	78	—	69	70	14
Canal Zone	3	1.50	1.50	—	3	—	—	1	2	—
Utah	19	10	8	1	13	6	—	5	14	—
Delaware	13	5.85	7.15	—	6.50	6.50	—	6.50	6.50	—
Rhode Island	22	20	2	—	22	—	—	7.09	14.91	—
Texas	130	34	96	—	34	96	—	96	34	—
West Virginia	35	13	22	—	15	20	—	24	11	—
South Dakota	17	17	—	—	17	—	—	—	17	—
Kansas	35	17	18	—	18	17	—	18	17	—
New York	278	269	9	—	267	11	—	20	256	2
Virginia	53	34.50	18.50	—	38.50	14.50	—	16.50	35.50	1
Wyoming	11	2.20	8.80	—	4.40	6.60	—	7.70	3.30	—
Arkansas	27	13	14	—	8	19	—	13	14	—
Indiana	76	18	58	—	33	43	—	53	23	—
Puerto Rico	7	6.50	0.50	—	6.50	0.50	—	0.50	6.50	—
Tennessee	49	22	27	—	23	26	—	20	29	—
Pennsylvania	182	55.50	126	0.50	72	105	5	106.50	62	13.50
Mississippi	25	20	5	—	19	6	—	—	25	—
Wisconsin	67	39	28	—	55	12	—	12	55	—
Illinois	170	79	90	1	114.50	55.50	—	76	30	64
Maine	20	1	19	—	—	20	—	13	7	—
Florida	81	1	80	—	3	78	—	80	1	—
New Hampshire	18	13.50	4.50	—	9.90	8.10	—	9	8.10	0.90
Arizona	25	15	10	—	12	13	—	4	21	—
North Carolina	64	6	58	—	21	43	—	39	23	2
Massachusetts	102	97	5	—	97	5	—	11	91	—
Nebraska	24	14	9	1	20	4	—	13	11	—
Georgia	53	5.50	47.50	—	21.75	31.25	—	24	27.50	1.50
North Dakota	14	7	6.30	0.70	8.40	5.60	—	2.10	11.90	—
Maryland	53	24	29	—	27.83	25.17	—	28.67	24.33	—
New Jersey	109	79	29	1	85.50	22.50	1	30	75.50	3.50
Vermont	12	7	5	—	11	1	—	2	10	—
Nevada	11	5.75	5.25	—	5.75	5.25	—	6.75	4.25	—
Michigan	132	51	81	—	55	76	1	85	47	—
Iowa	46	23	23	—	27	19	—	20	26	—
Colorado	36	23	13	—	27	9	—	5	31	—
Alabama	37	1	36	—	1	36	—	32	5	—
Alaska	10	6.75	3.25	—	7.25	2.75	—	4.75	5.25	—
Hawaii	17	2	15	—	7	10	—	17	—	—
Washington	52	—	52	—	—	52	—	52	—	—
Minnesota	64	56	8	—	29	35	—	32	32	—
Louisiana	44	25	19	—	22.50	21.50	—	9.50	32.50	2
Idaho	17	12.50	4.50	—	11.50	5.50	—	4	13	—
Montana	17	10	7	—	14.50	1	1.50	2.50	14.50	—
Connecticut	51	8	43	—	21	30	—	40	11	—
District of Columbia	15	12	3	—	13.50	1.50	—	1.50	13.50	—
Virgin Islands	3	1	2	—	2.50	0.50	—	3	—	—
Kentucky	47	10	37	—	11	36	—	36	10	1
Missouri	73	13.50	59.50	—	22.50	50.50	—	59	13	1
New Mexico	18	10	8	—	10	8	—	8	10	—
Guam	3	1.50	1.50	—	1.50	1.50	—	—	3	—
Oregon	34	16	18	—	33	1	—	2	32	—
Oklahoma	39	11	28	—	11	28	—	29	9	1
Total	3016	1429.05	1555.75	31.20	1618.28	1238.22	159.50	1371.56[a]	1486.04[b]	158.40

1. Delegations at this convention are listed in the order in which they voted. All fractional votes are expressed in decimals for consistency.

a. Sum of column; proceedings record, 1371.55.

b. Sum of column; proceedings record, 1486.05.

1972 Democratic

(Narrative, p. 135)

Minority Report Guaranteed Income			First Pres. Ballot[2] (Before shift)					First Pres. Ballot[3] (After shift)				
Yea	Nay	Not Voting	McGovern	Jackson	Wallace	Chisholm	Sanford	McGovern	Jackson	Wallace	Chisholm	Sanford
131	114	26	271	—	—	—	—	271	—	—	—	—
4	21	7	6	10	6	4	6	10	9	6	—	6
39	86	28	77	39	—	23	3	77	39	—	23	3
2.50	0.50	—	3	—	—	—	—	3	—	—	—	—
8	11	—	14	1	—	—	3	14	1	—	—	3
4.55	8.45	—	5.85	6.50	—	0.65	—	5.85	5.85	—	0.65	—
10.86	11.14	—	22	—	—	—	—	22	—	—	—	—
15	115	—	54	23	48	4	—	54	23	48	4	—
3	32	—	16	14	1	—	4	16	14	1	—	4
1	16	—	17	—	—	—	—	17	—	—	—	—
5	30	—	20	10	—	2	1	20	10	—	2	1
152	118	8	263	9	—	6	—	278	—	—	—	—
30	21	2	33.50	4	1	5.50	9	37	5	—	2.50	8.50
0.55	10.45	—	3.30	6.05	—	1.10	—	3.30	6.05	—	1.10	—
10	16	1	1	1	—	—	—	1	1	—	—	—
17	56	3	26	20	26	1	—	28	19	25	—	—
4	3	—	7	—	—	—	—	7	—	—	—	—
21	27	1	—	—	33	10	—	5	—	32	7	—
49.50	117.50	15	81	86.50	2	9.50	1	81	86.50	2	9.50	1
22	—	3	10	—	—	12	3	23	—	—	2	—
29	38	—	55	3	—	5	—	55	3	—	5	—
59	95	16	119	30.50	0.50	4.50	2	155	6	—	1	—
1	19	—	5	—	—	—	—	5	—	—	—	—
4	77	—	2	—	75	2	—	4	—	75	1	—
0.90	14.40	2.70	10.80	5.40	—	—	—	10.80	5.40	—	—	—
6	19	—	21	3	—	—	1	22	3	—	—	—
17	47	—	—	—	37	—	27	—	—	37	—	27
60	40	2	102	—	—	—	—	102	—	—	—	—
2	22	—	21	3	—	—	—	21	3	—	—	—
10.50	34	8.50	14.50	14.50	11	12	1	14.50	14.50	11	12	1
1.40	10.50	2.10	8.40	2.80	0.70	0.70	—	10.50	2.10	—	0.70	—
14.33	38.67	—	13	—	38	2	—	13	—	38	2	—
61.50	35.50	12	89	11.50	—	4	1.50	92.50	11	—	3.50	—
4	8	—	12	—	—	—	—	12	—	—	—	—
2.75	8.25	—	5.75	5.25	—	—	—	5.75	5.25	—	—	—
30.50	96.50	5	50.50	7	67.50	3	1	51.50	7	67.50	2	1
6	39	1	35	—	—	3	4	35	—	—	3	4
15	21	—	27	—	—	7	—	29	2	—	5	—
10	27	—	9	1	24	—	1	9	1	24	—	1
3	5.50	1.50	6.50	3.25	—	—	—	6.50	3.25	—	—	—
1.50	15.50	—	6.50	8.50	—	1	—	6.50	8.50	—	1	—
1	51	—	—	52	—	—	—	—	52	—	—	—
28	33	3	11	—	—	6	—	43	—	—	4	1
22	20	2	10.25	10.25	3	18.50	2	25.75	5.25	3	4	1
5	12	—	12.50	2.50	—	2	—	12.50	2.50	—	2	—
2	14	1	16	—	—	1	—	16	—	—	1	—
22	29	—	30	20	—	—	1	30	20	—	—	1
15	—	—	13.50	1.50	—	—	—	13.50	1.50	—	—	—
2.50	0.50	—	1	1.50	—	0.50	—	1	1.50	—	0.50	—
1	41	5	10	35	—	—	2	10	35	—	—	2
12	55	6	24.50	48.50	—	—	—	24.50	48.50	—	—	—
3	15	—	10	—	8	—	—	10	—	8	—	—
—	3	—	1.50	1.50	—	—	—	1.50	1.50	—	—	—
11	23	—	34	—	—	—	—	34	—	—	—	—
5.50	31.50	2	1.50	23.50	—	1	4	9.50	23.50	—	2	4
999.34	1852.86	163.80	1728.35	525.00	381.70	151.95	77.50	1864.95	485.65	377.50	101.45	69.50

2. Other candidates: Hubert H. Humphrey, 66.70 (46 in Minnesota, 4 in Ohio, 4 in Wisconsin, 3 in Michigan, 2 in Indiana, 2 in Pennsylvania, 2 in Florida, 1 in Utah, 1 in Chicago, 1 in Hawaii, 0.70 in North Dakota); Wilbur D. Mills, 33.80 (25 in Arkansas, 3 in Illinois, 3 in New Jersey, 2 in Alabama, 0.55 in Wyoming, 0.25 in Alaska); Edmund S. Muskie, 24.30 (15 in Maine, 5.50 in Illinois, 1.80 in New Hampshire, 1 in Texas, 1 in Colorado); Edward M. Kennedy, 12.70 (4 in Iowa, 3 in Illinois, 2 in Ohio, 1 in Kansas, 1 in Indiana, 1 in Tennessee, 0.70 in North Dakota); Wayne L. Hays, 5 (Ohio); Eugene J. McCarthy, 2 (Illinois); Mondale, 1 (Kansas); Clark, 1 (Minnesota); not voting, 5 (Tennessee).

3. Humphrey, 35 (16 in Minnesota, 4 in Ohio, 4 in Wisconsin, 3 in Indiana, 3 in Michigan, 2 in Pennsylvania, 1 in Utah, 1 in Florida, 1 in Hawaii); Mills, 32.80 (25 in Arkansas, 2 in Illinois, 2 in New Jersey, 2 in Alabama, 1 in South Carolina, 0.55 in Wyoming, 0.25 in Alaska); Muskie, 20.80 (15 in Maine, 3 in Illinois, 1.80 in New Hampshire, 1 in Texas); Kennedy, 10.65 (4 in Iowa, 2 in Ohio, 1 in Kansas, 1 in Indiana, 1 in Tennessee, 1 in Illinois, 0.65 in Delaware); Hays, 5 (Ohio); McCarthy, 2 (Illinois); Mondale, 1 (Kansas).

1972 Republican

(Narrative, p. 138)

| | | First Pres. Ballot | |
Delegation	Total Votes	Nixon	McCloskey
Alabama	18	18	—
Alaska	12	12	—
Arizona	18	18	—
Arkansas	18	18	—
California	96	96	—
Colorado	20	20	—
Connecticut	22	22	—
Delaware	12	12	—
Florida	40	40	—
Georgia	24	24	—
Hawaii	14	14	—
Idaho	14	14	—
Illinois	58	58	—
Indiana	32	32	—
Iowa	22	22	—
Kansas	20	20	—
Kentucky	24	24	—
Louisiana	20	20	—
Maine	8	8	—
Maryland	26	26	—
Massachusetts	34	34	—
Michigan	48	48	—
Minnesota	26	26	—
Mississippi	14	14	—
Missouri	30	30	—
Montana	14	14	—
Nebraska	16	16	—
Nevada	12	12	—
New Hampshire	14	14	—
New Jersey	40	40	—
New Mexico	14	13	1
New York	88	88	—
North Carolina	32	32	—
North Dakota	12	12	—
Ohio	56	56	—
Oklahoma	22	22	—
Oregon	18	18	—
Pennsylvania	60	60	—
Rhode Island	8	8	—
South Carolina	22	22	—
South Dakota	14	14	—
Tennessee	26	26	—
Texas	52	52	—
Utah	14	14	—
Vermont	12	12	—
Virginia	30	30	—
Washington	24	24	—
West Virginia	18	18	—
Wisconsin	28	28	—
Wyoming	12	12	—
District of Columbia	9	9	—
Guam	3	3	—
Puerto Rico	5	5	—
Virgin Islands	3	3	—
Total	1348	1347	1

1976 Democratic

(Narrative, p. 139)

		First Pres. Ballot[1] (Before shift)				First Pres. Ballot[2] (After shift)			
Delegation	Total Votes	Carter	Udall	Brown	Wallace	Carter	Udall	Brown	Wallace
Alabama	35	30	—	—	5	30	—	—	5
Alaska	10	10	—	—	—	10	—	—	—
Arizona	25	6	19	—	—	6	19	—	—
Arkansas	26	25	1	—	—	25	1	—	—
California	280	73	2	205	—	278	2	—	—
Colorado	35	15	6	11	—	15	6	11	—
Connecticut	51	35	16	—	—	35	16	—	—
Delaware	12	10.50	—	1.50	—	10.50	—	1.50	—
Florida	81	70	—	1	10	70	—	1	10
Georgia	50	50	—	—	—	50	—	—	—
Hawaii	17	17	—	—	—	17	—	—	—
Idaho	16	16	—	—	—	16	—	—	—
Illinois	169	164	1	2	1	164	1	2	1
Indiana	75	72	—	—	3	72	—	—	—
Iowa	47	25	20	1	—	25	20	1	—
Kansas	34	32	2	—	—	32	2	—	—
Kentucky	46	39	2	—	5	29	2	—	5
Louisiana	41	18	—	18	5	35	—	1	5
Maine	20	15	5	—	—	15	5	—	—
Maryland	53	44	6	3	—	44	6	3	—
Massachusetts[3]	104	65	21	—	11	65	21	—	11
Michigan	133	75	58	—	—	75	58	—	—
Minnesota	65	37	2	1	—	37	2	1	—
Mississippi	24	23	—	—	—	23	—	—	—
Missouri	71	58	4	2	—	58	4	2	—
Montana	17	11	2	—	—	11	2	—	—
Nebraska	23	20	—	3	—	20	—	3	—
Nevada	11	3	—	6.50	—	3	—	6.50	—
New Hampshire	17	15	2	—	—	15	2	—	—
New Jersey	108	108	—	—	—	108	—	—	—
New Mexico	18	14	4	—	—	14	4	—	—
New York	274	209.50	56.50	4	—	209.50	56.50	4	—
North Carolina	61	56	—	—	3	56	—	—	3
North Dakota	13	13	—	—	—	13	—	—	—
Ohio	152	132	20	—	—	132	20	—	—
Oklahoma	37	32	1	—	—	32	1	—	—
Oregon	34	16	—	10	—	16	—	10	—
Pennsylvania	178	151	21	6	—	151	21	6	—
Rhode Island	22	14	—	8	—	22	—	—	—
South Carolina	31	28	—	1	2	28	—	1	2
South Dakota	17	11	5	—	—	11	5	—	—
Tennessee	46	45	—	—	1	45	—	—	1
Texas	130	124	—	4	1	124	—	4	1
Utah	18	10	—	5	—	10	—	5	—
Vermont	12	5	4	3	—	5	4	3	1
Virginia	54	48	6	—	—	48	6	—	—
Washington	53	36	11	3	—	36	11	3	—
West Virginia	33	30	1	—	—	30	1	—	—
Wisconsin	68	29	25	—	10	29	25	—	10
Wyoming	10	8	1	1	—	8	1	1	—
District of Columbia	17	12	5	—	—	12	5	—	—
Puerto Rico	22	22	—	—	—	22	—	—	—
Canal Zone	3	3	—	—	—	3	—	—	—
Guam	3	3	—	—	—	3	—	—	—
Virgin Island	3	3	—	—	—	3	—	—	—
Democrats Abroad	3	2.50	—	0.50	—	2.50	—	0.50	—
Total	3008	2238.50	329.50	300.50	57.00	2468.50	329.50	70.50	57.00

1. Other candidates: Ellen McCormack, 22 (1 in Illinois, 2 in Massachusetts, 11 in Minnesota, 7 in Missouri, 1 in Wisconsin); Frank Church, 19 (3 in Colorado, 4 in Montana, 1 in Nevada, 8 in Oregon, 1 in Utah, 2 in Washington); Hubert H. Humphrey, 10 (9 in Minnesota, 1 in South Dakota); Henry M. Jackson, 10 (2 in Massachusetts, 4 in New York, 1 in Washington, 3 in Wisconsin); Fred Harris, 9 (2 in Massachusetts, 4 in Minnesota, 3 in Oklahoma); Milton J. Shapp, 2 (1 in Massachusetts, 1 in Utah); receiving one vote each: Robert C. Byrd (West Virginia); Cesar Chavez (Utah); Leon Jaworski (Texas); Barbara C. Jordan (Oklahoma); Edward M. Kennedy (Iowa); Jennings Randolph (West Virginia); Fred Stover (Minnesota); "nobody" (0.5 in Nevada); not voting, 3 (1 in Mississippi, 2 in North Carolina).

2. The rules were suspended after the switches and Carter was nominated by acclamation.

3. Massachusetts passed when originally called on and cast its votes at the end of the roll call, after vote switches.

1976 Republican

(Narrative, p. 142)

Delegation	Total Votes	Rule 16C[1]		First Pres. Ballot[2]	
		Yea	Nay	Ford	Reagan
Alabama	37	37	—	—	37
Alaska	19	2	17	17	2
Arizona	29	25	4	2	27
Arkansas	27	17	10	10	17
California	167	166	1	—	167
Colorado	31	26	5	5	26
Connecticut	35	—	35	35	—
Delaware	17	1	16	15	2
Florida	66	28	38	43	23
Georgia	48	39	7	—	48
Hawaii	19	1	18	18	1
Idaho	21	17	4	4	17
Illinois	101	20	79	86	14
Indiana	54	27	27	9	45
Iowa	36	18	18	19	17
Kansas	34	4	30	30	4
Kentucky	37	26	10	19	18
Louisiana	41	34	6	5	36
Maine	20	5	15	15	5
Maryland	43	8	35	43	—
Massachusetts	43	15	28	28	15
Michigan	84	29	55	55	29
Minnesota	42	5	35	32	10
Mississippi	30	—	30	16	14
Missouri	49	30	18	18	31
Montana	20	20	—	—	20
Nebraska	25	18	7	7	18
Nevada	18	15	3	5	13
New Hampshire	21	3	18	18	3
New Jersey	67	4	62	63	4
New Mexico	21	20	1	—	21
New York	154	20	134	133	20
North Carolina	54	51	3	25	29
North Dakota	18	6	12	11	7
Ohio	97	7	90	91	6
Oklahoma	36	36	—	—	36
Oregon	30	14	16	16	14
Pennsylvania	103	14	89	93	10
Rhode Island	19	—	19	19	—
South Carolina	36	25	11	9	27
South Dakota	20	11	9	9	11
Tennessee	43	17	26	21	22
Texas	100	100	—	—	100
Utah	20	20	—	—	20
Vermont	18	—	18	18	—
Virginia	51	36	15	16	35
Washington	38	31	7	7	31
West Virginia	28	12	16	20	8
Wisconsin	45	—	45	45	—
Wyoming	17	9	8	7	10
District of Columbia	14	—	14	14	—
Puerto Rico	8	—	8	8	—
Guam	4	—	4	4	—
Virgin Islands	4	—	4	4	—
Total	2259	1069	1180	1187	1070

1. Not voting, 10.
2. Other candidate: Elliot L. Richardson, 1 (New York); not voting, 1 (Illinois). The nomination was made unanimous at the end of the balloting.

1980 Republican

(Narrative, p. 144)

Delegation	Total Votes	First Pres. Ballot[1]		
		Reagan	Anderson	Bush
Alabama	27	27	—	—
Alaska	19	19	—	—
Arizona	28	28	—	—
Arkansas	19	19	—	—
California	168	168	—	—
Colorado	31	31	—	—
Connecticut	35	35	—	—
Delaware	12	12	—	—
District of Columbia	14	14	—	—
Florida	51	51	—	—
Georgia	36	36	—	—
Guam	4	4	—	—
Hawaii	14	14	—	—
Idaho	21	21	—	—
Illinois	102	81	21	—
Indiana	54	54	—	—
Iowa	37	37	—	—
Kansas	32	32	—	—
Kentucky	27	27	—	—
Louisiana	31	31	—	—
Maine	21	21	—	—
Maryland	30	30	—	—
Massachusetts	42	33	9	—
Michigan	82	67	—	13
Minnesota	34	33	—	—
Mississippi	22	22	—	—
Missouri	37	37	—	—
Montana	20	20	—	—
Nebraska	25	25	—	—
Nevada	17	17	—	—
New Hampshire	22	22	—	—
New Jersey	66	66	—	—
New Mexico	22	22	—	—
New York	123	121	—	—
North Carolina	40	40	—	—
North Dakota	17	17	—	—
Ohio	77	77	—	—
Oklahoma	34	34	—	—
Oregon	29	29	—	—
Pennsylvania	83	83	—	—
Puerto Rico	14	14	—	—
Rhode Island	13	13	—	—
South Carolina	25	25	—	—
South Dakota	22	22	—	—
Tennessee	32	32	—	—
Texas	80	80	—	—
Utah	21	21	—	—
Vermont	19	19	—	—
Virginia	51	51	—	—
Virgin Islands	4	4	—	—
Washington	37	36	1	—
West Virginia	18	18	—	—
Wisconsin	34	28	6	—
Wyoming	19	19	—	—
Total	1994	1939	37	13

1. Other candidates: Anne Armstrong, 1 (Michigan); not voting, 4.

1980 Democratic

(Narrative, p. 146)

Delegation	Total Votes	Minority Rule #5[1]		First Pres. Ballot[3] (Before shift)		First Pres. Ballot[4] (After shift)	
		Yea	Nay	Carter	Kennedy	Carter	Kennedy
Alabama	45	3	42	43	2	43	2
Alaska	11	6.11	4.89	8.40	2.60	8.40	2.60
Arizona	29	16	13	13	16	13	16
Arkansas	33	9	24	25	6	25	6
California	306	171	132[2]	140	166	140	166
Colorado	40	24	16	27	10	27	10
Connecticut	54	28	26	26	28	26	28
Delaware	14	6.50	7.50	10	4	14	—
District of Columbia	19	12	7	12	5	12	5
Florida	100	25	75	75	25	75	25
Georgia	63	1	62	62	—	62	—
Hawaii	19	4	15	16	2	16	2
Idaho	17	9	8	9	7	9	7
Illinois	179	26	153	163	16	163	16
Indiana	80	27	53	53	27	53	27
Iowa	50	21	29	31	17	33	17
Kansas	37	17	20	23	14	23	14
Kentucky	50	12	38	45	5	45	5
Louisiana	51	15	36	50	1	50	1
Maine	22	12	10	11	11	11	11
Maryland	59	27	32	34	24	34	24
Massachusetts	111	81	30	34	77	34	77
Michigan	141	71	70	102	38	102	38
Minnesota	75	30	45	41	14	41	14
Mississippi	32	—	32	32	—	32	—
Missouri	77	20	57	58	19	58	19
Montana	19	9	10	13	6	13	6
Nebraska	24	11	13	14	10	14	10
Nevada	12	6.47	5.53	8.12	3.88	8.12	3.88
New Hampshire	19	9	10	10	9	10	9
New Jersey	113	68	45	45	68	45	68
New Mexico	20	11	9	10	10	10	10
New York	282	163	118	129	151	129	151
North Carolina	69	13	56	66	3	66	3
North Dakota	14	10	4	5	7	5	7
Ohio	161	81	80	89	72	89	72
Oklahoma	42	9	33	36	3	36	3
Oregon	39	14	25	26	13	26	13
Pennsylvania	185	102	83	95	90	95	90
Puerto Rico	41	20	21	21	20	21	20
Rhode Island	23	17	6	6	17	6	17
South Carolina	37	6	31	37	—	37	—
South Dakota	19	10	9	9	10	9	10
Tennessee	55	8	47	51	4	51	4
Texas	152	47	105	108	38	108	38
Utah	20	12	8	11	4	11	4
Vermont	12	7.50	4.50	5	7	5	7
Virginia	64	7	57	59	5	59	5
Washington	58	24	34	36	22	36	22
West Virginia	35	16	19	21	10	21	10
Wisconsin	75	26	49	48	26	48	26
Wyoming	11	3.50	7.50	8	3	8	3
Virgin Islands	4	—	4	4	—	4	—
Guam	4	—	4	4	—	4	—
Latin America	4	4	—	4	—	4	—
Democrats Abroad	4	2.50	1.50	1.50	2	1.50	2
Total	3331	1390.58	1936.42	2123.02	1150.48	2129.02	1150.48

1. The vote was on a minority report by supporters of Sen. Edward M. Kennedy to overturn a proposed rule that would bind all delegates to vote on the first ballot for the presidential candidate under whose banner they were elected. a "yes" vote supported the Kennedy position while a "no" supported the Carter view that delegates should be bound.

2. Not voting, 1.

3. Other candidates: William Proxmire, 10 (Minnesota); Scott M. Matheson, 5 (Utah); Koryne Horbal, 5 (Minnesota); Ronald V. Dellums, 2.5 (2 in New York, 0.5 from Democrats Abroad); receiving 2 votes each: John C. Culver (Iowa); Warren Spannous (Minnesota); Alice Tripp (Minnesota); Kent Hance (Texas); Robert C. Byrd (West Virginia); receiving 1 vote each: Dale Bumpers (Arkansas); Edmund S. Muskie (Colorado); Walter F. Mondale (Minnesota); Hugh L. Carey (Oklahoma); Tom Steed (Oklahoma); Edmund G. Brown (Wisconsin); uncommitted, 10; not voting, 5: absent, 2.

4. Votes for other candidates remained the same except that Iowa switched its 2 votes for Culver to Carter. After the switches Carter was nominated by acclamation.

1984 Republican

(Narrative, p.152)

Delegation	Total Votes	First Pres. Ballot[1] Reagan
Alabama	38	38
Alaska	18	18
Arizona	32	32
Arkansas	29	29
California	176	176
Colorado	35	35
Connecticut	35	35
Delaware	19	19
District of Columbia	14	14
Florida	82	82
Georgia	37	37
Guam	4	4
Hawaii	14	14
Idaho	21	21
Illinois	93	92
Indiana	52	52
Iowa	37	37
Kansas	32	32
Kentucky	37	37
Louisiana	41	41
Maine	20	20
Maryland	31	31
Massachusetts	52	52
Michigan	77	77
Minnesota	32	32
Mississippi	30	30
Missouri	47	47
Montana	20	20
Nebraska	24	24
Nevada	22	22
New Hampshire	22	22
New Jersey	64	64
New Mexico	24	24
New York	136	136
North Carolina	53	53
North Dakota	18	18
Ohio	89	89
Oklahoma	35	35
Oregon	32	32
Pennsylvania	98	97
Puerto Rico	14	14
Rhode Island	14	14
South Carolina	35	35
South Dakota	19	19
Tennessee	46	46
Texas	109	109
Utah	26	26
Vermont	19	19
Virginia	50	50
Virgin Islands	4	4
Washington	44	44
West Virginia	19	19
Wisconsin	46	46
Wyoming	18	18
Total	2235	2233

1. Not voting, 2.

1984 Democratic

(Narrative, p. 150)

Delegation	Total Votes	No First Use of Nuclear Weapons Yea	Nay	Not Voting	Defense Spending Yea	Nay	Not Voting	Dual Primaries Yea	Nay	Not Voting	Military Force Restrictions Yea	Nay	Not Voting
Alabama	62	15	46	1	11	49	2	13	49	—	61	1	—
Alaska	14	7	7	—	1	13	—	2	12	—	13	1	—
Arizona	40	20	19	—	18	21	—	20	19	—	39	—	—
Arkansas	42	13	29	—	12	30	—	7	33	2	39	2	1
California	345	149	84	—	99	170	—	129	128	—	285	31	—
Colorado	51	31	16	4	5	45	1	26	24	1	51	—	—
Connecticut	60	28	24	8	32	27	1	27	33	—	60	—	—
Delaware	18	1	17	—	1	17	—	1	17	—	18	—	—
D.C.	19	15	4	—	17	2	—	14	5	—	6	12	—
Florida	143	47	76	20	42	81	20	27	110	6	95	25	23
Georgia	84	40	33	—	38	45	—	39	42	—	67	1	2
Hawaii	27	1	26	—	—	27	—	—	27	—	—	—	—
Idaho	22	9	—	—	10	11	—	9	13	—	22	—	—
Illinois	194	42	145	—	40	147	—	48	143	—	191	—	3
Indiana	88	31	46	—	18	64	—	23	64	—	88	—	—
Iowa	58	22	36	—	7	51	—	5	53	—	58	—	—
Kansas	44	14	29	1	6	38	—	10	34	—	44	—	—
Kentucky	63	14	48	—	10	52	—	15	47	—	55	8	—
Louisiana	69	24	32	—	30	39	—	44	22	—	44	22	—
Maine	27	7	16	—	3	23	—	10	16	—	23	1	—
Maryland	74	20	51	3	20	54	—	18	56	—	51	19	4
Massachusetts	116	89	24	—	69	43	1	82	31	1	112	—	—
Michigan	155	43	105	7	32	118	5	37	111	7	137	—	18
Minnesota	86	37	41	8	30	48	8	25	57	4	73	2	11
Mississippi	43	15	26	2	16	26	1	13	29	1	33	8	2
Missouri	86	20	62	4	22	62	2	24	61	1	70	—	16
Montana	25	8	15	2	4	21	—	5	20	—	25	—	—
Nebraska	30	2	25	3	2	25	3	10	17	3	24	—	6
Nevada	20	6	14	—	3	17	—	5	15	—	19	—	—
New Hampshire	22	10	12	—	5	17	—	1	21	—	22	—	—
New Jersey	122	9	113	—	9	113	—	7	115	—	116	6	—
New Mexico	28	7	19	2	2	26	—	3	25	—	27	1	—
New York	285	134	140	—	131	139	7	125	146	3	196	57	—
North Carolina	88	28	56	—	19	66	—	32	55	—	73	3	—
North Dakota	18	13	5	—	8	10	—	8	10	—	18	—	—
Ohio	175	71	103	—	47	122	6	40	133	2	173	—	2
Oklahoma	53	16	35	2	3	47	3	3	49	1	49	3	1
Oregon	50	32	13	5	26	21	3	24	24	2	49	—	1
Pennsylvania	195	42	153	—	39	156	—	53	142	—	195	—	—
Puerto Rico	53	—	53	—	—	53	—	—	53	—	10	43	—
Rhode Island	27	11	15	1	11	15	1	8	18	1	24	—	2
South Carolina	48	21	23	4	23	19	6	21	25	2	21	19	8
South Dakota	19	7	12	—	7	12	—	7	12	—	—	6	—
Tennessee	76	31	41	4	29	41	6	34	39	3	72	1	3
Texas	200	53	137	10	47	141	12	39	150	11	152	38	10
Utah	27	17	10	—	11	15	1	13	14	—	19	7	1
Vermont	17	11	4	—	10	4	—	10	4	—	12	3	—
Virginia	78	29	48	—	29	48	—	33	43	—	50	23	4
Washington	70	49	18	—	29	39	1	35	35	—	67	—	—
West Virginia	44	12	27	5	12	29	3	17	24	3	—	—	—
Wisconsin	89	28	45	16	26	57	6	31	54	4	83	6	—
Wyoming	15	2	12	—	2	12	—	13	1	—	13	1	—
Latin America	5	—	5	—	.5	4.5	—	—	5	—	5	—	—
Democrats Abroad	5	1.5	3.5	—	1.5	3.5	—	—	5	—	5	—	—
Virgin Islands	6	1.2	4.8	—	2.6	2.6	.6	1.2	4.8	—	4.8	1.2	—
American Samoa	6	—	6	—	—	6	—	—	6	—	6	—	—
Guam	7	—	7	—	—	7	—	7	—	—	7	—	—
Total	**3933**	**1405.7**	**2216.3**	**112**	**1127.6**	**2591.6**	**99.6**	**1253.2**	**2500.8**	**58**	**3271.8**	**351.2**	**118**

1984 Democratic

(Narrative, p. 150)

Delegation	Total Votes	First Pres. Ballot[1]		
		Mondale	Hart	Jackson
Alabama	62	39	13	9
Alaska	14	9	4	1
Arizona	40	20	16	2
Arkansas	42	26	9	7
California	345	95	190	33
Colorado	51	1	42	1
Connecticut	60	23	36	1
Delaware	18	13	5	0
D.C.	19	5	—	14
Florida	143	82	55	3
Georgia	84	40	24	20
Hawaii	27	27	—	0
Idaho	22	10	12	0
Illinois	194	114	41	39
Indiana	88	42	38	8
Iowa	58	37	18	2
Kansas	44	25	16	3
Kentucky	63	51	5	7
Louisiana	69	26	19	24
Maine	27	13	13	0
Maryland	74	54	3	17
Massachusetts	116	59	49	5
Michigan	155	96	49	10
Minnesota	86	63	3	4
Mississippi	43	26	4	13
Missouri	86	55	14	16
Montana	25	11	13	1
Nebraska	30	12	17	1
Nevada	20	9	10	1
New Hampshire	22	12	10	0
New Jersey	122	115	—	7
New Mexico	28	13	13	2
New York	285	156	75	52
North Carolina	88	53	19	16
North Dakota	18	10	5	1
Ohio	175	84	80	11
Oklahoma	53	24	26	3
Oregon	50	16	31	2
Pennsylvania	195	177	—	18
Puerto Rico	53	53	—	0
Rhode Island	27	14	12	0
South Carolina	48	16	13	19
South Dakota	19	9	10	0
Tennessee	76	39	20	17
Texas	200	119	40	36
Utah	27	8	19	0
Vermont	17	5	8	3
Virginia	78	34	18	25
Washington	70	31	36	3
West Virginia	44	30	14	0
Wisconsin	89	58	25	6
Wyoming	15	7	7	0
Latin American	5	5	—	0
Democrats Abroad	5	3	1.5	0.5
Virgin Islands	6	4	—	2
American Samoa	6	6	—	0
Guam	7	7	—	0
Total	3933	2191	1200.5	465.5

1. Other candidates: Thomas F. Eagleton, 18 (16 in Minnesota, 2 in North Dakota); George McGovern, 4 (3 in Massachusetts, 1 in Iowa); John Glenn, 2 (Texas); Joseph R. Biden Jr., 1 (Maine); Martha Kirkland, 1 (Alabama); not voting, 40 (27 in California, 7 Connecticut, 2 in Arizona, 2 in Florida, 1 in Vermont, 1 in Wyoming); absent, 10.

1988 Democratic

(Narrative, p. 154)

Delegation	Total Votes	Fair Tax[1]		No First Use of Nuclear Weapons[2]		First Pres. Ballot[3]	
		Yea	Nay	Yea	Nay	Dukakis	Jackson
Alabama	65	14	35	19	38	37	28
Alaska	17	5	7	8	8	9	7
Arizona	43	15	21	15	25	28	14
Arkansas	48	11	27	9	25	31	11
California	363	104	240	119.09	192.63	235	122
Colorado	55	20	31	20	32	37	18
Connecticut	63	16	42	21	39	47	16
Delaware	19	8	11	8	11	9	7
Florida	154	33	89	33	100	116	35
Georgia	94	30	43	36	43	50	42
Hawaii	28	8	19	8	19	19	8
Idaho	24	3	18	3	18	20	3
Illinois	200	28	75	40	62	138	57
Indiana	89	18	68	19	66	69.50	18
Iowa	61	11	48	21	38	49	12
Kansas	45	12	29.50	14.50	28.50	30	15
Kentucky	65	6	43	6	46	59	6
Louisiana	76	23	11	26	13	41	33
Maine	29	11	15	11	14	17	12
Maryland	84	21	58	21	58	59	25
Massachusetts	119	20	79	23	86	99	19
Michigan	162	78	77	78	77	80	80
Minnesota	91	36	45	42	46	57	29
Mississippi	47	24	15	27	16	19	26
Missouri	88	31	49	33	50	50	37
Montana	28	5	21	7	19	22	5
Nebraska	30	7	23	7	23	22	8
Nevada	23	5	15	6	15	16	5
New Hampshire	22	0	22	1	21	22	0
New Jersey	126	19	39	19	64	107	19
New Mexico	30	7	19	7	20	22	8
New York	292	90	181	108	173	194	97
North Carolina	95	36	51	37	51	58	35
North Dakota	22	46	131	5	11	17	3
Ohio	183	46	131	48	132	136	46
Oklahoma	56	4	44	4	46	52	4
Oregon	54	18	31	18	34	35	18
Pennsylvania	202	22	177	22	179	179	23
Rhode Island	28	3	15	4	16	24	3
South Carolina	53	29	19	30	23	22	31
South Dakota	20	2	16	2	17	19	1
Tennessee	84	12	54	15	57	63	20
Texas	211	72	123	72	121	135	71
Utah	28	3	18	5	20	25	3
Vermont	20	10	9	11	9	9	9
Virginia	86	37	46	41	44	42	42
Washington	77	27	46	29	42	50	27
West Virginia	47	0	44	1	43	47	0
Wisconsin	91	24	59	25	59	65	25
Wyoming	18	4	12	6	10	14	4
District of Columbia	25	13	6	16	8	7	18
Puerto Rico	57	3	53	8	48	48.50	8
Virgin Islands	5	5	0	5	0	0	5
American Samoa	6	0	6	0	6	6	0
Guam	4	0	4	0	4	4	0
Democrats Abroad	9	0.50	8.50	1	8	8.25	0.50
Total	4,162	1,091.50	2,499.00	1,220.59	2,474.13	2,876.25	1,218.50

1. Not voting, 90.
2. Not voting, 67.
3. Other candidates: Lloyd Bentsen, 1 (Alaska); Joseph R. Biden Jr., 2 (Delaware); Richard A. Gephardt, 2 (1 in Louisiana, 1 in Texas); Richard H. Stallings, 3 (Minnesota); Gary Hart, 1 (Vermont), absent, 44.25.

1988 Republican

(Narrative, p. 156)

Delegation	Total Votes	First Pres. Ballot Bush
Alabama	38	38
Alaska	19	19
Arizona	33	33
Arkansas	27	27
California	175	175
Colorado	36	36
Connecticut	35	35
Delaware	17	17
Florida	82	82
Georgia	48	48
Hawaii	20	20
Idaho	22	22
Illinois	92	92
Indiana	51	51
Iowa	37	37
Kansas	34	34
Kentucky	38	38
Louisiana	41	41
Maine	22	22
Maryland	41	41
Massachusetts	52	52
Michigan	77	77
Minnesota	31	31
Mississippi	31	31
Missouri	47	47
Montana	20	20
Nebraska	25	25
Nevada	20	20
New Hampshire	23	23
New Jersey	64	64
New Mexico	26	26
New York	136	136
North Carolina	54	54
North Dakota	16	16
Ohio	88	88
Oklahoma	36	36
Oregon	32	32
Pennsylvania	96	96
Rhode Island	21	21
South Carolina	37	37
South Dakota	18	18
Tennessee	45	45
Texas	111	111
Utah	26	26
Vermont	17	17
Virginia	50	50
Washington	41	41
West Virginia	28	28
Wisconsin	47	47
Wyoming	18	18
District of Columbia	14	14
Puerto Rico	14	14
Virgin Islands	4	4
Guam	4	4
Total	2,277	2,277

1992 Democratic

(Narrative, p. 158)

Delegation	Total Votes	Tax Fairness[1]		First Pres. Ballot[2]		
		Yes	Nay	Clinton	Brown	Tsongas
Alabama	67	0	67	67	0	0
Alaska	18	0	16	18	0	0
Arizona	49	29	15	23	12	14
Arkansas	48	0	48	48	0	0
California	406	96	176	211	160	0
Colorado	58	31	23	26	19	13
Connecticut	66	23	30	45	21	0
Delaware	21	8	8	17	3	1
Florida	167	50	71	141	3	15
Georgia	96	14	50	96	0	0
Hawaii	28	5	17	24	2	0
Idaho	26	5	17	22	0	1
Illinois	195	51	76	155	9	29
Indiana	93	21	68	73	20	0
Iowa	59	7	43	55	2	0
Kansas	44	5	38	43	0	0
Kentucky	64	3	53	63	0	0
Louisiana	75	0	75	75	0	0
Maine	31	18	2	14	13	4
Maryland	85	27	23	83	0	2
Massachusetts	119	97	0	109	6	1
Michigan	159	43	82	120	35	0
Minnesota	92	23	43	61	8	2
Mississippi	46	0	46	46	0	0
Missouri	92	6	46	91	1	0
Montana	24	0	19	21	2	0
Nebraska	33	10	14	24	9	0
Nevada	27	0	25	23	4	0
New Hampshire	24	10	10	17	0	7
New Jersey	126	12	76	102	24	0
New Mexico	34	3	27	30	3	0
New York	290	116	109	155	67	64
North Carolina	99	0	64	95	1	0
North Dakota	22	3	14	18	0	0
Ohio	178	37	141	144	34	0
Oklahoma	58	0	53	56	2	0
Oregon	57	14	38	38	19	0
Pennsylvania	194	21	78	139	43	4
Rhode Island	29	7	9	27	2	0
South Carolina	54	7	40	54	0	0
South Dakota	21	1	16	21	0	0
Tennessee	85	6	38	85	0	0
Texas	232	33	112	204	4	20
Utah	29	25	0	20	9	0
Vermont	21	11	6	14	7	0
Virginia	97	11	43	94	3	0
Washington	84	30	29	49	18	14
West Virginia	41	0	13	41	0	0
Wisconsin	94	29	61	46	30	18
Wyoming	19	5	8	18	1	0
District of Columbia	31	0	30	31	0	0
Puerto Rico	58	0	58	57	0	0
Virgin Islands	5	0	5	5	0	0
American Samoa	5	0	5	5	0	0
Guam	4	0	4	4	0	0
Democrats Abroad	9	0	8.75	9	0	0
Total	4,288	953.00	2,286.75	3,372	596	209

1. Not voting, 177.
2. Other candidates: Larry Agran, 3 (1 in Idaho, 2 in Minnesota); Robert P. Casey, 10 (Minnesota); Patricia Schroeder, 8 (Colorado); Albert Gore Jr., 1 (Pennsylvania); Joseph Simonetti, 1 (Pennsylvania); Others, 2 (1 in New Mexico, 1 in North Dakota). Not voting, 86.

1992 Republican

(Narrative, p. 160)

Delegation	Total Votes	First Pres. Ballot[1]	
		Bush	Buchanan
Alabama	38	38	0
Alaska	19	19	0
Arizona	37	37	0
Arkansas	27	27	0
California	201	201	0
Colorado	37	31	5
Connecticut	35	35	0
Delaware	19	19	0
Florida	97	97	0
Georgia	52	52	0
Hawaii	14	14	0
Idaho	22	22	0
Illinois	85	85	0
Indiana	51	51	0
Iowa	23	23	0
Kansas	30	30	0
Kentucky	35	35	0
Louisiana	38	38	0
Maine	22	22	0
Maryland	42	42	0
Massachusetts	38	35	1
Michigan	72	72	0
Minnesota	32	32	0
Mississippi	34	34	0
Missouri	47	47	0
Montana	20	20	0
Nebraska	24	24	0
Nevada	21	21	0
New Hampshire[2]	23	—	0
New Jersey	60	60	0
New Mexico	25	25	0
New York	100	100	0
North Carolina	57	57	0
North Dakota	17	17	0
Ohio	83	83	0
Oklahoma	34	34	0
Oregon	23	23	0
Pennsylvania	91	90	1
Rhode Island	15	15	0
South Carolina	36	36	0
South Dakota	19	19	0
Tennessee	45	34	11
Texas	121	121	0
Utah	27	27	0
Vermont	19	19	0
Virginia	55	55	0
Washington	35	35	0
West Virginia	18	18	0
Wisconsin	35	35	0
Wyoming	20	20	0
District of Columbia	14	14	0
Puerto Rico	14	14	0
Virgin Islands	4	4	0
American Samoa	4	4	0
Guam	4	4	0
Total	2,210	2,166	18

1. Other candidates: Howard Phillips, 2 (1 in Colorado; 1 in Massachusetts), Alan Keyes, 1 (Massachusetts).
2. Never voted.

1996 Republican

(Narrative, p. 163)

Delegation	Total Votes	First Pres. Ballot[1]	
		Dole	Buchanan
Alabama	40	40	0
Alaska	19	16	0
Arizona	39	37	0
Arkansas	20	16	0
California	165	165	0
Colorado	27	27	0
Connecticut	27	27	0
Delaware	12	12	0
Florida	98	98	0
Georgia	42	42	0
Hawaii	14	14	0
Idaho	23	19	0
Illinois	69	69	0
Indiana	52	52	0
Iowa	25	25	0
Kansas	31	31	0
Kentucky	26	26	0
Louisiana	30	17	10
Maine	15	15	0
Maryland	32	32	0
Massachusetts	37	37	0
Michigan	57	52	5
Minnesota	33	33	0
Mississippi	33	33	0
Missouri	36	24	11
Montana	14	14	0
Nebraska	24	24	0
Nevada	14	14	0
New Hampshire	16	16	0
New Jersey	48	48	0
New Mexico	18	18	0
New York	102	102	0
North Carolina	58	58	0
North Dakota	18	17	0
Ohio	67	67	0
Oklahoma	38	38	0
Oregon	23	18	5
Pennsylvania	73	73	0
Rhode Island	16	16	0
South Carolina	37	37	0
South Dakota	18	18	0
Tennessee	38	37	0
Texas	123	121	2
Utah	28	27	1
Vermont	12	12	0
Virginia	53	53	0
Washington	36	27	9
West Virginia	18	18	0
Wisconsin	36	36	0
Wyoming	20	20	0
District of Columbia	14	14	0
Puerto Rico	14	14	0
Virgin Islands	4	4	0
American Samoa	4	4	0
Guam	4	4	0
Total	1,990	1,928 ·	43

1. Other candidates: Phil Gramm, 2 (Louisiana); Alan Keyes, 1(Missouri); Robert Bork, 1 (Louisiana); not voting, 15.

1996 Democratic

(Narrative, p. 165)

Delegation	Total Votes	First Pres. Ballot[1] Clinton
Alabama	66	66
Alaska	19	19
Arizona	59	59
Arkansas	47	47
California	422	416
Colorado	56	56
Connecticut	67	67
Delaware	21	21
Florida	178	178
Georgia	91	91
Hawaii	30	29
Idaho	23	23
Illinois	193	193
Indiana	88	88
Iowa	56	56
Kansas	42	42
Kentucky	61	61
Louisiana	71	71
Maine	32	32
Maryland	88	88
Massachusetts	114	114
Michigan	156	156
Minnesota	92	92
Mississippi	47	47
Missouri	93	93
Montana	24	24
Nebraska	34	34
Nevada	26	26
New Hampshire	26	26
New Jersey	122	122
New Mexico	34	34
New York	289	289
North Carolina	99	99
North Dakota	22	21
Ohio	172	172
Oklahoma	52	52
Oregon	57	54
Pennsylvania	195	195
Rhode Island	32	31
South Carolina	51	51
South Dakota	22	22
Tennessee	80	80
Texas	229	229
Utah	31	31
Vermont	22	22
Virginia	97	97
Washington	90	90
West Virginia	43	43
Wisconsin	93	93
Wyoming	19	19
District of Columbia	33	33
Puerto Rico	58	58
Virgin Islands	4	4
American Samoa	6	6
Guam	6	6
Democrats Abroad	9	9
Total	4,289	4,277

1. Not voting, 12.

2000 Republican

(Narrative, p. 168)

Delegation	Total Votes	First Pres. Ballot Bush
Alabama	44	44
Alaska	23	23
Arizona	30	30
Arkansas	24	24
California	162	162
Colorado	40	40
Connecticut	25	25
Delaware	12	12
Florida	80	80
Georgia	54	54
Hawaii	14	14
Idaho	28	28
Illinois	74	74
Indiana	55	55
Iowa	25	25
Kansas	35	35
Kentucky	31	31
Louisiana	29	29
Maine	14	14
Maryland	31	31
Massachusetts	37	37
Michigan	58	58
Minnesota	34	34
Mississippi	33	33
Missouri	35	35
Montana	23	23
Nebraska	30	30
Nevada	17	17
New Hampshire	17	17
New Jersey	54	54
New Mexico	21	21
New York	101	101
North Carolina	62	62
North Dakota	19	19
Ohio	69	69
Oklahoma	38	38
Oregon	24	24
Pennsylvania	78	78
Rhode Island	14	14
South Carolina	37	37
South Dakota	22	22
Tennessee	37	37
Texas	124	124
Utah	29	29
Vermont	12	12
Virginia	56	56
Washington	37	37
West Virginia	18	18
Wisconsin	37	37
Wyoming	22	22
District of Columbia	15	15
Puerto Rico	14	14
Virgin Islands	4	4
American Samoa	4	4
Guam	4	4
Total	2,066	2,066

2000 Democratic

(Narrative, p. 170)

Delegation	Total Votes	First Pres. Ballot[1] Gore
Alabama	64	64
Alaska	19	19
Arizona	55	55
Arkansas	47	47
California	435	435
Colorado	61	61
Connecticut	67	67
Delaware	22	22
Florida	186	186
Georgia	92	92
Hawaii	33	33
Idaho	23	23
Illinois	190	190
Indiana	88	88
Iowa	57	57
Kansas	42	42
Kentucky	58	58
Louisiana	73	73
Maine	33	33
Maryland	95	95
Massachusetts	118	118
Michigan	157	157
Minnesota	91	91
Mississippi	48	48
Missouri	92	92
Montana	24	24
Nebraska	32	32
Nevada	29	29
New Hampshire	29	29
New Jersey	124	124
New Mexico	35	35
New York	294	294
North Carolina	103	103
North Dakota	22	22
Ohio	170	170
Oklahoma	52	52
Oregon	58	58
Pennsylvania	191	191
Rhode Island	33	33
South Carolina	52	52
South Dakota	22	22
Tennessee	81	81
Texas	231	231
Utah	29	29
Vermont	22	22
Virginia	95	95
Washington	94	94
West Virginia	42	42
Wisconsin	93	93
Wyoming	18	18
District of Columbia	33	33
Puerto Rico	58	58
Virgin Islands	6	6
American Samoa	6	6
Guam	6	6
Democrats Abroad	9	9
Total	4,339	4,339

1. Unofficial total. There may have been several delegates not voting.

2004 Republican

(Narrative, p. 176)

State	Total Allocated Votes	George W. Bush	Not Voting
Alabama	48	48	
Alaska	29	29	
American Samoa	9	9	
Arizona	52	52	
Arkansas	35	35	
California	173	173	
Colorado	50	50	
Connecticut	30	30	
Delaware	18	18	
District of Columbia	19	19	
Florida	112	112	
Georgia	69	69	
Guam	9	9	
Hawaii	20	20	
Idaho	32	32	
Illinois	73	73	
Indiana	55	55	
Iowa	32	31	1
Kansas	39	39	
Kentucky	46	46	
Louisiana	45	45	
Maine	21	21	
Maryland	39	39	
Massachusetts	44	44	
Michigan	61	61	
Minnesota	41	41	
Mississippi	38	38	
Missouri	57	57	
Montana	28	28	
Nebraska	35	35	
Nevada	33	33	
New Hampshire	32	32	
New Jersey	52	52	
New Mexico	24	24	
New York	102	102	
North Carolina	67	67	
North Dakota	26	26	
Ohio	91	91	
Oklahoma	41	41	
Oregon	31	31	
Pennsylvania	75	75	
Puerto Rico	23	23	
Rhode Island	21	21	
South Carolina	46	46	
South Dakota	27	27	
Tennessee	55	55	
Texas	138	138	
Utah	36	36	
Vermont	18	18	
Virgin Islands	9	9	
Virginia	64	64	
Washington	41	41	
West Virginia	30	30	
Wisconsin	40	40	
Wyoming	28	28	
Total	2,509	2,508	1

2004 Democratic

(Narrative, p. 174)

State	Total Allocated Votes	John Kerry	Present	Abstain
Alabama	62	62		
Alaska	18	17	1	
Arkansas	47	47		
Arizona	64	64		
California	441	441		
Colorado	63	50	13	
Connecticut	62	62		
Delaware	23	23		
Florida	201	201		
Georgia	101	98		3
Hawaii	29	17	8	4
Iowa	57	57		
Idaho	23	23		
Illinois	186	186		
Indiana	81	81		
Kansas	41	41		
Kentucky	57	57		
Louisiana	72	71		1
Massachusetts	121	121		
Maryland	99	99		
Maine	35	28	6	1
Michigan	155	155		
Minnesota	86	85	1	
Missouri	88	88		
Mississippi	41	40		1
Montana	21	21		
North Carolina	107	102	4	1
North Dakota	22	22		
Nebraska	31	31		
New Hampshire	27	26		1
New Jersey	128	116		12
New Mexico	37	37		
Nevada	32	32		
New York	284	284		
Ohio	159	159		
Oklahoma	47	47		
Oregon	59	56	3	
Pennsylvania	178	178		
Rhode Island	32	32		
South Carolina	55	55		
South Dakota	22	22		
Tennessee	85	85		
Texas	232	232		
Utah	29	28		1
Virginia	98	98		
Vermont	22	22		
Washington	95	88	7	
Wisconsin	87	87		
West Virginia	39	39		
Wyoming	19	19		
District of Columbia	39	39		
Puerto Rico	57	56		1
Virgin Islands	6	6		
American Samoa	6	6		
Guam	5	5		
Democrats Abroad	9	9		
Totals	4322	4253	43	26

Appendix: Political Parties and Candidates

U.S. Presidents and Vice Presidents

President and Political Party	Born	Died	Age at Inaugu-ration	Native of	Elected from	Term of Service	Vice President
George Washington (F)	1732	1799	57	Va.	Va.	April 30, 1789–March 4, 1793	John Adams
George Washington (F)			61			March 4, 1793–March 4, 1797	John Adams
John Adams (F)	1735	1826	61	Mass.	Mass.	March 4, 1797–March 4, 1801	Thomas Jefferson
Thomas Jefferson (DR)	1743	1826	57	Va.	Va.	March 4, 1801–March 4, 1805	Aaron Burr
Thomas Jefferson (DR)			61			March 4, 1805–March 4, 1809	George Clinton
James Madison (DR)	1751	1836	57	Va.	Va.	March 4, 1809–March 4, 1813	George Clinton
James Madison (DR)			61			March 4, 1813–March 4, 1817	Elbridge Gerry
James Monroe (DR)	1758	1831	58	Va.	Va.	March 4, 1817–March 4, 1821	Daniel D. Tompkins
James Monroe (DR)			62			March 4, 1821–March 4, 1825	Daniel D. Tompkins
John Q. Adams (DR)	1767	1848	57	Mass.	Mass.	March 4, 1825–March 4, 1829	John C. Calhoun
Andrew Jackson (D)	1767	1845	61	S.C.	Tenn.	March 4, 1829–March 4, 1833	John C. Calhoun
Andrew Jackson (D)			65			March 4, 1833–March 4, 1837	Martin Van Buren
Martin Van Buren (D)	1782	1862	54	N.Y.	N.Y.	March 4, 1837–March 4, 1841	Richard M. Johnson
W. H. Harrison (W)	1773	1841	68	Va.	Ohio	March 4, 1841–April 4, 1841	John Tyler
John Tyler (W)	1790	1862	51	Va.	Va.	April 6, 1841–March 4, 1845	
James K. Polk (D)	1795	1849	49	N.C.	Tenn.	March 4, 1845–March 4, 1849	George M. Dallas
Zachary Taylor (W)	1784	1850	64	Va.	La.	March 4, 1849–July 9, 1850	Millard Fillmore
Millard Fillmore (W)	1800	1874	50	N.Y.	N.Y.	July 10, 1850–March 4, 1853	
Franklin Pierce (D)	1804	1869	48	N.H.	N.H.	March 4, 1853–March 4, 1857	William R. King
James Buchanan (D)	1791	1868	65	Pa.	Pa.	March 4, 1857–March 4, 1861	John C. Breckinridge
Abraham Lincoln (R)	1809	1865	52	Ky.	Ill.	March 4, 1861–March 4, 1865	Hannibal Hamlin
Abraham Lincoln (R)			56			March 4, 1865–April 15, 1865	Andrew Johnson
Andrew Johnson (R)	1808	1875	56	N.C.	Tenn.	April 15, 1865–March 4, 1869	
Ulysses S. Grant (R)	1822	1885	46	Ohio	Ill.	March 4, 1869–March 4, 1873	Schuyler Colfax
Ulysses S. Grant (R)			50			March 4, 1873–March 4, 1877	Henry Wilson
Rutherford B. Hayes (R)	1822	1893	54	Ohio	Ohio	March 4, 1877–March 4, 1881	William A. Wheeler
James A. Garfield (R)	1831	1881	49	Ohio	Ohio	March 4, 1881–Sept. 19, 1881	Chester A. Arthur
Chester A. Arthur (R)	1830	1886	50	Vt.	N.Y.	Sept. 20, 1881–March 4, 1885	
Grover Cleveland (D)	1837	1908	47	N.J.	N.Y.	March 4, 1885–March 4, 1889	Thomas A. Hendricks
Benjamin Harrison (R)	1833	1901	55	Ohio	Ind.	March 4, 1889–March 4, 1893	Levi P. Morton
Grover Cleveland (D)	1837	1908	55	N.J.	N.Y.	March 4, 1893–March 4, 1897	Adlai E. Stevenson
William McKinley (R)	1843	1901	54	Ohio	Ohio	March 4, 1897–March 4, 1901	Garret A. Hobart
William McKinley (R)			58			March 4, 1901–Sept. 14, 1901	Theodore Roosevelt
Theodore Roosevelt (R)	1858	1919	42	N.Y.	N.Y.	Sept. 14, 1901–March 4, 1905	
Theodore Roosevelt (R)			46			March 4, 1905–March 4, 1909	Charles W. Fairbanks
William H. Taft (R)	1857	1930	51	Ohio	Ohio	March 4, 1909–March 4, 1913	James S. Sherman
Woodrow Wilson (D)	1856	1924	56	Va.	N.J.	March 4, 1913–March 4, 1917	Thomas R. Marshall
Woodrow Wilson (D)			60			March 4, 1917–March 4, 1921	Thomas R. Marshall
Warren G. Harding (R)	1865	1923	55	Ohio	Ohio	March 4, 1921–Aug. 2, 1923	Calvin Coolidge
Calvin Coolidge (R)	1872	1933	51	Vt.	Mass.	Aug. 3, 1923–March 4, 1925	
Calvin Coolidge (R)			52			March 4, 1925–March 4, 1929	Charles G. Dawes
Herbert Hoover (R)	1874	1964	54	Iowa	Calif.	March 4, 1929–March 4, 1933	Charles Curtis
Franklin D. Roosevelt (D)	1882	1945	51	N.Y.	N.Y.	March 4, 1933–Jan. 20, 1937	John N. Garner
Franklin D. Roosevelt (D)			55			Jan. 20, 1937–Jan. 20, 1941	John N. Garner
Franklin D. Roosevelt (D)			59			Jan. 20, 1941–Jan. 20, 1945	Henry A. Wallace
Franklin D. Roosevelt (D)			63			Jan. 20, 1945–April 12, 1945	Harry S. Truman
Harry S. Truman (D)	1884	1972	60	Mo.	Mo.	April 12, 1945–Jan. 20, 1949	
Harry S. Truman (D)			64			Jan. 20, 1949–Jan. 20, 1953	Alben W. Barkley
Dwight D. Eisenhower (R)	1890	1969	62	Texas	N.Y.	Jan. 20, 1953–Jan. 20, 1957	Richard Nixon
Dwight D. Eisenhower (R)			66		Pa.	Jan. 20, 1957–Jan. 20, 1961	Richard Nixon
John F. Kennedy (D)	1917	1963	43	Mass.	Mass.	Jan. 20, 1961–Nov. 22, 1963	Lyndon B. Johnson
Lyndon B. Johnson (D)	1908	1973	55	Texas	Texas	Nov. 22, 1963–Jan. 20, 1965	
Lyndon B. Johnson (D)			56			Jan. 20, 1965–Jan. 20, 1969	Hubert H. Humphrey
Richard Nixon (R)	1913	1994	56	Calif.	N.Y.	Jan. 20, 1969–Jan. 20, 1973	Spiro T. Agnew
Richard Nixon (R)			60		Calif.	Jan. 20, 1973–Aug. 9, 1974	Spiro T. Agnew / Gerald R. Ford
Gerald R. Ford (R)	1913		61	Neb.	Mich.	Aug. 9, 1974–Jan. 20, 1977	Nelson A. Rockefeller
Jimmy Carter (D)	1924		52	Ga.	Ga.	Jan. 20, 1977–Jan. 20, 1981	Walter F. Mondale
Ronald Reagan (R)	1911		69	Ill.	Calif.	Jan. 20, 1981–Jan. 20, 1985	George Bush
Ronald Reagan (R)			73			Jan. 20, 1985–Jan. 20, 1989	George Bush
George Bush (R)	1924		64	Mass.	Texas	Jan. 20, 1989–Jan. 20, 1993	Dan Quayle
Bill Clinton (D)	1946		46	Ark.	Ark.	Jan. 20, 1993–Jan. 20, 1997	Albert Gore Jr.
Bill Clinton (D)			50			Jan. 20, 1997–	Albert Gore Jr.
George W. Bush (R)	1946		54	Conn.	Texas	Jan. 20, 2001–Jan. 20, 2005	Richard B. Cheney
George W. Bush (R)			58			Jan. 20, 2005–	Richard B. Cheney

Note: D—Democrat; DR—Democratic–Republican; F—Federalist; R—Republican; W—Whig.

Historical Profiles of American Political Parties

ALTHOUGH POLITICAL PARTIES are not directly mentioned in the U.S. Constitution, they emerged in short order to become and remain an integral part of the American system of elected government. Today, as well as when they appeared in the 1790s, they satisfy an important need for U.S. democracy: bringing people with the same beliefs together to govern at the local and national levels. At nearly every moment in the nation's history there have been two major political parties in operation. Since the 1860s, the Democratic and Republican parties have been dominant.

Third parties also have had an important role in history: providing the forum for radical ideas, not accepted by the ruling parties of the day, to take root. Ideas such as the abolition of slavery, women's suffrage, minimum wages, and Social Security were first advocated by third parties before they were finally adopted by the major parties and accepted by the nation as a whole. This chapter examines the origins, development, and important policy ideas of all major parties and noteworthy third parties in U.S. history.

AMERICAN INDEPENDENT PARTY (1968–) AND AMERICAN PARTY (1972–)

Both the American Party and the American Independent Party descended from the American Independent Party that served as the vehicle for George C. Wallace's third-party presidential candidacy in 1968.

Wallace, governor of Alabama (1963–1967; 1971–1979), burst onto the national scene in 1964 as a Democratic presidential candidate opposed to the 1964 Civil Rights Act. Entering three primaries outside his native South—in Wisconsin, Indiana, and Maryland—he surprised political observers by winning between 30 percent and 43 percent of the Democratic primary vote in the three states. His unexpectedly strong showing brought the term "white backlash" into the political vocabulary as a description of the racial undertone of the Wallace vote.

In 1968 Wallace broke with the Democrats and embarked on his second presidential campaign as a third-party candidate under the American Independent Party label. His candidacy capitalized on the bitter reactions of millions of voters, especially white blue-collar workers, to the civil rights activism, urban riots, antiwar demonstrations, and heavy federal spending on Johnson administration "Great Society" programs that marked the mid-1960s. With the help of his Alabama advisers and volunteer groups, Wallace was able to get his party on the ballot in all fifty states.

The former governor did not hold a convention for his party, but in October he announced his vice-presidential running mate (retired air force general Curtis LeMay) and released a platform. In the November election the Wallace-LeMay ticket received 9,906,473 votes (13.5 percent of the popular vote), carried five southern states, and won forty-six electoral votes. The party's showing was the best by a third party since 1924, when Robert M. La Follette collected 16.6 percent of the vote on the Progressive Party ticket.

After his defeat in that election, Wallace returned to the Democratic Party, competing in Democratic presidential primaries in 1972 and 1976. Wallace's American Independent Party began to break into factions after the 1968 election but in 1972 united behind John G. Schmitz, a Republican U.S. representative from southern California (1970–1973), as its presidential nominee. Thomas J. Anderson, a farm magazine and syndicated news features publisher from Tennessee, was the party's vice-presidential candidate. In many states, the party shortened its name to American Party. In the November election, the Schmitz-Anderson ticket won 1,099,482 votes (1.4 percent of the popular vote) but failed to win any electoral votes. The ticket ran best in the West, taking 9 percent of the vote in Idaho, 7 percent in Alaska, and 6 percent in Utah.

In December 1972 a bitter fight occurred for the chairmanship of the American Independent Party between Anderson and William K. Shearer, the chairman of the party in California. Anderson defeated Shearer, retaining control of the party but re-

Sources

This section profiles all major and minor political parties that received a substantial presidential vote at some point in their history, generally 1 percent or more. The following sources were used: Congressional Quarterly, *CQ Weekly Report* (Washington, D.C.: Congressional Quarterly); *Dictionary of American History*, 8 vols. (New York: Scribner's, 1976); *Encyclopaedia Britannica* (Chicago: Encyclopaedia Britannica, 1980); *Encyclopedia Americana*, 30 vols. (Danbury, Conn.: Grolier Education, 1982); J. David Gillespie, *Politics at the Periphery: Third Parties in Two-Party America* (Columbia: University of South Carolina Press, 1993); Earl R. Kruschke, *Encyclopedia of Third Parties in the United States* (Santa Barbara, Calif.: ABC-CLIO, 1991); Arthur M. Schlesinger Jr., *History of U.S. Political Parties*, 1973 Reprint, (New York: Chelsea House, 1981); George W. Stimpson, *A Book About American Politics* (New York: Harper, 1952).

naming it the American Party. Shearer, over the following four years, expanded his California-based group into a new national party. He had kept the name American Independent Party in California and made that the name of the new nationwide group.

By 1976 there were two distinct entities: the American Party headed by Anderson and the American Independent Party headed by Shearer.

The 1976 American Party convention was held in Salt Lake City, Utah, in June. Anderson was nominated for president and Rufus Shackleford of Florida for vice president.

The party's nomination of Anderson followed its failure to enlist a prominent conservative to lead the ticket. Both Gov. Meldrim Thomson Jr. of New Hampshire and Sen. Jesse Helms of North Carolina were approached, but both decided to remain in the Republican Party. With well-known conservatives declining the party's overtures, the convention turned to Anderson. He easily won the nomination on the first ballot by defeating six party workers.

Anderson's campaign stressed the "permanent principles" of the party, augmented by the 1976 platform. These principles included opposition to foreign aid, U.S. withdrawal from the United Nations, and an end to trade with or recognition of communist nations. The platform included planks opposing abortion, gun control, the Equal Rights Amendment, and government-sponsored health care and welfare programs. In general, the party favored limits on federal power and was against budget deficits except in wartime.

The American Party was on the ballot in eighteen states, including eight states where the American Independent Party was also listed. In seven of those eight states, Anderson ran ahead of the American Independent Party ticket. Anderson's strength was spread fairly evenly across the country. His best showings were in Utah (2.5 percent of the vote) and Montana (1.8 percent). But Anderson's total of 160,773 popular votes (0.2 percent) placed him almost 10,000 votes behind the American Independent Party candidate nationally.

The American Independent Party convention met in Chicago in August 1976 and chose former Georgia governor Lester Maddox (1967–1971), a Democrat, as its presidential nominee and former Madison, Wisconsin, mayor William Dyke, a Republican, as its vice-presidential candidate. Maddox won a first-ballot nomination over Dallas columnist Robert Morris and former representative John R. Rarick, a Democrat of Louisiana (1967–1975).

At the convention, a group of nationally prominent conservatives made a bid to take over the party and use it as a vehicle to build a new conservative coalition. Richard Viguerie, a fundraiser for Wallace and a nationally known direct mail expert, was the leader of the group. He was joined at the convention by two leading conservatives—William Rusher, publisher of the *National Review,* and Howard Phillips, the former head of the Office of Economic Opportunity (1973) and leader of the Conservative Caucus, an activist conservative group. Viguerie, Phillips, and Rusher all argued that the American Independent Party should be overhauled, changed from a fringe group to a philosophical home for believers in free enterprise and traditional moral values. They also hoped they could attract Helms,

Thomson, or representative Philip M. Crane, R-Ill. When none of these men agreed to run on the American Independent Party ticket, Viguerie and his allies found themselves unable to successfully promote Morris, a lesser-known substitute.

Many American Independent Party members favored Maddox because they saw him as a colorful personality, one capable of drawing media attention and perhaps of picking up the 5 percent of the national vote needed to qualify the party for federal funding. Maddox never came close to that goal, however, achieving only 0.2 percent of the national vote (170,531). It was his 51,098 votes in California, where American Party nominee Anderson was not on the ballot, that enabled Maddox to run slightly ahead of Anderson nationally.

Despite the power struggle between Anderson and Shearer, there was little difference between their two party platforms. As did the American Party, the American Independent Party opposed abortion, gun control, forced busing, foreign aid, and membership in the United Nations.

By 1980 neither party was much of a force in American politics. Both retained the same basic platforms, but each was on the ballot in only a handful of states. The American Independent Party's nominee, former representative Rarick, ran in only eight states. Economist Percy L. Greaves Jr., the American Party candidate, was listed in just seven.

The American Independent Party did not field a presidential candidate in 1984, while the American Party placed Delmar Dennis, a book publisher from Pigeon Forge, Tennessee, on the ballot in six states.

Dennis also ran under the American Party banner in 1988 and, with his running mate, Earl Jeppson, received 3,475 votes. The American Independent Party fared better with their candidates, presidential nominee James C. Griffin and vice-presidential nominee Charles J. Morsa, receiving 27,818 votes.

By 1992 the fortunes for both parties had dwindled even further. American Party presidential nominee Robert J. Smith and running mate Doris Feimer were on the ballot only in Utah, where they received 292 votes. In 1996 the American Party ticket of Diane Beall Templin and Gary Van Horn made the ballot in two states, Colorado and Utah, and collected a total of 1,847 votes. The American Independent Party did not field a presidential ticket in the 1990s, nor did either party in 2000 or 2004.

ANTI-FEDERALISTS (1789–1796)

Never a formal party, the Anti-Federalists were a loosely organized group opposed to ratification of the Constitution. With the ratification of the Constitution in 1788, the Anti-Federalists served as the opposition to the Federalists in the early years of the Republic.

Anti-Federalists were primarily rural, agrarian men from inland regions who favored individual freedom and states' rights, which they felt would be jeopardized by the new Constitution. After ratification, the efforts of the Anti-Federalists led to adoption of the first ten amendments, the Bill of Rights, which spelled out the major limitations on federal power.

As the opposition faction in Congress during the formative years of the Republic, the Anti-Federalists basically held to a strict interpretation of the Constitution, particularly in regard to the various economic proposals of Treasury Secretary Alexander Hamilton to centralize more power in the federal government.

Although never the majority faction in Congress, the Anti-Federalists were a forerunner of Thomas Jefferson's Democratic-Republican Party, which came into existence in the 1790s and dominated American politics for the first quarter of the nineteenth century.

ANTI-MASONIC PARTY (1828–1836)

Born in the mid-1820s in upstate New York, the Anti-Masonic Party focused the strong, anti-elitist mood of the period on a conspicuous symbol of privilege, the Masons. The Masons were a secret fraternal organization with membership drawn largely from the upper class. Conversely, the appeal of the Anti-Masonic movement was to the common man—poor farmers and laborers especially—who resented the secrecy and privilege of the Masons.

The spark that created the party came in 1826, when William Morgan, a dissident Mason from Batavia, New York, allegedly on the verge of exposing the inner workings of the order, mysteriously disappeared and never was seen again. Refusal of Masonic leaders to cooperate in the inconclusive investigation of Morgan's disappearance led to suspicions that Masons had kidnapped and murdered him and were suppressing the inquiry.

From 1828 through 1831, the new Anti-Masonic Party spread through New England and the Middle Atlantic states, in many places establishing itself as the primary opposition to the Democrats. In addition to its appeal to the working classes, particularly in northern rural areas, and its opposition to Masonry, the Anti-Masons displayed a fervor against immorality, as seen not only in secret societies but also in slavery, intemperance, and urban life.

In September 1831 the party held the first national nominating convention in American history. One hundred and sixteen delegates from thirteen states gathered in Baltimore, Maryland, and nominated former attorney general William Wirt of Maryland for the presidency. In the 1832 elections, Wirt received only 100,715 votes (7.8 percent of the popular vote) and carried just one state, Vermont, but it was the first third party in U.S. politics to win any electoral college votes. The Anti-Masons did reasonably well at other levels, winning the Vermont governorship several years and competing in close elections in a few other states. In the U.S. House they had fifteen members in the Twenty-second Congress (1831–1833) and twenty-four in the Twenty-third Congress (1833–1835).

But the decline of Masonry, especially in New York, where the number of lodges dropped from 507 in 1826 to forty-eight six years later, robbed the Anti-Masons of an emotional issue and hastened their decline. The 1832 election was the high point for the Anti-Masons as a national party. In the 1836 campaign the party endorsed Whig candidate William Henry Harrison. Subsequently, the bulk of the Anti-Masonic constituency moved into the Whig Party. In 1836 the major parties also held their own conventions and wrote their own platforms. Despite its short life, the Anti-Masons were one of the most important American third parties, contributing to the openness of the system and establishing party platforms and conventions as part of modern political practices.

BRECKINRIDGE (SOUTHERN) DEMOCRATS (1860)

Agitation over the slavery issue, building for a generation, reached a climax in 1860 and produced a sectional split in the Democratic Party. Throughout the midnineteenth century the Democrats had remained unified by supporting the various pieces of compromise legislation that both protected slavery in the southern states and endorsed the policy of popular sovereignty in the territories. But in 1860 southern Democrats wanted the Democratic convention (meeting in Charleston, South Carolina) to insert a plank specifically protecting slavery in the territories. When their plank was defeated, delegates from most of the southern states walked out.

The northern wing of the party, after recessing for six weeks, reconvened in Baltimore, Maryland, where Sen. Stephen A. Douglas of Illinois was nominated as its presidential candidate. Most of the southern delegates, plus those from California and Oregon, nominated their own ticket in a rump convention held after Douglas's selection. John C. Breckinridge (1821–1875) of Kentucky, the incumbent vice president under President James Buchanan, accepted the southern wing's nomination. Joseph Lane, a states' rights advocate from Oregon, was selected as his running mate. After the formation of the two sectional tickets, two separate Democratic national committees operated in Washington, D.C., to oversee their campaigns.

The platforms of the Douglas and Breckinridge Democrats agreed that the Fugitive Slave Law must be enforced, but the Breckinridge Democrats also insisted on a federal slave code for the territories and on the right of slaveholders to take their slave property into the western territories, decisions that the Douglas platform said it would leave to the Supreme Court and that the Republican Party and its candidate, Abraham Lincoln, absolutely opposed. The four-way election also included John Bell of the Constitutional Union Party.

The Breckinridge ticket placed third in popular votes behind Lincoln and Douglas, receiving 848,019 votes (18.1 percent of the popular vote) and winning eleven of the fifteen slave states, which placed it second in electoral votes with seventy-two. Although the combined Douglas-Breckinridge vote amounted to a plurality of the ballots cast, the split in Democratic ranks was a boon to the campaign of the Republican candidate, Lincoln, who won with less than 40 percent of the vote. Lincoln's victory in the electoral college, however, did not depend on a divided opposition, for he took an absolute majority to win regardless. Breckinridge's support came mostly from the South, although it did not necessarily reflect the degree of proslavery sentiment in the region, since some voters who later supported secession voted for Douglas or Bell, and many of Breckinridge's supporters were traditional Democrats who did not see themselves as voting on secession. Indeed, Breckinridge saw himself as the only candidate who could prevent secession, since if he won, the South would happily remain in the Union.

Lincoln's election led to secession by seven Deep South states, and four more joined the Confederacy soon after his inauguration. Before Lincoln's inauguration, Vice President Breckinridge worked with other Democrats in Washington to fashion a compromise that might prevent a civil war. On the main point of contention, however, slavery in the territories, Lincoln would not budge, so no settlement could be reached. Breckinridge, while still vice president, had been elected to the U.S. Senate, his term to begin when his vice presidency ended. As a senator in 1861 he defended the right of southern states to secede and opposed Lincoln's efforts to raise an army.

By late 1861 Union and Confederate forces alike had entered Kentucky, and Breckinridge offered his services to the Confederacy. He resigned from the Senate before it expelled him for his pro-Confederate behavior. He served as a major general in the Confederate army and then as Confederate secretary of war. During the war the Southern Democrats provided much of the leadership for the Confederate government, including its president, Jefferson Davis.

When the war ended with the Confederacy's defeat and slavery's abolition, the particular issues that had animated Breckinridge's presidential bid in 1860 no longer mattered. The Southern Democrats made no attempt to continue as a separate sectional entity and rejoined the national Democratic Party.

CITIZENS PARTY (1979–1984)

Organized in 1979 as a coalition of dissident liberals and populists, the first Citizens Party convention chose author and environmental scientist Barry Commoner as its 1980 presidential candidate and La Donna Harris, wife of former Democratic senator Fred R. Harris of Oklahoma, as his running mate. The Citizens Party ticket ran on the central theme that major decisions in America were made to benefit corporations and not the average citizen. The party proposed public control of energy industries and multinational corporations; a halt to the use of nuclear power; a sharp cut in military spending; and price controls on food, fuel, housing, and health care.

Commoner ran in all of the large electoral vote states except Florida and Texas. He made his biggest push in California, Illinois, Michigan, New York, and Pennsylvania, where party leaders believed they could tap a "sophisticated working-class population" and appeal to political activists who had been involved in the environmental and antinuclear movements that sprang up in the late 1970s.

The Commoner-Harris ticket was on the ballot in twenty-nine states and the District of Columbia in 1980. Party leaders asserted that it was the largest number of ballot positions attained by any third party in its first campaign. In addition to its presidential ticket, the Citizens Party also fielded twenty-two candidates for other offices, including two for the U.S. Senate and seven for the House. The Citizens Party won 234,294 votes in the 1980 presidential election, or 0.3 percent of the vote.

As its 1984 presidential nominee, the Citizens Party chose outspoken feminist Sonia Johnson of Virginia. Johnson first attracted national attention in 1979, when the Mormon Church

excommunicated her for supporting the Equal Rights Amendment (ERA). In 1982 she staged a thirty-seven-day hunger strike in an unsuccessful effort to pressure the Illinois legislature to approve the ERA. The Citizens Party selected party activist Richard J. Walton of Rhode Island to accompany Johnson on the ticket. Winning 72,200 votes in 1984, the ticket garnered 0.1 percent of the vote. That was the last year that the Citizens Party fielded a national ticket.

COMMUNIST PARTY (1919–)

In 1919, shortly after the Russian Revolution, Soviet communists encouraged American left-wing groups to withdraw from the Socialist Party and to form a communist party in the United States. The party arose at that time as part of the social and economic turmoil that followed World War I and the Bolshevik Revolution in Russia. Two major organizations emerged from the American Socialist Party: the larger Communist Party of America and the Communist Labor Party. But both were aggressively prosecuted by the U.S. government in the period around 1920, causing a drop in their already small membership and forcing them underground.

By the mid-1920s, the Communist Party of the USA was formed to implant the revolutionary aims of the Soviet Union in America. William Z. Foster, a labor organizer, was the party's first presidential candidate, in 1924. National tickets were run every four years through 1940 and from 1968 through 1984, but the party's peak year at the polls was 1932, when Foster received 103,253 votes (0.3 percent of the popular vote).

The Communists have a distinctive place in American political history as the only party to have had international ties. In 1929 a party split brought the formal creation of the Communist Party of the United States, with acknowledged status as a part of the worldwide communist movement (the Communist International).

The Communist International terminated during World War II, and in 1944 the party's leader in America, Earl Browder, dissolved the party and committed the movement to operate within the two-party system. In the 1944 campaign the Communists endorsed President Franklin D. Roosevelt, who repudiated their support.

However, with the breakup of the U.S.–Soviet alliance after World War II, the Communists reconstituted themselves as a political party. They supported Henry Wallace's Progressive Party candidacy in 1948 but were limited in the cold war period of the 1950s by restrictive federal and state legislation that virtually outlawed the party.

With the gradual easing of restrictive measures, the Communist Party resumed electoral activities in the late 1960s. In a policy statement written in 1966, the party described itself as "a revolutionary party whose aim is the fundamental transformation of society."

The party's success at the polls, however, continued to be minimal. Its presidential candidates in 1968, 1972, 1976, 1980, and 1984—the last year that they appeared on the ballot—each received less than one-tenth of 1 percent of the vote.

CONSERVATIVE PARTY (1962–)

In 1962 the New York State Conservative Party began to take shape under the direction of J. Daniel Mahoney, a New York attorney, and his brother-in-law, Kieran O'Doherty. They were motivated primarily by the belief that real political alternatives were no longer being offered to the state electorate. They saw the three dominant parties in the state—the Liberal Party, the Democratic Party, and the Republican Party under Gov. Nelson A. Rockefeller and Sen. Jacob K. Javits—as offering a generally liberal agenda.

Although political commentators predicted the early demise of the party—particularly in the aftermath of Barry Goldwater's overwhelming defeat in the 1964 presidential elections—the party continued to grow both in membership and in candidate endorsements. In 1965 the nationally known columnist and intellectual William F. Buckley ran for mayor of New York City, generating national publicity for the party. One year later, the Conservative candidate for governor, Professor Paul Adams, outpolled Liberal Party candidate Franklin D. Roosevelt Jr., obtaining Row C of the ballot for the party. A party's position on the ballot is determined by the number of votes cast for its candidate for governor. Appearing in Row C is significant because the higher the row, the more notice voters are likely to take of the party's candidates. In 1970 James Buckley was elected to the U.S. Senate on Row C alone, winning nearly 2.3 million votes (38.8 percent of the total vote). From the mid-1970s onward few statewide Republican candidates gained office without a Conservative Party cross-endorsement.

Although the Conservative Party suffered some setbacks, such as the loss of Row C to the Independence (Reform) Party in 1996 and the siphoning off of some supporters to the Right to Life Party, it remains a major force in New York State politics. The Conservative Party has opposed abortion since it became a political issue; nonetheless, the party has occasionally backed abortion rights candidates whose conservative credentials were otherwise satisfactory. The Right to Life Party never backs candidates who support abortion.

Even though some members of the Conservative Party are Protestant fundamentalists, a large part of its membership and much of its leadership are traditionalist Roman Catholics. In a real sense, the rise of the party has mirrored the rise of the conservative movement in America—from Goldwater's capture of the 1964 Republican nomination to Ronald Reagan's electoral triumphs in 1980 and 1984. In addition, the party has successfully fought the image of extremism while generally remaining true to its core principles—tax limitation, education reform, and tough anticrime policies.

CONSTITUTIONAL UNION PARTY (1860)

The short-lived Constitutional Union Party was formed in 1859 to promote national conciliation in the face of rampant sectionalism, which included southern threats of secession. The party appealed to conservative remnants of the American (Know Nothing) and Whig parties, who viewed preservation of the Union as their primary goal.

The Constitutional Union Party held its first and only national convention in Baltimore, Maryland, in May 1860. For president the party nominated John Bell of Tennessee, a former senator and speaker of the House of Representatives, who previously had been both a Democrat and a Whig. The convention adopted a short platform, which intentionally avoided controversial subjects, most notably the divisive slavery issue. Instead, the platform simply urged support for "the Constitution, the Union and the Laws."

In the fall election, Bell received 590,901 votes (12.6 percent of the popular vote) and won Kentucky, Tennessee, and Virginia. However, the Bell ticket finished last in the four-way presidential race and, together with the sectional split in the Democratic Party, was a prominent factor in the victory of Republican Abraham Lincoln.

In the months after the 1860 election the Constitutional Union Party continued to urge national conciliation, but with the outbreak of the Civil War the party disappeared.

DEMOCRATIC PARTY (1828–)

The Democratic Party is the oldest political organization in the United States. Indeed, a history of the party is in some ways a political history of the nation. In the first few years of the Republic, political parties did not exist, although factions tied to issues and the personal ambitions of political leaders influenced elections and policies. The Democratic Party traces its roots to this factionalism, beginning with opposition to the Federalist policies of Alexander Hamilton in the first administration of George Washington.

Origins of the Democratic Party

Opposition to Federalist policies, organized by James Madison and Secretary of State Thomas Jefferson, first coalesced around Hamilton's proposal for a national bank, which Congress passed and Washington signed, over the strenuous objections of Jefferson and Madison. The two Virginians were more successful in preventing the adoption of Hamilton's larger plan for federal support for the development of U.S. industry. The Federalists, led by Hamilton and John Adams, favored a strong central government and a flexible interpretation of the Constitution. Key to their program was a national bank, which would facilitate economic growth and strengthen national and international commerce.

Jefferson's Democratic-Republicans advocated "strict construction" of the Constitution and opposed a national bank. Moreover, they favored friendly relations with France, while the Federalists sought to forge friendly diplomatic and commercial relations with England. Both parties had supporters throughout the country, but the Democratic-Republicans were strongest in the South and among slaveowners, and the Federalists were strongest in New England and among men with commercial and manufacturing interests. From the 1790s until the late 1820s various terms—Democratic-Republicans, Jeffersonian Republicans, Jeffersonian Democrats, and National Republicans—were applied to the people and leaders who, opposed to the Federalists, gradually became known as Democrats.

The Democratic-Republicans grew stronger as the Federalists began to fade during the presidency of Adams. A new alliance of agrarian southerners and urban northerners helped Jefferson defeat Adams in 1800 and win reelection in 1804. After Jefferson the presidency went to his friends and allies, Madison (1809–1817) and James Monroe (1817–1825). By 1820 the Federalist Party had all but disappeared, and Monroe won reelection with no opposition.

Indicative of the change in the party of Jefferson was its attitude toward the Bank of the United States. In 1791 Jefferson and Madison had vigorously opposed the creation of this bank, arguing that establishment of such a bank was unconstitutional. It is arguable that the genesis of the modern Democratic Party dates from that bank debate. In 1811 the bank's twenty-year charter expired, and the Democrats who controlled Congress and the presidency did not renew it. By 1816, however, Madison supported the creation of a new bank and renounced his former opposition to it. Congress, controlled by Democrats, passed the bill.

The inherent instability of one-party politics became clear in 1824, as four candidates—Andrew Jackson, John Quincy Adams, William Crawford, and Henry Clay, all claiming to represent the Jeffersonian tradition—ran for president. No candidate received a majority of popular or electoral votes, and the House of Representatives chose John Quincy Adams, although Jackson had received more popular votes and more electoral votes. After 1824 the old Jeffersonian party unraveled. John Quincy Adams had broken with the Federalist Party during the War of 1812 and had served as Monroe's secretary of state, but he was never a true "Jeffersonian." By the end of his administration in 1829 he and supporters such as Clay emerged as members of a faction that eventually became the Whig Party.

The Jackson Legacy

Jackson, hero of the War of 1812, defeated incumbent John Quincy Adams in 1828 and became the first president to represent the "Democratic Party." The party has maintained that name ever since, although it was often divided over issues such as slavery, economic policy, and national unity in the nineteenth century and foreign policy, civil rights, and economic policy in the twentieth.

Jackson, nominated in 1828 by the Tennessee legislature, led the Democrats to adopt a nominating convention as the method for choosing the party's future standard-bearers. The Democrats held their first national convention at Baltimore, Maryland, in 1832, eight months after the Anti-Masons held the first such convention, also in Baltimore. The 1832 Democratic convention adopted two rules that lasted more than a century. The two-thirds rule, requiring a two-thirds majority for nomination, led to numerous floor fights over the choosing of a Democratic presidential candidate. The unit rule allowed convention delegations to override minority objections within the delegation and to vote as a whole for one candidate or position.

From Jackson's election in 1828 through the end of James Buchanan's term in 1861, the Democrats dominated national politics. In this period the Democrats opposed any national bank, high tariffs, internal improvements, and even a uniform bankruptcy law. High points of Jackson's presidency included his veto of bills to support internal improvements and to extend the charter of the Second Bank of the United States. Jackson and other Democrats in this period vigorously supported territorial expansion through Native American removal, the annexation of Texas, and ultimately the Mexican-American War. Their support for territorial gains followed Jefferson's expansionist policies that led to the peaceful acquisition of Louisiana from France in 1803. Most Democrats, and almost all party leaders, supported the demands of the South between 1828 and 1861 on issues involving slavery. Meanwhile, Jackson's opponents—led by Clay, Daniel Webster, and William Henry Harrison—formed the Whig Party. The Whigs—who favored higher tariffs, a national bank, federally funded internal improvements, and a weak presidency—provided the main opposition to the Democrats until the emergence of the Republican Party in 1854.

Jackson's election ushered in an era known as "Jacksonian Democracy," which stressed political equality—for white men. Jacksonians throughout the country made war on black voters, taking away their voting rights in Pennsylvania, New Jersey, Tennessee, and North Carolina and opposing their voting rights elsewhere. Jackson himself led the movement to force Native Americans out of the states east of the Mississippi River.

Jefferson, already considered the "father" of the Democratic Party, had been the first president to remove officeholders and replace them with his supporters. Jackson renewed this policy through the "spoils system," a term that stemmed from the phrase "to the victors go the spoils." As the party in power during most of the period from 1829 to 1861, the Democrats controlled the growing bureaucracy and rewarded many supporters with patronage jobs.

Jackson's legacy was a Democratic Party that endured into the twenty-first century. Dominating national politics from its outset, the Democrats lost the presidential election only twice (in 1840 and 1848) between 1828 and 1860. From Jackson's inauguration in 1829 until 2005, the Democrats controlled the House of Representatives for fifty-five two-year sessions and the Senate for forty-six sessions (plus more than one and one-half years of the 107th Congress from 2001 to 2003). The number of years that the Democrats controlled the House or Senate during this period was more than the combined years of control by the Whig and Republican Parties.

Despite their long-term success, the Democrats barely survived their severest test, over slavery and secession. In 1846 northern Democrats supported the Wilmot Proviso, introduced in the House by Pennsylvania Democrat David Wilmot. The proviso would have prohibited slavery in any territory acquired during the Mexican-American War. Southern Democrats uniformly opposed the proviso. In 1848 many antislavery Democrats from New York, Pennsylvania, and New England voted for former president Martin Van Buren, who was running on the Free Soil Party ticket. These defections led to the election of the Whig candidate, Zachary Taylor. The Democrats regained the presidency in 1852, but slavery soon splintered the party. In 1856 Democrat Franklin

Pierce became the first elected president denied renomination by his party. He had alienated fellow northerners by signing legislation that allowed slavery into Kansas Territory, which in turn led it to become a battleground between pro- and antislavery forces. Another northerner, Buchanan, won the nomination but also was a one-term president. By 1860 many northern Democrats, among them Sens. Salmon P. Chase of Ohio and Hannibal Hamlin of Maine, had joined the new Republican Party.

At the 1860 convention in Charleston, South Carolina, northern and southern Democrats were divided over how much support to give slavery in the territories. Northerners, backing Stephen A. Douglas of Illinois, favored opening all territories to slavery under a system of popular sovereignty, in which settlers would decide for themselves whether to permit slavery. Most of the southerners bolted after the defeat of platform planks endorsing a federal slave code for the territories and guaranteeing the right of slaveowners to carry their human property into all federal territories. The northern delegates nominated Douglas for president, while the southern Democrats nominated John C. Breckinridge of Kentucky. Even had the Democrats remained united, it is doubtful they could have prevented the Republican candidate, Abraham Lincoln, from winning an electoral majority, as he swept every free state but New Jersey, which he split with Douglas. The split in the Democratic Party presaged the more important split in the nation, which occurred with the secession of eleven southern states in 1860–1861.

Decline and Resurgence

During the Civil War, northern Democrats remained divided. War Democrats generally supported the war effort and Lincoln's initial goal of bringing the South back into the Union, although they objected to Lincoln's emancipation policies and after 1863 were far less enthusiastic about the war or its goals. Throughout the war, by contrast, the Copperhead faction opposed the war effort and sought peace negotiations with the Confederacy.

Democrats came back together after the Civil War, but both their commitment to white supremacy and their image of disloyalty continued. During Reconstruction, Democrats opposed civil rights laws and the Fourteenth and Fifteenth Amendments, which were designed to establish citizenship for African Americans, recognize their civil rights, and guarantee their voting rights. As late as the 1880s, the Democrats were termed the party of "rum, romanism, and rebellion," because of the party's opposition to temperance laws, its support among Irish Catholics, and the fact that much of its support came from former Confederates.

In 1876 the Democratic governor of New York, Samuel J. Tilden, won the popular vote against Republican Rutherford B. Hayes, but Tilden lost the election when a congressional compromise awarded Hayes all the disputed electoral votes of three southern states. Election fraud, intimidation, and outright violence by white southern Democrats prevented thousands of blacks from voting. Had the election been run fairly, it is likely that Hayes would have won outright. As part of the compromise that brought Hayes to the White House, the new president promised to remove federal troops from the South, effectively

ending Reconstruction. Their removal led to a gradual disfranchisement of blacks in the South, which soon became solidly Democratic and would remain largely so until the presidential election of 1964. Despite a virtual lock on all southern electoral votes, the Democrats captured the presidency only twice between 1860 and 1912; New York governor Grover Cleveland won in 1884 and 1892.

By the late nineteenth century the Democratic Party's policies had changed somewhat from the antebellum period. Still a "white man's party," it was hostile to African Americans' civil rights and to Chinese immigration. With slavery ended, however, the party had dropped its aggressive expansionism of the earlier period. Cleveland refused to annex Hawaii, and some Democrats opposed the Spanish-American War in 1898. Democrats remained hostile to high tariffs, but they split on the issue of an expansive monetary policy; western Democrats favored the free coinage of silver, and eastern Democrats, among them Cleveland, opposed it. Most southern whites gave their allegiance to the Democrats, but in the North by the 1890s, and especially following the 1893 depression, economic and cultural issues outweighed memories of Civil War enmity in voter choices between the two major parties.

The GOP continued to dominate presidential politics for twelve years into the twentieth century. In 1912 the Republicans split when former president Theodore Roosevelt failed in his attempt to gain his party's nomination over the incumbent, William Howard Taft. Roosevelt ran in the general election anyway, on the Progressive—or Bull Moose—ticket, winning six states and 4.1 million votes. Roosevelt came in second, and Taft a distant third, but Taft and Roosevelt combined for 1.3 million more popular votes than the Democrat, New Jersey governor Woodrow Wilson. Had the Republicans been united, their candidate—either Roosevelt or Taft—would have won. But divided they enabled Wilson to carry forty states and the election, ending the Democrats' long presidential drought. Wilson demonstrated the Democrats' hostility to civil rights and racial equality, as he ordered the segregation of all federal facilities in Washington, D.C. He was a progressive reformer on many issues, however, and brought such innovations as the Federal Reserve System, in contrast to historic Democratic hostility to federal government intervention in the economy.

Wilson also led the Democrats to embrace a more internationally engaged foreign policy. Before the Civil War, the Democrats, in part spurred by the demands of the South for more territory for slavery, had pursued an aggressive policy of land acquisition, ultimately leading to war with Mexico. Pre–Civil War Democrats had had little interest in international affairs beyond the Western Hemisphere, however. In 1917, by contrast, Wilson successfully guided the American entry into World War I, and he continued his internationalist policies after the end of the war, as he vainly attempted to bring the United States into the League of Nations. For the next half-century the Democratic Party stood for intervention and international responsibility, while the Republicans retreated into a large measure of diplomatic isolationism.

After World War I the Republicans took back the White House in 1920, kept it in 1924, and won again with Herbert

Hoover's 1928 victory over Democrat Alfred E. Smith, the first Roman Catholic presidential nominee who was then governor of New York. After the stock market crashed in 1929, however, the Great Depression paved the way for a new Democratic dominance in the White House and an even longer one in Congress.

New Deal to Great Society

The election of Franklin D. Roosevelt—Smith's successor as governor of New York—in 1932 made a dramatic and lasting change in U.S. politics. Democrats sang "Happy Days Are Here Again" as they became the majority party and rallied behind FDR's bold New Deal programs. Democrats, long the party of states' rights and localism, became identified with national initiatives on economic and social issues. During the New Deal, rural electrification brought light and heat to much of the nation; a range of programs helped the poor and the unemployed; the nation's labor policy went through a sea change with the Wagner Labor Relations Act; and massive public works programs, such as the Tennessee Valley Authority, not only created jobs but constructed public buildings, roads, and dams. Once a party opposed to regulation, the Democrats helped create the regulatory state. Social programs, most notably Social Security, set the stage for the modern industrial state that provides a social safety net for citizens.

At Roosevelt's urging, the 1936 Democratic convention abolished the controversial two-thirds rule, which in effect had given the South a veto in choosing the national party ticket. Southern delegates agreed to a compromise, basing the size of future delegations on a state's Democratic voting strength instead of population size.

During the Roosevelt years and after, for the first time in its history, the Democratic Party welcomed African American support and even backed some civil rights legislation, and President Roosevelt and his successor, Harry S. Truman, issued executive orders to combat some types of racial segregation and other discrimination. The "New Deal coalition"—northern blacks, southern whites, farmers, labor unionists, intellectuals, and ethnic urban voters—kept Roosevelt and Truman in office for twenty consecutive years, ending in 1953.

Immediately before and during World War II, Roosevelt pushed an international agenda, building on Wilson's legacy. Here Roosevelt had the support of southern Democrats, who opposed some of his domestic agenda. Opposition came from Republican isolationists, but, unlike Wilson, FDR was able to bring the nation along with him, and the United States took the lead in establishing the United Nations (UN) after the war. Roosevelt died suddenly in 1945, three months into his record fourth term, turning the government abruptly over to his vice president, Truman. The new president continued Roosevelt's internationalist policy, first with the Marshall Plan to help Europe recover from World War II and then with the development of North Atlantic Treaty Organization (NATO) and other international defense pacts. In 1950 Truman pushed for UN intervention when North Korea attacked South Korea, and soon the United States was heavily involved in an Asian war.

In domestic politics, Truman pushed an activist agenda that he called the "Fair Deal" and called for expanded enforcement of African Americans' civil rights. Running for another term in 1948, he confronted schisms within his party from two quarters: the South and the left. Displeased with Truman's civil rights plank, conservative southerners bolted the Democratic Party in 1948 and ran J. Strom Thurmond of South Carolina as the States' Rights Democratic (Dixiecrats) nominee. Under the Progressive Party banner, Henry A. Wallace (Roosevelt's vice president before Truman) also challenged the incumbent. Thurmond won four states; Wallace took none. Despite the split, Truman defeated the Republican Party's overconfident candidate Thomas E. Dewey.

After Truman left office in 1953, a Republican, Dwight D. Eisenhower, served the next two terms, but then the Democrats took back the White House in 1960, as Sen. John F. Kennedy of Massachusetts narrowly defeated Eisenhower's vice president, Richard Nixon. Kennedy's slogan, "New Frontier," mirrored the candidate's youthfulness (he was forty-three years old when elected) as well as traditional Democratic slogans, such as Wilson's "New Freedom," FDR's "New Deal," and Truman's "Fair Deal." A pivotal issue in the 1960 campaign was religion, as Kennedy's Roman Catholic faith stirred strong debate as it did for Smith in 1928. But Kennedy weathered the controversy, in part because of his strong performance in a nationally televised series of presidential debates, the first ever in the nation's history. In office, Kennedy continued the Democratic agenda of internationalism, establishing the Peace Corps and providing aid to the pro-Western regime in South Vietnam, as well as fashioning an active domestic agenda, with a massive tax cut and federal programs in housing. Kennedy made tentative moves toward an expanded role for the national government in civil rights, but he moved cautiously because of the power of southern whites within the Democratic Party.

After Kennedy's assassination in November 1963, President Lyndon B. Johnson completed much of Kennedy's "New Frontier" agenda and called for additional programs in pursuit of the "Great Society," including a civil rights program that was termed by some a "Second Reconstruction." Applying all the skills he had learned as Senate majority leader (the position he held before becoming Kennedy's vice president), Johnson pushed through the Civil Rights Act of 1964. Johnson's support for civil rights ended the "solid South" as a Democratic stronghold. In 1964 Johnson won a full term in a landslide. Carrying all but six states, he took 61.1 percent of the popular vote, the largest share of the vote won by any presidential candidate in the nation's history. The Deep South, however, supported the Republican nominee, Sen. Barry Goldwater of Arizona, who had opposed the Civil Rights Act of 1964 and had flirted with the ultraright John Birch Society and segregationist White Citizens' Councils. Johnson's mandate enabled him to win passage of the Voting Rights Act of 1965, further solidifying Democratic support among African Americans although further undermining Democratic power among white southerners.

But the first two years of the Johnson presidency proved to be its high-water mark. As the president steadily expanded U.S. involvement in an increasingly unpopular war in Vietnam, the Democratic Party split openly. Johnson decided against running for reelection in 1968, while two antiwar senators, Robert F. Kennedy of New York, brother of the slain president, and Eugene J. McCarthy of Minnesota, mounted a dramatic duel for the nomination in scattered primaries across the nation that spring. But Kennedy was assassinated the night he won the California primary in early June, and McCarthy lacked the strength among party insiders to make a serious bid for the nomination at the Democratic convention in August. Held in Chicago, it was marred by police violence against antiwar demonstrators in downtown Chicago and turmoil within the convention hall. Vice President Hubert H. Humphrey, who had not entered any primaries, was nominated. But he faced an uphill fight during the fall, complicated by the American Independent candidacy of George C. Wallace, former Democratic governor of Alabama. In the end, Humphrey lost narrowly to Republican Nixon.

The Democratic Party Since 1968

Still chafing from the dissension and bossism at the 1968 convention and the subsequent loss to Nixon, the Democrats in the 1970s drastically reformed their delegate-selection and nominating rules, encouraging minority representation, dividing delegations equally between men and women, and awarding delegates to candidates in proportion to their primary votes. The party's 1972 candidate, Sen. George S. McGovern of South Dakota, had initially led the commission that drafted many of the reforms. The changes enhanced the role of primaries in the nominating process, leading to more primaries and fewer state caucuses.

The 1972 election was the last privately financed presidential election. Nixon raised $61.4 million versus McGovern's $21.2 million. McGovern, running as a peace candidate with a commitment to massive domestic spending, lost to Nixon in a landslide. The election-related Watergate scandal, however, drove Nixon from office two years later and brought Vice President Gerald R. Ford to the presidency. Evidence from the Watergate investigation showed that Nixon's operatives had used "dirty tricks" in the Democratic primaries to sabotage the candidacy of Sen. Edmund S. Muskie of Maine, who might have been a more formidable candidate than McGovern.

A fast start in the primaries in 1976, following Ford's unpopular full pardon of President Nixon for his criminal activities in the Watergate cover-up, helped the relatively unknown Jimmy Carter. The former Georgia governor won the Democratic nomination, then defeated incumbent Ford in the general election. Carter's primary strategy also served him in 1980, staving off a renomination challenge from Sen. Edward M. Kennedy, brother of the late president. But Carter's inability to curb inflation or obtain the release of American hostages held in Iran for 444 days doomed him to a one-term presidency and to defeat at the hands of Republican Ronald Reagan.

Although the popular Reagan handily won reelection in 1984, his vice president and successor, George Bush, fell victim in 1992 to Gov. Bill Clinton of Arkansas, as Democrats returned to the White House after twelve Republican years. As a presidential candidate Clinton addressed economic worries. His advisers reminded campaign workers, "It's the economy, stupid," and the strategy worked. He was the first Democrat to win the White House without taking Texas and, with Sen. Albert "Al" Gore Jr. of Tennessee as his running mate, the first president elected on an all-South ticket since 1828.

Clinton won as a moderate, declaring that "the era of big government is over." Behind him was a modified New Deal coalition that included "Reagan Democrats," union members, women, African Americans, Hispanics, Jews, a majority of Roman Catholics, public-sector employees, and intellectuals. But Clinton's presidency got off to a rocky start. In one of his first acts he instituted a controversial "don't ask, don't tell" policy toward homosexuals in the military. His convention call for a "new covenant with the American people" never caught on as a slogan, and he and First Lady Hillary Rodham Clinton failed in 1994 in an abortive attempt to reform the nation's health system. That fall, voters broke the Democratic lock on Congress, turning both chambers over to Republican control.

Two years later the electorate opted to continue a divided government, giving Clinton another four-year term in 1996 while leaving Congress in GOP hands. Although he was the first Democrat elected to a second full term since Franklin Roosevelt, Clinton again won with less than a majority of the popular vote. For the moment, Clinton's victories eased doubts that the Democrats' once-solid South had become a Republican bastion. Of the eleven states of the Old Confederacy, the Clinton-Gore ticket won four in 1992 and four in 1996. Unfortunately for the Democrats that success did not hold up four years later.

Democrats made history on various fronts from 1960 through the end of the century. In 1960 the party ran the nation's first successful Catholic presidential candidate in John Kennedy. In 1968 New York voters elected Democrat Shirley Chisholm as the first black woman member of the U.S. House, and in 1992 another Democrat, Carol Moseley-Braun of Illinois, became the first black woman U.S. senator. When former vice president Walter F. Mondale chose Geraldine A. Ferraro as his running mate against Reagan in 1984, she became the first woman in U.S. history to run on a major party ticket. In 1989 L. Douglas Wilder of Virginia became the first African American to be elected a state governor. In 2000 the Democratic nominee for president, Vice President Gore, chose Sen. Joseph I. Lieberman of Connecticut as his running mate. This was the first time a candidate of Jewish descent was on a national ticket. Also in 2000, Hillary Rodham Clinton became the first presidential wife to seek a major elective office, a U.S. Senate seat from New York, which she won.

Nevertheless, the 2000 elections were a major disappointment for Democrats. Gore lost a close and disputed election to Republican George W. Bush, son of the former president. Moreover, the Republicans retained control of both houses of Congress, although by the narrowest of margins. Still, it gave the GOP full control of the federal government for the first time in nearly a half century and sent the Democrats to the sidelines as the loyal opposition, but with little leverage to block the GOP program much less advance their own.

The 2000 presidential elections reasserted trends many noted in recent years. As political analyst Rhodes Cook put it: "Exit polls showed men favored Bush, women favored Gore; whites preferred Bush, non-whites preferred Gore; the more affluent voted strongly for Bush, the less affluent heavily favored Gore; rural and small town America went for Bush, urban America for Gore." In the South, the Republicans reasserted primacy, showing that this region was now the center of their party. Bush won the entire South—the eleven states of the Old Confederacy plus Kentucky and Oklahoma. Bush even won Gore's home state of Tennessee and Clinton's home state of Arkansas. The Democrats' strength was on the West and East Coasts, north of Virginia, and into the industrial heartland. The GOP dominated everywhere else—a giant "L"-shaped area from the South through the Plains states and Southwest and into the Mountain states.

Democrats gained some solace in June 2001 when Sen. James Jeffords of Vermont left the Republican Party to become an Independent, swinging control of the upper chamber to the Democrats for the rest of the 107th Congress. But the Democrats' success was short-lived, as Republicans recaptured the Senate in 2002 midterm elections and expanded their majorities in both houses of Congress in 2004.

The presidential election in 2004 proved to be a reprise of 2000. The nominating process was short for both parties. President Bush ran unopposed for the Republican nomination. Sen. John F. Kerry of Massachusetts quickly nailed down the Democratic nomination with critical victories in Iowa and New Hampshire at the start of the nominating season that produced an unstoppable wave of momentum behind his candidacy. By early March, Kerry had the nomination in hand, setting up an eight-month long general election campaign into which Democrats, Republicans, and allied interest groups poured hundreds of millions of dollars to influence the outcome.

But in spite of a record turnout of more than 122 million voters that fall—nearly 17 million more than in 2000—only three states switched party hands in 2004 from four years earlier, two of them going to the Republicans. It provided Bush with a more clear-cut victory than 2000, although still a tenuous one.

DEMOCRATIC-REPUBLICAN PARTY (1792–1828)

The Democratic-Republican Party developed in the early 1790s as the organized opposition to the incumbent Federalists and successor to the Anti-Federalists, who were a loose alliance of elements initially opposed to the ratification of the Constitution and subsequently to the policies of the George Washington administration, which were designed to centralize power in the federal government.

Thomas Jefferson was the leader of the new party, whose members as early as 1792 referred to themselves as Republicans. This remained their primary name throughout the party's history, although in some states they became known as Democratic-Republicans, the label used frequently by historians to avoid confusing Jefferson's party with the later Republican Party, which began in 1854. Party members were called Jeffersonian Republicans as well.

The Democratic-Republicans favored states' rights, a literal interpretation of the Constitution, and expanded democracy through extension of suffrage and popular control of the government. The party was dominated by rural, agrarian interests, intent on maintaining their dominance over the growing commercial and industrial interests of the Northeast. The principal strength of the party came from states in the South and Middle Atlantic.

The Democratic-Republicans first gained control of the federal government in 1800, when Jefferson was elected president and the party won majorities in both houses of Congress. For the next twenty-four years the party controlled both the White House and Congress, the last eight years virtually without opposition. For all but four years during this twenty-four-year period, there was a Virginia–New York alliance controlling the executive branch, with all three presidents from Virginia—Jefferson, James Madison, and James Monroe—and three of the four vice presidents from New York. Lacking an opposition party, the Democratic-Republicans in the 1820s became increasingly divided. In 1824, when four party leaders ran for president, John Quincy Adams won the election in the House of Representatives, although Andrew Jackson had received more popular votes.

The deep factionalism evident in the 1824 election doomed the Democratic-Republican Party. The two-party system revived shortly thereafter with the emergence of the National Republican Party, an outgrowth of the Adams faction, and the Democratic-Republican Party, the political organization of the Jackson faction. After 1830 the Jacksonians adopted the name Democratic Party.

DIXIECRATS (STATES' RIGHTS PARTY) (1948)

The States' Rights Democratic Party was a conservative southern faction that bolted from the Democrats in 1948. The immediate reason for the new party, popularly known as the Dixiecrats, was dissatisfaction with President Harry S. Truman's civil rights program. But the Dixiecrat effort to maintain a segregated way of life was also an attempt to demonstrate the political power of the twentieth-century southern Democrats and to reestablish their importance in the Democratic Party.

The Mississippi Democratic Party's state executive committee met in Jackson, Mississippi, in May 1948 to lay the groundwork for the Dixiecrat secession. The meeting called for a bolt by southern delegates if the Democratic National Convention endorsed Truman's civil rights program. When the convention did approve a strong civil rights plank, the entire Mississippi delegation and half the Alabama delegation left the convention. Gov. Fielding L. Wright of Mississippi invited all anti-Truman delegates to meet in Birmingham, Alabama, three days after the close of the Democratic convention to select a states' rights ticket.

Most southern Democrats with something at stake—national prominence, seniority in Congress, patronage privileges—shunned the new Dixiecrat Party. The party's leaders came from the ranks of southern governors and other state and local officials. The Birmingham convention chose two governors to lead the party: J. Strom Thurmond of South Carolina for president and Wright of Mississippi for vice president.

Other than the presidential ticket, the Dixiecrats did not run candidates for any office. Rather than try to develop an independent party organization, the Dixiecrats, whenever possible, used existing Democratic Party apparatus.

The party was on the ballot in only one state outside the South and in the November election received only 1,157,326 votes (2.4 percent of the popular vote). The Thurmond ticket carried four Deep South states where it ran under the Democratic Party label, but it failed in its basic objective to prevent the reelection of President Truman.

After the election the party ceased to exist almost as abruptly as it had begun, with most of its members returning to the Democratic Party. In a statement upon reentering the Democratic fold, Thurmond characterized the Dixiecrat episode as "a fight within our family." (While serving in the U.S. Senate sixteen years later, Thurmond switched to the Republican Party.)

FEDERALISTS (1792–1816)

Two related groups in late-eighteenth-century American politics called themselves Federalists. First were the proponents of ratifying the Constitution as framed in 1787, chief among them Alexander Hamilton and James Madison. They were successful. Next was the group that dominated national politics in the 1790s, as Americans began to form political parties.

The two groups were not identical. Madison, successful in promoting adoption of the new Constitution, led a political opposition that emerged in 1792. He, along with fellow Virginian Thomas Jefferson, argued for strict construction, or a narrow interpretation, of the powers of the new national government and organized a rival political party, the Democratic- (or Jeffersonian) Republicans, which came to power with Jefferson's election in 1800.

The Federalist Party, led by Hamilton as President George Washington's secretary of the Treasury, dominated national politics during the administrations of Washington and John Adams. The Federalists wanted to make the national government stronger by assuming state debts, chartering a national bank, and supporting manufacturing interests. In foreign affairs, they pursued policies that would protect commercial and political harmony with England, goals that led to ratification of Jay's Treaty in 1795. Under the treaty, England withdrew the last of its troops from American outposts and the United States agreed to honor debts owed to British merchants.

Though committed to a republican form of government, Federalists believed society to be properly hierarchical. Federalists such as William Cooper of New York and Henry Knox of Massachusetts professed that politics was an arena best left to the "natural aristocracy" of wealthy and talented men. Consequently, Federalists generally sought to limit suffrage, tighten naturalization policy, and silence antiadministration opinions. Recent examinations of the Federalists have disclosed a softer side to their conservatism, showing that, as self-proclaimed protectors of society, they sometimes sought to protect the basic rights of minorities. They tended to be more sympathetic than their Jeffersonian opponents to the plight of Native Americans and African Americans and less resistant to the inclusion of women in political processes.

Federalists drew their support primarily from the Northeast, where their procommercial and promanufacturing policies attracted merchants and businessmen. Although they had some southern strongholds in parts of Virginia and the Carolinas (especially Charleston), Federalists had considerably less success in attracting the support of western farmers and southern planters who opposed their elitism, antislavery bias, and promanufacturing economic policies.

Several factors contributed to the demise of the Federalist Party. Its passage of the highly unpopular Alien and Sedition Acts of 1798 served as a rallying cry for Jeffersonian Republicans. A more important factor may have been the Federalists' sharp division in the 1800 elections over Adams's foreign policy. Second-generation Federalists continued to mobilize regional support, mainly in New England, and, after Jefferson's unpopular embargo forbidding exports (1807–1809), they made a national comeback of sorts in the 1808 and 1812 elections. Many Federalists opposed the War of 1812, however, and in 1814 the Hartford Convention, a meeting of arch-Federalists, considered secession from the union, thereby permanently tainting the Federalist name and ending the party's legitimacy at the national level. Federalists continued to play a limited, though sometimes important, role in state and local politics into the 1820s, challenging for key offices in several states.

Federalist leadership during the nation's critical early years contributed greatly to preserving the American experiment. In large part they were responsible for laying the foundation for a national economy (later carried forward by the National Republicans and then the Whigs), a national foreign policy agenda, and creating a strong national judicial system. The last of these was perhaps the Federalists' most enduring legacy as John Marshall used his position as chief justice (1801–1835) to incorporate Federalist principles into constitutional law.

FREE SOIL PARTY (1848–1852)

Born as a result of opposition to the extension of slavery into the newly acquired southwest territories, the Free Soil Party was launched formally at a convention in Buffalo, New York, in August 1848. The Free Soilers were composed of antislavery elements from the Democratic and Whig parties as well as remnants of the Liberty Party. Representatives from all the northern states and three border states attended the Buffalo convention, where the slogan "Free Soil, Free Speech, Free Labor and Free Men" was adopted. This slogan expressed the antislavery sentiment of the Free Soilers as well as the desire for cheap western land.

Former Democratic president Martin Van Buren (1837–1841) was selected by the convention as the party's presidential candidate and Charles Francis Adams, the son of President John Quincy Adams (1825–1829), was chosen as his running mate.

In the 1848 election the Free Soil ticket received 291,501 votes (10.1 percent of the popular vote) but was unable to carry a single state. The party did better at the congressional level, winning nine House seats and holding the balance of power in the organization of the closely divided new Congress.

The 1848 election marked the peak of the party's influence. With the passage of compromise legislation on slavery in 1850, the Free Soilers lost their basic issue and began a rapid decline. The party ran its second and last national ticket in 1852, headed by John Hale, who received 155,210 votes (4.9 percent of the popular vote). As in 1848, the Free Soil national ticket failed to carry a single state.

Although the party went out of existence shortly thereafter, its program and constituency were absorbed by the Republican Party, whose birth and growth dramatically paralleled the resurgence of the slavery issue in the mid-1850s.

GREEN PARTY (1996–)

Although new to the United States, the Green Party was part of a decentralized worldwide movement for peace, social justice, and the environment. Until the collapse of international communism and the fall of the Berlin Wall, the Greens were best known for their political inroads in Germany. But the German party lost ground after opposing reunification and it only recently has returned to prominence as the junior coalition partner of Germany's left-of-center Social Democratic Party.

With famed consumer activist Ralph Nader heading its ticket, the Green Party made an impressive debut in U.S. presidential politics in 1996. Nader received 685,040 votes (0.7 percent of the popular vote) to finish fourth, albeit a distant fourth, behind the Reform Party's Ross Perot. Four years later, he made an even more impressive showing, winning 2,882,738 votes (2.7 percent of the total vote), and finished third, well ahead of other third-party candidates in the race. His showing probably tipped the outcome to the Republican Party in one or two states.

Nader received votes in every state except three (North Carolina, Oklahoma, and South Dakota), a significant increase from four years earlier when he was on the ballot in barely twenty states. As before, Nader ran best in New England and the West. As in 1996, his running mate in 2000 was Winona LaDuke of the White Earth reservation in Minnesota. A Harvard graduate, LaDuke was active as an advocate and writer on human rights and Native American environmental causes.

Unlike four years earlier, however, Nader and LaDuke in 2000 ran an aggressive and active campaign. He took his populist, anticorporate campaign to a variety of venues, ranging from TV studios to union meetings, in a bid to put together what he described as a "blue-green" coalition of disaffected voters. Nationwide polls in the summer of 2000 showed Nader drawing roughly 5 percent of the vote, and even more than that in several battleground states, including California. In the end, however, he received far fewer votes nationwide than expected. Nader was on the ballot in a number of closely contested states but most were won by the Democratic nominee, Al Gore, who was seen by analysts as the candidate most likely to be hurt by Nader's presence in the contest. Of these states, none was more important than Florida. In that state, Nader took more than 97,400 votes in a contest decided by a few hundred in favor of Republican George W. Bush. That win put Bush over the top in electoral votes and gave the White House back to the Republicans. Some political observers thought that had Nader not been on the ticket, Gore would have won Florida and the White House.

In 2004, Nader ran again for president, but as an independent. He sought the endorsement of the Green Party, although not its nomination. At their convention in Milwaukee, Wisconsin, in June, the Greens nominated a party activist, David Cobb of Texas, rather than endorse Nader's "no nomination" strategy. Patricia La Marche of Maine was chosen as Cobb's running mate.

The separate tickets did not turn out well for either candidate. Nader and his running mate, Peter Camejo of California, failed to make the ballot in almost one-third of the states and polled less than 500,000 votes nationwide. The Green Party ticket drew barely 100,000 votes and fell from third in the popular vote standings in 2000 to sixth in 2004.

GREENBACK PARTY (1874–1884)

The National Independent or Greenback-Labor Party, commonly known as the Greenback Party, was launched in Indianapolis in November 1874 at a meeting organized by the Indiana Grange. The party grew out of the Panic of 1873, a post–Civil War economic depression, which hit farmers and industrial workers particularly hard. Currency was the basic issue of the new party, which opposed a return to the gold standard and favored retention of the inflationary paper money (known as greenbacks), first introduced as an emergency measure during the Civil War.

In the 1876 presidential election the party ran Peter Cooper, a New York philanthropist, and drafted a platform that focused entirely on the currency issue. Cooper received 75,973 votes (0.9 percent of the popular vote), mainly from agrarian voters. Aided by the continuing depression, a Greenback national convention in 1878 effected the merger of the party with various labor reform groups and adopted a platform that addressed labor and currency issues. Showing voting strength in the industrial East as well as in the agrarian South and Midwest, the Greenbacks polled more than one million votes in the 1878 congressional elections and won fourteen seats in the U.S. House of Representatives. This marked the high point of the party's strength.

Returning prosperity, the prospect of fusion with one of the major parties, and a split between the party's agrarian and labor leadership served to undermine the Greenback Party. In the 1880 election the party elected only eight representatives and its presidential candidate, Rep. James B. Weaver of Iowa, received 305,997 votes (3.3 percent of the popular vote), far less than party leaders expected.

The party slipped further four years later, when the Greenbacks' candidate for president, former Massachusetts governor Benjamin F. Butler, received 175,096 votes (1.7 percent of the popular vote). With the demise of the Greenbacks, most of the party's constituency moved into the Populist Party, the agrarian reform movement that swept the South and Midwest in the 1890s.

KNOW NOTHING (AMERICAN) PARTY (1856)

The Know Nothing (or American) Party of the 1850s was the most formidable nativist political organization in American history; for two years in middle of that decade it was the nation's second-largest party. Nativism involved the fear of aliens and opposition to an internal minority believed to be un-American. Members of the American Party would be called Know Nothings because when asked about their organization they were instructed to say, "I know nothing." For them, fear and hatred of Catholics, particularly "papist conspirators," created this need for secrecy.

The Know Nothings emerged from one of the many nativist secret societies proliferating in the pre–Civil War period. The migration of millions of Catholics from Ireland and Germany stimulated an intense antialien activism in the United States. Key leaders of the Order of the Star Spangled Banner saw their group as a useful instrument for shaping a new political party in 1853. Like nativists of earlier decades, leaders of the Know Nothing Party accused Catholics of undermining the public school system and of being responsible for a host of social problems accompanying the influx of so many poverty-stricken newcomers into the great port cities.

The party emerged at a critical moment in U.S. political history. The slavery controversy was ripping apart the Whig Party, and the Democratic Party was suffering fissures in different states and sections. Out of this turmoil came a flood of members to the new nativist movement. For many people, a party organized around nativist themes—one that advanced "American" interests and stood for stability and union—offered a way out of the conflict between northerner and southerner, abolitionist and slaveholder. A common crusade against foreigners, they thought, could cement broken institutions and warring people.

The political divisions of the day meant that Know Nothing membership varied from section to section. In New York, where the party was born and had its strongest support, the leadership was composed of conservative Whig refugees, men who opposed free soil and antislavery elements in their former party. These included James Barker and Daniel Ullmann, the party candidate in the New York gubernatorial race in 1855. In New England the antislavery wing of the former Whig Party, "Conscience Whigs," played the key role. Leaders in Massachusetts included Henry Wilson, president of the state senate who was a U.S. senator in 1855, and Henry J. Gardner, elected governor in the Know Nothing landslide that year. Also swelling the party rolls in New England were abolitionists from the other major party, anti–Nebraska Act Democrats.

In the Midwest, where Know Nothings struggled to find support, nativists sought fusion with "Free Soil" activists in Indiana and Illinois, but in Wisconsin two factions (the Sams and the Jonathans) shared antialien attitudes yet split over slavery.

In the South, which contained a small immigrant population, nativism appealed to those who viewed "aliens" in the North as threatening to the southern way of life because it was assumed that newcomers would be opposed to slavery. The nativist party in the South represented an escape from the divisive struggle that threatened civil strife, but it had only limited impact.

Despite its political success in 1854 and 1855, the national Know Nothing Party could not survive the antislavery controversy. At the party gathering in Philadelphia in June 1855, a proslavery resolution led to wild debate and a massive defection led by Massachusetts nativists but including representatives from many other states. Further divisions in the party, including personal rivalries between New York leaders Barker and Ullmann, created more problems.

In 1856 the party nominated former president Millard Fillmore as its presidential candidate. But Fillmore—who had joined a Know Nothing lodge as a political maneuver and had never been a real nativist—failed at the polls, trailing in a three-way race with only 22 percent of the popular vote and taking only Maryland's eight electoral college votes. The Know Nothings did not recover, losing members rapidly in subsequent months. In 1857 the party held its last national council.

LIBERAL PARTY (1944–)

New York State's Liberal Party was founded in 1944 by anticommunist trade unionists and other politically liberal individuals who left communist-dominated political parties. Many of the state's labor and educational leaders were instrumental in creating the party, which for years billed itself as the nation's "longest existing third party." Yet by failing to win enough votes in the state's gubernatorial election in 2002, the Liberals lost their automatic ballot status, although voters could continue to register as Liberals in declaring their party affiliation.

The Liberal Party has played a major role in a number of New York elections. It provided crucial support for Franklin D. Roosevelt in 1944 and John F. Kennedy in 1960. Some political historians believe Roosevelt and Kennedy owed their national victories to the Liberal Party vote that carried New York for them. John Lindsay, nominally a Republican, won reelection in New York City's 1969 mayoral race as the Liberal Party candidate. In 2000 Democrat Hillary Rodham Clinton won the Liberal line in her campaign for the U.S. Senate, although the party continued to maintain its independence, describing itself in 2000 as an "alternative to a state Democratic Party dominated by local party machines rife with corruption and a Republican Party controlled by special interests."

The party proclaims to nominate candidates on the basis of "merit, independence, and progressive viewpoints." Many of the state's most prominent liberal politicians have sought and won the party's nomination for New York City mayor, governor, and U.S. senator, regardless of their major party affiliation. When the party has not run candidates of its own, it has usually been supportive of Democrats. Sometimes, however, the party's role has been that of a spoiler, particularly in close races, where its support represents the balance of power. In modern Senate races, for example, political analysts say Liberal Party endorsement of moderate or liberal candidates has sometimes drawn enough votes from Democratic candidates to throw the election to conservative Republicans.

The party is active in pushing its political agenda, which supports abortion rights, universal health care, and public education (it has aggressively opposed school voucher programs, for example). Its successful Supreme Court suit for congressional reapportionment contributed to the 1968 election of Shirley Chisholm of New York, the first African American woman elected to the House of Representatives.

Through the latter part of the twentieth century, the Liberal Party served as a counterweight in Empire State politics to New York's Conservative Party. In 1966, for instance, each party's gubernatorial candidate drew over a half million votes. The Liberal nominee was Franklin D. Roosevelt Jr.

Both parties have lost ground at the polls since then, the Liberals a bit more than the Conservatives (which have retained automatic ballot status). New York party enrollment figures in April 2005 showed the Conservatives with 156,186 registered voters, the Liberals with less than half as many (73,554).

LIBERAL REPUBLICAN PARTY (1872)

A faction of the Republican Party, dissatisfied with President Ulysses S. Grant's first term in office, withdrew from the party in 1872 to form a new party. Composed of party reformers, as well as anti-Grant politicians and newspaper editors, the new party focused on the corruption of the Grant administration and the need for civil service reform and for an end to the Reconstruction policy in the South.

The call for the Liberal Republican national convention came from the state party in Missouri, the birthplace of the reform movement. The convention, meeting in Cincinnati, Ohio, in May 1872, nominated Horace Greeley, editor of the *New York Tribune*, for president and Missouri governor B. Gratz Brown as his running mate. Greeley, the choice of anti-Grant politicians but suspect among reformers, was not popular among many Democrats either, who recalled his longtime criticism of the Democratic Party.

With the hope of victory in the fall election, however, the Democratic National Convention, meeting in July, endorsed the Liberal Republican ticket and platform. The coalition was an unsuccessful one, as many Democrats refused to vote for Greeley. He received 2,834,761 votes (43.8 percent of the popular vote) but carried only six states and lost to Grant by more than 750,000 votes out of nearly 6.5 million cast. Greeley died shortly after the election.

Underfinanced, poorly organized, and dependent on the Democrats for their success, the Liberal Republicans ceased to exist after the 1872 election.

LIBERTARIAN PARTY (1971–)

In the brief period of four years, 1972 to 1976, the Libertarian Party leaped from a fledgling organization on the presidential ballot in only two states to the nation's largest third party. They have largely retained that status ever since, when measured in terms of quantity of federal and nonfederal candidates and success in ballot access.

Formed in Colorado in 1971, the party nominated John Hospers of California for president in 1972. On the ballot only in Colorado and Washington, Hospers garnered 3,673 votes (including write-in votes from other states). But he received a measure of national attention when a Republican presidential elector from Virginia, Roger MacBride, cast his electoral vote for the Libertarian presidential nominee.

MacBride's action made him a hero in Libertarian circles, and the party chose him as its 1976 standard-bearer at its August 1975 convention in New York City. MacBride had served in the Vermont legislature in the 1960s and was defeated for the Republican gubernatorial nomination in that state in 1964. In the 1970s he settled on a farm near Charlottesville, Virginia, and devoted himself to writing and party affairs. He was cocreator of the television show *Little House on the Prairie*.

Making a major effort in 1976, the Libertarians got on the ballot in thirty-two states, more than Eugene J. McCarthy—who ran independent of any political party—or any other third-party candidate that year. The reward was a vote of 173,011, more than for any other minor party candidate but far below McCarthy's total and only 0.2 percent of the national vote. MacBride's strength was centered in the West; he received 5.5 percent of the vote in Alaska and 1 percent or more in Arizona, Hawaii, and Idaho. He also ran well ahead of his national average in California (0.7 percent) and Nevada (0.8 percent). His running mate was David P. Bergland, a California lawyer.

In 1980 the Libertarian Party appeared on the ballot in all fifty states and the District of Columbia for the first time. The party also fielded about 550 candidates for other offices, a number that dwarfed other third-party efforts. The party nominees, Edward E. Clark of California for president and David Koch of New York for vice president, garnered 921,299 votes or 1.1 percent of the vote nationwide. It was the highest vote total obtained by the Libertarian national ticket to date and would have been higher if not for the fact that the independent candidacy of John Anderson dominated media attention in 1980 that did not go to the two major parties. As in previous elections, the major support for the Libertarians came from western states.

Of all third-party presidential candidates running in 1984, the Libertarians appeared on the greatest number of ballots: thirty-eight states and the District of Columbia. David Bergland, who had run in 1976 for the second slot, was the party's presidential candidate, and Jim Lewis, a Connecticut business executive, his running mate. The ticket, though, received only 228,314 votes, less than one-fourth the number the Libertarians had garnered four years earlier. In 1988 the Libertarian presidential and vice-presidential nominees—Ron Paul (a Republican House member from Texas before and after he was a Libertarian) and Andre V. Marrou, respectively—were on the ballot in all fifty-one jurisdictions save four and received 432,179 votes.

In 1992 Nevada real estate broker Marrou was the presidential nominee with running mate Nancy Lord, a lawyer from Georgia. The pair was on the ballot in all states and the District of Columbia and had a campaign budget of $1 million. Marrou received 291,627 votes in a fourth-place finish behind H. Ross Perot, who stole most of the third-party candidates' thunder that year. The Libertarians maintained their strong base in the West, especially in California, Nevada, and Hawaii, where they also ran candidates in 1992 for most House seats.

In 1996 the Libertarians regained voting strength but nevertheless dropped to fifth place in the presidential race behind Perot and Ralph Nader of the newly formed Green Party. The Libertarian candidate, financial analyst Harry Browne of Tennessee, and running mate Jo Anne Jorgensen of South Carolina drew 485,798 votes or 0.5 percent of the total. It was the party's best showing since 1980.

The Libertarian result in the 2000 presidential race was similar but not as favorable. The party won votes in forty-nine states, but its candidates, again Browne and running mate Art Olivier of California, won just 386,024 votes, or 0.4 percent of all votes, down 20 percent from four years earlier.

The Libertarians fielded a new ticket in 2004, headed by computer programmer and constitutional scholar Michael Badnarik of Texas, with Richard Campagna of Iowa as his running mate. But the results were largely the same, with the Libertarian national ticket collecting roughly 400,000 ballots.

Yet while the Libertarians have yet to score a big breakthrough at the ballot box, they remain a role model for other third parties in their ability to get their candidates on the ballot. The party's presidential ticket in 2004 was listed in forty-eight states and the District of Columbia. Scores and scores of Libertarian candidates for other offices appeared on ballots across the country, winning a total of more than one million votes in U.S. House contests alone.

Individual responsibility and minimal government interference are the hallmarks of the Libertarian philosophy. The party has favored repeal of laws against so-called victimless crimes—such as pornography, drug use, and homosexual activity—the abolition of all federal police agencies, and the elimination of all government subsidies to private enterprise. In foreign and military affairs, the Libertarians have advocated the removal of U.S. troops from abroad, a cut in the defense budget, and the emergence of the United States as a "giant Switzerland," with no international treaty obligations. Libertarians also have favored repeal of legislation that they believe hinders individual or corporate action. They have opposed gun control, civil rights laws, price controls on oil and gas, labor protection laws, federal welfare and poverty programs, forced busing, compulsory education, Social Security, national medical care, and federal land-use restrictions.

LIBERTY PARTY (1839–1848)

Born in 1839, the Liberty Party was the product of a split in the antislavery movement between a faction led by William Lloyd Garrison that favored action outside the political process and a second led by James G. Birney that proposed action within the political system through the establishment of an independent antislavery party. The Birney faction launched the Liberty Party in November 1839. The following April a national convention with delegates from six states nominated Birney for the presidency.

Although the Liberty Party was the first political party to take an antislavery position, and the only one at the time to do so, most abolitionist voters in the 1840 election supported the Democratic or Whig presidential candidates. Birney received only 6,797 votes (0.3 percent of the popular vote).

Aided by the controversy over the annexation of slaveholding Texas, the Liberty Party's popularity increased in 1844. Birney, again the party's presidential nominee, received 62,103 votes (2.3 percent of the popular vote) but again, as in 1840, carried no states. The peak strength of the party was reached two years later in 1846, when in various state elections Liberty Party candidates received 74,017 votes.

In October 1847 the party nominated Sen. John P. Hale of New Hampshire for the presidency, but his candidacy was withdrawn the following year when the Liberty Party joined the broader-based Free Soil Party.

NATIONAL DEMOCRATIC PARTY (1896)

A conservative faction in favor of the gold standard, the National Democrats bolted the Democratic Party after the 1896 convention adopted a prosilver platform and nominated William Jennings Bryan for president. With the nation in the midst of a depression and the Populists in the agrarian Midwest and South demanding monetary reform, currency was the dominant issue of the 1896 campaign. This produced a brief realignment in U.S. politics.

The Republican Party was controlled by leaders who favored maintenance of the gold standard, a noninflationary currency. Agrarian midwestern and southern Democrats, reflecting a populist philosophy, gained control of the Democratic Party in 1896 and committed it to the free coinage of silver, an inflationary currency demanded by rural elements threatened by debts. The Democrats attracted prosilver bolters from the Republican Party, but gold standard Democrats, opposed to the Republicans' protectionist position on the tariff issue, established an independent party.

Meeting in Indianapolis, Indiana, in September 1896, the National Democrats adopted a platform favoring maintenance of the gold standard and selected a ticket headed by seventy-nine-year-old Illinois senator John M. Palmer. Democratic president Grover Cleveland and leading members of his administration, repudiated by the convention that chose Bryan, supported the National Democrats. During the campaign the National Democrats encouraged conservative Democrats to vote either for the National Democratic ticket or for the Republican candidate, William McKinley. The Palmer ticket received 133,435 votes (1.0 percent of the popular vote), and McKinley defeated Bryan.

In the late 1890s returning prosperity and the Spanish-American War overshadowed the currency issue, and the intense Democratic Party factionalism that produced the National Democratic Party faded.

NATIONAL REPUBLICAN PARTY (1828–1832)

The Democratic-Republican Party splintered after the 1824 election into two factions. The group led by Andrew Jackson retained the name Democratic-Republicans, which eventually was shortened to Democrats; the other faction, headed by President John Quincy Adams, assumed the name National Republicans. The new party supported a protective tariff, the Bank of the United States, federal administration of public lands, and national programs of internal improvements. But Adams's belief in a strong national government contrasted with the period's prevailing mood of populism and states' rights.

The Adams's forces controlled Congress for two years, 1825 to 1827, but as party structures formalized the National Republicans became a minority in Congress and suffered a decisive loss in the 1828 presidential election. Running for reelection, Adams was beaten by Jackson. Adams received 43.6 percent of the popular vote and carried eight states, none in the South. Henry Clay, the party's candidate against Jackson four years later, had even less success. He received only 37.4 percent of the popular vote and carried just six states, none of which, again, were in the South.

Poorly organized, with dwindling support and a heritage of defeat, the National Republicans went out of existence after the 1832 election, but their members provided the base for a new anti-Jackson party, the Whigs, which came into being in 1834.

NATIONAL UNITY PARTY (INDEPENDENT JOHN B. ANDERSON) (1980–1988)

Republican representative John B. Anderson of Illinois formed the National Unity Campaign as the vehicle for his independent presidential campaign in 1980. Anderson began his quest for the presidency by trying to win the Republican Party nomination. But as a moderate in a party becoming more and more conservative, he won no primaries and could claim only fifty-seven convention delegates by April 1980, when he withdrew from the Republican race and declared his independent candidacy.

Anderson focused his campaign on the need to establish a viable third party as an alternative to domination of the political scene by the Republican and Democratic parties. The National Unity Campaign platform touted the Anderson program as a "new public philosophy"—more innovative than that of the Democrats, who "cling to the policies of the New Deal," and more enlightened than that of the Republicans, who talk "incessantly about freedom, but hardly ever about justice." Generally, the Anderson campaign took positions that were fiscally conservative and socially liberal. He and his running mate, former Democratic governor Patrick J. Lucey of Wisconsin, tried to appeal to Republican and Democratic voters disenchanted with their parties and to the growing bloc of voters who classified themselves as independents.

The National Unity Campaign ticket was on the ballot in all fifty states in 1980, although Anderson had to wage costly legal battles in some states to ensure that result. In the end, the party won 6.6 percent of the presidential vote, more than the 5 percent necessary to qualify for retroactive federal campaign funding.

In April 1984 Anderson announced that he would not seek the presidency again. He said that instead he would focus his energies on building the National Unity Party, which he had established officially in December 1983. He planned to concentrate initially on running candidates at the local level. In August Anderson endorsed Walter F. Mondale, the Democratic nominee for president, and his running mate, Geraldine A. Ferraro.

The National Unity Party did not run a presidential candidate in the 1988 race and by 1992 was no longer a political party.

NATURAL LAW PARTY (1992–2004)

The Natural Law Party ran three presidential campaigns from 1992 to 2000, with John Hagelin of Iowa the party's standard-bearer each time. He drew 39,179 votes in 1992, 113,668 in 1996, and 83,520 in 2000. In the latter year Hagelin sought to broaden the scope of his campaign by challenging Patrick J. Buchanan for the Reform Party nomination. Losing that contest, Hagelin and his Reform Party supporters set up a splinter Reform Party that later joined in coalition with the Natural Law Party.

Hagelin, a Harvard-trained quantum physicist, was born in Pittsburgh in 1954 and grew up in Connecticut. He became as-

sociated with Maharishi International University in Iowa in 1983. His running mate on the Natural Law Party ticket in 1992 and 1996 was fellow Maharishi scientist Mike Tompkins, a Harvard graduate and specialist in crime prevention programs. In 2000, Hagelin was joined on the ticket by Nat Goldhaber of California.

The Natural Law Party once described itself as "the fastest growing grassroots party," standing for the environment, education, economic growth, job creation, and lower taxes. Despite its title, the party seemed to have little connection with the philosophic concept of natural law, which holds that some rules of society—such as the prohibition against murder—are so basic and inherent that they must be obeyed whether or not they are legislated. Hagelin and the party advocated prevention-oriented government and meditative, tension-relieving programs "designed to bring national life into harmony with natural law."

Hagelin was on the ballot in thirty-eight states in 2000. Because the Natural Law Party fulfilled the necessary requirements, it was assured automatic ballot access in ten states in the next presidential election. However, in April 2004 the party announced that it was closing its national headquarters and focusing its efforts on a new nonelectoral entity, the U.S. Peace Government, dedicated to creating permanent peace in the United States and the world.

NEW ALLIANCE PARTY (1988–1992)

The New Alliance Party formed in the late 1980s to promote a combination of minority interests. Self-described as "black-led, multiracial, pro-gay and pro-socialist," the party aggressively filed lawsuits to attain ballot access. In 1988 presidential candidate Lenora B. Fulani, a New York psychologist, drew 217,219 votes nationwide for a fourth-place finish. Her best showing was in the District of Columbia, where she received more than 1 percent of the vote.

In 1992, with the party qualifying for $1.8 million in federal matching funds, Fulani ran again, this time with California teacher Maria Munoz as a running mate. Fulani campaigned for equal employment for all. "I believe that a job at a union wage is the right of all Americans," she said. The New Alliance ticket appeared on the ballot in thirty-nine states and the District of Columbia and received 73,714 votes, slightly less than 0.1 percent nationwide.

PEACE AND FREEDOM PARTY (1967–)

Although founded in Michigan, the radical Peace and Freedom Party has been active largely in California—the only state where it appeared on the ballot in 2004. From the outset, the party worked with the California Black Panther Party to oppose U.S. involvement in the Vietnam War and espouse black nationalism and other so-called New Left causes. The first Peace and Freedom nominee for president, in 1968, was Black Panther leader Eldridge Cleaver. Running with various vice-presidential candidates, Cleaver received 36,563 votes.

Cleaver's autobiographical, antiracist polemic, *Soul on Ice*, was published in 1968. After the election Cleaver, a paroled convict awaiting trial for murder, went into exile. On his return years later, he became a born-again Christian.

Before the 1968 election, black activist-comedian Dick Gregory broke with the Peace and Freedom Party and set up the similarly named Freedom and Peace Party with himself as the presidential nominee. He received 47,133 votes.

After 1968 no Peace and Freedom candidate attracted significant numbers of presidential votes until 1980, when Maureen Smith and Elizabeth Barron received 18,116. In 1972, however, noted pacifist and pediatrician Benjamin Spock, the People's Party nominee, ran under the Peace and Freedom banner in California. He received 55,167 votes there and 23,589 votes in other states.

In 1974 the California Peace and Freedom Party declared itself to be socialist. In recent elections its presidential ticket has received at least 10,000 votes: 1988, Herbert Lewin and Vikki Murdock, 10,370; 1992, Ron Daniels and Asiba Tupahache, 27,961; 1996, Marsha Feinland and Kate McClatchy, 25,332; and 2004, Leonard Peltier and Janice Jordan, 27,607. In 2000 the party did not run a presidential candidate.

PEOPLE'S PARTY (1971–)

Delegates from activist and peace groups established the People's Party at a November 1971 convention held in Dallas, Texas. The initial cochairmen were pediatrician Benjamin Spock and author Gore Vidal.

The People's Party first ran a presidential candidate in 1972. They chose Spock for president and black activist Julius Hobson of Washington, D.C., for vice president. Despite hopes for widespread backing from the poor and social activists, the ticket received only 78,756 votes, 0.1 percent of the national total, with 55,167 of those votes from California alone.

At its convention, held in St. Louis, Missouri, August 31, 1975, the People's Party chose black civil rights activist Margaret Wright of California for president and Maggie Kuhn of Pennsylvania, a leader in the Gray Panthers movement for rights for the elderly, for vice president. Kuhn, however, declined the nomination and was replaced on the ticket by Spock.

The party platform focused on cutting the defense budget, closing tax loopholes, and making that money available for social programs. Other planks included redistribution of land and wealth, unconditional amnesty for war objectors, and free health care. In her campaign, Wright stressed the necessity for active participation by citizens in the governmental process, so that institutions and programs could be run from the grass roots up rather than from the top down.

As in 1972, the party's main backing came from California, where it was supported by the state Peace and Freedom Party. Wright's total national vote in 1976 was 49,024, and 85.1 percent (41,731 votes) of those votes came from California. The party has not fielded a presidential candidate since 1976.

POPULIST (PEOPLE'S) PARTY (1891–1908)

The Populist (or People's) Party, a third party founded in May 1891 in Cincinnati, Ohio, grew out of a period of agrarian revolt and remained politically active until 1908. Following the Civil War, farmers battled falling commodity prices, high railroad rates, and heavy mortgage debt. The Patrons of Husbandry (the Grange), organized in 1867 by Oliver Kelley, began as a group intent on improving educational and social opportunities for farmers and their families but soon adopted economic and political initiatives such as the cooperative movement of the 1870s. The inability of the Grange to give farmers an effective political voice led many Grangers in the 1880s to join the Farmers' Alliance, a precursor to the Populist Party. More aggressive and politically oriented, the Farmers' Alliance considered all agricultural problems as economic and pursued remedies such as political education and cooperative marketing, particularly in the South, as a means to break the grip of merchants who extended credit through crop liens.

Women, while active members, held far fewer offices in the Farmers' Alliance than those in the Grange. Existing racial prejudices led to the separate creation of a Colored Farmers' National Alliance in 1888.

In June 1890 Kansas farmers founded the People's Party based on the Southern Alliance platform, which included government ownership of railroads, free and unlimited coinage of silver, and a subtreasury (a system by which farmers could turn over a staple crop to a government warehouse and receive a loan for 80 percent of its value at 2 percent interest per month). As a national third party in 1891, the Populists also sought a farmer-laborer political coalition that championed the belief, expressed by Minnesota Populist Ignatius Donnelly, that the "public good is paramount to private interests."

For a time, the party attempted to bridge the racial gulf and recruited black farmers as well as white. Populism in the South, however, became mired in the volatility of race, epitomized by Georgia's Tom Watson and South Carolina's Benjamin Tillman. Although not immune to the negative racial and ethnic overtones of the period, the Populist Party was nevertheless more concerned with achieving economic reforms, a humane industrial society, and a just polity than it was with attacking cultural issues. The party's greatest support came from white land-owning cotton farmers in the South and wheat farmers in the West.

The Populists rallied behind a policy of monetary inflation in the expectation that it would increase the amount of currency in circulation, boost commodity prices, and ease farmers' indebtedness. In 1892, when the People's Party nominated James B. Weaver of Iowa as its presidential candidate, its demands included a graduated income tax, antitrust regulations, public ownership of railroads, and unlimited coinage of silver and gold at a ratio of sixteen to one. But Democrat Grover Cleveland was elected to a second term, with Weaver carrying only four states in the West. In 1896 the Populists nominated William Jennings Bryan, a free-silver candidate from Nebraska who was also the Democratic nominee, but the Republicans won with William McKinley.

Having lost on the silver issue and having lost their identity through a "fusion" with the Democrats, the Populists declined in strength and influence, particularly as new discoveries of gold eased the monetary crisis and agricultural conditions improved. Although the People's Party receded, some of the reforms it had championed, including a graduated income tax, were instituted during the Progressive era. The Populists' main significance lay in their visionary use of politics to turn a spotlight on the conditions facing farm families and thereby seek more democratic reform measures.

PROGRESSIVE (BULL MOOSE) PARTY (1912)

A split in Republican ranks, spurred by the bitter personal and ideological dispute between President William Howard Taft (1909–1913) and former president Theodore Roosevelt (1901–1909), resulted in the withdrawal of the Roosevelt forces from the Republican Party after the June 1912 GOP convention and the creation of the Progressive Party two months later. The new party was known popularly as the Bull Moose Party, a name resulting from Roosevelt's assertion early in the campaign that he felt as fit as a bull moose. While the Taft-Roosevelt split was the immediate reason for the new party, the Bull Moosers were an outgrowth of the Progressive movement that was a powerful force in both major parties in the early years of the twentieth century.

Roosevelt had handpicked Taft as his successor in 1908. But his disillusionment with Taft's conservative philosophy came quickly, and with the support of progressive Republicans Roosevelt challenged the incumbent for the 1912 Republican presidential nomination. Roosevelt outpolled Taft in nine of the ten presidential primaries where the two went head to head. Taft nevertheless won the nomination with nearly solid support in the South and among party conservatives, providing the narrow majority of delegates that enabled him to win the bulk of the key credentials challenges.

Although few Republican politicians followed Roosevelt in his bolt, the new party demonstrated a popular base at its convention in Chicago in August 1912. Thousands of delegates, basically middle- and upper-class reformers from small towns and cities, attended the convention that launched the party and nominated Roosevelt for president and California governor Hiram Johnson as his running mate. Roosevelt appeared in person to deliver his "Confession of Faith," a speech detailing his nationalistic philosophy and progressive reform ideas. The Bull Moose platform reflected key tenets of the Progressive movement, calling for more extensive government antitrust action and for labor, social, government, and electoral reform.

Roosevelt was wounded in an assassination attempt while campaigning in Milwaukee, Wisconsin, in October, but he finished the campaign. In the general election Roosevelt received more than 4 million votes (27.4 percent of the popular vote) and carried six states. His percentage of the vote was the highest ever received by a third-party candidate in U.S. history, but his candidacy split the Republican vote and enabled the Democratic nominee, Woodrow Wilson, to win the election. The Progressive Party had minimal success at the state and local levels, winning thirteen House seats but electing no senators or governors.

Roosevelt declined the Progressive nomination in 1916 and endorsed the Republican candidate, Charles Evans Hughes. With the defection of its leader, the decline of the Progressive movement, and the lack of an effective party organization, the Bull Moose Party ceased to exist.

PROGRESSIVE PARTY (LA FOLLETTE) (1924)

Similar to the Bull Moose Party of Theodore Roosevelt, the Progressive Party that emerged in the mid-1920s was a reform effort led by a Republican. Wisconsin senator Robert M. La Follette led the new Progressive Party, a separate entity from the Bull Moosers, which, unlike the middle- and upper-class Roosevelt party of the previous decade, had its greatest appeal among farmers and organized labor.

The La Follette Progressive Party grew out of the Conference for Progressive Political Action (CPPA), a coalition of railway union leaders and a remnant of the Bull Moose effort that was formed in 1922. The Socialist Party joined the coalition the following year. Throughout 1923 the Socialists and labor unions argued over whether their coalition should form a third party, with the Socialists in favor and the labor unions against it. It was finally decided to run an independent presidential candidate, La Follette, in the 1924 election but not to field candidates at the state and local levels. La Follette was given the power to choose his running mate and selected Montana senator Burton K. Wheeler, a Democrat.

Opposition to corporate monopolies was the major issue of the La Follette campaign, although the party advocated various other reforms, particularly aimed at farmers and workers, which were proposed earlier by either the Populists or Bull Moosers. But the Progressive Party itself was a major issue in the 1924 campaign, as the Republicans attacked the alleged radicalism of the party.

Although La Follette had its endorsement, the American Federation of Labor (AFL) provided minimal support. The basic strength of the Progressives, as with that of the Populists in the 1890s, derived from agrarian voters west of the Mississippi River. La Follette received 4,832,532 votes (16.6 percent of the popular vote) but carried just one state, his native Wisconsin. When La Follette died in 1925, the party collapsed as a national force. It was revived for a time by La Follette's sons on a statewide level in Wisconsin in the mid-1930s.

PROGRESSIVE PARTY (WALLACE) (1948)

Henry A. Wallace's Progressive Party resulted from the dissatisfaction of liberal elements in the Democratic Party with the leadership of President Harry S. Truman, particularly in the realm of foreign policy. The Progressive Party was one of two bolting groups from the Democratic Party in 1948; conservative southern elements withdrew to form the States' Rights Party.

Wallace, the founder of the Progressive Party, was secretary of agriculture, vice president, and finally secretary of commerce under President Franklin D. Roosevelt. He carried a reputation as one of the most liberal idealists in the Roosevelt administration. Fired from the Truman cabinet in 1946 after breaking with administration policy and publicly advocating peaceful coexistence with the Soviet Union, Wallace began to consider the idea of a liberal third-party candidacy. Supported by the American Labor Party, the Progressive Citizens of America, and other progressive organizations in California and Illinois, Wallace announced his third-party candidacy in December 1947.

The Progressive Party was launched formally the following July at a convention in Philadelphia, which ratified the selection of Wallace for president and Sen. Glen H. Taylor, D-Idaho, as his running mate. The party adopted a platform that emphasized foreign policy—opposing the cold war anticommunism of the Truman administration and specifically urging abandonment of the Truman Doctrine and the Marshall Plan. These measures were designed to contain the spread of communism and bolster noncommunist nations. On domestic issues the Progressives stressed humanitarian concerns and equal rights for both sexes and all races.

Representatives of women, youth, African Americans, Jews, and Hispanic Americans were active in the new party. But the openness of the Progressives brought Wallace a damaging endorsement from the Communist Party. Believing the two parties could work together, Wallace accepted the endorsement while characterizing his philosophy as "progressive capitalism."

In 1948 the Progressives appeared on the presidential ballot in forty-five states, but the Communist endorsement helped keep the party on the defensive the entire campaign. In the November election Wallace received only 1,157,326 votes (2.4 percent of the national popular vote), with nearly half of the votes from the state of New York. Not only were the Progressives unable to carry a single state, but President Truman won reelection. The Progressives had poor results in the congressional races as well, failing to elect a single representative or senator.

The Progressive Party's opposition to the Korean War in 1950 drove many moderate elements out of the party, including Wallace. The party ran a national ticket in 1952 led by Vincent Hallinan, but it received only 140,023 votes nationwide or 0.2 percent of the national popular vote. The party crumbled completely after the election.

PROHIBITION PARTY (1869–   )

Prohibition and temperance movements sought to legislate an end to consumption of intoxicating beverages. Colonial and early national Americans preferred alcohol to impure water or milk and more expensive coffee or tea. By 1825 those over fifteen years of age drank an average of seven gallons of pure alcohol per year, diluted in cider, beer, wine, and distilled liquor; white males typically consumed substantially more, women much less, and black slaves very little. Physicians, Protestant ministers, and temperance advocates concerned about damage to health, morals, and industrial production urged voluntary abstinence from drinking. After achieving remarkable success, the temperance movement sought legal banishment of liquor. During the 1850s a dozen states—led by Maine in 1851—adopted alcohol bans.

After the Civil War, temperance crusaders created effective political pressure groups: the Prohibition Party in 1869, the Woman's Christian Temperance Union in 1874, and the Anti-Saloon League of America in 1895. Their campaigns won adoption of numerous statewide prohibition and local option laws, the latter giving individual communities the right to outlaw the sale of alcohol. In 1913 Congress banned shipment of liquor into any state that chose to bar it. Dissatisfied by uneven and some-times short-lived state and local successes, goaded by rivalries between the Anti-Saloon League and competing temperance groups, and inspired by adoption of the first federal constitutional amendments in more than forty years (the income tax and direct Senate election amendments of 1913), reformers began calling for a total, permanent, nationwide solution to the liquor problem: a prohibition amendment to the Constitution.

National prohibition gathered support from evangelical Protestant denominations, feminists, nativists opposed to the recent flood of immigrants who drank, progressive social and political reformers, and industrial employers. Employing the unusual political tactic of pledging electoral support or punishment solely on the basis of a candidate's stand on the single issue of alcohol, proponents of Prohibition were able to get more and more supporters elected to Congress. U.S. entry into World War I against Germany added a final argument of patriotism, because the army needed the grain for bread and the troops needed to be sober to perform effectively. The Eighteenth (or Prohibition) Amendment was adopted with bipartisan backing in January 1919 and went into effect one year later; it operated with mixed success for fourteen years.

The Republicans, who were responsible for enforcement as the party in power throughout the 1920s, continued to defend Prohibition even as the Democrats' support was waning, especially in the urban North, as first Al Smith and later Franklin D. Roosevelt aligned with the repeal campaign. Differences regarding Prohibition were among the most clear-cut partisan divisions in the 1932 elections and helped account for the shift in the national political balance during the depths of the Great Depression. National Prohibition, widely viewed as a mistake, was repealed by the Twenty-first Amendment, which was ratified in December 1933.

The party remained after the repeal of Prohibition, however, becoming the longest running third party in American history in the twentieth century. The party has run a national ticket in every presidential election since 1872, but its candidates have never carried a single state. After the 1976 election, the Prohibition Party changed its name to the National Statesman Party, and its 1980 candidate registered using that party name. The 1984 candidate, Earl F. Dodge of Colorado, emphasized that his party—on the ballots once again as Prohibitionists—no longer focused on a single issue: the party backed religious liberty and an antiabortion amendment. Dodge ran again in 1988, 1992, 1996, 2000, and 2004. In 2000 the party could only muster 208 votes nationwide and fell short of that total four years later.

REFORM PARTY (INDEPENDENT ROSS PEROT) (1992–   )

The Reform Party emerged almost full grown from Texas billionaire Ross Perot's independent self-financed presidential candidacy of 1992. That year Perot drew the highest vote share of any independent or third-party candidate in eighty years. Relying heavily on his wealth and on grassroots volunteer efforts to get his name on the ballot in all fifty states and the District of Columbia, Perot received 19,741,657 votes or 18.9 percent of the nationwide vote. He did not win any sizable constituency or receive any electoral votes, but he drew a respectable 10 percent to 30 percent in popular voting across the nation.

Perot, who announced the possibility of his candidacy in February 1992, ran his early unofficial campaign mainly on one issue—eliminating the federal deficit. He had the luxury of personally funding his entire campaign, which included buying huge amounts of television time. He won additional exposure through participation in the fall presidential debates. Drawing on the disenchantment of voters, Perot and his folksy, nononsense approach to government reform struck a populist chord. But he also demonstrated his quirkiness by bizarrely withdrawing from the presidential race in mid-July and then reversing himself and reentering in October. He chose as his running mate retired admiral James B. Stockdale, who as a navy flier had been a prisoner during much of the Vietnam War.

United We Stand America (UWSA), formed from the ashes of Perot's candidacy, did not bill itself as an official political party. Promoting itself instead as a nonpartisan educational organization, UWSA called for a balanced budget, government reform, and health care reform. The group's leaders did not endorse candidates or offer them financial assistance.

In 1993 Perot, rather than UWSA, commanded considerable attention on Capitol Hill, from marshaling grassroots support on congressional reform to unsuccessfully opposing the North American Free Trade Agreement (NAFTA). Democrats and Republicans were unable to co-opt his following as they had those of major third-party movements in the past. Perot continued to use his supporters' anger with government and the political process to sustain himself as an independent political force. In the fall of 1995 Perot created a full-fledged political party, the Reform Party which qualified for federal funding in 1996 and went along with the limitations that acceptance of the money entailed. By garnering more than 5 percent of the 1992 presidential vote, Perot's party qualified in 1996 for some $30 million, less than half the amount he spent from his own pocket four years earlier.

Perot was challenged for the Reform Party nomination by Richard D. Lamm, a former Democratic governor of Colorado who had shown a willingness to risk voter displeasure. Lamm called, for example, for deep cuts in Medicare, the popular health care program for the elderly. Perot defeated Lamm in an unusual two-stage nominating procedure, starting with speeches by the candidates at a convention in Long Beach, California, followed by a mail, phone and computer vote with the winner announced a week later in Valley Forge, Pennsylvania. Ballots had been sent to 1.3 million voters who were registered party members or signers of its ballot access petitions. Less than 50,000 votes, though, were actually cast, with Perot a winner by a margin of nearly 2-to-1.

Perot again was on the general election ballot in all states. He chose as his running mate Pat Choate, a native Texan and economist who had coached Perot in his unsuccessful fight against NAFTA. The Reform Party also had congressional candidates in ten states.

Locked out of the presidential debates in 1996, Perot spent much of his campaign money on television "infomercials" es-

pousing the party's principles. Besides a balanced budget these included higher ethical standards for the White House and Congress, campaign and election reforms, a new tax system, and lobbying restrictions.

Even with his restricted campaign budget, Perot again placed third in the national election after the two major party candidates. However, his 8,085,402 votes, 8.4 percent of the total, came to less than half of his 1992 achievement of 18.9 percent, a third-party figure surpassed in the twentieth century only by former president Theodore Roosevelt and his Bull Moose candidacy of 1912. As in 1992, Perot won no electoral votes.

In 1998 the Reform Party scored a high-profile victory when former professional wrestler Jesse Ventura was elected governor of Minnesota running on the party label. Ventura's victory helped give the Reform Party the look of a growth stock, and several well-known personalities publicly considered running for the party's presidential nomination in 2000, including former Connecticut governor Lowell P. Weicker Jr. and financier Donald Trump. Ultimately, they did not run, although Patrick J. Buchanan did, bolting the Republican Party in October 1999.

Highly public party infighting followed, with Perot loyalists arrayed against Buchanan supporters. The latter claimed they offered the party energy and new blood; the former contended Buchanan was intent on a hostile takeover designed to give the Reform Party a socially conservative face.

Calling the party "dysfunctional," Ventura announced in February 2000 that he was leaving the national party and subsequently identified only with the Independence Party of Minnesota. In June Perot publicly distanced himself from his creation by declining to run against Buchanan in the party's mail-in primary in July. But John Hagelin, the candidate of the Natural Law Party in 1992 and 1996, did enter.

The Reform Party's convention in Long Beach, California, in August, disintegrated into two competing conclaves: one favorable to Buchanan, the other, dominated by Perot loyalists, favorable to Hagelin. After Buchanan wrested control of the party and nomination, the Hagelin forces set up a splinter Reform Party. Hagelin chose Nat Goldhaber of California for the vice-presidential spot on his ticket. In September the splinter group joined in coalition with the Natural Law Party, Hagelin's old party.

Nevertheless, Buchanan retained control of the Reform Party apparatus, and a federal court awarded him full use of the $12.6 million in federal funds that Perot's 1996 showing had qualified the party's 2000 nominee to receive. Buchanan chose Ezola Foster, a California teacher, for his running mate. The bipartisan Commission on Presidential Debates, however, denied Buchanan participation in the three presidential debates held in October, as his support in the polls stayed well under the 15 percent required by debate organizers to qualify.

The actual 2000 election results were a major disappointment to Reform Party supporters. Although commentators thought Buchanan's message would attract many social conservatives, the party garnered only 449,077 votes, just 0.4 percent of the total presidential vote. Some commentators, however, noted that Buchanan was on the ballot in four competitive states that were won by Democratic candidate Al Gore, in essence offsetting any damage done to Gore by the Green Party candidacy of Ralph Nader. In 2004, the Reform Party did not run a presidential candidate and endorsed the independent candidacy of Nader, providing him with their ballot line in a handful of states.

REPUBLICAN PARTY (1854–)

The Republican Party, founded in 1854, dominated national politics from 1860 to the New Deal era and presidential politics from 1968 to the present. The party emerged in 1854–1856 out of a political frenzy, in all northern states, revolving around the expansion of slavery into the western territories. The new party was so named because "republicanism" was the core value of American politics, and proponents of the new party argued that it was mortally threatened by the expanding "slave power." The enemy was not so much the institution of slavery or the mistreatment of the slaves. Rather, it was the political-economic system that controlled the South, exerted disproportionate control over the national government, and threatened to seize power in the new territories.

Origins Through Reconstruction

The party came into being in reaction to federal legislation allowing the new settlers of Kansas Territory to decide for themselves whether to adopt slavery or to continue the Compromise of 1820, which explicitly forbade slavery there. The new party lost on this issue, but in addition to bringing in most northern Whigs, it gained support from "Free Soil" northern Democrats who opposed the expansion of slavery. Only a handful of abolitionists joined. The Republicans adopted most of the modernization programs of the Whigs, favoring banks, tariffs, and internal improvements and adding, as well, a demand for a homestead law that would provide free farms to western settlers. In state after state, the Republicans outmaneuvered rival parties (the old Whigs, the Prohibitionists, and the Know Nothings), absorbing most of their supporters without accepting their doctrines.

The 1856 campaign, with strong pietistic, Protestant overtones, was a crusade for "Free Soil, Free Labor, Free Men, and Fremont!" John C. Fremont was defeated by a sharp countercrusade that warned against fanaticism and the imminent risk of civil war. By the late 1850s the new party dominated every northern state. It was well positioned to win the White House, despite its almost complete lack of support below the Mason-Dixon line. Leaders such as William H. Seward of New York and Salmon P. Chase of Ohio were passed over as presidential candidates in 1860 because they were too radical in their rhetoric and their states were safely in the Republican column. Abraham Lincoln was more moderate, and had more appeal in the closely divided midwestern states of Illinois and Indiana. With only 40 percent of the popular vote, Lincoln swept the North and easily carried the electoral college. Interpreting the Republican victory as a signal of intense, permanent Yankee hostility, seven states of the Deep South seceded and formed their own confederation.

The Republicans had not expected secession and were baffled by it. The Lincoln administration, stiffened by the unionist pleas of conservative northern Democrats, rejected both the suggestion of abolitionists that the slaveholders be allowed to depart in peace and the insistence of Confederates that they had a right to revolution and self-governance.

Lincoln proved brilliantly successful in uniting all the factions of his party to fight for the Union. Most northern Democrats were likewise supportive until fall 1862, when Lincoln added the abolition of slavery as a war goal. All the state Republican parties accepted the antislavery goal except Kentucky. In Congress the party passed major legislation to promote rapid modernization, including measures for a national banking system, high tariffs, homestead laws, and aid to education and agriculture. How to deal with the ex-Confederates was a major issue; by 1864 radical Republicans controlled Congress and demanded more aggressive action against slavery and more vengeance toward the Confederates. Lincoln held them off, but just barely. His successor, Andrew Johnson, proved eager to reunite the nation, but the radicals seized control of Congress, the party, and the army and nearly convicted Johnson on a close impeachment vote.

Ulysses S. Grant, former commander of the Union army, was elected president in 1868 with strong support from radicals and the new Republican regimes in the South. He in turn vigorously supported radical Reconstruction programs in the South, the Fourteenth Amendment, and equal civil and voting rights for the freedmen. Most of all, he was the hero of the war veterans, who gave him strong support. The party had become so large that factionalism was inevitable, hastened by Grant's tolerance of high levels of corruption. The Liberal Republicans split off in 1872 on the grounds that it was time to declare the war finished and bring the troops home from the occupied southern states.

Late Nineteenth Century

The 1873 depression energized the Democrats. They won control of the House and formed "Redeemer" coalitions that recaptured control of each southern state, often using threats and violence. The Compromise of 1877 resolved the disputed 1876 election by giving the White House to the Republicans and control of the southern states to the Democrats. The GOP, as it was now nicknamed, split into "Stalwart" and "Half-Breed" factions. In 1884, "Mugwump" reformers split off and helped elect Democrat Grover Cleveland.

In the North the Republican Party proved most attractive to men with an ambitious vision of a richer, more modern, and more complex society and economy. The leading modernizers were well-educated men from business, finance, and the professions. Commercial farmers, skilled mechanics, and office clerks largely supported the GOP, while unskilled workers and traditional farmers were solidly Democratic. The moral dimension of the Republican Party attracted pietistic Protestants, especially Methodists, Congregationalists, Presbyterians, Scandinavian Lutherans, and Quakers. By contrast, the high church or "liturgical" denominations (Roman Catholics, Mormons, German Lutherans, and Episcopalians) were offended by Republican crusaders who wanted to impose their moral standards, especially through prohibition and control over public schools.

Millions of immigrants entered the political system after 1850 and many started voting only a few years after arrival. The

Catholics (Irish, German, and Dutch) became Democrats, but the Republicans won majorities among the Protestant British, German, Dutch, and Scandinavian newcomers and among German Jews. After 1890 new, much poorer ethnic groups arrived in large numbers—especially Italians, Poles, and Yiddish-speaking Jews. For the most part they did not become politically active until the 1920s. After 1876 southern voting was quite distinct from the rest of America—with few white Republicans, apart from pockets of GOP strength in the Appalachian and Ozark Mountain counties. The party remained popular among black southerners, even as disenfranchisement minimized their political role. (They were allowed to select delegates to the Republican national convention.)

In the 1888 election, for the first time since 1872, the Republicans gained control of the White House and both houses of Congress. New procedural rules in the House gave the Republican leaders (especially Speaker Thomas Reed) the ability to pass major legislation. New spending bills, such as one that provided generous pensions to Civil War veterans, coupled with the new McKinley tariff, made the GOP the target of charges of "paternalism." Democrats ridiculed the "Billion Dollar Congress," to which Reed shot back, "It's a billion dollar country!"

At the grassroots level, militant pietists overcame the advice of more tolerant professionals to endorse statewide prohibition. In the Midwest, reformers declared war on the large German community, trying to shut down their parochial schools as well as their saloons. The Republicans, relying too much on the old-stock coalition that had always dominated the party's voting base, were badly defeated in the 1890 off-year election and the 1892 presidential contest, won by Cleveland. Alarmed professionals reasserted control over the local organizations, leading to a sort of "bossism" that (after 1900) fueled the outrage of progressives. Meanwhile, a severe economic depression struck both rural and urban America in 1893—on Cleveland's watch. The depression, combined with violent nationwide coal and railway strikes and snarling factionalism inside the Democratic Party, led to a sweeping victory for the GOP in 1894.

The party seemed invincible in 1896, until the Democrats unexpectedly selected William Jennings Bryan as their presidential candidate. Bryan's hugely popular crusade against the gold standard, financiers, railroads, and industrialists—indeed, against the cities—created a crisis for Republican candidate William McKinley and his campaign manager, Mark Hanna. Because of civil service reforms, parties could no longer finance themselves internally. Hanna solved that problem by directly obtaining $3.5 million from large corporations threatened by Bryan. During the next century, campaign finance would be hotly debated. McKinley promised prosperity for everyone and every group, with no governmental attacks on property or ethnic groups. The business community, factory workers, white-collar workers, and commercial farmers responded enthusiastically, becoming major components of the new Republican majority. As voter turnout soared to the 95 percent level throughout much of the North, Germans and other ethnic groups grew alarmed by Bryan's moralism and voted Republican.

Early Twentieth Century

Rejuvenated by their triumphs in 1894 and 1896 and by the glamour of a highly popular short war in 1898, against Spain over Cuba, the Philippines, and other Spanish possessions, the Republicans rolled to victory after victory. However, the party had again grown too large, and factionalism increasingly tore it apart.

The break within the party came in 1912 over the issue of progressivism. President William Howard Taft favored conservative reform controlled by the courts; former president Theodore Roosevelt found grassroots support in attacking Taft, bosses, courts, big business, and the "malefactors of great wealth." Defeated at the convention, Roosevelt bolted and formed a third party. The vast majority of progressive politicians refused to follow Roosevelt's action, which allowed the conservatives to seize control of the GOP which they kept for the next quarter century. Roosevelt's quixotic crusade also allowed Democrat Woodrow Wilson to gain the White House with only 42 percent of the vote. But after Wilson's fragile coalition collapsed in 1920, the GOP won three consecutive presidential contests.

Herbert Hoover, elected in 1928, represented the quintessence of the modernizing engineer, bringing efficiency to government and the economy. His poor skills at negotiating with politicians hardly seemed to matter when the economy boomed in the 1920s and Democrats were in disarray. However, when the Great Depression hit in the 1930s, his political ineptitude compounded the party's weaknesses. For the next four decades, whenever Democrats were at a loss for words, they could always ridicule Hoover.

New Deal and Democratic Dominance

The Great Depression sidelined the GOP for decades. The old conservative formulas for prosperity had lost their magic. The Democrats, by contrast, built up majorities that depended on labor unions, big-city machines, federal relief funds, and the mobilization of Catholics, Jews, and African Americans. However, middle-class hostility to new taxes, and fears about a repeat of the World War I, eventually led to a Republican rebound. Franklin D. Roosevelt's immense popularity gave him four consecutive victories, but by 1938 the GOP was doing quite well in off-year elections when FDR's magic was not at work.

In 1948 taxes were high, federal relief had ended, and big-city machines were collapsing, but union strength helped Harry S. Truman reassemble FDR's coalition for one last hurrah. The year 1948 proved to be the high-water mark of class polarization in American politics; afterward, the differences narrowed between the middle class and the working class.

The issues of Korea, communism, and corruption gave World War II hero Dwight D. Eisenhower a victory in 1952 for the Republicans, along with narrow control of Congress. However, the GOP remained a minority party and was factionalized, with a northeastern liberal element basically favorable to the New Deal welfare state and the policy of containing communist expansion, versus midwestern conservatives who bitterly opposed New Deal taxes, regulation, labor unions, and internationalism. Both factions used the issue of anticommunism and attacked the Democrats for harboring spies and allowing communist gains in China and Korea. New York governors Thomas E. Dewey and Nelson Rockefeller led the liberal wing, while senators Robert Taft of Ohio and Barry Goldwater of Arizona spoke for the conservatives. Eisenhower represented internationalism in foreign policy, and he sidetracked the isolationism represented by Taft and Hoover.

Richard Nixon, who was Eisenhower's vice president, was identified with the eastern wing of the GOP when he was nominated in 1960 to succeed Eisenhower. Nixon lost because the Democrats had a larger base of loyal supporters, especially among Catholics who turned out to support their candidate, John F. Kennedy. The defeat of yet another candidate sponsored by the eastern "establishment" opened the way for Goldwater's 1964 crusade against the New Deal and Kennedy's successor Lyndon B. Johnson's Great Society programs. Goldwater and his conservative supporters permanently vanquished the eastern liberals, but in turn his crushing defeat as the GOP presidential candidate in 1964 retired many old-line conservatives. Goldwater in 1964 and independent George Wallace in 1968 took southern whites and many northern Catholics away from their Democratic roots, while at the same time the Democratic commitment to civil rights won over nine-tenths of all African American voters.

Republican Revival

Democrat Johnson won an overwhelming victory in 1964 and brought with him a large Democratic majority in Congress that enacted sweeping social programs that Johnson called the Great Society. However, support for these programs collapsed in the mid-1960s in the face of violence and protest over racial anger as the civil rights movement gained steam, the increasingly unpopular Vietnam War, generational conflicts, the perception of increased crime, burning inner cities growing in part from the assassination of important civil rights leaders, and charges that the federal government was badly out of control.

Nixon seized the moment and ran again, winning narrowly in 1968. As president he largely ignored his party—his 1972 reelection campaign was practically nonpartisan but wildly successful as he buried his Democratic opponent. But Nixon was not to serve out his second term. The Watergate scandal, which revealed White House and presidential involvement in criminal activities, forced him to resign from office in the face of certain congressional impeachment and removal from office. Nixon's self-destruction wreaked havoc in the 1974 election, in which Democrats swept to a massive victory in off-year contests, and set the stage for the Carter interregnum.

Georgia governor Jimmy Carter won the White House for the Democrats in 1976 but his presidency crashed long before it expired in 1981. Foreign affairs were unusually salient, as public opinion saw failure in policy toward the Soviet Union, Middle Eastern nations that forced an energy crises by withholding oil supplies, and Iranian revolutionaries that held Americans hostage for months. "Stagflation" in the economy meant a combination of high unemployment and high inflation. Most of all

there was a sense of drift or, worse, of malaise. The country craved leadership.

Republican Ronald Reagan answered that need. A former movie actor and governor of California, Reagan had been a supporter of Goldwater and an articulate spokesperson for the conservative views that the 1964 presidential candidate set in motion. Reagan led a political revolution in 1980, capitalizing on grievances and mobilizing an entirely new voting bloc, the religious right. Southern Baptists and other fundamentalists and evangelicals had been voting Democratic since the New Deal. Suddenly they began to react strongly against a perceived national tolerance of immorality (especially regarding abortion and homosexuality), rising crime, and America's apparent rejection of traditional family values. Reagan had vision and leadership qualities that many in the political establishment did not initially understand. Reagan oversaw a massive military buildup, large tax cuts, and—inadvertently—a massive increase in the national debt.

By 1984 inflation had declined significantly, unemployment had eased, profits were soaring, some changes had been made in the Social Security system, and Reagan carried forty-nine states in winning reelection. Most astonishing of all was Reagan's aggressive pursuit of cold war policy, followed closely by the collapse of the Soviet Union and the end of international communism in most nations. The best issue for the Democrats was the soaring national debt—long a conservative theme. For the first time since 1932, the GOP pulled abreast of the Democrats in terms of party identification on the part of voters. A greater number of higher-income people were voting Republican, which was not offset by the lower-income groups that had always been the mainstay of the Democratic Party. By the 1980s a gender gap was apparent, with men and housewives more Republican while single, divorced, and professional women tended to be Democratic. Groups that were part of the religious right helped deliver to the GOP the votes of their membership. Those gains were largely offset by the Democratic increases among well-educated voters (those with college and postgraduate degrees) for the party's positions on social issues such as multiculturalism and a tolerance of homosexuality and abortion.

Vice President George Bush rode to the White House in 1988 on Reagan's popularity and could himself claim important victories in the cold war and in the Middle East, where the Persian Gulf War liberated Kuwait in 1991 after an invasion by neighboring Iraq. But Bush—so knowledgeable on international affairs—seemed unconcerned about taxes, deficits, and other domestic issues that bothered Americans far more. Most importantly, Bush was ambushed by the remnants of a nasty recession in 1990–1991 just as he was running for reelection in 1992, allowing Arkansas governor Bill Clinton to take back the White House for the Democrats.

The 1990s was a decade of travail for the Republican Party at the presidential level. It lost the 1992 and 1996 presidential elections to Clinton, the first time the GOP had lost successive White House elections since 1960 and 1964. Clinton proved a popular if controversial president, raising the specter that the generally Republican trend of recent decades had finally been broken. However, the GOP roared back in 1994, gaining control of Congress—both the House and Senate—for the first time since 1952 as well as control of governors' mansions in nearly all the major states. This remarkable achievement was engineered in important part by an ambitious Republican representative from Georgia, Newt Gingrich, who had worked his way into the GOP House leadership. As a result of the Republican victory in 1994, he became House Speaker but then proceeded to all but self-destruct through an aggressive and ultimately futile combat with Clinton over programs and policies.

The rancorous leadership of Gingrich soured politics in Washington, and he was unable to deliver on most of his conservative program that he called the "Contract with America." The Republican condition worsened when the party attempted to impeach and remove Clinton from office over a scandal that had its roots in a messy affair between the president and a young female intern in the White House that Clinton at first denied. The public, appalled at the scandal, never showed enthusiasm for removing Clinton and the Senate refused to convict the president after the House—in highly partisan proceedings—approved impeachment. This event, the Gingrich overreaching, and other missteps by Republicans gradually whittled down the Republican's control of Congress in the 1996 and 1998 elections.

Nevertheless, in the 2000 elections the Republican Party achieved a dream long thought impossible. In a contested election, former president Bush's son, George W. Bush, defeated Democrat Albert "Al" Gore Jr. This victory—although one of the most narrow in history—revived the GOP dominance of national-level politics that began with Nixon in 1968. Equally important, the GOP retained control of Congress, giving it complete control of the federal government for the first time since 1954. To be sure, their margin in the House was further eroded and the margin in the Senate evaporated entirely with an exact tie of fifty Democrats and fifty Republicans, with the GOP retaining control since the new vice president could break a tie vote. However, with the defection of moderate Republican senator Jim Jeffords of Vermont to the independent ranks in June 2001, the Senate reverted to Democratic control.

As the presidential party, the Republicans scored an unusual midterm success in 2002, regaining the Senate, expanding their margin in the House, and maintaining a majority of the nation's governorships. But that was merely a warm up for the presidential election of 2004. It was the first presidential contest to be held after the terrorist attacks of September 11, 2001; the first after the start of the war in Iraq; the first after a state court in Massachusetts approved gay marriage; and the first since Bush initially won the White House in 2000 on a split decision—winning the electoral vote but losing the popular vote.

To his critics, virtually everything about Bush was controversial—from the furor over his initial election to the president's embrace of an ideologically conservative agenda driven by an assertive leadership style. The 2004 campaign was waged against the backdrop of an uncertain economy, with both parties evenly matched—unified and well-financed. On Election Day, Repub-

licans were able to strengthen their grip on both ends of Pennsylvania Avenue. Bush was reelected with 51 percent of the vote. Republicans extended their majorities in the Senate and House. For good measure, the GOP maintained a clear majority of governorships in the election that produced the nation's highest voter turnout ever (more than 122 million votes).

SOCIALIST PARTY (1901–   )

The inception of the Socialist Party marked a unique, brief era of leftist organizational unity. Founded in 1901 by New York attorney Morris Hillquit and railroad worker and labor leader Eugene Debs, the Socialist Party brought together the Social Democratic Party; Social Laborites; Christian Socialists; a wing of the Socialist Labor Party; and followers of Henry George, Edward Bellamy, and assorted populist sympathizers. Rapid growth and early success continued through the 1912 presidential election, when Debs earned 6 percent of the votes cast and some 1,200 Socialist Party candidates won state and local elections, including seventy-nine mayoral races.

Despite the party's continued strong showing in the 1916 and 1920 elections, World War I took a toll on the Socialist Party. Although party members were already persecuted for their opposition to the war, the Sedition Act of 1918 resulted in additional arrests and prevented the Socialist Party from using the mail to communicate with branches beyond its East Coast and Midwest bases. While many, including Debs, were being sent to prison for either their pacifist views or Sedition Act violations, the 1917 Bolshevik Revolution in Russia led by Vladimir Lenin further hastened the party's demise.

By 1919, Leninist sympathizers threatened to take over the Socialist Party leadership. A schism ensued, resulting in the expulsion of radical party elements and the invalidation of the national executive committee elections. Thereafter, the Socialist Party and the Communist Party became two distinct organizations with decidedly different agendas. By breaking with its labor roots, the Socialist Party lost its legitimacy as an agent of radical social action. Debs's death in 1926 signaled the end of the worker-oriented party and the start of a more urban-middle-class-centered party under Norman Thomas's leadership. The Socialist Party, which had 9,500 members in 1929, experienced a revival between 1929 and 1934: membership increased during the Great Depression to almost 17,000 in 1932, when Thomas polled almost 900,000 votes in the presidential race, and to 20,000 members in 1934.

Many new members were young militants who increasingly disagreed with the party's old guard. Until Hillquit died in 1933, the old guard held their own, but they lost their grip thereafter. At the 1934 party convention in Detroit, the young militant wing, joined by Thomas and the Milwaukee mayor, Daniel W. Hoan, passed a new Socialist Party declaration of principles that the old guard believed encouraged too forcefully the nonelectoral seizure of power and sympathized too greatly with Soviet Russia. The old guard formally broke away in 1936 and formed the Social Democratic Federation (SDF). Party membership fell to 12,000 in 1936 and shrank to 6,500 the following year. More important, Thomas garnered only 187,000 votes during the 1936 presidential election and less than 100,000 in 1940.

From 1933 to 1940 the Socialist Party experienced further internal strains by criticizing President Franklin D. Roosevelt and the New Deal. Party members viewed New Deal programs as more sympathetic to corporate interests than to organized labor's concerns. Remaining party members split over wartime policy, with Thomas leading a pacifist faction; the party lost any influence it had as it was effectively co-opted by Roosevelt. Only in the cities of Bridgeport, Connecticut, and Milwaukee, Wisconsin, did the old Socialist Party maintain a real presence. However, Thomas continued to run as the Socialist presidential candidate through the 1948 election.

In the post–World War II era, all radicalism was suspect. Although the Socialists made inroads into the Congress of Industrial Organizations and helped organize Detroit autoworkers and southern sharecroppers, the party disintegrated as an organization. The party continued to field a presidential candidate until the 1960 election, when it failed to run a candidate. Radicals shifted their emphasis from organized labor to civil rights and, later, worked against the war in Vietnam.

In the early 1960s the Democratic Socialist Organizing Committee (DSOC), the New American Movement (NAM), and the Students for a Democratic Society (SDS) became the main organizational vehicles for the New Left—all working outside the constraints of third-party politics. The SDS faded after Martin Luther King's assassination in 1968 and the Paris Peace Accords in 1973. Meanwhile NAM devoted its energies to feminism, gay rights, and local community organizing into the early 1980s.

The DSOC continued to operate in the old socialist manner as the left wing of the New Deal coalition—not as a separate political party as much as a socialist force within the Democratic Party and the labor movement. The DSOC was successful in attracting activists such as machinist union leader William Winpisinger, feminist Gloria Steinem, and gay rights activist Harry Britt. Bernard Sanders, member of Congress from Vermont who was first elected in 1991, was the first self-avowed socialist elected to Congress in decades and perhaps the best known since Victor Berger served in the House of Representatives during the 1920s.

NAM and DSOC completed a formal merger in 1983 and emerged as the Democratic Socialists of America (DSA). The DSA brought together for the first time since World War I the disparate segments of leftist opinion, including the SDF and former socialists and communists. Although the American left was in disarray in the late 1960s and the administrations of Richard Nixon, Ronald Reagan, George Bush, and Bill Clinton were by and large conservative, a kind of socialist revival occurred at the end of the twentieth century. Although membership remained low, Socialist Party influences such as government-supported health care, minimum wage, and human rights were more apparent in the national political debate than at any time since the 1960s. In addition, the Socialist Party resumed running a presidential ticket in 1976 and has continued to do so in most elections since then, although the Socialists did not receive more than 15,000 votes in any of them.

SOCIALIST LABOR PARTY (1874–)

The Socialist Labor Party, the first national socialist party in the United States, ranks second only to the Prohibitionists among third parties in longevity. Formed in 1874 by elements of the Socialist International in New York, it was first known as the Social Democratic Workingmen's Party. In 1877 the group adopted the name Socialist Labor Party. Throughout the 1880s the party worked in concert with other left-wing third parties, including the Greenbacks.

The Socialist Labor Party ran national tickets in every presidential election from 1892 through 1976. The party collected its highest proportion of the national vote in 1896, when its candidate received 36,356 votes (0.3 percent of the popular vote).

Led by the autocratic Daniel DeLeon (1852–1914), a former Columbia University law lecturer, the Socialist Labor Party became increasingly militant and made its best showing in local races in 1898. But DeLeon's insistence on rigid party discipline and his opposition to the organized labor movement created a feeling of alienation among many members. Moderate elements bolted from the party, eventually joining the Socialist Party of Eugene V. Debs, which formed in 1901.

The Socialist Labor Party continued as a small, tightly organized far-left group bound to DeLeon's uncompromising belief in revolution. As late as 1976 the party advocated direct worker action to take over control of production and claimed 5,000 members nationwide, although it has not run a presidential ticket under the Socialist Labor banner since then.

SOCIALIST WORKERS PARTY (1938–)

The Socialist Workers Party was formed in 1938 by followers of the Russian revolutionary Leon Trotsky. Originally a faction within the U.S. Communist Party, the Trotskyites were expelled in 1936 on instructions from Soviet leader Joseph Stalin. A brief Trotskyite coalition with the Socialist Party ended in 1938 when the dissidents decided to organize independently as the Socialist Workers Party. Through its youth arm, the Young Socialist Alliance, the Socialist Workers Party was active in the anti–Vietnam War movement and contributed activists to civil rights protests.

Since 1948 the party has run a presidential candidate, but its entries have never received more than 0.1 percent of the popular vote. In 1992 presidential candidate James Warren was on the ballot in thirteen states and the District of Columbia and drew 23,096 votes nationwide. The party's 2004 candidate, James E. Harris Jr. of Georgia, received barely 7,000 votes.

UNION PARTY (1936)

Advocating more radical economic measures in light of the Great Depression, several early supporters of President Franklin D. Roosevelt broke with him and ran their own ticket in 1936 under the Union Party label. Largely an outgrowth of the Rev. Charles E. Coughlin's National Union for Social Justice, the new party also had the support of Dr. Francis E. Townsend, leader of a movement for government-supported old-age pensions, and Gerald L. K. Smith, self-appointed heir of Louisiana senator Huey P. Long's share-the-wealth program.

Father Coughlin was the keystone of the Union Party and was instrumental in choosing its presidential ticket in June 1936—Rep. William Lemke, R-N.D., for president and Thomas O'Brien, a Massachusetts railroad union lawyer, for vice president. The new party did not hold a convention. The party's platform reportedly was written by Coughlin, Lemke, and O'Brien and was similar to the program espoused by Coughlin's National Union. Among the features of the Union Party platform were proposals for banking and currency reform, a guaranteed income for workers, restrictions on wealth, and an isolationist foreign policy.

Lacking organization and finances during the campaign, the party further suffered from the increasingly violent and often anti-Semitic tone of the oratory of both Coughlin and Smith.

The Union Party failed miserably in its primary goal of defeating Roosevelt. Roosevelt won a landslide victory and the Lemke ticket received only 892,267 votes (2 percent of the popular vote). The party standard-bearers were unable to carry a single state, and the Union Party's candidates for the House and Senate all were defeated. The party continued on a local level until it was finally dissolved in 1939.

U.S. LABOR PARTY (INDEPENDENT LYNDON LAROUCHE) (1973–)

Formed in 1973 as the political arm of the National Caucus of Labor Committees (NCLC), the U.S. Labor Party made its debut in national politics in 1976. The NCLC, a Marxist group, was organized in 1968 by splinters of the radical movements of the 1960s. Lyndon H. LaRouche Jr., the party's chairman (then of New York) and a self-taught economist who worked in the management and computer fields, became its 1976 presidential nominee and Wayne Evans, a Detroit steelworker, his running mate.

The party directed much of its fire at the Rockefeller family. It charged that banks controlled by the Rockefellers were strangling the U.S. and world economies. In an apocalyptic vein, the party predicted a world monetary collapse by election day and the destruction of the country by thermonuclear war by summer 1977.

LaRouche's party developed a reputation for harassment because of its shouted interruptions and demonstrations against its political foes, including the Communist Party and the United Auto Workers. It accused some left-wing organizations and individuals, such as linguist Noam Chomsky and Marcus Raskin and his Institute for Policy Studies, of conspiring with the Rockefellers and the Central Intelligence Agency.

During the 1976 campaign, LaRouche was more critical of challenger Jimmy Carter than President Gerald R. Ford. He depicted Ford as a well-meaning man out of his depth in the presidency, but Carter as a pawn of nuclear war advocates and a disgracefully unqualified presidential candidate. LaRouche captured only 40,043 votes, less than 0.1 percent of the national vote. He was on the ballot in twenty-three states and the District of Columbia.

Although the U.S. Labor Party did not run a presidential candidate in the 1980 election, LaRouche ran a strident campaign—as a Democrat. By this time, LaRouche's politics had shifted to the right, and his speeches were fraught with warnings of conspiracy.

He continued his crusade in 1984 but as an "independent Democrat," dismissing Democratic presidential nominee Walter F. Mondale as an "agent of Soviet influence." LaRouche received 78,807 votes, or 0.1 percent of the vote, in the fall election.

In 1988 LaRouche again attempted to run as a Democrat but, failing the nomination, garnered 25,562 votes under the banner of the National Economic Recovery Party. On December 16, 1988, LaRouche and six of his associates were convicted on forty-seven counts of mail fraud and conspiracy to commit mail fraud. LaRouche was sentenced to fifteen years in prison.

In 1992 the unflagging LaRouche ran again for president from his jail cell. As a convicted felon, he no longer had the right to vote himself. LaRouche ran as an independent although his name appeared on several state ballots under various party names, including Economic Recovery. His supporters, experienced in winning ballot access, placed him on the ballot in seventeen states and the District of Columbia. He received 26,333 votes nationwide.

In 1996 LaRouche's name disappeared from the general election ballot, although he continued to be a quadrennial entry in the Democratic primaries. LaRouche ran in the party's primaries in every election from 1980 through 2004, with his best showing in 1996 when President Bill Clinton had no major opposition for renomination. That year, LaRouche drew nearly 600,000 Democratic primary votes (5.4 percent of the party's total primary ballots). In 2004 LaRouche received barely 100,000 votes in the Democratic primaries.

U.S. TAXPAYERS PARTY AND CONSTITUTION PARTY (1992–)

Making its second appearance in a presidential election, the U.S. Taxpayers Party was on the ballot in thirty-nine states in 1996. Its nominee, Howard Phillips of Virginia, drew 184,658 votes or more than four times his 1992 total of 43,434. Of the eighteen minor parties receiving at least 750 votes in 1996, the Taxpayers Party received the fourth highest total. In 2000 Phillips—running under the banner of several party labels—was on the ballot in 41 states. He won 98,004 votes, the sixth highest total of all presidential candidates in 2000.

Phillips, longtime chairman of the Conservative Caucus, founded the party to counter what he perceived to be a left-of-center movement by the Republican Party under George Bush. Failing to recruit rightist icons such as Patrick J. Buchanan, Oliver North, or Jesse Helms to be the party's nominee, Phillips ran himself as its standard-bearer. In addition to taxes the party opposed welfare, abortion, and affirmative action.

Phillips was nominated to run for president again in 2000, by which time the U.S. Taxpayers had changed its name to the Constitution Party, to more broadly reflect its conservative agenda. Phillips, though, was willing to step aside at several stages of the campaign when the prospect of the party nominating a more prominent politician was possible. First, it was Sen. Robert C. Smith of New Hampshire, a short-lived independent who returned to the Republican Party on the eve of the third party's convention in September 1999. Second, was Republican presidential contender Alan Keyes, who indicated in the spring of 2000 that he might bolt to the Constitution Party if the GOP weakened the antiabortion plank in the party's platform. It did not, and Keyes stayed in the Republican Party.

In 2004 Phillips did step aside in favor of Michael Peroutka, a lawyer and head of the state party in Maryland, who was paired on the Constitution Party ticket with Charles Baldwin of Florida. They made it on the presidential ballot in thirty-six states and received more than 140,000 votes, which placed the Constitution Party in fifth place in 2004 in the popular vote count.

WHIG PARTY (1834–1856)

Whigs were nineteenth-century modernizers who saw President Andrew Jackson (1829–1837) as a dangerous man with a reactionary opposition to the forces of social, economic, and moral change. As Jackson purged his opponents, vetoed internal improvements, and killed the Bank of the United States, alarmed local elites fought back.

The Whigs, led by Henry Clay, celebrated Clay's vision of the "American System." They demanded government support for a more modern, market-oriented economy, in which skill, expertise, and bank credit would count for more than physical strength or land ownership. They also sought to promote industrialization through high tariffs, a business-oriented money supply based on a national bank, and a vigorous program of government-funded "internal improvements," especially expansion of the road and canal systems. As well, the Whigs championed the creation of public schools, private colleges, charities, and cultural institutions.

The Democrats, by contrast, harkened back to the Jeffersonian ideal of an equalitarian agricultural society, insisting that traditional farm life bred republican simplicity, whereas modernization threatened to create a politically powerful caste of rich aristocrats who might subvert democracy. In general, the Democrats enacted their policies at the national level; the Whigs' greatest success was at the state level.

Although the Whigs won votes in every socioeconomic class, including the poorest, they appealed especially to more prosperous Americans. The Democrats likewise won support up and down the income ladder, but they often sharpened their appeals to the working class by ridiculing the aristocratic pretensions of the Whigs. Most bankers, storekeepers, factory owners, master mechanics, clerks, and professionals favored the Whigs. Moreover, commercially oriented farmers in the North voted Whig, as did most large-scale planters in the South.

In general, the commercial and manufacturing towns and cities were heavily Whig, save for Democratic wards filled with recent Irish Catholic and German immigrants. Waves of Protestant religious revivals in the 1830s injected a moralistic element into the Whig ranks. Nonreligious individuals who found themselves the targets of moral reform, such as calls for prohibition, denounced the Whigs as Puritans and sought refuge in the Democratic Party. Rejecting the automatic party loyalty that was the hallmark of the tight Democratic Party organization, the

Whigs suffered from factionalism. Yet the party's superb network of newspapers provided an internal information system.

Whigs clashed with Democrats throughout what historians term the "Second American Party System." When they controlled the Senate, Whigs passed a censure motion in 1834 denouncing Jackson's arrogant assumption of executive power in the face of the true will of the people as represented by Congress. Backing Henry Clay in 1832 and a medley of candidates in 1836, the opposition finally coalesced in 1840 behind a popular general, William Henry Harrison, and proved that the national Whig Party could win the White House. Moreover, in the 1840s Whigs won 49 percent of gubernatorial elections, with strong bases in the manufacturing Northeast and in the border states. Yet the party revealed limited staying power. Whigs were ready to enact their programs in 1841, but Harrison died and was succeeded by John Tyler, an old-line Democrat who never believed in Whiggery and was, in fact, disowned by the party while he was president. Factionalism helped defeat Henry Clay, the Whig presidential candidate, in 1844. In 1848 opportunity beckoned as the Democrats split. By ignoring Clay and nominating a famous war hero, Gen. Zachary Taylor, the Whigs papered over their deepening splits on slavery, and they won the White House for the second (and last) time. The trend, however, was for the Democratic vote to grow faster and for the Whigs to lose more and more marginal states and districts.

The Whigs were unable to deal with the slavery issue after 1850. Almost all of their southern leaders owned slaves. The northeastern Whigs, led by Daniel Webster, represented businessmen who loved the national flag and a national market but cared little about slavery one way or another. Many Whig voters in the North, however, felt slavery was incompatible with a free labor–free market economy, and the two sides were unable to find a compromise that would keep the party united. Furthermore, the burgeoning economy made full-time careers in business or law much more attractive than politics for ambitious young Whigs. For example, the party leader in Illinois, Abraham Lincoln, simply abandoned politics for several years after 1849. When new issues of nativism, prohibition, and antislavery burst on the scene in the mid-1850s, no one looked to the fast-disintegrating Whig Party for answers. In the North most ex-Whigs joined the new Republican Party, and in the South they flocked to a new, short-lived "American" (Know Nothing) Party. During the Lincoln administration (1861–1865), ex-Whigs enacted much of the "American System"; in the long run, America adopted Whiggish economic policies coupled with the Democrats' penchant for a strong presidency.

WORKERS WORLD PARTY (1959–)

With the Hungarian citizen revolt and other developments in eastern Europe providing some impetus, the Workers World Party in 1959 split off from the Socialist Workers Party. The party theoretically supports worker uprisings in all parts of the world. Yet it backed the communist governments that put down rebellions in Hungary during the 1950s, Czechoslovakia in the 1960s, and Poland in the 1980s. Workers World is an activist revolutionary group that, until 1980, concentrated its efforts on specific issues, such as the antiwar and civil rights demonstrations during the 1960s and 1970s. The party has an active youth organization, Youth Against War and Fascism.

In 1980 party leaders saw an opportunity, created by the weakness of the U.S. economy and the related high unemployment, to interest voters in its revolutionary ideas. That year it placed Deirdre Griswold, the editor of the party's newspaper and one of its founding members, on the presidential ballot in ten states. Together with her running mate Larry Holmes, a twenty-seven-year-old black activist, Griswold received 13,300 votes. In 1984 Holmes ran as the presidential candidate, getting on the ballot in eight states and receiving 15,329 votes. In 1988 Holmes ran with Gloria La Riva, and they garnered 7,846 votes. La Riva ran as the presidential candidate in 1992 and was on the ballot only in New Mexico, where she received 181 votes.

The Workers World Party dramatically improved its electoral fortunes in 1996. Its candidate, Monica Moorehead of New Jersey, was on the ballot in twelve states and received 29,082 votes. But the party's vote has plummeted sharply from even that modest total. In 2004, the Workers World ticket headed by John Parker, an antiwar activist from California, drew less than 2,000 votes.

Biographical Directory of Presidential and Vice-Presidential Candidates

THE NAMES in the directory include all persons who have received electoral votes for president or vice president since 1789. Also included are prominent third-party candidates who received popular votes but no electoral votes, and Nelson A. Rockefeller, appointed vice president by Gerald R. Ford, who became president following the resignation of Richard Nixon. For the 2004 election, only the presidential and vice-presidential candidates for the Democratic and Republican parties are included.

The material is organized as follows: name, state of residence in the year(s) the individual received electoral votes, party or parties with which the individual identified when he or she received electoral votes, date of birth, date of death (where applicable), major offices held, and the year(s) of candidacy.

For the elections of 1789 through 1800, presidential electors did not vote separately for president or vice president. It was, therefore, difficult in many cases to determine if an individual receiving electoral votes in these elections was a candidate for the office of president or vice president. Where no determination could be made from the sources consulted by Congressional Quarterly, the year in which the individual received electoral votes is given with no specification as to whether the individual was a candidate for president or vice president.

The following sources were used: *American Political Leaders, 1789–2000,* (Washington, D.C.: Congressional Quarterly, 2000); *Biographical Directory of the United States Congress, 1774–1989,* (Washington, D.C.: Government Printing Office, 1989); *Dictionary of American Biography,* (New York: Scribner's, 1928–36); John A. Garraty, ed., *Encyclopedia of American Biography,* (New York: Harper and Row, 1974); Jaques Cattell Press, ed., *Who's Who in American Politics, 1977–78,* 6th ed. (New York: R. R. Bowker, 1977); *Who Was Who in America, 1607–1968,* (Chicago: Marquis, 1943–68); Svend Petersen, *A Statistical History of the American Presidential Elections,* (Westport, Conn.: Greenwood Press, 1981); Richard M. Scammon, *America Votes 10* (Washington, D.C.: Congressional Quarterly, 1973); Richard M. Scammon and Alice V. McGillivray, *America Votes 12* (Washington, D.C.: Congressional Quarterly, 1977); *America Votes 14* (Washington, D.C.: Congressional Quarterly, *America Votes 18* (Washington, D.C.: Congressional Quarterly, *America Votes 20* (Washington, D.C.: Congressional Quarterly, 1993); Rhodes Cook, *America Votes 22* (Washington, D.C.: Congressional Quarterly, 1997); Rhodes Cook, *America Votes 24* (Washington, D.C.: CQ Press, 2001). Rhodes Cook, *America Votes 25* (Washington, D.C.: CQ Press, 2003). Rhodes Cook, *America Votes 26* (Washington, D.C.: CQ Press, 2005).

Adams, Charles Francis - Mass. (Free Soil) Aug. 18, 1807–Nov. 21, 1886; House, 1859–1861; minister to Great Britain, 1861–1868. Candidacy: VP - 1848.

Adams, John - Mass. (Federalist) Oct. 30, 1735–July 4, 1826; Continental Congress, 1774; signer of Declaration of Independence, 1776; minister to Great Britain, 1785; U.S. vice president, 1789–1797; U.S. president, 1797–1801. Candidacies: VP - 1789, 1792; P - 1796, 1800.

Adams, John Quincy - Mass. (Democratic-Republican, National Republican) July 11, 1767–Feb. 23, 1848; Senate, 1803–1808; minister to Russia, 1809–1814; minister to Great Britain, 1815–1817; secretary of state, 1817–1825; U.S. president, 1825–1829; House, 1831–1848. Candidacies: P - 1820, 1824, 1828.

Adams, Samuel - Mass. (Federalist) Sept. 27, 1722–Oct. 2, 1803; Continental Congress, 1774–1781; signer of Declaration of Independence; governor, 1793–1797. Candidacy: 1796.

Agnew, Spiro Theodore - Md. (Republican) Nov. 9, 1918–Sept. 17, 1996; governor, 1967–1969; U.S. vice president, 1969–1973 (resigned Oct. 10, 1973). Candidacies: VP - 1968, 1972.

Anderson, John B. - Ill. (Republican, Independent) Feb. 15, 1922– ; state's attorney, 1956–1960; House, 1961–1981. Candidacy: P - 1980.

Armstrong, James - Pa. (Federalist) Aug. 29, 1748–May 6, 1828; House, 1793–1795. Candidacy: 1789.

Arthur, Chester Alan - N.Y. (Republican) Oct. 5, 1830–Nov. 18, 1886; collector, Port of N.Y., 1871–1878; U.S. vice president, 1881; U.S. president, 1881–1885. Candidacy: VP - 1880.

Banks, Nathaniel Prentice - Mass. (Liberal Republican) Jan. 30, 1816–Sept. 1, 1894; House, 1853–1857, 1865–1873, 1875–1879, 1889–1891; governor, 1858–1861. Candidacy: VP - 1872.

Barkley, Alben William - Ky. (Democratic) Nov. 24, 1877–April 30, 1956; House, 1913–1927; Senate, 1927–1949, 1955–1956; Senate majority leader, 1937–1947; Senate minority leader, 1947–1949; U.S. vice president, 1949–1953. Candidacy: VP - 1948.

Bell, John - Tenn. (Constitutional Union) Feb. 15, 1797–Sept. 10, 1869; House, 1827–1841; Speaker of the House, 1834–1835; secretary of war, 1841; Senate, 1847–1859. Candidacy: P - 1860.

Benson, Allan Louis - N.Y. (Socialist) Nov. 6, 1871–Aug. 19, 1940; writer, editor; founder of *Reconstruction Magazine,* 1918. Candidacy: P - 1916.

Bentsen, Lloyd Millard Jr. - Texas (Democratic) Feb. 11, 1921– ; House 1948–1955; Senate 1971–1993; secretary of Treasury, 1993–1994. Candidacy: VP - 1988.

Bidwell, John - Calif. (Prohibition) Aug. 5, 1819–April 4, 1900; California pioneer; major in Mexican War; House, 1865–1867. Candidacy: P - 1892.

Birney, James Gillespie - N.Y. (Liberty) Feb. 4, 1792–Nov. 25, 1857; Kentucky Legislature, 1816–1817; Alabama Legislature, 1819–1820. Candidacies: P - 1840, 1844.

Blaine, James Gillespie - Maine (Republican) Jan. 31, 1830–Jan. 27, 1893; House, 1863–1876; Speaker of the House, 1869–1875; Senate, 1876–1881; secretary of state, 1881, 1889–1892; president, first Pan American Congress, 1889. Candidacy: P - 1884.

Blair, Francis Preston Jr. - Mo. (Democratic) Feb. 19, 1821–July 8, 1875; House, 1857–1859, 1860, 1861–1862, 1863–1864; Senate, 1871–1873. Candidacy: VP - 1868.

Bramlette, Thomas E. - Ky. (Democratic) Jan. 3, 1817–Jan. 12, 1875; governor, 1863–1867. Candidacy: VP - 1872.

Breckinridge, John Cabell - Ky. (Democratic, Southern Democratic) Jan. 21, 1821–May 17, 1875; House, 1851–1855; U.S. vice president, 1857–1861; Senate, 1861; major general, Confederacy, 1861–1865; secretary of war, Confederacy, 1865. Candidacies: VP - 1856; P - 1860.

Bricker, John William - Ohio (Republican) Sept. 6, 1893–March 22, 1986; attorney general of Ohio, 1933–1937; governor, 1939–1945; Senate, 1947–1959. Candidacy: VP - 1944.

Brown, Benjamin Gratz - Mo. (Democratic) May 28, 1826–Dec. 13, 1885; Senate, 1863–1867; governor, 1871–1873. Candidacy: VP - 1872.

Bryan, Charles Wayland - Neb. (Democratic) Feb. 10, 1867–March 4, 1945; governor, 1923–1925, 1931–1935; Candidacy: VP - 1924.

Bryan, William Jennings - Neb. (Democratic, Populist) March 19, 1860–July 26, 1925; House, 1891–1895; secretary of state, 1913–1915. Candidacies: P - 1896, 1900, 1908.

Buchanan, James - Pa. (Democratic) April 23, 1791–June 1, 1868; House, 1821–1831; minister to Russia, 1832–1834; Senate, 1834–1845; secretary of state, 1845–1849; minister to Great Britain, 1853–1856; U.S. president, 1857–1861. Candidacy: P - 1856.

Burr, Aaron - N.Y. (Democratic-Republican) Feb. 6, 1756–Sept. 14, 1836; attorney general of N.Y., 1789–1790; Senate, 1791–1797; U.S. vice president, 1801–1805. Candidacies: 1792, 1796, 1800.

Bush, George - Texas (Republican) June 12, 1924– ; House, 1967–1970; ambassador to the United Nations, 1971–1973; chairman of the Republican National Committee, 1973–1974; head of the U.S. liaison office in Peking, 1974–1975; director of the Central Intelligence Agency, 1976–1977; U.S. vice president, 1981–1989; U.S. president, 1989–1993. Candidacies: VP - 1980, 1984; P - 1988, 1992.

Bush, George W. - Texas (Republican) July, 6, 1946– ; governor, 1995–2000; U.S. president, 2001– . Candidacies: P - 2000, 2004.

Butler, Benjamin Franklin - Mass. (Greenback, Anti-Monopoly) Nov. 5, 1818–Jan. 11, 1893; House, 1867–1875, 1877–1879; governor, 1883–1884. Candidacy: P - 1884.

Butler, Nicholas Murray - N.Y. (Republican) April 2, 1862–Dec. 7, 1947; president, Columbia University, 1901–1945; president, Carnegie Endowment for International Peace, 1925–1945. Candidacy: VP - 1912. (Substituted as candidate after Oct. 30 death of nominee James S. Sherman.)

Butler, William Orlando - Ky. (Democratic) April 19, 1791–Aug. 6, 1880; House, 1939–1943. Candidacy: VP - 1848.

Byrd, Harry Flood - Va. (States' Rights Democratic, Independent Democratic) June 10, 1887–Oct. 20, 1966; governor, 1926–1930; Senate, 1933–1965. Candidacies: P - 1956, 1960.

Calhoun, John Caldwell - S.C. (Democratic-Republican, Democratic) March 18, 1782–March 31, 1850; House, 1811–1817; secretary of war, 1817–1825; U.S. vice president, 1825–1832; Senate, 1832–1843, 1845–1850; secretary of state, 1844–1845. Candidacies: VP - 1824, 1828.

Carter, James Earl Jr. - Ga. (Democratic) Oct. 1, 1924– ; Georgia Legislature, 1963–1967; governor, 1971–1975; U.S. president, 1977–1981. Candidacies: P - 1976, 1980.

Cass, Lewis - Mich. (Democratic) Oct. 9, 1782–June 17, 1866; military and civil governor of Michigan Territory, 1813–1831; secretary of war, 1831–1836; minister to France, 1836–1842; Senate, 1845–1848, 1849–1857; secretary of state, 1857–1860. Candidacy: P - 1848.

Cheney, Richard - Wyo. (Republican) Jan. 30, 1941– ; House 1979–1989; secretary of defense, 1989–1993; U.S. vice president, 2001– . Candidacies: VP - 2000, 2004.

Clay, Henry - Ky. (Democratic-Republican, National Republican, Whig) April 12, 1777–June 29, 1852; Senate, 1806–1807, 1810–1811, 1831–1842, 1849–1852; House, 1811–1814, 1815–1821, 1823–1825; Speaker of the House, 1811–1814, 1815–1820, 1823–1825; secretary of state, 1825–1829. Candidacies: P - 1824, 1832, 1844.

Cleveland, Stephen Grover - N.Y. (Democratic) March 18, 1837–June 24, 1908; mayor of Buffalo, 1882; governor, 1883–1885; U.S. president, 1885–1889, 1893–1897. Candidacies: P - 1884, 1888, 1892.

Clinton, Bill - Ark. (Democrat) Aug. 19, 1946– ; attorney general of Arkansas, 1977–1979; governor, 1979–1981, 1983–1992; U.S. president, 1993–2001. Candidacies: P - 1992, 1996.

Clinton, De Witt - N.Y. (Independent Democratic-Republican, Federalist) March 2, 1769–Feb. 11, 1828; Senate, 1802–1803; mayor of New York, 1803–1807, 1810, 1811, 1813, 1814; governor, 1817–1823, 1825–1828. Candidacy: P - 1812.

Clinton, George - N.Y. (Democratic-Republican) July 26, 1739–April 20, 1812; Continental Congress, 1775–1776; governor, 1777–1795, 1801–1804; U.S. vice president, 1805–1812. Candidacies: VP - 1789, 1792, 1796, 1804, 1808.

Colfax, Schuyler - Ind. (Republican) March 23, 1823–Jan. 13, 1885; House, 1855–1869; Speaker of the House, 1863–1869; U.S. vice president, 1869–1873. Candidacy: VP - 1868.

Colquitt, Alfred Holt - Ga. (Democratic) April 20, 1824–March 26, 1894; House, 1853–1855; governor, 1877–1882; Senate, 1883–1894. Candidacy: VP - 1872.

Coolidge, Calvin - Mass. (Republican) July 4, 1872–Jan. 5, 1933; governor, 1919–1921; U.S. vice president, 1921–1923; U.S. president, 1923–1929. Candidacies: VP - 1920; P - 1924.

Cox, James Middleton - Ohio (Democratic) March 31, 1870–July 15, 1957; House, 1909–1913; governor, 1913–1915, 1917–1921. Candidacy: P - 1920.

Crawford, William Harris - Ga. (Democratic-Republican) Feb. 24, 1772–Sept. 15, 1834; Senate, 1807–1813; president pro tempore of the Senate, 1812–1813; secretary of war, 1815–1816; secretary of Treasury, 1816–1825. Candidacy: P - 1824.

Curtis, Charles - Kan. (Republican) Jan. 25, 1860–Feb. 8, 1936; House, 1893–1907; Senate, 1907–1913, 1915–1929; president pro tempore of the Senate, 1911; Senate majority leader, 1925–1929; U.S. vice president, 1929–1933. Candidacies: VP - 1928, 1932.

Dallas, George Mifflin - Pa. (Democratic) July 10, 1792–Dec. 31, 1864; Senate, 1831–1833; minister to Russia, 1837–1839; U.S. vice president, 1845–1849; minister to Great Britain, 1856–1861. Candidacy: VP - 1844.

Davis, David - Ill. (Democratic) March 9, 1815–June 26, 1886; associate justice of U.S. Supreme Court, 1862–1877; Senate, 1877–1883; president pro tempore of the Senate, 1881. Candidacy: P - 1872.

Davis, Henry Gassaway - W.Va. (Democratic) Nov. 16, 1823–March 11, 1916; Senate, 1871–1883; chairman of Pan American Railway Committee, 1901–1916. Candidacy: VP - 1904.

Davis, John William - W.Va., N.Y. (Democratic) April 13, 1873–March 24, 1955; House, 1911–1913; solicitor general, 1913–1918; ambassador to Great Britain, 1918–1921. Candidacy: P - 1924.

Dawes, Charles Gates - Ill. (Republican) Aug. 27, 1865–April 3, 1951; U.S. comptroller of the currency, 1898–1901; first director of Bureau of the Budget, 1921–1922; U.S. vice president, 1925–1929; ambassador to Great Britain, 1929–1932. Candidacy: VP - 1924.

Dayton, William Lewis - N.J. (Republican) Feb. 17, 1807–Dec. 1, 1864; Senate, 1842–1851; minister to France, 1861–1864. Candidacy: VP - 1856.

Debs, Eugene Victor - Ind. (Socialist) Nov. 5, 1855–Oct. 20, 1926; Indiana Legislature, 1885; president, American Railway Union, 1893–1897. Candidacies: P - 1900, 1904, 1908, 1912, 1920.

Dewey, Thomas Edmund - N.Y. (Republican) March 24, 1902–March 16, 1971; district attorney, New York County, 1937–1941; governor, 1943–1955. Candidacies: P - 1944, 1948.

Dole, Robert Joseph - Kan. (Republican) July 22, 1923– ; House, 1961–1969; Senate, 1969–1996; Senate majority leader, 1985–1987, 1995–1996; Senate minority leader, 1987–1995; chairman of the Republican National Committee, 1971–1973. Candidacies: VP - 1976; P - 1996.

Donelson, Andrew Jackson - Tenn. (American "Know-Nothing") Aug. 25, 1799–June 26, 1871; minister to Prussia, 1846–1848; minister to Germany, 1848–1849. Candidacy: VP - 1856.

Douglas, Stephen Arnold - Ill. (Democratic) April 23, 1813–June 3, 1861; House, 1843–1847; Senate, 1847–1861. Candidacy: P - 1860.

Dukakis, Michael Stanley - Mass. (Democratic) Nov. 3, 1933– ; governor, 1975–1979, 1983–1991. Candidacy: P - 1988.

Eagleton, Thomas Francis - Mo. (Democratic) Sept. 4, 1929– ; attorney general of Missouri, 1961–1965; lieutenant governor, 1965–1968; Senate, 1968–1987. Candidacy: VP - 1972. (Resigned from Democratic ticket July 31; replaced by R. Sargent Shriver Jr.)

Edwards, John - N.C. (Democrat) June 10, 1953– ; Senate 1999–2005; Candidacy: VP - 2004.

Eisenhower, Dwight David - N.Y., Pa. (Republican) Oct. 14, 1890–March 28, 1969; general of U.S. Army, 1943–1948; Army chief of staff, 1945–1948; president of Columbia University, 1948–1951; commander of North Atlantic Treaty Organization, 1951–1952; U.S. president, 1953–1961. Candidacies: P - 1952, 1956.

Ellmaker, Amos - Pa. (Anti-Masonic) Feb. 2, 1787–Nov. 28, 1851; elected to the House for the term beginning in 1815 but did not qualify; attorney general of Pennsylvania, 1816–1819, 1828–1829. Candidacy: VP - 1832.

Ellsworth, Oliver - Conn. (Federalist) April 29, 1745–Nov. 26, 1807; Continental Congress, 1778–1783; Senate, 1789–1796; chief justice of United States, 1796–1800; minister to France, 1799. Candidacy: 1796.

English, William Hayden - Ind. (Democratic) Aug. 27, 1822–Feb. 7, 1896; House, 1853–1861. Candidacy: VP - 1880.

Everett, Edward - Mass. (Constitutional Union) April 11, 1794–Jan. 15, 1865; House, 1825–1835; governor, 1836–1840; minister to Great Britain, 1841–1845; president of Harvard University, 1846–1849; secretary of state, 1852–1853; Senate, 1853–1854. Candidacy: VP - 1860.

Fairbanks, Charles Warren - Ind. (Republican) May 11, 1852–June 4, 1918; Senate, 1897–1905; U.S. vice president, 1905–1909. Candidacies: VP - 1904, 1916.

Ferraro, Geraldine Anne - N.Y. (Democratic) Aug. 26, 1935– ; assistant district attorney, Queens County, 1974–1978; House, 1979–1985. Candidacy: VP - 1984.

Field, James Gaven - Va. (Populist) Feb. 24, 1826–Oct. 12, 1901; major in the Confederate Army, 1861–1865; attorney general of Virginia, 1877–1882. Candidacy: VP - 1892.

Fillmore, Millard - N.Y. (Whig, American "Know-Nothing") Jan. 7, 1800–March 8, 1874; House, 1833–1835, 1837–1843; N.Y. comptroller, 1847–1849; U.S. vice president, 1849–1850; U.S. president, 1850–1853. Candidacies: VP - 1848; P - 1856.

Fisk, Clinton Bowen - N.J. (Prohibition) Dec. 8, 1828–July 9, 1890; Civil War brevet major general; founder of Fisk University, 1866; member, Board of Indian Commissioners, 1874, president, 1881–1890. Candidacy: P - 1888.

Floyd, John - Va. (Independent Democratic) April 24, 1783–Aug. 17, 1837; House, 1817–1829; governor, 1830–1834. Candidacy: P - 1832.

Ford, Gerald Rudolph Jr. - Mich. (Republican) July 14, 1913– ; House, 1949–1973; House minority leader, 1965–1973; U.S. vice president, 1973–1974; U.S. president, 1974–1977. Candidacy: P - 1976.

Frelinghuysen, Theodore - N.J. (Whig) March 28, 1787–April 12, 1862; attorney general of New Jersey, 1817–1829; Senate, 1829–1835; president of Rutgers College, 1850–1862. Candidacy: VP - 1844.

Fremont, John Charles - Calif. (Republican) Jan. 21, 1813–July 13, 1890; explorer and Army officer in West before 1847; Senate, 1850–1851; governor of Arizona Territory, 1878–1881. Candidacy: P - 1856.

Garfield, James Abram - Ohio (Republican) Nov. 19, 1831–Sept. 19, 1881; major general in Union Army during Civil War; House, 1863–1880; U.S. president, 1881. Candidacy: P - 1880.

Garner, John Nance - Texas (Democratic) Nov. 22, 1868–Nov. 7, 1967; House, 1903–1933; House minority leader, 1929–1931; Speaker of the House, 1931–1933; U.S. vice president, 1933–1941. Candidacies: VP - 1932, 1936.

Gerry, Elbridge - Mass. (Democratic-Republican) July 17, 1744–Nov. 23, 1814; Continental Congress, 1776–1780, 1783–1785; signer of Declaration of Independence; Constitutional Convention, 1787; House, 1789–1793; governor, 1810–1812; U.S. vice president, 1813–1814. Candidacy: VP - 1812.

Goldwater, Barry Morris - Ariz. (Republican) Jan. 1, 1909–May 29, 1998; Senate, 1953–1965, 1969–1987. Candidacies: VP - 1960; P - 1964.

Gore, Albert Jr. - Tenn. (Democrat) March 31, 1948– ; House, 1977–1985; Senate, 1985–1993; U.S. vice president, 1993–2001. Candidacies: VP - 1992, 1996; P - 2000.

Graham, William Alexander - N.C. (Whig) Sept. 5, 1804–Aug. 11, 1875; Senate, 1840–1843; governor, 1845–1849; secretary of the Navy, 1850–1852; Confederate Senate, 1864. Candidacy: VP - 1852.

Granger, Francis - N.Y. (Whig) Dec. 1, 1792–Aug. 31, 1868; House, 1835–1837, 1839–1841, 1841–1843; postmaster general, 1841. Candidacy: VP - 1836.

Grant, Ulysses Simpson - Ill. (Republican) April 27, 1822–July 23, 1885; commander-in-chief, Union Army during Civil War; U.S. president, 1869–1877. Candidacies: P - 1868, 1872.

Greeley, Horace - N.Y. (Liberal Republican, Democratic) Feb. 3, 1811–Nov. 29, 1872; founder and editor, *New York Tribune*, 1841–1872; House, 1848–1849. Candidacy: P - 1872.

Griffin, S. Marvin - Ga. (American Independent) Sept. 4, 1907–June 13, 1982; governor, 1955–1959. Candidacy: VP - 1968. (Substituted as candidate until permanent candidate Curtis LeMay was chosen.)

Groesbeck, William Slocum - Ohio (Democratic) July 24, 1815–July 7, 1897; House, 1857–1859; delegate to International Monetary Conference in Paris, 1878. Candidacy: VP - 1872.

Hale, John Parker - N.H. (Free Soil) March 31, 1806–Nov. 19, 1873; House, 1843–1845; Senate, 1847–1853, 1855–1865; minister to Spain, 1865–1869. Candidacy: P - 1852.

Hamlin, Hannibal - Maine (Republican) Aug. 27, 1809–July 4, 1891; House, 1843–1847; Senate, 1848–1857, 1857–1861, 1869–1881; governor, 1857; U.S. vice president, 1861–1865. Candidacy: VP - 1860.

Hancock, John - Mass. (Federalist) Jan. 23, 1737–Oct. 8, 1793; Continental Congress, 1775–1778, 1785–1786; president of Continental Congress, 1775–1777; governor, 1780–1785, 1787–1793. Candidacy: 1789.

Hancock, Winfield Scott - Pa. (Democratic) Feb. 14, 1824 - Feb. 9, 1886; brigadier general, commander of II Army Corps, Civil War. Candidacy: P - 1880.

Harding, Warren Gamaliel - Ohio (Republican) Nov. 2, 1865–Aug. 2, 1923; lieutenant governor, 1904–1905; Senate, 1915–1921; U.S. president, 1921–1923. Candidacy: P - 1920.

Harper, Robert Goodloe - Md. (Federalist) January 1765–Jan. 14, 1825; House, 1795–1801; Senate, 1816. Candidacies: VP - 1816, 1820.

Harrison, Benjamin - Ind. (Republican) Aug. 20, 1833–March 13, 1901; Union officer in Civil War; Senate, 1881–1887; U.S. president, 1889–1893. Candidacies: P - 1888, 1892.

Harrison, Robert H. - Md. 1745–1790; chief justice, General Court of Maryland, 1781. Candidacy: 1789.

Harrison, William Henry - Ohio (Whig) Feb. 9, 1773–April 4, 1841; delegate to Congress from the Northwest Territory, 1799–1800; territorial governor of Indiana, 1801–1813; House, 1816–1819; Senate, 1825–1828; U.S. president, 1841. Candidacies: P - 1836, 1840.

Hayes, Rutherford Birchard - Ohio (Republican) Oct. 4, 1822–Jan. 17, 1893; major general in Union Army during Civil War; House, 1865–1867; governor, 1868–1872, 1876–1877; U.S. president, 1877–1881. Candidacy: P - 1876.

Hendricks, Thomas Andrews - Ind. (Democratic) Sept. 7, 1819–Nov. 25, 1885; House, 1851–1855; Senate, 1863–1869; governor, 1873–1877; U.S. vice president, 1885. Candidacies: P - 1872; VP - 1876, 1884.

Henry, John - Md. (Democratic-Republican) Nov. 1750–Dec. 16, 1798; Continental Congress, 1778–1780, 1785–1786; Senate, 1789–1797; governor, 1797–1798. Candidacy: - 1796.

Hobart, Garret Augustus - N.J. (Republican) June 3, 1844–Nov. 21, 1899; New Jersey Senate, 1876–1882; president of New Jersey Senate, 1881–1882; Republican National Committee, 1884–1896; U.S. vice president, 1897–1899. Candidacy: VP - 1896.

Hoover, Herbert Clark - Calif. (Republican) Aug. 10, 1874–Oct. 20, 1964; U.S. food administrator, 1917–1919; secretary of commerce, 1921–1928; U.S. president, 1929–1933; chairman, Commission on Organization of the Executive Branch of Government, 1947–1949, 1953–1955. Candidacies: P - 1928, 1932.

Hospers, John - Calif. (Libertarian) June 9, 1918– ; director of school of philosophy at University of Southern California. Candidacy: P - 1972.

Howard, John Eager - Md. (Federalist) June 4, 1752–Oct. 12, 1827; Continental Congress, 1788; governor, 1788–1791; Senate, 1796–1803. Candidacy: VP - 1816.

Hughes, Charles Evans - N.Y. (Republican) April 11, 1862–Aug. 27, 1948; governor, 1907–1910; associate justice of U.S. Supreme Court, 1910–1916; secretary of state, 1921–1925; chief justice of United States, 1930–1941. Candidacy: P - 1916.

Humphrey, Hubert Horatio Jr. - Minn. (Democratic) May 27, 1911–Jan. 13, 1978; mayor of Minneapolis, 1945–1948; Senate, 1949–1964, 1971–1978; U.S. vice president, 1965–1969. Candidacies: VP - 1964; P - 1968.

Huntington, Samuel - Conn., July 3, 1731–Jan. 5, 1796; Continental Congress, 1776, 1778–1781, 1783; president of the Continental Congress, 1779–1781; governor, 1786–1796. Candidacy: - 1789.

Ingersoll, Jared - Pa. (Federalist) Oct. 24, 1749–Oct. 31, 1822; Continental Congress, 1780–1781; Constitutional Convention, 1787. Candidacy: VP - 1812.

Iredell, James - N.C. (Federalist) Oct. 5, 1751–Oct. 20, 1799; associate justice of U.S. Supreme Court, 1790–1799. Candidacy: - 1796.

Jackson, Andrew - Tenn. (Democratic-Republican, Democratic) March 15, 1767–June 8, 1845; House, 1796–1797; Senate, 1797–1798, 1823–1825; territorial governor of Florida, 1821; U.S. president, 1829–1837. Candidacies: P - 1824, 1828, 1832.

Jay, John - N.Y. (Federalist) Dec. 12, 1745–May 17, 1829; Continental Congress, 1774–1776, 1778–1779; president of Continental Congress, 1778–1779; minister to Spain, 1779; chief justice of United States, 1789–1795; governor, 1795–1801. Candidacies: - 1789, 1796, 1800.

Jefferson, Thomas - Va. (Democratic-Republican) April 13, 1743–July 4, 1826; Continental Congress, 1775–1776, 1783–1784; author and signer of Declaration of Independence, 1776; governor, 1779–1781; minister to France, 1784–1789; secretary of state, 1790–1793; U.S. vice president, 1797–1801; U.S. president, 1801–1809. Candidacies: VP - 1792; P - 1796, 1800, 1804.

Jenkins, Charles Jones - Ga. (Democratic) Jan. 6, 1805–June 14, 1883; governor, 1865–1868. Candidacy: P - 1872.

Johnson, Andrew - Tenn. (Republican) Dec. 29, 1808–July 31, 1875; House, 1843–1853; governor, 1853–1857; Senate, 1857–1862, 1875; U.S. vice president, 1865; U.S. president, 1865–1869. Candidacy: VP - 1864.

Johnson, Herschel Vespasian - Ga. (Democratic) Sept. 18, 1812–Aug. 16, 1880; Senate, 1848–1849; governor, 1853–1857; senator, Confederate Congress, 1862–1865. Candidacy: VP - 1860.

Johnson, Hiram Warren - Calif. (Progressive) Sept. 2, 1866–Aug. 6, 1945; governor, 1911–1917; Senate, 1917–1945. Candidacy: VP - 1912.

Johnson, Lyndon Baines - Texas (Democratic) Aug. 27, 1908–Jan. 22, 1973; House, 1937–1949; Senate, 1949–1961; Senate minority leader, 1953–1955; Senate majority leader, 1955–1961; U.S. vice president, 1961–1963; U.S. president, 1963–1969. Candidacies: VP - 1960; P - 1964.

Johnson, Richard Mentor - Ky. (Democratic) Oct. 17, 1780–Nov. 19, 1850; House, 1807–1819, 1829–1837; Senate, 1819–1829; U.S. vice president, 1837–1841. Candidacies: VP - 1836, 1840.

Johnston, Samuel - N.C. (Federalist) Dec. 15, 1733–Aug. 17, 1816; Continental Congress, 1780–1781; governor, 1787–1789; Senate, 1789–1793. Candidacy: - 1796.

Jones, Walter Burgwyn - Ala. (Independent Democratic) Oct. 16, 1888–Aug. 1, 1963; Alabama Legislature, 1919–1920; Alabama circuit court judge, 1920–1935; presiding judge, 1935–1963. Candidacy: P - 1956.

Julian, George Washington - Ind. (Free Soil, Liberal Republican) May 5, 1817–July 7, 1899; House, 1849–1851, 1861–1871. Candidacies: VP - 1852, 1872.

Kefauver, Estes - Tenn. (Democratic) July 26, 1903–Aug. 10, 1963; House, 1939–1949; Senate, 1949–1963. Candidacy: VP - 1956.

Kemp, Jack F. - N.Y. (Republican) July 13, 1935– ; House, 1971–1989; secretary of Housing and Urban Development, 1989–1993. Candidacy: VP - 1996.

Kennedy, John Fitzgerald - Mass. (Democratic) May 29, 1917–Nov. 22, 1963; House, 1947–1953; Senate, 1953–1960; U.S. president, 1961–1963. Candidacy: P - 1960.

Kern, John Worth - Ind. (Democratic) Dec. 20, 1849–Aug. 17, 1917; Senate, 1911–1917; Senate majority leader, 1913–1917. Candidacy: VP - 1908.

Kerry, John F. - Mass. (Democrat) December 11, 1943– ; lieutenant governor of Massachusetts 1982–1984; Senate 1985– ; Candidacy: P - 2004.

King, Rufus - N.Y. (Federalist) March 24, 1755–April 29, 1827; Continental Congress, 1784–1787; Constitutional Convention, 1787; Senate, 1789–1796, 1813–1825; minister to Great Britain, 1796–1803, 1825–1826. Candidacies: VP - 1804, 1808; P - 1816.

King, William Rufus de Vane - Ala. (Democratic) April 7, 1786–April 18, 1853; House, 1811–1816; Senate, 1819–1844, 1848–1852; president pro tempore of the Senate, 1836, 1837, 1838, 1839, 1840, 1841, 1850; minister to France, 1844–1846; U.S. vice president, 1853. Candidacy: VP - 1852.

Knox, Franklin - Ill. (Republican) Jan. 1, 1874–April 28, 1944; secretary of the Navy, 1940–1944. Candidacy: VP - 1936.

La Follette, Robert Marion - Wis. (Progressive) June 14, 1855–June 18, 1925; House, 1885–1891; governor, 1901–1906; Senate, 1906–1925. Candidacy: P - 1924.

Landon, Alfred Mossman - Kan. (Republican) Sept. 9, 1887–Oct. 12, 1987; governor, 1933–1937. Candidacy: P - 1936.

Lane, Joseph - Ore. (Southern Democratic) Dec. 14, 1801–April 19, 1881; governor of Oregon Territory, 1849–1850, 1853; House (territorial delegate), 1851–1859; Senate, 1859–1861. Candidacy: VP - 1860.

Langdon, John - N.H. (Democratic-Republican) June 26, 1741–Sept. 18, 1819; Continental Congress, 1775–1776, 1787; governor, 1805–1809, 1810–1812; Senate, 1789–1801; first president pro tempore of the Senate, 1789. Candidacy: VP - 1808.

Lee, Henry - Mass. (Independent Democratic) Feb. 4, 1782–Feb. 6, 1867; merchant and publicist. Candidacy: VP - 1832.

LeMay, Curtis Emerson - Ohio (American Independent) Nov. 15, 1906–Oct. 1, 1990; Air Force chief of staff, 1961–1965. Candidacy: VP - 1968.

Lemke, William - N.D. (Union) Aug. 13, 1878–May 30, 1950; House, 1933–1941, 1943–1950. Candidacy: P - 1936.

Lieberman, Joseph I. - Conn. (Democratic) Feb. 24, 1942– ; Connecticut Legislature, 1971–1981; attorney general of Connecticut, 1983–1989; Senate 1989– . Candidacy: VP - 2000.

Lincoln, Abraham - Ill. (Republican) Feb. 12, 1809–April 15, 1865; House, 1847–1849; U.S. president, 1861–1865. Candidacies: P - 1860, 1864.

Lincoln, Benjamin - Mass. (Federalist) Jan. 24, 1733–May 9, 1810; major general in Continental Army, 1777–1781. Candidacy: - 1789.

Lodge, Henry Cabot Jr. - Mass. (Republican) July 5, 1902–Feb. 27, 1985; Senate, 1937–1944, 1947–1953; ambassador to United Nations, 1953–1960; ambassador to Republic of Vietnam, 1963–1964, 1965–1967. Candidacy: VP - 1960.

Logan, John Alexander - Ill. (Republican) Feb. 9, 1826–Dec. 26, 1886; House, 1859–1862, 1867–1871; Senate, 1871–1877, 1879–1886. Candidacy: VP - 1884.

Machen, Willis Benson - Ky. (Democratic) April 10, 1810–Sept. 29, 1893; Confederate Congress, 1861–1865; Senate, 1872–1873. Candidacy: VP - 1872.

Macon, Nathaniel - N.C. (Democratic-Republican) Dec. 17, 1757–June 29, 1837; House, 1791–1815; Speaker of the House, 1801–1807; Senate, 1815–1828; president pro tempore of the Senate, 1826, 1827. Candidacy: VP - 1824.

Madison, James - Va. (Democratic-Republican) March 16, 1751–June 28, 1836; Continental Congress, 1780–1783, 1787–1788; Constitutional Convention, 1787; House, 1789–1797; secretary of state, 1801–1809; U.S. president, 1809–1817. Candidacies: P - 1808, 1812.

Mangum, Willie Person - N.C. (Independent Democrat) May 10, 1792–Sept. 7, 1861; House, 1823–1826; Senate, 1831–1836, 1840–1853. Candidacy: P - 1836.

Marshall, John - Va. (Federalist) Sept. 24, 1755–July 6, 1835; House, 1799–1800; secretary of state, 1800–1801; chief justice of United States, 1801–1835. Candidacy: VP - 1816.

Marshall, Thomas Riley - Ind. (Democratic) March 14, 1854–June 1, 1925; governor, 1909–1913; U.S. vice president, 1913–1921. Candidacies: VP - 1912, 1916.

McCarthy, Eugene Joseph - Minn. (Independent) March 29, 1916– ; House, 1949–1959; Senate, 1959–1971. Candidacy: P - 1976.

McClellan, George Brinton - N.J. (Democratic) Dec. 3, 1826–Oct. 29, 1885; general-in-chief of Army of the Potomac, 1861; governor, 1878–1881. Candidacy: P - 1864.

McGovern, George Stanley - S.D. (Democratic) July 19, 1922– ; House, 1957–1961; Senate, 1963–1981. Candidacy: P - 1972.

McKinley, William Jr. - Ohio (Republican) Jan. 29, 1843–Sept. 14, 1901; House, 1877, 1885–1891; governor, 1892–1896; U.S. president, 1897–1901. Candidacies: P - 1896, 1900.

McNary, Charles Linza - Ore. (Republican) June 12, 1874–Feb. 25, 1944; state Supreme Court judge, 1913–1915; Senate, 1917–1918, 1918–1944; Senate minority leader, 1933–1944. Candidacy: VP - 1940.

Miller, William Edward - N.Y. (Republican) March 22, 1914–June 24, 1983; House, 1951–1965; chairman of Republican National Committee, 1960–1964. Candidacy: VP - 1964.

Milton, John - Ga. circa 1740–circa 1804; secretary of state, Georgia, circa 1778, 1781, 1783. Candidacy: - 1789.

Mondale, Walter Frederick - Minn. (Democratic) Jan. 5, 1928– ; Senate, 1964–1976; U.S. vice president, 1977–1981; ambassador to Japan, 1993–1996. Candidacies: VP - 1976, 1980; P - 1984.

Monroe, James - Va. (Democratic-Republican) April 28, 1758–July 4, 1831; Continental Congress, 1783–1786; Senate, 1790–1794; minister to France, 1794–1796, 1803; minister to England, 1803–1807; governor, 1799–1802, 1811; secretary of state, 1811–1814, 1815–1817; U.S. president, 1817–1825. Candidacies: VP - 1808; P - 1816, 1820.

Morton, Levi Parsons - N.Y. (Republican) May 16, 1824–May 16, 1920; House, 1879–1881; minister to France, 1881–1885; U.S. vice president, 1889–1893; governor, 1895–1897. Candidacy: VP - 1888.

Muskie, Edmund Sixtus - Maine (Democratic) March 28, 1914–March 26, 1996; governor, 1955–1959; Senate, 1959–1980; secretary of state, 1980–1981. Candidacy: VP - 1968.

Nathan, Theodora Nathalia - Ore. (Libertarian) Feb. 9, 1923– ; broadcast journalist; National Judiciary Committee, Libertarian Party, 1972–1975; vice chairperson, Oregon Libertarian Party, 1974–1975. Candidacy: VP - 1972.

Nixon, Richard Milhous - Calif., N.Y. (Republican) Jan. 9, 1913–April 22, 1994; House, 1947–1950; Senate, 1950–1953; U.S. vice president, 1953–1961; U.S. president, 1969–1974. Candidacies: VP - 1952, 1956; P - 1960, 1968, 1972.

Palmer, John McAuley - Ill. (Democratic, National Democratic) Sept. 13, 1817–Sept. 25, 1900; governor, 1869–1873; Senate, 1891–1897. Candidacies: VP - 1872; P - 1896.

Parker, Alton Brooks - N.Y. (Democratic) May 14, 1852–May 10, 1926; chief justice of N.Y. Court of Appeals, 1898–1904. Candidacy: P - 1904.

Pendleton, George Hunt - Ohio (Democratic) July 19, 1825–Nov. 24, 1889; House, 1857–1865; Senate, 1879–1885; minister to Germany, 1885–1889. Candidacy: VP - 1864.

Perot, H. Ross - Texas (Independent, Reform) June 27, 1930– ; business executive and owner. Candidacies: P - 1992, 1996.

Pierce, Franklin - N.H. (Democratic) Nov. 23, 1804–Oct. 8, 1869; House, 1833–1837; Senate, 1837–1842; U.S. president, 1853–1857. Candidacy: P - 1852.

Pinckney, Charles Cotesworth - S.C. (Federalist) Feb. 25, 1746–Aug. 16, 1825; president, state senate, 1779; minister to France, 1796. Candidacies: VP - 1800; P - 1804, 1808.

Pinckney, Thomas - S.C. (Federalist) Oct. 23, 1750–Nov. 2, 1828; governor, 1787–1789; minister to Great Britain, 1792–1796; envoy to Spain, 1794–1795; House, 1797–1801. Candidacy: - 1796.

Polk, James Knox - Tenn. (Democratic) Nov. 2, 1795–June 15, 1849; House, 1825–1839; Speaker of the House, 1835–1839; governor, 1839–1841; U.S. president, 1845–1849. Candidacies: VP - 1840; P - 1844.

Quayle, Dan - Ind. (Republican) Feb. 4, 1947– ; House, 1977–1981; Senate, 1981–1989; U.S. vice president, 1989–1993. Candidacies; VP - 1988, 1992.

Reagan, Ronald Wilson - Calif. (Republican) Feb. 6, 1911– ; governor, 1967–1975; U.S. president, 1981–1989. Candidacies: P - 1980, 1984.

Reid, Whitelaw - N.Y. (Republican) Oct. 27, 1837–Dec. 15, 1912; minister to France, 1889–1892; editor-in-chief, *New York Tribune*, 1872–1905. Candidacy: VP - 1892.

Robinson, Joseph Taylor - Ark. (Democratic) Aug. 26, 1872–July 14, 1937; House, 1903–1913; governor, 1913; Senate, 1913–1937; Senate minority leader, 1923–1933; Senate majority leader, 1933–1937. Candidacy: VP - 1928.

Rockefeller, Nelson Aldrich - N.Y. (Republican) July 8, 1908–Jan. 26, 1979; governor, 1959–1973; U.S. vice president, 1974–1977 (nominated under the provisions of the 25th Amendment).

Rodney, Daniel - Del. (Federalist) Sept. 10, 1764–Sept. 2, 1846; governor, 1814–1817; House, 1822–1823; Senate, 1826–1827. Candidacy: VP - 1820.

Roosevelt, Franklin Delano - N.Y. (Democratic) Jan. 30, 1882–April 12, 1945; assistant secretary of the Navy, 1913–1920; governor, 1929–1933; U.S. president, 1933–1945. Candidacies: VP - 1920; P - 1932, 1936, 1940, 1944.

Roosevelt, Theodore - N.Y. (Republican, Progressive) Oct. 27, 1858–Jan. 6, 1919; assistant secretary of the Navy, 1897–1898; governor, 1899–1901; U.S. vice president, 1901; U.S. president, 1901–1909. Candidacies: VP - 1900; P - 1904, 1912.

Ross, James - Pa. (Federalist) July 12, 1762–Nov. 27, 1847; Senate, 1794–1803. Candidacy: VP - 1816.

Rush, Richard - Pa. (Democratic-Republican, National-Republican) Aug. 29, 1780–July 30, 1859; attorney general, 1814–1817; minister to Great Britain, 1817–1824; secretary of Treasury, 1825–1829. Candidacies: VP - 1820, 1828.

Rutledge, John - S.C. (Federalist) Sept. 1739–July 23, 1800; Continental Congress, 1774–1775, 1782–1783; governor, 1779–1782; Constitutional Convention, 1787; associate justice of U.S. Supreme Court, 1789–1791; chief justice of United States, 1795. Candidacy: - 1789.

Sanford, Nathan - N.Y. (Democratic-Republican) Nov. 5, 1777–Oct. 17, 1838; Senate, 1815–1821, 1826–1831. Candidacy: VP - 1824.

Schmitz, John George - Calif. (American Independent) Aug. 12, 1930– ; House, 1970–1973. Candidacy: P - 1972.

Scott, Winfield - N.J. (Whig) June 13, 1786–May 29, 1866; general-in-chief of U.S. Army, 1841–1861. Candidacy: P - 1852.

Sergeant, John - Pa. (National-Republican) Dec. 5, 1779–Nov. 23, 1852; House, 1815–1823, 1827–1829, 1837–1841. Candidacy: VP - 1832.

Sewall, Arthur - Maine (Democratic) Nov. 25, 1835–Sept. 5, 1900; Democratic National Committee member, 1888–1896. Candidacy: VP - 1896.

Seymour, Horatio - N.Y. (Democratic) May 31, 1810–Feb. 12, 1886; governor, 1853–1855, 1863–1865. Candidacy: P - 1868.

Sherman, James Schoolcraft - N.Y. (Republican) Oct. 24, 1855–Oct. 30, 1912; House, 1887–1891, 1893–1909; U.S. vice president, 1909–1912. Candidacies: VP - 1908, 1912. (Died during 1912 campaign; Nicholas Murray Butler replaced Sherman on the Republican ticket.)

Shriver, Robert Sargent Jr. - Md. (Democratic) Nov. 9, 1915– ; director, Peace Corps, 1961–1966; director, Office of Economic Opportunity, 1964–1968; ambassador to France, 1968–1970. Candidacy: VP - 1972. (Replaced Thomas F. Eagleton on Democratic ticket Aug. 8.)

Smith, Alfred Emanuel - N.Y. (Democratic) Dec. 30, 1873–Oct. 4, 1944; governor, 1919–1921, 1923–1929. Candidacy: P - 1928.

Smith, William - S.C., Ala. (Independent Democratic-Republican) Sept. 6, 1762–June 26, 1840; Senate, 1816–1823, 1826–1831. Candidacies: VP - 1828, 1836.

Sparkman, John Jackson - Ala. (Democratic) Dec. 20, 1899–Nov. 16, 1985; House, 1937–1946; Senate, 1946–1979. Candidacy: VP - 1952.

Stevenson, Adlai Ewing - Ill. (Democratic) Oct. 23, 1835–June 14, 1914; House, 1875–1877, 1879–1881; assistant postmaster general, 1885–1889; U.S. vice president, 1893–1897. Candidacies: VP - 1892, 1900.

Stevenson, Adlai Ewing II - Ill. (Democratic) Feb. 5, 1900–July 14, 1965; assistant to the secretary of Navy, 1941–1944; assistant to the secretary of state, 1945; governor, 1949–1953; ambassador to United Nations, 1961–1965. Candidacies: P - 1952, 1956.

Stockton, Richard - N.J. (Federalist) April 17, 1764–March 7, 1828; Senate, 1796–1799; House, 1813–1815. Candidacy: VP - 1820.

Taft, William Howard - Ohio (Republican) Sept. 15, 1857–March 8, 1930; secretary of war, 1904–1908; U.S. president, 1909–1913; chief justice of United States, 1921–1930. Candidacies: P - 1908, 1912.

Talmadge, Herman Eugene - Ga. (Independent Democratic) Aug. 9, 1913– ; governor, 1947, 1948–1955; Senate, 1957–1981. Candidacy: VP - 1956.

Taylor, Glen Hearst - Idaho (Progressive) April 12, 1904–April 28, 1984; Senate, 1945–1951. Candidacy: VP - 1948.

Taylor, Zachary - La. (Whig) Nov. 24, 1784–July 9, 1850; major general, U.S. Army; U.S. president, 1849–1850. Candidacy: P - 1848.

Tazewell, Littleton Waller - Va. (Democratic) Dec. 17, 1774–May 6, 1860; House, 1800–1801; Senate, 1824–1832; president pro tempore of the Senate, 1832; governor, 1834–1836. Candidacy: VP - 1840.

Telfair, Edward - Ga. (Democratic-Republican) 1735–Sept. 17, 1807; Continental Congress, 1778, 1780–1782; governor, 1789–1793. Candidacy: - 1789.

Thomas, Norman Mattoon - N.Y. (Socialist) Nov. 20, 1884–Dec. 19, 1968; Presbyterian minister, 1911–1931; author and editor. Candidacies: P - 1928, 1932, 1936, 1940, 1944, 1948.

Thurman, Allen Granberry - Ohio (Democratic) Nov. 13, 1813–Dec. 12, 1895; House, 1845–1847; Ohio Supreme Court, 1851–1856; Senate, 1869–1881; president pro tempore of the Senate, 1879, 1880. Candidacy: VP - 1888.

Thurmond, James Strom - S.C. (States' Rights Democrat) Dec. 5, 1902– ; governor, 1947–1951; Senate, 1954–1956, 1956– ; president pro tempore of the Senate, 1981–1987; 1995– . Candidacies: P - 1948.

Tilden, Samuel Jones - N.Y. (Democratic) Feb. 9, 1814–Aug. 4, 1886; governor, 1875–1877. Candidacy: P - 1876.

Tompkins, Daniel D. - N.Y. (Democratic-Republican) June 21, 1774–June 11, 1825; elected to the House for the term beginning in 1805 but resigned before taking seat; governor, 1807–1817; U.S. vice president, 1817–1825. Candidacies: VP - 1816, 1820.

Truman, Harry S. - Mo. (Democratic) May 8, 1884–Dec. 26, 1972; Senate, 1935–1945; U.S. vice president, 1945; U.S. president, 1945–1953. Candidacies: VP - 1944; P - 1948.

Tyler, John - Va. (Whig) March 29, 1790–Jan. 18, 1862; governor, 1825–1827; Senate, 1827–1836; U.S. vice president, 1841; U.S. president, 1841–1845. Candidacies: VP - 1836, 1840.

Van Buren, Martin - N.Y. (Democratic, Free Soil) Dec. 5, 1782–July 24, 1862; Senate, 1821–1828; governor, 1829; secretary of state, 1829–1831; U.S. vice president, 1833–1837; U.S. president, 1837–1841. Candidacies: VP - 1824, 1832; P - 1836, 1840, 1848.

Wallace, George Corley - Ala. (American Independent) Aug. 25, 1919–Sept. 13, 1998; governor, 1963–1967, 1971–1979, 1983–1989. Candidacy: P - 1968.

Wallace, Henry Agard - Iowa (Democratic, Progressive) Oct. 7, 1888–Nov. 18, 1965; secretary of agriculture, 1933–1940; U.S. vice president, 1941–1945; secretary of commerce, 1945–1946. Candidacies: VP - 1940; P - 1948.

Warren, Earl - Calif. (Republican) March 19, 1891–July 9, 1974; governor, 1943–1953; chief justice of United States, 1953–1969. Candidacy: VP - 1948.

Washington, George - Va. (Federalist) Feb. 22, 1732–Dec. 14, 1799; First and Second Continental Congresses, 1774, 1775; commander-in-chief of armed forces, 1775–1783; president of Constitutional Convention, 1787; U.S. president, 1789–1797. Candidacies: P - 1789, 1792, 1796.

Watson, Thomas Edward - Ga. (Populist) Sept. 5, 1856–Sept. 26, 1922; House, 1891–1993; Senate, 1921–1922. Candidacies: VP - 1896; P - 1904, 1908.

Weaver, James Baird - Iowa (Greenback, Populist) June 12, 1833–Feb. 6, 1912; House, 1879–1881, 1885–1889; Candidacies: P - 1880, 1892.

Webster, Daniel - Mass. (Whig) Jan. 18, 1782–Oct. 24, 1852; House, 1813–1817, 1823–1827; Senate, 1827–1841, 1845–1850; secretary of state, 1841–1843, 1850–1852. Candidacy: P - 1836.

Wheeler, Burton Kendall - Mont. (Progressive) Feb. 27, 1882–Jan. 6, 1975; Senate, 1923–1947. Candidacy: VP - 1924.

Wheeler, William Almon - N.Y. (Republican) June 30, 1819–June 4, 1887; House, 1861–1863, 1869–1877; U.S. vice president, 1877–1881. Candidacy: VP - 1876.

White, Hugh Lawson - Tenn. (Whig) Oct. 30, 1773–April 10, 1840; Senate, 1825–1835, 1835–1840. Candidacy: P - 1836.

Wilkins, William - Pa. (Democratic) Dec. 20, 1779–June 23, 1865; Senate, 1831–1834; minister to Russia, 1834–1835; House, 1843–1844; secretary of war, 1844–1845. Candidacy: VP - 1832.

Willkie, Wendell Lewis - N.Y. (Republican) Feb. 18, 1892–Oct. 8, 1944; utility executive, 1933–1940. Candidacy: P - 1940.

Wilson, Henry - Mass. (Republican) Feb. 16, 1812–Nov. 22, 1875; Senate, 1855–1873; U.S. vice president, 1873–1875. Candidacy: VP - 1872.

Wilson, Woodrow - N.J. (Democratic) Dec. 28, 1856–Feb. 3, 1924; governor, 1911–1913; U.S. president, 1913–1921. Candidacies: P - 1912, 1916.

Wirt, William - Md. (Anti-Masonic) Nov. 8, 1772–Feb. 18, 1834; attorney general, 1817–1829. Candidacy: P - 1832.

Wright, Fielding Lewis - Miss. (States' Rights Democratic) May 16, 1895–May 4, 1956; governor, 1946–1952. Candidacy: VP - 1948.

Political Party Nominees, 1831–2004

Following is a comprehensive list of major and minor party nominees for president and vice president from 1831, when the first nominating convention was held by the Anti-Masonic Party, to 2004. In many cases, minor parties made only token efforts at a presidential campaign. Often, third-party candidates declined to run after being nominated by the convention, or their names appeared on the ballots of only a few states. In some cases the names of minor candidates did not appear on any state ballots and they received only a scattering of write-in votes, if any.

The basic source for the 1832 to 1972 elections was Joseph Nathan Kane, *Facts About the Presidents*, 6th ed. (New York: H. W. Wilson Co., 1993). To verify the names appearing in Kane, Congressional Quarterly consulted the following additional sources: Richard M. Scammon, *America at the Polls* (Pittsburgh: University of Pittsburgh Press, 1965); Richard M. Scammon, *America Votes 8* (Washington, D.C.:

Congressional Quarterly, 1969); Richard M. Scammon, *America Votes 10* (Washington, D.C.: Congressional Quarterly, 1973); Richard B. Morris, ed. *Encyclopedia of American History*, (New York: Harper and Row, 1965); *Dictionary of American Biography*, (New York: Scribner's, 1928–1936); *Facts on File* (New York: Facts on File Inc., 1945–1975); Arthur M. Schlesinger, ed., *History of U.S. Political Parties*, Vols. I–IV, (New York: McGraw Hill, 1971); and *Who Was Who in America, 1607–1968*, Vols. I–V (Chicago: Marquis Co., 1943–1968). The source for the 1976 to 2004 elections was Congressional Quarterly's *America Votes* series, Vols. 12 (1977), 14 (1981), 16 (1985), 18 (1989), 20 (1993), 22 (1997), 24 (2001), and 26 (2005) published in Washington, D.C.

In cases where these sources contain information in conflict with Kane, the conflicting information is included in a footnote. Where a candidate appears in Kane *but could not be verified in another source,* an asterisk appears beside the candidate's name on the list.

1832 ELECTION

Democratic Party
President: Andrew Jackson, Tennessee
Vice president: Martin Van Buren, New York

National Republican Party
President: Henry Clay, Kentucky
Vice president: John Sergeant, Pennsylvania

Independent Party
President: John Floyd, Virginia
Vice president: Henry Lee, Massachusetts

Anti-Masonic Party
President: William Wirt, Maryland
Vice president: Amos Ellmaker, Pennsylvania

1836 ELECTION

Democratic Party
President: Martin Van Buren, New York
Vice president: Richard Mentor Johnson, Kentucky

Whig Party
President: William Henry Harrison, Hugh Lawson White, Daniel Webster
Vice president: Francis Granger, John Tyler

> The Whigs nominated regional candidates in 1836 hoping that each candidate would carry his region and deny Democrat Van Buren an electoral vote majority. Webster was the Whig candidate in Massachusetts; Harrison in the rest of New England, the Middle Atlantic states, and the West; and White in the South.
>
> Granger was the running mate of Harrison and Webster. Tyler was White's running mate.

1840 ELECTION

Whig Party
President: William Henry Harrison, Ohio
Vice president: John Tyler, Virginia

Democratic Party
President: Martin Van Buren, New York

> The Democratic convention adopted a resolution that left the choice of vice-presidential candidates to the states. Democratic electors divided their vice-presidential votes among incumbent Richard M. Johnson (forty-eight votes), Littleton W. Tazewell (eleven votes), and James K. Polk (one vote).

Liberty Party
President: James Gillespie Birney, New York
Vice president: Thomas Earle, Pennsylvania

1844 ELECTION

Democratic Party
President: James Knox Polk, Tennessee
Vice president: George Mifflin Dallas, Pennsylvania

Whig Party
President: Henry Clay, Kentucky
Vice president: Theodore Frelinghuysen, New Jersey

Liberty Party
President: James Gillespie Birney, New York
Vice president: Thomas Morris, Ohio

National Democratic Party
President: John Tyler, Virginia
Vice president: None

> Tyler withdrew in favor of the Democrat, Polk.

1848 ELECTION

Whig Party
President: Zachary Taylor, Louisiana
Vice president: Millard Fillmore, New York

Democratic Party
President: Lewis Cass, Michigan
Vice president: William Orlando Butler, Kentucky

Free Soil Party
President: Martin Van Buren, New York
Vice president: Charles Francis Adams, Massachusetts

Free Soil (Barnburners—Liberty Party)
President: John Parker Hale, New Hampshire
Vice president: Leicester King, Ohio
Later John Parker Hale relinquished the nomination.
National Liberty Party
President: Gerrit Smith, New York
Vice president: Charles C. Foote, Michigan

1852 ELECTION

Democratic Party
President: Franklin Pierce, New Hampshire
Vice president: William Rufus De Vane King, Alabama
Whig Party
President: Winfield Scott, New Jersey
Vice president: William Alexander Graham, North Carolina
Free Soil
President: John Parker Hale, New Hampshire
Vice president: George Washington Julian, Indiana

1856 ELECTION

Democratic Party
President: James Buchanan, Pennsylvania
Vice president: John Cabell Breckinridge, Kentucky
Republican Party
President: John Charles Fremont, California
Vice president: William Lewis Dayton, New Jersey
American (Know-Nothing) Party
President: Millard Fillmore, New York
Vice president: Andrew Jackson Donelson, Tennessee
Whig Party (the "Silver Grays")
President: Millard Fillmore, New York
Vice president: Andrew Jackson Donelson, Tennessee
North American Party
President: Nathaniel Prentice Banks, Massachusetts
Vice president: William Freame Johnson, Pennsylvania
Banks and Johnson declined the nominations and gave their support to the Republicans.

1860 ELECTION

Republican Party
President: Abraham Lincoln, Illinois
Vice president: Hannibal Hamlin, Maine
Democratic Party
President: Stephen Arnold Douglas, Illinois
Vice president: Herschel Vespasian Johnson, Georgia
Southern Democratic Party
President: John Cabell Breckinridge, Kentucky
Vice president: Joseph Lane, Oregon
Constitutional Union Party
President: John Bell, Tennessee
Vice president: Edward Everett, Massachusetts

1864 ELECTION

Republican Party
President: Abraham Lincoln, Illinois
Vice president: Andrew Johnson, Tennessee
Democratic Party
President: George Brinton McClellan, New York
Vice president: George Hunt Pendleton, Ohio
Independent Republican Party
President: John Charles Fremont, California
Vice president: John Cochrane, New York

Fremont and Cochrane declined the nominations and gave their support to the Republicans.

1868 ELECTION

Republican Party
President: Ulysses Simpson Grant, Illinois
Vice president: Schuyler Colfax, Indiana
Democratic Party
President: Horatio Seymour, New York
Vice president: Francis Preston Blair Jr., Missouri

1872 ELECTION

Republican Party
President: Ulysses Simpson Grant, Illinois
Vice president: Henry Wilson, Massachusetts
Liberal Republican Party
President: Horace Greeley, New York
Vice president: Benjamin Gratz Brown, Missouri
Independent Liberal Republican Party (Opposition Party)
President: William Slocum Groesbeck, Ohio
Vice president: Frederick Law Olmsted, New York
Democratic Party
President: Horace Greeley, New York
Vice president: Benjamin Gratz Brown, Missouri
Straight-Out Democratic Party
President: Charles O'Conor, New York
Vice president: John Quincy Adams, Massachusetts
Prohibition Party
President: James Black, Pennsylvania
Vice president: John Russell, Michigan
People's Party (Equal Rights Party)
President: Victoria Claflin Woodhull, New York
Vice president: Frederick Douglass
Labor Reform Party
President: David Davis, Illinois
Vice president: Joel Parker, New Jersey
Liberal Republican Party of Colored Men
President: Horace Greeley, New York
Vice president: Benjamin Gratz Brown, Missouri
National Working Men's Party
President: Ulysses Simpson Grant, Illinois
Vice president: Henry Wilson, Massachusetts

1876 ELECTION

Republican Party
President: Rutherford Birchard Hayes, Ohio
Vice president: William Almon Wheeler, New York
Democratic Party
President: Samuel Jones Tilden, New York
Vice president: Thomas Andrews Hendricks, Indiana
Greenback Party
President: Peter Cooper, New York
Vice president: Samuel Fenton Cary, Ohio
Prohibition Party
President: Green Clay Smith, Kentucky
Vice president: Gideon Tabor Stewart, Ohio
American National Party
President: James B. Walker, Illinois
Vice president: Donald Kirkpatrick, New York

1880 ELECTION

Republican Party
President: James Abram Garfield, Ohio
Vice president: Chester Alan Arthur, New York

Democratic Party
President: Winfield Scott Hancock, Pennsylvania
Vice president: William Hayden English, Indiana

Greenback Labor Party
President: James Baird Weaver, Iowa
Vice president: Benjamin J. Chambers, Texas

Prohibition Party
President: Neal Dow, Maine
Vice president: Henry Adams Thompson, Ohio

American Party
President: John Wolcott Phelps, Vermont
Vice president: Samuel Clarke Pomeroy, Kansas *

1884 ELECTION

Democratic Party
President: Grover Cleveland, New York
Vice president: Thomas Andrews Hendricks, Indiana

Republican Party
President: James Gillespie Blaine, Maine
Vice president: John Alexander Logan, Illinois

Anti-Monopoly Party
President: Benjamin Franklin Butler, Massachusetts
Vice president: Absolom Madden West, Mississippi

Greenback Party
President: Benjamin Franklin Butler, Massachusetts
Vice president: Absolom Madden West, Mississippi

Prohibition Party
President: John Pierce St. John, Kansas
Vice president: William Daniel, Maryland

American Prohibition Party
President: Samuel Clarke Pomeroy, Kansas
Vice president: John A. Conant, Connecticut

Equal Rights Party
President: Belva Ann Bennett Lockwood, District of Columbia
Vice president: Marietta Lizzie Bell Stow, California

1888 ELECTION

Republican Party
President: Benjamin Harrison, Indiana
Vice president: Levi Parsons Morton, New York

Democratic Party
President: Grover Cleveland, New York
Vice president: Allen Granberry Thurman, Ohio

Prohibition Party
President: Clinton Bowen Fisk, New Jersey
Vice president: John Anderson Brooks, Missouri *

Union Labor Party
President: Alson Jenness Streeter, Illinois
Vice president: Charles E. Cunningham, Arkansas *

United Labor Party
President: Robert Hall Cowdrey, Illinois
Vice president: William H. T. Wakefield, Kansas *

American Party
President: James Langdon Curtis, New York
Vice president: Peter Dinwiddie Wigginton, California *

Equal Rights Party
President: Belva Ann Bennett Lockwood, District of Columbia
Vice president: Alfred Henry Love, Pennsylvania *

Industrial Reform Party
President: Albert E. Redstone, California *
Vice president: John Colvin, Kansas *

1892 ELECTION

Democratic Party
President: Grover Cleveland, New York
Vice president: Adlai Ewing Stevenson, Illinois

Republican Party
President: Benjamin Harrison, Indiana
Vice president: Whitelaw Reid, New York

People's Party of America
President: James Baird Weaver, Iowa
Vice president: James gaven Field, Virginia

Prohibition Party
president: John bidwell, California
Vice president: James Britton Cranfill, Texas

Socialist Labor Party
President: Simon Wing, Massachusetts
Vice president: Charles Horatio Matchett, New York *

1896 ELECTION

Republican Party
President: William McKinley, Ohio
Vice president: Garret Augustus Hobart, New Jersey

Democratic Party
President: William Jennings Bryan, Nebraska
Vice president: Arthur Sewall, Maine

People's Party (Populist)
President: William Jennings Bryan, Nebraska
Vice president: Thomas Edward Watson, Georgia

National Democratic Party
President: John McAuley Palmer, Illinois
Vice president: Simon Bolivar Buckner, Kentucky

Prohibition Party
President: Joshua Levering, Maryland
Vice president: Hale Johnson, Illinois *

Socialist Labor Party
President: Charles Horatio Matchett, New York
Vice president: Matthew Maguire, New Jersey

National Party
President: Charles Eugene Bentley, Nebraska
Vice president: James Haywood Southgate, North Carolina *

National Silver Party (Bi-Metallic League)
President: William Jennings Bryan, Nebraska
Vice president: Arthur Sewall, Maine

1900 ELECTION

Republican Party
President: William McKinley, Ohio
Vice president: Theodore Roosevelt, New York

Democratic Party
President: William Jennings Bryan, Nebraska
Vice president: Adlai Ewing Stevenson, Illinois

Prohibition Party
President: John Granville Wooley, Illinois
Vice president: Henry Brewer Metcalf, Rhode Island

Social-Democratic Party
President: Eugene Victor Debs, Indiana
Vice president: Job Harriman, California

People's Party (Populist—Anti-Fusionist faction)
President: Wharton Barker, Pennsylvania
Vice president: Ignatius Donnelly, Minnesota

Socialist Labor Party
President: Joseph Francis Malloney, Massachusetts
Vice president: Valentine Remmel, Pennsylvania

Union Reform Party
President: Seth Hockett Ellis, Ohio
Vice president: Samuel T. Nicholson, Pennsylvania

United Christian Party
President: Jonah Fitz Randolph Leonard, Iowa
Vice president: David H. Martin, Pennsylvania

People's Party (Populist—Fusionist faction)
President: William Jennings Bryan, Nebraska
Vice president: Adlai Ewing Stevenson, Illinois

Silver Republican Party
President: William Jennings Bryan, Nebraska
Vice president: Adlai Ewing Stevenson, Illinois

National Party
President: Donelson Caffery, Louisiana
Vice president: Archibald Murray Howe, Massachusetts *

1904 ELECTION

Republican Party
President: Theodore Roosevelt, New York
Vice president: Charles Warren Fairbanks, Indiana

Democratic Party
President: Alton Brooks Parker, New York
Vice president: Henry Gassaway Davis, West Virginia

Socialist Party
President: Eugene Victor Debs, Indiana
Vice president: Benjamin Hanford, New York

Prohibition Party
President: Silas Comfort Swallow, Pennsylvania
Vice president: George W. Carroll, Texas

People's Party (Populist)
President: Thomas Edward Watson, Georgia
Vice president: Thomas Henry Tibbles, Nebraska

Socialist Labor Party
President: Charles Hunter Corregan, New York
Vice president: William Wesley Cox, Illinois

Continental Party
President: Austin Holcomb
Vice president: A. King, Missouri

1908 ELECTION

Republican Party
President: William Howard Taft, Ohio
Vice president: James Schoolcraft Sherman, New York

Democratic Party
President: William Jennings Bryan, Nebraska
Vice president: John Worth Kern, Indiana

Socialist Party
President: Eugene Victor Debs, Indiana
Vice president: Benjamin Hanford, New York

Prohibition Party
President: Eugene Wilder Chafin, Illinois
Vice president: Aaron Sherman Watkins, Ohio

Independence Party
President: Thomas Louis Hisgen, Massachusetts
Vice president: John Temple Graves, Georgia

People's Party (Populist)
President: Thomas Edward Watson, Georgia
Vice president: Samuel Williams, Indiana

Socialist Labor Party
President: August Gillhaus, New York
Vice president: Donald L. Munro, Virginia

United Christian Party
President: Daniel Braxton Turney, Illinois
Vice president: Lorenzo S. Coffin, Iowa

1912 ELECTION

Democratic Party
President: Woodrow Wilson, New Jersey
Vice president: Thomas Riley Marshall, Indiana

Progressive Party ("Bull Moose" Party)
President: Theodore Roosevelt, New York
Vice president: Hiram Warren Johnson, California

Republican Party
President: William Howard Taft, Ohio
Vice president: James Schoolcraft Sherman, New York
    Sherman died October 30; he was replaced by Nicholas Murray
Butler, New York.

Socialist Party
President: Eugene Victor Debs, Indiana
Vice president: Emil Seidel, Wisconsin

Prohibition Party
President: Eugene Wilder Chafin, Illinois
Vice president: Aaron Sherman Watkins, Ohio

Socialist Labor Party
President: Arthur Elmer Reimer, Massachusetts
Vice president: August Gillhaus, New York[1]

1916 ELECTION

Democratic Party
President: Woodrow Wilson, New Jersey
Vice president: Thomas Riley Marshall, Indiana

Republican Party
President: Charles Evans Hughes, New York
Vice president: Charles Warren Fairbanks, Indiana

Socialist Party
President: Allan Louis Benson, New York
Vice president: George Ross Kirkpatrick, New Jersey

Prohibition Party
President: James Franklin Hanly, Indiana
Vice president: Ira Landrith, Tennessee

Socialist Labor Party
President: Arthur Elmer Reimer, Massachusetts *
Vice president: Caleb Harrison, Illinois *

Progressive Party
President: Theodore Roosevelt, New York
Vice president: John Milliken Parker, Louisiana

1920 ELECTION

Republican Party
President: Warren Gamaliel Harding, Ohio
Vice president: Calvin Coolidge, Massachusetts

Democratic Party
President: James Middleton Cox, Ohio
Vice president: Franklin Delano Roosevelt, New York

Socialist Party
President: Eugene Victor Debs, Indiana
Vice president: Seymour Stedman, Illinois

Farmer Labor Party
President: Parley Parker Christensen, Utah
Vice president: Maximilian Sebastian Hayes, Ohio

Prohibition Party
  President: Aaron Sherman Watkins, Ohio
  Vice president: David Leigh Colvin, New York
Socialist Labor Party
  President: William Wesley Cox, Missouri
  Vice president: August Gillhaus, New York
Single Tax Party
  President: Robert Colvin Macauley, Pennsylvania
  Vice president: R. G. Barnum, Ohio
American Party
  President: James Edward Ferguson, Texas
  Vice president: William J. Hough

1924 ELECTION

Republican Party
  President: Calvin Coolidge, Massachusetts
  Vice president: Charles Gates Dawes, Illinois
Democratic Party
  President: John William Davis, West Virginia
  Vice president: Charles Wayland Bryan, Nebraska
Progressive Party
  President: Robert La Follette, Wisconsin
  Vice president: Burton Kendall Wheeler, Montana
Prohibition Party
  President: Herman Preston Faris, Missouri
  Vice president: Marie Caroline Brehm, California
Socialist Labor Party
  President: Frank T. Johns, Oregon
  Vice president: Verne L. Reynolds, New York
Socialist Party
  President: Robert La Follette, New York
  Vice president: Burton Kendall Wheeler, Montana
Workers Party (Communist Party)
  President: William Zebulon Foster, Illinois
  Vice president: Benjamin Gitlow, New York
American Party
  President: Gilbert Owen Nations, District of Columbia
  Vice president: Charles Hiram Randall, California[2]
Commonwealth Land Party
  President: William J. Wallace, New Jersey
  Vice president: John Cromwell Lincoln, Ohio
Farmer Labor Party
  President: Duncan McDonald, Illinois *
  Vice president: William Bouck, Washington *
Greenback Party
  President: John Zahnd, Indiana *
  Vice president: Roy M. Harrop, Nebraska *

1928 ELECTION

Republican Party
  President: Herbert Clark Hoover, California
  Vice president: Charles Curtis, Kansas
Democratic Party
  President: Alfred Emanuel Smith, New York
  Vice president: Joseph Taylor Robinson, Arkansas
Socialist Party
  President: Norman Mattoon Thomas, New York
  Vice president: James Hudson Maurer, Pennsylvania
Workers Party (Communist Party)
  President: William Zebulon Foster, Illinois
  Vice president: Benjamin Gitlow, New York

Socialist Labor Party
  President: Verne L. Reynolds, Michigan
  Vice president: Jeremiah D. Crowley, New York
Prohibition Party
  President: William Frederick Varney, New York
  Vice president: James Arthur Edgerton, Virginia
Farmer Labor Party
  President: Frank Elbridge Webb, California
  Vice president: Will Vereen, Georgia[3]
Greenback Party
  President: John Zahnd, Indiana *
  Vice president: Wesley Henry Bennington, Ohio *

1932 ELECTION

Democratic Party
  President: Franklin Delano Roosevelt, New York
  Vice president: John Nance Garner, Texas
Republican Party
  President: Herbert Clark Hoover, California
  Vice president: Charles Curtis, Kansas
Socialist Party
  President: Norman Mattoon Thomas, New York
  Vice president: James Hudson Maurer, Pennsylvania
Communist Party
  President: William Zebulon Foster, Illinois
  Vice president: James William Ford, New York
Prohibition Party
  President: William David Upshaw, Georgia
  Vice president: Frank Stewart Regan, Illinois
Liberty Party
  President: William Hope Harvey, Arkansas
  Vice president: Frank B. Hemenway, Washington
Socialist Labor Party
  President: Verne L. Reynolds, New York
  Vice president: John W. Aiken, Massachusetts
Farmer Labor Party
  President: Jacob Sechler Coxey, Ohio
  Vice president: Julius J. Reiter, Minnesota
Jobless Party
  President: James Renshaw Cox, Pennsylvania
  Vice president: V. C. Tisdal, Oklahoma
National Party
  President: Seymour E. Allen, Massachusetts

1936 ELECTION

Democratic Party
  President: Franklin Delano Roosevelt, New York
  Vice president: John Nance Garner, Texas
Republican Party
  President: Alfred Mossman Landon, Kansas
  Vice president: Frank Knox, Illinois
Union Party
  President: William Lemke, North Dakota
  Vice president: Thomas Charles O'Brien, Massachusetts
Socialist Party
  President: Norman Mattoon Thomas, New York
  Vice president: George A. Nelson, Wisconsin
Communist Party
  President: Earl Russell Browder, Kansas
  Vice president: James William Ford, New York

Prohibition Party
President: David Leigh Colvin, New York
Vice president: Alvin York, Tennessee
Socialist Labor Party
President: John W. Aiken, Massachusetts
Vice president: Emil F. Teichert, New York
National Greenback Party
President: John Zahnd, Indiana *
Vice president: Florence Garvin, Rhode Island *

1940 ELECTION

Democratic Party
President: Franklin Delano Roosevelt, New York
Vice president: Henry Agard Wallace, Iowa
Republican Party
President: Wendell Lewis Willkie, New York
Vice president: Charles Linza McNary, Oregon
Socialist Party
President: Norman Mattoon Thomas, New York
Vice president: Maynard C. Krueger, Illinois
Prohibition Party
President: Roger Ward Babson, Massachusetts
Vice president: Edgar V. Moorman, Illinois
Communist Party (Workers Party)
President: Earl Russell Browder, Kansas
Vice president: James William Ford, New York
Socialist Labor Party
President: John W. Aiken, Massachusetts
Vice president: Aaron M. Orange, New York
Greenback Party
President: John Zahnd, Indiana *
Vice president: James Elmer Yates, Arizona *

1944 ELECTION

Democratic Party
President: Franklin Delano Roosevelt, New York
Vice president: Harry S. Truman, Missouri
Republican Party
President: Thomas Edmund Dewey, New York
Vice president: John William Bricker, Ohio
Socialist Party
President: Norman Mattoon Thomas, New York
Vice president: Darlington Hoopes, Pennsylvania
Prohibition Party
President: Claude A. Watson, California
Vice president: Andrew Johnson, Kentucky
Socialist Labor Party
President: Edward A. Teichert, Pennsylvania
Vice president: Arla A. Albaugh, Ohio
America First Party
President: Gerald Lyman Kenneth Smith, Michigan
Vice president: Henry A. Romer, Ohio

1948 ELECTION

Democratic Party
President: Harry S. Truman, Missouri
Vice president: Alben William Barkley, Kentucky
Republican Party
President: Thomas Edmund Dewey, New York
Vice president: Earl Warren, California

States' Rights Democratic Party
President: James Strom Thurmond, South Carolina
Vice president: Fielding Lewis Wright, Mississippi
Progressive Party
President: Henry Agard Wallace, Iowa
Vice president: Glen Hearst Taylor, Idaho
Socialist Party
President: Norman Mattoon Thomas, New York
Vice president: Tucker Powell Smith, Michigan
Prohibition Party
President: Claude A. Watson, California
Vice president: Dale Learn, Pennsylvania
Socialist Labor Party
President: Edward A. Teichert, Pennsylvania
Vice president: Stephen Emery, New York
Socialist Workers Party
President: Farrell Dobbs, New York
Vice president: Grace Carlson, Minnesota
Christian Nationalist Party
President: Gerald Lyman Kenneth Smith, Missouri
Vice president: Henry A. Romer, Ohio
Greenback Party
President: John G. Scott, New York
Vice president: Granville B. Leeke, Indiana *
Vegetarian Party
President: John Maxwell, Illinois
Vice president: Symon Gould, New York *

1952 ELECTION

Republican Party
President: Dwight David Eisenhower, New York
Vice president: Richard Milhous Nixon, California
Democratic Party
President: Adlai Ewing Stevenson II, Illinois
Vice president: John Jackson Sparkman, Alabama
Progressive Party
President: Vincent William Hallinan, California
Vice president: Charlotta A. Bass, New York
Prohibition Party
President: Stuart Hamblen, California
Vice president: Enoch Arden Holtwick, Illinois
Socialist Labor Party
President: Eric Hass, New York
Vice president: Stephen Emery, New York
Socialist Party
President: Darlington Hoopes, Pennsylvania
Vice president: Samuel Herman Friedman, New York
Socialist Workers Party
President: Farrell Dobbs, New York
Vice president: Myra Tanner Weiss, New York
America First Party
President: Douglas MacArthur, Wisconsin
Vice president: Harry Flood Byrd, Virginia
American Labor Party
President: Vincent William Hallinan, California
Vice president: Charlotta A. Bass, New York
American Vegetarian Party
President: Daniel J. Murphy, California
Vice president: Symon Gould, New York *
Church of God Party
President: Homer Aubrey Tomlinson, New York
Vice president: Willie Isaac Bass, North Carolina *

Constitution Party
    President: Douglas MacArthur, Wisconsin
    Vice president: Harry Flood Byrd, Virginia
Greenback Party
    President: Frederick C. Proehl, Washington
    Vice president: Edward J. Bedell, Indiana
Poor Man's Party
    President: Henry B. Krajewski, New Jersey
    Vice president: Frank Jenkins, New Jersey

1956 ELECTION

Republican Party
    President: Dwight David Eisenhower, Pennsylvania
    Vice president: Richard Milhous Nixon, California
Democratic Party
    President: Adlai Ewing Stevenson II, Illinois
    Vice president: Estes Kefauver, Tennessee
States' Rights Party
    President: Thomas Coleman Andrews, Virginia
    Vice president: Thomas Harold Werdel, California
        Ticket also favored by Constitution Party.
Prohibition Party
    President: Enoch Arden Holtwick, Illinois
    Vice president: Edward M. Cooper, California
Socialist Labor Party
    President: Eric Hass, New York
    Vice president: Georgia Cozzini, Wisconsin
Texas Constitution Party
    President: William Ezra Jenner, Indiana *
    Vice president: Joseph Bracken Lee, Utah *
Socialist Workers Party
    President: Farrell Dobbs, New York
    Vice president: Myra Tanner Weiss, New York
American Third Party
    President: Henry Krajewski, New Jersey
    Vice president: Ann Marie Yezo, New Jersey
Socialist Party
    President: Darlington Hoopes, Pennsylvania
    Vice president: Samuel Herman Friedman, New York
Pioneer Party
    President: William Langer, North Dakota *
    Vice president: Burr McCloskey, Illinois *
American Vegetarian Party
    President: Herbert M. Shelton, California *
    Vice president: Symon Gould, New York *
Greenback Party
    President: Frederick C. Proehl, Washington
    Vice president: Edward Kirby Meador, Massachusetts *
States' Rights Party of Kentucky
    President: Harry Flood Byrd, Virginia
    Vice president: William Ezra Jenner, Indiana
South Carolinians for Independent Electors
    President: Harry Flood Byrd, Virginia
Christian National Party
    President: Gerald Lyman Kenneth Smith
    Vice president: Charles I. Robertson

1960 ELECTION

Democratic Party
    President: John Fitzgerald Kennedy, Massachusetts
    Vice president: Lyndon Baines Johnson, Texas

Republican Party
    President: Richard Milhous Nixon, California
    Vice president: Henry Cabot Lodge, Massachusetts
National States' Rights Party
    President: Orval Eugene Faubus, Arkansas
    Vice president: John Geraerdt Crommelin, Alabama
Socialist Labor Party
    President: Eric Hass, New York
    Vice president: Georgia Cozzini, Wisconsin
Prohibition Party
    President: Rutherford Losey Decker, Missouri
    Vice president: Earle Harold Munn, Michigan
Socialist Workers Party
    President: Farrell Dobbs, New York
    Vice president: Myra Tanner Weiss, New York
Conservative Party of New Jersey
    President: Joseph Bracken Lee, Utah
    Vice president: Kent H. Courtney, Louisiana
Conservative Party of Virginia
    President: C. Benton Coiner, Virginia
    Vice president: Edward M. Silverman, Virginia
Constitution Party (Texas)
    President: Charles Loten Sullivan, Mississippi
    Vice president: Merritt B. Curtis, District of Columbia
Constitution Party (Washington)
    President: Merritt B. Curtis, District of Columbia
    Vice president: B. N. Miller
Greenback Party
    President: Whitney Hart Slocomb, California *
    Vice president: Edward Kirby Meador, Massachusetts *
Independent Afro-American Party
    President: Clennon King, Georgia
    Vice president: Reginald Carter
Tax Cut Party (America First Party; American Party)
    President: Lar Daly, Illinois
    Vice president: Merritt Barton Curtis, District of Columbia
Theocratic Party
    President: Homer Aubrey Tomlinson, New York
    Vice president: Raymond L. Teague, Alaska *
Vegetarian Party
    President: Symon Gould, New York
    Vice president: Christopher Gian-Cursio, Florida

1964 ELECTION

Democratic Party
    President: Lyndon Baines Johnson, Texas
    Vice president: Hubert Horatio Humphrey, Minnesota
Republican Party
    President: Barry Morris Goldwater, Arizona
    Vice president: William Edward Miller, New York
Socialist Labor Party
    President: Eric Hass, New York
    Vice president: Henning A. Blomen, Massachusetts
Prohibition Party
    President: Earle Harold Munn, Michigan
    Vice president: Mark Shaw, Massachusetts
Socialist Workers Party
    President: Clifton DeBerry, New York
    Vice president: Edward Shaw, New York
National States' Rights Party
    President: John Kasper, Tennessee
    Vice president: J. B. Stoner, Georgia

Constitution Party
President: Joseph B. Lightburn, West Virginia
Vice president: Theodore C. Billings, Colorado

Independent States' Rights Party
President: Thomas Coleman Andrews, Virginia
Vice president: Thomas H. Werdel, California *

Theocratic Party
President: Homer Aubrey Tomlinson, New York
Vice president: William R. Rogers, Missouri *

Universal Party
President: Kirby James Hensley, California
Vice president: John O. Hopkins, Iowa

1968 ELECTION

Republican Party
President: Richard Milhous Nixon, New York
Vice president: Spiro Theodore Agnew, Maryland

Democratic Party
President: Hubert Horatio Humphrey, Minnesota
Vice president: Edmund Sixtus Muskie, Maine

American Independent Party
President: George Corley Wallace, Alabama
Vice president: Curtis Emerson LeMay, Ohio
 LeMay replaced S. Marvin Griffin, who originally had been selected.

Peace and Freedom Party
President: Eldridge Cleaver
Vice president: Judith Mage, New York

Socialist Labor Party
President: Henning A. Blomen, Massachusetts
Vice president: George Sam Taylor, Pennsylvania

Socialist Workers Party
President: Fred Halstead, New York
Vice president: Paul Boutelle, New Jersey

Prohibition Party
President: Earle Harold Munn Sr., Michigan
Vice president: Rolland E. Fisher, Kansas

Communist Party
President: Charlene Mitchell, California
Vice president: Michael Zagarell, New York

Constitution Party
President: Richard K. Troxell, Texas
Vice president: Merle Thayer, Iowa

Freedom and Peace Party
President: Richard Claxton (Dick) Gregory, Illinois
Vice president: Mark Lane, New York

Patriotic Party
President: George Corley Wallace, Alabama
Vice president: William Penn Patrick, California

Theocratic Party
President: William R. Rogers, Missouri

Universal Party
President: Kirby James Hensley, California
Vice president: Roscoe B. MacKenna

1972 ELECTION

Republican Party
President: Richard Milhous Nixon, California
Vice president: Spiro Theodore Agnew, Maryland

Democratic Party
President: George Stanley McGovern, South Dakota
Vice president: Thomas Francis Eagleton, Missouri

Eagleton resigned and was replaced on August 8, 1972, by Robert Sargent Shriver Jr., Maryland, selected by the Democratic National Committee.

American Independent Party
President: John George Schmitz, California
Vice president: Thomas Jefferson Anderson, Tennessee

Socialist Workers Party
President: Louis Fisher, Illinois
Vice president: Genevieve Gunderson, Minnesota

Socialist Labor Party
President: Linda Jenness, Georgia
Vice president: Andrew Pulley, Illinois

Communist Party
President: Gus Hall, New York
Vice president: Jarvis Tyner

Prohibition Party
President: Earle Harold Munn Sr., Michigan
Vice president: Marshall Uncapher

Libertarian Party
President: John Hospers, California
Vice president: Theodora Nathan, Oregon

People's Party
President: Benjamin McLane Spock
Vice president: Julius Hobson, District of Columbia

America First Party
President: John V. Mahalchik
Vice president: Irving Homer

Universal Party
President: Gabriel Green
Vice president: Daniel Fry

1976 ELECTION

Democratic Party
President: James Earl (Jimmy) Carter Jr., Georgia
Vice president: Walter Frederick Mondale, Minnesota

Republican Party
President: Gerald Rudolph Ford, Michigan
Vice president: Robert Joseph Dole, Kansas

Independent candidate
President: Eugene Joseph McCarthy, Minnesota
Vice president: none[4]

Libertarian Party
President: Roger MacBride, Virginia
Vice president: David P. Bergland, California

American Independent Party
President: Lester Maddox, Georgia
Vice president: William Dyke, Wisconsin

American Party
President: Thomas J. Anderson, Tennessee
Vice president: Rufus Shackleford, Florida

Socialist Workers Party
President: Peter Camejo, California
Vice president: Willie Mae Reid, California

Communist Party
President: Gus Hall, New York
Vice president: Jarvis Tyner, New York

People's Party
President: Margaret Wright, California
Vice president: Benjamin Spock, New York

U.S. Labor Party
President: Lyndon H. LaRouche Jr., New York
Vice president: R. W. Evans, Michigan

Prohibition Party
  President: Benjamin C. Bubar, Maine
  Vice president: Earl F. Dodge, Colorado
Socialist Labor Party
  President: Jules Levin, New Jersey
  Vice president: Constance Blomen, Massachusetts
Socialist Party
  President: Frank P. Zeidler, Wisconsin
  Vice president: J. Quinn Brisben, Illinois
Restoration Party
  President: Ernest L. Miller
  Vice president: Roy N. Eddy
United American Party
  President: Frank Taylor
  Vice president: Henry Swan

1980 ELECTION[5]

Republican Party
  President: Ronald Wilson Reagan, California
  Vice president: George Herbert Walker Bush, Texas
Democratic Party
  President: James Earl (Jimmy) Carter Jr., Georgia
  Vice president: Walter Frederick Mondale, Minnesota
National Unity Campaign
  President: John B. Anderson, Illinois
  Vice president: Patrick Joseph Lucey, Wisconsin
Libertarian Party
  President: Edward E. Clark, California
  Vice president: David Koch, New York
Citizens Party
  President: Barry Commoner, New York
  Vice president: LaDonna Harris, New Mexico
Communist Party
  President: Gus Hall, New York
  Vice president: Angela Davis, California
American Independent Party
  President: John Richard Rarick, Louisiana
  Vice president: Eileen M. Shearer, California
Socialist Workers Party
  President: Andrew Pulley, Illinois
  Vice president: Matilde Zimmermann
  President: Clifton DeBerry, California
  Vice president: Matilde Zimmermann
  President: Richard Congress, Ohio
  Vice president: Matilde Zimmermann
Right to Life Party
  President: Ellen McCormack, New York
  Vice president: Carroll Driscoll, New Jersey
Peace and Freedom Party
  President: Maureen Smith, California
  Vice president: Elizabeth Barron
Workers World Party
  President: Deirdre Griswold, New Jersey
  Vice president: Larry Holmes, New York
Statesman Party
  President: Benjamin C. Bubar, Maine
  Vice president: Earl F. Dodge, Colorado
Socialist Party
  President: David McReynolds, New York
  Vice president: Diane Drufenbrock, Wisconsin
American Party
  President: Percy L. Greaves, New York
  Vice president: Frank L. Varnum, California

President: Frank W. Shelton, Utah
  Vice president: George E. Jackson
Middle Class Party
  President: Kurt Lynen, New Jersey
  Vice president: Harry Kieve, New Jersey
Down With Lawyers Party
  President: Bill Gahres, New Jersey
  Vice president: J. F. Loghlin, New Jersey
Independent Party
  President: Martin E. Wendelken
Natural Peoples Party
  President: Harley McLain, North Dakota
  Vice president: Jewelie Goeller, North Dakota

1984 ELECTION[6]

Republican Party
  President: Ronald Wilson Reagan, California
  Vice president: George Herbert Walker Bush, Texas
Democratic Party
  President: Walter Fritz Mondale, Minnesota
  Vice president: Geraldine Anne Ferraro, New York
Libertarian Party
  President: David P. Bergland, California
  Vice president: Jim Lewis, Connecticut
Independent Party
  President: Lyndon H. LaRouche Jr., Virginia
  Vice president: Billy Davis, Mississippi
Citizens Party
  President: Sonia Johnson, Virginia
  Vice president: Richard Walton, Rhode Island
Populist Party
  President: Bob Richards, Texas
  Vice president: Maureen Kennedy Salaman, California
Independent Alliance Party
  President: Dennis L. Serrette, New Jersey
  Vice president: Nancy Ross, New York
Communist Party
  President: Gus Hall, New York
  Vice president: Angela Davis, California
Socialist Workers Party
  President: Mel Mason, California
  Vice president: Andrea Gonzalez, New York
Workers World Party
  President: Larry Holmes, New York
  Vice president: Gloria La Riva, California
  President: Gavrielle Holmes, New York
  Vice president: Milton Vera
American Party
  President: Delmar Dennis, Tennessee
  Vice president: Traves Brownlee, Delaware
Workers League Party
  President: Ed Winn, New York
  Vice presidents: Jean T. Brust, Helen Halyard, Edward Bergonzi
Prohibition Party
  President: Earl F. Dodge, Colorado
  Vice president: Warren C. Martin, Kansas

1988 ELECTION[7]

Republican Party
  President: George Herbert Walker Bush, Texas
  Vice president: James "Dan" Quayle, Indiana

Democratic Party
President: Michael Stanley Dukakis, Massachusetts
Vice president: Lloyd Millard Bentsen Jr., Texas

Libertarian Party
President: Ronald E. Paul, Texas
Vice president: Andre V. Marrou, Nevada

New Alliance Party
President: Lenora B. Fulani, New York
Vice president: Joyce Dattner

Populist Party
President: David E. Duke, Louisiana
Vice president: Floyd C. Parker

Consumer Party
President: Eugene Joseph McCarthy, Minnesota
Vice president: Florence Rice

American Independent Party
President: James C. Griffin, California
Vice president: Charles J. Morsa

National Economic Recovery Party
President: Lyndon H. LaRouche Jr., Virginia
Vice president: Debra H. Freeman

Right to Life Party
President: William A. Marra, New Jersey
Vice president: Joan Andrews

Workers League Party
President: Edward Winn, New York
Vice president: Barry Porster

Socialist Workers Party
President: James Warren, New Jersey
Vice president: Kathleen Mickells

Peace and Freedom Party
President: Herbert Lewin
Vice president: Vikki Murdock

Prohibition Party
President: Earl F. Dodge, Colorado
Vice president: George D. Ormsby

Workers World Party
President: Larry Holmes, New York
Vice president: Gloria La Riva, California

Socialist Party
President: Willa Kenoyer, Minnesota
Vice president: Ron Ehrenreich

American Party
President: Delmar Dennis, Tennessee
Vice president: Earl Jepson

Grassroots Party
President: Jack E. Herer, California
Vice president: Dana Beal

Independent Party
President: Louie Youngkeit, Utah

Third World Assembly
President: John G. Martin, District of Columbia
Vice president: Cleveland Sparrow

1992 ELECTION[8]

Democratic Party
President: Bill Clinton, Arkansas
Vice president: Albert Gore Jr., Tennessee

Republican Party
President: George Herbert Walker Bush, Texas
Vice president: James "Dan" Quayle, Indiana

Independent
President: H. Ross Perot, Texas
Vice president: James Stockdale, California

Libertarian Party
President: Andre V. Marrou, Nevada
Vice president: Nancy Lord, Georgia

America First Party (Populist)
President: James "Bo" Gritz, Nevada
Vice president: Cyril Minett

New Alliance Party
President: Lenora B. Fulani, New York
Vice president: Maria E. Munoz, California

U.S. Taxpayers Party
President: Howard Phillips, Virginia
Vice president: Albion W. Knight, Maryland

Natural Law Party
President: John Hagelin, Iowa
Vice president: Mike Tompkins, Iowa

Peace and Freedom Party
President: Ron Daniels, California
Vice president: Asiba Tupahache

Independent
President: Lyndon H. LaRouche Jr., Virginia
Vice president: James L. Bevel

Socialist Workers Party
President: James Warren, New Jersey
Vice president: Willie Mae Reid

Independent
President: Drew Bradford

Grassroots Party
President: Jack E. Herer, California
Vice president: Derrick P. Grimmer

Socialist Party
President: J. Quinn Brisben, Illinois
Vice president: Barbara Garson

Workers League Party
President: Helen Halyard, Michigan
Vice president: Fred Mazelis, Michigan

Take Back America Party
President: John Yiamouyiannas
Vice president: Allen C. McCone

Independent
President: Delbert L. Ehlers
Vice president: Rick Wendt

Prohibition Party
President: Earl F. Dodge, Colorado
Vice president: George D. Ormsby

Apathy Party
President: Jim Boren
Vice president: Will Weidman

Third Party
President: Eugene A. Hem
Vice president: Joanne Roland

Looking Back Party
President: Isabell Masters, Oklahoma
Vice president: Walter Masters, Florida

American Party
President: Robert J. Smith
Vice president: Doris Feimer

Workers World Party
President: Gloria La Riva, California
Vice president: Larry Holmes, New York

1996 ELECTION[9]

Democratic Party
President: Bill Clinton, Arkansas
Vice president: Albert Gore Jr., Tennessee

Republican Party
President: Robert Dole, Kansas
Vice president: Jack Kemp, New York

Reform Party
President: H. Ross Perot, Texas
Vice president: Pat Choate, District of Columbia

Green Party
President: Ralph Nader, District of Columbia
Vice president: Winona LaDuke, Minnesota

Libertarian Party
President: Harry Browne, Tennessee
Vice president: Jo Anne Jorgensen, South
Carolina

U.S. Taxpayers Party
President: Howard Phillips, Virginia
Vice president: Herbert W. Titus, Virginia

Natural Law Party
President: John Hagelin, Iowa
Vice president: Mike Tompkins, North Carolina

Workers World Party
President: Monica Moorehead, New York
Vice president: Gloria La Riva, California

Peace and Freedom Party
President: Marsha Feinland, California
Vice president: Kate McClatchy, Massachusetts

Independent
President: Charles E. Collins, Florida
Vice president: Rosemary Giumarra

Socialist Workers Party
President: James E. Harris Jr., Georgia
Vice president: Laura Garza, New York

Grassroots Party
President: Dennis Peron, Minnesota
Vice president: Arlin Troutt, Arizona

Socialist Party
President: Mary Cal Hollis, Colorado
Vice president: Eric Chester, Massachusetts

Socialist Equality Party
President: Jerome White, Michigan
Vice president: Fred Mazelis, Michigan

American Party
President: Diane Beall Templin, California
Vice president: Gary Van Horn, Utah

Prohibition Party
President: Earl F. Dodge, Colorado
Vice president: Rachel Bubar Kelly, Maine

Independent Party of Utah
President: A. Peter Crane, Utah
Vice president: Connie Chandler, Utah

America First Party
President: Ralph Forbes, Arkansas

Independent Grassroots Party
President: John Birrenbach, Minnesota
Vice president: George McMahon, Iowa

Looking Back Party
President: Isabell Masters, Oklahoma
Vice president: Shirley Jean Masters, California

Independent
President: Steve Michael, District of Columbia

2000 ELECTION

Republican Party
President: George W. Bush, Texas
Vice president: Richard Cheney, Wyoming

Democratic Party
President: Albert Gore Jr., Tennessee
Vice president: Joseph Lieberman, Connecticut

Green Party
President: Ralph Nader, District of Columbia
Vice president: Winona LaDuke, Minnesota

Reform Party
President: Patrick J. Buchanan, Virginia
Vice president: Ezola Foster, California

Libertarian Party[10]
President: Harry Browne, Tennessee
Vice president: Art Olivier, California
President: L. Neil Smith, Arizona

Constitution Party
President: Howard Phillips, Virginia
Vice president: J. Curtis Frazier II, Missouri

Natural Law Party
President: John Hagelin, Iowa
Vice president: Nat Goldhaber, California

Socialist Workers Party
President: James E. Harris Jr., Georgia
Vice president: Margaret Trowe, Minnesota

Socialist Party
President: David McReynolds, New York
Vice president: Mary Cal Hollis, Colorado

Workers World Party
President: Monica Moorehead, New Jersey
Vice president: Gloria La Riva, California

Independent
President: Cathy Gordon Brown, Tennessee
Vice president: Sabrina R. Allen, Tennessee

Vermont Grassroots Party
President: Dennis I. Lane, Vermont
Vice president: Dale Wilkinson, Minnesota

Independent
President: Randall A. Venson, Tennessee
Vice president: Gene Kelley, Tennessee

Prohibition Party
President: Earl F. Dodge, Colorado
Vice president: W. Dean Watkins, Arizona

Independent
President: Louie Youngkeit, Utah
Vice president: Robert Leo Beck, Utah

2004 ELECTION[11]

Republican Party
President: George W. Bush, Texas
Vice President: Richard B. Cheney, Wyoming

Democratic Party
President: John Kerry, Massachusetts
Vice President: John Edwards, North Carolina

Independent
President: Ralph Nader, District of Columbia
Vice President: Peter Miguel Camejo, California

Libertarian Party
President: Michael Badnarik, Texas
Vice President: Richard V. Campagna, Iowa

Constitution Party
President: Michael Peroutka, Maryland
Vice President: Chuck Baldwin, Florida

Green Party
President: David Cobb, Texas
Vice President: Patricia LaMarche, Maine

Peace and Freedom Party
President: Leonard Peltier, Kansas
Vice President: Janice Jordan, California

Socialist Party
President: Walter F. Brown, Oregon
Vice President: Mary Alice Herbert, Vermont

Socialist Workers Party
President: James Harris, Georgia
Vice President: Margaret Trowe, Minnesota

Socialist Workers Party
President: Roger Calero, New York
Vice President: Arrin Hawkins, New York

Christian Freedom Party
President: Thomas J. Harens, Minnesota
Vice President: Jennifer A. Ryan, Minnesota

Concerns of People Party
President: Gene Amondson, Alaska
Vice President: Leroy Pletten, Michigan

Socialist Equality Party
President: Bill Van Auken, New York
Vice President: Jim Lawrence, Ohio

Workers World Party
President: John Parker, California
Vice President: Teresa Gutierrez, New York

Personal Choice Party
President: Charles Jay, Indiana
Vice President: Marilyn Chambers Taylor, California

Unaffiliated
President: Stanford E. "Andy" Andress, Colorado
Vice President: Irene M. Deasy, Colorado

Prohibition Party
President: Earl F. Dodge, Colorado
Vice President: Howard F. Lydick, Texas

NOTES

* Candidates appeared in Joseph Nathan Kane, *Facts About the Presidents*, 4th ed. (New York: H. W. Wilson, 1981), but could not be verified in another source.

1. 1912: Arthur M. Schlesinger's History of American Presidential Elections (New York: McGraw-Hill, 1971) lists the Socialist Labor Party vice-presidential candidate as Francis. No first name is given.

2. 1924: Richard M. Scammon's *America at the Polls* (Pittsburgh: University of Pittsburgh Press, 1965) lists the American Party vice-presidential candidate as Leander L. Pickett.

3. 1928: *America at the Polls* lists the Farmer Labor Party vice-presidential candidate as L. R. Tillman.

4. 1976: McCarthy, who ran as an independent with no party designation, had no national running mate, favoring the elimination of the office. But as various state laws required a running mate, he had different ones in different states, amounting to nearly two dozen, all political unknowns.

5. 1980: In several cases vice-presidential nominees were different from those listed for most states, and the Socialist Workers and American Party nominees for president varied from state to state. For example, because Pulley, the major standard-bearer for the Socialist Workers Party was only twenty-nine years old, his name was not allowed on the ballot in some states (the Constitution requires presidential candidates to be at least thirty-five years old). Hence, the party ran other candidates in those states. In a number of states, candidates appeared on the ballot with variants of the party designations listed, without any party designation, or with entirely different party names.

6. 1984: Both Larry Holmes and Gavrielle Holmes were standard-bearers of the Workers World Party. Of the two, Larry Holmes was listed on more state ballots. Milton Vera was Gavrielle Holmes's vice-presidential running mate in Ohio and Rhode Island. The Workers League Party had three vice-presidential candidates: Jean T. Brust in Illinois; Helen Halyard in Michigan, New Jersey, and Pennsylvania; and Edward Bergonzi in Minnesota and Ohio.

7. 1988: The candidates listed include all those who appeared on the ballot in at least one state. In some cases, a party's vice-presidential candidate varied from state to state. Candidates' full names and states were not available from some parties.

8. 1992: The candidates listed include all those who appeared on the ballot in at least one state. In some cases a party's vice-presidential candidate varied from state to state. Candidates' states were not available from some parties.

9. 1996: The candidates listed include all those who appeared on the ballot in at least one state. In some cases a party's vice-presidential candidate varied from state to state. Candidates' states were not available from some parties.

10. 2000: L. Neil Smith ran as the Libertarian Party's presidential candidate in Arizona only. Harry Browne ran as the party's candidate in the other forty-nine states.

11. 2004: The candidates listed include all who appeared on the ballot in at least one state. In many states various third party candidates appeared on the ballot with variations of the party designations, were carried with entirely different party labels, or were listed as "Independent".

Bibliography

Aldrich, John H. *Before the Convention: Strategies and Choices in Presidential Nomination Campaigns.* Chicago: University of Chicago Press, 1980.

Alexander, Herbert E., and Anthony Corrado. *Financing the 1992 Election.* Armonk, N.Y.: M. E. Sharpe, 1995.

Arnett, A. M. *The Populist Movement in Georgia.* 1922. Reprint. New York: Columbia University Press, 1971.

Bain, Richard C., and Judith H. Parris. *Convention Decisions and Voting Records.* 2nd ed. Washington, D.C.: Brookings, 1975.

Bartels, Larry M. *Presidential Primaries and the Dynamics of Public Choice.* Princeton, N.J.: Princeton University Press, 1988.

Bibby, John F. *Politics, Parties, and Elections in America.* 4th ed. Chicago: Nelson-Hall, 1999.

Bibby, John F., and L. Sandy Maisel. *Two Parties—Or More? The American Party System.* Boulder, Colo.: Westview, 1998.

Blue, Frederick J. *The Free Soilers: Third Party Politics, 1848–1854.* Urbana: University of Illinois Press, 1973.

Borden, Morton. *Parties and Politics in the Early Republic, 1789–1815.* Arlington Heights, Ill.: Davidson, Harlan, 1967.

Brock, William. *Parties and Political Conscience: American Dilemmas, 1840–1850.* Millwood, N.Y.: Kraus International Publications, 1979.

Brown, Stuart G. *First Republicans: Political Philosophy and Public Policy in the Party of Jefferson and Madison.* 1954. Reprint. Westport, Conn.: Greenwood Press, 1977.

Buell, Emmett H., Jr., and Lee Sigelman. *Nominating the President.* Knoxville: University of Tennessee Press, 1991.

Burner, David. *The Politics of Provincialism: The Democratic Party in Transition, 1918–1932.* 1968. Reprint. Cambridge: Harvard University Press, 1986.

Byrne, Gary C., and Paul Marx. *The Great American Convention: A Political History of Presidential Elections.* Palo Alto, Calif.: Pacific Books, 1977.

Cannon, James P. *The History of American Trotskyism from Its Origin in 1928 to the Founding of the Socialist Labor Workers Party.* New York: Pathfinders Press, 1972.

Chambers, William N., and Walter D. Burnham, eds. *The American Party Systems: Stages of Political Development.* 2nd ed. New York: Oxford University Press, 1975.

Chase, James S. *Emergence of the Presidential Nominating Convention: 1789–1832.* Urbana: University of Illinois Press, 1973.

Conway, M. Margaret. *Political Participation in the United States.* 3rd ed. Washington, D.C.: CQ Press, 2000.

Congressional Quarterly. *Presidential Elections 1789–1996.* Washington, D.C.: Congressional Quarterly, 1997.

Congressional Quarterly. *Selecting the President: From 1789–1996.* Washington, D.C.: Congressional Quarterly, 1997.

Cook, Rhodes. *Race for Presidency: Winning the 2000 Nomination.* Washington, D.C.: CQ Press, 2000.

Cook, Rhodes. *U.S. Presidential Primary Elections, 1968–1996.* Washington, D.C.: CQ Press, 2000.

Cotter, Cornelius P. *Party Organization in American Politics.* Pittsburgh: University of Pittsburgh Press, 1989.

Cunningham, Noble E. *Jeffersonian Republicans: The Formation of Party Organization, 1789–1801.* Chapel Hill: University of North Carolina Press, 1967.

Davis, James W., and Robert E. DiClerico. *Choosing Our Choices: Debating the Presidential Nominating Process.* New York: Rowman and Littlefield, 2000.

de Tocqueville, Alexis. *Democracy in America.* Reprint. New York: Vintage, 1990.

Dinkin, Robert J. *Voting in Revolutionary America: A Study of Elections in the Original Thirteen States, 1776–1789.* Westport, Conn.: Greenwood Press, 1982.

Durbin, Thomas, ed. *Nomination and Election of the President and Vice President of the United States, 1992, Including the Manner of Selecting Delegates to National Party Conventions.* Washington, D.C.: U.S. Government Printing Office, 1992.

Eldersveld, Samuel J., Hanes Walton, and Hanes Walton Jr. *Political Parties in American Society.* New York: St. Martin's Press, 1999.

Fairlie, Henry. *The Parties: Republicans and Democrats in this Century.* New York: St. Martin's Press, 1978.

Farley, James A. *Behind the Ballots: the Personal History of a Politician.* 1938. Reprint. New York: Da Capo Press, 1973.

Fleishman, Joel L. *The Future of American Political Parties.* Englewood Cliffs, N.J.: Prentice-Hall, 1982.

Foner, Eric. *Free Soil, Free Labor, Free Men: The Ideology of the Republican Party Before the Civil War.* Rev. ed. New York: Oxford University Press, 1995.

Gillespie, J. David. *Politics at the Periphery: Third Parties in Two-Party America.* Columbia: University of South Carolina Press, 1993.

Goldstein, Michael L. *Guide to the 2000 Presidential Election.* Washington, D.C.: CQ Press, 1999.

Green, John C., and Daniel M. Shea, eds. *The State of the Parties: The Changing Role of Contemporary American Politics.* 3rd ed. Lanham, Md.: Rowman and Littlefield, 1999.

Halstead, Murat. *Trimmers, Trucklers and Temporizers: Notes of Murat Halstead from the Political Convention of 1856.* Madison: Wisconsin Historical Society Press, 1961.

Haskell, John. *Fundamentally Flawed: Understanding and Reforming Presidential Primaries.* New York: Rowman and Littlefield, 1996.

Hertzke, Allen D. *Echoes of Discontent: Jesse Jackson, Pat Robertson, and the Resurgence of Populism.* Washington, D.C.: CQ Press, 1993.

Hicks, John D. *The Populist Revolt: A History of the Farmer's Alliance in the People's Party.* Reprint. Minneapolis: University of Minnesota Press, 1981.

Hofstadter, Richard. *The Idea of a Party System: The Rise of Legitimate Opposition in the United States, 1780–1840.* Berkeley: University of California Press, 1969.

Holcombe, Arthur N. *Political Parties of Today: A Study in Republican and Democratic Politics.* New York: Harper and Row, 1974.

Jackson, John S., and William Crotty. *The Politics of Presidential Selection.* New York: HarperCollins, 1996.

Jones, Charles O. *The Republican Party in American Politics.* New York: Macmillan, 1965.

Keech, William R., and Donald R. Matthews. *The Party's Choice: With an Epilogue on the 1976 Nominations.* Washington, D.C.: Brookings, 1977.

Keefe, William J. *Parties, Politics, and Public Policy in America.* 8th ed. Washington, D.C.: CQ Press, 1997.

Kent, Frank R. *The Democratic Party: A History.* 1928. Reprint. New York: Johnson Reprint, 1968.

Kessel, John H. *Presidential Campaign Politics.* 4th ed. Pacific Grove, Calif.: Brooks-Cole, 1992.

Kipnis, Ira. *American Socialist Movement, 1897–1912.* Westport, Conn.: Greenwood Press, 1968.

Kraut, Alan M., ed. *Crusaders and Compromisers: Essays on the Relationship of Antislavery Struggle to the Antebellum Party System.* Westport, Conn.: Greenwood Press, 1983.

Kruschke, Earl R. *Encyclopedia of Third Parties in the United States.* Santa Barbara, Calif.: ABC-CLIO, 1991.

Ladd, Everett C., Jr. *Where Have All the Voters Gone? The Fracturing of American Political Parties.* 2nd ed. New York: Norton, 1982.

Ladd, Everett C., Jr., and Charles D. Hadley. *Transformations of the American Party System: Political Coalitions from the New Deal to the 1970s.* 2nd ed. New York: Norton, 1978.

Lamis, Alexander P. *The Two-Party South.* 2nd ed. New York: Oxford University Press, 1990.

Lawrence, David G. *The Collapse of the Democratic Presidential Majority: Realignment, Dealignment, and Electoral Change from Franklin Roosevelt to Bill Clinton.* Boulder, Colo.: Westview, 1996.

Lee, John H. *The Origin and Progress of the American Party in Politics: Embracing a Complete History of the Philadelphia Riots in May and July, 1844.* Reprint. Salem, N.H.: Ayer, 1977.

Livermore, Shaw, Jr. *Twilight of Federalism: The Disintegration of the Federalist Party, 1815–1830.* Staten Island, N.Y.: Gordian Press, 1972.

Main, Jackson T. *Political Parties Before the Constitution.* New York: Norton, 1974.

Maisel, L. Sandy, ed. *The Parties Respond: Changes in American Parties and Campaigns.* 3rd ed., Boulder, Colo.: Westview, 1998.

Matthews, Donald R. *Perspectives on Presidential Selection.* Washington, D.C.: Brookings, 1973.

McCormick, Richard P. *The Second American Party System: Party Formulation in the Jacksonian Era.* Chapel Hill: University of North Carolina Press, 1973.

McKay, Kenneth. *The Progressive Movement of 1924.* New York: Octagon Books, 1966.

McKee, Thomas H. *The National Conventions and Platforms of All Political Parties, 1789–1905: Convention, Popular and Electoral Vote.* New York: AMS Press, 1971.

Milkis, Sidney M. *The President and the Parties: The Transformation of the American Party System Since the New Deal.* New York: Oxford University Press, 1993.

Moore, John L. *Elections A to Z.* Washington, D.C.: CQ Press, 1999.

Morgan, Wayne. *From Hayes to McKinley: National Party Politics, 1877–1896.* Syracuse, N.Y.: Syracuse University Press, 1969.

Nichols, Roy F. *The Invention of the American Political Parties: A Study of Political Improvisation.* New York: Free Press, 1972.

Overacker, Louise. *The Presidential Primary.* 1926. Reprint. New York: Arno, 1974.

Parris, Judith H. *The Convention Problem: Issues in Reform of Presidential Nominating Procedures.* Washington, D.C.: Brookings, 1972.

Pika, Joseph H., and Richard Watson. *The Presidential Contest.* 5th ed. Washington, D.C.: CQ Press, 1995.

Pinchot, Amos R. E. *History of the Progressive Party, 1912–1916.* 1958. Reprint. New York: Westport, Conn.: Greenwood Press, 1978.

Pomper, Gerald M. *Nominating the President: The Politics of Convention Choice.* New York: Dodd, Mead, 1975.

———. *Voters, Elections, and Parties: The Practice of Democratic Theory.* New Brunswick, N.J.: Transaction Books, 1988.

Porter, Kirk H., and Donald Bruce Johnson. *National Party Platforms, 1840–1972.* Urbana: University of Illinois Press, 1973.

Reeves, Richard. *Convention.* New York: Harcourt Brace Jovanovich, 1977.

Reichley, A. James. *The Life of the Parties: A History of American Political Parties.* New York: Rowman and Littlefield, 2000.

Robinson, Edgar E. *The Evolution of American Political Parties.* 1924. Reprint. New York: Harcourt Brace Jovanovich, 1971.

Roseboom, Eugene H. *A History of Presidential Elections: From George Washington to Jimmy Carter.* 4th ed. New York: Macmillan, 1979.

Rosenstone, Steven J., Ray L. Behr, and Edward H. Lazarus. *Third Parties in America: Citizen Response to Major Party Failure.* Princeton, N.J.: Princeton University Press, 1996.

Ross, Earle D. *The Liberal Republican Movement.* New York: AMS Press, 1971.

Rossiter, Clinton. *Parties and Politics in America.* Ithaca, N.Y.: Cornell University Press, 1960.

Sanford, Terry. *A Danger of Democracy: The Presidential Nominating Process.* Boulder, Colo.: Westview, 1981.

Schefter, Martin. *Political Parties and the State: The American Historical Experience.* Princeton, N.J.: Princeton University Press, 1994.

Schlesinger, Arthur M., Jr. *History of U.S. Political Parties.* 4 vols. 1973. Reprint. New York: Chelsea House, 1981.

———, ed. *The Coming to Power: Critical Presidential Elections in American History.* New York: Chelsea House, 1981.

Schlesinger, Joseph A. *Political Parties and the Winning of Office.* Ann Arbor: University of Michigan Press, 1991.

Shafer, Byron. *Bifurcated Politics: Evolution and Reform in the National Party Convention.* Cambridge, Mass.: Harvard University Press, 1988.

Shafritz, Jay M. *The Dorsey Dictionary of American Government and Politics.* Chicago: Dorsey Press, 1988.

Smallwood, Frank. *The Other Candidates: Third Parties in Presidential Elections.* Hanover, N.H.: University Press of New England, 1983.

Smith, Theodore C. *Liberty and Free Soil Parties in the Northwest.* Reprint. New York: Arno Press, 1970.

Stedman, Murray S., Jr., and Susan W. Stedman. *Discontent at the Polls: A Study of Farmer and Labor Parties, 1827–1948.* New York: Russell and Russell Publishers, 1967.

Sundquist, James L. *Dynamics of the Party System: Alignment and Realignment of Political Parties in the United States.* Rev. ed. Washington, D.C.: Brookings, 1983.

Timberlake, James H. *Prohibition and the Progressive Movement, 1912–1925.* New York: Random House, 1969.

Van Buren, Martin. *Inquiry into the Origin and Course of Political Parties in the United States.* 1867. Reprint. New York: A. M. Kelley, 1967.

Wattenberg, Martin P. *The Decline of the American Political Parties 1952 to 1992.* Boston: Harvard University Press, 1994.

Wayne, Steven. *The Road to the White House 2000: The Politics of Presidential Elections.* New York: St. Martin's Press, 2000.

White, Theodore H. *America in Search of Itself: The Making of the President, 1956–1980.* New York: Harper and Row, 1982.

———. *The Making of the President, 1960.* New York: Atheneum, 1961.

Wilson, Woodrow. "There Ought Never to Be Another Presidential Nominating Convention: Excerpts from a Letter, February 5, 1913." *U.S. News & World Report,* Oct. 23, 1967, 124.

Index

Note: Italic numbers refer to photographs or illustrations.

DATE DUE

GAYLORD   PRINTED IN U.S.A.